CANADIAN POLITICS AND GOVERNMENT

IN THE CHARTER ERA

Heather MacIvor

University of Windsor

THOMSON

NELSON

Australia   Canada   Mexico   Singapore   Spain   United Kingdom   United States

THOMSON

NELSON

Canadian Politics and Government in the Charter Era

Heather MacIvor

**Associate Vice-President,
Editorial Director:**
Evelyn Veitch

Publisher:
Chris Carson

**Senior Executive Marketing
Manager:**
Don Thompson

Senior Developmental Editor:
Rebecca Rea

Photo Researcher:
Amie Plourde

Permissions Coordinator:
Kristiina Bowering

Production Editor:
Tammy Scherer

Copy Editor:
Eliza Marciniak

Proofreader:
Mariko Obokata

Indexer:
Edwin Durbin

Senior Production Coordinator:
Helen Locsin

Creative Director:
Angela Cluer

Interior Design:
Sarah Battersby

Cover Design:
Roxanna Bennett

Cover Image:
© Ron Fehling/Masterfile

Compositors:
Pamela Clayton/Janet Zanette

Printer:
Transcontinental

**Library and Archives Canada
Cataloguing in Publication**

MacIvor, Heather, 1964-

Canadian politics and government in the Charter era / Heather MacIvor.

Includes index.

ISBN 0-17-641589-0

1. Canada. Canadian Charter of Rights and Freedoms.
2. Canada—Politics and government—1984–1993.
3. Canada—Politics and government—1993- I. Title.

KE4381.5.M42 2005
KF4483.C519M34 2005
342.7108'5   C2004-907275-7

Contents

Preface

Introduction

The Canadian Charter of Rights and Freedoms has been part of our constitution for over twenty years. Most Canadians (at least those outside Quebec) have forgotten the bitter controversies that attended its creation. When it took effect in 1982, the Charter had few cheerleaders and innumerable critics. Opponents claimed that it would destroy the British tradition of parliamentary supremacy, which gives elected legislators the last word on public policy. That power would pass to appointed judges, who would use it to shape the law in accordance with their personal opinions. Other critics dismissed the Charter as a cynical power grab by Prime Minister Pierre Trudeau. The federally appointed Supreme Court would use the Charter to restrict the latitude of provincial governments, especially in the fields of minority language rights and social policy. A third anti-Charter argument condemned its "Americanizing" impact on Canadian politics and culture. Its proponents feared that the U.S. Bill of Rights, and the extensive jurisprudence arising from its provisions, would be imported into Canada without regard for our unique history and culture. Moreover, the judicial review of legislation on the basis of rights and freedoms would allow "special interests" to override Parliament and fragment the body politic.

Two decades later, most Canadians have embraced the Charter. According to opinion surveys, a large majority of us appreciate our entrenched rights and freedoms and approve of their enforcement by the courts. But the critics have not been silenced. They maintain that Canada has been transformed from a democracy governed by elected legislators to a "jurocracy" ruled by unelected judges. Many argue that the political balance has tipped too far in the direction of "rights," particularly the rights of accused or convicted criminals. They also claim that special interests have used the Charter and the courts to override the policy preferences of the majority. Some hot-button issues, like abortion and same-sex marriage, have been framed as clashes between Charter rights (as interpreted by "elitist" judges) and traditional social values.

These controversies, which had simmered for years, flared up during the 2004 federal election campaign. Liberal leader Paul Martin accused Conservative leader Stephen Harper of a hidden agenda. According to Martin, a Harper government would use the notwithstanding clause in the Charter to take away protected rights and freedoms. These allegations, which Harper condemned as "fearmongering," appeared to be supported by comments from some Conservative candidates. In a videotaped interview, veteran MP Randy White chuckled, "To heck with the courts, eh?" Former Justice critic Vic Toews and Ontario MP Cheryl Gallant claimed that a Conservative government would repeal a recent amendment to the hate-crimes law, which made it illegal to incite hatred against gays and lesbians. Harper himself pledged that he would allow free votes on private members' bills concerning social issues, including abortion. Although the precise impact of Charter issues on the election outcome may never be known, the Liberals' surprisingly strong result was widely attributed (in part) to a last-minute switch by voters who feared the Conservatives' social and judicial agenda. If this is accurate, the message seems to be that Charter critics are out of step with majority opinion. Public attacks on entrenched rights and freedoms, and the judges who interpret them, appeal strongly to a minority of Canadians; but they risk alienating many more.

One striking aspect of the 2004 campaign was the frequency of uninformed public comment about the Charter and the courts. There was considerable confusion, among politicians and journalists alike, about whether the Charter protects gays and lesbians from discrimination. Few people seemed to grasp the purpose and effect of the notwithstanding clause. The relationship between the courts and Parliament was often portrayed, inaccurately, as an unequal struggle between powerless MPs and almighty judges. Whatever else one might say about the recent campaign, this much is clear: most Canadians, inside and outside the political arena, need to learn more about government and politics in the Charter era.

The Purposes of This Book

This book is intended to serve two purposes. First, it seeks to provide a comprehensive picture of the Charter and its impact on our political system. Second, it offers students and instructors an alternative to the existing political science texts dealing with the Charter. These books have many virtues. They are well-researched, well-written, and provocative. However, most of them portray the Charter in a consistently negative light. The authors raise legitimate and often unanswerable criticisms, especially about the policy-making power of judges. But there is little attempt to examine the positive effects of the Charter, or to present a balanced analysis of the jurisprudence on rights and freedoms. In my experience, most students share the general view that the Charter is a good thing. Instead of insisting (implicitly) that their perceptions are misguided, this book is designed to give readers the information they need to reach their own conclusions.

Using the Book: A Note to Readers

The topics discussed in this book are wide-ranging and often complicated. Each chapter contains several features that will help you master the material. Every Dossier provides an in-depth analysis of an individual case, or a specific issue, to illustrate the general points made in the regular text. Where appropriate, technical terms are presented in **boldface** and defined in the Glossary of Key Terms at the end of the chapter. You should use the Discussion and Review Questions to test your understanding of the material in each chapter. This will allow you to gauge your progress, and it will help you prepare for classroom discussions and tests. The list of Suggested Readings will be particularly useful to those who plan to write papers on the Charter; these readings should give you a head start as you begin your search for source materials. Some readings, particularly those from legal journals, may be available only in hard copy at a law library. If your university does not have a law school, you may

be able to access most of the recommended articles online. Consult the reference librarians at your campus library for assistance.

This book summarizes a number of important rulings from the Supreme Court of Canada (often referred to, in shorthand terms, as "the Court"). The emphasis on the Supreme Court reflects its status as the final judicial authority in Canada. While every effort has been made to ensure the accuracy of these summaries, they are no substitute for the rulings themselves. The complete text of every Charter ruling from the Supreme Court is available online. Go to the Supreme Court website (www.scc-csc.gc.ca) and click on "Judgments." Follow the links to the LexUM website at the Université de Montréal. You will find a chronological listing of Charter rulings, along with a searchable database. The LexUM site is a superb resource for researchers.

Many important Charter rulings have been issued by provincial Courts of Appeal. Their databases are not as comprehensive, but you can usually find recent decisions online. (If you have access to a law library, you can also consult the *Dominion Law Reports* in bound volumes.) Most of the senior courts in Canada can be accessed through the website of the Canadian Legal Information Institute (www.canlii.org). This site is a gold mine for legal research: it provides searchable access to laws and regulations as well as court rulings.

Most Supreme Court opinions are written in clear and accessible language, although the inherent complexity of the law and the prevalence of legal jargon may pose a few problems for a reader without legal training. (The Glossaries appended to each chapter of this book are intended to clarify the jargon.) The box on page xi offers some advice.

The case summaries in this book use a standard legal citation style. Each citation presents the name of the case (first in full, then with reference to one of the parties), then the paragraph number of the citation (where appropriate), and finally the name of the Justice who authored the particular opinion to which the citation refers. (Where the name of the author is provided in the text, it may not appear in the citation.)

Whether you intend to pursue a political or legal career, or you wish to become better informed about your rights and freedoms, I hope that you will find a

HOW TO READ A SUPREME COURT RULING

When you read a Supreme Court ruling, ask yourself the questions listed below. You may wish to enter these questions into your computer, to use as a template for writing notes on each case. By answering each question, you will create a clear and concise summary of the case, which will make it much easier to write papers or study for tests.

(1) *Facts*
- How many judges are on the panel? (This is usually an odd number, to avoid a tie vote.)
- Who are they?
- What are the dates on which the case was heard and the ruling issued? (Earlier Charter cases tend to be the most influential precedents; later cases contain either a reformulation of an earlier Charter doctrine or a particularly useful application of an existing precedent.)
- Who is the appellant, and who is the respondent? (See the Glossary of Key Terms for Chapter 1 pages 37–38.)
- Are there any intervenors? If so, who are they?
- What are the facts of the case at bar?
- How many opinions does the ruling contain? (These will fall into as many as three categories: the *majority* opinion, one or more *concurring* opinions, and one or more *dissenting* opinions—see the Glossary of Key Terms for Chapter 1 pages 37–38.)

(2) *Issue(s) of Law*
- Which law, policy, or police action is being impugned (i.e., challenged as unconstitutional)?
- Which Charter section(s) is (are) allegedly violated by the impugned law, policy, or police action, and what form does that alleged violation take?
- What is the core issue of law that forms the ground for the appeal to the Supreme Court? (Alternatively, what is/are the constitutional question(s) answered in the ruling?)
- Is a s. 1 analysis required?

(3) *Disposition*
- Is the lower-court ruling upheld, or the appeal dismissed by the majority?
- Is the law, policy, or police action constitutional or unconstitutional?
- What remedy, if any, does the majority impose in the event of a finding of unconstitutionality?

(4) *Reasons*
- What are the key reasons of the majority for their disposition of the case?
- What are the key reasons in the concurring opinion(s), if any? How do they differ from those of the majority?
- What are the key reasons in the dissenting opinion(s), if any? How do they differ from those of the majority?
- What new law, if any, does the majority opinion add to the existing body of Charter jurisprudence?

(5) *Conclusion*
- In a sentence or two, what is the key interpretation (or reinterpretation) of the Charter that emerges from this ruling?
- What precedent(s) does (do) the ruling set for the future?
- What messages or instructions does the majority ruling send to Crown attorneys, defence counsel, police, the lower courts, Canadian citizens, and/or legislators?

useful introduction to the Charter in these pages. The meaning of the entrenched guarantees and their impact on our politics and government are too important to be left to the "experts"—not to mention the misleading rhetoric of politicians and pundits, both pro- and anti-Charter. If this book helps you become a more critical consumer of such rhetoric, then it will have served its primary purpose.

Acknowledgments

This book was inspired by the students in my Charter courses at the University of Windsor. I am grateful for their curiosity, their probing questions, and their willingness to challenge preconceived notions about rights and freedoms. The writing was made possible by the excellent research assistance of Mark Chalmers, a gifted student of law and politics in his own right, and by the generosity and support of friends and family. Kendal McKinney provided the love and encouragement that every writer needs. I am particularly grateful for his patient willingness to discuss obscure points of law and his tolerance for a preoccupied spouse. Thanks to Victoria Cross, and to the organizers of two conferences on the Charter, for giving me the opportunity to present and refine my ideas. Finally, I wish to express my appreciation to the team at Thomson Nelson Publishing, especially Chris Carson and Rebecca Rea, and to the following reviewers for their constructive and helpful suggestions: James Lawson, Memorial University of Newfoundland; Jay Haaland, Kwantlen University College; and Karman Kawchuk, University of Saskatchewan.

This book is dedicated to two new Canadians: Laura and Emily Cabral. May their adopted country give them everything they need to thrive and prosper, and may they enjoy their rights and freedoms (and every other good thing) for many, many years to come.

Introduction

Chapter 1

An Introduction to the Charter

Prime Minister Trudeau looks on as Queen Elizabeth II signs Canada's constitutional proclamation in Ottawa on April 17, 1982.
CP PHOTO

INTRODUCTION

The Canadian Charter of Rights and Freedoms makes up Schedule I of the Appendix to the Constitution Act, 1982. The act came into force on April 17, 1982, with two exceptions: section (s.) 15 of the Charter was delayed for three years, to give the federal and provincial governments time to bring their laws into conformity with it, and the effect of s. 23(1)(a) was suspended until its ratification by a given province (see Chapter 7, pages 224–27). There are 34 sections in the Charter, not including the preamble. The subsequent sections of the Constitution Act, 1982 contain a formula for future amendments, special protections for Aboriginal rights, and an amendment to the division of powers in the Constitution Act, 1867. The act concludes with Part VII, which sets out technical rules for the enforcement and application of the Constitution. The crucial section is 52(1), which declares the Constitution to be "the supreme law of Canada" and directs the courts to strike down laws that conflict with its provisions.[1]

The Constitution Act, 1982 is by far the most important constitutional amendment since Confederation in 1867. It is not, as some people believe, a "new Constitution"; most previous constitutional documents remain in force. The 1982 package is best understood as a supplement to the existing "supreme law," albeit a highly significant supplement. For the first time, the Constitution explicitly empowers the courts to strike down laws that infringe rights and freedoms. In consequence, the relationships between the judiciary and the other branches of government are changing. Policy-makers are now required to take rights and freedoms into account; if they do not, they risk judicial nullification or amendment of their laws. Interest groups with the resources to engage in Charter litigation have influenced public policy, especially in relation to equality rights. The **entrenchment** of rights and freedoms has affected the daily lives of many Canadians in subtle ways. For some, particularly those involved with the criminal justice system, those alterations have been particularly marked.

It would be a mistake, however, to attribute these effects to the Charter alone. The entrenchment of rights and freedoms, in and of itself, changes nothing. Its impact depends on the presence or absence of several other variables:

- a "support structure for legal mobilization," which funds and pursues strategic rights-based litigation on behalf of interest groups and/or individual clients;[2]
- a capable and aggressive judiciary, ready and willing to challenge the other branches of government over the protection of rights and freedoms, and free to set its own agenda;[3]
- policy-makers who take their "first-order" Charter duties seriously, ensuring that proposed laws are compatible with the protected rights and freedoms;[4]
- a political culture that recognizes the importance of rights and freedoms, and broadly accepts the need for judicial intervention where appropriate;[5] and
- implementation mechanisms to give effect to court rulings, which might otherwise be mere paper shields against Charter violations.[6]

To a greater or lesser degree, the first four variables were already present in Canada when the Charter was proclaimed in 1982. Some interest groups, frustrated at their failure to secure policy gains from the legislative and executive branches, began to seek judicial relief in the 1960s and 1970s (and a few even earlier).[7] The rapid expansion of legal education in Canada in the 1960s brought hundreds of young professors into law faculties across the country, many of them products of American graduate schools that emphasized the Bill of Rights. They were liberal in orientation and activist by inclination. Some pursued their interest in rights and freedoms by establishing support networks

for interest litigation.[8] Those networks were fostered and reinforced by the establishment of the Law Reform Commission of Canada and other government agencies, which provided administrative assistance and funding. These developments are discussed in greater detail in Chapter 6.

Meanwhile, Prime Minister Trudeau had given the Supreme Court of Canada greater control over its **docket**, and appointed judges who—unlike their predecessors—did not shrink from questions of public policy.[9] When the Charter took effect, the Court was ready to use it to strike down laws that infringed the protected rights and freedoms (see Chapter 3, pages 93–95). Although policy-makers in the executive branch were initially reluctant to give lawyers too much influence over their decisions, former deputy minister of justice Roger Tassé made sure that a Charter review mechanism (the Human Rights Law Branch) was in place in April 1982.[10] The changing roles of Parliament and the executive under the Charter are explained in Chapters 4 and 5 respectively. Finally, the political culture that would legitimize judicial review on Charter grounds evolved throughout the second half of the twentieth century and coalesced during the 1980–82 hearings of the Special Joint Committee on Constitution of Canada (see Chapter 2, pages 69–76).

The missing element, both before and since 1982, is the implementation of Court rulings. Chapter 3, pages 126–28, takes a look at the various populations that are affected by a particular judgment, and the ways in which they can, if they choose, prevent Charter remedies from being put into effect. While it is often tempting to assume that a particular court ruling—e.g., *Brown v. Board of Education* and *Miranda v. Arizona* in the United States, *R. v. Stinchcombe* and *R. v. Sparrow* in Canada[11]—has had an enormous and positive impact on the lives of the people whom it affects, the reality is more complex. We cannot automatically assume that either the Charter or its interpretation by the courts has magically transformed social policy, criminal justice, or the lives of Aboriginal Canadians.

This chapter provides a brief primer on the Charter: what it says, what it means, and how it works. We begin with the concepts of constitutionalism and the rule of law, and their expression in a written constitution. Among other things, written constitutions are intended to restrain the power of the legislative and executive branches of government. They cannot serve this purpose unless they are interpreted and enforced by a strong judiciary. Therefore, the Charter's impact cannot be understood without a discussion of judicial review. The chapter also offers a brief summary of what the Charter says, and explains why it applies to some people and agencies but not to others. The chapter concludes with a brief discussion of the Canadian controversy over judicial review in the Charter era and a preview of the rest of the book.

THE NATURE AND PURPOSES OF A WRITTEN CONSTITUTION

Constitutionalism and the Rule of Law

The Charter of Rights and Freedoms is a part of Canada's Constitution. In the simplest terms, the **constitution** of a given country is the set of binding norms and principles that regulate the legitimate exercise of political power.[12] If we dissect this definition into its various components, we find that a constitution is supposed to do at least four things:

1. It establishes the institutions of government, defines the powers and responsibilities of each one, and prescribes the relationships among them.
2. It describes, in broad outlines, the processes by which binding rules may be made, applied, and interpreted; in so doing, it translates raw power into legitimate authority.
3. It restricts the power of the state vis-à-vis the citizens over whom it governs.
4. It expresses the shared values of the population, symbolizing the political community which has—at least in theory—agreed to be bound by its terms.

The distinction between arbitrary power and legitimate authority underpins the very idea of a constitution. Dossier 1.1 summarizes the Canadian **jurisprudence** on two related concepts: constitutionalism and the rule of law.

DOSSIER 1.1

CONSTITUTIONALISM AND THE RULE OF LAW IN CANADA

In 1998, in response to a reference question from the federal government, the Supreme Court of Canada ruled on the constitutionality of a unilateral declaration of independence (UDI) by a province.[1] The separatist government of Quebec had long claimed that a majority decision in a provincial referendum would be sufficient to legitimize the province's secession from Canada. In the *Secession Reference* decision, the Supreme Court identified four "organizing principles" of the Canadian Constitution: "federalism, democracy, constitutionalism and the rule of law, and respect for minority rights."[2] While these unwritten principles cannot override the written Constitution, which "promotes legal certainty and predictability, and ... provides a foundation and a touchstone for the exercise of

constitutional judicial review,"[3] judges should refer to them when they interpret entrenched constitutional laws.[4] When necessary, the "organizing principles" should be used to "fill gaps" in those laws.[5]

The Court identified three elements in the rule of law principle:

- the supremacy of law over both private citizens and public officials, which prohibits the arbitrary exercise of power;[6]
- "the creation and maintenance of an actual order of positive laws which preserves and embodies the more general principle of normative order";[7] and
- the idea that "the exercise of all public power must find its ultimate source in a legal rule."[8]

(continued)

The third element, which the Court dubbed "constitutionalism," demands that "all government action comply with the Constitution."[9]

> This Court has noted on several occasions that with the adoption of the *Charter*, the Canadian system of government was transformed to a significant extent from a system of Parliamentary supremacy to one of constitutional supremacy. The Constitution binds all governments, both federal and provincial, including the executive branch.... They may not transgress its provisions: indeed, their sole claim to exercise lawful authority rests in the powers allocated to them under the Constitution, and can come from no other source.[10]

In effect, constitutionalism serves as a constraint on democratic government. That constraint is reflected in the process of entrenchment, which safeguards the rule of law from the ambitions of the powerful and the passing whims of the majority. The procedures for amending the entrenched written constitution are necessarily more demanding than the rules for amending ordinary legislation, as a brake on democratic "majority rule": "By requiring broad support in the form of an 'enhanced majority' to achieve constitutional change, the Constitution ensures that minority interests must be addressed before proposed changes which would affect them may be enacted."[11] In general, "Constitutionalism facilitates—indeed, makes possible—a democratic political system by creating an orderly framework within which people may make political decisions."[12] Therefore, the Court concluded that democracy alone, as reflected by a majority vote for sovereignty in a provincial referendum, would be insufficient to legitimize a UDI. The principles of federalism, constitutionalism, and the rule of law require an orderly process of political negotiation among the ten provinces and the national government, culminating in a formal amendment to the written Constitution, before a province could legally separate from Canada.

ENDNOTES

1. *Reference re Secession of Quebec*, [1998] 2 S.C.R. 217.

2. Ibid., paragraph 49, *per curiam*.

3. Ibid., paragraph 53.

4. See also *Re Manitoba Language Rights*, [1985] 1 S.C.R. 721, paragraph 67, *per curiam*.

5. *Reference re Remuneration of Judges of the Provincial Court (P.E.I.)*, [1997] 3 S.C.R. 3, paragraph 104, per Lamer C.J.

6. *Re Manitoba Language Rights, paragraph 59, per curiam*. In this case, the Court ruled that the guarantee of bilingualism in the Manitoba Act, 1870 had been violated whenever the provincial legislature adopted a law in English only. Hundreds of unilingual, and hence unconstitutional, statutes were declared null and void. However, the Court suspended the effect of the declaration to give the government of Manitoba time to readopt bilingual versions of the impugned laws. Had the declaration taken effect immediately, the ruling would have created a legal vacuum and effectively suspended the rule of law in the province. As explained in Chapter 12, page 375, this case did not engage the Charter.

7. *Re Manitoba Language Rights*, paragraphs 59 and 60, *per curiam*.

8. *Reference re Remuneration of Judges of the Provincial Court (P.E.I.), per* Lamer C.J. This ruling defined the sources and scope of judicial independence from the other two branches of government.

9. *Reference re Secession of Quebec*, paragraph 72, *per curiam*.

10. Ibid., paragraph 72.

11. Ibid., paragraph 77, *per curiam*.

12. Ibid., paragraph 78.

The rule of law principle is a central theme in Western political thought. The idea that law, not men, should rule goes all the way back to the *Politics* of Aristotle (written in the fourth century B.C.E.). The importance of law as a civilizing force, and as a bulwark of societal peace and order, was also recognized by the ancient Greeks. Aristotle wrote that the man who lives outside the state, and outside the law, is a beast. Man may be born with the potential for goodness and reason, but this potential cannot develop in the absence of good laws (both written and unwritten). Finally, the claim that "public power" should arise from law, not from arbitrary seizure or brutal oppression, is a central component of liberal political theory, from John Locke in the late seventeenth century to John Stuart Mill in the nineteenth century and beyond.

The basic premise of constitutionalism—that the actions of rulers can and should be judged by a higher standard than mere expediency or self-interest[13]—is grounded in the ancient notion of natural law.[14] The core premise of natural law is that every human being is bound by a set of unwritten rules that transcend human-made, or positive, law. These rules are generally attributed to a divine lawgiver (e.g., the Judeo-Christian God). They are discoverable by human reason; they are morally binding on all people, including rulers; and they are the same everywhere, at least in broad outline, although the details of their application may vary in different societies. Where a positive law conflicts with the natural law, the former is deemed to be unjust.[15] It follows that a human-made law that violates universal moral principles may be disobeyed, if such disobedience does not cause greater harm than the law itself.

The idea of a natural law has great appeal for critics of the legal and political status quo. It can also be a useful tool for rulers who wish to legitimate their power, as the Roman emperors discovered. They turned the broad principles of Stoic natural law into the *jus gentium* ("law of the peoples"), a set of flexible legal rules that united the far-flung and diverse Empire under a single code of law. But natural law has never been particularly effective in restricting the power of rulers, for at least two reasons.[16] First, its content is inherently and inescapably subjective.[17]

You and I may agree, for example, that it is wrong for one human being to kill another, but we may differ profoundly over the practical application of that rule. Does it apply to active euthanasia? What about passive euthanasia? What about abortion, self-defence, or a "just war"? Because it lacks the clarity and precision of written law, natural law cannot establish clear limits on state power. Second, natural law cannot be enforced. Whereas the state can deploy police and bureaucrats to enforce its laws, and send violators to prison, those who infringe the natural law face no such organized sanction. When that infringement has been committed by a powerful ruler, who will punish him or her for it?

Since the eighteenth century, these criticisms have been supplemented by a growing attack on the very sources and moral legitimacy of natural law. If I believe that these unwritten moral principles are laid down by my God, and that their binding force ultimately derives from religious teachings, can I impose them on people who do not share my faith? In a diverse society—indeed, in any society where religion and politics are separate—unwritten moral rules grounded in sacred dogma cannot provide a sound basis for political and legal consensus. A secular replacement must be found. Ideally, this will consist of written principles with some kind of enforcement mechanism. The alternative, to abandon the idea of a "higher law" altogether, risks unrestrained tyranny.

In 1787, the framers of the American Constitution set out to create a "higher law" with the precision of positive law. In the process, they created the modern doctrine of constitutionalism: the effective restraint on government power through a written document.[18] The framers were influenced by John Locke and other liberal thinkers: they located the source of legitimate authority, not in divine Providence, but in the consent of the governed. They addressed the problem of subjectivity by crafting a written statement of principles, including a Bill of Rights that would limit legitimate state interference with individual rights and freedoms. But one problem remained: the Constitution lacked an "effective institutional means for enforcing the positively embodied higher principles of law within the polity."[19] If the legislative branch (Congress) or the executive branch (the president and cabinet) overreached the powers assigned to them in articles 1 and 2 respectively, where was the remedy?

The answer, according to one of the framers, lay in article 3: "the judicial Power of the United States, shall be vested in one supreme Court." In the *Federalist Papers*, a series of newspaper articles written in defence of the new Constitution, Alexander Hamilton argued that an independent judiciary would be the bulwark of the "higher law." The duty of the courts "must be to declare all acts contrary to the manifest tenor of the Constitution void. Without this, all the reservations of particular rights or privileges would amount to nothing."[20] Acknowledging that this argument appeared to place the appointed judiciary above the elected legislature, Hamilton explained that none of the three branches of government—legislative, executive, or judicial—would be supreme over the others. Rather, the role of the courts was to ensure that other two branches obeyed the will of the people as embodied in their Constitution.

> The interpretation of the laws is the proper and peculiar province of the courts. A constitution is, in fact, and must be regarded by the judges as, fundamental law. It therefore belongs to them to ascertain its meaning as well as the meaning of any particular act proceeding from the legislative body. If there should happen to be an irreconcilable variance between the two ... the Constitution ought to be preferred to the statute, the intention of the people to the intention of their agents.[21]

Taken literally, this argument suggested that the new United States would be governed not by the Constitution but by the judges who interpreted it. Seeking to assuage fears of judicial supremacy, Hamilton pointed out that the courts had "no influence over either the sword or the purse" and could "take no active resolution whatever." Even the Supreme Court "must ultimately depend upon the aid of the executive arm ... for the efficacy of its judgements."[22] Nonetheless, Hamilton implied that the moral authority of the Constitution would become a vital resource for its judicial interpreters; as long as they expounded the Constitution in a manner consistent with "the intention of the people," the Justices of the Supreme Court would be capable of restraining the other two branches.

Hamilton's hopes for the new Supreme Court went unfulfilled for almost two decades. Finally, in 1803, Chief Justice John Marshall laid the legal foundations of judicial review. Writing for the Court in the case of *Marbury v. Madison*, Marshall repeated Hamilton's claim that the ultimate authority in the new Republic lay in the people whose will was expressed in the Constitution. The proper interpretation of that Constitution was vested in the courts, not in the elected Congress:

> The powers of the Legislature are defined and limited; and that those limits may not be mistaken or forgotten, the Constitution is written. To what purpose are powers limited, and to what purpose is that limitation committed to writing, if these limits may at any time be passed by those intended to be restrained? The distinction between a government with limited and unlimited powers is abolished if those limits do not confine the persons on whom they are imposed, and if acts prohibited and acts allowed are of equal obligation. It is a proposition too plain to be contested that the Constitution controls any legislative act repugnant to it....
>
> Certainly all those who have framed written Constitutions contemplate them as forming the fundamental and paramount law of the nation, and consequently the theory of every such government must be that an act of the Legislature repugnant to the Constitution is void.... It is emphatically the province and duty of the Judicial Department to say what the law is.[23]

Sixteen years later, still Chief Justice of the United States, Marshall delivered another seminal opinion. In discussing the principles of constitutional drafting and interpretation, he wrote the following:

> A Constitution, to contain an accurate detail of all the subdivisions of which its great powers will admit, and of all the means by which they may be carried into execution, would partake of the prolixity of a legal code, and could scarcely be embraced by the human mind. It would prob-

ably never be understood by the public. Its nature, therefore, requires that only its great outlines should be marked, its important objects designated, and the minor ingredients which compose those objects be deduced from the nature of the objects themselves. That this idea was entertained by the framers of the American Constitution is not only to be inferred from the nature of the instrument, but from the language.... In considering this question, then, we must never forget that it is a Constitution we are expounding.[24]

To have prescribed the means by which Government should, in all future time, execute its powers would have been to change entirely the character of the instrument and give it the properties of a legal code. It would have been an unwise attempt to provide by immutable rules for exigencies which, if foreseen at all, must have been seen dimly, and which can be best provided for as they occur.[25]

In these two decisions, Marshall staked a daring claim for his Court. He argued that "the people" had entrusted it with three crucial tasks: (1) to enforce limits on the power of the other two branches of government; (2) to strike down laws "repugnant to the Constitution"; and (3) to "deduce" specific principles from the general language of its provisions. By grounding the power of judicial review in the Constitution's status as supreme law, rather than the division of powers among the three branches of the federal government, Marshall gave the legal profession an interpretive monopoly over its meaning. The Constitution would belong, not to the "political branches" or the citizenry, but to judges and lawyers.[26] Over time, Marshall's doctrine of judicial review has been embraced by his successors on the U.S. Supreme Court. Today, many observers argue that the Court has distorted the original intent of the Founding Fathers by creating judicial supremacy in the guise of constitutionalism: "By treating the Constitution mainly as a set of legal restraints rather than an instrument enabling self-government, the Court has made more plausible the idea that constitutional interpretation is exclusively the province of lawyers."[27]

Until recently, Canada's political tradition has been more deeply imprinted by the British experience than by the American example. Before the proclamation of the Charter, the guiding principle of our Constitution was the supremacy of Parliament. True, the Constitution Act, 1867 divided legislative powers between the federal and provincial governments; but within its proper sphere, the House of Commons or a provincial legislature could legislate as it pleased. The courts could strike down laws, but only when those laws had been enacted by the "wrong" level of government —say, a provincial law that created a serious criminal offence, or a federal law concerning "property and civil rights." In principle, any law that was found to be *ultra vires* (beyond the power of) the sponsoring legislature could be validly enacted by the other level of government. We will return to the history of pre-Charter judicial review in Chapter 2, pages 49–67.

Perhaps the most significant change wrought by the Constitution Act, 1982 is the remedial power conferred on the courts by ss. 24(1) and 52(1). Section 24(1) allows anyone whose Charter rights have been infringed—by the wording of a law, by the decision of a public official, or by a process of government—to seek a remedy in the courts. Section 52(1) declares that any law that conflicts with the Constitution, the "supreme law of Canada," is null and void "to the extent of the inconsistency." Although the two sections may appear to overlap, the distinction is clear in practice. Imagine that X has been unjustly convicted of a criminal offence. At the appellate stage, X has two remedial options under the Charter: to have the law under which he was convicted declared unconstitutional, or to seek a new trial on the grounds that the first was procedurally flawed. Recourse to s. 52(1) makes it unnecessary to invoke s. 24, according to the Supreme Court of Canada: "The supremacy of the Constitution declared in s. 52 dictates that no one can be convicted under an unconstitutional law."[28] In the absence of a challenge to the specific statute, X may still find a remedy in the due-process guarantees of legal rights.

Both sections derive their power from the doctrine of judicial review. The judicial branch of government decides whether, and to what extent, a law or action is "inconsistent with" the Constitution. In the process, it identifies the proper limits to the authority of the legislative and executive branches and imposes remedies for the arbitrary use of power. This is the same type of judicial review envisaged by Chief Justice Marshall two centuries ago. Some observers argue that the Charter has imported American-style "judicial supremacy" into Canada; others claim that the Constitution, not the judges, is supreme. That controversy is discussed at the end of this chapter.

Written versus Unwritten Constitutional Rules

A constitution is more than a set of entrenched written rules. Although this book focuses on entrenched constitutional text, three additional elements of a constitution bear mention:

1. nonentrenched written law;
2. unwritten constitutional conventions; and
3. the common law (also called case law).

Nonentrenched written laws are sometimes called quasi-constitutional documents. In form, they are ordinary statutes, but their purpose—to regulate the legitimate operation of political institutions—elevates them above regular legislation. Canadian examples include the 1960 Bill of Rights[29] and the 2000 Clarity Act.[30] **Constitutional conventions** are unwritten rules of political procedure that are morally and politically binding on governments. Unlike written laws, they are not enforceable by the courts.[31] Because they evolve over time, conventions allow the constitution to "[adapt] to changes in the general political principles and values of the day, without the need for formal amendment of existing positive law."[32] Some Canadian constitutional conventions are markedly different from the entrenched text. For example, the Constitution Act, 1867 vests executive power in the Queen and, for day-to-day purposes, in the "Governor in Council." In reality, executive power is exercised by the prime minister and cabinet, neither of which is mentioned in the document.

The **common law**, like constitutional conventions, evolves and builds up over time. As Justice Marshall pointed out, a constitution is necessarily written in very broad and general language. The drafters cannot predict the future; they cannot foresee the social and economic development of their societies, or the constitutional adaptations that such development will demand. This difficulty is not unique to constitutions. Every law must be written broadly enough to cover unexpected circumstances, while specifying clearly which actions are permitted and which are not. Over two millennia ago, Aristotle identified the solution: to give judges the power to interpret broadly worded laws and apply them to the facts of individual cases.[33] This principle of judicial interpretation, which Aristotle called "equity," remains at least as important today as it was in ancient Athens.

As the courts interpret the constitution, applying it to case after individual case, consistent principles emerge. The principles enshrined in these precedents are binding on lower courts. The rulings of the Supreme Court of Canada cannot be disregarded by the trial or appeal courts in the provinces and territories. (See the discussion of *stare decisis* in Chapter 3, pages 103–4.) To understand the binding force of precedents, we must understand what an appellate judge is doing when she writes a decision. First, and most important, the judge must dispose of the case at bar. Except in reference cases, the adversarial system in Canadian courts requires the judge to resolve a dispute between two parties. In division-of-powers cases, the parties are the federal government and one or more provinces. Charter challenges to the validity of a law, or the constitutionality of a state action, pit the responsible government against the plaintiff(s). Civil disputes embroil two private parties. Where the judge finds that one of the parties is at fault, she may grant a remedy to the other party. This process is called **adjudication**.

Second, an appeals judge must be mindful of the precedent that her ruling will set for the future. What she considers to be the proper resolution of an individual case may establish a principle of law that could be harmful if applied in different circumstances—hence the old saying that "hard cases make bad law."[34] The higher the court, the more weight must be given to the precedential impact of the ruling. A poorly reasoned ruling from the Supreme Court of Canada could (and occasionally does[35]) create legal and administrative problems across the country. So the reasons for the disposition—the *ratio decidendi*—must be stated as precisely, and their application limited as narrowly, as possible. This is particularly true when the judge is writing a **majority opinion**. Appellate panels are always odd-numbered, to ensure a clear majority for either the **appellant** or the **respondent**. When the court issues two or more judgments in a particular case, only the one that is formally endorsed by the majority of the panel sets a binding legal precedent. A minority opinion may be either a **concurring judgment**, in which one or more judges agrees with the disposition of the case for reasons that differ from those of the majority, or a **dissenting judgment**. In the latter instance, a judge rejects both the disposition of the case and the reasoning on which it rests. While dissents do not set binding legal precedents, it is a mistake to dismiss them as pointless or self-indulgent. Today's dissent may become tomorrow's majority opinion.[36] Even in the relatively brief history of the Charter, a few dissenting judgments have subsequently been adopted by Supreme Court majorities and thus transformed into binding law.[37] Other dissents have been enacted into statute law by Parliament, as we will see in Chapter 4.

Third, a judge may wish to comment on some aspect of law or public policy that does not bear directly on the disposition of the case at bar but raises the same or similar issues. Consequently, many appellate judgments contain two distinct types of argument. The *ratio decidendi* ("reasons for judgment") is the argument in support of the judge's disposition of the case. The *ratio* contains the principles of law through which the common law evolves—those that bind lower courts and set the legal direction for the future. *Obiter dicta* ("marginal comments") allow the judge to air her views on the issues of the case in a way that will not tie the hands of future courts. By distinguishing clearly between *ratio* and *obiter*, a judge can settle the dispute at bar and contribute to public debate without setting a dangerous legal precedent. However, this distinction is not always clear; lower courts can find it difficult to determine which statements in a Supreme Court ruling are binding and which are not.[38]

When lawyers raise constitutional issues in court, they rely on precedents to support their claims on behalf of their clients. Take the example of a lawyer whose client endured a three-year wait between a formal criminal charge and the start of his trial. The lawyer knows that in the 1990 *Askov* ruling,[39] the Supreme Court of Canada held that an excessive delay between the preliminary hearing and the start of trial violated s. 11(b) of the Charter (see Dossier 3.4, pages 120–21). She also knows that the remedy in that case was a **stay** of all charges against the accused. Based on that precedent, the lawyer submits a motion to the trial judge—an "*Askov* application"—for a stay of proceedings against her client. Unless the facts of the case at bar are so significantly different from those in *Askov* that the judge can **distinguish the precedent**, he may have no choice but to dismiss the charges.

The *Askov* example illustrates the importance of case law in interpreting the Charter. The words on the page tell us relatively little about the content of the rights and freedoms protected therein. As we have seen, this uncertainty arises from the vagueness of constitutional language. What does the word "unreasonable" mean in s. 8? Does it mean the same thing in s. 11(a)? What is a "reasonable limit prescribed by law" (s. 1), and how would we know one if we saw it? These broad outlines are filled in by judicial reasoning, one case at a time. Critics argue that the words in the Charter mean whatever the judges want them to mean,[40] just as the similarly vague expressions in the American Bill of Rights have gradually acquired meaning over two centuries of judicial interpretation:

> Nonlawyers may not know the meaning of the term "freedom of speech" because they are not part of the community that defines this term, with its accepted prototypical cases and its shared but contingent background assumptions about substantive issues. Any particular understanding of the words "freedom of speech" or "equal" will require much more than a dictionary or a language lesson.[41]

As Chapter 3, pages 102–4, explains, a judge cannot twist the words in a constitution to suit his own personal preferences. He is constrained by precedent, written and unwritten rules of legal interpretation, and the need to win the backing of other judges on the court. On the other hand, judges are required to apply the often vague Charter guarantees to individual cases and, in the process, they may infer meanings that a nonlawyer could not have gleaned from the text. It was argued earlier that one cannot understand the day-to-day operation of the Canadian government from reading the text of the Constitution Act, 1867. The unwritten conventions inherited from Britain, including responsible cabinet government and the office of prime minister, must be taken into consideration. Similarly, one cannot fully grasp the meaning of a particular Charter guarantee without some knowledge of the cases discussed in Part 3 of this book.

THE CONTENT OF THE CHARTER

Table 1.1 **Categorizing the Sections in the Charter**

Category	Relevant Charter Sections
Rights	3–23 (plus ss. 35 and 35.1 of the Constitution Act, 1982)
Freedoms	2
Rules of Interpretation	1, 25–31
Remedies	24 (plus s. 52(1) of the Constitution Act, 1982)
Miscellaneous	32–34

The content of the Charter may be divided into five categories: rights, freedoms, rules of interpretation, remedies, and miscellaneous provisions.

Rights and Freedoms

In theory, a right implies a positive entitlement, while a freedom implies an absence of external restraint. In other words, my right to vote entitles me to demand certain things—such as a public polling place and a secret ballot—from the state. My right creates a corresponding government duty. In contrast, my freedom to express my political opinions exists independently of any state action. To respect my freedom, all the government has to do is refrain from censoring me or punishing me for expressing an unpopular viewpoint; it is not required to provide me with a platform and a megaphone.[42]

In common language, the distinction between rights and freedoms is not entirely clear. Some "fundamental freedoms" or "civil liberties" are also referred to as "human rights." Nor is the difference necessarily apparent in the Charter itself. For example, the section on mobility rights (s. 6) protects the "right" of Canadian citizens and permanent residents to live and work in any province. But is choosing a place of residence a "right"—which implies positive state action of some sort—or a "freedom" with which no government can legitimately interfere? Other rights are easier to distinguish. The guarantees of legal due process and minority language education are clearly intended to serve a remedial purpose. They require government actors to do certain things that they might not otherwise do, or to perform their existing duties in particular ways.

In an ordered society, rights and freedoms cannot trump all other considerations. They must not be exercised without regard for (1) the rights and freedoms of others or (2) other social values that are not expressed in the language of rights. For example, the Charter guarantee of free expression does not license Canadians to incite hatred or violence against a particular group of people. A Charter guarantee does not trump the moral obligation of each individual to respect the needs and the human dignity of others. In general, "rights talk" offers a partial, and arguably misleading, picture of human nature. It emphasizes the "lone rights-bearer," and overlooks the complex web of emotional attachments that gives meaning to our lives.[43] Bills of rights are mere legal instruments; they cannot cure all social ills.

Within their limitations, constitutional guarantees of rights and freedoms serve a useful purpose. They require policy-makers to consider a variety of differing needs and perspectives, and to balance them against other imperatives (e.g., administrative expediency or fiscal constraints). They restrain the arbitrary power of the state, by requiring it to justify incursions into the sphere of individual conscience. Perhaps most important, bills of rights set a moral standard for the treatment of individuals and groups that—although not binding on private actors—symbolizes the equal worth and dignity of each person. For hundreds of years, these advantages have inspired demands for the legal recognition of rights and freedoms.

Human rights claims are often divided into three "generations," based on a rough chronology of their origins. Some "first-generation rights," those pertaining to citizenship and basic liberties, are perhaps better understood as freedoms; others, which relate to the status of a person suspected of a criminal offence, involve claims against the state and are thus clearly in the "rights" category. The first-generation rights include:

> freedom of personal conscience and expression; freedom of movement and association; freedom to vote and run for public office; reliable legal protection against violence; and the various due process rights, like the right to be considered innocent before proven guilty of a crime and the right to a public trial before an impartial jury.[44]

These are the classic liberal claims against the state, grounded in the Enlightenment belief that each man was entitled to certain rights and liberties by virtue of his reason. In its origins—the writings of John Locke,[45] the natural-law tradition, and the American Revolution[46]—liberalism was a struggle against the arbitrary and irresponsible power of kings and queens. The emphasis on individual freedom from government interference was entirely appropriate under those circumstances.

By the late nineteenth century, much of the first-generation agenda had been completed—at least in Britain, the "white dominions," and the United States. Although there were still, even in these countries, millions of people who could not vote and for whom "due process" was an unattainable ideal, some progress had been made. At this juncture, claims for what are now called "second-generation" rights—economic, social, and cultural claims against the state—gained public attention.[47] These were inspired less by the liberal emphasis on liberty and private property than by socialist demands for equality and social justice. Second-generation rights include "a subsistence level of income, basic level of education and health care, clean water and air, and equal opportunity at work."[48] The notion of an economic "right" is controversial, largely because of its financial implications. If each and every Canadian has a "right" to these material benefits, with the same moral weight as his or her "right" to free speech or a fair trial, a government that does not provide them—or that provides them to some citizens but not to others—may violate the Constitution. Moreover, the entrenchment of economic "rights" could shift fiscal decision-making from the legislature to the judiciary and open up private transactions to constitutional review. (For this reason, the proposal to entrench property rights in the Charter failed.)

In the twentieth century, a "third generation" of rights claims emerged. These claims to "equality and recognition"[49] do not merely engage national governments; they challenge the world to respond. The list includes "national self-determination, economic development, a clean environment, affirmative action programs, the survival of one's mother tongue as a functioning language, parental leave benefits, [and] various minority group rights."[50] The idea that every human being has the right to be valued and respected, that each has an inherent dignity that no public authority may legitimately damage, lies at the heart of third-generation claims. Such claims were inspired, in part, by the American civil rights movement of the late 1950s and 1960s. Although the movement began with African-Americans demanding their first- and second-generation rights—voting and access to public education—it quickly came to focus on the human dignity and worth of "Negroes." When Rosa Parks refused to give up her seat on a Montgomery bus to a white man, she implicitly demanded that her society and government recognize her as a human being worthy of respect. That emphasis on human dignity and recognition inspired activists around the world, from the women's and "gay liberation" movements in North America and *souverainisme* in Quebec to anti-colonialism in Africa and Asia.

Whereas the first-generation rights pertain to the individual (apart from the right to physical security), those in the second generation are primarily collective rights. It would be absurd for me to claim an individual right to clean air or a fully staffed hospital; these are common goods, which we expect governments to provide to everyone. Most third-generation rights, by their very nature, are collective. If I am Cree, I may claim an entitlement to speak my ancestral language, but that entitlement is meaningless without other Cree-speakers who can understand what I am saying. A "right" to national self-determination can be exercised only by a group of people large enough to sustain the costs and the responsibilities of a sovereign state. The distinction between individual and collective rights is rarely clear-cut, but the following formula may be helpful: I can claim an individual right by virtue of my status as a human being, whereas a collective right attaches to my status as a member of a particular group (e.g., an Aboriginal nation or an official-language minority).

All three "generations" appear in the United Nations documents on human rights, from the Universal Declaration of 1948 to the two Covenants—on Civil and Political Rights, and on Economic, Social and Cultural Rights—ratified in 1976. They can also be found in Canada's Charter. The first-generation rights are guaranteed by ss. 2, 3–5, and 7–14: fundamental freedoms, democratic rights, and legal rights. The principal second-generation right, equality before and under the law, is located in s. 15(1). Third-generation rights are located in ss. 15(2) (affirmative action), 16–23 (minority language rights), 25 and 35 (Aboriginal and treaty rights), 27 (multiculturalism), and 28 (gender). This categorization is not water-tight, because some Charter sections overlap two or more "generations"; for example, s. 14—guaranteeing an interpreter in court proceedings—touches on both legal rights and minority language or multicultural rights. But it is important to distinguish among the various generations of rights. The features that make our Charter unique—the language and mobility rights—belong to the third generation. Those claims have not been fully accepted by jurists, perhaps because they lack the centuries of common-law grounding and tradition that underlie the first-generation guarantees. Conse-quently, as Chapters 7, pages 224–29 and 12, pages 375–77 explain, they have left a smaller footprint on Charter jurisprudence than the sections with longer pedigrees.

A final comment about the rights in the Charter concerns the obligations that each imposes on the state. Most of the first-generation rights are "negative": they merely restrain the government from doing particular things. Conversely, many of the second- and third-generation rights impose "positive" duties on the state to provide social, economic, and cultural benefits. Despite the inclusion of these rights in the Charter, there is as yet no consensus about the balance between "negative" and "positive" rights. With some

exceptions,[51] the Supreme Court has interpreted the entrenched rights and freedoms as constraints on government power.[52] However, the Justices appear to be increasingly sympathetic to claims that the Charter requires the state to provide certain goods; see the discussion of the *Gosselin* case in Chapter 13, page 394.

Rules of Interpretation

Rules of interpretation instruct judges to read and apply entrenched rights and freedoms in particular ways. By far, the most important of the interpretive clauses is s. 1, the external limitation clause, which we will discuss below. Sections 25, 27, and 28 instruct courts to take particular interests into account—Aboriginal, multicultural, and gender respectively—when they interpret the rights and freedoms in the Charter. Of the three, s. 27 appears to have had some impact on the Supreme Court's approach to rights and freedoms;[53] ss. 25 and 28 have been all but ignored in Charter jurisprudence (see Chapter 12, pages 377–79). Section 26 protects non-Charter rights from derogation on the grounds of their omission. It may have the effect of entrenching those sections of the 1960 Bill of Rights that were not replicated in the Charter (see Dossier 2.9, pages 68–69). Section 29 protects the historic rights of Catholic and other denominational schools against the potential impact of ss. 2(a) and 15(1).[54] Sections 30–32 clarify the relationship between the Charter and the existing division of powers, not just between the federal and provincial governments but among the various branches of government.

In practice, an interpretive clause is only one factor to be taken into account when a judge makes a Charter ruling. The Supreme Court has adopted its own rules of Charter interpretation, which are discussed in Chapter 3. Judges are also guided by common-law rules of construction (e.g., the "mischief rule" discussed in Dossier 1.6, pages 27–30.[55] Despite their entrenchment, the interpretive clauses in the Charter do not "trump" alternative approaches to the language of the guarantees.

Remedies and Enforcement

The two key remedial sections are s. 24 of the Charter and s. 52(1) of the Constitution Act, 1982. Section 24(1) allows anyone whose rights and freedoms have been infringed to seek a remedy from the courts. Section 24(2) is narrower in scope: it requires judges to exclude evidence from a criminal trial if its admission would "bring the administration of justice into disrepute." In practice, s. 24 is most often used to enforce the legal rights in ss. 7–14: if a police officer, Crown prosecutor, or trial judge acts in a way that violates Charter guarantees of due process, an appellate court can quash the resulting conviction and order a new trial. If the Charter infringement has tainted some or all of the evidence against the accused,

that evidence may not be admitted at the retrial. In extreme cases, appeals judges may stay the charges against the accused.

The broad language of s. 24(1) authorizes courts to impose creative remedies for Charter violations, so long as these are "appropriate and just in the circumstances." They may not trespass on the legitimate powers of the legislative and executive branches of government, except where absolutely necessary.[56] Dossier 1.2 summarizes a recent case dealing with the limits of the courts' remedial power under s. 24(1).

DOSSIER 1.2

DOUCET-BOUDREAU V. NOVA SCOTIA (2003)

In November 2003, the Supreme Court of Canada upheld a remedial order issued by a superior-court judge in Nova Scotia. That judge had ordered the provincial government to provide the necessary accommodations for francophone students, as a remedy for violations of the minority language education rights in the Charter. More controversially, he had added an unusual requirement: the provincial authorities responsible for providing the French-language programs under his order would continue to report to him on their progress until all elements of the remedial order had been completed. In most cases, judges issue orders but stop short of enforcing them. The case of *Doucet-Boudreau v. Nova Scotia* is unusual, because the judge of first instance decided that his orders would not be properly carried out unless he retained the jurisdiction to monitor compliance and issue further orders if necessary.

The Nova Scotia Court of Appeal upheld most of the earlier judgment, but overturned the enforcement order. That reversal was appealed to the Supreme Court of Canada, which split 5-4 over the question of continuing judicial involvement in remedial enforcement. For the majority, Justices Iacobucci and Arbour declared that s. 24(1) gave courts the power to do whatever

was "appropriate and just" to ensure that Charter remedies were carried out. They argued that "The requirement of a generous and expansive interpretive approach holds equally true for Charter remedies as for Charter rights,"[1] citing the ancient rule of *ubi jus, ibi remedium* ("Where there is a right, there must be a remedy"). These principles apply with particular force to the guarantee of minority language rights in s. 23, which was expressly intended to redress the lack of educational facilities for official-language minorities (see Chapter 7, pages 224–27). While acknowledging that "courts must be sensitive to their role as judicial arbiters and not fashion remedies which usurp the role of the other branches of governance,"[2] Iacobucci and Arbour asserted that "Deference ends ... where the constitutional rights that the courts are charged with protecting begin."[3] In the context of the case at bar, and in light of the historic inadequacy of francophone schooling in Nova Scotia, the extraordinary jurisdiction assumed by the trial judge fell within the scope of the powers granted to the judicial branch by the Charter.

In the course of their ruling, the two Justices set out five criteria for an "appropriate and just" remedy under s. 24(1):

(continued)

- First, the remedy must "meaningfully vindicate" the violated Charter right or freedom. A judicial remedy whose practical effect is blunted by "procedural delays and difficulties" is neither appropriate nor just.[4]

- Second, the remedy must respect the constitutional division of powers, although the degree of respect should vary with the subject matter of the case: "A remedy may be appropriate and just notwithstanding that it might touch on functions that are principally assigned to the executive. The essential point is that the courts must not, in making orders under s. 24(1), depart unduly or unnecessarily from their role of adjudicating disputes and granting remedies that address the matter of those disputes."[5]

- Third, the remedy must reflect the specific institutional expertise and responsibilities of the judicial branch: "It will not be appropriate for a court to leap into the kinds of decisions and functions for which its design and expertise are manifestly unsuited."[6]

- Fourth, the remedy must be fair to both parties to the litigation; it must not "impose substantial hardships that are unrelated to securing the right."[7]

- Fifth and finally, "tradition and history cannot be barriers to what reasoned and compelling notions of appropriate and just remedies demand. In short, the judicial approach to remedies must remain flexible and responsive to the needs of a given case."[8]

In a vigorous dissent, Justices LeBel and Deschamps argued that "constitutional remedies should be designed keeping in mind ... a proper awareness of the nature of the role of courts in our democratic political regime, a key principle of which remains the separation of powers."[9] They objected to the majority's claim that a judge could retain jurisdiction over the case at bar after he had issued his final ruling. Finally, they asserted that "Courts should not unduly encroach on areas which should remain the responsibility of public administration and should avoid turning themselves into managers of the public service."[10] Citing the trial judge's order, which they found to be deeply flawed, Justices LeBel and Deschamps implied that the courts were always "manifestly unsuited" to "engage in administrative supervision and decision making."[11] They pointed out that the Court had frequently given legislators a wide latitude to replace laws that had been nullified on Charter grounds and argued that the executive branch should also "retain autonomy in administering government policy that conforms with the Charter."[12]

The case raises important questions about the relationships among the three branches of government under the Charter. As we will see in Chapter 3, the courts lack the institutional capacity to make and implement policy effectively. They should be mindful of their limitations when they exercise their remedial powers, as both the majority and the dissenters pointed out. On the other hand, the Charter requires judges to review the decisions of the other two branches; where legislators or administrators have failed in their duty to protect entrenched rights and freedoms, the courts have little choice but to enforce the guarantees in the Constitution. That duty is especially clear in relation to s. 23, which is explicitly remedial in its purpose (see the discussion in Chapter 7, pages 224–27). The precedential impact of *Doucet-Boudreau* will depend on the willingness of future Justices to assert their remedial powers in the face of resistance from other government actors. Its critics might be reassured by the recent departure from the Court of the two Justices who wrote the majority ruling; if Justices Abella and Charron sympathize with the dissenting judgment, *Doucet-Boudreau* may become a jurisprudential dead end instead of a blank cheque for judicial activism.[13]

ENDNOTES

1. *Doucet-Boudreau v. Nova Scotia (Minister of Education)*, [2003] 3 S.C.R. 3 paragraph 24.

2. Ibid., paragraph 34.

3. Ibid., paragraph 36.

4. Ibid., paragraph 55, quoting McLachlin C.J. in *R. v. 974649 Ontario Inc.*, [2001] 3 S.C.R. 575 (*"Dunedin"*), paragraph 20.

5. *Doucet-Boudreau*, paragraph 56.

6. Ibid., paragraph 57.

7. Ibid., paragraph 58.

8. Ibid., paragraph 59.

9. Ibid., paragraph 94.

10. Ibid., paragraph 91.

11. Ibid., paragraph 125.

12. Ibid., paragraph 124.

13. Lorne Gunter, "Judicial Arrogance Borders on the Monarchical," *National Post*, Thursday, November 20, 2003, accessed online at www.nationalpost.com.

Miscellaneous

Of the "miscellaneous" sections in the Charter, the best-known is the notwithstanding clause in s. 33. Chapter 12 provides an extensive discussion of s. 33. The other section of note is 32, which restricts the application of the Charter to the acts of governments. It is discussed in the following section.

Comparing the Charter

Our Charter blends uniquely Canadian provisions—the language and mobility rights, and the derogation powers in s. 33—with universally recognized rights and freedoms. As we will see in Chapter 2, the content of the Charter was influenced by the American Bill of Rights, the 1948 Universal Declaration on Human Rights, the International Covenant on Civil and Political Rights (ratified in 1976), and the 1950 European Convention on Human Rights.

When the Charter first took effect, some observers predicted that Canadian courts would borrow heavily from American Bill of Rights jurisprudence. Others anticipated that our judges would rely on international human rights law, mostly from Europe.[57] At the beginning of Charter jurisprudence, some appellate judges did refer to American constitutional doctrines. But even as early as 1985, the Supreme Court was warning against an uncritical importation of U.S. common law into Canada.[58] That warning arose from the profound differences between the two constitutions. The Constitution Act, 1982 contains several features—the external limitation clauses (ss. 1 and 33), the explicit remedial powers (s. 24), and the declaration of legal supremacy (s. 52)—that have no parallel in American law. Moreover, the Charter omits the right to property, which is protected in the Fifth and Fourteenth Amendments to the U.S. Constitution (collectively, these amendments constitute the American Bill of Rights).[59] Finally, the U.S. Bill of Rights is an exclusively "first-generation" document, concerned with "negative" rights, whereas some of the rights and freedoms protected in the Charter may create positive obligations for governments. Despite its uniquely Canadian character, the Charter has become a model for some new democracies. It has also influenced established states that have recently amended their constitutions. The post-apartheid constitution of South Africa guarantees many of the same rights and freedoms, and judges in that country have often cited the Supreme Court of Canada as an authority in their rulings on those guarantees.

THE SCOPE AND APPLICATION OF CHARTER REVIEW

Although most Canadians know the Charter exists, few understand how far it goes and how it works. Some may believe that their rights are constitutionally protected in all areas of life, such as private relationships with their landlords or employers. Others might assume that the Charter covers only Canadian citizens, or that it applies to written laws passed by legislators and not to the judge-made common law. The text of the Charter itself does little to clarify these issues. For example, s. 32(1) appears to restrict the Charter to the acts of governments, and specifically to the laws passed by federal and provincial legislatures. As we have seen, however, s. 24 allows the courts to remedy *procedural* violations of rights and freedoms. Nor, despite the broad language of some Charter sections—e.g., "Everyone has the following fundamental freedoms" or "Everyone has the right to life, liberty and security of the person"—are such remedies automatic. In reality, the entrenched rights and freedoms may legitimately be restricted by governments where they conflict with competing social goals (see Chapter 4).

To understand how the Charter works, we must begin by understanding the questions it raises and the ways in which judges seek to answer them. Dossier 1.3 analyzes the basic structure of a Charter challenge in the courts.

DOSSIER 1.3

THE NUTS AND BOLTS OF A CHARTER CHALENGE

At the most fundamental level, a Charter case requires judges—particularly at the Supreme Court level—to answer three questions:

- Can the state do X?[1]
- If the answer to the first question is "yes," or "maybe," by what means and under what circumstances can the state do X?
- When the state is found to have violated the Charter by doing X, or by doing it in an inappropriate way, what is the proper judicial remedy?

We will consider each question separately.

The first question identifies the central issue in any Charter appeal. The meaning of "the state" is specific to each individual case. Where a particular law is alleged to infringe the Charter, "the state" refers to the legislature that passed the law. For example, a challenge to a section of the Criminal Code of Canada questions whether the federal Parliament violated legal rights when it adopted that particular provision. In contrast, a procedural appeal asks the court to determine the constitutionality of a particular action by a public official. Can a police officer interrogate a suspect without first giving her the opportunity to obtain legal advice? (No.) Can a federal adjudicator deport a refugee claimant to his home country if he is certain to be tortured there? (No.) Can a prosecutor in a criminal trial withhold evidence from the defence that might prove the innocence of the accused? (No.)[2]

The meaning of "X" is equally case-specific. Can Parliament deny prison inmates the right to vote in federal elections? (No.) Can a provincial government deny benefits to common-law couples that it provides automatically to married couples? (No.) Can it give public money to Catholic schools while withholding funds from Muslim and Jewish schools? (Yes.)[3]

The above examples notwithstanding, the answer to this first question is rarely a straightforward yes or no. The most frequent answers are "sometimes" or "it depends." Can the state restrict the right of an individual to express his or her political views in a nonviolent way? (Yes, but only where such restrictions are necessary to prevent the rich from monopolizing electoral discourse.) Can Parliament prohibit the defence from cross-examining the complainant in a sexual-assault trial about her sexual history? (Yes, but not in all circumstances.) Can the federal Department of Indian and Northern Affairs seize reserve land and sell it to a private developer? (No, unless it compensates the band fairly for the loss of its land.)[4] This brings us to the second question: by what means and under what circumstances can the state do X?

To answer this question with respect to statute law, the courts usually turn to the limitation clause. Section 1 of the Charter requires judges to balance the protected rights and freedoms (1) against each other, and (2) against competing social values. The *Oakes* test (Dossier 1.6, pages 27–30) established several criteria for judges to apply when deciding whether a particular state action violates the Charter. In general, a law or action that infringes a protected right or freedom will be found to be justified if it is necessary to achieve a pressing policy objective, and if the harm caused by the infringement is proportional to the benefit flowing from the impugned state action.

For example, the Supreme Court has found that the "hate speech" provision in the Criminal Code—which makes it a criminal offence to incite hatred against a particular group, even through nonviolent means—infringes the guarantee of free expression in s. 2(b). However, a majority of the Justices upheld the law because Parliament had a legitimate interest in suppressing hate speech, and because the harm caused by restricting a largely worthless type of expression was outweighed by the value of protecting vulnerable groups.[5]

If the alleged Charter violation arises from the action of a public official, s. 1 does not apply. Instead, the court may examine internal limitations within a particular Charter guarantee to determine whether or not the impugned action was justified. Most of the legal rights contain internal qualifications—for example, the protection against "*unreasonable* search and seizure" in s. 8. Because most of the legal rights are essentially procedural, not substantive, the internal limitations come into play when a court is asked to evaluate a state action rather than the law that authorized it.[6] The Supreme Court of Canada has turned these internal limitations into specific tests that lower courts should apply when evaluating a procedural infringement. The criteria for a valid search or seizure under s. 8 criteria include the requirement of prior legislative authorization and the degree to which the complainant's "reasonable expectation of privacy" has been violated.[7]

If a court determines that the state has violated the Charter by doing X in an inappropriate way, it must answer a third question: what is the appropriate judicial remedy? As we have seen, ss. 24 and 52(1) give judges a wide range of remedial options. An impugned state action will normally trigger a remedy under s. 24. A law that infringes the Charter, and cannot be saved under s. 1, will generally trigger one of four remedies under s. 52(1): an immediate nullification of the impugned provision; a suspended nullification; "reading in"; or "reading down." These are discussed in greater detail later in this chapter.

ENDNOTES

1. This question should not be confused with the central issue in federalism jurisprudence: "Can *this particular level of government* do X?" As Chapter 2, page 49, explains, the 1867 Constitution divides the power to legislate between the federal and provincial governments. If the federal Parliament passes a law dealing with a purely provincial field of jurisdiction, that law may be struck down by the courts as a violation of the division of powers. Before the Charter, the federal and provincial legislatures were collectively supreme: if one level of government was constitutionally prohibited from passing a particular law, the other faced no such restriction. Since 1982, the Charter has restricted *both* levels of government. For the first time, there are things that neither level of government may do (e.g., imprisoning an individual for several months without a formal charge or a hearing before a judge).

2. See, e.g., *R. v. Manninen*, [1987] 1 S.C.R. 1233; *Suresh v. Canada (Minister of Citizenship and Immigration)*, [2002] 1 S.C.R. 3; *R. v. Stinchcombe*, [1991] 3 S.C.R. 326.

3. *Sauvé v. Canada (Chief Electoral Officer)*, [2002] 3 S.C.R. 519; *Miron v. Trudel*, [1995] 2 S.C.R. 418; *Reference re Bill 30, An Act to Amend the Education Act (Ont.)*, [1987] 1 S.C.R. 1148 and *Adler v. Ontario*, [1996] 3 S.C.R. 609.

(continued)

4. *Libman v. Quebec (Attorney General)*, [1997] 3 S.C.R. 569; *R. v. Seaboyer; R. v. Gayme*, [1991] 2 S.C.R. 577 and *R. v. Darrach*, [2002] 2 S.C.R. 443; *Blueberry River Indian Band v. Canada (Department of Indian Affairs and Northern Development)*, [1995] 4 S.C.R. 344.

5. *R. v. Keegstra*, [1990] 3 S.C.R. 697.

6. Justice Gérald V. La Forest, "The Balancing of Interests under the Charter," *National Journal of Constitutional Law* 2 (1992), p. 151.

7. *Hunter v. Southam Inc.* [1984] 2 S.C.R. 145.

Having established the broad structure of a Charter case, we will now consider the scope and limits of Charter guarantees. These have been defined by the Supreme Court over time, as individual cases raise unforeseen issues of Charter application.

Does the Charter Apply to the Common Law?

At first glance, this question appears technical and legalistic—the sort of issue that only a lawyer could love. In reality, the answers carry significant practical consequences. Common-law rules apply both in public law (e.g., criminal trials) and private disputes (property rights, contracts). While the province of Quebec relies on a written civil code, the other nine provinces and the three territories are bound by the English common law as developed and elaborated in the Canadian setting. If the Charter applied only to statute law, its impact on our daily lives would be considerably reduced.

As Dossier 1.4, pages 22–24, explains, the Supreme Court first addressed the relationship between the Charter and the common law in the 1986 *Dolphin Delivery* case.[60] Writing for the majority, Justice McIntyre found that s. 52(1) of the Constitution Act, 1982 applied to both statute law and common law. He wrote: "To adopt a construction of s. 52(1) which would exclude from Charter application the whole body of the common law which in great part governs the rights and obligations of the individuals in society, would be wholly unrealistic and contrary to the clear language employed in s. 52(1) of the Act."[61] In a later part of the ruling, however, McIntyre modified this blanket importation of the

common law into the ambit of the Charter: "the Charter will apply to the common law, whether in public or private litigation. It will apply to the common law, however, only in so far as the common law is the basis of some governmental action which, it is alleged, infringes a guaranteed right or freedom."[62]

If McIntyre's ruling was unclear about the precise extent of Charter application to the common law, it was equally confusing on another issue: whether or not the decisions of the judicial branch were subject to Charter review in the same manner as those of the legislative and executive branches. This question is relevant to the topic of the common law, for the very simple reason that common law is made by judges. McIntyre expressly excluded some activities of the judicial branch from Charter review: "To regard a court order as an element of governmental intervention necessary to invoke the Charter would, it seems to me, widen the scope of Charter application to virtually all private litigation."[63]

The immunization of court orders from Charter scrutiny worries critics of "judicial supremacy." Christopher Manfredi interprets it as a claim that "courts are somehow above the constitutional documents they enforce," and ultimately that "courts must monopolise the process of constitutional interpretation."[64] Similarly, Rainer Knopff and F.L. Morton interpret *Dolphin Delivery* to mean that the courts cannot be bound by the Charter, because "the courts and the Charter are one."[65] These concerns should have been assuaged by subsequent rulings, in which court orders in both criminal and private litigation have been subjected to Charter review.[66] In the 1988 *BCGEU* case, the Supreme Court upheld a lower-court injunction against union picketing at the

Vancouver courthouse despite finding that it infringed s. 7.[67] In the 1994 *Dagenais* case, the Court determined that a publication ban issued by a trial judge infringed the guarantee of free expression.[68] As these examples indicate, McIntyre's ruling on court orders has not inhibited the Court from applying the Charter to the acts of judges.

Finally, in the 1995 case of *Hill v. Church of Scientology*, the Court clarified the Charter's application to the common law in purely private litigation. Writing for the majority, Justice Cory situated the Charter within the historic tradition of the common law:

> Historically, the common law evolved as a result of the courts making those incremental changes which were necessary in order to make the law comply with current societal values. The *Charter* represents a restatement of the fundamental values which guide and shape our democratic society and our legal system. It follows that it is appropriate for the courts to make such incremental revisions to the common law as may be necessary to have it comply with the values enunciated in the *Charter*.[69]

The distinction between implicit Charter *values* and explicit Charter *rights* underlies Cory's approach to the common law.

> Private parties owe each other no constitutional duties and cannot found their cause of action upon a Charter right. The party challenging the common law cannot allege that the common law violates a Charter *right* because, quite simply, Charter rights do not exist in the absence of state action. The most that the private litigant can do is argue that the common law is inconsistent with Charter *values*.... Therefore, in the context of civil litigation involving only private parties, the Charter will "apply" to the common law only to the extent that the common law is found to be inconsistent with Charter values.[70]

These "Charter values" have not yet been spelled out in any definitive way. However, the following statement from former Chief Justice Dickson provides some useful clues:

> The Court must be guided by the values and principles essential to a free and democratic society which I believe embody, to name but a few, respect for the inherent dignity of the human person, commitment to social justice and equality, accommodation of a wide variety of beliefs, respect for cultural and group identity, and faith in social and political institutions which enhance the participation of individuals and groups in society. The underlying values and principles of a free and democratic society are the genesis of the rights and freedoms guaranteed by the Charter and the ultimate standard against which a limit on a right or freedom must be shown, despite its effect, to be reasonable and demonstrably justified.[71]

In addition to these broad principles, each individual Charter section enshrines a particular set of values. Since its earliest Charter rulings, the Supreme Court has taken a **purposive approach** to interpreting Charter guarantees.[72] As explained in Chapter 3, pages 104–5, this approach requires the Justices to determine the reasons for entrenching each specific right or freedom. In the process, they have identified core values specific to each section. For example, the Court has inferred that the guarantee of free expression in s. 2(b) protects the search for truth, artistic self-fulfilment, and participation in social and political life.[73] The guarantee of equality in s. 15(1) "entails the promotion of a society in which all are secure in the knowledge that they are recognized at law as human beings equally deserving of concern, respect and consideration" and "prevent[s] the infringement of essential human dignity."[74] The "principles of fundamental justice" in s. 7 incorporate common-law standards of *mens rea*, the right to make a full answer and defence, and protections against self-incrimination. In these instances, the Justices have "read in" specific Charter values in the course of interpreting the broad guarantees. While this may raise some concerns for critics of judicial power, the fact that the Justices have relied on the existing common law to determine the purpose of entrenched rights and freedoms suggests that the Charter promotes legal continuity, not a judge-made "Charter Revolution."[75]

The Public Sector versus the Private Sector

In the early years of Charter review, one of the key questions was whether—and to what extent—it applied to the private sector. Left-wing critics argued that if the Charter's only function was to restrain governments, it would have no impact on the most serious social injustices.[76] Landlords and employers could still discriminate against gay or visible-minority tenants and employees; the rich would still oppress the poor. While this argument overlooks the existence of statutory human rights codes, whose purpose is to protect individuals from mistreatment in the private sector, it raises an important question: what good is a Charter of Rights that merely protects the wealthy from state intervention? More broadly, why shouldn't Canadians be "as secure against unreasonable searches and seizures by beverage-room bouncers as by police officers"?[77]

The Supreme Court's decisions on this issue are neither as clear nor as consistent as one might wish. The majority in *Dolphin Delivery* held that the Charter did not apply to private activity, such as contracts between landlord and tenant or employer and worker. Nonetheless, as we have seen, Justice McIntyre's majority ruling imposed a duty on judges to interpret and develop the common law in ways consistent with the Charter. This duty implied that some private transactions might be subject to Charter review.[78]

In practice, the distinction between the public and private sectors is not always clear. Hundreds of thousands of Canadians are employed in what might be called the "para-public" sector: institutions such as universities, colleges, public schools, and hospitals. These institutions are governed by community boards, heavily subsidized by provincial (and sometimes federal) governments, and regulated by provincial statutes. To this extent, they are part of the government sector. But unlike the federal Department of Finance, or a provincial ministry of education, universities and hospitals are not part of the structure of government. They are separate and self-governing institutions. Does the Charter apply to their activities and, if so, to what extent? The answer, as Dossier 1.4 explains, has not been entirely consistent.

DOSSIER 1.4

THE CHARTER'S APPLICATION TO THE PUBLIC AND PRIVATE SECTORS OF THE ECONOMY

The case of *RWDSU v. Dolphin Delivery* arose from a 1982 labour dispute between Purolator and its unionized employees. The Retail, Wholesale and Department Store Union, Local 580, was the bargaining agent for the locked-out Purolator workers. Dolphin Delivery, a local firm in Vancouver, carried out some of Purolator's business in that area during the labour dispute. The RWDSU wanted to set up a secondary picket at the headquarters of Dolphin Delivery, but it could not do so until the legality of such a picket was determined. The determination would be based on the common law because there was no federal or provincial statute governing the issue at bar.

In 1986, the case was finally settled by the Supreme Court of Canada. Writing for the majority, Justice McIntyre set out three constitu-tional questions: (1) whether the injunction against secondary picketing infringed the guarantee of free expression under s. 2(b); (2) whether common-law rules were reviewable under the Charter; and (3) the extent of the Charter's application to private litigation. Although he answered the first question in the negative, thus dismissing the union's appeal, McIntyre went on to discuss the second and third questions. (See page 21 for the answer to the second question.)

The third question was the most complex. McIntyre determined that the purpose of a con-stitution was to restrain governments in their dealings with private individuals and groups. He then turned to the wording of s. 32(1), and found that the words "Parliament" and "govern-ment" referred to the legislative and executive branches respectively.[1] Consequently, the Charter "will apply to those branches of government whether ... their action is invoked in public or private litigation."[2] McIntyre concluded that where some degree of "governmental action" is present—such as an enabling statute or regulation—"and where one private party invokes or relies upon it to produce an infringement of the *Charter* rights of another, the *Charter* will be applicable."[3]

The 1990 *McKinney* ruling dealt with university mandatory-retirement policies for faculty and librarians. The question raised by the plaintiffs was whether such policies discriminated on the basis of age, and thereby violated s. 15(1) of the Charter (see Chapter 11, page 341). In the words of Justice La Forest, writing on this issue for the majority, "the respondent universities do not form part of the government apparatus, so their actions, as such, do not fall within the ambit of the Charter. Nor in establishing mandatory retirement for faculty and staff were they implementing a governmental policy."[4] In effect, the entire para-public sector of the economy—apart from community colleges, which are "emanations of government"[5]—was exempt from Charter review. The plaintiffs lost.

The *McKinney* distinction between the public and private activities of para-public institutions was most recently revisited in the 1997 *Eldridge* case.[6] Three appellants, all of whom were deaf and preferred to communicate in sign language, took the British Columbia government to court over the failure to provide sign-language interpreters in hospitals. They argued, and the Supreme Court agreed, that this failure effectively discriminated against patients with a particular physical disability, and thus violated s. 15(1) of the Charter. The real question was whether the remedy lay with the provincial legislature—in other words, whether the two provincial statutes that governed the delivery of health-care services were unconstitutional because they did not require sign-language interpretation—or with the hospitals themselves.

A unanimous Court, led once again by Justice La Forest, found that the violation, and hence the remedy, lay with the hospitals. Although these were para-public institutions, and should therefore have been exempt from Charter review under the *McKinney* doctrine, the Court found that the impugned activity in *Eldridge* directly affected the delivery of health-care services, and hence the "implementation of government policy." In other words, the impugned policy lay within the implicit exception that La Forest had established in *McKinney*. Moreover, the treatment of deaf patients lay within the administrative discretion given to the hospitals under the two provincial statutes governing the delivery of hospital care, and thus "engaged the Charter" under the test laid down by Justice McIntyre in *Dolphin Delivery*. For a unanimous court, Justice La Forest wrote that "a private entity may be subject to the *Charter* in respect of certain inherently governmental actions"[7]—in this case, the provision of medical services under the statutory authority of the provincial government.

The Court's distinction between the internal employment policies of para-public institutions and their "inherently governmental actions" is questionable. La Forest himself blurred the distinction in the 1991 *Lavigne* case.[8] He rejected the argument that the Charter should not apply to government activities that were "private, commercial, contractual or non-public [in] nature."[9] La Forest argued that modern governments have a significant and legitimate role to play in stimulating and directing the economy.

> In such circumstances, government activities which are in form "commercial" or "private" transactions are in reality expressions of government policy, be it the support of a particular region or industry, or the enhancement of Canada's overall international competitiveness. In this context, one has to ask: why should our concern that government conform to the principles set out in the Charter not extend to these aspects of its contemporary mandate? To

(continued)

say that the Charter is only concerned with government as law maker is to interpret our Constitution in light of an understanding of government that was long outdated even before the Charter was enacted.[10]

ENDNOTES

1. *RWDSU v. Dolphin Delivery Ltd.*, [1986] 2 S.C.R. 573, paragraphs 26–34, *per* McIntyre J.

2. Ibid., *paragraph 34, per* McIntyre J.

3. Ibid., *paragraph 39, per* McIntyre J.

4. *McKinney v. University of Guelph*, [1990] 3 S.C.R. 229, *per* La Forest J.

5. *Douglas/Kwantlen Faculty Association v. Douglas College*, [1990] 3 S.C.R. 570. See also *Lavigne v. Ontario Public Service Employees Union*, [1991] 2 S.C.R. 211.

6. *Eldridge v. British Columbia (Attorney General)*, [1997] 3 S.C.R. 624.

7. Ibid., *paragraph 39, per* La Forest J.

8. *Lavigne v. Ontario Public Service Employees Union*, [1991] 2 S.C.R. 211.

9. Ibid., *per* La Forest J.

10. Ibid., *per* La Forest J.

In summary, the Charter applies to any action that is empowered by, and undertaken in direct consequence of, a particular statute.[79] Purely private actions and those that do not engage the relationship between the state and an individual (e.g., labour relations within a university) are not subject to Charter review. However, the resolution of private disputes under the common law must conform to Charter values, as defined by the courts.

Citizens and Noncitizens

The language of the Charter signals that some of the protected rights and freedoms apply to all persons on Canadian soil, while others do not. The fundamental freedoms and legal rights are guaranteed to "everyone," whereas democratic rights (s. 3), mobility rights (s. 6), and minority language education rights (s. 23) are restricted to "every citizen of Canada." In an early Charter case, the Supreme Court had to decide whether the word "everyone" in s. 7 referred only to Canadian citizens, or whether it guaranteed "fundamental justice" to noncitizens as well. The stakes were high, particularly for refugee claimants who faced deportation if their claims failed. Dossier 1.5, page 25, summarizes the Court's judgment.

While noncitizens may claim a degree of Charter protection, they are not necessarily entitled to the full degree of protection afforded to Canadian citizens. In a subsequent case, a unanimous Court ruled that "non-citizens do not have an unqualified right to enter or remain in the country."[80] In the context of immigration law, where both legal and mobility rights are at stake, the word "everyone" in s. 7 does not trump the "distinction between citizens and non-citizens" in s. 6: "While permanent residents are given the right to move to, take up residence in, and pursue the gaining of a livelihood in any province in s. 6(2), only citizens are accorded the right 'to enter, remain in and leave Canada' in s. 6(1)."[81] So while the Charter protects noncitizens, its full benefits are reserved for native-born and naturalized Canadians.

Laws versus Executive Decrees

As we have already seen, s. 32 of the Charter defines the scope of Charter review by the courts. The wording explicitly refers to "all matters within the authority of Parliament," in contrast to "the legislatures *and governments* of each province." Did the exclusion of "the government of Canada" insulate orders-in-council, decrees, treaties, and other acts of the federal executive branch from Charter review? The answer, according to a majority of the Supreme Court, is no. Since *Operation Dismantle* (Dossier 5.2, pages 187–88), the Court has claimed the power to review cabinet orders and other executive decrees. Such cases are relatively infrequent. As explained in Chapter 5, pages 188–93, most arise from appeals to deportation

DOSSIER 1.5

SINGH V. MINISTER OF EMPLOYMENT AND IMMIGRATION (1985)

In 1984, the Supreme Court heard appeals from seven people whose claims to refugee status had been denied.[1] The appellants had petitioned the Immigration Appeal Board under the provisions of the Immigration Act, seeking to have their denials overturned. Section 71(1) of the act allowed the Board to dismiss appeals on the basis of written evidence alone; it did not require an oral hearing, where the applicants could argue their case for refugee status in person, nor did it require the government to disclose the reasons for denying refugee claims. Before the Court, the appellants argued that the refugee determination process infringed s. 7 of the Charter. They claimed that deportation to their home country—where they feared persecution on political and religious grounds—violated their right to life, liberty, and security of the person in a manner that did not conform to fundamental justice.

Before the Court could determine the merits of the appeals, it first had to decide whether noncitizens were entitled to protection under s. 7. Justice Wilson, writing for the three Justices who addressed the Charter issues in the appeal, concluded that the word "everyone" includes "every human being who is physically present in Canada and by virtue of such presence amenable to Canadian law."[2] In other words, the legal rights in s. 7 are not restricted to Canadian citizens; they may be claimed by visitors, international students, refugee claimants, and landed immigrants. (Note, however, that these rights are denied to any entity that is not a "human being" at common law, including corporations[3] and fetuses.[4]) Justice Wilson found that the refugee-determination system violated the procedural guarantees in s. 7 and struck down the relevant section of the Immigration Act.

ENDNOTES

1. *Singh v. Minister of Employment and Immigration*, [1985] 1 S.C.R. 177.

2. Ibid., paragraph 35.

3. In *Irwin Toy Ltd. v. Quebec (Attorney General)*, [1989] 1 S.C.R. 927, former Chief Justice Dickson defined "everyone" to "exclude corporations and other artificial entities incapable of enjoying life, liberty or security of the person, and include only human beings." This interpretation of s. 7 has been upheld in subsequent cases; see, e.g., *Canadian Egg Marketing Agency v. Richardson*, [1998] 3 S.C.R. 157, paragraph 36, *per* Iacobucci and Bastarache JJ. But the Court has subsequently upheld the Charter rights of corporations under s. 2(b) (*RJR-MacDonald Inc. v. Canada (Attorney General)*, [1995] 3 S.C.R. 199) and s. 8 (e.g., *Hunter v. Southam Inc.*, [1984] 2 S.C.R. 145).

4. *Winnipeg Child and Family Services (Northwest Area) v. G. (D.F.)*, [1997] 3 S.C.R. 925, paragraphs 11–17, *per* McLachlin J. (as she then was).

orders. As a general rule, cabinet ministers and administrators must exercise their discretionary powers in conformity to the Charter; in particular, they must ensure that any decision affecting "liberty and security of the person" must be made "in accord with the principles of fundamental justice."

LIMITS ON RIGHTS

The rights and freedoms guaranteed in the Charter are not absolute. They must be balanced against each other, and against competing social interests, by policy-makers and implementers in all three branches of government. The inherent difficulty of "balancing individual and social interests"[82]—of deciding, for example, whether freedom of expression should outweigh the protection of vulnerable minorities from hate speech—is partially alleviated by formal limitations on rights. The most extreme limit is derogation, which permits a government to restrict or even deny a particular right under unusual circumstances—say, a national emergency. (See the discussion of s. 33 in Chapter 12, pages 379–83.)

In most instances, judges and lawmakers rely on less drastic methods to limit rights and freedoms. The Charter contains two such methods: internal limitations and external limitations. As previously discussed, internal limitations are contained within the text of individual sections.

When a court is called upon to interpret an internally limited right, it usually begins by identifying the purpose of the guarantee. In his first Charter ruling, former Chief Justice Dickson declared the purpose of s. 8 to be the protection of individual privacy, or at least a reasonable expectation thereof.[83] Having done so, he turned to the central question: how to balance the "reasonable expectation of privacy" against the competing social value of law enforcement. Following the standard practice, Dickson interpreted the limiting language with reference to existing common-law principles. At common law, the police have the power to search private premises for evidence, but that power may be exercised only with the prior authorization of a legislature (by an explicit statutory provision) and/or a judge (via a warrant). Dickson concluded that the warrantless search of the plaintiff's premises had been unconstitutional.

The key external limitation is found in s. 1, which guarantees the rights and freedoms in the Charter "subject only to such reasonable limits prescribed by law as can be demonstrably justified in a free and democratic society." The presence of an external limitation clause has profoundly affected the development of Charter jurisprudence. Instead of construing the various rights and freedoms narrowly, in order to balance them against competing social values (and each other), the courts have given each guarantee a "large and liberal interpretation"[84] and left the proper balance to be struck under s. 1. "This broad and generous interpretation of rights in the initial stage of judicial review has the consequence of subjecting a far greater range of legislative activities to Charter review than if the Court had developed internal limitations."[85]

Initially, government lawyers tasked with defending legislation against Charter challenges struggled to understand the requirements of a s. 1 analysis. In the earliest Charter ruling from the Supreme Court, the May 1984 *Skapinker* judgment, Justice Estey gently chastised the lawyers for all parties (and the intervenor) for failing to provide sufficient evidentiary basis for a s. 1 analysis:

> As experience accumulates, the law profession and the courts will develop standards and practices which will enable the parties to demonstrate their position under s. 1 and the courts to decide issues arising under that provision. May it only be said here, in the cause of being helpful to those who come forward in similar proceedings, that the record on the s. 1 issue was indeed minimal, and without more, would have made it difficult for a court to determine the issue as to whether a reasonable limit on a prescribed right had been demonstrably justified. Such are the problems of the pioneer and such is the clarity of hindsight.[86]

Shortly thereafter, in the July 1984 *Quebec Protestant School Boards* ruling that struck down part of Quebec's French-language education law, the Court (***per curiam***) made it clear that s. 1 was not an all-purpose escape clause for governments seeking to minimize the effect of the Charter: "Whatever their scope, the limits which s. 1 allows cannot be equated with exceptions to the rights and freedoms guaranteed by the Charter and may not be treated as amendments to the Charter."[87] Justice Dickson gave another hint in the October 1984 *Hunter v. Southam* ruling: "The phrase 'demonstrably justified' puts the onus of justifying a limitation on a right or freedom set out in the Charter on the party seeking to limit."[88] Finally, in 1985, Dickson (now Chief Justice) began to lay the foundations for an explicit approach to s. 1:

> [N]ot every government interest or policy objective is entitled to s. 1 consideration. Principles will have to be developed for recognizing which government objectives are of sufficient impor-

tance to warrant overriding a constitutionally protected right or freedom. Once a sufficiently significant government interest is recognized then it must be decided if the means chosen to achieve this interest are reasonable—a form of proportionality test. The court may wish to ask whether the means adopted to achieve the end sought do so by impairing as little as possible the right or freedom in question.[89]

In his 1986 ruling in *R. v. Oakes*, Dickson finally fleshed out the skeletal hints given in previous judgments. The "*Oakes* test" has become a cornerstone of Charter jurisprudence, at least where the plaintiff seeks to impugn a federal or provincial statute. Dossier 1.6 summarizes the ruling, which may well be the most important in the recent history of the Supreme Court.

DOSSIER 1.6

THE *OAKES* TEST AND THE "CHARTER TWO-STEP"[1]

In 1981, police in London, Ontario, arrested David Edwin Oakes outside a tavern. Oakes was found to be in possession of a considerable quantity of cash and several vials of hashish oil.[2] Under s. 8 of the Narcotics Control Act, Oakes had to prove that he was not engaged in drug trafficking—a more serious offence than simple possession. The law imposed a "reverse onus," requiring the accused to demonstrate his innocence instead of requiring the Crown to prove guilt beyond a reasonable doubt.[3] Oakes challenged the constitutional validity of the reverse onus, arguing that it violated the presumption of innocence as guaranteed in s. 11(d) of the Charter. The trial judge agreed, striking down the impugned provision. The Crown appealed to the Ontario Court of Appeal. When the ruling was upheld, the Crown appealed again to the Supreme Court of Canada.

After the oral hearing, the Justices met in conference to discuss the case. (This process is described in Chapter 3, page 101.) Although they all agreed with the disposition of the case by Judge Martin of the Ontario Court of Appeal, there was some concern about Martin's approach to s. 1. Instead of interpreting s. 11(d) broadly and then considering the issue of limitation separately, Justice Martin had applied s. 1 as an interpretive clause to determine the meaning of the presumption of inno-

cence.[4] The Supreme Court had already established a "two-step" procedure for settling Charter challenges to statute law. At the first stage, the plaintiff (the person or entity seeking to **impugn** the law) had to demonstrate that the law infringed one or more Charter rights or freedoms. If the plaintiff met this burden of proof, the onus shifted to the sponsoring government for the second stage of inquiry. The question to be answered at this point was whether the infringement could be justified under s. 1. To date, however, the Court had not clarified the means by which that question should be answered. The *Oakes* conference did not discuss a specific "test" for applying s. 1; it merely authorized Chief Justice Dickson to write an opinion on the presumption of innocence.[5]

As he drafted his judgment, Dickson decided that he could not resolve the issues raised by the case without a more extensive discussion of s. 1 than any yet issued by the Court. He sought the assistance of his law clerks, asking them to research the American and European approaches to limiting rights. Together, they drafted "five of the most important pages ever written in Canadian constitutional law."[6]

Dickson began by discussing the purpose of s. 1. He observed that "It may become necessary to limit rights and freedoms in circumstances where their exercise would be inimical

(continued)

to the realization of collective goals of fundamental importance."[7] However, such limits must be considered not as standard operating procedure but as "exceptions to their general guarantee. The presumption is that the rights and freedoms are guaranteed unless the party invoking s. 1 [i.e., the sponsoring government] can bring itself within the exceptional criteria which justify their being limited."[8] To do this, the government seeking to uphold the law must demonstrate, on the civil standard of a balance of probabilities, that the provision is "justified in a free and democratic society" despite its adverse impact on a protected right or freedom. Dickson then elaborated on Estey's statement in *Skapinker* about the evidentiary requirements of s. 1:

> Where evidence is required in order to prove the constituent elements of a s. 1 inquiry, and this will generally be the case, it should be cogent and persuasive and make clear to the Court the consequences of imposing or not imposing the limit.... A court will also need to know what alternative measures for implementing the objective were available to the legislators when they made their decisions. I should add, however, that there may be cases where certain elements of the s. 1 analysis are obvious or self-evident.[9]

Having established the responsibilities of both parties to a Charter case, Dickson went on to prescribe a four-stage "proportionality test" for courts to use at the s. 1 stage of analysis.

- First, the court must be satisfied that the objective of the impugned law is—to quote *Big M Drug Mart*—"of sufficient importance to warrant overriding a constitutionally protected right or freedom." Dickson argued that s. 1 was not intended to protect "objectives which are trivial or discordant with the principles integral to a free and democratic society." At the very least, the objective must "relate to concerns which are pressing

and substantial in a free and democratic society"; if it does not, the law will fail at this first stage of analysis.[10] In practice, the Court sometimes substitutes a modified version of the common-law "mischief rule": what is the harm (mischief) which the law seeks to cure?

- Second, "the measures adopted must be carefully designed to achieve the objective in question. They must not be arbitrary, unfair or based on irrational considerations. In short, they must be rationally connected to the objective."[11] Although Dickson did not explicitly say so, this second criterion cannot be answered by resort to the standard tools of legal analysis. It is a question of policy, pure and simple. The Court must evaluate the design and effectiveness of a particular law or program: does it address the "mischief" that it was designed to remedy? This question can rarely be resolved by referring to the words of the statute or the specific facts of the case at bar. It demands the submission and consideration of social-science data and competent policy analysis. What is the real-world impact of this policy on those whom it was meant to assist, to exclude, or to punish? Does it achieve the objective in practice or only in theory? As we will see in Chapter 3, page 108, the Supreme Court has not always handled this prong of the *Oakes* test competently. In some cases, the Justices have simply deferred to the sponsoring government and accepted its claims of policy effectiveness at face value; elsewhere, they have made factual claims in support of a particular policy that do not withstand empirical scrutiny. The Supreme Court, as an institution, is not equipped to evaluate public policy on nonlegal grounds.

- Third, the law must infringe the protected right or freedom "as little as possible" (quoting *Big M Drug Mart*). This is called the "minimal impairment" branch of the *Oakes* test. Like the "rational connection" standard, this criterion requires the Court to go beyond legal analysis and assess the wisdom of policy-makers. In conducting the "minimal impairment" review, judges often invoke Dickson's reference to "alternative measures for implementing the objective." If those who designed the impugned policy chose among a range of alternative means for achieving the objective, did they pick the right one? Some Justices, notably La Forest, were uncomfortable with the implications of the phrase "as little as possible." La Forest was concerned that the Court should "avoid rigid and inflexible standards" that could tie the hands of governments.[12] He persuaded Dickson to modify this prong of the *Oakes* test: a few months later, in *Edwards Books and Art*, Dickson adopted the wording "as little as is *reasonably* possible," in an effort to address La Forest's concerns.[13] The modified version has usually been applied in subsequent cases. Even so, it has not been easy for governments to defend their laws even against the less stringent *Edwards* standard: in the eleven years following *Oakes*, the vast majority of the laws that were found to be unjustified under s. 1 failed the "minimal impairment" test.[14]

- Dickson defined the fourth and final prong of the proportionality test as follows: "there must be a proportionality between the *effects* of the measures which are responsible for limiting the Charter right or freedom, and the objective which has been identified as of 'sufficient importance.'"[15] He explained that a law that passed the first three stages of the proportionality test could still fail to satisfy s. 1 if its "**deleterious** effects" on

"individuals or groups" were sufficiently serious. "The more severe the deleterious effects of a measure, the more important the objective must be if the measure is to be reasonable and demonstrably justified in a free and democratic society."[16] In practice, this element of *Oakes* has had little impact on Charter jurisprudence; as of 1997, no single law had ever been struck down for failing this fourth criterion.[17] Dickson's initial formulation, requiring courts to evaluate the proportionality between the law's harmful effects on the Charter and its beneficial purpose, was amended by the Court in 1994. Chief Justice Lamer reformulated it as follows: "there must be a proportionality between the deleterious effects of the measures which are responsible for limiting the rights or freedoms in question and the objective, *and there must be a proportionality between the deleterious and the salutary effects of the measures*."[18] This new version finally came into its own in 1999, when the Court found that the legislated denial of legal aid to plaintiffs in child custody cases violated the Charter: "Assuming without deciding that the policy of not providing state-funded counsel to respondents in custody applications was a limit prescribed by law, that the objective of this policy—controlling legal aid expenditures—is pressing and substantial, that the policy is rationally connected to that objective, and that it constitutes a minimal impairment of s. 7, I find that the deleterious effects of the policy far outweigh the salutary effects of any potential budgetary savings."[19]

ENDNOTES

1. The phrase "Charter two-step" is borrowed from Rainer Knopff and F.L. Morton, *Charter Politics* (Scarborough: Nelson, 1992), Chapter 3.

(continued)

2. Robert J. Sharpe and Kent Roach, *Brian Dickson: A Judge's Journey* (Toronto: University of Toronto Press/Osgoode Society for Canadian Legal History, 2003), p. 332.

3. See Chapter 10, page 324, for a more extensive discussion of "reverse onus" provisions.

4. Ibid., *Brian Dickson*, p. 333.

5. Ibid., *Brian Dickson*, p. 333.

6. Ibid., *Brian Dickson*, p. 333. While there is nothing unusual in a close working relationship between a Supreme Court Justice and his or her law clerks, Morton and Knopff argue that their influence on *Oakes* was disproportionately great. One in particular, Joel Bakan, went on to become a law professor and a leading left-wing critic of judicial conservatism. Morton and Knopff, who have consistently argued that the Supreme Court is overly sympathetic to progressive and "post-materialist" plaintiffs (the so-called "Court Party"), portray Bakan as a bad influence on Dickson, and his work on *Oakes* as an unjustified exercise of power by the secretive and unaccountable "jurocracy." It should be noted that Morton and Knopff themselves rely on secretive "unnamed sources" for their attack on Bakan and his work. See *The Charter Revolution and the Court Party*, p. 111, 141, and 191 n. 18. According to one former clerk, the argument that Canadian Justices are captives of their clerks is grossly overstated: "the clerks' lack of experience and lack of tenure ensures that the influence of any one clerk on any one Justice's decision making will be fleeting at best" (Lorne Sossin, "The Sounds of Silence: Law Clerks, Policy-Making and the Supreme Court of Canada," *University of British Columbia Law Review* 30 [1996], p. 308).

7. *R. v. Oakes*, [1986] 1 S.C.R. 103, paragraph 65.

8. Ibid., paragraph 66.

9. Ibid., paragraph 68.

10. Ibid., paragraph 69.

11. Ibid., paragraph 70.

12. Sharpe and Roach, *Brian Dickson*, p. 355; see also p. 323.

13. *R. v. Edwards Books and Art Ltd.*, [1986] 2 S.C.R. 713, paragraph 113 [emphasis added]. On the other side of the issue, Justice Wilson fought to preserve the minimal-impairment criterion in its full rigour. She dissented from Dickson's majority judgment in *Edwards*, which upheld Ontario's Sunday-closing laws as a "reasonable limit" on freedom of religion. According to Dickson's biographers, "La Forest more or less wanted to overrule *Oakes*," while "Wilson was prepared to defend a strict test for laws that impinged upon protected rights" (Sharpe and Roach, *Brian Dickson*, p. 356).

14. Leon Trakman, William Cole-Hamilton, and Sean Gatien, "*R. v. Oakes* 1986–1997: Back to the Drawing Board," *Osgoode Hall Law Journal* 36 (1998), p. 100.

15. *Oakes*, paragraph 70.

16. Ibid., paragraph 71.

17. Trakman, Cole-Hamilton, and Gatien, "*R. v. Oakes*," p. 103. See also Peter W. Hogg, "Section 1 Revisited," *National Journal of Constitutional Law* 1 (1991), p. 23: "So far as I can tell, [the requirement of proportionate effect] has never had any influence on the outcome of any case. I think the reason for this is that it is redundant."

18. *Dagenais v. Canadian Broadcasting Corp.*, [1994] 3 S.C.R. 835, paragraph 95 (emphasis in original).

19. *New Brunswick (Minister of Health and Community Services) v. G. (J.)*, [1999] 3 S.C.R., paragraph 98, *per* Lamer C.J.

Before a court can proceed to the four steps of the *Oakes* test outlined by Dickson, an analysis under s. 1 requires it to answer two preliminary questions: (1) is the Charter infringement "a limit prescribed by law," and (2) what is the objective of the law? In most cases, the answer to the first question is obvious: any statute passed by Parliament or a provincial legislature and any regulation issued by a cabinet is a "law" by definition.[90] In rare cases, however, a vague or poorly worded law may fail at this preliminary stage of s. 1 analysis: "where there is no intelligible standard and where the legislature has given a plenary discretion to do whatever seems best in a wide set of circumstances, there is no 'limit prescribed by law.'"[91]

On its face, identifying the objective of a law may appear straightforward. In practice, this is not always the case. The government that seeks to justify a law that infringes the Charter must state the purpose of that law as clearly and precisely as possible. But in some instances, especially where pre-Charter laws are involved, the historical record does not readily disclose such an objective.[92] The lawyers are forced to fall back on "vague and symbolic" objectives, which do not always find favour with the Court.[93]

Dickson did not intend the *Oakes* test to be applied rigidly or mechanically.[94] He did not anticipate that courts (including his own) would come to rely exclusively on *Oakes*, instead of using the language of s. 1 itself as a standard for evaluating Charter infringements.[95] Within a short time of its issue, the judgment had "taken on some of the character of holy writ"[96]—to the dismay of some judges, including Dickson himself. In the 1992 *Keegstra* ruling, he warned against this tendency:

> The analytical framework of *Oakes* has been continually reaffirmed by this Court, yet it is dangerously misleading to conceive of s. 1 as a rigid and technical provision, offering nothing more than a last chance for the state to justify incursions into the realm of fundamental rights. From a crudely practical standpoint, Charter litigants sometimes may perceive s. 1 in this manner, but in the body of our nation's constitutional law it plays an immeasurably richer role, one of great magnitude and sophistication.[97]

Justice La Forest, who questioned the wisdom of creating inflexible rules for Charter interpretation, tried to discourage the rigid application of *Oakes*. In *RJR-MacDonald* (1995), dissenting on the application of s. 1, he criticized the reasoning of the trial judge:

> Throughout his judgment, Chabot J. referred to the requirements set forth in *Oakes* as a "test." In so doing, he adopted the view, unfortunately still held by some commentators, that the proportionality requirements established in *Oakes* are synonymous with, or have even superseded, the requirements set forth in s. 1. This view is based upon a misperception of this Court's jurisprudence. The appropriate "test" to be applied in a s. 1 analysis is that found in s. 1 itself, which makes it clear that the court's role in applying that provision is to determine whether an infringement is reasonable and can be demonstrably justified in a "free and democratic society." In *Oakes*, this Court established a set of principles, or guidelines, intended to serve as a framework for making this determination. However, these guidelines should not be interpreted as a substitute for s. 1 itself. It is implicit in the wording of s. 1 that the courts must, in every application of that provision, strike a delicate balance between individual rights and community needs. Such a balance cannot be achieved in the abstract, with reference solely to a formalistic "test" uniformly applicable in all circumstances.[98]

Justice McLachlin endorsed La Forest's argument in her concurring judgment.[99] Those opinions, together with the concurring judgment of Justice Sopinka in *Egan* (1995),[100] heralded a new era in s. 1 jurisprudence. The Court has returned to the normative language of s. 1, using *Oakes* to clarify the issues at bar but without automatically employing it to determine the constitutionality of a particular law.[101] According to some observers, the more flexible standard of justification adopted in 1995 has required (or permitted) the Court to defer more readily to the legislative branch.[102] Chapter 4 discusses the controversy over this deferential approach.

CHARTER REMEDIES

As Dossier 1.2, pages 15–17, explains, sections 24 and 52 of the Constitution Act, 1982 empower the courts to remedy Charter violations. While the remedies in sections 24(2) and 52(1) are relatively narrow—respectively, excluding evidence in a criminal trial and nullifying the offending legal provision(s)—s. 24(1) allows judges to choose from a wide range: overturning a conviction (with or without a new trial), staying criminal charges, reducing a prison sentence, revising a common-law rule, or creating new administrative procedures.[103] Over time, the Supreme Court has given a similarly broad interpretation to its remedial powers under s. 52(1). It has supplemented the "blunt instrument" of immediate nullification with three subtler remedies: (1) "reading in," (2) "reading down," and (3) issuing a suspended decree of nullification, with guidelines for legislators should they decide to reenact the impugned law.[104] The declaration of nullity usually takes effect on a specific date named by the Court. In the 2003 *Figueroa* ruling, for example, Parliament was given twelve months from the date of issue to amend the party-registration rules in the Canada Elections Act. The majority in *M. v. H.* (1999) gave the Ontario legislature six months' grace to bring the Family Law Act into conformity with its ruling that same-sex couples must have the same legal status as heterosexual common-law couples.[105] In effect, the Justices set a deadline for the sponsoring legislature to adopt a suitable replacement for the unconstitutional provision; if it fails to meet that deadline, the law ceases to have effect and a "legal vacuum" occurs.

The remedy of suspended nullification is controversial. On the one hand, it keeps an unconstitutional law in force, at least temporarily. According to former Chief Justice Lamer, this is "a serious matter from the point of view of the enforcement of the Charter."[106] On the other hand, a declaration of immediate invalidity may pose risks to public safety[107] and/or the rule of law. As discussed earlier in this chapter, the rule of law principle requires "the creation and maintenance of an actual order of positive laws."[108] Striking down a legal provision leaves a gap that can cause serious problems for those charged with administering and enforcing the law. In these circumstances,

suspending the decree of invalidity permits a transitional period in which the executive branch can adjust to the new legal situation. Suspended nullification also respects the role of the legislative branch, by giving it an opportunity to address the public-policy issues arising from the Court's reasoning instead of imposing an immediate judicial remedy.[109] Finally, the Court is wary of "fixing" social programs that deny benefits to deserving recipients in a discriminatory manner (thus violating s. 15) by striking down the enabling legislation immediately and thereby depriving *all* recipients.[110] By declaring the law unconstitutional and leaving it in place for a period of time, judges can avoid such a damaging result.

When a law fails the "minimal impairment" criterion in *Oakes*, the Court often advises the legislature to adopt a different means for achieving the legislative objective. The Court rarely condemns the objective itself: in a study of Charter cases decided between 1986 and 1997, only three percent of nullified laws were rejected on the ground that their purposes violated the Charter.[111] Judges are far more likely to conclude that the means chosen to achieve the objective infringe the Charter more than "reasonably necessary."[112] In such cases, the Justices often identify alternative policy mechanisms with less impact on protected rights and freedoms. In the 1998 *Thomson Newspapers* case, for instance, the Court found that a section of the Canada Elections Act that prohibited the publication of new polling results during the 72 hours immediately before voting day failed the "minimal impairment" prong of the *Oakes* test. Justice Bastarache declared, for the majority, that "a provision which prohibited the publication of opinion polls without methodological information would be less intrusive to freedom of expression than a ban on publication of polling information during a crucial period."[113] Parliament subsequently amended the Canada Elections Act to ban the publication of polling results during the last 24 hours of the campaign period; news outlets are now required to publish basic methodological information about each survey.[114]

Defenders of the Charter and its interpretation by the courts interpret these "legislative sequels"—new laws enacted by Parliament in response to judicial nullification—as the products of a "dialogue" between the two branches of government.[115] In effect, the Court gives Parliament a range of acceptable options that would bring its legislation within the bounds of the Charter, and Parliament has the freedom to choose among those options. Critics of the Court argue that such judicial "advice" gives the judges the upper hand over legislators, and violates the separation of powers between the two branches. As F.L. Morton put it, "If I go into a restaurant, order a sandwich, and the waiter brings me the sandwich I ordered, I would not count this as a 'dialogue.'"[116] Similarly, Manfredi argues that "policy distortion occurs whenever a legislature must subordinate its understanding of constitutionally permissible policy to that articulated by a court, even when legislative objectives are not at issue."[117] We will return to the debate over the "dialogue" metaphor in Chapter 4, pages 150–56.

In principle, "reading in" and "reading down" are the least drastic remedies for Charter violations. In essence, they are rules of statutory interpretation. Such rules are generally based on the presumption that the legislature does not intend to violate the Constitution when it enacts a law.[118] Therefore, "If words [in a statute] can be read in two ways, the court will choose the way that produces harmony between the legislation and established legal principles."[119] Because the judgments of the Supreme Court of Canada are binding on all lower courts, its interpretations of statutory language effectively amend impugned laws. "Reading in" amends by addition, usually to remedy "underinclusiveness." Most commonly, an "underinclusive" law withholds public benefits from possible recipients on discriminatory grounds and thus violates s. 15 of the Charter. By reinterpreting the statute to cover a wider range of beneficiaries, the Court remedies the infringement of equality rights. In *Vriend*, for example, the Supreme Court "read in" sexual orientation to the list of prohibited grounds of discrimination in Alberta's Individual Rights Protection Act (see Dossier 1.8, pages 36–37). The principles that courts must apply when determining whether to "read in" as the appropriate Charter remedy are set out in Dossier 1.7.

DOSSIER 1.7

SCHACHTER V. CANADA (1992) AND THE RULES FOR "READING IN"

In 1992, the Supreme Court issued a definitive statement on Charter remedies. The *Schachter* case challenged the constitutionality of the parental benefits scheme under the Unemployment Insurance Act. The law gave adoptive fathers, but not natural fathers, the choice to stay home with their new children for up to fifteen weeks while receiving UI payments. Shalom Schachter argued that the law discriminated against natural fathers like himself. The Supreme Court eventually agreed. Before the appeal reached the top court, the federal government amended the impugned provisions by extending them to all parents. For budgetary reasons, however, the government did not extend the full fifteen weeks of paid leave to natural parents; it reduced the benefit to ten weeks for adoptive and natural parents alike.

Even though the policy issue in the case was now moot, the Court took the opportunity to address one of the constitutional questions raised by the litigation: "whether s. 52(1) of the *Constitution Act, 1982* required that s. 32 of the *Unemployment Insurance Act, 1971*, given an unequal benefit contrary to s. 15(1) of the Charter, be declared of no force or effect."[1] For the majority, then–Chief Justice Lamer determined that "reading in" was an appropriate Charter remedy where the resulting statute is "as faithful as possible within the requirements of the Constitution to the scheme enacted by the Legislature."[2] In other words, the power to "read in" should be only exercised "to fulfil the purposes of the Charter and at the same time minimize the interference of the court with the parts of legislation that do not themselves violate the Charter."[3] If "the question of how the statute ought to be extended in order to comply with the Constitution cannot be answered with a sufficient degree of precision" by the Court,

(continued)

the sponsoring legislature must be allowed to amend the statute instead.[4]

Lamer acknowledged that "reading in" raised difficult questions about the proper scope of judicial power, particularly where it extended public benefits to a new set of recipients. Under the separation of powers doctrine, the judiciary cannot intervene in the spending decisions of the legislative and executive branches of government. (Recall Alexander Hamilton's remark that the courts had no influence over the "purse.") But even while advising courts not to impose heavy costs on governments—for example, by extending a benefit intended for a small minority of the population to tens of millions of Canadians—Lamer rejected the claim that courts must never interfere with budgetary priorities. He argued that "Any remedy granted by a court will have some budgetary repercussions whether it be a saving of money or an expenditure of money.... In determining whether reading in is appropriate then, the question is not whether courts can make decisions that impact on budgetary policy; it is to what degree they can appropriately do so."[5]

ENDNOTES

1. *Schachter v. Canada*, [1992] 2 S.C.R. 679, paragraph 20, *per* Lamer C.J.

2. Ibid., paragraph 35.

3. Ibid., paragraph 40.

4. Ibid., paragraph 50; see also paragraph 54.

5. Ibid., paragraph 61.

If "reading in" to statutes is controversial, the Court's decision to "read in" to the Charter itself is even more so. A judicially amended statute that does not find favour with the sponsoring legislature can be repealed or amended by a simple majority vote. The Constitution is not so flexible. For the reasons discussed at the beginning of this chapter, entrenched constitutional documents are purposely difficult to amend. So when a court determines that a particular personal characteristic—be it sexual orientation, marital status, or citizenship—constitutes an "analogous ground" of discrimination under s. 15(1), that determination amends the Charter effectively and perhaps permanently. The debate over the recognition of "analogous grounds" is covered in Chapter 11.

"Reading down" amends by subtraction. The Court declares that the words of the statute must be interpreted narrowly, to exclude particular meanings that may violate the Charter. In practice, the distinction between "reading in" and "reading down" is not always clear. In the 2002 *Sharpe* ruling, Chief Justice McLachlin "read in" two exemptions to the law against possessing child pornography.[120] Although she described her approach as "reading in," the actual effect of the ruling is to "read down" the law in order to ensure that its provisions do not inadvertently criminalize behaviour that causes no provable harm to others. The same principles that restrict "reading in" also apply to "reading down": the remedy is available only in the clearest of cases; it may not alter the objective of the impugned law; and it must not extend to "judicial rewriting of the legislation."[121]

THE CONTROVERSY OVER JUDICIAL SUPREMACY

Despite the caution with which the Court has fashioned its various Charter remedies, its critics are convinced that judges have usurped the proper policy-making role of the other branches of government. The most prominent of these critics are Rainer Knopff and F.L. Morton, who argue that judges have become too "activist" since 1982. They define "judicial activism" as "the disposition to interpret rights broadly and to enforce them vigorously against the other branches of government, usually by striking down statutes or excluding evidence in criminal cases."[122] For Knopff and Morton, this disposition constitutes a threat to democratic self-government and an illegitimate usurpation of policy-making power by unelected judges. In a similar vein,

Christopher Manfredi suggests that the courts have used the broad language of Charter guarantees to elevate themselves above legislators and executives. They have distorted constitutional supremacy into judicial supremacy.[123]

In response, Kent Roach argues that critics of "judicial activism" have inappropriately injected an American debate into Canadian politics. He dismisses claims of judicial activism as "myths" based on mistaken assumptions about the proper role of courts in a constitutional democracy. Roach portrays the Charter as "a continuation of a common law tradition that enhances democracy by requiring legislatures to consider rights, but does not impose the Court's judgments about rights as the absolute final word."[124]

Both the critics and the defenders of the Charter offer valid arguments, although neither perspective is entirely accurate. Morton and Knopff are correct inasmuch as the judicial remedies in the Charter have allowed judges to veto the choices made by other political actors. As Chapter 3 explains, the Justices of the Supreme Court are neither elected nor accountable. Moreover, they lack the expertise to make effective public policy (except perhaps in the field of criminal law). However, one may question the claim that the protection of minority rights should always be left to legislative majorities. The history of human rights in Canada, which is briefly summarized in Chapter 2, reveals that legislators and administrators do not always take rights as seriously as they should. They have now been forced to do so, by the very "judicial activism" that the critics decry (see Chapters 4 and 5).

On the other side of the issue, Roach is correct to argue that democracy is enhanced (rather than negated) by strong protections for rights and freedoms. But he assumes, wrongly, that judges are the only public officials who can be trusted to interpret Charter guarantees and to translate them into policy. For example, Roach argues that "legislative sequels"— laws enacted in response to a prior nullification— should not be upheld by the courts unless "the legislature has refined the law so that it is justified under section 1 of the Charter."[125] There is an obvious problem with this claim: it implies that the "refinement" of the law must follow the guidelines set out by the court in the previous ruling, and that the judges are solely responsible for determining whether or not the law is "justified." The legislative branch must defer to the judicial branch, and not the other way around.

In a parliamentary democracy, this suggestion is problematic. Surely the elected branch should be permitted to reach its own conclusions about the Charter. Indeed, it is required to do so by the rule of law. As Chapter 4 points out, those who would defend the court against charges of "judicial activism" often fail to distinguish between the Charter itself and its interpretation by the courts. If the Charter means *only* what the judges say it means, then we have indeed abandoned constitutional supremacy for "judicial supremacy." Fortunately, as we will see in Part 2, this scenario is overdrawn. The courts, including the Supreme Court, have become less assertive and more deferential to legislators in recent years. There are exceptions to this trend, the 1998 *Vriend* ruling among them. In that decision, former Justice Iacobucci delivered a strong defence of the court's "activism" under the Charter. That defence, reproduced in Dossier 1.8, pages 36–37, has attracted the ire of Court critics; Manfredi, for one, refers to Iacobucci's ruling as a prime example of "judicial hubris" cloaked in the language of deference.[126]

The debate over "judicial activism" tells us relatively little about the day-to-day reality of politics in the Charter era. How have entrenched rights and freedoms altered the relationships among the three branches of government? How do they affect the policy-making process? Are judges distorting the meaning of the Charter to enhance their own policy-making authority, or are they obeying the will of the framers? How has the common law shaped the meaning of the individual guarantees?

The following chapters attempt to answer these questions. They are intended to provide a complete and balanced account of Canadian government and politics in the Charter era. The next chapter discusses the history of rights and freedoms in Canada and the factors that led to the adoption of the Constitution Act, 1982. Part 2 analyzes the Charter's impact on our institutions of government and the process of policy-making. Part 3 summarizes the leading cases on the Charter and evaluates their effects on Canadian law. The concluding chapter identifies some recent trends and speculates about their evolution over the next twenty years.

DOSSIER 1.8

THE COURT DEFENDS ITSELF IN *VRIEND*

Background: In 1998, the Supreme Court of Canada ruled that Alberta's human rights law violated s. 15 of the Charter because it did not explicitly protect gays and lesbians from discrimination.[1] The majority chose to remedy the violation by "reading in" sexual orientation to the Individual Rights Protection Act. There was an alternative remedy available: to strike down the impugned sections of the IRPA altogether, and then to suspend the effect of the ruling to give the Alberta legislature a chance to amend the legislation. This might have been the more prudent choice, especially since the Alberta cabinet and legislature had deliberately refused to include sexual orientation in the law. Because the clash between the legislature and the Court was unusually stark in this case, the majority judgment devoted considerable space to a discussion of the proper relationship between the two branches of government. The following are excerpts from Justice Iacobucci's ruling, paragraphs 130–36 and 174–75 (citations omitted).

Much was made in argument before us about the inadvisability of the Court interfering with or otherwise meddling in what is regarded as the proper role of the legislature, which in this case was to decide whether or not sexual orientation would be added to Alberta's human rights legislation. Indeed, it seems that hardly a day goes by without some comment or criticism to the effect that under the *Charter* courts are wrongfully usurping the role of the legislatures. I believe this allegation misunderstands what took place and what was intended when our country adopted the *Charter* in 1981–82.

When the *Charter* was introduced, Canada went, in the words of former Chief Justice Brian Dickson, from a system of Parliamentary supremacy to constitutional supremacy. Simply put, each Canadian was given individual rights and freedoms which no government or legislature could take away. However, as rights and freedoms are not absolute, governments and legislatures could justify the qualification or infringement of these constitutional rights under s. 1.... Inevitably disputes over the meaning of the rights and their justification would have to be settled and here the role of the judiciary enters to resolve these disputes.... We should recall that it was the deliberate choice of our provincial and federal legislatures in adopting the *Charter* to assign an interpretive role to the courts and to command them under s. 52 to declare unconstitutional legislation invalid.

... it should be emphasized again that our *Charter*'s introduction and the consequential remedial role of the courts were choices of the Canadian people through their elected representatives as part of a redefinition of our democracy. Our constitutional design was refashioned to state that henceforth the legislatures and executive must perform their roles in conformity with the newly conferred constitutional rights and freedoms. That the courts were the trustees of these rights insofar as disputes arose concerning their interpretation was a necessary part of this new design. So courts in their trustee or arbiter role must perforce scrutinize the work of the legislature and executive not in the name of the courts, but in the interests of the new social contract that was democratically chosen. All of this is implied in the power given to the courts under s. 24 of the *Charter* and s. 52 of the *Constitution Act, 1982*.

Because the courts are independent from the executive and legislature, litigants and citizens generally can rely on the courts to make reasoned and principled decisions according to the dictates of the constitution even though specific decisions may not be universally acclaimed. In carrying out their duties, courts are not to second-guess legislatures and the executives; they are not to make value judgments on what they regard as the proper policy choice; this is for the other branches. Rather, the courts are to uphold the Constitution and have been expressly invited to perform that role by the Constitution itself. But respect by the courts for the legislature and executive role is as important as ensuring that the other branches respect each others' role and the role of the courts....

In my view, the process by which the Alberta Legislature decided to exclude sexual orientation from the *IRPA* was inconsistent with democratic principles.... In my view, a democracy requires that legislators take into account the interests of majorities and minorities alike, all of whom will be affected by the decisions they make. Where the interests of a minority have been denied consideration, especially where that group has historically been the target of prejudice and discrimination, I believe that judicial intervention is warranted to correct a democratic process that has acted improperly.

ENDNOTES

1. *Vriend v. Alberta*, [1998] 1 S.C.R. 493.

GLOSSARY OF KEY TERMS

adjudication The process by which judges resolve a dispute between two parties, by applying rules of law to the facts of the particular case.

appellant The party to a court case who seeks to overturn a lower-court ruling by appealing to a higher court. For example, a man who has been convicted of a criminal offence by a trial court may appeal the conviction to the provincial court of appeal; if his case is heard, he is designated as the appellant. If the appellate court grants his appeal, the Crown (the official representative of the government) can ask the Supreme Court of Canada to overturn that decision. If the Supreme Court agreed, the Crown would be designated as the appellant; the individual seeking to uphold his victory at the court of appeal would be designated as the respondent.

common law The corpus of judicial decisions on a particular topic (e.g., the interpretation of a particular constitutional provision). Each prior decision sets a precedent for subsequent cases on the same topic. Over time, the common law (also called the case law) yields consistent rules or principles whose application is intended to produce just results (e.g., the right to silence).

concurring judgment A written opinion by a judge who agrees with the majority on the disposition of the case at bar but disagrees with some or all of the *ratio decidendi*.

constitution The set of binding norms and principles that regulate the legitimate exercise of political power in a country.

constitutional conventions Unwritten rules of political practice that, over time, acquire binding moral force.

deleterious Harmful or damaging.

dissenting judgment A written opinion by a judge who disagrees with the majority ruling on the disposition of the case at bar.

distinguish the precedent A court can try to evade a prior precedent by distinguishing it from the case at bar, either on the facts or on the law. For example, the Supreme Court has often distinguished Charter cases from similar cases decided under the 1960 Bill of Rights (for an example, see Dossier 2.12, pages 77–79).

docket The shorthand term for the agenda of cases heard by a particular court.

entrenchment The process of inserting a written law into the constitution of a country. The Charter, like the rest of Canada's written constitution, can be amended only through the special procedures set out in ss. 38–48 of the Constitution Act, 1982.

impugn To challenge the constitutionality of a particular law or a section of a law.

jurisprudence The body of case law that interprets and applies a particular law or constitutional provision. Canadian lawyers often refer broadly to "Charter jurisprudence," and more narrowly to "the jurisprudence on s. 2" or "legal-rights jurisprudence."

majority opinion The opinion signed by a majority of the judges on a particular panel. It becomes part of the common law and establishes a binding precedent for future rulings on the same issue. Other opinions, whether they are concurring or dissenting, do not have the force of law.

mens rea Latin for "guilty mind." See the discussion of the mental elements of a criminal offence in Chapter 10, pages 308–11.

nonentrenched written laws Statutes whose purpose—to regulate the legitimate operation of political institutions—elevates them above regular legislation; they are sometimes called quasi-constitutional documents.

obiter dicta Portions of a judgment that do not pertain directly to the case at bar but convey a judge's view of a related topic. Unlike the *ratio decidendi*, an *obiter dictum* (the singular form of *dicta*) does not necessarily bind lower courts or future courts.

per curiam Latin for "by the court." A judgment may be issued *per curiam* instead of being signed by one or more Justices, but only so long as all of the Justices have had some hand in drafting it.[127] Attributing a judgment to the entire Court sends a clear message of unanimity. It may also shield individual Justices from the political fallout of individual authorship in politically sensitive cases; for example, the 1998 *Secession Reference*—which dealt with the contentious issue of Quebec's right to separate from Canada—was a *per curiam* ruling.

purposive approach A technique of constitutional interpretation in which the judge seeks to identify the interests that a particular constitutional provision was intended to protect or promote. For example, the Supreme Court has determined that the purpose of s. 2(b) of the Charter (freedom of expression) is to protect certain types of message (political debate) but not others (violent protest).

ratio decidendi Latin for "the reasons for decision."

respondent The party to a court case who contests the appeal filed by the appellant.

stay of charges When a judge decides to stay the charges against an accused, she forbids the Crown to prosecute those particular charges in court. If he chooses, a Crown prosecutor can seek a reversal of the stay from a higher court. If the Supreme Court of Canada upholds the stay, the charges are quashed. A stay of charges should not be confused with an acquittal. It does not mean that the accused has been found innocent; it simply means that a judge has determined that the further prosecution of the case would be either ineffective or unjust.

DISCUSSION AND REVIEW QUESTIONS

1. In your own words, explain the difference between "positive rights" and "negative rights." Identify one example of each in the Charter.

2. Explain the "two-step" process of Charter analysis. How has the inclusion of s. 1 in the Charter affected the interpretation of the subsequent sections?

3. Briefly explain the term "common law" (or "case law"). How does it relate to the written text of the Charter?

4. The Charter is often described as a "liberal" document. What does this mean?

5. In your own words, explain the rule of law. What are its principal elements, according to the Supreme Court of Canada?

6. Identify two of the judicial remedies in the Constitution Act, 1982. Briefly explain how each of them works in practice.

7. Summarize the four main elements of the *Oakes* test. Which of the four has had the greatest impact on Canadian law, and why?

SUGGESTED READINGS

Beaudoin, Gérald-A., and Ed Ratushny, eds. *The Canadian Charter of Rights and Freedoms.* 2nd ed. Toronto: Carswell, 1989.

Bogdanor, Vernon, ed. *Constitutions in Democratic Politics.* Aldershot, U.K.: Gower/Policy Studies Institute, 1988.

Canon, Bradley C., and Charles A. Johnson. *Judicial Policies: Implementation and Impact.* 2nd ed. Washington: CQ Press, 1999.

Epp, Charles R. "Do Bills of Rights Matter? The Canadian Charter of Rights and Freedoms." *American Political Science Review* 90, no. 4 (December 1996), pp. 765–79.

———. *The Rights Revolution: Lawyers, Activists, and Supreme Courts in Comparative Perspective.* Chicago: University of Chicago Press, 1998.

Glendon, Mary Ann. *Rights Talk: The Impoverishment of Political Discourse.* New York: Free Press, 1991.

Heard, Andrew. *Canadian Constitutional Conventions: The Marriage of Law and Politics.* Toronto: Oxford University Press, 1991.

Hiebert, Janet L. *Limiting Rights: The Dilemma of Judicial Review.* Montreal and Kingston: McGill-Queen's University Press, 1996.

Howe, Paul, and Peter H. Russell, eds. *Judicial Power and Canadian Democracy.* Montreal and Kingston: McGill-Queen's University Press/Institute for Research on Public Policy, 2001.

Knopff, Rainer, and F.L. Morton. *Charter Politics.* Scarborough: Nelson, 1992.

Manfredi, Christopher P. *Judicial Power and the Charter: Canada and the Paradox of Liberal Constitutionalism.* 2nd ed. Toronto: Oxford University Press, 2001.

Morton, F.L., and Rainer Knopff. *The Charter Revolution and the Court Party.* Peterborough: Broadview Press, 2002.

Orend, Brian. *Human Rights: Concept and Context.* Peterborough: Broadview Press, 2002.

Roach, Kent. *The Supreme Court on Trial: Judicial Activism or Democratic Dialogue?* Toronto: Irwin Law, 2001.

Sharpe, Robert J., Katherine E. Swinton, and Kent Roach. *The Charter of Rights and Freedoms.* 2nd ed. Toronto: Irwin Law, 2002.

Sigurdson, Richard. "Left- and Right-Wing Charterphobia in Canada: A Critique of the Critics." *International Journal of Canadian Studies* 7–8 (Spring–Fall 1993), pp. 95–115.

Slattery, Brian. "A Theory of the Charter." *Osgoode Hall Law Journal* 25 (1987), pp. 701–47.

ENDNOTES

1. As then–Chief Justice Dickson put it in *R. v. Big M Drug Mart Ltd.*, [1985] 1 S.C.R. 295, paragraph 143: "If a court or tribunal finds any statute to be inconsistent with the Constitution, the overriding effect of the *Constitution Act, 1982*, s. 52(1), is to give the Court not only the power, but the duty, to regard the inconsistent statute, to the extent of the inconsistency, as being no longer 'of force or effect.'"

2. Charles R. Epp, "Do Bills of Rights Matter? The Canadian Charter of Rights and Freedoms," *American Political Science Review* 90, no. 4 (December 1996), p. 765; Charles R. Epp, *The Rights Revolution: Lawyers, Activists, and Supreme Courts in Comparative Perspective* (Chicago: University of Chicago Press, 1998), Chapter 1.

3. Epp, "Do Bills of Rights Matter," p. 765; Epp, *The Rights Revolution*, pp. 14–15.

4. Brian Slattery, "A Theory of the Charter," *Osgoode Hall Law Journal* 25 (1987), pp. 701–47; Janet L. Hiebert, *Charter Conflicts: What Is Parliament's Role?* (Montreal and Kingston: McGill-Queen's University Press, 2002).

5. Joseph F. Fletcher and Paul Howe, "Public Opinion and the Courts," *Choices* 6, no. 3 (Montreal: Institute for Research on Public Policy, May 2000); available online at www.irpp.org.

6. Gerald N. Rosenberg, *The Hollow Hope: Can Courts Bring About Social Change?* (Chicago: University of Chicago Press, 1991); Bradley C. Canon and Charles A. Johnson, *Judicial Policies: Implementation and Impact*, 2nd ed. (Washington: CQ Press, 1999); W.A. Bogart, *Courts and Country: The Limits of Litigation and the Social and Political Life of Canada* (Toronto: Oxford University Press, 1994), Chapter 2.

7. Kent Roach, "The Role of Litigation and the Charter in Interest Advocacy," in F. Leslie Seidle, ed., *Equity and Community: The Charter, Interest Advocacy and Representation* (Montreal: Institute for Public Policy, 1993), pp. 160–65; Miriam Smith, *Lesbian and Gay Rights in Canada: Social Movements and Equality-Seeking, 1971–1995* (Toronto: University of Toronto Press, 1999), Chapter 3; Ian Brodie, *Friends of the Court: The Privileging of Interest Group Litigants in Canada* (Albany: State University of New York Press, 2002), Chapter 2.

8. Epp, "Do Bills of Rights Matter," pp. 770–71; F.L. Morton and Rainer Knopff, *The Charter Revolution and the Court Party* (Peterborough: Broadview Press, 2000), Chapter 6.

9. Brodie, *Friends of the Court*, p. 25.

10. Roger Tassé, interview with the author, June 17, 2003.

11. The 1954 U.S. Supreme Court ruling in *Brown v. Board of Education* overturned the "separate but equal" doctrine, under which Black children were educated in segregated schools with fewer resources than those available to white children. *Miranda v. Arizona* established the famous "*Miranda* rules" requiring police officers to inform criminal suspects of their due-process rights under the Fourth Amendment to the American Constitution. *Stinchcombe* requires Crown prosecutors to disclose all relevant information to the defence in a criminal trial. *Sparrow* extended constitutional protection to Aboriginal fishing rights, and by extension to hunting and logging rights.

12. The literature on the meaning and purposes of constitutions is vast and varied. See, e.g., R.C. van Caenegem, *An Historical Introduction to Western Constitutional Law* (Cambridge: Cambridge University Press, 1995), especially Chapter 5; Gerald L. Gall, *The Canadian Legal System* (Toronto: Carswell, 1995).

13. In the words of British scholar Christopher Hughes, "[An] appeal to a pre-existing law is the essence of constitutionalism." See his chapter on the Swiss Constitution in Vernon Bogdanor, ed., *Constitutions in Democratic Politics* (Aldershot, U.K.: Gower/Policy Studies Institute, 1988), p. 277.

14. For a brief and lucid introduction, see Brian Rix, "Natural Law Theory," in Dennis Patterson, ed., *A Companion to Philosophy of Law and Legal Theory* (Oxford: Blackwell, 1999), pp. 223–40. See also Paul E. Sigmund, ed., *Natural Law in Political Thought* (Lanham, MD: University Press of America, 1971).

15. As St. Thomas Aquinas put it in the thirteenth century C.E., "[T]he force of a law depends on the extent of its justice.... Consequently every human law has just so much of the nature of law, as it is derived from the law of nature. But if in any point it deflects from the law of nature, it is no longer a law but a perversion of law." *Summa Theologica* I–II, Question 95, Article 2; reproduced in Ralph McInerny, ed., *Treatise on Law* (Washington, DC: Regnery Gateway, 1996).

16. Mark E. Brandon, "Constitutionalism and Constitutional Failure," in Sotirios A. Barber and Robert P. George, eds., *Constitutional Politics: Essays on Constitution Making, Maintenance, and Change* (Princeton: Princeton University Press, 2001), pp. 300–1.

17. John Hart Ely, *Democracy and Distrust: A Theory of Judicial Review* (Cambridge, MA: Harvard University Press, 1980), pp. 48–54.

18. Brandon, "Constitutionalism," p. 301–3.

19. Ibid., p. 302.

20. Alexander Hamilton, "Federalist No. 78," in Alexander Hamilton, James Madison, and John Jay, *The Federalist Papers*, ed. Clinton Rossiter (New York: New American Library, 1961 [1787–88]), p. 466.

21. Hamilton, "Federalist No. 78," p. 467.

22. Ibid., p. 465.

23. *Marbury v. Madison*, 5 U.S. 137 (1803), pp. 176–77.

24. *McCulloch v. Maryland*, 17 U.S. 316 (1819), p. 407.

25. Ibid., p. 415.

26. John E. Finn, "The Civic Constitution: Some Preliminaries," in Barber and George, *Constitutional Politics*, pp. 47–48.

27. Christopher L. Eisgruber, "Judicial Supremacy and Constitutional Distortion," in Barber and George, *Constitutional Politics*, p. 71.

28. *Big M Drug Mart*, headnotes.

29. See the late Justice Laskin's dissent in *Hogan v. the Queen*, [1975] 2 S.C.R. 574, reprinted in Peter H. Russell, Rainer Knopff, and Ted Morton, eds., *Federalism and the Charter: Leading Constitutional Decisions* (Ottawa: Carleton University Press, 1989), p. 383.

30. Bill C–20, An Act to Give Effect to the Requirement for Clarity as Set Out in the Opinion of the Supreme Court of Canada in the Quebec Secession Reference, 36th Parliament, 2nd Session, 1999–2000.

31. See Andrew Heard, *Canadian Constitutional Conventions: The Marriage of Law and Politics* (Toronto: Oxford University Press, 1991), Chapter 1; the *Patriation Reference*, reprinted in Russell, Knopff, and Morton, *Federalism and the Charter*, pp. 736–41. More recently, however, the Supreme Court may have rendered certain constitutional conventions justiciable—i.e., enforceable by the courts—by effectively entrenching them in the Preamble of the Constitution Act, 1867 and/or s. 52(1) of the Constitution Act, 1982. See Mark D. Walters, "The Common Law Constitution in Canada: Return of *Lex Non Scripta* as Fundamental Law," *University of Toronto Law Journal* 51 (2001), pp. 91–141.

32. Heard, *Canadian Constitutional Conventions*, p. 5.

33. Aristotle, *The Nicomachean Ethics* (Oxford University Press, 1980), p. 133.

34. On this point, see former U.S. Supreme Court Justice Benjamin Cardozo: "Our jurisprudence ... has refused to sacrifice the larger and more inclusive good to the narrower and smaller." In other words, justice in the case at bar—while crucially important—must not be done at the expense of the larger principles that give order to a society. See Cardozo, *The Nature of the Judicial Process* (New Haven: Yale University Press, 1921), p. 139.

35. In this connection, critics of the Supreme Court often mention the *Singh* and *Askov* cases (discussed elsewhere in this book).

36. Recently retired Justice Claire L'Heureux-Dubé, nicknamed "The Great Dissenter" for the frequency of her minority opinions, has called dissenting judgments "the seeds of innovation." See her article "The Dissenting Opinion: Voice of the Future?" *Osgoode Hall Law Journal* 38 (2000), pp. 495–517.

37. One example is the dissent of former Chief Justice Brian Dickson in the 1987 *Alberta Labour Reference*. Dickson declared that labour is more than a mere economic interest; it affects an individual's entire life. Organized labour

(i.e., unions) is essential to the protection of human dignity and fairness. Although the majority rejected this approach in 1987, the Court has since repudiated the majority ruling and adopted Dickson's dissent as binding law. See Dossier 8.11, pages 273–75.

38. In a pre-Charter case, the Supreme Court of Canada relied on an *obiter dictum* in a previous case to settle a criminal appeal. In so doing, it effectively gave its own *dicta* the force of binding precedent. See *R. v. Sellars*, [1980] 1 S.C.R. 527. For commentary on this ruling, see F.L. Morton and Rainer Knopff, *The Charter Revolution and the Court Party* (Peterborough: Broadview Press, 2000), p. 56.

39. *R. v. Askov*, [1990] 2 S.C.R. 1199.

40. Former American Justice Charles Evan Hughes is quoting as saying that "the constitution is what the judges say it is." Quoted in Rainer Knopff and F.L. Morton, *Charter Politics* (Scarborough: Nelson, 1992), p. 190.

41. Cass R. Sunstein, *Legal Reasoning and Political Conflict* (New York: Oxford University Press, 1996), p. 123.

42. This illustration is borrowed from the decision of Justice L'Heureux-Dubé in *Haig v. Canada; Haig v. Canada (Chief Electoral Officer)*, [1993] 2 S.C.R. 995.

43. See Mary Ann Glendon, *Rights Talk: The Impoverishment of Political Discourse* (New York: Free Press, 1991), especially Chapters 3 and 4.

44. Brian Orend, *Human Rights: Concept and Context* (Peterborough: Broadview Press, 2002), p. 30.

45. John Locke (1632–1704) is widely regarded as the greatest exponent of classical liberalism. His most important works in this regard are the *Letter on Toleration*, which argued for religious freedom, and the *Second Treatise on Government*, in which Locke argued that men should live in a "civil society," bound by nothing but the rule of law and respect for each others' rights. See John Gray, *Liberalism*, 2nd ed. (Minneapolis: University of Minnesota Press, 1995), Chapter 2, and John Dunn, *The Political Thought of John Locke: An Historical Account of the Argument of the "Two Treatises of Government"* (Cambridge: Cambridge University Press, 1969).

46. The 1776 Declaration of Independence, written by Thomas Jefferson, is the perfect encapsulation of classic liberal ideas: "We hold these Truths to be self-evident, that all Men are created equal, that they are endowed by their Creator with certain inalienable Rights, that among these are Life, Liberty, and the Pursuit of Happiness ..." Pauline Maier, ed., *The Declaration of Independence and the Constitution of the United States* (New York: Bantam, 1998), p. 53.

47. Orend, *Human Rights*, p. 30.

48. Ibid., p. 30.

49. Ibid., p. 30.

50. Ibid., p. 110.

51. These include the right to legal counsel (s. 10(b)), the provision of adequate trial facilities (s. 11(b)), and the establishment of special mechanisms to enable prison inmates to vote (s. 3).

52. In the 1984 *Hunter* ruling (*Hunter v. Southam Inc.*, [1984] 2 S.C.R. 145, p. 156), Justice Dickson (as he then was) declared that the Charter "is intended to constrain governmental action inconsistent with those rights and freedoms; it is not in itself an authorization for governmental action."

53. See, for example, *Big M Drug Mart, per* Dickson J. (as he then was); *R. v. Edwards Books and Art Ltd.*, [1986] 2 S.C.R. 713, *per* Dickson C.J. and *per* Wilson J.; *R. v. Keegstra*, [1990] 3 S.C.R. 697, *per* Dickson C.J.

54. *Reference re Bill 30, An Act to Amend the Education Act (Ont.)*, [1987] 1 S.C.R. 1148, *per* Wilson J.; *Adler v. Ontario*, [1996] 3 S.C.R. 609, *per* Iacobucci J.

55. However, statutory rules of interpretation (e.g., the federal Interpretation Act) do not apply to the Charter, because of its unique character as an entrenched law. See the ruling of Estey J. in *Skapinker*.

56. *Doucet-Boudreau v. Nova Scotia (Minister of Education)*, [2003] 3 S.C.R. 3, *per* Iacobucci and Arbour JJ.

57. M. Ann Hayward, "International Law and the Interpretation of the Canadian Charter of Rights and Freedoms: Uses and Justifications," *University of Western Ontario Law Review* 23 (1985), pp. 9–20; Maxwell Cohen and Anne F. Bayefsky, "The Canadian Charter of Rights and Freedoms and Public International Law," *Canadian Bar Review* 61 (March 1983), pp. 265–313; Graham Zellick, "The European Convention on Human Rights: Its Significance for Charter Litigation." in Robert J. Sharpe, ed., *Charter Litigation* (Toronto: Carswell, 1987), pp. 97–130; Jamie Cameron, "The Motor Vehicle Reference and the Relevance of American Doctrine in Charter Interpretation," in Sharpe, *Charter Litigation*, pp. 69–96.

58. *Re B.C. Motor Vehicle Act*, [1985] 2 S.C.R. 486, paragraph 18, *per* Lamer J. (as he then was).

59. Paul Bender, "The Canadian Charter of Rights and Freedoms and the United States Bill of Rights: A Comparison," *McGill Law Journal* 28, no. 4 (1983), p. 821.

60. *RWDSU v. Dolphin Delivery Ltd.*, [1986] 2 S.C.R. 573.

61. Ibid., paragraph 25, *per* McIntyre J.

62. Ibid., paragraph 34, *per* McIntyre J.

63. Ibid., paragraph 36, *per* McIntyre J.

64. Christopher P. Manfredi, *Judicial Power and the Charter: Canada and the Paradox of Liberal Constitutionalism*, 2nd ed. (Toronto: Oxford University Press, 2001), p. 46.

65. Knopff and Morton, *Charter Politics*, p. 190.

66. For a general discussion of the Court's approach to the common law under the Charter, see Robert J. Sharpe, Katherine E. Swinton, and Kent Roach, *The Charter of Rights and Freedoms*, 2nd ed. (Toronto: Irwin Law, 2002), pp. 91–94.

67. *BCGEU v. British Columbia (Attorney General)*, [1988] 2 S.C.R. 214.

68. *Dagenais v. Canadian Broadcasting Corp.*, [1994] 3 S.C.R. 835. At issue was the CBC docudrama *The Boys of St. Vincent*, which portrayed child sexual abuse by the Christian Brothers in Newfoundland. The show was scheduled to air during or shortly before the trials of four Christian Brothers on similar charges in Ontario. By a 5-4 majority, the Court held that a lower-court judge had erred in law when he granted an injunction preventing the CBC from airing the show. While the common-law rule protected the right to a fair trial, which is also a Charter value (s. 11(d)), it had to be applied in a manner consistent with the guarantee of free expression. The majority reformulated the common-law rule in order to balance the competing values at stake.

69. *Hill v. Church of Scientology of Toronto*, [1995] 2 S.C.R. 1130, paragraph 92, *per* Cory J.

70. Ibid., paragraph 95, *per* Cory J. (emphasis in original).

71. *R. v. Oakes*, [1986] 1 S.C.R. 103, paragraph 64, *per* Dickson C.J.

72. *Hunter v. Southam*, *per* Dickson J.; *Big M Drug Mart*, paragraph 117, *per* Dickson J.

73. See, e.g., *Keegstra*, paragraphs 88–89, *per* Dickson C.J.

74. *Andrews v. Law Society of British Columbia*, [1989] 1 S.C.R. 143, paragraph 34, *per* McIntyre J.; *Egan v. Canada*, [1995] 2 S.C.R. 513, paragraph 171, *per* Cory J.; *Law v. Canada (Minister of Employment and Immigration)*, [1999] 1 S.C.R. 497, paragraphs 48–50, *per* Iacobucci J.

75. The phrase "Charter Revolution" is taken from the work of Rainer Knopff and F.L. Morton. On the continuity between the Charter and the common law, see Kent Roach, *The Supreme Court on Trial: Judicial Activism or Democratic Dialogue?* (Toronto: Irwin Law, 2001).

76. See, e.g., Allan C. Hutchinson and Andrew Petter, "Private Rights/Public Wrongs: The Liberal Lie of the Charter," *University of Toronto Law Journal* 38 (1988), pp. 278–97. See also Richard Sigurdson's summary and critique of this view in "Left- and Right-Wing Charterphobia in Canada: A Critique of the Critics," *International Journal of Canadian Studies* 7–8 (Spring–Fall 1993), pp. 95–115.

77. Dale Gibson, *The Law of the Charter: General Principles* (Toronto: Carswell, 1986), p. 110.

78. *RWDSU v. Dolphin Delivery*, paragraph 39, *per* McIntyre J.

79. *Slaight Communications Inc. v. Davidson*, [1989] 1 S.C.R. 1038, *per* Dickson C.J.

80. *Canada (Minister of Employment and Immigration) v. Chiarelli*, [1992] 1 S.C.R. 711, paragraph 22, *per* Sopinka J.

81. Ibid., paragraph 24.

82. La Forest, "The Balancing of Interests," p. 134.

83. *Hunter v. Southam*, *per* Dickson J. (as he then was). The case arose from the warrantless search of a newspaper's offices by investigators of the Combines Investigation Branch. In this instance, the issue was not whether the investigators had followed improper procedure, but whether the authorizing section of the Combines Investigation Act violated s. 8.

84. *Edwards v. Attorney-General for Canada*, [1930] A.C. 124, *per* Viscount Sankey, at p. 136, quoted by Dickson J. (as he then was) in *Hunter v. Southam*, at p. 156. Note that the Court has not been entirely consistent in this approach; until recently, it construed "freedom of association" in s. 2(d) very narrowly (see Chapter 8, pages 272–78). See Chapter 3 for a more extensive analysis of the "large and liberal" approach to Charter guarantees.

85. Janet L. Hiebert, *Limiting Rights: The Dilemma of Judicial Review* (Montreal and Kingston: McGill-Queen's University Press, 1996), p. 6.

86. *Law Society of Upper Canada v. Skapinker*, [1984] 1 S.C.R. 358, p. 384.

87. *A.G. Quebec v. Quebec Association of Protestant School Boards*, [1984] 2 S.C.R. 66, headnotes. The case is discussed more fully in Chapter 7, pages 224–27.

88. *Hunter v. Southam*, p. 169.

89. *Big M Drug Mart*, paragraph 139.

90. *R. v. Thomsen*, [1988] 1 S.C.R. 640, *per* Le Dain J.

91. See, e.g., *Irwin Toy Ltd. v. Quebec (Attorney General)*, [1989] 1 S.C.R. 927, paragraph 62, *per* Dickson C.J. and Wilson J. See also *Reference re ss. 193 and 195.1(1)(c) of the Criminal Code (Man.)*, [1990] 1 S.C.R. 1123, *per* Dickson C.J. (the *Prostitution Reference*); *Committee for the Commonwealth of Canada v. Canada*, [1991] 1 S.C.R. 139, *per* L'Heureux-Dubé J.; *Osborne v. Canada (Treasury Board)*, [1991] 2 S.C.R. 69, *per* Sopinka J.; and *R. v. Nova Scotia Pharmaceutical Society*, [1992] 2 S.C.R. 606, *per* Gonthier J.

92. See the discussion of the *Figueroa* ruling in Dossier 9.3, pages 296–97.

93. In the 2002 *Sauvé* ruling on prisoner voting, Chief Justice McLachlin scolded the Department of Justice for advancing broad objectives that were of no assistance to the Court in its s. 1 analysis. See *Sauvé v. Canada (Chief Electoral Officer)*, paragraphs 16 and 20–26. See also *U.F.C.W., Local 1518 v. KMart Canada*, [1999] 2 S.C.R. 1083, paragraph 59, *per* Cory J.

94. Robert J. Sharpe and Kent Roach, *Brian Dickson: A Judge's Journey* (Toronto: University of Toronto Press/Osgoode Society for Canadian Legal History, 2003), p. 354. See also Dickson's judgment in *Edwards Books and Art*, especially paragraph 122: "Both in articulating the standard of proof and in describing the criteria comprising the proportionality requirement the Court has been careful to avoid rigid and inflexible standards."

95. Leon Trakman, William Cole-Hamilton, and Sean Gatien, "*R. v. Oakes* 1986–1997: Back to the Drawing Board," *Osgoode Hall Law Journal* 36 (1998), p. 85.

96. Peter W. Hogg, "Section 1 Revisited," *National Journal of Constitutional Law* 1 (1991), p. 3; see also Trakman, Cole-Hamilton, and Gatien, "*R. v. Oakes*," p. 85.

97. *Keegstra*, paragraph 42.

98. *RJR-MacDonald Inc. v. Canada (Attorney General)*, [1995] 3 S.C.R. 199, paragraph 62.

99. *RJR-MacDonald*, paragraphs 126–29.

100. *Egan v. Canada*, paragraphs 104–11. Justice L'Heureux-Dubé explicitly condemned Sopinka's approach to s. 1 at paragraph 100, arguing that it "undermines the very values which our Charter, including s. 1, seeks to preserve."

101. Trakman, Cole-Hamilton, and Gatien refer to this body of jurisprudence as "*Oakes*-plus"; see "*R. v. Oakes*," p. 108.

102. Trakman, Cole-Hamilton, and Gatien, "*R. v. Oakes*," p. 137; Martha Jackman, "Protecting Rights and Promoting Democracy: Judicial Review under Section 1 of the Charter," *Osgoode Hall Law Journal* 34 (1996), p. 661.

103. For a discussion of the impact of s. 24(1) on public law, see Christopher P. Manfredi, "*Re Lavigne and Ontario Public Service Employees Union*: Public Administration and Remedial Decree Litigation under the Charter of Rights and Freedoms," *Canadian Public Administration* 34, no. 3 (Autumn 1991), pp. 395–416.

104. *Schachter v. Canada*, [1992] 2 S.C.R. 679, paragraph 23, *per* Lamer C.J.

105. *Figueroa v. Canada (Attorney General)*, [2003] 1 S.C.R. 912, paragraph 93, *per* Iacobucci J.; *M. v. H.*, [1999] 2 S.C.R. 3, paragraphs 145–47, *per* Iacobucci J. The former case is analyzed in Dossier 9.3, pages 296–97; Dossier 11.4, pages 359–62, provides an extensive discussion of the latter.

106. *Schachter*, paragraph 79.

107. *R. v. Swain*, [1991] 1 S.C.R. 933, *per* Lamer C.J. See also the discussion of the *Feeney* ruling in Chapter 4, pages 161–64.

108. *Re Manitoba Language Rights*, [1985] 1 S.C.R. 721, paragraph 60, *per* Dickson C.J.

109. *Egan v. Canada*, paragraph 226, *per* Iacobucci J. (dissenting); *M. v. H.*, paragraph 146, *per* Iacobucci J. (for the majority). This position contradicts the reasoning of Lamer C.J. in *Schachter*, where he declared that "The question whether to delay the application of a declaration of nullity should therefore turn not on considerations of the role of the courts and the legislature" (paragraph 81), but it is consistent with the Court's recent emphasis on a "dialogue" with Parliament, as discussed in Chapter 4. See also Roach, *The Supreme Court on Trial*, pp. 200–4.

110. In the 1986 *Phillips* case, the Nova Scotia Court of Appeal struck down the provincial law that guaranteed welfare benefits to single parents, on the ground that it violated s. 15 by providing more generous welfare benefits to single mothers than to single fathers. This drastic remedy left all single parents in the province without welfare benefits, until such time as the provincial legislature could enact a new law. *Phillips* illustrates the problems inherent in a conservative judicial approach to equality rights: the Nova Scotia court did not wish to intrude into the budgetary prerogatives of the other two branches of government by ordering equal benefits for all single parents, and it saw no alternative to an immediate declaration of invalidity. See the discussion of *Phillips* in *Schachter*, at paragraph 38.

111. Trakman, Cole-Hamilton, and Gatien, "*R. v. Oakes*," p. 95.

112. "Reasonably necessary": *Edwards Books and Art*, paragraph 113, *per* Dickson C.J.; *RJR-MacDonald*, paragraph 149, *per* McLachlin J. Trakman, Cole-Hamilton, and Gatien found that eighty-six percent of nullified laws failed the "minimal impairment" test ("*R. v. Oakes*," p. 100).

113. *Thomson Newspapers Co. v. Canada (Attorney General)*, [1998] 1 S.C.R. 877, paragraph 120. Note, however, that the majority voted to strike down the offending provision immediately.

114. The new provisions were contained in sections 326 and 328 of Bill C-2, the revised Canada Elections Act adopted in 2000.

115. Peter W. Hogg and Allison A. Bushell, "The Charter Dialogue between Courts and Legislatures (Or Perhaps the Charter Isn't Such a Bad Thing After All)," *Osgoode Hall Law Journal* 35 (1997), p. 75–124; Roach, *The Supreme Court on Trial*, Chapter 10.

116. F.L. Morton, "Dialogue or Monologue?" in Paul Howe and Peter H. Russell, eds., *Judicial Power and Canadian Democracy* (Montreal and Kingston: McGill-Queen's University Press/Institute for Research on Public Policy, 2001), p. 111.

117. Manfredi, *Judicial Power*, p. 179. See also Mark Tushnet, "Policy Distortion and Democratic Debilitation: Comparative Illumination of the Countermajoritarian Difficulty," *Michigan Law Review* 94 (1995–96), especially pp. 247 and 250.

118. Although the Supreme Court has explicitly declared the presumption of constitutionality inapplicable in Charter cases—because its strict application would render the remedial power in s. 52(1) meaningless—it has nonetheless imported the rules of statutory interpretation into its Charter jurisprudence at the remedial stage of analysis. See *Manitoba (A.G.) v. Metropolitan Stores Ltd.*, [1987] 1 S.C.R. 110, paragraphs 12–26, *per* Beetz J.

119. Ruth Sullivan, *Statutory Interpretation* (Toronto: Irwin Law, 1997), p. 179.

120. *R. v. Sharpe*, 2001 SCC 2, paragraphs 114–27, *per* McLachlin C.J.

121. *R. v. Heywood*, [1994] 3 S.C.R. 761, paragraph 70, *per* Cory J.

122. Knopff and Morton, *Charter Politics*, p. 98. See also Morton and Knopff, *The Charter Revolution and the Court Party*, pp. 15–16.

123. Manfredi, *Judicial Power*, Chapters 1 and 7.

124. Roach, *The Supreme Court on Trial*, p. 220.

125. Ibid., p. 251.

126. Manfredi, *Judicial Power*, p. 134.

127. Ian Greene, Carl Baar, Peter McCormick, George Szablowski, and Martin Thomas, *Final Appeal: Decision-Making in Canadian Courts of Appeal* (Toronto: Lorimer, 1998), p. 121.

Chapter 2

The Origins and Development of the Charter

The late Ivan Rand was the leading defender of civil rights on the Supreme Court in the 1940s and 1950s.

Photographer unknown, Supreme Court of Canada Collection. Reprinted with permission.

THE JUDICIAL ENFORCEMENT OF HUMAN RIGHTS: FROM FEDERALISM AND THE COMMON LAW TO THE CHARTER

The creation of the Canadian Charter of Rights and Freedoms was a lengthy and controversial process. There was strong resistance to the constitutional entrenchment of rights, particularly from those provincial governments that feared the erosion of their legislative and administrative powers. In Canada, unlike the United States, there was no indigenous tradition of judicially enforceable rights. On the contrary, Canadian judges and politicians clung to the British principle of **parliamentary supremacy**—even as that principle began to lose its political legitimacy in the second half of the twentieth century.[1] But by the mid-1980s, a majority of Canadians believed that the courts should have the final say on laws that infringed rights and freedoms. Most voters no longer perceived Parliament as the best safeguard against violations of their human rights.[2]

The gradual loss of faith in parliamentary supremacy requires some explanation. There is nothing wrong with the claim that elected legislators, and the cabinets that are formally accountable to them, should have the final word on public policy. As we will see in Part 2, the federal executive branch—unlike the Supreme Court—employs experts who can assess the practical impact of a proposed law. The administrative arm of the executive has the tools to implement policy effectively. Parliamentarians, unlike judges, are directly elected by the citizens. When MPs and public servants have to balance rights and freedoms against competing social values, they have the institutional capacity to respect both the fiscal constraints of government and the political preferences of the electorate. These are strong arguments in favour of parliamentary supremacy and against the judicial enforcement of entrenched rights and freedoms.

In the early 1980s, political resistance to an entrenched Charter finally yielded to three countervailing forces. The first was the growing perception that existing protections for civil liberties were inadequate. While elected legislators and public servants may have enjoyed the political and institutional capacity to balance rights against other social goals, some observers argued that their choices—especially those taken under conditions of crisis—gave short shrift to individual liberties. The apparent ineffectiveness of the 1960 Bill of Rights, an ordinary federal statute, strengthened the argument for entrenchment. The second force was a new international focus on human rights, fostered by the United Nations and other supranational bodies. Canada was not immune to this trend: after 1945, a growing chorus of lawyers, politicians, and interest groups demanded that our federal and provincial governments live up to their commitments under the Universal Declaration of Human Rights and subsequent international agreements. Third, Canadians elected a prime minister with the determination and the political resources to entrench a strong Charter of Rights with explicit judicial remedies for its violation. For Pierre Elliott Trudeau, constitutional protection for language and mobility rights was the best defence against provincial demands for autonomy—and, in particular, the separatist movement in Quebec. The confluence of these three forces in 1980–82 finally overcame the principle of parliamentary supremacy.

We may conveniently divide the history of civil rights in Canada into three periods:

- From 1867 to 1960, the courts had the power to interpret and apply written statutes. They also had the power to make policy, as they interpreted statutes and adapted British common-law principles to new circumstances. In most instances, they refrained from striking down laws that violated rights and freedoms. Parliament was supreme, and if it chose to pursue other social goals at the expense of civil liberties, there was little the courts could (or would) do about it.

- From 1960 until 1982, the Supreme Court had the power to "construe and apply" federal laws in conformity to the Bill of Rights. Had they chosen to do so, they might have used the Bill as both a shield against discrimination and a sword to defend rights and freedoms. With one notable exception (see Dossier 2.8, pages 65–66), they chose instead to defer to Parliament—even in instances when the contradiction between the statute and the Bill was too obvious to ignore.

- The third period began in 1982, when Canadian courts were given the explicit right and responsibility to make and unmake law as required by the Charter of Rights.

In legal and constitutional terms, 1982 was a watershed. In practical terms, the impact of the Charter is less clear. While some areas of public policy—notably criminal justice and election law—have been transformed by the judicial application of the Charter, others have remained relatively unchanged. Many of the factors that have enhanced the impact of entrenched rights and freedoms were already in place before 1982: a Supreme Court with control over its own docket and a preference for public-law appeals; a growing cadre of rights-minded lawyers, legal scholars, and judges; a political culture influenced by American "rights talk"; and a willingness by some interest groups to pursue their policy goals through litigation.[3] All of these factors helped create the Charter, instead of being created by it. Therefore, it is more accurate to say that the Charter reflected and reinforced preexisting trends than to claim that the entrenchment of rights and freedoms transformed Canadian politics and government.

This does not mean, however, that the events of April 17, 1982, have left no traces on our politics and government. The entrenchment of judicial remedies, and the willingness of the Supreme Court to use those remedies, has forced the other branches of government to take their Charter duties seriously. Given the minority status of some "Charter groups" (e.g., Aboriginal Canadians or gays and lesbians) and the unpopularity of others (e.g., suspected or convicted criminals), it is unlikely that either Parliament or the executive branch would have struck the same balance between rights and competing social values as the courts have done. If we compare the pre-Charter record of rights protection by Canadian governments to the jurisprudence discussed in Part 3, the Charter's impact on Canadian law is clearly evident.

JUDICIAL PROTECTION OF HUMAN RIGHTS IN CANADA, 1867–1960

The Judicial Committee of the Privy Council, 1867–1949

The Charter of Rights did not introduce the concept of judicial review into Canada. Since Confederation, our courts have been asked to rule on the constitutional validity of federal and provincial laws. The Supreme Court was established in 1875, by an ordinary act of Parliament, under the authority granted by s. 101 of the British North America Act (now called the Constitution Act, 1867). However, the Court was supreme in name only: as subjects of the British Crown, Canadian citizens had the right of appeal to the Judicial Committee of the Privy Council (JCPC) in London.[4] Until such appeals were abolished in 1949, a plaintiff who lost in Ottawa could take his case to the JCPC, hoping for a more positive result.

But if our hypothetical plaintiff asked the JCPC to protect his rights and freedoms, he was almost certain to be disappointed. Neither the JCPC nor the Supreme Court paid much attention to the civil liberties of Canadian citizens, for three reasons. First, the British North America (BNA) Act recognizes only a few rights, most of which apply to relatively small groups. Examples include s. 133 (the right to use either English or French in legislatures and courts), s. 93 (protection for denominational schools), and s. 50 (a five-year limit on the length of a Parliament between general elections). Before 1982, there was no broad guarantee of rights and freedoms in the Canadian Constitution.

Second, the vast majority of constitutional cases were brought by one level of government against the other. Few private individuals could afford to seek judicial recognition of their common-law rights. Consequently, most constitutional rulings from Ottawa and London dealt with the division of powers between the federal and provincial governments, as set out in ss. 91–95 of the BNA Act.

Third, both the Justices and the Law Lords were bound by the principle of parliamentary supremacy. In the British tradition, Parliament's lawmaking power is almost limitless. In Canada, that broad discretion is divided between the federal Parliament and the provincial legislatures. A national law concerning primary education would be unconstitutional, as would a provincial law on banking or currency. (Primary education is a provincial responsibility under s. 93 of the Constitution Act, 1867; banking and currency are federal matters under s. 91.) If either law were challenged in court, it would be declared ***ultra vires*** (beyond the power of) the sponsoring legislature.

Before 1982, the federal and provincial legislatures were collectively supreme: what one level of government could not do, the other could. The effect, as lawyer and civil libertarian F.R. Scott pointed out in 1949, was to leave rights and freedoms at the mercy of legislators.

> No acts of any parliament in Canada can be held *ultra vires* just because they punish a man without trial ... or because they confiscate his property without compensation or interfere with his private contracts. We can create *ex post facto* crimes, we can prescribe cruel and unusual punishments, and can do many things which are denied to American legislatures.... The courts are only called upon to see that the boundaries of Dominion and provincial jurisdiction are not crossed, and may not decide upon the morality or justice of the law. Their sole function is to ensure that the law in question has been enacted by the proper legislature.[5]

Much of the time, the legislators did their jobs well. But they could not always be relied on to defend the liberties of unpopular or frightening groups against a hostile public opinion. They knew that the JCPC would not invalidate a law that violated human rights, because their constitutional mandate restricted the Law Lords to determining whether the law had been passed by the appropriate level of government. Dossier 2.1 describes one such case.

DOSSIER 2.1

CUNNINGHAM V. TOMEY HOMMA (1903)

In 1900, a Japanese-born Canadian citizen named Tomey Homma applied for inclusion on the voters' list in Vancouver. His application was rejected. Under British Columbia's Provincial Elections Act, it was a criminal offence to register a "Chinaman, Japanese, or Indian" to vote, even if he was a Canadian citizen.[1] The law defined a "Japanese" as "any person of the Japanese race naturalized or not." Homma took the province to court. Although he was clearly a victim of racial discrimination, such treatment was perfectly legal under the Constitution. So Homma argued instead that the law was *ultra vires* the British Columbia legislature because it dealt with a matter of federal jurisdiction—in this instance, "Naturalization and Aliens" (s. 91(25) of the BNA Act). The provincial government replied that the law was *intra vires* because it pertained to provincial elections (s. 92(1)). The County Court and the Supreme Court of Canada agreed with Homma, and voted to invalidate the law. The province appealed to the JCPC.

The Law Lords appear to have disapproved of the discriminatory law. They pointedly stated that "the policy or impolicy of such an enactment as that which excludes a particular race from the franchise is not a topic which their Lordships are entitled to consider."[2] All that they could do was to decide whether the law trenched on federal jurisdiction. The JCPC found that it did not. The Law Lords held that the deliberate disenfranchisement of racial minorities by a province was a matter falling within provincial jurisdiction. The lower-court rulings were overturned and the law was upheld.

ENDNOTES

1. *Cunningham and Attorney General for British Columbia v. Tomey Homma*, JCPC 1903, reprinted in Richard A. Olmstead, ed., *Decisions of the Judicial Committee of the Privy Council*, vol. 1 (Ottawa: Queen's Printer, 1954), p. 481.

2. *Tomey Homma*, p. 484.

The influence of the JCPC on Canadian law is still hotly debated.[6] In general, its impact on Canadian rights and freedoms was negligible. But there is one striking exception: its 1929 ruling in the "Persons Case." As Dossier 2.2 points out, however, the issue in that case had nothing to do with the division of powers; their Lordships accordingly had no choice but to confront the problem of discrimination directly.

DOSSIER 2.2

THE "PERSONS CASE"

By 1921, most Canadian women were eligible to vote in federal elections and to contest seats in the House of Commons.[1] But no woman had ever been appointed to the Senate. When, in 1921, five Alberta women asked the prime minister to appoint Emily Murphy,[2] he refused. King pointed out that s. 24 of the BNA Act—the section empowering him to appoint Senators—

referred to "Qualified Persons" and argued that women were not "Persons" in the legal sense. The "Famous Five" would not take no for an answer.[3] They petitioned the federal government to refer the question to the Supreme Court of Canada. In 1928, a unanimous Court rejected their claim. The nine (male) Justices ruled that women were not legal "Persons" for the purposes of s. 24 because they had not enjoyed that status when the BNA Act took effect in 1867.

The Five appealed to the JCPC. On October 18, 1929, the Law Lords delivered a judgment that has become a keystone of Canadian constitutional law.[4] The ruling was a victory for the Five: "Their Lordships are of opinion that the word 'persons' in s. 24 does include women, and that women are eligible to be summoned to and become members of the Senate of Canada."[5] The Law Lords were careful to limit the scope of their decision, insisting that they were not "deciding any question as to the rights of women."[6] Nonetheless, the "Persons Case" is a landmark in the history of Canadian women. "Persons Day" is celebrated every October 18, to celebrate the Famous Five and their achievements. On October 18, 2000, a monument to the Five was unveiled on Parliament Hill—just a few yards away from the Senate chamber. Ironically, none of the Five came so close to the Senate doors in real life; when King finally appointed a woman Senator in 1930, he chose Liberal Cairine Wilson.

The broader impact of the ruling lies in the Lords' sweeping declaration of the purposes of Canada's Constitution, and the proper approach to its interpretation:

> The British North America Act planted in Canada a living tree capable of growth and expansion within its natural limits.... Their Lordships do not conceive it to be the duty of this Board—it is certainly not their desire—to cut down the provisions of the Act by a narrow and technical construction, but rather to give it a large and liberal interpretation...[7]

From the very beginning of Charter jurisprudence, these words have guided the Supreme Court in its interpretation of the protected rights and freedoms.[8]

ENDNOTES

1. Many men and women of East Asian ancestry could not vote, regardless of citizenship, until 1948. "Indians" who lived on-reserve were disenfranchised until 1960; before that date, they could not vote unless they gave up their tax-exempt status. See Elections Canada, *A History of the Vote in Canada* (Ottawa: Minister of Public Works and Government Services, 1997), pp. 80–83 and 85–89.

2. Emily Murphy (1868–1933) was the first female magistrate in the British Empire. She was also a best-selling author and prominent social activist. See Grant MacEwan, *Mighty Women: Stories of Western Canadian Pioneers* (Vancouver: GreyStone, 1995 [1975]), pp. 127–37.

3. In addition to Murphy, they included: Henrietta Muir Edwards (1849–1931), a lifelong advocate of legal reforms for women and children; Louise C. McKinney (1868–1931), the first woman in the British Empire to take her seat in an elected legislature; Irene Parlby (1868–1965), founding president of the United Alberta Farm Women and the second female cabinet minister in Canada; and Nellie McClung (1873–1951), the leader of the crusade for women's voting rights in Manitoba and the only woman to represent Canada at the League of Nations in 1918. For further information, see the website of the Famous 5 Foundation (www.famous5.org).

4. *Henrietta Muir Edwards v. Attorney-General for Canada*, JCPC, 1929; reprinted in Olmstead, *Decisions*, vol. 2, pp. 630–48.

5. Ibid., p. 633.

6. Ibid., p. 642.

7. Ibid., pp. 641–42.

8. *Law Society of Upper Canada v. Skapinker*, [1984] 1 S.C.R. 357, p. 365, *per* Estey J.

The Supreme Court of Canada, 1867–1960: The Failure of the "Implied Bill of Rights"

With the abolition of appeals to the JCPC in 1949, the Supreme Court became the final court of appeal for Canadians. Despite its newfound legal supremacy, the Court remained as deferential to Parliament as it had always been. Its constitutional mandate had not changed: the Justices were still required to enforce the division of powers, not the rights of citizens.

Nonetheless, a handful of Justices were willing to challenge legislators who disregarded common-law rights. In 1938, then–Chief Justice Lyman Duff—with the support of his brethren—declared that the BNA Act (The Constitution Act, 1867) contained an "implied bill of rights." The "Duff Doctrine" relied on the traditional common-law techniques of interpretation. Had it commanded majority support in subsequent rulings, the "implied bill of rights" might have forced federal and provincial governments to weigh the political balance more heavily in favour of common-law liberties. But as Dossier 2.3 explains, the "Duff Doctrine" foundered on the rocks of parliamentary supremacy.

DOSSIER 2.3

THE "IMPLIED BILL OF RIGHTS" IN THE CONSTITUTION ACT, 1867

In 1935, in the depths of the Great Depression, the voters of Alberta elected their first Social Credit government. The Social Credit Party based its platform on the economic theory of social credit, which originated in England in the 1920s and which promised to end the Depression through monetary reform.[1] The government would distribute "purchasing power" among the population by means of "social credit." In so doing, it would enable everyone to buy more goods and services, thus stimulating the economy and putting the unemployed back to work. The source of the purchasing power lay in the unused capacity of the industrial economy. In its simplest terms, social credit was a "demand-side" solution to the problems of capitalism. By taking credit away from the banks and putting it in the hands of the people, the new government of Alberta hoped to release pent-up demand among the poor and thus trigger an economic boom in the province.

In 1937, the Aberhart government moved to put its social credit policies into effect. As part of a comprehensive legislative program, it adopted the Bank Taxation Act, the Credit of Alberta Regulations Act, and the Accurate News and Information Act. The first two statutes were designed to eliminate the private banking industry in the province and to establish a mechanism for turning industrial capacity into purchasing power. The third statute required every newspaper in Alberta to publish, in its entirety and without amendment, any statement by the chairman of the Social Credit Board concerning the operation of the new economic system. The Accurate News and Information Act (the Alberta Press Bill, for short) also obliged publishers to disclose the name, address, and occupation of anyone who criticized the government's policies in print. The federal government used its power under the BNA Act to disallow three of the other laws in the social credit package, and to reserve the three laws listed above for review by the Supreme Court. It asked the Court whether the three laws were *ultra vires* the legislature of Alberta.

The Court found the first two laws *ultra vires*, as intrusions on the federal power to regulate banking, trade, and commerce. Because its operation presumed their validity, the Alberta Press Bill was automatically *ultra vires* too. But Chief Justice Duff went beyond the division of powers. On two separate grounds, he found that the BNA Act contained an implied bill of rights that was violated by the Press Bill. In the first place, the BNA Act "contemplates a parliament working under the influence of public opinion and public discussion."

> There can be no controversy that such institutions derive their efficacy from the free public discussion of affairs, from criticism and answer and counter-criticism, from attack upon policy and administration and defence and counter-attack; from the freest and fullest analysis and examination from every point of view of political proposals.... [I]t is axiomatic that the practice of this right of free public discussion of public affairs, notwithstanding its incidental mischiefs, is the breath of life for parliamentary institutions.[2]

Second, the **Preamble** to the BNA Act—which gave Canada "a Constitution similar in Principle to that of the United Kingdom"—did more than import the unwritten conventions of English parliamentary government. It also guaranteed the historic rights of British subjects to the citizens of the new Dominion. Although Duff focused on freedom of speech and worship, later commentators on the "implied bill of rights" added peaceful participation in politics, security from arbitrary government power (i.e., the rule of law), and the assurance of fair treatment by the justice system.[3]

Duff concluded that the subject matter of the Accurate News and Information Act—the fundamental civil liberties of Canadians—lay within federal jurisdiction. He held that freedom of the press was a universal concern, not a "purely local" matter assigned to provincial jurisdiction. Therefore, the law was *ultra vires* the Alberta legislature. But the "Duff Doctrine" left one crucial question unanswered: were some rights and freedoms beyond the reach of both levels of government? In other words, could an "implied bill of rights" ever trump the supremacy of Parliament?

Duff never stated explicitly that the rights in the BNA Act were immune from legislative interference. However, he hinted that a law that "effects such a curtailment of the exercise of the right of public discussion as substantially to interfere with the working of the parliamentary institutions of Canada" might well run afoul of the courts, which have a responsibility to ensure that those institutions have sufficient "scope" to perform properly.[4] His colleague Justice Cannon, who found the law *ultra vires* the province on other grounds,[5] disagreed with the implication that free expression should be beyond the reach of both levels of government: "The federal parliament is the sole authority to curtail, if deemed expedient and in the public interest, the freedom of the press."[6]

For better or worse, the "Duff Doctrine" never swayed a majority of Justices on the Supreme Court. The danger of an "implied bill of rights," visible only to the judicial eye, is that no one—Parliament, citizens, or police officers—can anticipate which laws or actions will violate its terms and which will not. The Doctrine was in direct conflict with other aspects of the Constitution, particularly the supremacy of Parliament.[7] But had the Supreme Court been willing and able to clarify and enforce the "Duff Doctrine," it might have changed Canadian history. Would the federal government have interned innocent Japanese Canadians during World War II? Would Canadians of Asian ancestry have been barred from voting in federal elections until 1947, and Aboriginal Canadians on reserves until 1960? And would either the 1960 Bill of Rights or the 1982 Charter have been necessary?[8]

ENDNOTES

1. C.B. Macpherson, *Democracy in Alberta: Social Credit and the Party System*, 2nd ed. (Toronto: University of Toronto Press, 1962), Chapter 4.

2. *Reference re Alberta Statutes*, [1938] S.C.R. 100, p. 133, *per* Duff C.J.

3. Comprehensive lists of the rights in the BNA Act can be found in Scott, "Dominion Jurisdiction over Human Rights and Fundamental Freedoms," pp. 213–14; and Walter Surma Tarnopolsky, *The Canadian Bill of Rights*, 2nd rev. ed. (Toronto: McClelland and Stewart, 1975), p. 29.

(continued)

4. *Reference re Alberta Statutes*, pp. 134–35, *per* Duff C.J.

5. Cannon ruled that the Press Bill was a criminal statute, because it identified offences for which an accused could be found guilty and incarcerated. Because the criminal law is a federal power under s. 91(27), the bill was *ultra vires*.

6. *Reference re Alberta Statutes*, p. 146, *per* Cannon J.

7. Ian Greene, *The Charter of Rights* (Toronto: Lorimer, 1989), p. 20.

8. Peter H. Russell, Rainer Knopff, and Ted Morton, eds., *Federalism and the Charter: Leading Constitutional Decisions* (Ottawa: Carleton University Press, 1989), p. 318.

The abolition of appeals to the JCPC coincided with the growing international consciousness of human rights after World War II. Under the circumstances, the Supreme Court might have carved out a bold new Canadian jurisprudence of civil liberties. Most Justices refused to do so. The exceptions were younger Justices with American training in the law of entrenched rights. One of these, Ivan Rand, tried repeatedly to attract majority support for the "Duff Doctrine." But as Dossier 2.4 explains, not even the blatant disregard of basic rights by an autocratic premier could convince the Court to compromise parliamentary supremacy.

DOSSIER 2.4

PREMIER DUPLESSIS VERSUS THE COMMUNISTS AND THE JEHOVAH'S WITNESSES

The Union Nationale under Maurice Duplessis governed Quebec for almost twenty years (1936–39, 1944–60). Premier Duplessis was an autocrat, a staunch supporter of the Catholic Church, and a man deeply suspicious of "alien" ideas.[1] He waged a bitter campaign against two groups that he perceived as mortal enemies of Quebec: Communists and Jehovah's Witnesses. The latter drew his particular wrath because of their intemperate anti-Catholic rhetoric, vividly expressed in the pamphlets that they handed out in the streets. Duplessis was not the only public official in the province who disliked the Witnesses. As early as 1933, the City of Quebec had adopted a bylaw that required anyone who wished to distribute literature in a public place to secure the written permission of the chief of police before doing so. While other religious and secular groups had no difficulty winning police approval, every application by the Witnesses was turned down.

In 1953, the Supreme Court heard an appeal arising from a lawsuit against the City of Quebec.[2] Laurier Saumur, an active Witness, sought a judicial declaration that the bylaw was *ultra vires* both the municipal government and the province (the city bylaws were given force by a provincial statute). Saumur argued that the real purpose of the bylaw was to censor free expression and to prohibit the religious activities of his faith, not (as the city claimed) to prevent littering, traffic congestion, and public nuisance. He further argued that freedom of expression and religion were matters falling under federal jurisdiction, insofar as they were not expressly mentioned in s. 92 of the British North America Act.[3]

Four of the Justices agreed that the bylaw was *ultra vires*, although for differing reasons, and declared it invalid. They found that freedom of religion was not a "civil right," which would make it a provincial matter, but a natural right of all Canadians:

Strictly speaking, civil rights arise from positive law; but freedom of speech, religion and the inviolability of the person, are original freedoms which are at once the necessary attributes and modes of self-expression of human beings and the primary conditions of their community life within a legal order.... That legislation "in relation" to religion and its profession is not a local or private matter would seem to me to be self-evident.[4]

Following Chief Justice Duff's ruling in the *Alberta Press* case, Justices Rand, Kellock, and Locke found protection for expressive and religious freedom in the Preamble to the BNA Act. Justice Estey did not take this view, preferring instead to identify statutory sources for a federal power to regulate religious freedom. A fifth Justice concluded that religion fell under "Property and Civil Rights" in s. 92(13) of the BNA Act, and was therefore a matter for the province to regulate as it saw fit.[5] However, he found that the treatment of the Witnesses violated Quebec's Freedom of Worship Act, and so he "read down" the bylaw to exclude religious groups from the requirement to seek prior permission. The other four Justices, including the three from Quebec,[6] dissented: they would have upheld the bylaw as a valid exercise of municipal and provincial powers.

Because only four of the nine Justices held that religion was a federal responsibility, the ruling gave provincial governments—including that of Duplessis—the power to restrict religious freedom. The Duplessis government subsequently amended the Freedom of Worship Act, expressly excluding Jehovah's Witnesses from statutory protection. Saumur's attempt to have the revised provincial statute declared unconstitutional was dismissed on technical grounds.[7] So Rand's attempt to revive the "implied bill of rights" failed.

Four years later, the Justices revisited the Duplessis government's record on civil liberties. This time, the impugned statute was the notorious 1937 "Padlock Law" (formally entitled

An Act to Protect the Province against Communistic Propaganda). The law permitted the police to seize and secure any private premises that had been used by professed or alleged Communists. In January 1949, John Switzman was caught storing and distributing Communist literature in his rented apartment. He was locked out, and his landlady (Freda Elbling) took him to court to cancel his lease and cover her damages. Switzman fought the lawsuit by challenging the constitutionality of the "Padlock Law." He argued that the law was *ultra vires* the provincial legislature because it was criminal law in pith and substance. Eight of the nine Justices agreed; only Justice Taschereau dissented on the grounds that the law was a legitimate exercise of the province's authority over "Property and Civil Rights." Of the eight Justices in the majority, five relied solely on the division-of-powers argument. The other three—Rand, Kellock, and Abbott—also condemned the law as a violation of expressive freedom. According to Justice Rand:

Parliamentary government postulates a capacity in men, acting freely and under self-restraints, to govern themselves; and that advance is best served in the degree achieved of individual liberation from subjective as well as objective shackles.... Liberty in [political expression] is little less vital to man's mind and spirit than breathing is to his physical existence.[8]

Justice Abbott went even further. He declared that the right of free political expression was *ultra vires* not only the provincial legislature but Parliament as well.[9] But despite this bold—and historically unique—assertion of human rights over parliamentary supremacy, the "Duff Doctrine" was again rejected by a majority of the Court.

The final round in the battle between the Court and the Duplessis government came in 1959, with the case of *Roncarelli v. Duplessis*. Frank Roncarelli was a successful Montreal restaurateur and a devout Jehovah's Witness.

(continued)

He posted bail for hundreds of his fellow Witnesses who were arrested for distributing their religious tracts in public. All of the charges were later dropped. When Duplessis learned that the man who was frustrating his persecution of the Witnesses happened to hold a provincial liquor licence for his restaurant, he ordered Quebec's liquor commissioner to cancel that licence immediately and to inform Roncarelli that it would never be renewed. This arbitrary action drove Roncarelli into bankruptcy. He sued Duplessis personally, arguing that the premier (who was also the attorney general) had abused the power of his office and was liable for damages.

In 1959, a six-Justice majority agreed with Roncarelli. The evidence of Duplessis's personal interference in the commission's decision-making, and his intent to ruin Roncarelli because of his ties to the Witnesses, was overwhelming. Justice Rand's remarks were particularly scathing. He observed that when "administration according to law" is replaced by "action dictated by and according to the arbitrary likes, dislikes and irrelevant purposes of public officers," the rule of law is coming to an end.[10] The majority awarded Mr. Roncarelli substantial damages and ordered his liquor licence restored. Unfortunately, the passage of time made the victory hollow: Roncarelli had lost his restaurant years before the Court ruled in his favour.

ENDNOTES

1. Kenneth McRoberts, *Quebec: Social Change and Political Crisis*, 3rd ed. (Toronto: McClelland and Stewart, 1988), Chapters 3 and 4.

2. *Saumur v. City of Quebec* [1953], 2 S.C.R. 299.

3. Now the Constitution Act, 1867.

4. *Saumur v. Quebec*, p. 329, *per* Rand J.

5. Ibid., p. 323, *per* Kellock J.

6. Indeed, Chief Justice Rinfret—one of the two Justices from Montreal—seems to have been personally offended by the Witness tracts that were entered into evidence. After quoting two particularly virulent anti-Catholic passages, he asked: "Quel tribunal condemnerait un conseil municipal qui empêcherait la circulation de pareilles déclarations?" [What court would condemn a city council which prohibited the circulation of such statements?] *Saumur v. Quebec*, p. 318, *per* Rinfret C.J.

7. Peter H. Russell, Rainer Knopff, and Ted Morton, eds., *Federalism and the Charter: Leading Constitutional Decisions* (Ottawa: Carleton University Press, 1989), p. 300.

8. *Switzman v. Elbling*, [1957] S.C.R. 285, p. 306, *per* Rand J.

9. Ibid., p. 328, *per* Abbott J.

10. *Roncarelli v. Duplessis*, [1959] S.C.R. 121, p. 142, *per* Rand J.

Paradoxically, the claim of an "implied bill of rights" in the BNA Act had little effect until *after* the Charter provided explicit constitutional protection for rights and freedoms. The contrast between the *Dupond* and *OPSEU* rulings is instructive. In the *Dupond* case, decided by the Supreme Court in 1978, a majority rejected the claim that a Quebec City bylaw prohibiting public meetings should be struck down on the basis of *Saumur* and *Switzman*. For the majority, Justice Beetz ruled that freedoms of expression, association, and assembly were not "so enshrined in the Constitution as to be beyond the reach of competent [i.e., *intra vires*] legislation." Nor were they common-law English freedoms that could be "read into" the 1867 Preamble.[7]

Although the *OPSEU* ruling was issued in 1987, the dispute between the Ontario government and its employees predated the Charter. Provincial public servants challenged an Ontario law that forbade them to participate in politics, arguing that it violated the common-law freedoms protected by the 1867 Preamble. Although the Supreme Court dismissed their appeal, the majority—led by, of all people, Justice Beetz—explicitly endorsed the "implied bill of rights."[8] For the first time in almost half a century, the "Duff Doctrine" commanded the support of a majority on the Court. More recently, the Court has identified the 1867 Preamble as the wellspring not only of parliamentary democracy but of political accountability, judicial independence, and the foundational principles of our entire system of government.[9] The Charter appears to have breathed new life into the approach used to create the "implied bill of rights," despite rendering its content redundant.[10]

Before 1982, the courts had good reason to take a cautious approach to rights and freedoms. Judges had no clear constitutional mandate to evaluate the impact of laws on civil liberties, or to fashion judicial remedies for infringements. As discussed in Chapter 3, there was little support for judicial policy-making among lawyers, interest groups, or judges themselves. By the 1950s, however, the intellectual climate was beginning to change. Justice Rand's eloquent defence of rights and freedoms commanded wide support among a younger generation of lawyers and academics. The Universal Declaration of Human Rights and the civil-rights jurisprudence of the American Supreme Court—especially *Brown v. Board of Education*,[11] which declared racially segregated schools to be unconstitutional—threw a harsh light on Canada's rights record. The internment of Japanese Canadians, the suspension of legal rights during the "red scares" of the 1930s and late 1940s, the denial of basic human dignity and recognition to Aboriginal Canadians—these and other shameful episodes in Canadian history inspired demands for enforceable guarantees of rights and freedoms.[12] A small but growing cadre of progressive lawyers and academics found a more receptive audience for their claim that legislators could not always be trusted to defend civil liberties against a hostile or fearful majority.

The Bill of Rights, 1960–82

The postwar years brought a newly heightened awareness of civil rights, both in the United States and in Canada. Several provinces enacted anti-discrimination laws and human rights codes.[13] In 1945, MP Alistair

Stewart put a motion on the Commons floor calling for a constitutional bill of rights.[14] The following year, a new Citizenship Act prompted calls for a new and uniquely Canadian identity, distinct from Britain, which could educate and inspire recent arrivals to Canada.[15] John Diefenbaker, a Progressive Conservative MP and future prime minister, tried to amend the Citizenship Act to include a bill of rights. In 1947, the federal government set up a Joint Committee of the Senate and House of Commons on Human Rights and Fundamental Freedoms to study the idea.[16] The creation of the Universal Declaration of Human Rights in 1948 heightened global awareness of rights and freedoms and placed new responsibilities on Canada's governments.

Unlike the opposition parties in the House of Commons, the Liberal government was not enthusiastic about a bill of rights. Its spokesmen claimed that the British tradition of parliamentary supremacy was the best protection for civil liberties, especially when combined with a federal division of powers.[17] Despite repeated calls from the Canadian Bar Association and other interest groups, and the moral obligations arising from Canada's participation in the United

Former prime minister John Diefenbaker was the chief advocate of a Canadian bill of rights. He achieved his goal in 1960.

CP PHOTO/Ted Grant

Nations, the Liberals refused to enact statutory protection for rights and freedoms. A bill of rights had to wait until after 1957, when the Conservatives under Diefenbaker defeated the Liberals. With a huge majority in the 1958 election, Diefenbaker had the perfect opportunity to achieve his highest political priority. But one problem remained: the question of whether or not to entrench the proposed bill of rights in the Constitution. An entrenched bill would apply to, and override, both federal and provincial laws. In other words, a federal or provincial statute that conflicted with an entrenched bill could be invalidated by a court. In 1950, a special Senate committee concluded that an entrenched bill would be the most effective way to protect rights and freedoms. But for both practical and political reasons, it recommended against entrenchment until such time as the Constitution could be amended in Canada. (See the discussion of **patriation**, below.) However, "as an interim measure, the Canadian Parliament [should] adopt a Declaration of Human Rights to be strictly limited to its own legislative jurisdiction."[18]

The Diefenbaker government tabled its draft bill in 1958, then withdrew it to give interested groups and individuals a chance to study and comment on it. When the bill was reintroduced in 1960, a House of Commons special committee held hearings and proposed amendments. Despite these opportunities, there was little public discussion. The 1960 committee hearings attracted only sixteen witnesses, one of whom was the sponsoring minister of justice.[19] The Bill of Rights was passed unanimously by the House of Commons, and it passed quickly through the remaining legislative stages. It received royal assent in August 1960. (See Dossier 2.5 for the full text of the 1960 Bill of Rights.)

DOSSIER 2.5

THE 1960 BILL OF RIGHTS

AN ACT FOR THE RECOGNITION AND PROTECTION OF HUMAN RIGHTS AND FUNDAMENTAL FREEDOMS

Preamble

The Parliament of Canada, affirming that the Canadian Nation is founded upon principles that acknowledge the supremacy of God, the dignity and worth of the human person and the position of the family in a society of free men and free institutions;

Affirming also that men and institutions remain free only when freedom is founded upon respect for moral and spiritual values and the rule of law;

And being desirous of enshrining these principles and the human rights and fundamental freedoms derived from them, in a Bill of Rights which shall reflect the respect of Parliament for its constitutional authority and which shall ensure the protection of these rights and freedoms in Canada:

Therefore Her Majesty, by and with the advice and consent of the Senate and House of Commons of Canada, enacts as follows:

PART I • BILL OF RIGHTS

Recognition and declaration of rights and freedoms

1. It is hereby recognized and declared that in Canada there have existed and shall continue to exist without discrimination by reason of race, national origin, colour, religion or sex, the following human rights and fundamental freedoms, namely,

(a) the right of the individual to life, liberty, security of the person and enjoyment of property, and the right not to be deprived thereof except by due process of law;

(b) the right of the individual to equality before the law and the protection of the law;

(c) freedom of religion;

(d) freedom of speech;

(e) freedom of assembly and association; and

(f) freedom of the press.

Construction of law

2. Every law of Canada shall, unless it is expressly declared by an Act of the

Parliament of Canada that it shall operate notwithstanding the Canadian Bill of Rights, be so construed and applied as not to abrogate, abridge or infringe or to authorize the abrogation, abridgment or infringement of any of the rights or freedoms herein recognized and declared, and in particular, no law of Canada shall be construed or applied so as to

(a) authorize or effect the arbitrary detention, imprisonment or exile of any person;

(b) impose or authorize the imposition of cruel and unusual treatment or punishment;

(c) deprive a person who has been arrested or detained
  (i) of the right to be informed promptly of the reason for his arrest or detention,
  (ii) of the right to retain and instruct counsel without delay, or
  (iii) of the remedy by way of *habeas corpus* for the determination of the validity of his detention and for his release if the detention is not lawful;

(d) authorize a court, tribunal, commission, board or other authority to compel a person to give evidence if he is denied counsel, protection against **self crimination** or other constitutional safeguards;

(e) deprive a person of the right to a fair hearing in accordance with the principles of fundamental justice for the determination of his rights and obligations;

(f) deprive a person charged with a criminal offence of the right to be presumed innocent until proved guilty according to law in a fair and public hearing by an independent and impartial tribunal, or of the right to reasonable bail without just cause; or

(g) deprive a person of the right to the assistance of an interpreter in any proceedings in which he is involved or in which he is a party or a witness, before a court, commission, board or other tribunal, if he does not understand or speak the language in which such proceedings are conducted.

Duties of Minister of Justice

3. (1) Subject to subsection (2), the Minister of Justice shall, in accordance with such regulations as may be prescribed by the Governor in Council, examine every regulation transmitted to the Clerk of the Privy Council for registration pursuant to the Statutory Instruments Act and every Bill introduced in or presented to the House of Commons by a Minister of the Crown, in order to ascertain whether any of the provisions thereof are inconsistent with the purposes and provisions of this Part and he shall report any such inconsistency to the House of Commons at the first convenient opportunity.

Exception

(2) A regulation need not be examined in accordance with subsection (1) if prior to being made it was examined as a proposed regulation in accordance with section 3 of the Statutory Instruments Act to ensure that it was not inconsistent with the purposes and provisions of this Part.

1960, c. 44, s. 3; 1970-71-72, c. 38, s. 29; 1985, c. 26, s. 105; 1992, c. 1, s. 144(F).

Short title

4. The provisions of this Part shall be known as the Canadian Bill of Rights.

PART II
Savings

5. (1) Nothing in Part I shall be construed to abrogate or abridge any human right or fundamental freedom not enumerated therein that may have existed in Canada at the commencement of this Act.

"Law of Canada" defined

(2) The expression "law of Canada" in Part I means an Act of the Parliament of Canada enacted before or after the coming into force of this Act, any order, rule or

(continued)

regulation thereunder, and any law in force in Canada or in any part of Canada at the commencement of this Act that is subject to be repealed, abolished or altered by the Parliament of Canada.

Jurisdiction of Parliament

(3) The provisions of Part I shall be construed as extending only to matters coming within the legislative authority of the Parliament of Canada.

The Bill of Rights and the Supreme Court

The Bill of Rights was intended to affect federal laws in three ways. First, s. 3(1) required the minister of justice to scrutinize all proposed laws and regulations[20] for conformity to the Bill of Rights.[21] Implicitly, therefore, it prohibited Parliament from adopting laws that violated the protected rights and freedoms—unless, as provided in s. 2, the law contained an explicit notwithstanding clause. An earlier draft of the bill had required the minister of justice to "ensure" compliance, not just to evaluate and report inconsistencies. Under the weaker version enacted into law, the minister had only to scrutinize draft laws and regulations at the earliest opportunity; if they were found to be compatible with the Bill of Rights, the Department of Justice would attach a certificate to that effect and send them to the clerks of the Privy Council and the House of Commons. There was no requirement that the minister advise the House when a draft law had been found to be consistent with the Bill, or that any report of inconsistency be made available to MPs before their final vote. Only one such report was ever made.[22] Section 3 of the Bill of Rights was repealed in 1985, and the Department of Justice Act amended to require a similar review in accordance with the Charter (see Chapter 5).[23]

According to Elmer Driedger, a former deputy minister of justice, the Bill had a major influence on the drafting of federal laws and regulations. In 1977, he claimed that "A bill or regulation patently in violation of the Bill of Rights and lacking, in the case of a bill, the declaration contemplated by section 2, has almost no chance of becoming law."[24] Although the Bill did not give courts a clear "second-order" duty to invalidate other laws, it did impose a "first-order" duty on Parliament and the federal executive branch to ensure conformity with its provisions.[25] Driedger went so far as to claim that "No government would be

so foolish or stupid as to submit to Parliament a bill obviously in conflict with the Bill of Rights [without invoking the notwithstanding clause]."[26]

Second, s. 2 of the Bill stipulated that federal laws must not be applied in such a way as to infringe protected rights and freedoms, with particular emphasis on the existing common-law rights against unfair or arbitrary treatment by the justice system. Under this provision, police, Crown prosecutors, and judges were responsible for enforcing the Criminal Code of Canada in accord with the due-process rights of suspects. Here, the impact of the Bill appears to have been minimal. Police misconduct—ranging from the treatment of suspects by local police officers[27] to the notorious barn-burnings by rogue Mounties in Quebec[28]—went on undeterred. In general, the due-process guarantees in the Bill were trumped by the crime-control emphasis of police, prosecutors, and legislators.[29] Police powers of search and seizure, aided by general "writs of assistance," were almost unlimited. Evidence obtained in violation of the Bill of Rights could not be excluded at trial. Overall, the Supreme Court and lower courts refused "to use section 2 to impose minimum procedural safeguards on the exercise of administrative power under federal statutes."[30]

Third, s. 2 instructed courts to interpret federal laws—whether passed before or after 1960—in a manner which protected the rights and freedoms listed in the Bill. The only exceptions were laws that Parliament designated as "notwithstanding" the Bill. The derogation clause was invoked precisely once: in the November 1970 Public Order (Temporary Measures) Act,[31] which extended the "emergency" measures taken during the October Crisis.[32] In October 1970, a small terrorist group calling itself the Front de Libération du Québec (FLQ) kidnapped a British diplomat and a Quebec cabinet minister in Montreal. The latter was later found murdered. The provincial government asked the federal cabinet to invoke the War Measures Act, which would allow Parliament to suspend civil liberties for a specified period of time. During that time, police and military officers would be empowered to search premises, take suspects into custody without explanation, and detain them in prison without formal charges.[33] For obvious reasons, the act was formally exempted from ss. 1 and 2 of the Bill of Rights—in particular, the strictures against arbitrary detention and denial of bail.[34]

In practice, the Bill of Rights had less impact on Canadian law than its champions had hoped. There are at least four reasons. First, it contained no clear judicial remedies for rights violations. In their absence, most judges assumed that Parliament did not intend them to strike down or amend laws that conflicted with its provisions. Second, the Bill was an ordinary federal statute. Unlike the entrenched Charter, it was not automatically paramount over laws with which it conflicted. At best, it was "a quasi-constitutional instrument."[35]

Third, the Bill applied only to federal laws and regulations. It had no impact on provincial law. Because Canada's court system is divided between the two levels of government, many provincial officials—police, prosecutors, trial judges—were responsible for its implementation. But statutes adopted by provincial legislators were immune from judicial or ministerial review on the basis of the Bill. Many areas of public policy with particular relevance to rights and freedoms fall under provincial jurisdiction, including social welfare and education. Moreover, as the previous discussion of civil rights in Quebec suggests, some provincial governments may have been more willing than Parliament to adopt discriminatory laws. Therefore, the restricted scope of the Bill greatly reduced its potential effect.

Fourth and finally, the Bill was poorly drafted.[36] For example, s. 1 declares that the protected rights "have existed and shall continue to exist." As Dossier 2.6 explains, a majority of the Supreme Court interpreted this phrase to mean that the content of the Bill was "frozen" at the moment of its adoption. The Bill of Rights would be a museum piece, not "a living tree, capable of growth and expansion" (see Dossier 2.2, pages 50–51). The framers of the Charter learned from this mistake: they defined the various rights and freedoms in that document in clear and open-ended language, without reference to the past.

DOSSIER 2.6

"FROZEN RIGHTS"

Robertson and Rosetanni v. the Queen[1] was the first Bill of Rights case at the Supreme Court of Canada. Walter Robertson and Fred Rosetanni were the proprietors of a bowling alley in Hamilton, Ontario. They were convicted of operating their business on a Sunday, contrary to the federal Lord's Day Act. The impugned section of the law required that all businesses close on the Christian **Sabbath**, with no allowance for those whose day of rest fell on a different day of the week. Robertson and Rosetanni appealed their conviction, arguing that the law violated the guarantee of religious freedom in s. 1(c) of the Bill of Rights; therefore, under s. 2 of the Bill, it should be declared invalid. After the Ontario Court of Appeal dismissed their argument, Robertson and Rosetanni took their case to the Supreme Court.

Unfortunately for the plaintiffs—and for almost all subsequent Bill of Rights appellants—the top court dismissed their argument. Writing for the majority, Justice Ritchie adopted a narrow construction of the religious freedom protected by the Bill.

> ... the Canadian Bill of Rights is not concerned with "human rights and fundamental freedoms" in any abstract sense, but rather with such "rights and freedoms" as they existed in Canada immediately before the statute was enacted. It is therefore the "religious freedom" then existing in this country that is safe-guarded by the provisions of s. 2...[2]

(continued)

In other words, the Bill would not be interpreted broadly, with reference to universal notions of rights and freedoms. Nor would its content grow and change with evolving social needs. Instead, the substance of the Bill was "frozen" at the moment of its proclamation. Whatever statutory limits then existed on the rights and freedoms of Canadians would be preserved—not removed—by judicial review. Those preexisting limits were effectively "read in" to the Bill, as qualifications on the rights and freedoms therein. Ritchie's interpretation was consistent with the common-law approach to civil liberties, which holds that whatever is not expressly forbidden by law is tacitly permitted. But for advocates of the Bill, who had not been entirely satisfied with common-law protections for rights and freedoms, the "frozen rights" approach was a major disappointment.[3]

Ritchie went on to declare that "the *effect* of the *Lord's Day Act*, rather than its *purpose* must be looked to in order to determine whether its application involves the abrogation, abridgment or infringement of religious freedom."[4] This approach, which runs counter to the usual purpose-oriented construction of statutes,[5] yielded a predictable result:

> I can see nothing in [the Lord's Day Act] which in any way affects the liberty of religious thought and practice of any citizen of this country.... The practical result of this law on those whose religion requires them to observe a day of rest other than Sunday, is a purely secular and financial one.[6]

By ignoring the religious purpose of a law whose clear and obvious intent was to enforce the Christian Sabbath on all Canadians, Justice Ritchie was able to convince himself (and three other members of the Court) that the impugned provision did not conflict with the Bill of Rights. Even if such a conflict did exist, it would not render the law invalid; after all, "legislation for the preservation of the sanctity of Sunday has existed in this country from the earliest times." (One might well wonder, however, how or why someone might construe "legislation for the preservation of the sanctity of Sunday" as non-religious in either purpose or effect.)

In dissent, Justice Cartwright found that the impugned law did indeed infringe religious freedom, and that the "frozen rights" approach was expressly contradicted by section 5(2) of the Bill. He also declared that "where there is irreconcilable conflict between another Act of Parliament and the *Canadian Bill of Rights* the latter must prevail."[7] Like the "Duff Doctrine," this activist approach to the Bill of Rights would remain a minority viewpoint.

ENDNOTES

1. [1963] S.C.R. 651.

2. *Robertson and Rosetanni v. the Queen*, [1963] S.C.R. 651, p. 654, *per* Ritchie J.

3. Ritchie's subsequent pronouncements on the "frozen rights" approach are inconsistent and confusing. In the 1970 *Drybones* case, he denied that he had intended to incorporate existing statutory limitations on rights and freedoms into the Bill of Rights. In the 1975 *Lavell* and *Bedard* case ([1974] S.C.R. 1349), he returned to his approach in *Robertson and Rosetanni*: "In my view the meaning to be given to the language employed in the Bill of Rights is the meaning which it bore in Canada at the time when the Bill was enacted."

4. *Robertson and Rosetanni*, p. 657, *per* Ritchie J. (emphasis in original).

5. Ruth Sullivan, *Statutory Interpretation* (Toronto: Irwin Law, 1997), Chapter 9.

6. *Robertson and Rosetanni*, p. 657, *per* Ritchie J.

7. Ibid., p. 662, *per* Cartwright J.

The wording of s. 2 posed even bigger problems for advocates of human rights. It did not require or authorize courts to strike down laws that infringed the protected rights and freedoms. Most judges declined to "read in" remedies, a choice that would have contradicted the British tradition of parliamentary supremacy. They reasoned that if Parliament had wanted or expected judges to strike down laws that conflicted with the Bill, it would have said so explicitly in the text of the Bill itself.[37]

In practice, s. 2 operated as an interpretive rule. If a court had to choose between two alternative constructions of a particular law, only one of which was consistent with the Bill of Rights, it was required to apply the one that was consistent.[38] For example, the Supreme Court ruled that the denial of legal counsel (s. 2(c)(ii) of the Bill) constituted a "reasonable excuse" for failing to provide a breathalyzer sample. It therefore interpreted the offence of refusing to provide a sample without a reasonable excuse in a way that respected the right to counsel declared in the Bill.[39] However, the Court did not consider itself bound to apply s. 2 consistently. In a subsequent case, a majority of Justices refused to exclude breathalyzer evidence at trial despite a clear violation of its own precedent.[40] The message was clear: the Supreme Court was not prepared to stand by its own interpretations of the legal rights in the Bill. Nor would it seek to enforce them by devising an exclusionary rule to punish and deter police misconduct (see Dossier 2.7).

DOSSIER 2.7

"THE FRUIT OF THE POISONED TREE"

Under English common law, there was little support for the idea that "a court should exclude real evidence because it was improperly obtained."[1] While judges were concerned about the voluntariness and reliability of confessions, "real" evidence—fingerprints, a murder weapon, bloodstains—was admissible even if the police had violated the rights of the suspect in gathering it. The American approach was very different. Since the early twentieth century, and especially since the 1960s, the U.S. Supreme Court had carved out a strict exclusionary rule known as the "fruit of the poisoned tree." A violation of the suspect's due-process rights during the investigation or prosecution of a crime could taint any evidence gathered as a result of the violation; tainted evidence could not be admitted at trial, whatever its **probative** value might be.[2] The Court declared that, in the absence of such a strong sanction and deterrent for police misconduct, "the protection of the 4th Amendment, declaring [a] right to be secure against such searches and seizures, is of no value, and, so far as those thus placed are concerned, might as well be stricken from the Constitution."[3]

Under the Bill of Rights, the English approach to evidence prevailed in Canada.[4] In the notorious *Wray* case, a murder suspect endured ten hours of police interrogation—without benefit of legal counsel—before being coerced into confessing. The suspect subsequently told the police where to find the rifle used in the shooting; he led them to the place where he had discarded it, and the police duly recovered the murder weapon. Because of the manifest abuses of police power that produced it, the confession was ruled inadmissible at trial. That was not particularly surprising. But the rifle, which was "real" evidence, was also excluded, to the chagrin of the police and Crown. With no solid evidence of guilt, Wray was acquitted.

The Crown appealed the acquittal, and the Supreme Court eventually overturned the trial judge's ruling: "There is no judicial authority in this country or in England which supports the proposition that a trial judge has a discretion to exclude admissible evidence because, in his opinion, its admission would be calculated to bring the administration of justice into disrepute."[5] The Court could have relied on s. 2(f) to exclude evidence that might taint the fairness of

(continued)

a criminal proceeding, but it refused to do so. (Although Wray's defence counsel did not cite the Bill of Rights in his arguments, the language of s. 2 clearly instructed the Court to interpret the law—in this case, the common law of evidence—in a manner consistent with the right to a fair trial.)

Section 24(2) of the Charter was the federal government's response to the inconsistent common-law protections for the due-process rights of criminal suspects. The provinces feared "importing American jurisprudence relating to due process of law and non-admissibility of illegally obtained evidence."[6] In their draft Charter of August 1980, the premiers inserted the following clause: "Nothing in this Charter affects the admissibility of evidence or the ability of Parliament or a legislature to legislate thereon."[7] The federal government included a slightly modified version of this clause in its September 1980 draft, and retained it (as s. 26) in the October 1980 version that was tabled in Parliament. Following intense criticism from some witnesses before the Special Joint Committee on Constitution of Canada, the federal government deleted the clause in January 1981. The existing s. 24(2) first appeared in its current form in the February 1981 version of the Charter. Its wording appears to be a deliberate repudiation of the majority judgment in *Wray*.

The entrenchment of an exclusionary rule was strongly opposed by the Canadian Association of Chiefs of Police and by Crown prosecutors. Their views made little impression on the committee, partly because "most of their provincial employers opposed patriation."[8] The wording of the section reflects an attempt to avoid the extreme application of the "fruit of the poisoned tree" doctrine. Section 24(2) requires judges to consider "all the circumstances" before determining admissibility. According to the drafters in the Department of Justice, judges would consider both the seriousness of the crime and the severity of the Charter breach.[9] In other words, they would balance the safety of the community against the importance

of due-process rights. Murderers would not be set free because of technical errors in the collection of evidence, as allegedly happened in the United States.

The drafters also predicted that the exclusionary rule would be used only in very rare cases. This expectation, which may have reflected a rosy view of Canadian police practice, was refuted almost immediately. As early as 1984, the following comment appeared in a Canadian legal journal:

> It is ... plausible that the frequency of illegality in police investigations never really came to the attention of the courts or the public because Canadian courts, until 1982, did not exclude improperly obtained evidence. The large number of reported cases which in recent months have involved illegalities, some rather serious, in routine police investigations, offers an indication of what reality actually held in store.

The author concluded, "In this regard, the Charter has been an eye-opener."[10]

One year later, in *Therens*, the Supreme Court signalled that it would take an unexpectedly strict approach to the exclusion of evidence. (See Dossier 2.11, pages 75–76.) In 1995, the Supreme Court "disapproved" its decision in *Wray*, at least with regard to the admissibility of unconstitutionally obtained evidence.[11] According to Ontario appellate judge Marc Rosenberg, "The express exclusionary rule in s. 24(2) has been the most important effect of the Charter and represents its most tangible measurable impact."[12]

ENDNOTES

1. Yves-Marie Morissette, "The Exclusion of Evidence under the Canadian Charter of Rights and Freedoms: What to Do and What Not to Do," *McGill Law Journal* 29 (1983–84), p. 523.

2. See *Weeks v. U.S.*, 232 U.S. 383 (1914), and *Mapp v. Ohio*, 367 U.S. 643 (1961). Both rulings are available online at www.findlaw.com.

3. *Weeks v. U.S.*, p. 393, *per* Day J.

4. See Ritchie's rather contemptuous dismissal of the American jurisprudence in *Hogan v. the Queen*, [1975] 2 S.C.R. 574.

5. *R. v. Wray*, [1971] S.C.R. 272, pp. 287, *per* Martland J.

6. "Report by the Sub-Committee of Officials on a Charter of Rights," July 24, 1980; reprinted in Anne F. Bayefsky, ed., *Canada's Constitution Act, 1982 and Amendments: A Documentary History* (Toronto: McGraw-Hill Ryerson, 1989), vol. 2, p. 662.

7. "The Canadian Charter of Rights and Freedoms, Provincial Proposal (In the Event that There Is Going to Be Entrenchment," August 28, 1980, reprinted in Bayefsky, *Canada's Constitution Act*, vol. 2, p. 678, clause 22(b).

8. Kent Roach, *Due Process and Victims' Rights: The New Law and Politics of Criminal Justice* (Toronto: University of Toronto Press, 1999), p. 47.

9. E.G. Ewaschuk, Department of Justice, Minutes of Proceedings and Evidence of the Special Joint Committee on the Constitution of Canada, January 29, 1981, p. 48:123. Ewaschuk's prediction was technically correct, insofar as the Supreme Court identified these factors (among others) as those that a judge must take into consideration when weighing an application for exclusion under s. 24(2). See *R. v. Collins*, [1987] 1 S.C.R. 265, *per* Lamer J. (as he then was). However, critics—including former Justice L'Heureux-Dubé—argue that the Court has placed too much weight on the due-process rights of the accused and insufficient emphasis on the severity of the crime and the Charter violation. See, e.g., F.L. Morton and Rainer Knopff, *The Charter Revolution and the Court Party* (Peterborough: Broadview Press, 2000), pp. 39–40, and Alex Macdonald, *Outrage: Canada's Justice System on Trial* (Vancouver: Raincoast, 1999).

10. Morissette, "The Exclusion," p. 535.

11. *R. v. Burlingham*, [1995] 2 S.C.R. 206, paragraph 147, *per* Sopinka J. The other part of the *Wray* doctrine, the rule that evidence will be admissible unless its prejudicial effect outweighs its probative value, has been retained.

12. Marc Rosenberg, "The Impact of the Charter on the Law of Evidence in Criminal Cases," in Jamie Cameron, ed., *The Charter's Impact on the Criminal Justice System* (Toronto: Carswell, 1996), p. 199.

Treating s. 2 as a mere interpretive rule was consistent with parliamentary supremacy. Most Justices accepted the principle that Parliament had the right to make and unmake laws, and the Court did not. But what happened if an impugned law could not be "so construed and applied as not to abrogate, abridge or infringe" the rights and freedoms in s. 1? Could s. 2 be interpreted to allow a court to invalidate such a law, on the grounds of its inconsistency with the Bill of Rights? In every case but one, the majority on the Supreme Court answered no. That single exception was the 1970 *Drybones* case, discussed in Dossier 2.8.

DOSSIER 2.8

R. V. DRYBONES (1970)

In 1970, the Supreme Court heard an appeal from the Northwest Territories. Joe Drybones, a status Indian, was found intoxicated in a Yellowknife hotel. Under s. 94(b) of the Indian Act, it was unlawful for an Indian to be intoxicated off-reserve. As Justice Ritchie pointed out in his majority ruling, "an Indian who is intoxicated in his own home 'off a reserve' is guilty of

(continued)

an offence and subject to a minimum fine of not less than $10 or a term of imprisonment not exceeding three months or both, whereas all other citizens in the Territories may, if they see fit, become intoxicated otherwise than in a public place without committing any offence at all."[1] Therefore, s. 94(b) clearly violated the nondiscrimination clause in s. 1 of the Bill of Rights. Moreover, the law could not possibly be interpreted in a manner consistent with s. 2 of the Bill. So what should the Court do?

Justice Ritchie set out two alternative courses of action. The first, arising from a 1962 British Columbia case, was to abandon the Bill of Rights as inapplicable in the circumstances.[2] Ritchie rejected this approach, which "strike[s] at the very foundations of the Bill of Rights," in favour of the dissenting opinion of Justice Cartwright (as he then was) in *Robertson and Rosetanni*: "In my opinion where there is irreconcilable conflict between another Act of the Parliament and the Canadian Bill of Rights the latter must prevail." He argued that if s. 2 were simply an interpretive clause, it would not include the phrase "unless it is expressly declared by an Act of the Parliament of Canada that it shall operate notwithstanding the Canadian Bill of Rights." Ritchie construed the Bill differently:

> s. 2 is intended to mean and does mean that if a law of Canada cannot be "sensibly construed and applied" so that it does not abrogate, abridge or infringe one of the rights and freedoms recognized and declared by the Bill, then such law is inoperative "unless it is expressly declared by an Act of the Parliament of Canada that it shall operate notwithstanding the Canadian Bill of Rights."

By "inoperative," Ritchie did not mean "invalid," He was not arguing that the Bill of Rights empowered the courts to strike down legislation, but that s. 94(b) of the Indian Act should not apply to "the particular circumstances of the case." This distinction is difficult to understand: if the law is not to apply to intoxicated Indians off-reserve, and the only people who can be convicted under it are intoxicated Indians off-reserve, then the law is clearly invalid for all practical purposes. It appears that Ritchie meant to exempt Indians from the effect of s. 94(b) in jurisdictions where there is no comparable prohibition for non-Indians (e.g., the Territories).

Ironically, at the same moment that Justice Ritchie abandoned his restrictive approach to the Bill of Rights in favour of Chief Justice Cartwright's more assertive stance, the latter repudiated his activist ruling in *Robertson and Rosetanni*—in favour of Ritchie's previous doctrine! Cartwright asked "whether or not it is the intention of Parliament to confer the power and impose the responsibility upon the Courts of declaring inoperative any provision in a statute of Canada" that cannot be "construed" to make it consistent with the Bill. He continued, "If it were intended that the question should be answered in the affirmative there would, in my opinion, have been added after the word 'declared' in the seventh line of the opening paragraph of s. 2 of the Bill some such words as the following 'and if any law of Canada cannot be so construed and applied it shall be regarded as inoperative or *pro tanto* repealed.'"[3] In the absence of any such indicator of legislative intent, Cartwright rejected Ritchie's activist ruling.

ENDNOTES

1. *R. v. Drybones*, [1970] S.C.R. 282, *per* Ritchie J.

2. *R. v. Gonzales* (1962), 32 D.L.R. (2d) 290 at p. 292, *per* Davey J.A.

3. *R. v. Drybones*, *per* Cartwright C.J.C.

With the exception of *Drybones*, most members of the Court refused to challenge the supremacy of Parliament even when interpreting laws that clearly violated s. 1 of the Bill.[41] The lengths to which they would go to avoid invalidating laws are sometimes amusing and occasionally appalling. In the *Lavell and Bedard*[42] case, a majority of the Justices upheld a section of the Indian Act that deprived Indian women of their band status—including the right to live on-reserve—if they married non-Indian men. Their children also lost any claim to Indian status and its accompanying benefits. On the other hand, Indian men who married non-Indian women automatically conferred their band status on their wives and children. The Court held that the law did not discriminate against Indian women, within the meaning of the Bill of Rights, because it did not affect the exercise of an enumerated right or freedom in the Bill itself. The ubiquitous Justice Ritchie claimed that whereas the law invalidated in *Drybones* imposed a legal disadvantage on Indians, "no such inequality of treatment between Indian men and women flows as a necessary result of the application of s. 12(1)(b) of the *Indian Act*."[43] This absurd result may have been intended to shield the Court from political controversy; the federal government and some Indian bands feared that the restoration of Indian status to thousands of women and children would overwhelm the resources of poor reserves.[44] While the *Lavell* ruling may have pleased the federal government, it infuriated advocates of women's rights.

In 1979, the Court tied itself in similar logical knots when it dismissed the claim of Stella Bliss for Unemployment Insurance (UI) payments under the Unemployment Insurance Act. The period of work required to qualify for maternity benefits, which paid a higher weekly rate, was longer than the qualification period for ordinary UI benefits. Under s. 46 of the act, pregnant women (like Bliss) who did not qualify for maternity benefits—but who would have qualified for regular UI payments—were expressly denied access to the UI program. In other words, they were denied benefits to which they would have been entitled had they not been pregnant. Bliss argued that the discrepancy discriminated against women. The Court unanimously disagreed. In the words, once again, of Justice Ritchie, "Any inequality between the sexes in this area is created not by legislation but by nature."[45] Moreover, the law did not discriminate against women per se, but against pregnant "persons."[46] Because all pregnant "persons" were treated identically under the act, there was no discrimination and no violation of the Bill. The fact that all "pregnant persons" happen to be women, recent advances in medical technology notwithstanding, appears to have eluded the Court. (As we will see in Chapter 11, page 343, the "similarly situated" test that permitted the Court to reach this decision was expressly repudiated by the wording of s. 15 of the Charter.)

If the Bill of Rights had been intended to protect Canadians from legislative and administrative violations of their civil liberties, it was largely a failure. Its shortcomings, coupled with the judicial conservatism of the Supreme Court, gave a powerful impetus to the growing campaign for an entrenched and judicially enforceable Charter. Bill of Rights jurisprudence also affected the way in which the Charter was drafted, both in the individual guarantees of rights and freedoms and in the judicial remedies for violation. The Bill remains in force under s. 26 of the Charter, and some observers have argued that those elements of it that were not incorporated in the Charter—the property rights in s. 1(a) and the right to a fair hearing in s. 2(e)[47]—are still available to any plaintiff who wishes to use them in court.[48] But as Dossier 2.9, pages 68–69 explains, the persistence of the "frozen rights" approach to the Bill raises doubts about its practical effect.

DOSSIER 2.9

THE *AUTHORSON* CASE (2000)

Thousands of Canadian men fought for the Allies in World War II. Of those who survived the war, many were so traumatized by their experience of battle that they became mentally ill. When a returning war veteran was hospitalized for psychological reasons, the federal government became the guardian of his military benefits. These were paid into a special fund, which was administered by the Veterans Affairs Canada (as it is now called). These monies, which eventually amounted to hundreds of millions of dollars, were never invested or properly managed. As a result, the veterans who were released from psychiatric institutions were never paid interest on the money administered by the government. For many, the resulting financial loss was catastrophic.

One such veteran was Joseph Authorson. In 1999, he became the representative plaintiff in a class-action suit against Veterans Affairs. The disabled veterans claimed millions of dollars in back interest, arguing that the federal government had breached its fiduciary duty when it failed to manage their money appropriately. In response, the government pointed out that it had passed a law in 1990 that initiated the payment of interest on the funds held in trust for these veterans. At the same time, the law immunized the federal government against claims for interest that would otherwise have accrued before 1990. So before the class-action could proceed, the courts had to determine whether or not this law was valid. If it was, then Authorson and his fellow plaintiffs would have a much harder time winning their case against Veterans Affairs.

In 2000, the lawsuit came to trial in Windsor, Ontario. Judge Brockenshire found for the plaintiffs, on the grounds that the Bill of Rights forbade the government from seizing the property of Canadians without due process of law.[1] Brockenshire ruled that the 1990 law did not meet normal standards of due process. He noted that, in 1986, the auditor general had expressed serious concerns about the violation of fiduciary duty and the government's unfunded liability to veterans, which—according to a secret government document written in 1987—exceeded $1 billion. When the Veterans' Affairs Act was amended in 1990 to retroactively eliminate the government's liability, the minister never drew Parliament's attention to the real reasons for changing the law (i.e., the wish to avoid paying $1 billion in back interest). Relying on the reasoning of Justice Ritchie in *Drybones*, Brockenshire concluded that the impugned law could only be "sensibly construed" as a violation of the property guarantee in the Bill of Rights, and that the law as it existed in 1960 (when the Bill took effect) recognized a fiduciary duty on the part of government agencies toward those persons whose funds they managed. Therefore, Brockenshire declared "that s. 5.1(4) of the *Department of Veterans' Affairs Act* is inoperative in barring the claim raised by the plaintiff class in this action."[2]

The Ontario Court of Appeal upheld Brockenshire's ruling in its entirety.[3] The federal government appealed to the Supreme Court of Canada, which heard the case in April 2003. The unanimous ruling, written by Justice Major, overturned the two lower-court rulings and declared the 1990 law to be valid. Justice Major acknowledged that "Where federal legislation conflicts with the protections of the Bill of Rights, unless the conflicting legislation expressly declares that it operates notwithstanding the Bill of Rights as required by s. 2, the Bill of Rights applies and the legislation is inoperative."[4] However, he rejected Brockenshire's argument that the passage of the 1990 law violated the Bill's "due process" guarantee, on the ground that Parliament is not bound by these provisions.

Major also dismissed the suggestion that the Bill protects "substantive due process" rights of individuals, specifically the right not to have their property seized by the Crown. He observed that "The Bill of Rights protects only rights that existed at the time of its passage, in 1960. At that time it was undisputed, as it continues to be today, that Parliament had the right to expropriate property if it made its intention clear."[5] Major appears to have overlooked the evidence, cited by both Brockenshire and the Court of Appeal, that the federal government had deliberately misled Parliament as to its intentions toward the disabled veterans. He concluded: "Since [Authorson] would have had no substantive right against a clear and unambiguous expropriation in 1960, the *Bill of Rights* can offer him no such protection today."[6]

Nowhere in his reasons does Justice Major address the concept of fiduciary duty, which played a key role in the two previous rulings on the case. Major may have ignored this issue because the concept was recognized by the Supreme Court of Canada only in 1984. Consequently, there was no room for fiduciary duty in the "frozen rights" approach to the Bill.

All that remained was the power of the Crown to expropriate property as it saw fit, and the immunity of Parliament from due-process considerations, both of which were established in Canadian law before 1960.

ENDNOTES

1. *Authorson (Litigation Guardian of) v. Canada (Attorney General)*, 84 C.R.R. (2d) 211, [2000] O.J. No. 3768, 53 O.R. (3d) 221.

2. *Authorson (Litigation Guardian of) v. Canada (A.G.)* [2000], paragraph 101.

3. *Authorson (Guardian of) v. Canada (Attorney General)*, (2002-03-12) ONCA C35254; C35835; available at www.canlii.org/on/cas/onca/2002/2002onca10119.html.

4. *Authorson v. Canada (Attorney General)*, [2003] 2 S.C.R. 40, paragraph 32.

5. Ibid., paragraph 52.

6. Ibid., paragraph 57.

THE ORIGINS OF THE CHARTER

Although it is usually misleading to overstate the historic influence of an individual, it is no exaggeration to say that the Charter of Rights owes its existence to the late prime minister Pierre Elliott Trudeau (1921–2000). Even before Trudeau entered federal politics in 1965, he publicly advocated an entrenched charter of civil and linguistic rights.[49] His faith in a charter sprang from three primary sources. First, he was a trained lawyer and political philosopher. A classical liberal, with a passion for individual liberty and a loathing of tribal nationalism, Trudeau was a natural advocate of constitutional protection for rights and freedoms. Second, he was well aware of the growing international emphasis on human rights.[50] He must have been less than impressed by the Supreme Court's refusal to interpret the Bill of Rights more aggressively.

Third, and most important, Trudeau was utterly opposed to the separatist movement in his native Quebec.[51] He was equally hostile to demands for decentralization of federal power from other provinces. He would not give in to provincial calls for greater autonomy. Instead, he would counter their province-building with a grand project of nation-building, creating a country where French- and English-language speakers could feel at home everywhere. The culmination of that project would be an entrenched Charter of Rights, which would protect mobility and language rights from provincial legislation.[52] In addition, Trudeau was determined to "patriate" the Constitution. A century after Confederation, the BNA Act was still a British statute; it could not be changed without the participation of the Parliament in London. Because there was no amending formula in the BNA Act, Canada was denied the full constitutional independence granted to other British Dominions by the 1931 Statute of Westminster. So while an entrenched Charter was the prime minister's top constitutional priority, patriation and an amending formula were also high on the list.

Soon after he was sworn in as federal justice minister in 1967, Trudeau addressed the annual meeting of the Canadian Bar Association. He advocated the entrenchment of "a constitutional Bill of Rights—a Bill that would guarantee the fundamental freedoms of the citizen from interference, whether federal or provincial."[53] The content of his proposed Bill bore a striking resemblance to the actual 1982 Charter:

> ... we envision a Bill of Rights which will be broader in scope than the existing legislation. We all agree on the familiar basic rights— freedom of belief and expression, freedom of association, the right to a fair trial and to fair legal procedures generally. We would also expect a guarantee against discrimination on the basis of race, religion, sex, ethnic or national origin.[54]

In addition to these universal human rights, Trudeau wanted to entrench uniquely Canadian guarantees of linguistic equality. Without entrenched constitutional protection for linguistic minorities,

> we cannot assure every Canadian of an equal opportunity to participate in the political, cultural, economic, and social life of this country. I venture to say that, if we are able to reach agreement on this vital aspect of the over-all problem, we will have found a solution to a basic issue facing Canada today.[55]

In his 1967 speech, Trudeau identified an entrenched Charter as "the best basis on which to begin a dialogue of constitutional reform between the federal government and the provincial governments."[56] He believed—erroneously, as it turned out—that the entrenchment of rights was "the basis most likely to find a wide degree of acceptance."[57] Beginning a comprehensive program of constitutional reform with entrenched rights and freedoms also made practical sense: one could not devise a new division of powers between the federal and provincial governments before determining the scope of legislative power per se.[58]

In January 1968, at a First Ministers' Meeting on the Constitution, the justice minister unveiled his proposals for "a constitutional bill of rights" that would apply to both levels of government.[59] A more seasoned politician might have anticipated the premiers' hostile reaction. Most of them wanted to expand their legislative jurisdictions, not to constrict them by adopting an entrenched Charter. In response to provincial concerns, Trudeau repeatedly stressed that the Charter would not transfer power from one level of government to the other; rather, "it would involve a common agreement to restrict the power of [all] governments" in the name of protecting rights and freedoms.[60] He did not repeat his earlier acknowledgment that an entrenched Charter would inevitably compromise parliamentary supremacy—both federal and provincial—by giving the Courts a wider scope for reviewing legislation:

> A constitutional Bill of Rights would modify even further the concept of parliamentary sovereignty in Canada. Once fundamental rights are guaranteed, they will be beyond the reach of government at all levels. This will confer new and very important responsibilities on the courts, because it will be up to the courts to interpret the Bill of Rights, to decide how much scope should be given to the protected rights and to what extent the power of government should be curtailed.[61]

During the three rounds of constitutional negotiation that followed—the 1968–71 Victoria Round, the introduction of Bill C-60 in 1978, and the 1980–82 Patriation Round—Trudeau would learn to avoid such explicit statements about a Charter's potential impact on the relationship between courts and legislatures.

Although the Charter proposal was the centrepiece of Trudeau's constitutional strategy from the very beginning of his prime ministership, he had to wait for over a decade to achieve it. The biggest obstacle was the reluctance of most provincial premiers to accept entrenched—and judicially enforced—limits on their legislative and administrative capacities. A few were strongly opposed to entrenchment on principle: they did not want to replace the British tradition of parliamentary sovereignty with the American practice of judicial review.[62] Others feared that an entrenched Charter, as interpreted by a federally appointed Supreme Court, would inevitably centralize power in the national government. There were also specific concerns about the impact of legal rights, equality rights, and some fundamental freedoms. On the whole, however, most premiers were simply uninterested in the Trudeau proposals. They wanted a decentralized division of powers, reforms to central institutions (particularly the Senate), and greater fiscal autonomy. Entrenched rights and freedoms were useless abstractions at best, and threats to provincial jurisdiction at worst. Although there was no amending formula in the 1867 Constitution, most participants in the process assumed that major constitutional change would require the unanimous consent of the provinces. These conflicting constitutional agendas, and the presumption of unanimity, led to repeated stalemates.

Quebec premiers—whether separatist or federalist—faced a particular problem: unless they extracted major concessions from Ottawa on the division of powers, their participation in constitutional negotiations risked enraging nationalist voters.[63] Such concessions were not forthcoming from Prime Minister Trudeau. Even after the election of a federalist Quebec government in 1970, there was little intergovernmental consensus on constitutional reform. That lack of agreement doomed the 1971 Victoria Charter, which was hammered out at the First Ministers' Meeting after three years of consultations and discussions. The Victoria Charter contained an amending formula, a watered-down bill of rights, and some minor transfers of power to the provinces. All eleven governments agreed to ratify the deal in their respective legislatures as quickly as possible. But when Quebec Premier Robert Bourassa returned home, he was shocked by the strength of local opposition to the agreement.[64] He quickly withdrew his support for the deal, effectively ending the first round of Trudeau's constitutional-reform project.

The content of the 1971 Victoria Charter illustrates the gulf between the Trudeau government and most of the provinces. In 1969, Trudeau had published a draft Charter of Rights.[65] It is a comprehensive catalogue of rights and freedoms, similar to the 1982 Charter in many respects. But the premiers refused to accept the legal and equality rights, and could agree only on the entrenchment of a few strictly limited freedoms. The weakness of the Victoria rights reflects provincial reservations about judicial power under an entrenched Charter.[66] Consequently, the Victoria document contained only "Political Rights" and a watered-down list of language rights.[67]

Article 1 effectively entrenched sections 1 and 2 of the Bill of Rights and applied the interpretive provisions to provincial laws. Article 2 went slightly further than the Bill: instead of telling judges how to "construe and apply" laws, it imposed a duty on legislators to make no law abrogating or abridging the fundamental freedoms. Unlike Trudeau's 1969 draft, however, it did not authorize judges to invalidate such laws. Another five articles guaranteed the rights to vote and to seek office; imposed five-year limits on federal and provincial legislatures; and required every legislature to meet at least once every twelve months. With some modifications, these provisions were ultimately included in the 1982 Charter (ss. 3–5). Article 9 declared that the "Political Rights" would not be "deemed to confer any legislative power on the Parliament of Canada"—an attempt to reassure premiers who feared that entrenched rights would centralize power in Ottawa.

Finally, article 3 of the Victoria Charter was a response to provincial concerns about "absolute" rights:

> Nothing in this Part shall be construed as preventing such limitations on the exercise of the fundamental freedoms as are reasonably justifiable in a democratic society in the interests of public safety, order, health or morals, of national security, or of the rights and freedoms of others, whether imposed by the Parliament of Canada or the Legislature of a Province, within the limits of their respective legislative powers, or by the construction or application of any law.

Given this broad derogation clause, and the weakness of the protected rights themselves, it is difficult to imagine a law that could not have been justified under the Victoria formula.

The weakness of the Victoria Charter, and its quick demise at the hands of the Quebec government, boded ill for the future of entrenched rights. But when Bourassa's federalist Liberal government lost to the separatist Parti Québécois in 1976, English Canada was shocked into action. In June 1978, Trudeau tabled Bill C-60—the Constitutional Amendment Bill—in the House of Commons. Bill C-60 was an attempt to address some of Quebec's constitutional demands, thus ensuring that the separatists would lose their promised referendum on sovereignty, while securing some elements of Trudeau's own agenda. The draft Charter of Rights reproduced much of the 1969 version, with the addition of stronger judicial remedies (an early version of the present s. 24(1)) and the first mention of entrenched Aboriginal rights.[68]

There would be no negotiations with the provinces on a package of amendments. Instead, the elements of the proposed Charter of Rights that lay within federal jurisdiction would take effect as soon as it was adopted by Parliament. Those that directly affected the provincial governments would take effect only after ratification by each legislature.[69] For example, the rights contained in the Bill would become binding on the government of Nova Scotia as soon as the House of Assembly in Halifax formally agreed to accept its terms. In exchange for ratifying the Bill, Trudeau promised to repeal the hated federal powers of disallowance and reservation. Although C-60 was a bold initiative to break the constitutional deadlock, it was opposed by several provinces[70] and by the other parties in the Commons.

The bill was sent to a special joint committee of the House of Commons and Senate, where it stalled. It died on the order paper when the House of Commons was dissolved for the 1979 general election. In 1980, the Supreme Court of Canada ruled the proposed Senate amendments unconstitutional, on the grounds that the federal government could not unilaterally "change the character" of the Upper House.[71] It looked as though the constitution could not be patriated without significant concessions from the federal government to the provinces. Although intergovernmental meetings on constitutional reform continued through 1979 and early 1980, the prospects for Trudeau's Charter looked bleak.

The political climate changed in May 1980, when Quebec's Parti Québécois Premier René Lévesque lost a provincial referendum on sovereignty. Shortly before the vote, Prime Minister Trudeau addressed a "No" rally in Montreal:

> I know that I can make a most solemn commitment that following a "No" vote we will immediately take action to renew the constitution and we will not stop until we have done that. And I make a solemn declaration to all Canadians in the other provinces: we, the Quebec MPs, are laying ourselves on the line, because we are telling Quebecers to vote "No" and telling you in the other provinces that we will not agree to your interpreting a "No" vote as an indication that everything is fine and can remain as it was before.[72]

The day after the referendum, Trudeau told the House of Commons that he would do whatever was necessary to keep his promise to Quebec. Although he would not compromise on the Charter of Rights, everything else—including the division of powers—was open for negotiation.[73]

Within a few weeks, the federal and provincial governments reestablished the Continuing Committee of Ministers on the Constitution (CCMC). The CCMC had been created in late 1978, as the debate raged over Bill C-60; it had not met since October 1979, when the short-lived Clark government had been in power.[74] The reconstituted committee was chaired by federal Justice Minister Jean Chrétien and his Saskatchewan counterpart Roy Romanow. During the summer of 1980, the two men toured provincial capitals discussing the elements of a constitutional agenda. On July 4, the federal government issued a "discussion draft" of an entrenched Charter. The form and content had evolved over two years of drafting and redrafting. The various rights and freedoms were now grouped into categories—fundamental freedoms, democratic rights, and so forth; this structure was later incorporated into the 1982 Charter.

The general limitation clause in the Victoria Charter had been replaced by internal limitations within the text of each section. For example, the right to vote was guaranteed "without unreasonable distinction or limitation"; property rights could be infringed only "in accordance with law and for reasonable compensation."[75] (Property rights were eventually deleted from the Charter at the insistence of several provinces.[76]) The July meeting of the CCMC, and subsequent discussions by the Sub-Committee of Officials on a Charter of Rights, revealed considerable confusion over the meaning and purpose of these various limitation clauses. To address this problem, federal officials proposed a return to the 1971 Victoria formula: "an opening clause in the Charter that would indicate that none of the rights and freedoms were absolute but must be balanced against the interests of an organized free and democratic society operating under the rule of law."[77] Such clauses had been included in the 1950 European Convention on Human Rights and the 1966 International Convention on Civil and Political Rights. Although provincial officials were not enthusiastic about this suggestion, the August 22 federal draft omitted the internal limitations and incorporated a new section 1 (for details, see Dossier 2.10).

DOSSIER 2.10

THE EVOLUTION OF SECTION 1

August 22, 1980

(federal draft)

The Canadian Charter of Rights and Freedoms recognizes the following rights and freedoms subject only to such reasonable limits as are generally accepted in a free and democratic society.

September 3, 1980

(federal draft)

The Canadian Charter of Rights and Freedoms recognizes the following rights and freedoms subject only to such reasonable limits as are generally accepted in a free and democratic society *with a parliamentary system of government.*

April 17, 1982

(final version)

The Canadian Charter of Rights and Freedoms *guarantees* the rights and freedoms set out in it subject only to such reasonable limits *prescribed by law* as can be *demonstrably justified* in a free and democratic society.

The reference to "a parliamentary system of government" was added at the insistence of the eight dissenting premiers,[1] who wanted to protect parliamentary supremacy from unbridled judicial discretion in applying the Charter. From the federal government's perspective, a concession on this score appeared to be the best way to prevent the provinces from imposing a blanket override on Charter rights.[2] Many of the witnesses before the Special Joint Committee in 1980–81 condemned the phrase, arguing that it would require judges to defer to Parliament's chosen balance between Charter rights and competing social values. After months of criticism from rights advocates, the federal government deleted the reference to parliamentary government.[3] In response, the "Gang of Eight" forced Trudeau to accept the notwithstanding clause (s. 33; see Chapter 12, pages 379–83). But given its unpopularity, it can hardly be considered as a counterweight to s. 1.

The other changes in wording are equally important. The change from "recognizes" to "guarantees" strengthens the Charter significantly; it transforms the protection of rights from passive recognition to an active duty. It signals to legislators, administrators, and judges that they must go beyond the simple acknowledgment of rights and freedoms; they must, wherever possible, protect and promote those rights and freedoms. The new phrase "demonstrably justified" puts the onus on governments to justify infringements on Charter rights. In contrast, the words "generally accepted" might have shielded time-honoured rights violations—e.g., discrimination against gays and lesbians—from judicial remedy.

(continued)

Unlike the other two amendments, the insertion of the phrase "prescribed by law" tends to limit the scope of s. 1. It means that rights violations arising from official acts—e.g., mistreatment of criminal suspects by the police—are exempt from the external limitation. Consequently, internal limits remain in the Charter's legal rights, which are procedural as well as statutory (e.g., the right to be secure against *unreasonable* search and seizure in s. 8).[4] Because s. 1 does not apply, the procedural rights must be subject to internal limitations.

The deletion of internal limits in ss. 2, 3, and 15 has shaped the judicial interpretation of the Charter. The courts do not have to "read in" limitations to these sections, because they know that the s. 1 stage of analysis will give them an opportunity to balance rights against the social interests served by an impugned law. (See Dossier 1.6, pages 27–30.) The result has been a "large and liberal" interpretation of rights and freedoms—precisely what the provincial opponents of entrenchment had hoped to avoid.

ENDNOTES

1. "The Canadian Charter of Rights and Freedoms, Provincial Proposal (In the Event that There Is Going to be Entrenchment)," August 28, 1980, reprinted in Anne F. Bayefsky, ed., *Canada's Constitution Act, 1982 and Amendments: A Documentary History* (Toronto: McGraw-Hill Ryerson, 1989), vol. 2, p. 678, clause 1: "The Canadian Charter of Rights and Freedoms recognizes the following rights and freedoms subject only to such reasonable limits as are generally accepted in a free society living under a parliamentary democracy."

2. Janet L. Hiebert, *Limiting Rights: The Dilemma of Judicial Review* (Montreal and Kingston: McGill-Queen's University Press, 1996), p. 29.

3. "Consolidation of Proposed Resolution and Possible Amendments as Placed before the Special Joint Committee by the Minister of Justice, January 12, 1981," reprinted in Bayefsky, *Canada's Constitution Act*, vol. 2, p. 766.

4. Justice Gerard V. La Forest, "The Balancing of Interests under the Charter," *National Journal of Constitutional Law* 2 (1992), p. 151.

The September 1980 First Ministers' Meeting broke up in acrimony and mutual recriminations after the Quebec delegation leaked a federal strategy paper laying out a plan for **unilateral patriation**.[78] The federal government put an end to intergovernmental negotiations, and moved quickly to put its plan into effect. In early October, Prime Minister Trudeau announced to the country that he would ask the British Parliament to pass the Canada Act—comprising a patriation provision, an amending formula, and a Charter of Rights—with the support of only two provinces: Ontario and New Brunswick. Shortly thereafter, he tabled his draft constitutional package in the House of Commons. By the end of that month, three provincial governments had referred the constitutionality of unilateral patriation to their respective courts. Meanwhile, the parliamentary debate at second reading was cut short and the draft Canada Act sent to the Special Joint Committee of the Senate and House of Commons. After several days of resistance, the Liberals agreed to televise all of the committee's proceedings. In hindsight, their initial reluctance is puzzling. Opening the deliberations to a national audience allowed the evolving Charter to capture the imagination of Canadians, and it gave the Trudeau government the political resources to strengthen the guarantees of rights and freedoms.

Once the federal government decided to proceed without provincial consent, it was free to restore the Charter of Rights to its original strength. Since the heady days of January 1968, when the newly minted justice minister predicted that the virtues of entrenched rights and freedoms would be self-evident to the provincial governments, Trudeau had learned some hard political lessons. He had been forced to water down his proposed charter at the 1971 Victoria meeting, and again in Bill C-60 and the October 1980 draft. When witnesses before the Special Joint

Committee called for stronger guarantees of rights and freedoms, the federal government was more than willing to cooperate.

In January 1981, Justice Minister Jean Chrétien tabled a set of amendments to the October draft of the Charter.[79] Most incorporated suggestions from witnesses who had called for stronger guarantees. Two examples are presented here; the evolution of specific Charter sections will be further discussed in Part 3. The new version of s. 8 guaranteed "the right to be secure against unreasonable search and seizure," deleting the earlier qualification "except on grounds, and in accordance with procedures, established by law." The effect of the deletion was to give courts full discretion to weigh violations against the guaranteed right itself, without reference to any legislated limitations. The October 1980 version of s. 10(b) guaranteed that anyone who was arrested or detained would have "the right to retain and instruct counsel without delay"; the January 1981 version added the crucial phrase, "and to be informed of that right." This addition, presumably inspired by the famous *Miranda* ruling from the U.S. Supreme Court,[80] strengthened both the content of the guaranteed rights and the remedies available to judges.

The legal impact of the stronger due-process guarantees in the amended Charter became clear in 1985, when the Supreme Court upheld a dismissal of drunk-driving charges because the accused had not been informed of his right to counsel (Dossier 2.11).

DOSSIER 2.11

R. V. THERENS (1985)

In April 1982, shortly after the proclamation of the Charter, Paul Therens was arrested for impaired driving. The arresting officer did not inform him of his right to speak to a lawyer before providing a breathalyzer sample, and Therens did not request legal counsel on his own initiative. At trial, the judge excluded the results of the breathalyzer—which showed that he had, in fact, been legally impaired—because the officer had violated Therens' rights under s. 10(b). The Crown appealed the exclusion to the Ontario Court of Appeal, without success. When the Supreme Court of Canada ruled on the case in 1985, it agreed with the lower courts. Writing for the majority on this issue, Justice Estey was uncompromising: "To do otherwise than reject this evidence on the facts and circumstances in this appeal would be to invite police officers to disregard Charter rights of the citizens and to do so with an assurance of impunity."[1] Justice Le Dain agreed on this point, stressing the fundamental importance of the right to counsel in the criminal process. Any denial of that right "must *prima facie* discredit the administration of justice."[2]

The ruling overturned the 1979 *Chromiak* judgment,[3] which had been decided under the Bill of Rights. In that case, the Court had held that a person who was requested by police to provide a breathalyzer sample was not thereby "detained" within the meaning of s. 2(c) of the Bill. Therefore, his right to counsel under s. 2(c)(ii) was not engaged. The Crown had argued in *Therens* that the word "detained" in s. 10 of the Charter should be interpreted in the same way. Despite the similarity in language between the relevant sections of the Bill and the Charter, the Justices rejected the claim that their Charter jurisprudence should be bound by Bill of Rights precedents. In the first place, the Charter was a constitutional provision and the Bill a mere statute. The permanency of a constitution, which could not be amended as easily as a statute, required a broader and more liberal interpretation of its wording.[4] Second, the Charter required the courts to impose remedies for rights violations; no such requirement had been imposed by the Bill.

> ... the *Charter* must be regarded, because of its constitutional character, as a new affirmation of rights and freedoms and of judicial power and responsibility in relation to their protection. This results from s. 52 of the *Constitution Act, 1982,* which

(continued)

removes any possible doubt or uncertainty as to the general effect which the *Charter* is to have by providing that it is part of the supreme law of Canada and that any law that is inconsistent with its provisions is to the extent of such inconsistency of no force and effect, and from s. 24 of the *Charter*, which provides that anyone whose guaranteed rights or freedoms have been infringed or denied may apply to a court of competent jurisdiction to obtain such remedy as the court considers appropriate and just in the circumstances. In considering the relationship of a decision under the *Canadian Bill of Rights* to an issue arising under the *Charter*, a court cannot, in my respectful opinion, avoid bearing in mind an evident fact of Canadian judicial history, which must be squarely and frankly faced: that on the whole, with some notable exceptions, the courts have felt some uncertainty or ambivalence in the application of the *Canadian Bill of Rights* because it did not reflect a clear constitutional mandate to make judicial decisions having the effect of limiting or qualifying the traditional sovereignty of Parliament.[5]

Third, the Charter went beyond the simple guarantee of counsel in the Bill by requiring police to make suspects aware of that guarantee. "This, in my opinion, shows the additional importance which the *Charter* attaches to the right to counsel."[6] Fourth, the inclusion of s. 1 in the Charter must be taken to mean that the rights contained therein are to be interpreted broadly, without judicially created internal limitations. Conversely, the rights in the Bill—which contained no general limitation clause—had to be construed narrowly, to avoid conflicting with each other (and with social values not protected in the Bill).[7] (Despite this discussion of the relationship between s. 1 and the rest of the Charter, the Justices determined that s. 1 did not apply in this case, because the violation arose from the police officer's actions and not from a written statute.[8])

The Court expanded the interpretation of the word "detention" to include roadside breathalyzer testing. The Justices also made it clear that they would repudiate their own pre-Charter precedents whenever it seemed appropriate to do so. Finally, they declared—though not unanimously—that the exclusion of evidence under s. 24(2) was the proper remedy for Charter violations in the criminal investigative process. The probative value of tainted evidence must be balanced against "the maintenance of respect for and confidence in the administration of justice, as that may be affected by the violation of constitutional rights and freedoms."[9] Moreover, "the relative seriousness of the constitutional violation"—taking into account "whether it was committed in good faith, or was inadvertent or of a merely technical nature, or whether it was deliberate, wilful or flagrant"—must be weighed against "the relative seriousness of the criminal charge."[10] As noted above, the seriousness of a s. 10(b) violation was found by the majority to require an automatic exclusion of evidence resulting therefrom. Dissenting on this issue, Justice McIntyre argued that probative evidence—such as an incriminating breathalyzer result—should not be excluded automatically on Charter grounds: "The exclusion of the evidence in the circumstances of this case would itself go far to bring the administration of justice into disrepute."[11]

ENDNOTES

1. *R. v. Therens*, [1985] 1 S.C.R. 613, paragraph 11.

2. *Therens*, paragraph 77.

3. *Chromiak v. The Queen*, [1980] 1 S.C.R. 471.

4. *Therens*, paragraph 48, *per* Le Dain J.

5. Ibid., *per* Le Dain J.

6. Ibid., *per* Le Dain J.

7. Ibid., *per* Le Dain J.

8. Ibid., *per* Le Dain J.

9. Ibid., *per* Le Dain J.

10. Ibid., *per* Le Dain J.

11. Ibid., *per* McIntyre J.

The *Therens* ruling reveals the importance of the January 1981 amendments to the Charter. It also illustrates the significance of explicit judicial remedies for infringements of rights and freedoms. Finally, it demonstrates how judicial interpretation shapes the meaning of the entrenched guarantees. Had the majority of Justices agreed with McIntyre's approach to s. 24(2), legal-rights jurisprudence might have evolved very differently (see Chapter 10, pages 312–15).

WAS AN ENTRENCHED CHARTER NECESSARY?

As we have seen, Trudeau's proposal for an entrenched Charter of Rights drew strong criticism from several provincial governments. Some opponents suggested that the Bill of Rights was sufficient, at least in the federal sphere, especially if it were amended to incorporate a stronger declaration of invalidity.[81] They also pointed out that the federal and provincial governments had adopted human rights codes, which provided administrative remedies for discrimination in the public and private sectors. Defenders of the Charter argued that the Bill and the statutory codes were insufficient protection against governments bent on discriminating against particular groups, and that explicit judicial remedies for unjust laws were the best protection against hostile majorities.

To understand the differences between pre-Charter and post-Charter judicial review, it is useful to compare the outcomes of two rulings on the same issue. Dossier 2.12 contrasts the pre-Charter and post-Charter decisions of the Supreme Court on the constitutionality of Canada's abortion law, to illustrate the impact of explicit judicial remedies and constitutional entrenchment.[82] It also reveals a change in judicial attitudes: after 1982, deference to a supreme Parliament was replaced by a willingness to strike down laws that—in the opinion of a majority of Justices—infringed protected rights and freedoms.

DOSSIER 2.12

THE BILL OF RIGHTS VERSUS THE CHARTER IN THE *MORGENTALER* RULINGS

In 1975, the Supreme Court of Canada upheld section 251 of the Criminal Code, which prohibited abortion. The only exceptions to the law were "therapeutic abortions": those performed in a hospital with the approval of a Therapeutic Abortion Committee (TAC) made up of three doctors (not including the doctor who would perform the actual procedure).

In the mid-1970s, one-quarter of Canadian hospitals had fewer than four doctors on staff; these hospitals were therefore unable to establish TACs. In larger hospitals, political pressure forced administrators either to forbid the creation of TACs or to disband existing committees. By 1982, only one in five Canadian hospitals had functioning TACs. Under the law, a TAC could authorize an abortion only if the continuation of the pregnancy "would or would be likely to endanger [the] life or health" of the woman. Some doctors interpreted the word "health" broadly, to include mental and emotional well-being, while others would not permit abortions except in medical emergencies. The procedural flaws in section 251 were serious: not only did access to abortion vary widely across the regions, but the bureaucracy and arbitrariness inherent in the committee system delayed abortion procedures—often by eight weeks or more. The result was a grave risk to the life and health of women seeking abortions.

Dr. Henry Morgentaler fought to change the law, largely through a one-man civil disobedience campaign. In 1973, he was charged with performing an illegal abortion in his Montreal clinic. The procedure violated s. 251 because it did not take place in a hospital, and there was no TAC approval. He was acquitted by a jury, even though he was clearly in violation of the law; the Quebec Court of Appeal overturned the verdict and imposed a conviction. That decision

(continued)

was appealed to the Supreme Court in 1975.

The Justices refused to consider Morgentaler's argument that the flawed TAC system violated the due-process guarantee in the Bill of Rights. Chief Justice Laskin did address the Bill of Rights arguments, but only for the purpose of debunking them. In the first place, he rejected Morgentaler's request for an American-style judicial review of the abortion law: "any interference by a court with the substantive content of legislation" would be "foreign to our constitutional traditions, to our constitutional law and to our conceptions of judicial review."[1] Canada, unlike the United States, did not have a "constitutionally entrenched Bill of Rights";[2] as a federal statute, the 1960 Bill did not give the courts the power to strike down other federal laws. Second, Laskin insisted that the courts could not second-guess Parliament or usurp its power to make and amend laws.

> I do not regard s. 1(b) of the Canadian Bill of Rights as charging the courts with supervising the administrative efficiency of legislation or with evaluating the regional or national organization of its administration... Parliament has made a judgement which does not admit of any interference by the court.... Any unevenness in the administration of the relieving provisions is for Parliament to correct and not for the courts to monitor as being a denial of equality before the law and the protection of the law.[3]

Morgentaler's conviction was upheld and he went to prison.

After his release, Morgentaler continued to challenge the abortion law. In 1984, he was arrested in Toronto; once again a jury acquitted him and an appeals court convicted him. In 1986, he returned to the Supreme Court, hoping that the entrenched Charter would embolden the Justices to strike down the law. He argued that because the delays imposed by the TACs threatened "life" and "security of the person," the abortion law violated the rights guaranteed in section 7 of the Charter. Chief Justice Dickson, who had participated in the 1975 ruling, made it clear from the outset that the Court would treat the Charter very differently from the Bill of Rights:

> [S]ince 1975, and the first *Morgentaler* decision, the Court has been given added responsibilities.... Although no doubt it is still fair to say that courts are not the appropriate forum for articulating complex and controversial programmes of public policy, Canadian courts are now charged with the crucial obligation of ensuring that the legislative initiatives pursued by our Parliament and legislatures conform to the democratic values expressed in the *Canadian Charter of Rights and Freedoms*.... It is in this latter sense that the current *Morgentaler* appeal differs from the one we heard a decade ago.[4]

Justice McIntyre shared this view of the Court's "second-order" Charter duties, even while warning against an overly broad interpretation of protected rights.

> Before the adoption of the *Charter*, there was little question of the limits of judicial review of the criminal law. For all practical purposes it was limited to a determination of whether the impugned enactment dealt with a subject which could fall within the criminal law power in s. 91(27) of the *Constitution Act, 1867*.... The adoption of the *Charter* brought a significant change. The power of judicial review of legislation acquired greater scope but, in my view, that scope is not unlimited and should be carefully confined to that which is ordained by the *Charter*. I am well aware that there will be disagreement about what was ordained by the *Charter* and, of course, a measure of interpretation of the *Charter* will be required in order to give substance and reality to its provisions. But the courts must not, in the guise of interpretation, postulate rights and freedoms which do not have a firm and a reasonably identifiable base in the *Charter*.[5]

Five of the seven Justices on the panel voted to strike down the abortion law, although for varying reasons. The four male Justices in the majority agreed with Morgentaler that the TACs violated section 7 of the Charter because they threatened both the physical and psychological well-being of women seeking abortions. The law did not operate "in accordance with the principles of fundamental justice." Madam Justice Wilson, in a separate opinion, found that the law violated the right to liberty, as well as the other rights in section 7: "the right to liberty contained in s. 7 guarantees to every individual a degree of personal autonomy over important decisions intimately affecting their private lives."[6] She also found that the law violated section 2(a) of the Charter: "I believe that the decision whether or not to terminate a pregnancy is essentially a moral decision, a matter of conscience."[7]

Finally, the Court used the Charter to evaluate the application of the impugned law—a deviation from the previous Morgentaler ruling.

> Although the mandate given to the courts under the Charter does not, generally speaking, enable the judiciary to provide remedies for administrative inefficiencies, when denial of a right as basic as security of the person is infringed by the procedure and administrative structures created by the law itself, the courts are empowered to act.... If section 251 of the Criminal Code does indeed breach s. 7 of the Charter through its general effects, that can be sufficient to invalidate the legislation under s. 52.[8]

ENDNOTES

1. *Morgentaler v. the Queen*, [1976] S.C.R. 632.

2. Ibid.

3. Ibid.

4. *R. v. Morgentaler*, [1998] S.C.R. 30, paragraph 3.

5. Ibid., paragraph 185.

6. Ibid., paragraph 237.

7. Ibid., paragraph 246.

8. Ibid., paragraphs 31 and 32.

The reversal of the 1975 *Morgentaler* ruling illustrates several important features of Canadian politics and government in the Charter era. Whereas the 1975 judgment preserved the policy status quo, the 1988 ruling forced legislators to grapple with an issue that most would prefer to avoid. The ensuing legislative battle over a replacement law—which ultimately died in the Senate—attracted the participation of several interest groups, most of whom spoke in the language of rights rather than the political language of compromise. Some provincial governments and anti-abortion activists tried to restrict abortion, highlighting the inability of judges to implement their rulings.

Finally, the 1988 ruling drew the ire of critics who bemoaned "judicial activism" and argued—incorrectly—that the Court had tried to have the last word on the abortion issue. For them, the ruling was proof that an entrenched Charter was neither necessary nor beneficial. At the same time, *Morgentaler* delighted groups and individuals who had grown impatient with Parliamentary reluctance to amend the abortion laws, and those who believed that entrenched rights should weigh heavily in the policy-making balance. For supporters of the ruling, the Court had demonstrated that an entrenched Charter was indeed necessary.

The entrenchment of the Charter, in concert with the evolving support structure for rights mobilization, produced significant changes in Canadian politics and government. If they chose, judges could use their new remedial powers to invalidate or amend laws; after 1982, many did choose to do so. The legislative and executive branches at both levels of government had to review their existing laws and scrutinize new ones in order to eliminate potential Charter violations. Early rulings from the courts reinforced this imperative: it quickly became clear that judges would no longer defer to legislators as they had under the Bill of

Rights. Nor did it take long for existing interest groups—particularly those that had been most visible at the Special Joint Committee hearings—to turn to the courts, or for new groups to form for the express purpose of using the Charter to secure their policy goals. Although the mobilization of First Nations, women's groups, official-language minorities, and reform-minded lawyers began well before 1982, the entrenchment of rights and freedoms gave them a new legal status and a powerful political resource.

Part 2 of this book traces these trends and evaluates the Charter's impact on key players in Canada's political system. It argues that the shift of policy-making power to the courts has not been accompanied by an increase in their capacity to make and enforce good public policy. On a more positive note, judicial assertiveness in the early years of the Charter gave the other two branches of government a strong incentive to weigh protected rights and freedoms more heavily in their own lawmaking processes.

Part 3 explores the Charter's impact on Canadian law and policy. It concludes that the entrenchment of rights and freedoms, together with explicit judicial remedies, has made a significant difference in many areas of law. But its tangible day-to-day impact is harder to determine. The reach of a law, whether statutory or judge-made, is usually limited. Changing the law does not automatically produce a better quality of life for the poor, fairer treatment for minorities, genuine due-process safeguards for criminal suspects, or a more vibrant democracy. Recalcitrant parliamentarians or public officials can blunt the impact of a Charter ruling, as can stubborn social prejudices and stereotypes. Nonetheless, there can be little doubt that the third period of human rights protection in Canada has brought important and generally positive changes to our politics and government. We will explore those changes in the remainder of this book.

GLOSSARY OF KEY TERMS

parliamentary supremacy A central principle of the parliamentary system that Canada inherited from Britain. In theory, the laws passed by elected legislators cannot be struck down or amended by the courts. In practice, judges make incremental changes to written statutes in the process of interpreting and applying them to particular disputes. Canadian judges have long held the power to nullify laws that are found to be *ultra vires* the sponsoring government.

patriation Literally, "bringing home." In the context of the 1980–82 constitutional negotiations, "patriation" referred to the process by which the 1867 Constitution would cease to be a British statute and become a purely Canadian law. The British Parliament would lose its power to amend Canada's constitution.

preamble A statement of facts and/or principles that appears at the very beginning of a written law (entrenched or nonentrenched). It consists of one or more clauses, each of which normally begins with the word "Whereas" (the 1960 Bill of Rights is an exception). For example, the Preamble to the Constitution Act, 1982 reads: "Whereas Canada is founded upon the principles that recognize the supremacy of God and the rule of law." In general, the Preamble to a law is not enforceable, either by the courts or by the executive branch. The Preamble to the Constitution Act, 1867 is a partial exception, as this chapter explains.

probative A legal term describing the value of a particular piece of evidence to the trier of fact in a criminal proceeding. Reliable evidence that tends to prove the guilt or innocence of the accused (e.g., fingerprints on a murder weapon or a DNA sample found near the body) will generally be considered to have high probative value. When a judge decides whether to admit a particular piece of evidence at trial, she must weigh its probative value against any prejudicial effect that it may have. For example, testimony about the prior sexual history of the victim of an alleged sexual assault may be prejudicial if it plays into social stereotypes about "loose" or dishonest women. On the other hand, according to the Court in *Seaboyer*, such evidence might be probative if it demonstrates that the accused might reasonably (though mistakenly) have believed that the alleged victim consented to the sexual activity in question.

Sabbath The weekly holy day of a particular religion. The faithful are expected to refrain from paid work on that day and to participate in their worship rituals (whether public or private). Christians observe the Sabbath on Sundays, Jews on Saturdays, and Muslims on Fridays.

self crimination The same as self-incrimination, that is, any statement or other evidence that may lead to an inference of guilt against that person.

ultra vires Latin for "beyond the power of." When a court rules that a particular law is *ultra vires*, it means that the legislature that passed that law went beyond the powers assigned to it by the Constitution Act, 1867 (the BNA Act). Before the Charter, a law that was *ultra vires* one level of government could be validly enacted by the other level (where it would be *intra vires*— "within the power of").

unilateral patriation The approach adopted by the Trudeau government after the failure of the September 1980 First Ministers' Meeting. Trudeau would present a package of proposed constitutional reforms—a Charter, an amending formula, and a statement of patriation—to Parliament; after they received the approval of both Houses, he would take the package to the British Parliament and ask it to amend the BNA Act without provincial consent. Trudeau gambled that the lack of a written amending formula in the 1867 Constitution would allow him to proceed with the support of only two provincial governments (New Brunswick and Ontario). In September 1981, the Supreme Court of Canada declared that unilateral patriation was technically legal, but that it violated the convention of "substantial provincial consent" for constitutional amendments affecting the division of powers. Trudeau was forced to return to the bargaining table, which he did in November 1981.

DISCUSSION AND REVIEW QUESTIONS

1. Identify and explain two important changes in Canadian judicial review since 1982.

2. Identify and explain two arguments for and two arguments against the principle of parliamentary supremacy.

3. Why did civil libertarians like Trudeau believe that an entrenched charter of rights was necessary?

4. Identify and describe two international influences on the Charter.

5. Summarize the key events that led up to the proclamation of the Charter. How did each affect the final wording of its guarantees?

SUGGESTED READINGS

Bayefsky, Anne F., ed. *Canada's Constitution Act, 1982 and Amendments: A Documentary History.* Toronto: McGraw-Hill Ryerson, 1989.

Cairns, Alan C. *Charter versus Federalism: The Dilemmas of Constitutional Reform.* Montreal and Kingston: McGill-Queen's University Press, 1992.

———. *Disruptions: Constitutional Struggles, from the Charter to Meech Lake.* Ed. Douglas E. Williams. Toronto: McClelland and Stewart, 1991.

———. "The Judicial Committee and Its Critics." In Douglas E. Williams, ed., *Constitution, Government, and Society in Canada: Selected Essays by Alan C. Cairns.* Toronto: McClelland and Stewart, 1988, pp. 43–85.

Greene, Ian. *The Charter of Rights.* Toronto: Lorimer, 1989.

McWhinney, Edward. *Canada and the Constitution, 1979–1982: Patriation and the Charter of Rights.* Toronto: University of Toronto Press, 1982.

Romanow, Roy, John Whyte, and Howard Leeson. *Canada ... Notwithstanding: The Making of the Constitution, 1976–1982.* Toronto: Carswell/Methuen, 1984.

Russell, Peter H. *Constitutional Odyssey: Can Canadians Become a Sovereign People?* 2nd ed. Toronto: University of Toronto Press, 1993.

———. "The Political Purposes of the Canadian Charter of Rights and Freedoms." *Canadian Bar Review* 61, no. 1 (March 1983), pp. 30–54.

———, Rainer Knopff, and F.L. Morton, eds. *Federalism and the Charter: Leading Constitutional Decisions.* Ottawa: Carleton University Press, 1989.

Scott, F.R. *Essays on the Constitution: Aspects of Canadian Law and Politics.* Toronto: University of Toronto Press, 1977.

Sheppard, Robert, and Michael Valpy. *The National Deal: The Fight for a Canadian Constitution.* Toronto: Macmillan, 1982.

Tarnopolsky, Walter Surma. *The Canadian Bill of Rights.* 2nd rev. ed. Toronto: McClelland and Stewart, 1975.

Trudeau, Pierre Elliott. *Federalism and the French Canadians.* Ed. John Saywell. Toronto: Macmillan, 1968.

Williams, Cynthia. "The Changing Nature of Citizen Rights." In Alan C. Cairns and Cynthia Williams, eds., *Constitutionalism, Citizenship and Society in Canada, vol. 33 of the collected research studies for the Royal Commission on the Economic Union and Development Prospects for Canada.* Toronto: University of Toronto Press, 1985, pp. 99–132.

ENDNOTES

1. Alan C. Cairns, *Charter versus Federalism: The Dilemmas of Constitutional Reform* (Montreal and Kingston: McGill-Queen's University Press, 1992), p. 22.

2. Joseph F. Fletcher and Paul Howe, "Canadian Attitudes toward the Charter and the Courts in Comparative Perspective," *Choices* 6, no. 3 (Montreal: Institute for Research on Public Policy, May 2000), p. 11, Figure 7; available online at www.irpp.org.

3. Charles R. Epp, "Do Bills of Rights Matter? The Canadian Charter of Rights and Freedoms," *American Political Science Review* 90, no. 4 (December 1996), pp. 765–79; Epp, *The Rights Revolution: Lawyers, Activists, and Supreme Courts in Comparative Perspective* (Chicago: University of Chicago Press, 1998), Chapters 2 and 9–10.

4. This right was grounded in Britain's Colonial Laws Validity Act, passed in 1865, which made the laws of the British Parliament paramount over those passed by Dominion legislatures. Canada's first Constitution, the British North America Act of 1867, was an act of the British Parliament (until it was patriated in 1982). Consequently, the "Law Lords" on the Judicial Committee of the Privy Council—Britain's highest court of appeal—were empowered to resolve conflicts between ordinary statutes and the BNA Act.

5. F.R. Scott, "Dominion Jurisdiction over Human Rights and Fundamental Freedoms," in F.R. Scott, *Essays on the Constitution: Aspects of Canadian Law and Politics* (Toronto: University of Toronto Press, 1977), p. 213 (emphasis added).

6. See, e.g., Alan C. Cairns, "The Judicial Committee and Its Critics," in Douglas E. Williams, ed., *Constitution, Government, and Society in Canada: Selected Essays by Alan C. Cairns* (Toronto: McClelland and Stewart, 1988), pp. 43–85, and Miriam Smith, "Ghosts of the Judicial Committee of the Privy Council: Groups, Politics and Charter Litigation in Canadian Political Science," *Canadian Journal of Political Science* 35 (2002), pp. 3–29.

7. *A.G. (Canada) and Dupond v. Montreal,* [1978] 2 S.C.R. 770, pp. 796–97, *per* Beetz J.

8. *Ontario (Attorney General) v. OPSEU,* [1987] 2 S.C.R. 2, paragraphs 151–52, *per* Beetz J.

9. See, e.g., *New Brunswick Broadcasting Co. v. Nova Scotia (Speaker of the House of Assembly),* [1993] 1 S.C.R. 319, *per* McLachlin J.; *Reference re Remuneration of Judges of the Provincial Court (P.E.I.),* [1997] 3 S.C.R. 3, paragraphs 99–104, *per* Lamer C.J.; *Reference re Secession of Quebec,* [1998] 2 S.C.R. 217, paragraph 53, *per curiam.*

10. *OPSEU,* paragraph 152, *per* Beetz J.

11. 347 U.S. 483 (1954); available online at www.law.cornell.edu.

12. Cynthia Williams, "The Changing Nature of Citizen Rights," in Alan C. Cairns and Cynthia Williams, eds., *Constitutionalism, Citizenship and Society in Canada,* vol. 33 of the collected research studies for the Royal Commission on the Economic Union and Development Prospects for Canada (Toronto: University of Toronto Press, 1985), pp. 100–4.

13. Noel A. Kinsella, "Tomorrow's Rights in the Mirror of History," in Gerald L. Gall, ed., *Civil Liberties in Canada: Entering the 1980s* (Toronto: Butterworths, 1982), pp. 34–35.

14. The rights and freedoms listed in Stewart's motion included "minority rights," the standard civil liberties of speech and opinion, and "equal treatment before the law of all citizens, irrespective of race, nationality or religious or political beliefs." See *Hansard,* 1945, p. 900, reproduced in Walter Surma Tarnopolsky, *The Canadian Bill of Rights,* 2nd rev. ed. (Toronto: McClelland and Stewart, 1975), pp. 11–12. Stewart was a member of the Co-operative Commonwealth Federation (CCF), the forerunner of today's New Democratic Party.

15. Williams, "The Changing Nature," p. 102.

16. Tarnopolsky, *The Canadian Bill of Rights,* p. 8.

17. Cairns, *Charter versus Federalism,* p. 28; Williams, "The Changing Nature," p. 103.

18. 1950 Senate Committee *Proceedings,* p. 301; reproduced in Tarnopolsky, *The Canadian Bill of Rights,* p. 13.

19. Tarnopolsky, *The Canadian Bill of Rights,* p. 14. Note that the committee gave potential witnesses only a day or two to prepare their briefs, which may have limited the number of participants; see Williams, "The Changing Nature," p. 105.

20. When Parliament passes a law, it usually authorizes the cabinet to make whatever detailed regulations are necessary for its implementation. Ideally, draft regulations are submitted to Parliament together with the draft law. Before order-in-council regulations can take effect, they are reviewed by the Privy Council Office, one or more of the standing committees of cabinet, and any other agency required by law.

21. The most comprehensive discussion of the ministerial review process is in Tarnopolsky, *The Canadian Bill of Rights,* pp. 125–28.

22. Peter W. Hogg, "A Comparison of the Canadian Charter of Rights and Freedoms with the Canadian Bill of Rights," in Gérald-A. Beaudoin and Ed Ratushny, eds., *The Canadian Charter of Rights and Freedoms,* 2nd edition (Toronto: Carswell, 1989), p. 13, note 39.

23. Ibid., p. 13.

24. Elmer A. Driedger, "The Meaning and Effect of the Canadian Bill of Rights: A Draftsman's Viewpoint," *Ottawa Law Review* 9 (1977), p. 306.

25. For a discussion of first- and second-order Charter duties, see Brian Slattery, "A Theory of the Charter," *Osgoode Hall Law Journal* 25 (1987), pp. 701–47; see also Chapter 4 in this book.

26. Driedger, "The Meaning," p. 311. Similarly, the late Walter Tarnopolsky—the leading expert on the Bill and later a judge of the Ontario Court of Appeals—suggested that the potential embarrassment arising from an unfavourable ministerial report would motivate the legislative drafters in the Department of Justice to "resolve any inconsistency between the Bill of Rights and a draft Bill" long before the latter could be introduced into the Commons. See Tarnopolsky, *The Canadian Bill of Rights*, p. 128.

27. The wrongful convictions of Donald Marshall, Jr., in Nova Scotia, and David Milgaard in Saskatchewan are perhaps the best known examples of police and prosecutorial misconduct during the Bill of Rights period. Despite their notoriety, it seems clear that these were not isolated examples. See the *Report of the Royal Commission on the Donald Marshall, Jr., Prosecution* (Halifax: Province of Nova Scotia, 1989), and Dianne L. Martin, "The Police Role in Wrongful Convictions: An International Comparative Study," in Saundra D. Westervelt and John A. Humphrey, eds., *Wrongly Convicted: Perspectives on Failed Justice* (New Brunswick, NJ: Rutgers University Press, 2001), pp. 77–95.

28. See the various *Reports* of the Commission of Inquiry Concerning Certain Activities of the Royal Canadian Mounted Police (Ottawa: Minister of Supply and Services, 1981).

29. Kent Roach, *Due Process and Victims' Rights: The New Law and Politics of Criminal Justice* (Toronto: University of Toronto Press, 1999), pp. 38–41.

30. Berend Hovius and Robert Martin, "The Canadian Charter of Rights and Freedoms in the Supreme Court of Canada," *Canadian Bar Review* 61, no. 1 (March 1983), p. 357.

31. Bill C-181, 28th Parliament, 2nd Session, November 1970, Chapter 2. The act expired on April 30, 1971. See Hogg, "A Comparison," p. 10, note 32.

32. Tarnopolsky, *The Canadian Bill of Rights*, p. 346.

33. As Tarnopolsky points out, very few of the 497 people arrested during these "sweeps" were ever convicted of a criminal offence. See also Denis Smith, *Bleeding Hearts ... Bleeding Country* (Edmonton: Hurtig, 1971), for a critique of the federal government's response and its effects on civil liberties.

34. Bill C-181, section 12.

35. *Hogan v. the Queen*, [1975] 2 S.C.R. 680, p. 597, *per* Laskin C.J.

36. Driedger, who helped craft the Bill, argued that the fault lay with poor judging and not poor drafting. See "The Meaning," p. 307.

37. See, for example, *R. v. Drybones*, [1970] S.C.R. 282, *per* Cartwright C.J.C.

38. This approach follows three preexisting rules of statutory interpretation: the presumption that Parliament did not intend to violate the Constitution, the presumption of congruence with common law, and the inapplicability of legislation in particular cases (e.g., retroactivity or extraterritoriality). See Ruth Sullivan, *Statutory Interpretation* (Toronto: Irwin Law, 1997), pp. 177–97.

39. *Brownridge v. the Queen*, [1972] S.C.R. 926.

40. *Hogan v. the Queen*, [1975] 2 S.C.R. 680.

41. The late Chief Justice Laskin, a proponent of civil liberties, tried to use *Drybones* as a binding precedent in later Bill of Rights cases—at least those involving the due-process rights of criminal suspects. He was unable to win the support of his colleagues. His dissents appear to have had some influence on the federal government when it drafted the Charter. The best example is *Hogan v. the Queen*, [1975] 2 S.C.R. 574.

42. *Attorney General of Canada v. Lavell and Bedard*, [1974] S.C.R. 1349.

43. *Lavell and Bedard, per* Ritchie J.

44. Peter H. Russell, Rainer Knopff, and Ted Morton, eds., *Federalism and the Charter: Leading Constitutional Decisions* (Ottawa: Carleton University Press, 1989), p. 360.

45. *Bliss v. Attorney General of Canada,* [1979] 1 S.C.R. 183, p. 190, *per* Ritchie J. (for a unanimous Court).

46. Ritchie cited, approvingly, the ruling of Justice Pratte of the Federal Court of Appeal: "If section 46 treats unemployed pregnant women differently from other unemployed persons, be they male or female, it is, it seems to me, because they are pregnant and not because they are women." Cited at pp. 190–91 of *Bliss.*

47. *Singh v. Minister of Employment and Immigration,* [1985] 1 S.C.R. 177, paragraphs 84–85, *per* Beetz J.

48. Hogg, "A Comparison," pp. 3–4.

49. See Pierre Elliott Trudeau, "Quebec and the Constitutional Problem," a paper prepared for the Constitution Committee of Quebec's Legislative Assembly in 1965. Reprinted in Pierre Elliott Trudeau, *Federalism and the French Canadians,* ed. John Saywell (Toronto: Macmillan, 1968), pp. 3–51. Trudeau's comments about an entrenched Charter appear on pp. 44–45. See also Trudeau's suggestion, made in 1955, that Quebec should accept "the incorporation of a declaration of human rights in the constitution on the condition that the rights of disallowance and reservation be done away with." Trudeau, "A Constitutional Declaration of Rights," in *Federalism and the French Canadians,* p. 53.

50. On the influence of the Universal Declaration on Human Rights and other international treaties on Canadian attitudes toward an entrenched Charter, see Cairns, *Charter versus Federalism,* Chapter 1. See also Williams, "The Changing Nature," pp. 99–111.

51. Peter H. Russell, *Constitutional Odyssey: Can Canadians Become a Sovereign People?,* 2nd ed. (Toronto: University of Toronto Press, 1993), pp. 76–77.

52. Scholarly analyses of Trudeau's constitutional project include Peter H. Russell, "The Political Purposes of the Canadian Charter of Rights and Freedoms," *Canadian Bar Review* 61, no. 1 (March 1983), pp. 30–54; Russell, *Constitutional Odyssey;* Edward McWhinney, *Canada and the Constitution 1979–1982: Patriation and the Charter of Rights* (Toronto: University of Toronto Press, 1982); and Alan C. Cairns, *Disruptions: Constitutional Struggles, from the Charter to Meech Lake,* ed. Douglas E. Williams (Toronto: McClelland and Stewart, 1991), Chapters 1–3. The most comprehensive memoir by participants in the 1980–82 process is Roy Romanow, John Whyte, and Howard Leeson, *Canada ... Notwithstanding: The Making of the Constitution, 1976–1982* (Toronto: Carswell/Methuen, 1984). Finally, reporters Robert Sheppard and Michael Valpy wrote a useful journalistic account of the 1980–82 round: *The National Deal: The Fight for a Canadian Constitution* (Toronto: Macmillan, 1982).

53. Trudeau, "A Constitutional Declaration of Rights," p. 54.

54. Ibid., p. 55.

55. Ibid., p. 56.

56. Ibid., p. 54.

57. Ibid., p. 54.

58. Pierre Elliott Trudeau, "The Constitution and the People of Canada: An Approach to the Objectives of Confederation, the Rights of People and the Institutions of Government," 1968, reprinted in Anne F. Bayefsky, ed., *Canada's Constitution Act, 1982 and Amendments: A Documentary History* (Toronto: McGraw-Hill Ryerson, 1989), vol. 1, p. 82.

59. Pierre Elliott Trudeau, "A Canadian Charter of Human Rights," January 1968, in Bayefsky, *Canada's Constitution Act*, vol. 1, p. 52.

60. Ibid., p. 54. See also Lester B. Pearson, "Federalism for the Future: A Statement of Policy by the Government of Canada," 1968, in Bayefsky, *Canada's Constitution Act*, vol. 1, p. 66.

61. Trudeau, "A Constitutional Declaration of Rights," pp. 57–58. See also Trudeau, "A Canadian Charter of Human Rights," p. 52.

62. The staunchest defenders of parliamentary supremacy were Manitoba's Sterling Lyon and Saskatchewan's Allan Blakeney; see Romanow et al., *Canada*, p. 110, and Russell, *Constitutional Odyssey*, p. 120.

63. Claude Morin, *Quebec versus Ottawa: The Struggle for Self-Government, 1960–72* (Toronto: University of Toronto Press, 1976), Chapter 9; Edward McWhinney, *Quebec and the Constitution, 1960–1978* (Toronto: University of Toronto Press, 1979).

64. Morin, *Quebec versus Ottawa*, pp. 68–69; Russell, *Constitutional Odyssey*, pp. 90–91.

65. Reprinted in Bayefsky, *Canada's Constitution Act*, vol. 1, pp. 90–93.

66. R.G. Robertson, "Report of the Continuing Committee of Officials to the Federal–Provincial First Ministers' Conference," December 4, 1968, reprinted in Bayefsky, *Canada's Constitution Act*, vol. 1, pp. 113–15.

67. For the text of the "Political Rights" in the Victoria Charter, see Bayefsky, *Canada's Constitution Act*, vol. 1, p. 214.

68. Section 26 of the draft Charter shielded rights arising from the Royal Proclamation of 1763 from any possible conflict with the other rights and freedoms listed therein.

69. Bill C-60, reprinted in Bayefsky, *Canada's Constitution Act*, vol. 1, p. 348. See also Romanow et al., *Canada*, p. 9.

70. The strongest opponents were the governments of British Columbia and Alberta. Ontario, New Brunswick, and Prince Edward Island supported an entrenched Charter. The other provinces either expressed no opinion or were unclear. See Canadian Intergovernmental Conference Secretariat, *Proposals on the Constitution, 1971–1978* (Ottawa: CICS, December 1978), pp. 73–81.

71. *Reference re Legislative Authority of Parliament to Alter or Replace the Senate*, [1980] 1 S.C.R. 54.

72. Quoted in Sheppard and Valpy, *The National Deal*, p. 33.

73. Romanow et al., *Canada*, p. 61.

74. Trudeau's Liberals lost the May 1979 federal election. The Progressive Conservatives under Joe Clark formed a minority government, which was defeated in the House of Commons on a budget vote in December 1979. That defeat triggered the February 1980 general election. Trudeau, who had announced his retirement from politics, was persuaded to resume the leadership of the federal Liberal Party shortly after the governor general dissolved Parliament. The Liberals went on to win a majority under his leadership.

75. "Rights and Freedoms within the Canadian Federation," Discussion Draft Tabled by the Delegation of the Government of Canada, July 4, 1980, reprinted in Bayefsky, *Canada's Constitution Act*, vol. 2, pp. 299 and 601 [sections 3 and 9 respectively].

76. See the "Report by the Sub-Committee of Officials on a Charter of Rights," July 24, 1980, in Bayefsky, *Canada's Constitution Act*,

vol. 2, p. 662, for a summary of provincial objections to the entrenchment of property rights.

77. "Report by the Sub-Committee of Officials on a Charter of Rights," July 24, 1980, in Bayefsky, *Canada's Constitution Act*, vol. 2, p. 662.

78. See Romanow et al., *Canada*, pp. 94–103; Sheppard and Valpy, *The National Deal*, pp. 15 and 54–64.

79. Bayefsky, *Canada's Constitution Act*, vol. 2, pp. 765–800.

80. In *Miranda v. Arizona*, 384 U.S. 436 (1966), the Court imposed a constitutional duty on the police to inform suspects that they had a right to speak to a lawyer before making any statements. This right was grounded on the Fifth Amendment right to remain silent and the common-law right against self-incrimination. See also *Escobedo v. Illinois*, 378 U.S. 478 (1964). Unlike the American rule, s. 10(b) applies from the moment a person comes into contact with the police; it does not take effect upon entering the police station.

81. See, e.g., Tarnopolsky, *The Canadian Bill of Rights*, Chapters 1 and 4; "Report by the Sub-Committee of Officials on a Charter of Rights" (July 1980), in Bayefsky, *Canada's Constitution Act*, vol. 2, p. 661 (reflecting Manitoba's preference for an amended Bill of Rights over an entrenched Charter); "Co-Chairman's Summary of Consensus Reached by Ministers on Committee Reports" (July 1980), in Bayefsky, *Canada's Constitution Act*, vol. 2, p. 665 (Manitoba's request to consider whether the Bill could be given an enhanced status without formal entrenchment).

82. These particular rulings were chosen not because they concern the legality of abortion, but because they reached opposite conclusions based on almost identical facts. Consequently, they make the independent impact of the Charter and other factors clearer than other examples could do.

The Charter's Impact on Canadian Political Institutions

The Supreme Court of Canada

The Supreme Court of Canada at work, 2003.

CP PHOTO/Fred Chartrand

A statute defines present rights and obligations. It is easily enacted and as easily repealed. A constitution, by contrast, is drafted with an eye to the future. Its function is to provide a continuing framework for the legitimate exercise of governmental power and, when joined by a Bill or a Charter of Rights, for the unremitting protection of individual rights and liberties. Once enacted, its provisions cannot easily be repealed or amended. It must, therefore, be capable of growth and development over time to meet new social, political and historical realities often unimagined by its framers. The judiciary is the guardian of the constitution and must, in interpreting its provisions, bear these considerations in mind.[1]

What the public doesn't understand is that the role of the judge is to look at legislation in regard to the Constitution. Is that legislation constitutional? That's what we did before [the Charter]; that's what we do now. We do it [with] different criteria. Before it was either the provincial or the federal government impinged on the powers of the other. Now it's just more fundamental rights. That role has never changed, the role of the courts to decide whether that legislation is in conformity with the Constitution.[2]

INTRODUCTION: FROM ADJUDICATION TO POLICY-MAKING

The Charter's impact on Canadian politics and government was not predetermined at the moment of its proclamation. As we saw in Chapter 1, bills of rights are not self-enforcing. Their effectiveness depends on a strong judiciary with the courage and the will to challenge the other branches of government. The 1960 Bill of Rights had little impact, partly because it was a regular federal statute and partly because the Supreme Court almost always deferred to Parliament and the federal executive. As discussed in Chapter 2, the Court rejected the doctrine of parliamentary supremacy only once: it struck down a discriminatory section of the Indian Act in the 1970 *Drybones* case. In other cases, the Justices went to remarkable lengths to avoid overruling the elected legislature. As we saw in Chapter 2, few Justices perceived themselves as policy-makers. As an institution, the Court was committed to the principle of parliamentary supremacy.

Whether or not they cared to admit it, judges in the pre-Charter era did make public policy.[3] In the English-speaking provinces, common-law rules in criminal and civil proceedings evolved as judges adapted them to new situations. What has changed since 1982 is the scope and the assertiveness of the courts' lawmaking role. Judges can no longer pretend that they do not legislate. The Supreme Court, in particular, is now a central institution in the policy-making apparatus of government. As Part 3 of this book demonstrates, there are few areas of public policy that have remained unaffected by judicial review on Charter grounds. It does no good to ask whether judges *should* make policy; the real question, which is explored in this chapter, is whether they make *good* policy.

If, as I argue, the Charter has transformed the Supreme Court from a primarily **adjudicative** body to a policy-making body, how well has the Court adapted? In theory, a policy-making body should have the institutional capacity to gather and process the social facts on which effective policies are based. Its decisions should be based on established principles; arbitrary choices and personal preferences cannot be

allowed to trump the rule of law. Its internal decision-making processes should be sufficiently transparent to legitimize the results. It need not be formally accountable to the electorate—under Canada's system of cabinet government, the executive branch is accountable only to Parliament—so long as its members are chosen in a way that is consistent with accepted norms of democratic procedure. Finally, it should have some means of implementing and enforcing the policies it makes, to ensure their effectiveness in the real world outside the courtroom.

As this chapter demonstrates, the Supreme Court has not yet acquired these characteristics of an effective policy-generating institution. The adjudicative role, with which judges are comfortable and familiar, does not lend itself to the informational demands of policy-making. Judgments are made in secret, often—as in the case of leave applications—without written reasons. This secrecy makes it impossible to gauge the relative influence of legal principle and personal preference on policy outcomes, although it is likely that the attitudes of individual Justices do affect their rulings to some degree. At the time of writing, Justices were chosen and appointed by the prime minister in roughly the same closed-door process used since 1875. Implementation of Supreme Court rulings is a hit-and-miss affair, varying with the capacity of the affected agencies to resist policies that limit their discretion. While the Court has taken some steps to enhance its policy capacity, and minor reforms have been undertaken by the current prime minister, the mismatch between its policy-making responsibility and its institutional limitations will persist for the foreseeable future.

This chapter begins with a discussion of the early Charter era, when the Supreme Court embraced its expanded policy-making role with considerable (and to some, alarming) gusto. It argues that this "Charter honeymoon" ended quickly, and that the Court has become increasingly deferential to the legislative and executive branches over the past fifteen years. The next section describes the day-to-day work of the Court. Because the Justices work behind closed doors, this account of the decision-making process is necessarily incomplete and often anecdotal. However, it does illuminate the creation of judicial policy. The fourth section identifies the principles that guide the

Court in interpreting the Charter. These principles may have been intended to reduce uncertainty and arbitrariness in judicial review; whether they have had this effect is an open question. The fifth section analyzes the policy-making capacity of the court on three fronts: its use of policy-relevant evidence, its relations with the media, and the appointment process. The sixth section describes the limited power of courts to implement their decisions. The conclusion discusses possible reforms to enhance the policy-making capacity of the Supreme Court (and, by extension, other courts of appeal).

PATTERNS OF JUDICIAL POLICY-MAKING IN THE CHARTER ERA

[T]here has prevailed in certain quarters an assumption that all but a narrow construction of [the Charter] will inexorably lead the courts to "question the wisdom of enactments," to adjudicate upon the merits of public policy. From this have sprung warnings of the dangers of a judicial "super-legislature" beyond the reach of Parliament, the provincial legislatures and the electorate.... This is an argument which was heard countless times prior to the entrenchment of the Charter but which has in truth, for better or for worse, been settled by the very coming into force of the *Constitution Act, 1982.* It ought not to be forgotten that the historic decision to entrench the Charter in our Constitution was taken not by the courts but by the elected representatives of the people of Canada. It was those representatives who extended the scope of constitutional adjudication and entrusted the courts with this new and onerous responsibility. Adjudication under the Charter must be approached free of any lingering doubts as to its legitimacy.[4]

Because of the time lag arising from the appellate process (explained below), the Supreme Court of Canada did not issue its first major Charter rulings until 1984. Over the next few years, most of the Justices embraced their new responsibilities with

enthusiasm. They invalidated laws that conflicted with the Charter, declared their independence from its framers, and made it clear that the cautious and deferential approach was a thing of the past. This "judicial activism" was particularly marked in 1985 and 1986, when 64 percent of rights claimants (9 out of 14) succeeded before the Supreme Court—a more than fourfold increase over the 15 percent success rate in Bill of Rights cases (5 out of 34).[5] Moreover, a majority of these early Charter rulings were unanimous.[6] The Court's message was clear: it understood its new responsibility to protect rights and freedoms, and it was not afraid to exercise its new remedial powers to the full. Critics of judicial power were understandably alarmed. Had the Court staged a *coup d'état,* overthrowing Parliament and claiming dictatorial power over Canadian policy-making?

In retrospect, this initial period of "activism"—the "Charter honeymoon," as some observers have called it[7]—may not have been as threatening as it appeared. The phrase "judicial activism" implies a power-grab by judges who refuse to respect the legitimate policy-making role of the executive and legislative branches of government. Morton and Knopff argue that the Supreme Court has used the Charter to transform itself from an adjudicative institution, whose primary job is to resolve particular disputes in narrow legal terms, into the supreme policy-making body in Canada:

> If newly created judicial standards are to have widespread effect on public policies, they must apply well beyond the confines of the particular case before the court.... [The Supreme Court] now sees itself as the authoritative oracle of the constitution, whose main job is to develop constitutional standards for society as a whole, rather than just for the litigants before it. The establishment of constitutional policy comes first, the concrete dispute second.[8]

Instead of being derided as "oracular" or "activist," the Court's early approach to the Charter may be more accurately described as "maximalist." A maximalist Court ruling, in Cass Sunstein's phrase, answers broad questions that are not strictly necessary to resolve the specific dispute. In the process, it may provide a wide-ranging, philosophical basis for rights jurisprudence, instead of adhering to the facts of the particular case.[9] Conversely, a "minimalist" ruling answers as few questions as possible. It is intended to address the case at bar, without laying down rules that would bind future courts and legislators.[10] The Charter jurisprudence from the Supreme Court of Canada was clearly maximalist in the early years. As the Justices grappled with their new responsibilities, they often felt compelled to go beyond the facts of the case at bar. Former Chief Justice Dickson believed that the Court had a duty to create a "distinctively Canadian jurisprudence," which would guide legislators and lower-court judges in a period of intense legal uncertainty.[11] Canada, unlike its southern neighbour, had little experience with constitutionally entrenched rights and freedoms or their judicial review. Therefore, the Dickson Court (1984–1990) often engaged in wide-ranging discussions of Charter values—e.g., "liberty," "freedom of religion," and "fundamental justice"—in an effort to establish clear principles of Charter interpretation.

Once the broad questions arising from a particular Charter section have been addressed, the Justices have adopted a more minimalist approach to each individual case dealing with that guarantee. As a rule, the Court rarely indulges in "oracular" pronouncements when these are inappropriate.[12] In the first major Charter case to come before the Supreme Court, Justice Estey set the tone:

> The development of the Charter, as it takes its place in our constitutional law, must necessarily be a careful process. Where issues do not compel commentary on these new Charter provisions, none should be undertaken. There will be occasion when guidance by *obiter* or anticipation of issues will serve the Canadian community, and particularly the evolving constitutional process. On such occasions, the Court might well enlarge its reasons for judgment beyond that required to dispose of the issues raised.[13]

A careful reading of the Court's Charter jurisprudence reveals that the Justices normally refuse to answer questions that are not necessary to resolve the instant dispute. At the early stages of an appeal, the Chief Justice often states specific constitutional questions to guide the counsel for the parties as they prepare their arguments. Justices also use these questions to structure their written opinions. The phrase "It is not necessary to answer this question" appears regularly in the text of opinions. Most often, a Justice will dispose of an appeal as narrowly as possible and leave extraneous issues to be resolved in a future case. (The jurisprudence on s. 3 is an exception, as we will see in Chapter 9, pages 290–92.)

If the "oracular" view of the Court is misleading, so is the assumption that the early Charter jurisprudence demonstrates a general pattern of "judicial activism." It is certainly true that the Justices struck down a relatively high proportion of impugned laws in its early years. Of the first one hundred Charter cases analyzed by Morton, Russell, and Withey, twenty-four involved challenges to federal statutes.[14] One-third of those challenges were successful.[15] The Court's decision to strike down eight federal laws on Charter grounds prompted the authors to question its "competitive relationship" with the legislative branch and the legitimacy of judicial policy-making.[16] Similar complaints have continued ever since.[17]

On the other hand, it is worth pointing out that seven of the eight statutes[18] struck down between 1984 and 1988 were found to violate the legal rights in ss. 7–14 of the Charter (the exception, *Big M Drug Mart*, will be discussed later in this chapter). Only two of the cases dealt with the substance of the law itself; the others concerned the procedures established by the impugned statutes. All of the nullified laws predated the Charter—indeed, one had been enacted in 1892, another in 1906. Some were clearly out of step with the evolving values of Canadian society (e.g., the Lord's Day Act); others, such as the "reverse onus" in the Narcotics Control Act, were patently incompatible with the protected rights in the Charter. So instead of portraying the Court's early Charter jurisprudence as a worrisome power grab, we might classify the outcome of these cases as a belated legal "housecleaning," which Parliament should have done years earlier.

Since the mid-1980s, the success rate of plaintiffs who challenge statutes and regulations has fallen from 38 percent to 30 percent.[19] Federal laws passed since 1988 are almost always upheld, either because they do not infringe the Charter or because any infringement is justified under s. 1. Kelly attributes this trend to the growing effectiveness of the "Charter-proofers" in the federal Department of Justice.[20] As we will see in Chapters 4 and 5, the legislative and executive branches of government have been forced by the courts to take their "first-order" Charter duties seriously. The "first-order" responsibility of government institutions is "to assess the reasonableness of *their own* anticipated acts in light of fundamental rights and to act accordingly."[21] When those who make and ratify public policy strive to bring the substance of laws into conformity with the requirements of the Charter, the "second-order" duties of the judicial branch—the review and remedy of statutes—are reduced.

It has also been argued that fewer statutes are nullified nowadays because the Supreme Court has become more deferential to Parliament.[22] Although this apparent diffidence may be related to the previous argument—i.e., courts are, and should be, more willing to defer to Parliament when it takes rights seriously[23]—it may also be a reaction to public criticism of "judicial activism," or the natural consequence of turnover on the Court. In the latter context, it is instructive to consider three Justices appointed after the "Charter honeymoon": Gonthier (appointed in 1989), Iacobucci (1991), and Major (1992). All three, and especially Gonthier and Major, have been reluctant to countenance what they perceive as judicial intrusions on the province of the legislative branch. Gonthier's **dissent** in the 2002 *Sauvé* ruling, which was signed by Major, is premised on the belief that the Court should defer to any reasonable "social or political philosophy" advanced by Parliament to justify limiting Charter rights.[24] Major was the lone dissenter in the 1998 *Vriend* case; he agreed with the majority that the exclusion of sexual orientation from Alberta's human rights legislation violated s. 15 of the Charter, but he refused to endorse the remedy of "reading in" sexual orientation to the impugned law.

> ... it should lie with the elected Legislature to determine this issue. They are answerable to the electorate of that province and it is for them to choose the remedy whether it is changing the legislation or using the notwithstanding clause.

That decision in turn will be judged by the voters.

> The responsibility of enacting legislation that accords with the rights guaranteed by the Charter rests with the legislature. Except in the clearest of cases, courts should not dictate how underinclusive legislation must be amended. Obviously, the courts have a role to play in protecting Charter rights by deciding on the constitutionality of legislation. Deference and respect for the role of the legislature come into play in determining how unconstitutional legislation will be amended where various means are available.[25]

All three Justices endorsed the majority ruling in *Mills* (1999), which explicitly deferred to the legislative branch despite Parliament's deliberate rejection of the Court's own reasoning in a prior case, as well as the majority in *Gosselin* (2002), which found no Charter violation in a Quebec law that reduced welfare benefits to recipients under the age of thirty.[26] In these and other cases, the deferential approach endorsed by Gonthier and Major (and to a lesser degree by Iacobucci) may have made the difference between upholding and nullifying a law.[27] While it would be a mistake to give too much weight to the preferences of individual Justices (a point to which we will return later in this chapter), it is nonetheless likely that changes in the membership of the Court have reinforced the recent trend toward judicial self-restraint.

The Court's growing deference to Parliament is often overlooked by critics of "judicial activism," as is the trend toward minimalism in Charter interpretation. There can be no doubt of the Justices' aggressive and maximalist stance in the first few years of the Charter era. It is equally clear, however, that the Court has become more aware of its limitations in recent years. Those limitations are not purely constitutional, despite the judicial recognition that some issues are best left to be resolved by the legislative and executive branches. They also arise from the structures and processes of the Court itself.

THE SUPREME COURT AT WORK

Managing the Appellate Process

The workload of the Supreme Court of Canada is immense. In any given year, the nine Justices issue between 70 and 150 rulings, of which anywhere from 15 to 25 percent raise Charter issues.[28] As many as one-third are brief oral judgments from the bench. The rest are written decisions of varying length and complexity. In a given year, the annual Supreme Court Reports fill an average of over 3000 pages.[29] The number of Justices who write opinions in a particular case varies from one (in a unanimous judgment) to four or even five, depending on the controversial nature of the issues and the success of the Chief Justice in fostering consensus.[30] Between 1984 and 1997, the Court produced an average of 2.22 written opinions per Charter case.[31] Where a case generates two separate rulings, these are usually the majority opinion—which settles the case and sets a precedent for the future—and the minority opinion (also called the dissent). Particularly divisive cases may generate two or more separate opinions on each side. Opinions that support the **disposition** of the case but not the reasons given by the majority—the *ratio decidendi*—are called concurring opinions. Dissenters may differ from the majority, and from each other, on either the disposition or the *ratio*.

Ideally, all Supreme Court rulings would be unanimous.[32] Such rulings send a strong signal to the lower courts, the other branches of government, and future Justices, that the Court will not water down or reverse this particular decision. Unanimity reinforces the rule of law by creating clear and predictable constitutional interpretations. But given the divisive nature of many constitutional issues, especially those arising from the Charter, unanimity is often difficult to achieve.[33] In the mid-1980s, two-thirds of Charter rulings commanded the support of the entire Court; that percentage fell to 56 percent in 1990–92.[34] Between 1993 and 2003, the annual unanimity rate in Charter rulings rose from 67 to 76 percent,[35] reflecting both the stable membership of the Court during that period and the declining frequency of challenges to statute law. The latter are more divisive than appeals arising from procedural violations because they "raise questions about the legitimacy of the Court's invalidation of the decisions of legislative majorities."[36] Justices who take a deferential approach toward Parliament are more likely to dissent from rulings that nullify statutes, even if they agree with the legal reasoning of the majority; in these instances, the justification analysis under s. 1 is the usual crux of controversy.[37]

The outcome of a case is determined by the number of Justices finding for the appellant (the party that lost at the previous court of appeal and seeks a different verdict from the Supreme Court) and for the respondent (the party seeking to uphold the prior decision). (For definitions of the terms "appellant" and "respondent," see the Glossary for Chapter 1, pages 37–38.) Whichever party persuades a majority of the Justices on the panel wins. When possible, cases are heard by the entire Court. Until recently, panels of five or seven Justices were fairly common. Between 1984 and 1989, roughly three-quarters of Charter cases were handled by panels of seven Justices or fewer.[38] The prevalence of seven-judge panels provoked considerable criticism from academics and other observers, who argued that a majority of four Justices in a particular case could have been a dissenting minority on a nine-judge panel.[39] In other words, the decision to strike a smaller panel might have decided the outcome of the case. (For a possible example, see Dossier 8.10, pages 271–72.)

In fairness, there were good reasons for the scarcity of nine-judge panels in the mid-1980s. Justice Dickson, who took over as Chief Justice following the death of Bora Laskin in 1984, was faced with a difficult situation: while the Court's docket was starting to fill up with complex and challenging Charter cases, the active membership of the Court was dwindling. Even before the proclamation of the Charter in April 1982, the Supreme Court had a backlog of undecided appeals because two Justices—Laskin and Ritchie—were incapacitated by illness.[40] Matters grew steadily worse over the next few years. Justice Estey left the court in 1985 to preside over a public inquiry (the last Supreme Court Justice to do so); he eventually quit the Court in 1988, leaving twenty-five appeals in limbo and failing to keep his promise that he would deal with them in the six months following his departure.[41] Justices Beetz and Le Dain were notorious perfectionists who tinkered with their draft judgments for months at a time and agonized over the judgments written by their colleagues. Both became seriously ill in 1988 and were forced to retire from the Court.[42] Justice Chouinard was diagnosed with cancer in 1987. At a time when Dickson needed all hands on deck, the ship seemed to be sinking. A disproportionate share of the workload fell on Dickson and Justices Wilson, Lamer, and La Forest (appointed in 1985 to replace Ritchie).[43] The Court did not achieve its full complement of nine active Justices until around the time that Antonio Lamer was appointed Chief Justice in 1990, a change that also heralded a period of stability in the membership of the institution. (See Dossier 3.1 for a complete list of Justices of the Supreme Court since 1960.)

DOSSIER 3.1

THE MEMBERSHIP OF THE SUPREME COURT OF CANADA, 1960–2004[1]

Name	Region/Province	Dates of Service
Patrick Kerwin	Ontario	1935–63 Chief Justice 1954–63
Robert Taschereau	Quebec	1940–67 Chief Justice 1963–67
Charles Holland Locke	West (British Columbia)	1947–62
John Robert Cartwright	Ontario	1949–70 Chief Justice 1967–70
Joseph Honoré Gérald Fauteux	Quebec	1949–73 Chief Justice 1970–73
Douglas Charles Abbott	Quebec	1954–73
Ronald Martland	West (Alberta)	1958–82
Wilfred Judson	Ontario	1958–77
Roland Almon Ritchie	Atlantic (Nova Scotia)	1959–84
Emmett Matthew Hall	West (Saskatchewan)	1962–73
Wishart Flett Spence	Ontario	1963–78
Louis-Philippe Pigeon	Quebec	1967–80
Bora Laskin	Ontario	1970–84 Chief Justice 1973–84
Robert George Brian Dickson	West (Manitoba)	1973–91 Chief Justice 1984–91
Jean Beetz	Quebec	1974–88
Louis-Philippe de Grandpré	Quebec	1974–77
Willard Zebedee Estey	Ontario	1977–88
Yves Pratte	Quebec	1977–79
William Rogers McIntyre	West (British Columbia)	1979–89
Julien Chouinard	Quebec	1979–87
Antonio Lamer	Quebec	1980–2000 Chief Justice 1990–2000
Bertha Wilson	Ontario	1982–91

(continued)

Name	Region/Province	Dates of Service
Gerald Eric LeDain	Ontario	1984–88
Gérard V. La Forest	Atlantic (New Brunswick)	1985–97
Claire L'Heureux-Dubé	Quebec	1987–2002
John Sopinka	Ontario	1988–97
Charles Doherty Gonthier	Quebec	1989–2003
Peter deCarteret Cory	Ontario	1989–99
Beverley McLachlin	West (British Columbia)	1989– Chief Justice 2000–
William Stevenson	West (Alberta)	1990–92
Frank Iacobucci	Ontario	1991–2004
John C. Major	West (Alberta)	1992–
Michel Bastarache	Atlantic (New Brunswick)	1997–
William Ian Corneil Binnie	Ontario	1998–
Louise Arbour	Ontario	1999–2004
Louis LeBel	Quebec	2000–
Marie Deschamps	Quebec	2002–
Morris J. Fish	Quebec	2003–
Louise Charron	Ontario	2004–
Rosalie Silberman Abella	Ontario	2004–

ENDNOTES

1. Sources: For Justices appointed before 1987, the Appendix to James G. Snell and Frederick Vaughan, *The Supreme Court of Canada:* *History of the Institution* (Toronto: University of Toronto Press/Osgoode Society, 1985). For subsequent Justices, the Supreme Court of Canada website (www.scc-csc.gc.ca).

In response to complaints that the composition of the panels might decide the outcome of appeals, Lamer ensured that the entire Court worked on particularly important or divisive appeals.[44] Between 1991 and 1996, the percentage of cases heard by all nine Justices rose from fewer than one in ten to over half.[45] Chief Justice McLachlin, who took over in 2000, has followed Lamer's practice: today, it is rare for a major case on the Charter to be heard by seven Justices, except in unusual circumstances (e.g., the sudden death of Justice Sopinka in 1997). Less weighty or controversial matters, such as criminal appeals "as of right" on which the Court has a unanimous opinion, may be heard by a five-judge panel to avoid wasting scarce judicial time.[46] Panels are almost always odd-numbered, to ensure a clear numerical victory for one party or the other.

Most Charter cases before the Supreme Court originate as appeals from a provincial appellate court, although a few concern reference questions from a provincial or federal government.[47] Unlike the constitutional courts that operate in some West European countries, our Supreme Court is not exclusively concerned with issues of public law. It is the highest court of appeal in civil, criminal and administrative cases. Over the years, the Court's control over its caseload—

also called the docket—has steadily increased. Since 1975, when **appeals by right** in civil cases were abolished by an amendment to the Supreme Court Act, the majority of cases on the Court's docket are **appeals by leave**.[48] The exceptions are criminal appeals as of right, which the Court must hear but which it usually deals with as quickly as possible.[49] The number of such appeals has fallen sharply in recent years, from 56 (42 percent of the docket) in 1993 to 16 (19.5 percent) in 2003.[50]

The implications of the Court's control over its own docket are significant. Judicial time and energy are limited resources. If the Justices are forced to hear dozens of trivial appeals, they will have few opportunities to grant leave in cases that raise important legal and/or constitutional issues. The greater the docket discretion, the greater the Court's emphasis on Charter rights and freedoms.[51] At the same time that civil appeals were reduced, the Supreme Court Act was also amended to provide broad criteria for granting leave to appeal. According to s. 40(1) of the act, the Court should restrict its attention to those cases that raise important legal issues whose resolution properly falls to the highest national tribunal.[52]

The law does not define the "public importance" of individual applications for leave, which can make it difficult for attorneys to predict which particular issues will seize the Court's fancy. However, the late Justice Sopinka suggested that he and his colleagues would be most likely to hear an appeal that raised a fresh constitutional issue, gave the Court a chance to revisit an earlier decision that had proved troublesome in practice, or allowed it to settle a dispute among lower courts. Challenges to trivial or narrowly applied statutes, whether federal or provincial, are less likely to proceed than those affecting important areas of law.[53] Finally, the fact that the Court overturns almost forty percent of provincial appellate rulings suggests that the Justices focus on cases that they perceive as having been wrongly decided in the lower courts.[54]

Motions for leave to appeal—between 500 and 650 in any given year[55]—are filed with the Court by lawyers for the appellant. Each motion is vetted for conformity to the Court's rules of practice and then summarized by the legal services section of the Registrar's Office. The summary is sent to the appropriate Justices for review. The Court is divided into three-judge panels, called *corams*, to review the motions for leave and decide which they will accept. The Chief Justice appoints the *corams* at the start of the Court's term, usually in November. While the Justices are usually rotated among the various *corams* each year,[56] the membership of the *corams* is not random. Since 1994, a special panel consisting of the three Quebec Justices has been assigned to review motions from that province.[57] Unlike the other nine provinces, which rely on the common-law tradition inherited from Britain, Quebec uses a distinct civil code to regulate private law (e.g., contracts and torts). It makes sense for the Justices from the Quebec bar, who possess a particular expertise in civil law, to pronounce on leave applications from that system. Additionally, particular types of motions—those dealing with commercial law, for example—are often assigned to *corams* whose members have special expertise in those fields of law.[58] Otherwise, the motions are divided more or less equally among the various panels.

Each application for leave is reviewed by the clerks assigned to the Justices on the relevant *coram*. A Justice of the Supreme Court hires three clerks every year, from a pool of twenty-seven recent law graduates hired by the Court.[59] The number of clerks grew from one per Justice in 1982 to two in 1984 and three in 1989, in response to the growing workload imposed by the Charter.[60] Each clerk reviews about two dozen leave applications. He or she writes a fifteen-page memo to the appropriate panel, summarizing the issues in the case and recommending acceptance or rejection.[61] A one-page summary is prepared for the other six Justices, to keep them abreast of the issues considered for leave. When the panels decide which cases will be granted leave, they rarely meet face to face. More often, a Justice will review his or her *coram*'s list of motions in isolation and then memo his or her two colleagues. If the three Justices agree that the application should be granted or rejected, that decision is binding on the whole Court; if the *coram*'s decision is not unanimous, it is referred to the conference described in the following paragraph.[62] On occasion, a single Justice with a strong commitment to a particular issue can persuade reluctant colleagues to grant leave,[63] but given the recent emphasis on reducing the Court's workload to more manageable levels, this probably happens rarely.

After the panels have processed a sufficient number of applications, the entire Court meets in conference to finalize its docket for the term. Most of the time, the conference will approve panel decisions to accept or dismiss; it will generally endorse the leave decision of a two-judge majority on a divided *coram*.[64] A Justice who wishes to hear a case that was denied leave by another *coram* can argue against dismissal, although there are no data about the frequency with which this happens.[65] After the conference ends, the leave decisions are finalized and made public.

Until recently, the percentage of successful leave applications averaged around 15 percent.[66] Since 1994, it has hovered around 12 percent.[67] The approval rate of individual *corams* varies, which implies that an applicant's chances of success may depend on the panel that hears his or her motion. The Court rarely gives reasons for granting or denying leave to appeal, so we have no way of knowing why a *coram* or conference makes a particular decision.

Once leave has been granted, the appellant and respondent are notified and a date is set for an oral hearing before the Court. Before the hearing, each party is required to submit a factum summarizing their argument, together with written evidence to support their various points. The appellant's factum sets out the facts of the case and the issues of law, and it explains why the previous court ruling should be overturned. The respondent's factum counters the appellant's case for overruling the prior judgment. Generally speaking, the Court may not overturn the factual analysis of a lower court, unless it is obviously mistaken.[68] It must confine itself to correcting errors of law, for the reasons spelled out by Justices Iacobucci and Bastarache in 2002:

> ... while the primary role of trial courts is to resolve individual disputes based on the facts before them and settled law, the primary role of appellate courts is to delineate and refine legal rules and ensure their universal application. In order to fulfill the above functions, appellate courts require a broad scope of review with respect to matters of law.[69]

In addition to the actual parties to the case, the Court may agree to consider arguments from *amici curiae*—literally, "friends of the Court"—more commonly called **intervenors** in Canada. Intervenors are not directly involved in the case at bar. They are governments, groups, and individuals with a particular interest in the issues raised by the appellant and/or the respondent. As we will see in Chapter 6, intervenor status has become a crucial legal and political resource for some Canadian interest groups. Although some members of the Court initially welcomed, even encouraged, policy-oriented interventions, others— notably former Chief Justice Dickson—were less enthusiastic.[70] By 1986, the Court had adopted a fairly liberal policy toward intervenors. In 1999, for example, the Court received 113 applications for intervenor status (24 from the federal and provincial attorneys general, and 89 from nongovernmental groups), of which it accepted 89 percent. Intervenors may not present oral arguments at Court hearings; they are restricted to written briefs, which may be no longer than twenty pages.[71] Most such briefs focus on the broader policy issues raised by the case at bar, not on the specific parties to the case. We will return to the topic of intervenors in Chapter 6.

When the Supreme Court is in session, it alternates between "sitting weeks" (when the Justices hear appeals) and "judgment weeks" for writing and research.[72] (Leave applications are also handled on "judgment weeks.") The Court usually hears ten cases on every "sitting week"—two per day. As part of its overall strategy to keep its workload manageable, the Supreme Court has set a one-hour time limit on oral arguments.[73] Before the oral hearing, each Justice assigns one of his or her clerks to prepare a "bench memo" based on the documents filed by the parties and intervenors. These include briefs and factums from the parties and intervenors, trial records and lower-court rulings, and any other evidence that may have been submitted for their consideration. The bench memo, typically twenty to forty-five pages in length, contains a summary of the contending arguments and "recommendations based on a thorough review of the applicable law."[74] According to former Justice Claire L'Heureux-Dubé, most Justices arrive at the hearing with "a good idea of the law and of where the case should go." This does not mean, however, that the hearings are irrelevant. L'Heureux-Dubé recently told a Commons committee that a good oral presentation by a particular advocate can influence the outcome of the appeal: "between 15 percent and 25 percent of the time we change our minds."[75] The Justices take "bench notes" during hearings. They often interrupt the attorneys to ask questions or to draw them out on particular points of law. The purpose is to clarify the issues that could not be definitively resolved on the basis of the written record.

Immediately after the hearing in the main courtroom, the Justices withdraw to a conference room to discuss the case. Each Justice states his or her opinion in turn, beginning with the most junior (recently appointed) judge and ending with the Chief Justice. This conference indicates "whether there is any prospect of unanimity or whether there is clearly going to be more than one judgment."[76] The Court usually holds one official conference on a particular case, although Justices often meet informally to compare notes and hash out difficult issues. During the early years of the Charter, when the Court was struggling to create a new jurisprudence from scratch, it deviated from this practice: "the Court seems often to have held more than one conference to discuss a case or group of cases under consideration. The judges were conscious that their early Charter pronouncements would set the tone for the future, and they wanted to sound as clear, confident, and unanimous as possible."[77]

Although these conferences are confidential, scholars have been able to discern their inner workings by reading conference notes and interviewing judges. The post-conference memos that Justices circulate among themselves also contain hints. The Chief Justice tries to broker whatever compromises are necessary to produce a unanimous judgment. If this is impossible, he or she will attempt to minimize the number of dissenting and concurring judgments. If a majority emerges, one member of this group will volunteer (or be assigned by the Chief Justice) to draft an opinion. While the authoring Justice normally follows the line of analysis that he or she presented at the conference, changes of mind can occur during the drafting process. These may arise from a reconsideration of the issues, discussions with clerks, or consultations with other members of the Court.[78]

According to L'Heureux-Dubé, the conference sometimes produces an unexpected result: "We have had a few cases where we unanimously said we would reject an appeal, and then eventually we unanimously allowed it."[79] One example was the 1989 *Daigle* case, in which a pregnant woman who had been abused by her ex-boyfriend asked the Court to overturn an injunction preventing her from obtaining an abortion. Then–Chief Justice Dickson ordered a rare August sitting of the Court to hear the appeal, conscious of the time pressures that Chantal Daigle faced. He called the Justices back from their holidays for a hurriedly arranged hearing. During the lunch break, Daigle's lawyer was informed that she had obtained the abortion that morning in an American clinic. When Dickson heard that the extraordinary hearing was now moot, he was furious. He adjourned the hearing and called a conference, where he insisted that the Court drop the case immediately and hinted that Daigle might face contempt charges. The most junior Justice at the time, now Chief Justice Beverley McLachlin, asked Dickson and his colleagues to "put themselves

Chief Justice Beverley McLachlin became Canada's highest judge in 2000.

CP PHOTO/Tom Hanson

in Daigle's shoes." She reminded them that Daigle could not wait for the Court to issue a ruling several months after the hearing. Dickson changed his mind, resumed the hearing, and announced the Court's decision immediately: Daigle's appeal was allowed.[81] The Court's unanimous written reasons, authored by Dickson but issued *per curiam*, were issued in November.[81]

When the first draft is completed, weeks or months later, it is circulated to the other eight judges. Those who concur with the draft may suggest changes or clarifications, either with or without the implicit threat of dissent should the changes be rejected by the author. If a particular Justice cannot concur with the draft reasons, he or she writes a memo to the rest of the Court setting out the intention to dissent. "This grinds the process of concurring to a halt since it is viewed as 'bad form' to concur with the original reasons until you have seen the dissent."[82] After the draft dissent is circulated, the other Justices must decide whether or not to propose amendments. The decision can be held up for months, as memos fly back and forth among the members of the Court. Former Justice Cory described the process in colourful terms: "Memos are circulated to everybody. You will get one back saying: 'I agree to A and to B, but not to C—and over my dead body to D.'"[83]

Given the Court's heavy caseload, and the pressure to issue judgments in a timely fashion, most of its members tend to concentrate on their own writing and give their colleagues' drafts the benefit of the doubt whenever possible. The late Chief Justice Laskin described this tendency as "an institutional preference to support a majority result by reasons acceptable to a majority."[84] Former Justice Wilson was critical of that "institutional preference":

> Under the pressure of a heavy caseload the delicate balance which should exist between judicial independence and collegiality may be displaced and collegiality may give way to expediency. This is an extremely serious matter for an appellate tribunal because the integrity of the process itself is threatened.[85]

In other words, a Justice may go along with a decision that he or she does not really support, simply because he or she lacks the time to write a dissent or to propose changes. This runs counter to Wilson's belief that each judge has a duty to reach his or her own independent conclusion on difficult legal issues, and her conviction that "multiple judgments made an important contribution to the rolling evolution of the common law."[86] Even worse, in her view, was the tendency for judges to "lobby for support of their own reasons," partly along ideological lines.[87] This lobbying becomes particularly intense when the panel members are evenly divided at conference, leaving one or two undecided Justices—the "swing votes"—to determine the outcome of the appeal.[88]

After the draft judgments in a particular case are complete, they are reviewed by every member of the panel that heard the case. Each must sign on to one of the opinions (or to *the* opinion, where the Court is unanimous). Once this has been done, and the judgment has been translated into both official languages, it is issued to the parties and the public. Judgments are usually released on Thursday and Friday mornings. The length of time between hearing and judgment varies with the number of opinions.[89] The state of the law also affects the gestation period of a ruling: cases that can be resolved by applying well-established principles of law are processed more quickly than those that require the Justices to craft new doctrines.[90] In recent years, an increasingly unified Court has relied on its established body of Charter precedents to settle cases expeditiously: over the past decade, the average length of time between hearing and judgment has varied between three and five months.[91]

Judicial Reasoning: The Sources of the Common Law

> Judges have a professional obligation to deny the fact that their decisions are based on factors other than law, because their authority comes from the perception that it is rule-driven, not result-driven, but in their more candid moments even Supreme Court judges admit that it's not quite that way.[92]

In theory, judicial rulings in constitutional cases arise solely from established rules of legal interpretation.

The judge elicits the meaning of a law, compares it to the relevant section(s) of the written constitution, and determines whether the two conflict. This rule-driven model implies that the meaning of a law—entrenched or statutory—is always clear. Any two judges, whatever their personal beliefs, can look at the same legal provisions and interpret them in precisely the same way. There is no room for **extrinsic** influences, whether personal or institutional. The judge cannot choose his or her preferred result and tailor the law to fit. To adopt a result-oriented approach in constitutional cases is to substitute judicial whim for the will of the majority, a profound violation of the rule of law and democratic legitimacy.[93]

As discussed in Chapter 1, the Supreme Court is expected to follow its own prior precedents when it decides cases. Because the Supreme Court is the highest tribunal in Canada, its decisions are binding on lower courts. The common-law doctrine of precedent is called *stare decisis et non quieta movere*.[94] Roughly translated from the Latin, it means "the decision stands and should not be disturbed." The *stare decisis* rule has several advantages in a common-law system (although its utility in Quebec's civil-law tradition is less clear). First, it adds to the stability and continuity of the rule of law. Instead of resolving disputes according to the whim of the moment, judges apply established principles in prescribed ways. Second, *stare decisis* allows the legislative and executive branches to predict, with some degree of certainty, how the courts will interpret the laws that come before them. Third, the doctrine of precedent makes the task of judging manageable: instead of thrashing about blindly in a legal thicket, the judge uses the relevant case law to carve a path through the complexities of justice. Finally, the principle of *stare decisis* is intended to limit the discretion of individual judges; instead of imposing their personal preferences, they must apply the established common-law rules to resolve the cases that come before them.

Whatever the normative appeal of the rule-driven model of judging, there are good empirical reasons to question its accuracy. In the first place, judges are human beings. Despite their intensive training and lengthy experience in the law, they are not reasoning machines devoid of feelings and values.[95] Like it or not, the varied backgrounds and personal characteristics of judges must have some influence.[96] The late American Justice Benjamin Cardozo put it this way:

> There is in each of us a stream of tendency, whether you choose to call it philosophy or not, which gives coherence and direction to thought and action. Judges cannot escape that current any more than other mortals. All their lives, forces which they do not recognize and cannot name, have been tugging at them—inherited instincts, traditional beliefs, acquired convictions; and the resultant is an outlook on life, a conception of social needs ... which, when reasons are nicely balanced, must determine where choice shall fall.... We may try to see things as objectively as we please. None the less, we can never see them with any eye except our own.[97]

In the second place, the frequency of dissenting (and concurring) opinions on the Supreme Court belies the suggestion that judges mechanically apply impartial rules of construction or precedential dogma. It is simply inconceivable that broad, normative terms like "reasonable" and "just" will mean precisely the same thing to different people. As Cardozo's description implies, "inherited instincts" and "acquired convictions" vary from judge to judge. Left-wing critics often point out that the vast majority of Canadian judges are drawn from the upper strata of society; hence, they argue, the judiciary shares the assumptions and prejudices of other rich white people.[98] This reasoning overstates the ideological conformity among Justices, perhaps because it overlooks the fact that some were born in relatively humble circumstances.[99] More to the point, it assumes that all of the Justices have drawn the same lessons from their shared experience of power and privilege.

Anyone who studies Supreme Court rulings on gender, social equality, or the rights of criminal suspects quickly realizes that this assumption is incorrect.[100] Members of the Supreme Court often stake out distinct and consistent positions on divisive issues, whether as individuals[101] or in relatively stable "voting blocs."[102] This does not mean, however, that the Justices are simply substituting their personal preferences for a principled reading of the law. As Roach points out, individual judges make a difference but "the text of the Charter still matters."[103] Whatever her own values may be, a Justice cannot simply ignore precedents and constitutional language in the pursuit of a preferred result. At the very least, she is bound by the institutional nature of the Court to justify the disposition of the case on legal grounds; if she cannot do so, her colleagues will not support her reasoning and it will have no force in law.

In the third place, *stare decisis* does not bind the Supreme Court of Canada as firmly as it does the lower courts.[104] In some instances, a majority of Justices will refuse to follow the reasoning of their predecessors (some of whom may be their colleagues). This can happen in one of two ways: a judge can distinguish the case at bar from a prior case (see the Glossary of Key Terms for Chapter 1, pages 37–38 for a definition), or she can explicitly overturn the previous ruling. The latter option is extremely rare. In constitutional cases, distinguishing may be the only way to solve problems created by an earlier ruling. In the early years of the Charter, for example, the Court made it clear that it would not be bound by its Bill of Rights jurisprudence when handling appeals arising from the newly entrenched rights and freedoms. (See Dossiers 2.11 and 2.12, pages 75–79.)

Finally, courts are collegial institutions. The influence of personal relationships among the Justices is difficult to measure, but it cannot be discounted. A well-respected jurist who finds himself in the minority at the post-hearing conference may, if his colleagues in the majority are sufficiently open-minded, build a new consensus around his approach to the case.[105] The *Daigle* appeal, discussed earlier, illustrates this process. Institutional norms of mutual respect and cooperation, combined with the preference of Chief Justices for unanimous rulings, can outweigh individual preferences—whether for particular outcomes, legal doctrines, or approaches to constitutional interpretation. Where those preferences are firmly held, dissents or concurrences will result. But in the absence of strong views on either side, the desire for legal clarity and collegiality will often produce unanimity.

In the absence of hard empirical data about judicial decision-making, the relative influence of legal principles, judicial ideology, and collegiality cannot be determined with any precision or generality. It is probably safe to conclude that where the law is clear, judges will apply it as impartially as they can; where it is not clear, or where the strict application of a precedent will produce an unjust result, judges must fashion new legal rules that will, in their view, further the cause of justice.[106] Given the inherently subjective nature of "justice," both the disposition of the case and the *ratio decidendi* used to justify it will attract criticism from those who do not share the judge's perspective.

CHARTER INTERPRETATION AT THE SUPREME COURT: FULFILLING THE "SECOND-ORDER DUTY"

The Supreme Court has issued hundreds of Charter rulings since 1984. Although the sheer volume of the jurisprudence makes it difficult to discern general principles of interpretation, the Justices have made a consistent effort to identify and apply five basic rules.

- First, as discussed in Chapter 1, the entrenched rights and freedoms must be given a "large and liberal interpretation." If limits must be placed on Charter guarantees, to prevent them from overriding other important social values, this may only be done at the s. 1 stage of inquiry.
- Second, the Court interprets the various rights and freedoms in a purposive manner; it must infer the reasons why these particular guarantees were entrenched in the Constitution.
- Third, rights and freedoms must be interpreted in the context of each individual case, not in the abstract.
- Fourth, the various sections of the Charter must not be interpreted in isolation from each other; the values that inform specific guarantees illuminate the purpose of the entrenched rights and freedoms as a whole.
- Fifth and finally, the Court must consider both the purpose and the effect of a particular law in order to determine its constitutionality.

We will consider each of the last four rules of interpretation separately.

The purposive approach was first articulated by former Chief Justice Dickson in *Hunter v. Southam* (1984). The case, discussed in more detail in Chapter 10, turned on the constitutionality of a provision in the federal Combines Investigation Act that permitted warrantless searches of business premises. The plaintiff, the Southam newspaper chain, argued that the provision violated s. 8 of the Charter. In his first Charter ruling, Dickson set out his interpretive approach:

> The Canadian Charter of Rights and Freedoms is a purposive document. Its purpose is to guarantee and to protect, within the limits of reason, the enjoyment of the rights and freedoms it enshrines. It is intended to constrain governmental action inconsistent with those rights and freedoms; it is not in itself an authorization for governmental action.... Since the proper approach to the interpretation of the Charter of Rights and Freedoms is a purposive one, before it is possible to assess the reasonableness or unreasonableness of the impact of a search or of a statute authorizing a search, it is first necessary to specify the purpose underlying s. 8: in other words, to delineate the nature of the interests it is meant to protect.[107]

Dickson elaborated on the techniques of purposive analysis the following year, in *Big M Drug Mart*:

> In my view this analysis is to be undertaken, and the purpose of the right or freedom in question is to be sought by reference to the character and the larger objects of the Charter itself, to the language chosen to articulate the specific right or freedom, to the historical origins of the concepts enshrined, and where applicable, to the meaning and purpose of the other specific rights and freedoms with which it is associated within the text of the Charter. The interpretation should be, as the judgment in *Southam* emphasizes, a generous rather than a legalistic one, aimed at fulfilling the purpose of the guarantee and securing for individuals the full benefit of the Charter's protection. At the same time it is important not to overshoot the actual purpose of the right or freedom in question, but to recall that the Charter was not enacted in a vacuum, and must

therefore ... be placed in its proper linguistic, philosophical and historical contexts.[108]

As this passage indicates, Dickson cast a wide evidentiary net. He implied that judges should consider various forms of **intrinsic evidence**, specifically the wording of the Charter itself, as well as **extrinsic evidence** about the development of particular concepts of individual liberty. Although Dickson hints here that the intent of the framers is an important interpretive aid—how else to place the Charter in "its proper linguistic, philosophical and historical contexts"?—the Court subsequently refused to be bound by the views of the Charter's drafters (see the discussion of framers' intent, pages 109–110). The purposive analysis is especially important where the wording of the guarantee is too broad to be easily applied to discrete cases, e.g., the "principles of fundamental justice" in s. 7. It is generally less extensive in relation to such phrases as "freedom of the press" (s. 2(b)) or "a fair trial" (s. 11(d)), the meanings of which are clear and well-established elements of the common law.

The contextual approach to the Charter was introduced by former Justice Wilson. She believed that the only way to balance a just outcome in an individual case against the development of broad common-law principles was to interpret the relevant right or freedom in the context of each unique set of facts. In other words, an abstract interpretation of "freedom of expression"—such as that yielded by a purposive analysis alone—would not necessarily lead to justice in a particular dispute; but a purely case-specific (i.e., minimalist) approach would not provide sufficient guidance for future courts or the other branches of government. If, however, one were to interpret freedom of expression differently in different circumstances, one might provide a useful precedent for similar cases in the future while resolving the case at bar fairly—especially where the court had to balance competing rights or social values at the s. 1 stage. Wilson explained this approach in her majority judgment in *Edmonton Journal* (1989):

> One virtue of the contextual approach, it seems to me, is that it recognizes that a particular right or freedom may have a different value depending on the context. It may be, for example, that freedom of expression has greater

value in a political context than it does in the context of disclosure of the details of a matrimonial dispute. The contextual approach attempts to bring into sharp relief the aspect of the right or freedom which is truly at stake in the case as well as the relevant aspects of any values in competition with it. It seems to be more sensitive to the reality of the dilemma posed by the particular facts and therefore more conducive to finding a fair and just compromise between the two competing values under s. 1.

It is my view that a right or freedom may have different meanings in different contexts. Security of the person, for example, might mean one thing when addressed to the issue of overcrowding in prisons and something quite different when addressed to the issue of noxious fumes from industrial smoke-stacks. It seems entirely probable that the value to be attached to it in different contexts for the purpose of the balancing under s. 1 might also be different. It is for this reason that I believe that the importance of the right or freedom must be assessed in context rather than in the abstract and that its purpose must be ascertained in context. This having been done, the right or freedom must then, in accordance with the dictates of this Court, be given a generous interpretation aimed at fulfilling that purpose and securing for the individual the full benefit of the guarantee.[109]

The contextual approach has found its greatest influence in freedom-of-expression cases, where the content of the expression at issue has been held to determine the degree of protection merited under s. 1.[110] The distinction between "core" and "peripheral" expression is discussed at greater length in Chapter 8, pages 259–65.

The principle that a specific guarantee should be interpreted in relation to the Charter as a whole was established in the 1985 *Dubois* ruling. A man who had been convicted of second-degree murder at his second trial, partly on the strength of his testimony at the first trial, argued (successfully) that his right against self-incrimination under s. 13 of the Charter had been violated. For the majority, then–Justice Lamer illuminated the meaning of s. 13 with reference to ss. 11(c) and (d).[111] His analysis demonstrated that courts

should not merely refer to the interpretive sections of the Charter (ss. 25 and 27–31); where appropriate, they should use the values underlying one substantive guarantee to clarify the meaning of another. In *Keegstra*, Chief Justice Dickson held that the guarantee of equality in s. 15 should be taken into consideration when weighing the degree to which s. 2(b) protected "hate speech" against legislative restriction.[112] In *Thomson Newspapers* (1998), the Supreme Court interpreted the democratic rights in s. 3 in relation to the freedom of political expression in s. 2(b).[113]

The first four principles apply to the interpretation of the Charter. The fifth applies to the interpretation of regular statutes. When the meaning of the guarantee at issue has been discerned, the judges must then determine whether the impugned law violates that guarantee. To answer that question, they must consider both its purpose and its effect. Because relatively few laws are expressly designed to conflict with the Charter (unless they incorporate the notwithstanding clause in s. 33), the guarantees would have little practical impact unless courts considered their effects—both deliberate and unanticipated—when assessing constitutionality.[114]

The emphasis on both purpose and effect was established early in the Charter era. In *Big M Drug Mart*, Chief Justice Dickson found that the purpose of the Lord's Day Act violated the guarantee of religious freedom (see Dossier 8.2, pages 252–53). Because the case could be settled on this basis, Dickson was initially reluctant to address the law's effects. Justice Wilson urged him to make it clear that both purpose and effect were relevant to a Charter inquiry.[115] Dickson tried to accommodate her concerns. Although Wilson ultimately wrote a separate concurring judgment, the Chief Justice's attempt to build consensus produced a key principle of Charter jurisprudence:

In my view, both purpose and effect are relevant in determining constitutionality; either an unconstitutional purpose or an unconstitutional effect can invalidate legislation. All legislation is animated by an object the legislature intends to achieve. This object is realized through the impact produced by the operation and application of the legislation. Purpose and effect respectively, in the sense of the legislation's object and its ultimate impact, are clearly linked, if not indivisible. Intended and actual effects have often been looked to for guidance in assessing the legislation's object and thus, its validity.

... the legislation's purpose is the initial test of constitutional validity and its effects are to be considered when the law under review has passed or, at least, has purportedly passed the purpose test. If the legislation fails the purpose test, there is no need to consider further its effects, since it has already been demonstrated to be invalid. Thus, if a law with a valid purpose interferes by its impact, with rights or freedoms, a litigant could still argue the effects of the legislation as a means to defeat its applicability and possibly its validity. In short, the effects test will only be necessary to defeat legislation with a valid purpose; effects can never be relied upon to save legislation with an invalid purpose.[116]

Although this rule—like the others just discussed—has not always been explicitly invoked in Court rulings, it has played a key role in the evolution of Charter jurisprudence. In the 1989 *Irwin Toy* ruling, the majority applied the "purpose and effects" test to a Quebec law that prohibits advertising to children.[117] In the process, it laid the foundation for all subsequent interpretation of s. 2(b). (See Dossier 8.4, pages 257–59.) The *Irwin* majority found that the *purpose* of the law infringed the Charter, although it was saved by s. 1. In the 1988 *Morgentaler* case, Chief Justice Dickson and Justice Lamer found that the *purpose* of the abortion law was valid, but that its *effects* violated the right to "security of the person" in s. 7.[118] The law was struck down.

These judge-made rules of Charter interpretation have attracted considerable criticism. Morton and Knopff argue that the "purposive approach" allows judges to pick and choose among the alternative meanings of a particular Charter guarantee; they will generally opt for the meaning that gives the broadest scope for "judicial creativity."[119] Russell adds that the "purposive" approach is a recipe for judicial disagreement, not for jurisprudential certainty.[120] The subjectivity inherent in allowing judges to determine the meaning of a protected right or freedom on whatever basis they choose may undermine the legitimacy of

Charter rulings. In a similar vein, Manfredi claims that Wilson's "effects-oriented" and contextual approach has "considerably broadened the scope of judicial review" and allowed judges to substitute their personal policy preferences for the intent of the Charter's framers.[121] Hawkins and Martin have gone further in their critique of Wilson, and her contextual approach in particular: "She was prepared to give those words [in the Charter] whatever meaning was required in the factual context before her to promote the social objectives to which she was personally committed." At bottom, they argue, the contextual approach is nothing more than an assertion of the right to legislate from the bench.[122]

Many of these criticisms arise from a profound discomfort with the interpretive latitude that the Charter has conferred on the judicial branch. Inasmuch as they reflect concerns about personal subjectivity and inconsistency in the development of the common law, they are worthy of serious consideration. On the other hand, the framers of the Charter deliberately phrased the guarantees in broad terms. Phrases such as "fundamental justice" and "unreasonable search and seizure" cannot be used to resolve specific disputes unless judges interpret and apply them to the facts of each case. Russell himself has described the entrenched rights and freedoms as "limp balloons which the constitution-makers have handed to the judiciary; the judges must now decide how much air to blow into them."[123] The remedies included in the Charter also indicate the framers' intent to give the courts more power to evaluate and, where necessary, alter public policies. The real issue, as stated earlier, is not the legitimacy of judicial review. It is the institutional capacity of the courts—and, in particular, the Supreme Court of Canada—to do their job appropriately. The interpretive rules adopted by the Court require all parties to a case to answer key questions: what did the legislature think it was doing when it passed this law? how does the law affect protected rights and freedoms in practice? does it cure the mischief at which it was aimed? In the absence of persuasive answers to these questions, the Justices may be forced to resort to their own subjective notions of justice in order to settle the dispute at bar. Under those circumstances, the fault lies not with the judges but with the parties who brought and argued the case.

THE POLICY CAPACITY OF THE SUPREME COURT OF CANADA

Courts, and the judges who compose them, are comfortable with legal analysis. They have evolved, or were designed, to answer questions of law arising from particular disputes. In a word, they are adjudicative institutions. Since 1982, Canada's courts—and the Supreme Court in particular—have been forced to undertake a new policy-making function, for which they are not well suited.[124] The word "forced" is contentious: critics of judicial power argue that judges should have adhered to their purely adjudicative role under the Charter, leaving issues of public policy to the legislative and executive branches.[125] Manfredi points out that the *Oakes* test for justifying laws (Dossier 1.6, pages 27–30) is a purely judicial creation, which gives judges free rein to substitute their policy preferences for those of elected legislators.[126] Similarly, Morton and Knopff charge that the Supreme Court has, without any clear basis in the Charter itself, transformed itself into "a *de facto* third chamber of the legislature."[127]

In self-defence, some judges have pointed out (rightly) that the line between law and policy is not always clear, especially where rights and freedoms are at stake. In an article pointedly titled "We Didn't Volunteer," former Justice Wilson argued that the Charter was drafted and ratified by legislators and public administrators in the full knowledge that it would require the courts to enforce its guarantees. "What right have [judges] to frustrate the will of the people's duly elected representatives? None, I would say, except for the fact that in enacting the Charter these same duly elected representatives conferred not just that right but that duty upon them."[128] Although Wilson's frank acknowledgment of the Court's policy-making role made her a target for critics of "judicial activism," she was surely correct to claim that the Charter requires the courts to evaluate and, where necessary, to create, public policy.

The real issue, as noted at the beginning of this chapter, is the capacity of the judicial branch to perform this duty effectively. Can judges reasonably be expected to assess the quality of extrinsic evidence—what Manfredi calls "social or legislative facts"—when their training equips them to deal solely with "adjudicative facts"?[129] Should the Supreme Court be bound by the intent of those who drafted the Charter—most of whom, unlike the framers of the American Constitution, are still available for consultation—when it interprets the guarantes of rights and freedoms? Have the Court's procedures, and the appointment of its members, become more transparent as its policy-making power grows? Finally, does the Court rely too heavily on interventions by interest groups, or deprive itself of useful policy perspectives by restricting interest-group access? These issues go to the heart of the legitimacy of the judicial branch. This section asks whether the Supreme Court possesses the institutional competence to carry out the duties assigned to it in 1982. More than two decades later, its record is mixed.

Extrinsic Evidence in Charter Cases: Framers' Intent and Social Science

From the very beginning, the Supreme Court has insisted that Charter arguments be based on thorough and reliable evidence. At first, the Justices complained of receiving insufficient information at the s. 1 stage of analysis.[130] Later, the Court demanded that every element of a Charter case rest on solid proof. In *Edwards Books and Art* (1986), Chief Justice Dickson refused to answer questions about the impact of Sunday-closing laws on Hindu and Muslim retailers because there was no factual foundation in the record that would permit him to do so.[131] In a unanimous 1989 judgment dismissing an appeal for lack of evidence, Justice Cory established the following principles:

> Charter cases will frequently be concerned with concepts and principles that are of fundamental importance to Canadian society. For example, issues pertaining to freedom of religion, freedom of expression and the right to life, liberty and the security of the individual will have to be considered by the courts. Decisions on these issues must be carefully considered as they will profoundly affect the lives of Canadians and all residents of Canada. In light of the importance and the impact that these decisions may have in the future, the courts have every right to expect and indeed to insist upon the careful preparation and presentation of a factual basis in most Charter

cases. The relevant facts put forward may cover a wide spectrum dealing with scientific, social, economic and political aspects. Often expert opinion as to the future impact of the impugned legislation and the result of the possible decisions pertaining to it may be of great assistance to the courts.

Charter decisions should not and must not be made in a factual vacuum. To attempt to do so would trivialize the Charter and inevitably result in ill-considered opinions. The presentation of facts is not, as stated by the respondent, a mere technicality; rather, it is essential to a proper consideration of Charter issues. A respondent cannot, by simply consenting to dispense with the factual background, require or expect a court to deal with an issue such as this in a factual void. Charter decisions cannot be based upon the unsupported hypotheses of enthusiastic counsel.[132]

To fill the "factual void," lawyers can choose among several types of extrinsic evidence. We will focus here on three of these:

- the intent of the Charter's framers;
- the legislative history of an impugned law; and
- social-science data.

The Framers' Intent

The degree to which the framers' intent—also called "original intent"—should bind on judges is a matter of controversy, both in Canada and in the United States. Manfredi distinguishes between two general approaches: interpretivism (also called "originalism") and noninterpretivism.[133] When an interpretivist judge seeks to determine the meaning of a particular constitutional provision, she relies on the text of the provision itself; the only permissible extrinsic evidence is that which demonstrates the meaning intended by those who wrote it.[134] A noninterpretivist judge will examine the text, and may consider the intent of the framers, but only as one possible source of meaning. He will rely on a wide range of materials—historical, philosophical, or socioeconomic—to help him construe the provision. He will not be bound by the intent of the framers where that intent appears to him

to be out of step with changing social conditions or contrary to contemporary notions of justice.[135]

Defenders of the interpretivist approach argue that judges who deviate from the framers' intent undermine the legitimacy of judicial review. Because a constitution, in theory, reflects the will of the majority (at least at the time when it took effect), nonelected judges who reinterpret that will to suit changing conditions are behaving anti-democratically.[136] They are also guilty of violating the separation of powers that the constitution prescribes. Critics of the interpretivist approach counter that judges should not be bound by the ideas of constitutional drafters who did their work decades, even centuries, earlier.[137] They argue that the constitution is a "living tree" that must be allowed to grow and develop along with the society that it governs. (See Dossier 2.2, pages 50–51.)

As Morton and Knopff have argued, the growth of the "living tree" must be constrained by judicial self-restraint. The courts cannot turn an elm tree into a willow, metaphorically speaking; the rights enshrined in the Constitution may be applied to new facts as these arise, but they must not be transformed out of all recognition, or have new rights grafted on, by the courts.[138] Even former Justice Wilson, the most outspoken proponent of noninterpretivism on the Supreme Court, recognized the perils of unconstrained judicial creativity:

> While things are slowly changing, it cannot be said that judges in Canada are broadly representative of the general public. There is, therefore, no plausible justification for us to substitute our personal values and our moral choices for those of the elected legislature. The metaphor of the living tree is a harmless one so long as it is used merely to suggest that a constitution must adapt and grow to meet modern realities. It could, however, become dangerous and anti-democratic if it were used to justify the shaping of the constitution according to the personal values of individual judges.[139]

Whether or not one accepts the normative case for relying solely on the framers' intent, those who advocate its adoption face serious practical difficulties. Hogg identifies three barriers to the use of "framers' intent" in constitutional interpretation: identifying which of the many "framers" should have the greatest authority; trying to discern a single "intent" among the members of a single legislature, let alone several; and (in the case of the Constitution Act, 1867) trying to reconstruct the motivations of men who wrote a constitution decades ago.[140] Even if these difficulties could be resolved, there remains the problem of distinguishing actual intent from political "spin." Canadian courts have never given much weight to parliamentary speeches, whether by ministers of the Crown or backbench MPs.[141]

In a general sense, the Court and its defenders have long claimed fidelity to the general intent of the framers. That intent, they argue, was that judges would and should use the Charter to identify and remedy violations of protected rights and freedoms.[142] They cite the open-ended language of the individual guarantees, together with the explicit judicial remedies, as proof that the framers wanted and expected the courts to carve out their own path.[143] On the other hand, as Roach argues, "It will not do to say simply that elected governments agreed to entrench the Charter. The governments that agreed to the Charter may not have foreseen the evolution of judicial review in Canada."[144] In several instances, the Supreme Court has interpreted the text of the Charter in ways that conflict with the clearly expressed preferences of (some of) the framers. Morton and Knopff point to its rulings on s. 24(2) (exclusion of evidence), abortion, Aboriginal rights,

and same-sex rights, none of which appear to reflect the policy goals of the Trudeau government or the premiers who participated in the 1980–82 constitutional negotiations.[145]

Within a few years of the Charter's proclamation, the Supreme Court signalled that it would not be bound by the framers' intent when it interpreted specific Charter guarantees. (See Dossier 3.2.) This approach was consistent with the Court's pre-Charter jurisprudence in federalism cases. The judges rarely admitted historical data about the intent of the Fathers of Confederation; when they did, such data carried little weight in the interpretive process.[146] There is, of course, one major difference between the 1867 Constitution and the Charter: as interpretivists were quick to point out, the framers of the Constitution Act, 1982 were still available for consultation. There was no necessity for historical research; if lawyers or jurists wished to abide by the intended meaning of the protected rights and freedoms, all they had to do was pick up the phone. Nor was there any shortage of documentary evidence about the 1980–82 negotiations—unlike in the case of the 1864 conferences in Quebec City and Charlottetown, which left few written traces.[147] As it turned out, the Court was unimpressed by this difference between the two Constitution Acts. It has applied the same evidentiary principles to both documents, admitting the evidence of the framers' intent where relevant but giving it little weight in the interpretive process.

DOSSIER 3.2

THE *B.C. MOTOR VEHICLE REFERENCE* AND THE INTENT OF THE FRAMERS

In 1985, the Supreme Court grappled with the meaning of s. 7 for the first time. The Justices had to decide whether a British Columbia law violated the guarantee of liberty in a manner that was not "in accordance with the principles of fundamental justice." Before they could answer this question, the Court had to determine the meaning of the latter phrase. Was it purely procedural in nature, or did it allow the courts to evaluate the substance of laws as well? Some lower courts had ruled that "the principles of fundamental justice" were intended to apply

only to the processes by which individuals were investigated, charged, tried, and sentenced. In support of this claim, they referred to the testimony of former federal Justice officials before the Standing Joint Committee on the Constitution. The relevant testimony is reproduced here, beginning with the words of then–assistant deputy minister Barry Strayer:

> Mr. Chairman, it was our belief that the words "fundamental justice" would cover the same thing as what is called procedural due process, that is the meaning of due

process in relation to requiring fair procedure. However, it in our view does not cover the concept of what is called substantive due process, which would impose substantive requirements as to policy of the law in question.

This has been most clearly demonstrated in the United States in the area of property, but also in other areas such as the right to life. The term due process has been given the broader concept of meaning both the procedure and substance. Natural justice or fundamental justice in our view does not go beyond the procedural requirements of fairness.[1]

Strayer's then-boss, deputy minister Roger Tassé, echoed the view that "fundamental justice" meant the same thing as "natural justice," a purely procedural concept:

We assume that the Court would look at that much like a Court would look at the requirements of natural justice, and the concept of natural justice is quite familiar to courts and they have given a good deal of specific meaning to the concept of natural justice. We would think that the Court would find in that phraseology principles of fundamental justice a meaning somewhat like natural justice or inherent fairness.

Courts have been developing the concept of administrative fairness in recent years and they have been able to give a good deal of consideration, certainly to these sorts of concepts and we would expect they could do the same with this.[2]

The justice minister at the time, Jean Chrétien, also believed that natural and fundamental justice were essentially the same concept.[3]

This was clear evidence of the framers' intent. Tassé and Strayer were the two most important federal officials in the 1980–82 constitutional negotiations; Chrétien had been the sponsoring minister and chief federal negotiator. If anyone knew the intended meaning of the phrase "fundamental justice," they did. Faced with this evidence, Lamer had to decide

(1) whether it was admissible and (2) how much weight it should have in the Court's deliberations. On the issue of admissibility, he noted that the Court had recently modified the strict rule against admitting such evidence; by the 1970s, former Chief Justice Laskin had adopted a case-by-case approach, where the substance of the issue would determine the value of the framers' intent.[4] Because the testimony of the Justice officials was relevant in the case at bar, Lamer ruled it admissible.

Like his predecessors on the Court, Lamer found that "speeches and declarations by prominent figures are inherently unreliable."[5] The Charter, he observed, had engaged the efforts of dozens, perhaps hundreds of people inside and outside the eleven senior governments of Canada. Under those circumstances, even the testimony of central figures like Strayer and Tassé could give only a partial picture. The intent of the framers was "a fact which is nearly impossible of proof"; in the absence of proof, it could not be given much evidentiary weight.[6] In other words, the legislative history of the Charter might be admissible, but it would not be allowed to determine the Court's interpretation of the guarantees.

This practical argument against taking the comments of the justice officials at face value was followed by a second, normative argument, which has attracted considerably more attention from critics of the Court:

Another danger with casting the interpretation of s. 7 in terms of the comments made by those heard at the Special Joint Committee Proceedings is that, in so doing, the rights, freedoms and values embodied in the Charter in effect become frozen in time to the moment of adoption with little or no possibility of growth, development and adjustment to changing societal needs. Obviously, in the present case, given the proximity in time of the Charter debates, such a problem is relatively minor, even though it must be noted that even at this early stage in the life of the Charter, a host of issues and questions have been

(continued)

raised which were largely unforeseen at the time of such proceedings. If the newly planted "living tree" which is the Charter is to have the possibility of growth and adjustment over time, care must be taken to ensure that historical materials, such as the Minutes of Proceedings and Evidence of the Special Joint Committee, do not stunt its growth.[7]

Lamer concluded that the standard of "fundamental justice" applies both to the procedural aspects of the legal system and to the substance of the laws by which it is regulated. He struck down the law.

In a 2003 interview, Tassé expressed his disappointment with Lamer's treatment of his testimony. While he was not surprised that the minister's statements were given short shrift, he and his officials had assumed that their perspective on the Charter's wording would have a greater influence on judicial interpretation. He acknowledged, however, that this was "the risk all the constituents were taking when they gave the courts the responsibility to interpret the rights in the Charter."[8]

ENDNOTES

1. Barry L. Strayer, testimony before the Special Joint Committee on the Constitution, January 27, 1980 (available in the *Minutes of Proceedings and Evidence* at p. 46:32; reproduced in *Re B.C. Motor Vehicle Act*, [1985] 2 S.C.R. 486, paragraph 36, *per* Lamer J.

2. Roger Tassé, testimony before the Special Joint Committee on the Constitution, November 12, 1980 (available in the *Minutes of Proceedings and Evidence* at p. 3:79, reproduced in *Re B.C. Motor Vehicle Act*, paragraph 36, *per* Lamer J.

3. *Re B.C. Motor Vehicle Act*, paragraph 37.

4. *Re Anti-Inflation Act*, [1976] 2 S.C.R. 373, p. 389, *per* Laskin C.J., quoted in *B.C. Motor Vehicle*, paragraph 40, *per* Lamer J.

5. *Re B.C. Motor Vehicle Act*, paragraph 50.

6. Ibid., paragraph 52.

7. Ibid., paragraph 53.

8. Roger Tassé, interview with the author, June 17, 2003.

Legislative History

A second category of extrinsic evidence that may be useful in Charter cases is the legislative history of an impugned law. Hogg identifies five categories of legislative history: reports by law commissions or other investigative bodies, recommending the adoption of a particular statute; government policy documents from the early stages of policy-making; previous drafts of the **bill**; testimony by department officials (including the minister) before a parliamentary committee studying the bill; and speeches by legislators during debate on the bill.[148] A 1993 study by Morton and Brodie found that almost half of Charter factums to the Supreme Court cited reports by commissions and parliamentary committees, while fewer than ten percent referred to parliamentary debates.[149]

Legislative history may be useful to the Court where the meaning of the statute cannot be definitively ascertained from its wording.[150] It is also helpful at the s. 1 stage of analysis, when the Court has to determine (1) the objective of an impugned law; (2) whether that objective is "pressing and substantial"; and (3) whether the sponsoring government considered alternative policy mechanisms to achieve that objective, which would have a lesser impact on protected rights and freedoms. (See Dossier 1.6, pages 27–30.) In recognition of this fact, Parliament and the federal Department of Justice have become more assiduous in compiling legislative histories for bills that are likely to face Charter challenges.[151] Such bills often include preambles that identify and justify the objective of the law, in an effort to preempt a judicial analysis under s. 1.[152] (See Chapter 4, page 160.)

Older laws, especially those passed before the Charter came into effect, are rarely accompanied by such extensive records. There may be little, other than the statements of parliamentarians, to show why the law was passed or what alternatives its authors may have considered. In such cases, lawyers for the sponsoring government find themselves in considerable difficulty. If they cannot identify a clear legislative purpose, the Court may be left to infer the objective from the wording of the law itself. In rare cases, even when the purpose is established by the evidence, the Court may choose to "read in" an objective that makes the law easier to justify (see Dossier 3.3).

DOSSIER 3.3

R. V. BUTLER AND THE "SHIFTING PURPOSES" DOCTRINE

When a court applies the *Oakes* test (Dossier 1.6, pages 27–30), it must determine the objective of the legislature that passed the impugned law and weigh it against the harm caused by a Charter infringement. The Supreme Court insists that the intent of the legislature must be interpreted accurately, in the context of the time at which the law was passed. In *Big M Drug Mart* (1985), Chief Justice Dickson struck down the 1906 Lord's Day Act as an unjustified infringement on freedom of religion. He dismissed the federal government's claim that the original objective of the law—the enforcement of the Christian faith—had changed over the years, and that the act had become a secular measure for guaranteeing workers a weekly day of rest (which just happened to be Sunday, the Christian Sabbath). Dickson rejected this "shifting purposes" doctrine on two grounds:

> First, there are the practical difficulties. No legislation would be safe from a revised judicial assessment of purpose. Laws assumed valid on the basis of persuasive and powerful authority could, at any time, be struck down as invalid. Not only would this create uncertainty in the law, but it would encourage re-litigation of the same issues and, it could be argued, provide the courts with a means by which to arrive at a result dictated by other than legal considerations.... Furthermore, the theory of a shifting purpose stands in stark contrast to fundamental notions developed in our law concerning the nature of "Parliamentary intention." Purpose is a function of the intent of those who drafted and enacted the legislation at the time, and not of any shifting variable.[1]

In effect, Dickson required the courts to stick to whatever legislative intent could be teased out of the contemporaneous record, and not to attribute objectives of their own devising. Objective lies in the factual record, not in the eye of the beholder.

Six years later, Justice Sopinka wrote the majority opinion in the *Butler* case, which concerned the constitutionality of the obscenity provisions in the Criminal Code. Canada does not have a general law restricting the sale or production of pornography; instead, it has a patchwork of laws on child pornography, the importation of obscene materials, and related matters. In the absence of a general law, the sections of the Criminal Code regulating obscene writings and images—which were passed in 1959, and never subsequently amended—must be used to charge purveyors of pornography who do not fall under the other laws. Donald Butler, the owner of a Winnipeg "adult" store, had been convicted on several counts of possessing and distributing obscene materials. He appealed, arguing that the law was unconstitutional because it infringed the guarantee of free expression in s. 2(b) of the Charter. The Manitoba Court of Appeal rejected his argument, whereupon he appealed to the Supreme Court of Canada.

The legislative history of the obscenity provisions posed a problem for the Court, which appeared keen to uphold them if it could find a way to do so. The evidence showed that Parliament's intent when it passed the original obscenity law in 1892, and refined it in 1949, had been to restrict the circulation of books and

(continued)

images that could degrade the morals of Canadians. The earlier legislation contained the words "disgusting," "indecent," and "tending to corrupt morals."[2] There was no evidence that Parliament had repudiated this objective when it replaced the law in 1959. Sopinka acknowledged that had he relied on the legislative history in the manner prescribed by Dickson in *Big M Drug Mart*, he would have to strike the law down: "The prevention of 'dirt for dirt's sake' is not a legitimate objective which would justify the violation of one of the most fundamental freedoms enshrined in the Charter."[3]

Instead, Sopinka crafted a wholly new objective for the impugned provisions: "the avoidance of harm to society."[4] The specific harm to be avoided, he argued, was "the desensitization of individuals exposed to materials which depict violence, cruelty, and dehumanization in sexual relations."[5] While admitting that there was no solid proof that consumers of "degrading and dehumanizing" pornography were more likely to commit sexual crimes, Sopinka nevertheless asserted that such material "predisposes persons to act in an anti-social manner as, for example, the physical or mental mistreatment of women by men."[6] He then determined that the objective that he had devised was "pressing and substantial." Moreover, he concluded that the prohibition of such materials was "rationally connected" to the objective, on the ground that "Parliament was entitled to have a 'reasoned apprehension of harm'" in light of the connection between pornography and violence against women.[7] This statement overlooks the fact that Parliament had no such apprehension when it enacted the 1959 law; the claim that pornography promotes sexual crime is a product of the 1970s and 1980s, not the 1950s.

Critics of the *Butler* ruling, with considerable understatement, have called Sopinka's s. 1 analysis "somewhat intellectually dishonest."[8] Sopinka himself denied that he had resurrected the "shifting purposes" doctrine after its demise in *Big M Drug Mart*. He insisted that the objective of the law had always been "to avoid harm,"

but that Canadians' understanding of the nature of that "harm" had evolved since 1959.[9] In effect, he had not changed the purpose of the law, but merely given that purpose a more up-to-date meaning. This "shifting emphasis" doctrine put the Court in a difficult position. Six months after *Butler*, the Court issued its ruling in *Zundel* (Dossier 8.10, pages 271–72). The majority found that the Criminal Code section prohibiting the spread of "false news" could not survive Charter scrutiny. The minority, represented by Justices Cory and Iacobucci, argued that the law should be upheld under s. 1. They reasoned that the original purpose of the law—to protect the political elite from public criticism—had now evolved into something more "pressing and substantial": the protection of vulnerable groups from hate speech, and the protection of society at large from "internecine hostilities between and among social groups."[10] They relied on *Butler* to defend this "shifting emphasis" approach.[11] Justice McLachlin, writing for the majority, was forced to counter this argument without repudiating *Butler* (which she had signed). In a rather tortuous passage, McLachlin attempted to distinguish Sopinka's reasoning from the "shifting purposes" doctrine forbidden by *Big M Drug Mart*:

> In determining the objective of a legislative measure for the purposes of s. 1, the Court must look at the intention of Parliament when the section was enacted or amended. It cannot assign objectives, nor invent new ones according to the perceived current utility of the impugned provision.... Although the application and interpretation of objectives may vary over time, new and altogether different purposes should not be invented. The case is quite different from the anti-obscenity legislation in *Butler* where the goal historically and to the present day is the same—combatting the "detrimental impact" of obscene materials on individuals and society—even though our understanding or conception of that detrimental impact (a "permissible shift in emphasis") may have evolved, as Sopinka J. noted.[12]

This attempt to distinguish between "shifting purposes" and "shifting emphasis" is unconvincing. What Cory and Iacobucci did in their *Zundel* dissent is precisely what Sopinka had done in *Butler*: they drew the vague outlines of a "public interest" objective for the impugned law, and then filled it in with their own content. In both cases, the effect was the same: to divorce legislative intent from legislative history.

ENDNOTES

1. *Big M Drug Mart*, paragraphs 90–91.

2. Reproduced in *R. v. Butler*, [1992] 1 S.C.R. 452, paragraphs 31–32.

3. Ibid., paragraph 78.

4. Ibid., paragraph 81. Such vague objectives are generally rejected out of hand when proffered by the parties and not by a member of the Court; see Dossier 1.6, pages 27–30.

5. Ibid., paragraph 106.

6. Ibid., paragraph 93.

7. Ibid., paragraph 106.

8. D.F. Bur and J.K. Kehoe, "Developments in Constitutional Law: The 1992–1993 Term," *Supreme Court Law Review* 5 (2d) (1993), p 86. See also Peter W. Hogg, *Constitutional Law of Canada*, 2002 student ed. (Toronto: Carswell, 2002), p. 788; Richard Moon, *The Constitutional Protection of Freedom of Expression* (Toronto: University of Toronto Press, 2000), Chapter 4.

9. *Butler*, paragraph 84.

10. *R. v. Zundel*, [1992] 2 S.C.R. 731, paragraph 129, *per* Cory and Iacobucci JJ.

11. Ibid., paragraphs 188–90, *per* Cory and Iacobucci JJ.

12. Ibid., paragraph 45.

In addition to the intended purpose or objective of the law, judges may rely on legislative history to determine whether the sponsoring government had considered alternatives to the impugned policy. (See Dossier 1.6, pages 27–30.) If the lawyers tasked with defending the law do not present evidence of such deliberations, the Court may conclude that no "rational connection" exists between the objective of the law and the means chosen to achieve it. As Justice McLachlin put it in *RJR-MacDonald*, evidence of alternatives can make the difference between upholding a law under s. 1 and striking it down:

> The tailoring process seldom admits of perfection and the courts must accord some leeway to the legislator. If the law falls within a range of reasonable alternatives, the courts will not find it overbroad merely because they can conceive of an alternative which might better tailor objective to infringement.... On the other hand, if the government fails to explain why a significantly less intrusive and equally effective measure was not chosen, the law may fail.[153]

To identify alternative policy measures, Justices may turn to similar laws in other countries—e.g., Justice Wilson's reference to the American case *Roe v. Wade* in her concurring opinion in *Morgentaler*[154]— or to the recommendations of experts who have studied the issue.[155] If they identify a less intrusive means of achieving the objective, and have not been told why the means chosen by the sponsoring government are more effective, they are more likely to strike down the law.

Social-Science Data

Whereas legislative history can help to determine the purpose of an impugned law, it offers little assistance in evaluating the effects. Here the courts may turn to the third type of extrinsic evidence: social science. The data generated by social scientists include survey results, policy analyses, statistics, anthropological narratives, philosophical arguments, and comparisons of law and policy in different countries. With the exception of law journals, which are cited in most Charter cases,[156] the type of data used varies with the subject matter of the case at bar. In the 1988 *Morgentaler* ruling on Canada's abortion law, the Court cited works in moral philosophy, annual reports from Statistics Canada, articles from medical journals, and comparative studies of abortion laws in Western states. Judgments on Aboriginal rights often cite anthropological studies of traditional band practices. Rulings on election law rely heavily on the work of political scientists. The jurisprudence on s. 15(1) is replete with references to psychologists, economists, and sociologists.

Before 1982, the Supreme Court rarely considered extrinsic evidence pertaining to social or legislative facts.[157] The Justices applied the traditional techniques of statutory interpretation to derive meaning from the words of the law or constitutional provision themselves. The Charter requires a more generous approach to evidence, for at least two reasons. First, the language of its guarantees is too broad for ***prima facie*** application. A judge, confronted with phrases like "existing Aboriginal and treaty rights" or "where numbers warrant," cannot be expected to resolve the dispute at bar without reliable social-science information.[158] Second, the task of determining whether a law infringes the Charter, and whether that infringement can be justified in "a free and democratic society," imposes a duty on judges to evaluate the substance of public policy—and, where appropriate, to create new policy.[159] As we saw earlier, this duty has been "amplified by judicial interpretation"—in particular, by the "effects-oriented" and "contextual" approaches to statutory interpretation and the formulation of the *Oakes* test (Dossier 1.6, pages 27–30).[160]

The U.S. Supreme Court, with its long tradition of interpreting entrenched rights, has admitted social-science evidence in constitutional cases since the late nineteenth century. Its infamous 1896 ruling in *Plessy v. Ferguson*, which approved "separate but equal" treatment for Black and white Americans, was influenced by the racial theories of the day.[161] When the Court finally overturned *Plessy* in *Brown v. Board of Education* (1954), it cited a written statement from thirty-two prominent social scientists attacking the factual premises on which the earlier ruling had been based.[162] In the past half-century, the volume of "social facts" before the court has increased dramatically. A comparison of two major cases on abortion

illustrates the trend. In *Roe v. Wade* (1973) the Court received fewer than twenty social-science briefs; when it revisited the legality of abortion in *Webster v. Reproductive Health Services* (1989), almost eighty briefs were submitted.[163]

Although the *Brown* judgment itself was obviously correct, it illustrates three serious problems with the judicial use of social-science data.

- First, constitutional interpretation should (ideally) be informed by stable and widely held norms of justice and fairness; it should not shift with the prevailing winds of academic opinion.
- Second, the American Justices appear to have been influenced not only by the statement referred to above, but by other social-science studies of dubious merit. One study in particular, whose methodology and conclusions were deeply flawed, was taken seriously by the Court. This may have happened, in part, because "counsel for the school board [which was defending "separate but equal"] either treated it as trivial or chose to make racial attacks rather than to cross-examine about the studies."[164] In the absence of the quality control afforded by cross-examination, the Justices had no way to evaluate the evidence presented by the two contending parties and the intervenors (the *amici curiae*). They could not, or did not, assess the validity of the social-science data for themselves, or determine whether any or all of it provided a sound basis for public policy.
- Third, we will never know whether the social-science data actually determined the outcome of *Brown*, or whether the Justices made up their minds on the basis of other factors—e.g., legal analysis, political pressure, or personal preference—and simply used the empirical studies to rationalize the outcome that they wanted to reach.[165]

These are three aspects of a general problem: the capacity of lawyers and judges to deal competently and responsibly with "social facts."

The introduction of the Charter brought these issues to Canada. The broad question of institutional competence has received considerable attention, both from outside observers and from legal practitioners.[166] As Horowitz points out, the adjudicative process by which courts have traditionally resolved disputes "is ill-adapted to the ascertainment of social facts."[167] Lawyers are advocates for one side or the other. They present the facts of their case narrowly, in a manner that is designed to persuade the court that their cause is just—or, at the very least, that the relevant legal precedents point to a victory for their client. Few lawyers are equipped, by education or professional training, to evaluate the validity of social-science data. They cannot predict what will happen if their client's victory produces a change in the law, nor (in most cases) can they give the court a complete and accurate account of the effects of an impugned policy on society at large. Their appointment to the bench does nothing to remedy these deficiencies.

Members of the Supreme Court of Canada have often acknowledged their disadvantage, relative to the legislative and executive branches of government, in the making and assessment of public policy. In the pre-Charter era, that awareness inhibited the Court from answering broad questions extending beyond the narrow province of law. In a 1978 case involving the right of striking workers to trespass on private property, then–Justice Dickson issued a warning against judicial legislation:

> The submission that this court should weigh and determine the respective values to society of the right to property and the right to picket raises important and difficult political and socio-economic issues, the resolution of which must, by their very nature, be arbitrary and embody personal economic and social beliefs. It raises also fundamental questions as to the role of this Court under the Canadian constitution. The duty of the Court, as I envisage it, is to proceed in the discharge of the adjudicative function in a reasoned way from principled decision and established concepts. I do not for a moment doubt the power of the court to act creatively—it has done so on countless occasions; but manifestly one must ask—what are the limits of the judicial function?[168]

The proclamation of the Charter appears to have changed Dickson's perspective. Seven years after writing the above, in a speech to law students, he said, "When the occasion cries out for new law, let us dare to make it."[169] While conscious that the Court's

capacity to process "statistical, economic and sociological data" had not been magically improved by the Charter, Dickson encouraged lawyers and intervenors to educate judges about the "social context and legislative effect which are necessary for policy making."[170]

The tension between institutional incapacity and lofty goals, implicit in Dickson's remarks, has not yet been resolved. Some Justices have explicitly acknowledged that the courts are ill-equipped to second-guess the policy choices made by legislators and political executives, although their reluctance to do so varies with the subject matter of the policy in question. In *Irwin Toy*, the majority distinguished between social policy and criminal law, arguing that courts should show more deference to legislative choices in the former area than the latter. The making of social policy forces legislators (and executives) to "mediat[e] between the claims of competing groups" on the basis of "conflicting scientific evidence and differing justified demands on scarce resources." When assessing the constitutionality of the compromises thus reached, the courts "must be mindful of the legislature's representative function"—and, by implication, of its greater capacity to acquire and process empirical data.[171] On the other hand, the courts enjoy greater expertise in the field of criminal justice, where the state is "the singular antagonist of the individual."[172] The statutory definition of criminal offences, and the procedures by which suspects are investigated and tried, "do not lie in the realm of general public policy but in the inherent domain of the judiciary as guardian of the justice system."[173]

In *McKinney*, the majority repeated its caution against undue judicial interference in social policy. At the same time, however, Justice La Forest asserted that "In performing their functions of ensuring compliance with the constitutional norms in these amorphous areas, courts must of necessity turn to such available knowledge as exists and, in particular, to social science research, both of a particular and general nature."[174]

La Forest returned to the *Irwin* distinction in his dissenting judgment in *RJR-MacDonald*. In the course of arguing that the federal law prohibiting tobacco advertising should be upheld under s. 1, he discussed the "fundamental institutional distinction between the legislative and judicial functions that lies at the very heart of our political and constitutional system":

> Courts are specialists in the protection of liberty and the interpretation of legislation and are, accordingly, well placed to subject criminal justice legislation to careful scrutiny. However, courts are not specialists in the realm of policy-making, nor should they be. This is a role properly assigned to the elected representatives of the people, who have at their disposal the necessary institutional resources to enable them to compile and assess social science evidence, to mediate between competing social interests and to reach out and protect vulnerable groups. In according a greater degree of deference to social legislation than to legislation in the criminal justice context, this Court has recognized these important institutional differences between legislatures and the judiciary.
>
> Seen in this way, it is clear that the *Act* is the very type of legislation to which this Court has generally accorded a high degree of deference. In drafting this legislation, which is directed toward a laudable social goal and is designed to protect vulnerable groups, Parliament was required to compile and assess complex social science evidence and to mediate between competing social interests. Decisions such as these are properly assigned to our elected representatives, who have at their disposal the necessary resources to undertake them, and who are ultimately accountable to the electorate.[175]

La Forest was more deferential to Parliament than to the trial judge. He held that trial courts are entitled to deference on questions of adjudicative fact, but not social or legislative fact:

> [T]he privileged position of the trial judge does not extend to the assessment of "social" or "legislative" facts that arise in the law-making process and require the legislature or a court to assess complex social science evidence and to draw general conclusions concerning the effect of legal rules on human behaviour.... In my view, the causal connection between tobacco advertising and consumption, or the lack thereof, is a

paradigm example of a legislative or social fact.... Moreover, given the intimate relation that exists between legislative facts and the creation of legal rules, there is also a strong policy reason for suspending the non-interference rule with respect to legislative or social facts.[176]

In effect, La Forest argued that the Supreme Court is a policy-making institution that may assert primacy over the information on which policies are based, whereas the lower courts are essentially adjudicative institutions whose policy views are not binding. This is not entirely consistent with his claim that the judicial branch is ill-equipped to handle the kind of social-science evidence on which public policies are based.

In her majority opinion, Justice McLachlin disagreed with both of La Forest's conclusions about the use of social-science evidence. In the first place, she rejected the suggestion that the courts should automatically lower the standard of s. 1 justification when assessing the constitutionality of social policies:

> Deference must not be carried to the point of relieving the government of the burden which the Charter places upon it of demonstrating that the limits it has imposed on guaranteed rights are reasonable and justifiable. Parliament has its role: to choose the appropriate response to social problems within the limiting framework of the Constitution. But the courts also have a role: to determine, objectively and impartially, whether Parliament's choice falls within the limiting framework of the Constitution. The courts are no more permitted to abdicate their responsibility than is Parliament. To carry judicial deference to the point of accepting Parliament's view simply on the basis that the problem is serious and the solution difficult, would be to diminish the role of the courts in the constitutional process and to weaken the structure of rights upon which our constitution and our nation is founded.[177]

Second, she questioned the distinction between legislative and adjudicative facts, and pointed out that trial courts may be better placed than appellate courts to evaluate social-science data.

[T]he distinction between legislative and adjudicative facts may be harder to maintain in practice than in theory. Suffice it to say that in the context of the s. 1 analysis, more deference may be required to findings based on evidence of a purely factual nature whereas a lesser degree of deference may be required where the trial judge has considered social science and other policy oriented evidence. As a general matter, appellate courts are not as constrained by the trial judge's findings in the context of the s. 1 analysis as they are in the course of non-constitutional litigation, since the impact of the infringement on constitutional rights must often be assessed by reference to a broad review of social, economic and political factors in addition to scientific facts. At the same time, while appellate courts are not bound by the trial judge's findings in respect of social science evidence, they should remain sensitive to the fact that the trial judge has had the advantage of hearing competing expert testimony firsthand. The trial judge's findings with respect to the credibility of certain witnesses may be useful when the appeal court reviews the record.[178]

McLachlin's reference to "competing expert testimony" raises another issue: the various means by which social-science data are presented in court. In general, "legislative" or "social facts" may be introduced into evidence in three ways:

- by counsel for the parties to the case (the appellant and respondent);
- by intervenors; or
- by judicial notice.

Until recently, it was rare for a Canadian lawyer to address policy issues in a factum to the Court—which makes sense, given the restrictive attitude toward admitting extrinsic evidence. In contrast, the U.S. Supreme Court was well acquainted with policy-related factums—known in American parlance as "Brandeis briefs," after the lawyer (later a Supreme Court Justice himself) who pioneered the technique in 1907. The case of *Error Muller v. Oregon* concerned the appeal from conviction of a laundry owner who had violated state law by forcing a female employee to work longer than ten hours a day. Louis Brandeis, the counsel for the state of Oregon, argued that the law advanced important social goals. His 113-page brief consisted largely of quotations from government reports, both domestic and foreign, and references to learned journals. In its unanimous judgment affirming the law, the Court cited this evidence approvingly.[179]

A few Canadian lawyers experimented with "Brandeis briefs" before 1982, with mixed success.[180] Post-Charter courts have been more receptive to policy-based arguments for or against the constitutionality of laws and government acts. They have also been more willing to hear *viva voce* testimony, and receive written affidavits, from expert witnesses. Each of these techniques has its advantages and disadvantages.[181] Because appeal courts cannot summon witnesses, *viva voce* testimony must be introduced at the trial phase or not at all. The advantage of calling expert witnesses to testify in person, as Justice McLachlin noted, is that they can be cross-examined and the validity of their data tested through the adversarial process. On the downside, the cost of hiring experts can be prohibitive for most defendants. Moreover, a lawyer may not anticipate a particular constitutional issue until it is too late to gather extrinsic evidence.[182] If this happens, and the case goes to appeal, counsel can file written submissions that address the constitutional issues directly. In many instances, as we will see in Chapter 6, outside groups and individuals with a particular interest in the policy issue at bar are permitted to submit their own briefs. However, these materials—affidavits, interventions and "Brandeis briefs"—are not automatically subject to cross-examination.[183] In effect, there are few quality controls on social-science data. Unless the judges can spot methodological problems for themselves—which, as we have seen, is not always the case—they may be misled by flaws in the empirical evidence (accidental or otherwise).

The term "judicial notice" refers to "the acceptance by the court of a matter of fact or law without the necessity of formal proof in the form of evidence adduced by one of the parties."[184] In practice, a judge can simply assume certain facts to be true, without solid proof; he may even base his ruling on that assumption. Occasionally, if he believes that the written record does not permit him to answer an important question, he may try to gather evidence on his own initiative.[185] Judges are not supposed to do their own research; they are expected to base their rulings on the evidence tendered by the parties to the dispute.[186] As Dossier 3.4 suggests, there are other arguments to be made against judicial research—particularly the analytical incompetence previously discussed.

DOSSIER 3.4

ASKOV, MORIN, AND THE ABUSE OF SOCIAL SCIENCE

In the 1990 *Askov* ruling, the Supreme Court stayed criminal charges against four Ontario men who had been charged with conspiracy to commit extortion and other serious crimes. The majority, led by Justice Cory, found that the courts in Peel Region had violated the appellants' right to trial within a reasonable time (s. 11(b) of the Charter). The four men had been arrested in November 1983. Three were held in custody until May 1984. The preliminary hearing began on July 4, 1984. It could not be completed in one day; the resumption was set for September 21. The trial was scheduled for the earliest available date, which was October 15, 1985. It was delayed because there was no courtroom available on that day. On October 25, 1985, the trial was delayed until September 2, 1986—almost three years after the initial arrest. When it finally began, defence lawyers moved for a stay of charges on the ground of unreasonable delay. The stay was granted. The Crown successfully appealed the stay to the Ontario Court of Appeal, which ordered that the trials proceed. The four accused then appealed the reversal to the Supreme Court of Canada, which overturned the Court of Appeal and restored the stay order.

Justice Cory determined that the elapsed time between the preliminary hearing and the trial was "unreasonable" within the meaning of s. 11(b) of the Charter. In previous rulings on this issue, the Court had refrained from setting a mathematical standard of "reasonableness"; while it required judges to take the length of the delay into account in assessing prejudice against the accused, it did not specify a time limit beyond which a declaration of "unreasonableness" would be automatic. (See Chapter 10, pages 322–23.) In *Askov*, however, Cory determined that the delay was caused by factors intrinsic to the court system itself, specifically the underfunding of the justice system in the Peel Region of Ontario. To prove his point, and to bolster his critique of successive provincial governments for their failure to invest in the court system, Cory conducted his own comparative analysis of trial delays in several Canadian jurisdictions.

In fairness to Cory, the analysis was inspired by the lawyer for one of the appellants. The lawyer had heard through the legal grapevine that Carl Baar, a professor of political science, had compiled statistics on trial delays in Ontario, New Brunswick, and British Columbia.[1] He commissioned Baar to prepare an affidavit for the Supreme Court, which showed that the courts in Peel Region were particularly slow to dispose of cases. Partly on the basis of these social-science data, Cory concluded that "a period of delay in a range of some six to eight months between committal and trial might be deemed to be the outside limit of what is reasonable."[2]

In his affidavit, Baar observed that "If Canadian courts were required to set cases for trial within six months, they could almost universally do so," with the sole exception of Peel Region.[3] However, he did not suggest that a six-month deadline should be imposed on courts, nor did he intend his statistics to become the foundation for judicial policy-making. The affidavit was submitted solely to demonstrate that the systemic underfunding of Ontario courts had caused the violation of the appellants' Charter rights. The facts therein were adjudicative, not legislative.[4]

Askov is an object lesson for judges in how not to use social-science data. Not only did Cory misinterpret Baar's affidavit; he also indulged in some freelance fact-finding that led him into further error. Apparently on his own initiative, Cory gathered statistics on trial delays in Quebec. These data were not made known to the lawyers for the appellants or to the Crown. There was no opportunity for either party to clarify what the statistics actually meant, or to examine their validity.[5] Cory concluded, on the basis of his own research, that the average time to dispose of a trial in three Quebec districts ranged from 63.5 days to 84.3 days.[6] He used these figures to calculate the six- to eight-month "guideline," by a statistical process that had no empirical basis. He then imposed the "guideline" immediately, without giving the courts an opportunity to adjust or "grandfather" cases that were already in process.[7]

The result was, or should have been, predictable. Over the next several months, more than 50 000 criminal charges were stayed or withdrawn, together with another 64 000 regulatory charges. Although 90 percent of ongoing criminal charges in Ontario were unaffected by the ruling, the news media—with the assistance of an outraged provincial attorney general—portrayed the ruling as a wholesale "amnesty for criminals."[8] Apparently alarmed by the fallout, and stung by the criticism, the Supreme Court returned to the issue of trial delays in the 1992 *Morin* ruling.[9] Justice Sopinka declared that the *Askov* guideline was "neither a limitation period nor a fixed ceiling on delay," and he gave the task of making case-by-case adjustments to the provincial courts of appeal.[10] He placed the blame for the errors in *Askov* not on his colleague Justice Cory, but on a "misleading" comparison between Montreal and Peel Region in the affidavit of Professor Baar. In fact, Baar never mentioned Quebec in his affidavit; he believed that the differences between the civil-law system in that province and the common-law systems elsewhere in Canada made such a comparison invalid.[11]

Sopinka went on to suggest an eight- to ten-month guideline for cases in provincial courts, relying (once again) on Cory's faulty statistical analysis of Baar's data in *Askov*. This is a classic apples-and-oranges mistake: Baar's data applied to superior courts, which are entirely distinct from the provincial courts at issue in *Morin*.[12] As it had in *Askov*, a majority of the Supreme Court of Canada endorsed a judge-made public policy based on a misreading of social-science data.

ENDNOTES

1. Carl Baar, "Social Facts, Court Delay and the Charter," in F.L. Morton, ed., *Law, Politics and the Judicial Process in Canada*, 2nd ed. (Calgary: University of Calgary Press, 1992), pp. 293–94.

2. *R. v. Askov*, [1990] 2 S.C.R. 1199, paragraph 89, *per* Cory J.

3. Affidavit of Carl Baar in the case of *Askov v. the Queen* (Supreme Court of Canada), sworn 16, January, 1990, reproduced in *Askov*, paragraph 76, *per* Cory J.

4. Christopher P. Manfredi, *Judicial Power and the Charter: Canada and the Paradox of Liberal Constitutionalism*, 2nd ed. (Toronto: Oxford University Press, 2001), p. 160.

5. Baar, "Social Facts," p. 295.

6. *Askov*, paragraph 88.

7. Baar, "Social Facts," p. 296.

8. Kent Roach, *Due Process and Victims' Rights: The New Law and Politics of Criminal Justice* (Toronto: University of Toronto Press, 1999), p. 92.

9. *R. v. Morin*, [1992] 1 S.C.R. 771.

10. *Morin*, paragraphs 48 and 57.

11. Baar, "Social Facts," p. 295.

12. F.L. Morton, "Editor's Note," in Morton, ed., *Law, Politics*, pp. 298–99.

The *Askov* and *Morin* cases illustrate the chief failing of judicial notice: unlike parties or intervenors, judges cannot be cross-examined on their facts. There is no quality control, either on the data that judges collect or on the techniques by which they interpret those data and apply them to policy problems.

Overall, the Court's handling of extrinsic evidence—particularly the "social facts" that must guide effective public policy—suggests that it has yet to become a fully competent policy-making institution. Even when it makes good choices—as it arguably did in *Butler*, by upholding the general law against pornography—it can reach them in a way that flouts the accepted rules of judicial decision-making. When it makes poor choices, as it did in *Askov*, its limitations as a policy-making body are starkly revealed. This evaluation should not be taken to suggest that the Justices "get it wrong" most of the time. Indeed, as Part 3 of this book demonstrates, the Court's overall record under the Charter is a good one. The problem lies not with the Justices themselves, but with the lack of fit between their post-1982 policy-making responsibilities and an institution that evolved to deal with very different kinds of issues.

The Supreme Court and the News Media

It was suggested at the beginning of this chapter that a policy-making institution should conduct its business in a reasonably open and transparent way. As we have seen, the Supreme Court does not meet this standard. The Justices never give reasons for their decisions on leave applications. Nor do their judgments fully explain how they reach their conclusions on cases. The written reasons in Court judgments are often lengthy and detailed, but the suspicion lingers that they sometimes rationalize in legal terms a decision that was reached on other grounds. Since 1982, the Court has assumed a central place in Canadian politics and government. Its traditional aloofness and obscurity have no place in the Charter era.

To his credit, former Chief Justice Dickson recognized that the Court had to adapt to its newly acquired public prominence. Under his administration, and those of Chief Justices Lamer and

McLachlin, the Supreme Court of Canada has become "an international trailblazer in terms of media relations."[187] Shortly after the Charter's proclamation, Dickson introduced two innovations at the Court: the new position of executive legal officer (ELO) and a Media Relations Committee made up of Justices and reporters. The ELO is the official liaison between the Court and the parliamentary press gallery. He or she holds off-the-record briefings on important cases, helping reporters (few of whom have any legal background) to understand complex legal issues. The purpose is not to "spin" the rulings but to provide accurate information to the public.[188]

The Media Relations Committee meets once or twice a year to resolve issues pertaining to media access and technology. One perennial issue is the scope and accommodation of television coverage. Since 1995, Supreme Court hearings have been recorded and broadcast by the Cable Public Affairs Channel (CPAC). The exceptions are hearings covered by a publication ban, or those in which the participants object to the cameras (which they rarely do).[189] The Court has come a long way since September 1981, when the first-ever live broadcast in the courtroom turned into a technical nightmare.[190] Since then, the Justices have grown accustomed to appearing on television, although they have imposed strict rules on the camera operators during hearings. Outside the courtroom itself, the growing public and media interest in Charter rulings has turned the lobby of the Supreme Court building into a press theatre on judgment days. Participants in a newly decided case are "scrummed" by reporters, while representatives of interest groups jockey for "face time" on camera.

The Justices themselves rarely make public comments about their work. They do not give interviews about cases, relying on the rulings to speak for themselves.[191] Although the current members of the Court are less reticent toward journalists than their predecessors,[192] most hold themselves aloof from the media (at least until after their retirement from the bench). The late Justice Sopinka was an exception: he cultivated informal contacts with reporters, a practice that at least one former journalist wishes were more widespread: "More judges should make themselves available and break their silence to assist the public in understanding the process."[193]

Despite his institutional reforms and his efforts to build positive relationships between the Court and the media, Dickson was highly sensitive to public criticism. He appears to have relaxed the strict *Oakes* standard of justification in subsequent cases, in part, because of negative comments from the media.[194] More recently, the Court has faced sustained criticism from the *National Post* and other media outlets. Shortly before he retired as Chief Justice, Antonio Lamer expressed the fear that "as a result of virulent or harsh comments by the press or public, the most popular thing to do might become the outcome."[195] In the late 1990s, it appeared that hostile media reaction to the Court's due-process rulings on legal rights might have sapped its determination to protect the rights of accused criminals.[196] Championing unpopular minorities, a job requirement under the Charter, does not always make for glowing news coverage.

In its efforts to become more open with the media, the Supreme Court has probably gone about as far as it can without sacrificing judicial neutrality, collegiality, and confidentiality. In this respect, it has adapted fairly well to the institutional demands of its expanded policy-making role. The U.S. Supreme Court, whose status as a policy-making institution has been acknowledged for decades, shuns news coverage. Its Public Information Office issues a constant stream of written material to journalists, keeping them too busy to penetrate the secrecy that surrounds the institution.[197] There are no off-the-record briefings; there is no Media Relations Committee. Compared to Canadians, Americans receive less information, and less accurate information, about their highest court and its impact on their lives. In the words of a former ELO, "The Supreme Court of Canada goes to quite extraordinary lengths to accommodate the media."[198] In this respect, it is a more effective policy-making agency than its American counterpart. Despite these efforts, evidence suggests that few Canadians are well informed about the Court and its decisions. In a 1999 survey, fewer than half of the respondents had heard of the 1998 *Vriend* case.[199] Unlike most Supreme Court rulings, *Vriend* had prompted a political firestorm (especially in Alberta) and attracted much critical comment across the country (see Dossier 1.8, pages 36–37). The fact that this unusually high-profile ruling was unknown to a majority of Canadians suggests a failure (by the Court and the news media) to inform the public about the important work of judges in the Charter era.

The Appointment Process

Before the Charter, the Supreme Court of Canada toiled in relative obscurity. The process by which its members were chosen and appointed was a matter of public indifference. No one seemed to care that appointed judges with life tenure were refereeing political disputes between federal and provincial governments. This began to change in 1980–82, when the proposed Charter drew the attention of individuals and interest groups. Grafting a "citizens' constitution" onto the "governments' constitution" raised the profile of the Court and raised doubts about the legitimacy of the secretive appointment process.[200]

Judicial appointments to Canada's senior courts are regulated by ss. 96 and 101 of the Constitution Act, 1867. Section 96 provides that all judges, except those working in provincial courts, will be appointed by the governor general of Canada. In practice, this power is exercised by the federal cabinet, which appoints the candidates proposed by the minister of justice. Section 101 permits the federal government to "provide for the Constitution, Maintenance, and Organization of a General Court of Appeal for Canada." Pursuant to this section, the Supreme Court of Canada was established in 1875. Its structure and powers are set out in the Supreme Court Act, which is a regular federal statute—quasi-constitutional at best, and certainly not entrenched. By extension, the power of the federal cabinet to appoint federal judges under s. 96 applies to the Supreme Court as well. Reflecting the political importance of the highest court, the prime minister of the day rarely leaves the choice to the minister of justice; he or she regularly intervenes in the appointment process.

Until the late 1960s, Justices were often appointed on partisan grounds. Historians of the Court have described Prime Minister Mackenzie King's criteria as follows: "no preference for judicial experience, considerable weight to service to the Liberal Party, some minimum level of ability, and influential friends."[201] Under Pierre Trudeau, party patronage gave way to academic credentials and other indicia of actual merit.[202] Although the short-lived Progressive Conservative government of Joe Clark briefly revived partisanship as a criterion of appointment,[203] the growing public and media scrutiny of the Court in the Charter era has led prime ministers to avoid overt patronage.

Whatever the other criteria for appointment may have been, the convention of regional representation has imposed the primary constraint on prime ministerial choice. Of the nine members of the Court, three are appointed from the civil bar of Quebec. (As noted above, this provision in the Supreme Court Act ensures the presence of a *coram* equipped to assess the merits of leave applications from that province.) Another three come from Ontario, one from the Atlantic provinces, and two from the Prairies and British Columbia. When a Justice steps down, he or she must be replaced by an appointee from the same region.[204] The first woman, Bertha Wilson, was appointed to the Court in 1982; this appointment established a new convention of gender representation. There have been as many as four female Justices at one time, although it is not clear whether that number has acquired the same normative force as the regional distribution. As of September 1, 2004, there were an unprecedented four women on the Court; two female Justices were appointed in August 2004 to replace a retiring male and a female judge.

Until recently, the process by which the prime minister chose the members of the Supreme Court was shrouded in secrecy. In a 1999 survey, 13 percent of respondents knew that the prime minister picked the Justices; another 8 percent named the federal government or cabinet. Fully two-thirds had no idea.[205] The veil was finally pierced in March 2004, when federal Justice Minister Irwin Cotler explained the consultation process to a House of Commons standing committee.[206] At the first stage, the minister of justice identifies possible candidates. The pool of potential Justices includes the members of provincial courts of appeal, "senior members of the Bar," and prominent legal academics. The minister consults with the Chief Justice of the Supreme Court, the Chief Justices of the provincial courts in the region, provincial attorneys general, the Canadian Bar Association, and the local law societies. This informal process yields a shortlist of candidates. The second stage involves the assessment

of the candidates by the minister and the prime minister. Cotler identified three criteria: "professional capacity, personal characteristics, and diversity." The minister relies on his informal contacts and written profiles prepared by the Department of Justice to determine which candidate best meets these criteria. The prime minister is consulted throughout the process and participates in the final decision. His or her preferred candidate is recommended to cabinet and appointed by an order-in-council.

Responding to growing criticism of this process,[207] Prime Minister Paul Martin promised in December 2003 to give parliamentarians a role in the selection of future Supreme Court Justices. The Standing Committee on Justice had already begun an examination of the appointments process, pursuant to a motion adopted by the House of Commons in October 2003.[208] In March 2003, following the announcement that Justices Arbour and Iacobucci would be leaving the Court unexpectedly, the committee returned to the appointment issue as a matter of urgency. Over the next few weeks, it heard from the minister of justice, academic experts, the Canadian Bar Association, and retired Justice L'Heureux-Dubé. None of the witnesses expressed support for the secretive and informal process by which the Court had traditionally been appointed. Most recommended two specific reforms: the establishment of a commission to identify and evaluate potential Justices, and/or parliamentary scrutiny of the prime minister's candidate prior to the official appointment. Although few witnesses were comfortable with parliamentary ratification of Court appointments—largely because of the damaging political battles over recent American Supreme Court nominees—most believed that a public hearing where MPs could interview the preferred candidate would make the process more transparent. In the process, it could give the Court and its rulings greater public legitimacy.[209]

One promising model for the nominating commission is the existing procedure for choosing the judges appointed under s. 96. Since 1989, judicial advisory committees have operated in each province and territory.[210] Each has seven members: one representative each from the Canadian Bar Association, the provincial/territorial law society, and the federal Department of Justice; the chief justice and the attorney general for the province or territory; and two laypeople from outside the legal profession. The committees review applications from lawyers with at least ten years' professional experience. Each application is accompanied by a questionnaire about the personal history of the aspiring judge, to screen out those with personal or other problems that might impair their ability to function on the bench. The committees evaluate the applications, focusing on "professional competence and overall merit."[211] They must assign each application to one of three categories: "highly recommended," "recommended," or "unable to recommend." When a judicial vacancy occurs, the minister of justice must appoint a replacement from among the applicants on the "highly recommended" or "recommended" list for that province or territory.[212] He or she cannot go outside the process to find a politically palatable candidate or veto the committee's findings and tell them to start over.

The Standing Committee on Justice issued four reports—one each from the Liberal majority and the three opposition parties—in early May 2004. The majority report recommended that the two impending vacancies on the Court be filled as soon as possible, using an interim procedure. The informal consultation process would be retained and the two candidates chosen under the existing process; the minister of justice would then appear before the committee to explain how they had been selected.[213] For the longer term, the majority proposed that an advisory committee similar to those used for other federal judicial appointments be established each time a vacancy occurs on the Supreme Court. Its membership would be drawn from the official parties in the House of Commons, the provinces, judges, lawyers, and laypeople. Its first task would be to prepare a list of candidates from the affected province or region, from a pool of names submitted by the federal and provincial governments and other, unspecified sources. The committee would then narrow down the list of candidates, producing a shortlist of three to five names that would be forwarded to the minister of justice. This process would be based entirely on written documentation; "we would not support the interviewing of candidates." If the cabinet "did not wish to appoint any of the individuals on the short list, a new short list would be prepared by the advisory committee." In other words, the minister of justice would not be bound by the committee's recommendations.

As required by the Constitution and the Supreme Court Act, the final decision would rest with the cabinet. Once the appointment had been announced, the chair of the advisory committee and/or the justice minister would appear before the Standing Committee on Justice to explain the basis for the choice (ideally, without compromising confidentiality). The nominee him- or herself would not be subject to parliamentary scrutiny or ratification.

The Conservative members of the committee demanded a more public and transparent process. They called for both "a public review of a short list of the nominees before a parliamentary committee" and a form of parliamentary ratification that would be compatible with the cabinet's power to appoint Justices.[214] The Bloc Québécois dissented from the majority report in two respects: it demanded that the pool of candidates be determined solely by the government(s) of the province(s) affected by the vacancy, and that the federal government confine its choices to the shortlist prepared by the advisory committee. It further recommended that the cabinet refrain from filling the two vacancies on the Court until after a new permanent process had been put in place, suggesting that seven Justices were more than sufficient to make up a quorum.[215] Finally, the NDP complained about the vagueness of the majority's recommendations and argued that "the Minister's appearance should take place *before* the actual appointment is made."[216]

The justice committee report was issued shortly before Parliament was dissolved for a general election. The selection of Justices became a campaign issue, albeit a minor one. Conservative leader Stephen Harper promised that, if he became prime minister, he would give provincial governments a veto over nominations to the Court from their regions. He also pledged to subject nominees to parliamentary ratification, although MPs would not have the power to veto appointments.[217] In an editorial, *The Globe and Mail* expressed concern that Harper would "attempt to remake the Supreme Court by appointing tame judges who would defer to Parliament when constitutional rights were at stake." The writer noted Harper's earlier allegations that the current Court was biased toward the Liberal government, and pointed out that the next prime minister would fill at least three seats on the Court (the two Ontario vacancies, plus the Western seat left vacant by Justice Major's anticipated 2006 retirement).[218] Despite the Conservatives' ultimate loss to the Liberals, it is unlikely that these concerns had any impact on the election outcome. In August 2004, Justice Minister Cotler appointed Judges Rosalie Abella and Louise Charron from the Ontario Court of Appeal to fill the two vacancies. Pursuant to an all-party agreement, Cotler appeared before an Interim Ad Hoc Committee on the Appointment of Supreme Court Judges; it included seven MPs, a member of the Law Society of Upper Canada (representing Ontario lawyers), and a representative from the Canadian Judicial Council. The purpose of the hearing was to allow the MPs to question the minister about the qualifications of the two nominees; instead, the opposition MPs spent most of their time complaining that the process was too rushed and arguing that the judges should have appeared in person.[219] The two new Justices were approved, despite the political wrangling (although it does not appear that the committee could have vetoed their appointments). They officially joined the Court on August 30.

IMPLEMENTING COURT DECISIONS

Discussions of the Charter's effects on public policy, both positive and negative, are usually premised on the belief that Court rulings have a direct impact on the lives of Canadians. This is a questionable assumption. Appellate courts lack the means to implement their own policies: they control neither the sword (law enforcement) nor the purse (the expenditure of public funds). Courts must rely on other agencies and individuals to put their rulings into effect, a fact which the advent of the Charter did nothing to change. So before we conclude that the entrenchment of rights and freedoms has directly affected the lives of all Canadians, it is as well to take a closer look at the implementation of judicial rulings.[220]

One influential theory of judicial impact focuses on the implementation of Court rulings by other agencies.[221] The authors distinguish among four pop-

ulations that may be affected by a particular judgment: interpreters, implementers, consumers, and the secondary population. Interpreters, as the name implies, are responsible for translating broadly worded judicial opinions into practical rules for conduct. For example, a ruling that changes Canada's election law—e.g., the British Columbia ruling that struck down the election-night "blackout"—is carefully analyzed by the legal experts at Elections Canada. In this instance, they advised the chief electoral officer (CEO) that he could not enforce the "blackout" provisions in the Canada Elections Act while the B.C. ruling was under appeal. Those provisions prohibit the transmission of results from Eastern Canada to Alberta and British Columbia until after the end of voting in those provinces. As a result of the CEO's decision, which was based on the advice of his interpreters, voters on the West coast knew that the Liberals were doing better than expected in the Atlantic and central provinces while they still had time to vote.[222]

Implementers are the individuals and organizations responsible for actually putting court rulings into effect. Lower courts are the most visible implementers of Supreme Court rulings, especially (although not exclusively) in the area of criminal law. If, for example, the Supreme Court decrees that evidence obtained in consequence of a Charter violation is to be excluded, trial judges and provincial appeal courts are expected to comply. In practice, lower courts can find ways to distinguish precedents if they so choose.[223] Outright defiance is rare in Canada, but it has occurred in the United States: judges in some Southern states refused to enforce *Brown v. Board of Education* (discussed earlier) in their local jurisdictions.[224]

Depending on the subject matter of the ruling, other key implementers may include Parliament, a federal government department, police, or immigration officials. Most are situated within the federal or provincial public sector. Although they are bound by their offices to uphold the rule of law, implementers may be unwilling or unable to implement judicial policies. Even if they agree with the spirit of a ruling that directly affects their operations, they may lack the resources to carry it out. In the 1985 *Singh* ruling, the Supreme Court told the federal Department of

Immigration that its refugee-determination procedures did not meet Charter standards of due process. The judgment halted the refugee process in its tracks, created a large backlog of refugee claims (which prompted the government to award landed-immigrant status to 15 000 claimants), and ultimately forced the federal government to spend over $100 million to set up a new system along the lines suggested by the Court.[225]

Consumers are the private individuals or groups who may benefit or suffer from a particular ruling. Some are more directly affected than others. In the 1990 *Rocket* case, for example, the Supreme Court struck down a law that forbade dentists to advertise their services. Dentists who wished to advertise were the direct consumers of the ruling; potential clients who wanted to know which dental services were locally available were the indirect consumers. The impact of a particular ruling on the consumer population varies: some decisions *require* or *forbid* them to do certain things, while others—like the *Rocket* decision—simply *allow* them to do certain things if they so choose. The more people wish to take advantage of new, judicially created opportunities, the greater the real-world impact of the ruling.[226] The size of the potential market for the ruling is determined not by the Court itself, but by social and economic factors beyond its control. It is incorrect, for example, to suggest that hundreds of same-sex couples in Ontario and British Columbia rushed to get married in the summer of 2003[227] *because* courts in those provinces had struck down the common-law rule restricting marriage to heterosexual couples. It is more correct to claim that these couples already wanted to get married, and the court rulings simply removed the legal obstacles.

Finally, the secondary population includes all of the groups and individuals who may (or may not) be interested in a particular ruling, but whose lives are in no way affected by it. Where the consumer population is very small, the secondary population is much larger. The 2002 *Sauvé* ruling from the Supreme Court, which gave federal prisoners the right to vote in national elections, directly affected the approximately 30 000 inmates of Canadian penitentiaries (at least those who were willing and able to cast ballots). The consuming population was a small fraction of the secondary population, although the latter included a lot

of people who were offended by the ruling. In contrast, the 1998 *Thomson Newspapers* ruling, striking down the 72-hour publication ban on polling data immediately before election day, affected every Canadian who watches television news or reads the daily paper. (The secondary population, it is to be hoped, was relatively small.)

The practical impact of a judicial policy depends most heavily on the implementers and the direct consumers. Their attitudes toward a particular ruling will determine whether or not it has any real effect beyond the pages of the Supreme Court Reports. If the implementers tasked with putting a ruling into effect refuse to comply, either wholly or in part, its impact will be blunted.[228] Similarly, consumers who see no need to avail themselves of the opportunities afforded by the Supreme Court will simply ignore a ruling that was intended to help them in some way. The attitudes of implementers and consumers are beyond the control of the Justices. It is therefore doubtful whether most, or indeed any, of the Court's Charter rulings have changed the world in the way their authors may have expected.

Even in the realm of criminal law, which the Court has identified as its own "inherent domain," enforcement of its rulings is far from automatic. In a speech on the occasion of the Charter's twentieth anniversary, then–Justice Iacobucci described its impact on the criminal law from a judicial perspective. He cited the rulings in *Stinchcombe* (requiring full Crown disclosure to the defence), *Askov*, and the Court's jurisprudence on s. 8. Iacobucci was particularly proud of the Court's approach to the exclusionary rule in s. 24(2).[229] The thrust of his remarks was that the Court's Charter rulings had greatly improved both the substance of laws and the procedures of criminal justice.

Unfortunately, the empirical evidence that could either prove or disprove Iacobucci's claims does not exist in Canada. One exception is a study of the *Stinchcombe* ruling, which found that it had "added greatly to the expenses and labours of prosecutors and police."[230] (*Stinchcombe* requires Crown prosecutors in criminal trials to disclose all relevant information to the defence in a timely manner; see Chapter 10, page 312.) In complex criminal cases, disclosure entails photocopying hundreds of pages of documents. Some Crown prosecutors refuse to bear the cost, telling defence attorneys—including those employed by poorly funded legal aid programs—to come to their offices and do the copying themselves. Even if the defence lawyers are willing and able to perform this task, the documents may not provide sufficient information for them to gauge the full nature of the Crown's case—e.g., the credibility of prosecution witnesses or the strategy that prosecutors plan to use in court.

Apart from this study, the only way to estimate the practical effect of the Court's due-process rulings is to study comparable judgments from the U.S. Supreme Court. Like the *Collins* case (Chapter 10, pages 312–15), which set out a strict test for the admissibility of evidence tainted by Charter violations, the 1964 American case of *Mapp v. Ohio* required trial courts to exclude evidence obtained in consequence of a constitutional violation. In its wake, police in some U.S. cities made fewer arrests, fearing that if they took a weak case to trial their evidence would be excluded and the suspect freed. They turned instead to informal techniques of harassment, hoping to discourage crime by making their presence felt. There are anecdotal reports that police officers perjured themselves on the witness stand, concealing the truth about searches and seizures to avoid exclusion.[231] Such behaviour, where it happened, was more likely to be rewarded by police officials than punished. Rosenberg argues that "Supreme Court decisions that impose procedural rules on the police are often seen as aiding criminals and making police work more difficult." Consequently, "any pressure stemming from *Mapp* would most likely be to circumvent rather than to implement the exclusionary rule.... [P]olice organizations have not created incentives for observing the exclusionary rule, or imposed costs for violating it."[232] There are reasons to suspect a similar reaction to *Collins* on this side of the border. In Canada, too, the "police culture" may lead investigators to assume that "the law can be ignored while they are pursuing convictions."[233]

American police forces also found ways to evade the policy established in *Miranda v. Arizona*. The top U.S. court required arresting officers to inform suspects of their rights, emphasizing the right to remain silent and to obtain legal advice before being interrogated. Many police forces quickly issued "caution cards" for officers to read to suspects, to insure compliance with *Miranda*. In some cases, officers complied with the letter of the ruling but not the spirit: they read the "caution card" in a tone that implied that the suspect should not take the contents seriously or were less than cooperative when a suspect asked to call a lawyer.[234] In place of the physical intimidation that the Court had condemned, some officers became skilled in applying psychological pressure during interrogation.[235] The consumers of the ruling were no more likely than the implementers to follow the Court's instructions: instead of remaining silent, most suspects (at least those studied by researchers) believed that invoking their due-process rights "would be a tacit admission of guilt." They thought that it was in their best interests to cooperate with the police.[236] These findings should raise doubts about the efficacy of *Manninen*, *Therens*, *Brydges*, and other Canadian rulings on s. 10(b) of the Charter (discussed in Chapter 10, pages 318–21).[237]

If we accept the premise that a policy-making institution should be able to implement its own policies, the toothlessness of the Supreme Court suggests that its policy reach exceeds its grasp. There is no reason to anticipate that its enforcement powers will increase in the foreseeable future, unless one interprets the recent *Doucet-Boudreau* ruling as a sign that judges have lost patience with implementers and decided to take matters into their own hands. (See Dossier 1.2, pages 15–17.) While some Justices have publicly expressed their dismay at the apparent misinterpretation of their policies,[238] there is no reason to believe that the Supreme Court will embark on a new policy of judicial enforcement. The most that the courts can do is to issue clear reasons for judgment, accompanied by precise remedies that leave little "wiggle room" for reluctant implementers.[239] In so doing, courts must be careful not to intrude inappropriately on the powers of the legislative and executive branches of government. As Chapters 4 and 5 demonstrate, the final word on public policy still issues from the cabinet, which is—at least in principle—accountable to the elected representatives of the people.

CONCLUSION: THE LEGITIMACY OF THE SUPREME COURT IN THE CHARTER ERA

This chapter has suggested that the Supreme Court is not well suited to its expanded policy-making role under the Charter. It further argues that the legitimacy of the institution may depend, in part, on its capacity to adapt to that role. In the Charter's third decade, Canadians seem to hold a generally positive opinion of the Court. Surveys taken in 1987 and 1999 posed the following question: "When the legislature passes a law but the courts say it is unconstitutional on the grounds that it conflicts with the Charter of Rights, who should have the final say, the legislature or the courts?" In both surveys, a little over sixty percent of respondents thought the Court should have the last word.[240] (In reality, as we will see in Chapter 4, this is not always the case.) Canadians, particularly those outside Quebec, were more satisfied with the performance of the highest court than respondents in other Western countries, including the United States.[241]

On the negative side, respondents to the Canadian survey were divided over the Court's "right to decide certain controversial issues"; equal numbers thought it should or should not be reduced. This suggests that the Canadian Court's legitimacy as a policy-making institution is less firmly established than that of its American counterpart. This may be attributed, in part, to the relative novelty of the Charter and to lingering regional distaste for a federally appointed umpire in intergovernmental contests.[242] However, it could also reflect the fact that some Court rulings—particularly those that defend the due-process rights of criminal suspects—conflict with majority opinion (or perhaps with the strongly held views of vocal minorities). At present, Canadians who disagree with specific rulings do not appear to lose faith in the Court as an institution. Over the long term, however, the Court may lose some of its legitimacy if it consistently flouts public opinion.[243]

The problem is that protecting the rights of unpopular minorities is precisely what the Charter requires the Court to do. As Justice Lamer put it, "The Charter is designed to protect the accused from the majority, so the enforcement of the Charter must not be left to that majority."[244] If the legitimacy of the Supreme Court rests, to a degree, on its reflection of popular opinion, it seems to be in a no-win situation. One possible solution is to improve the Court's policy-making capacity by improving its use of extrinsic evidence. Another is to admit a wide range of opinion by granting leave to public-interest intervenors (although this may be problematic; see Chapter 6). A third is to make the appointment process more transparent, perhaps by involving Parliament in the actual choice, so that Canadians who care about our political institutions can feel reassured that the best possible candidates are chosen.

The Court's ability to adapt its decision-making procedures to the demands of the Charter is limited by its primary adjudicative function and by the adversarial norms of the common law. Some important reforms have already been made with regard to the news media and intervenors. More remains to be done. The Court may wish to create a research office, where trained social scientists can assess the credibility of extrinsic evidence. For the reasons given earlier, judicial notice of social facts should be limited; but if a Justice believes that the existing evidentiary record is inadequate to resolve a constitutional or policy question, the research office could provide valuable assistance. It could also assist in implementing Court rulings by clarifying ambiguities in the Court's reasoning. Finally, a dedicated research office could give the Justices a clearer sense of the possible implications of a particular ruling, thus avoiding unpleasant surprises (e.g., the fallout from *Singh* and *Askov*).

In the Charter era, the debate about whether courts should make public policy is moot. Judicial policy-making is a reality. The real issue is whether the policies resulting from Charter challenges are well suited to the realities of Canadian government and society. As Charter jurisprudence matures, and judges become ever more accustomed to the policy challenges posed by entrenched rights and freedoms, there is reason to hope that the quality and implementation of judicial policy will improve. Additionally, as Chapters 4 and 5 demonstrate, the evolving relationship among the three branches of government may reduce the policy-making burden on the courts. Legislators, cabinet ministers, and civil servants are taking their "first-order" Charter duties more seriously than they did in the early years of the Charter. If this trend continues, the "spectre of a judicial 'super-legislature'" may be laid to rest.[245]

GLOSSARY OF KEY TERMS

adjudicative   An adjective used to describe an institution that resolves legal disputes in a definitive manner. When two parties take their dispute before a court, they are asking the court to apply principles of law (whether long-established or new) to their specific case. As mentioned in Chapter 1, page 10, the process of applying broad legal rules to a particular case is called adjudication. It is distinct from legislation, which creates broad rules that will apply to a wide range of circumstances. As discussed in Chapter 1, page 10, the fit between a general rule and a specific circumstance may not be perfect; unless the rule is tailored to fit, injustice may result. That tailoring (which Aristotle termed "equity") is undertaken by adjudicative institutions—e.g., courts and tribunals—on a case-by-case basis. In the process of adjudication, courts establish common-law rules that provide some flexibility in the application of written statutes (just as unwritten constitutional conventions afford necessary flexibility in the operation of a written constitution).

appeals by leave   When an appellate court grants leave to hear an appeal, it chooses to hear a case that raises important legal or constitutional issues. The higher the court, the greater its discretion over its docket and the higher the proportion of appeals by leave. Conversely, a court must hear **appeals by right**; as the term suggests, appellate courts must hear any appellant who is legally entitled to pursue his or her case to the highest level.

bill   The official term for a draft law. When a proposed law is introduced in the legislature by the sponsoring minister, it is given an official number (e.g., Bill C-3 or Bill 101). It is known by that number until it has passed through the legislative process, received royal assent, and been proclaimed into law.

disposition   The outcome of a particular dispute at bar. For example, if a man convicted of a crime wins his appeal at a higher court, the judges will dispose of the case by declaring that his conviction is overturned. In the text of a ruling from the Supreme Court of Canada, the disposition appears in the headnotes immediately after the statement of facts (it is signalled by the word "Held.")

dissent   A judgment, endorsed by a minority of the Justices on a particular panel, that offers a different disposition of the case from that provided by the majority. A minority opinion which accepts the disposition, but reaches it by a different route, is called a concurrence.

extrinsic   Meaning "originating outside of"; in other words, any idea or fact derived from a source other than the text of the Constitution or the impugned statute/action.

extrinsic evidence   Claims of fact presented in litigation that do not arise from the adjudicative record of the case at bar. Examples include the legislative history of an impugned law; historical materials intended to demonstrate the intent of those who drafted a particular constitutional provision; and social-science data concerning the need for, or the practical impact of, a given policy. On the other hand, **intrinsic evidence** is found in the facts of the case at bar or in the wording of a law (which is assumed to be sufficiently clear without reference to the stated intentions of those who drafted it).

intervenors   Groups or individuals with a particular interest in the issues raised by an appeal. Although they are not direct parties to the case, they may seek leave to present written arguments to the court. (See Chapter 6.)

intrinsic evidence   See *extrinsic evidence.*

prima facie   Literally, "on the face of it." When a judge interprets a fact or a phrase *prima facie*, he or she takes its meaning to be self-evident and does not look for extrinsic evidence to support her interpretation.

viva voce A Latin term meaning, roughly, "live and in person." In legal terms, it refers to the testimony of a witness who appears in the courtroom and may be cross-examined by opposing counsel.

DISCUSSION AND REVIEW QUESTIONS

1. Identify three types of extrinsic evidence that may be used in Charter cases. Give one example of each type of evidence, using the cases discussed in this book.

2. This chapter argues that the Supreme Court of Canada lacks the institutional capacity to make and enforce good public policy. Identify and briefly explain two of the problems discussed in this chapter. How, if at all, can these problems be fixed?

3. Briefly describe the progress of a case through the Supreme Court of Canada, from the motion seeking leave to appeal through to the disposition and the remedy.

4. Explain the traditional process of appointment to the Supreme Court of Canada. In your view, should the process be changed? If so, how and why?

5. What is the role of implementers in relation to a particular court ruling? Do they always carry out their court-imposed duties as expected? Why or why not? If they do not, what are the implications for judicial policy-making?

6. Is it appropriate for a judge to bring his or her own experiences and viewpoint to bear in interpreting the Charter? Why or why not?

7. Briefly define the term "judicial activism." Is the Supreme Court of Canada an "activist" court in your view? Why or why not?

8. Identify and briefly describe four major principles of Charter interpretation, as developed by the Supreme Court of Canada. In your opinion, do any or all of these principles give the Justices too much influence over the substance of public policy? Why or why not?

SUGGESTED READINGS

Anderson, Ellen. *Judging Bertha Wilson: Law as Large as Life.* Toronto: University of Toronto Press/Osgoode Society for Canadian Legal History, 2001.

Bogart, W.A. *Courts and Country: The Limits of Litigation and the Social and Political Life of Canada.* Toronto: Oxford University Press, 1994.

Cardozo, Benjamin N. *The Nature of the Judicial Process.* New Haven: Yale University Press, 1921.

Golding, Martin P. *Legal Reasoning.* Peterborough: Broadview Press, 2001.

Greene, Ian, Carl Baar, Peter McCormick, George Szablowski, and Martin Thomas. *Final Appeal: Decision-Making in Canadian Courts of Appeal.* Toronto: Lorimer, 1998.

Horowitz, Donald L. *The Courts and Social Policy.* Washington, DC: Brookings Institution, 1977.

Howe, Paul, and Peter H. Russell, eds. *Judicial Power and Canadian Democracy.* Montreal and Kingston: McGill-Queen's University Press/ Institute for Research in Public Policy, 2001.

Kelly, James B. "The Charter of Rights and Freedoms and the Rebalancing of Liberal Constitutionalism in Canada, 1982–1997." *Osgoode Hall Law Journal* 37 (1999), pp. 625–91.

Magnet, Joseph Eliot, Gérald-A. Beaudoin, Gerald Gall, and Christopher Manfredi, eds. *The Canadian Charter of Rights and Freedoms: Reflections on the Charter after Twenty Years.* Toronto: Butterworths, 2003.

McAllister, Debra M. *Taking the Charter to Court: A Practitioner's Analysis.* Victoria: Trafford, 2001.

McCormick, Peter. *Supreme at Last: The Evolution of the Supreme Court of Canada.* Toronto: Lorimer, 2000.

Mellon, Hugh, and Martin Westmacott, eds. *Political Dispute and Judicial Review: Assessing the Work of the Supreme Court of Canada.* Toronto: Nelson, 2000.

Monahan, John, and Laurens Walker, eds. *Social Science in Law.* 5th ed. New York: Foundation Press, 2002.

Rosenberg, Gerald N. *The Hollow Hope: Can Courts Bring about Social Change?* Chicago: University of Chicago Press, 1991.

Russell, Peter H. "The Effect of a Charter of Rights on the Policy-Making Role of Canadian Courts." *Canadian Public Administration* 25, no. 1 (Spring 1982), pp. 2–13.

Sharpe, Robert J., ed. *Charter Litigation.* Toronto: Butterworths, 1987.

————, and Kent Roach. *Brian Dickson: A Judge's Journey.* Toronto: University of Toronto Press/ Osgoode Society for Canadian Legal History, 2003.

Snell, James G., and Frederick Vaughan. *The Supreme Court of Canada: History of the Institution.* Toronto: University of Toronto Press/Osgoode Society, 1985.

Sunstein, Cass R. *One Case at a Time: Judicial Minimalism on the Supreme Court.* Cambridge, MA: Harvard University Press, 1999.

Wilson, Bertha. "Decision-Making in the Supreme Court." *University of Toronto Law Journal* 36 (1986), pp. 227–48.

ENDNOTES

1. *Hunter v. Southam Inc.,* [1984] 2 S.C.R. 145, p. 155, *per* Dickson J. (as he then was).

2. Retired Supreme Court Justice Claire L'Heureux-Dubé, testifying before the House of Commons Standing Committee on Justice, Human Rights, Public Safety and Emergency Preparedness, March 30, 2004, available online at www.parl.gc.ca.

3. Peter H. Russell, "The Effect of a Charter of Rights on the Policy-Making Role of Canadian Courts," *Canadian Public Administration* 25, no. 1 (Spring 1982), pp. 2–13; Kent Roach, *The Supreme Court on Trial: Judicial Activism or Democratic Dialogue?* (Toronto: Irwin Law, 2001), pp. 254–63.

4. *Re B.C. Motor Vehicle Act,* [1985] 2 S.C.R. 486, paragraphs 15–16, *per* Lamer J. (as he then was).

5. F.L. Morton, Peter H. Russell, and Troy Riddell, "The Canadian Charter of Rights and Freedoms: A Descriptive Analysis of the First Decade, 1982–1992," *National Journal of Constitutional Law* 5 (1995), p. 5.

6. All four of the Charter rulings issued in 1984 were signed by every Justice on the panel (although the full complement of nine Justices did not sit on any of these appeals). That unanimity rate of 100 percent fell to 82 percent for the eleven rulings issued in 1985. In 1986, the rate sank to 55 percent, as the Court struggled to build consensus among judges with very different approaches to the Charter. See F.L. Morton, Peter H. Russell, and Michael J. Withey, "The Supreme Court's First One Hundred Charter of Rights Decisions: A Statistical Analysis," *Osgoode Hall Law Journal* 30 (1992), p. 37, Table 11.

7. Morton, Russell, and Withey, "The Supreme Court's First One Hundred," p. 10.

8. F.L. Morton and Rainer Knopff, *The Charter Revolution and the Court Party* (Peterborough: Broadview Press, 2000), pp. 53–54.

9. Cass R. Sunstein, *One Case at a Time: Judicial Minimalism on the Supreme Court* (Cambridge, MA: Harvard University Press, 1999), pp. 9–10.

10. Sunstein, *One Case,* Chapter 1. Although Sunstein argues that judicial minimalism is, on the whole, more consistent with the separation of powers in the American Constitution (because it leaves as much as possible to be decided by the elected branches), he acknowledges that it is not entirely compatible with the common-law tradition that the United States (and Canada) inherited from Great Britain.

11. Robert J. Sharpe and Kent Roach, *Brian Dickson: A Judge's Journey* (Toronto: University of Toronto Press/Osgoode Society for Canadian Legal History, 2003), pp. 310–13.

12. There are, of course, notable exceptions. Some individual Justices, particularly Dickson, Wilson, and L'Heureux-Dubé, took a consistently maximalist approach. For example, Wilson often cited philosophers (especially John Stuart Mill) in her rulings. More recently, former Justice Arbour tried to carve out new realms of jurisprudence by questioning the fundamental principles adopted in earlier cases— for example, the assumption that s. 7 does not impose positive duties on the state. Her inability to persuade the rest of the Court may have prompted her to resign from the Court in 2004 to take up a senior position at the United Nations.

13. *Law Society of Upper Canada v. Skapinker*, [1984] 1 S.C.R. 358, p. 383.

14. Their analysis of the twenty-six cases involving provincial laws will not be discussed here because of the methodological problems discussed in Chapter 7, pages 232–34.

15. Morton, Russell, and Withey, "The Supreme Court's First One Hundred," p. 25, Table 7.

16. Ibid., p. 25.

17. See, e.g., Christopher P. Manfredi, *Judicial Power and the Charter: Canada and the Paradox of Liberal Constitutionalism*, 2nd ed. (Toronto: Oxford University Press, 2001); Rainer Knopff and F.L. Morton, *Charter Politics* (Scarborough: Nelson, 1992); Morton and Knopff, *The Charter Revolution and the Court Party*.

18. Three sections of the Narcotics Control Act were nullified. They dealt with the reverse onus on persons suspected of trafficking (*R. v. Oakes*), the "writs of assistance" that permitted warrantless searches for drugs (*R. v. Hamill*), and the minimum sentences for drug offences (*R. v. Smith*). Two sections of the Criminal Code—the offence of "constructive murder" and the law regulating abortion—met the same fate (in *R. v. Vaillancourt* and *R. v. Morgentaler*, respectively). The Court also struck down a section of the Combines Investigation Act that permitted warrantless search and seizure (*Hunter v. Southam*); parts of the Immigration Act dealing with the procedure for handling refugee claims (*Singh*); and the Lord's Day Act, which forced retail businesses to close on Sundays (*Big M Drug Mart*). Morton, Russell, and Withey, "The Supreme Court's First One Hundred," p. 27, Table 8.

19. James B. Kelly, "The Charter of Rights and Freedoms and the Rebalancing of Liberal Constitutionalism in Canada, 1982–1997," *Osgoode Hall Law Journal* 37 (1999), pp. 625–91.

20. James B. Kelly, "Bureaucratic Activism and the Charter of Rights and Freedoms: The Department of Justice and Its Entry into the Centre of Government," *Canadian Public Administration* 42, no. 4 (Winter 1999), p. 506.

21. Brian Slattery, "A Theory of the Charter," *Osgoode Hall Law Journal* 25 (1987), p. 707 (emphasis in original).

22. See, e.g., Kelly, "The Charter of Rights and Freedoms," p. 683; Roach, *The Supreme Court on Trial*, pp. 89–95 and 284; David M. Paciocco, "Competing Constitutional Rights in an Age of Deference: A Bad Time to Be Accused," *Supreme Court Law Review* 14 (2d) (2001), pp. 111–37.

23. Janet L. Hiebert, *Limiting Rights: The Dilemma of Judicial Review* (Montreal and Kingston: McGill-Queen's University Press, 1996), p. 125.

24. *Sauvé v. Canada (Chief Electoral Officer)*, [2002] 3 S.C.R. 519.

25. *Vriend v. Alberta*, [1998] 1 S.C.R. 493, paragraphs 198–99.

26. *R. v. Mills*, [1999] 3 S.C.R. 668; *Gosselin v. Quebec (Attorney General)*, [2002] 4 S.C.R. 429.

27. See, e.g., *Egan v. Canada*, [1995] 2 S.C.R. 513; *Rodriguez v. British Columbia (Attorney General)*, [1993] 3 S.C.R. 519.

28. Patrick J. Monahan, "Constitutional Cases 2000: An Overview," *Supreme Court Law Review* 14 (2d) (2001), p. 1; Kelly, "The Charter of Rights and Freedoms," p. 639, Table 1. In 2003, Charter cases accounted for only sixteen percent of all appeals heard by the Court. See Supreme Court of Canada, "Statistics: 1993 to 2003" (Bulletin of Proceedings Special Edition), available on the Court's website (www.scc-csc.gc.ca).

29. Supreme Court of Canada, "Statistics," p. 9.

30. Appeals in which the plaintiff alleges an infringement of s. 15 (equality rights) have been particularly divisive. The 1995 *Egan* case (the entitlement of same-sex couples to pension benefits) generated no fewer than five separate decisions, as did the 2002 *Gosselin* case (age discrimination in entitlement to welfare benefits). See the discussion in Chapter 11, pages 346–50.

31. Kelly, "The Charter of Rights and Freedoms," p. 668, Table 12.

32. This is the view of several past Supreme Court Justices, including former Chief Justices Laskin and Dickson and former Justices McIntyre and Cory. See Ellen Anderson, *Judging Bertha Wilson: Law as Large as Life* (Toronto: University of Toronto Press/Osgoode Society for Canadian Legal History, 2001), pp. 154–55; Sharpe and Roach, *Brian Dickson*, p. 312. See also the views of recently retired Justice Frank Iacobucci, in his article "The Charter: Twenty Years Later," in Joseph Eliot Magnet, Gérald-A. Beaudoin, Gerald Gall, and Christopher Manfredi, eds., *The Canadian Charter of Rights and Freedoms: Reflections on the Charter after Twenty Years* (Toronto: Butterworths, 2003), p. 395.

33. Some Justices argue that unanimity should not be achieved at the expense of individual conscience and flexibility in the development of the common law. See Anderson, *Judging Bertha Wilson*, p. 154. See also Ian Greene, Carl Baar, Peter McCormick, George Szablowski, and Martin Thomas, *Final Appeal: Decision-Making in Canadian Courts of Appeal* (Toronto: Lorimer, 1998), p. 121.

34. Morton, Russell, and Riddell, "The Canadian Charter of Rights and Freedoms," p. 33, Table 11.

35. Supreme Court of Canada, "Statistics," p. 4.

36. Kelly, "The Charter of Rights and Freedoms," p. 666.

37. See, for example, the debate between Chief Justice McLachlin and former Justice Gonthier in *Sauvé v. Canada (Chief Electoral Officer)*, and the conflict between Justices Sopinka and Cory in *Egan v. Canada*.

38. Morton, Russell, and Withey, "The Supreme Court's First One Hundred," p. 47.

39. Greene et al., *Final Appeal*, p. 115; Andrew Heard, "The Charter in the Supreme Court of Canada: The Importance of Which Judges Hear an Appeal," *Canadian Journal of Political Science* 24, no. 2 (June 1991), pp. 289–307.

40. Sharpe and Roach, *Brian Dickson*, p. 371.

41. Ibid., pp. 372–73 and 427–30.

42. Ibid., pp. 374–75.

43. The immensity of the task undertaken by these four Justices can be fully appreciated only if one understands that Dickson was an amputee—he had lost a leg in World War II—who had difficulty walking, and Wilson was plagued with severe arthritis that hampered her mobility as well.

44. Greene et al., *Final Appeal*, p. 115.

45. Ibid., p. 115; Kelly, "The Charter of Rights and Freedoms," p. 684, Table 19.

46. Greene et al., *Final Appeal*, p. 115.

47. Notable examples include the 1987 *Alberta Labour Reference* (1 S.C.R. 313), the 1990 *Prostitution Reference* (1 S.C.R. 1123), and the 2003 reference on same-sex marriage (which had not been heard at the time of writing).

48. F.L. Morton, "Judicial Decision-Making," in F.L. Morton, ed., *Law, Politics and the Judicial Process in Canada*, 2nd ed. (Calgary: University of Calgary Press, 1992), p. 438; James G. Snell and Frederick Vaughan, *The Supreme Court of Canada: History of the Institution* (Toronto: University of Toronto Press/Osgoode Society, 1985), p. 233.

49. Anyone convicted of a criminal offence may seek leave to appeal to the provincial appellate court. If the conviction is upheld unanimously, there is no right of appeal to the Supreme Court of Canada (although the plaintiff may seek leave to appeal). However, if one or more provincial appeal judges dissents on a question of law, or the appeal court has entered a conviction following the Crown's appeal of an acquittal at trial, the plaintiff has the right to appeal the majority ruling to the highest court without seeking leave. Criminal Code of Canada, ss. 675 and 691.

50. Supreme Court of Canada, "Statistics," p. 4.

51. Charles R. Epp, "Do Bills of Rights Matter? The Canadian Charter of Rights and Freedoms," *American Political Science Review* 90, no. 4 (December 1996), pp. 768, 771, and 775; Charles R. Epp, *The Rights Revolution: Lawyers, Activists, and Supreme Courts in Comparative Perspective* (Chicago: University of Chicago Press, 1998), pp. 14–15.

52. Roy B. Flemming, "Processing Appeals for Judicial Review: The Institutions of Agenda Setting in the Supreme Courts of Canada and the United States," in Hugh Mellon and Martin Westmacott, eds., *Political Dispute and Judicial Review: Assessing the Work of the Supreme Court of Canada* (Toronto: Nelson, 2000), p. 42.

53. Paraphrased in Flemming, "Processing Appeals," pp. 44–45.

54. Kelly, "The Charter of Rights and Freedoms," pp. 641–43; Morton, Russell, and Riddell, "The Canadian Charter of Rights and Freedoms," p. 10.

55. Greene et al., *Final Appeal*, p. 107; Supreme Court of Canada, "Statistics," p. 4.

56. Flemming, "Processing Appeals," p.50.

57. Ibid., p. 53.

58. Ibid., p. 53.

59. Ibid., p. 53.

60. Anderson, *Judging Bertha Wilson*, p. 156; Lorne Sossin, "The Sounds of Silence: Law Clerks, Policy-Making and the Supreme Court of Canada," *University of British Columbia Law Review* 30 (1996), p. 284.

61. Sossin, "The Sounds of Silence," p. 289.

62. Greene et al., *Final Appeal*, p. 110.

63. Anderson cites the example of Bertha Wilson, who fought for leave to hear a case involving the adoption of a young Indian child by a mixed-race couple (*Judging Bertha Wilson*, p. 189).

64. Greene et al., *Final Appeal*, pp. 110–11.

65. Flemming, "Processing Appeals," p. 57.

66. Ibid., p. 48.

67. Supreme Court of Canada, "Statistics," p. 4.

68. For a useful discussion of this principle, see the majority opinion of Justices Iacobucci and Bastarache in *Housen v. Nikolaisen*, [2002], 2 S.C.R. 235.

69. *Housen v. Nikolaisen*, paragraph 9.

70. The Court's internal battle over intervenors is described in Sharpe and Roach, *Brian Dickson*, pp. 383–89.

71. Ian Brodie, *Friends of the Court: The Privileging of Interest-Group Litigants in Canada* (Albany: State University of New York Press, 2002), p. 35; "Rules of the Supreme Court of Canada," section 42(5), available online at www.scc-csc.gc.ca.

72. Greene et al., *Final Appeal*, p. 230, note 13.

73. Ibid., p. 118.

74. Sossin, "The Sounds of Silence," p. 292.

75. L'Heureux-Dubé, testifying, March 30, 2004. The same figure is cited by the Justices interviewed by Greene et al., *Final Appeal* (p. 123).

76. Bertha Wilson, "Decision-Making in the Supreme Court," *University of Toronto Law Journal* 36 (1986), p. 236.

77. Sharpe and Roach, *Brian Dickson*, p. 312.

78. Sharpe and Roach relate a story about former Justice Wilson, whose approach to the *Operation Dismantle* case (Dossier 5.2, pages 187–88) changed significantly after she had been assigned to write the majority opinion. At the post-hearing conference, she had argued that the issues raised by the plaintiffs were "non-justiciable" and that the Court had no business dealing with them. As she considered her reasons, she "reversed her position at conference" and decided to issue "a strong assertion of the Court's power to vindicate Charter rights even where highly contentious political issues were at play." (*Brian Dickson*, p. 329) After exchanging a flurry of memos, Chief Justice Dickson decided that he could not support her reasoning; he authored the majority judgment and Wilson's opinion was left as a solo concurrence.

79. L'Heureux-Dubé, testifying, March 30, 2004.

80. Sharpe and Roach, *Brian Dickson*, pp. 393–94.

81. *Tremblay v. Daigle*, [1989] 2 S.C.R. 530.

82. Wilson, "Decision-Making," p. 237. However, at least one of Wilson's colleagues felt differently; former Justice McIntyre recalled that he read and signed judgments whenever they reached his desk, without regard for "who was agreeing and who was disagreeing." Quoted in Anderson, *Judging Bertha Wilson*, p. 163.

83. Kirk Makin, "Top Court Judge Defends Bench: Retiring Justice Peter Cory Speaks Out against Grilling of Potential Jurists," *The Globe and Mail*, March 3, 1999, p. A5, quoted in Hugh Mellon, "Introduction: Appreciating the Supreme Court's National Significance," in Mellon and Westmacott, *Political Dispute*, p. 13.

84. Quoted in Wilson, "Decision-Making," p. 237.

85. Wilson, "Decision-Making," p. 237.

86. Anderson, *Judging Bertha Wilson*, p. 162.

87. Ibid., pp. 162 and 164–65.

88. Sossin, "The Sounds of Silence," p. 295, note 48.

89. The 1988 *Morgentaler* ruling, which contained four separate opinions, was finally issued fifteen months after the hearing; even taking into account the illness of two Justices on the panel (Beetz and Estey), much of that delay can be attributed to the divisiveness of the abortion issue. The five rulings in *Gosselin* (2002) were issued almost fourteen months after the hearing, at a time when the Court's membership was stable and all the Justices were apparently healthy.

90. The *Law* ruling, in which Iacobucci J. attempted to create a consensus on s. 15 of the Charter, took fifteen months from the first hearing to the judgment. Seven Justices attended the first hearing in January 1998. A

second hearing, attended by all nine Justices, was held in December 1998. The opinion appeared in March 1999. In contrast, the 2003 *Malmo-Levine* and *Clay* rulings upholding the law against marijuana possession appeared seven and a half months after the hearings. Even though the issue was hotly debated among Canadians, and had divided provincial appellate judges, the Supreme Court relied on the established jurisprudence on s. 7 to resolve the cases quickly.

91. Supreme Court of Canada, "Statistics," p. 4.

92. Peter McCormick, testimony before the House of Commons Standing Committee on Justice, Human Rights, Public Safety and Emergency Preparedness, April 1, 2004.

93. On this point, see Robert H. Bork, "Neutral Principles and Some First Amendment Problems," *Indiana Law Journal* 47 (1971–72), pp. 2–3.

94. Martin P. Golding, *Legal Reasoning* (Peterborough: Broadview Press, 2001), p. 98.

95. For the classic arguments on this point, see Jerome Frank, *Law and the Modern Mind* (New York: Anchor/Doubleday, 1963 [1930]). See also Jerome Frank, *Courts on Trial: Myth and Reality in American Justice* (Princeton: Princeton University Press, 1949), especially Chapters 10 and 11.

96. For one particularly striking example, see the discussion of Justice Bastarache's ruling in *Beaulac* (Chapter 12, page 376).

97. Benjamin N. Cardozo, *The Nature of the Judicial Process* (New Haven: Yale University Press, 1921), pp. 12–13.

98. See, e.g., Robert Martin, "Ideology and Judging," *Osgoode Hall Jaw Journal* 26 (1988), pp. 803–06; Michael Mandel, *The Charter of Rights and the Legalization of Politics in Canada*, 3rd ed. (Toronto: Thompson, 1994).

99. Greene et al., *Final Appeal*, pp. 23–24.

100. Bertha Wilson, "Will Women Judges Make a Difference?" *Osgoode Hall Law Journal* 26 (1990), pp. 507–22.

101. C.L. Ostberg, Matthew E. Wetstein, and Craig R. Ducat, "Attitudinal Dimensions of Supreme Court Decision Making in Canada: The Lamer Court, 1991–1995," *Political Research Quarterly* 55, no. 1 (March 2002), pp. 235–56.

102. Peter McCormick, *Supreme at Last: The Evolution of the Supreme Court of Canada* (Toronto: Lorimer, 2000), pp. 134–38.

103. Roach, *The Supreme Court on Trial*, p. 213.

104. Greene et al., *Final Appeal*, pp. 104–5. The authors point out that even lower-court judges will avoid following Supreme Court precedents in cases where *stare decisis* would produce an unjust result; see p. 201.

105. Greene et al., *Final Appeal*, pp. 207–8.

106. Ibid., p. 199; Cardozo, *The Nature*, pp. 20–21.

107. *Hunter v. Southam Inc.*, pp. 156–57.

108. *R. v. Big M Drug Mart Ltd.*, [1985] 1 S.C.R. 295, paragraph 117.

109. *Edmonton Journal v. Alberta (Attorney General)*, [1989] 2 S.C.R. 1326, paragraphs 51–52.

110. See, e.g., *R. v. Keegstra*, [1990] 3 S.C.R. 697, *per* Dickson C.J.; *Rocket v. Royal College of Dental Surgeons of Ontario*, [1990] 2 S.C.R. 232, *per* McLachlin J. (as she then was); *Thomson Newspapers Co. v. Canada (Attorney General)*, [1998] 1 S.C.R. 877, *per* Bastarache J.

111. *Dubois v. The Queen*, [1985] 2 S.C.R. 350, paragraph 9.

112. *Keegstra*, paragraphs 75–76.

113. *Thomson Newspapers* (1998), *per* Bastarache J.

114. The insistence on evaluating the effects of legislation is most associated with former Justice Wilson. Her strongest argument in favour of the "effects-oriented" approach can be found in her article "The Making of a Constitution: Approaches to Judicial Interpretation," *Public Law* (Autumn 1988), pp. 370–401.

115. Sharpe and Roach, *Brian Dickson*, p. 352.

116. *Big M Drug Mart*, paragraphs 80 and 88.

117. *Irwin Toy Ltd. v. Quebec (Attorney General)*, [1989] 1 S.C.R. 927, paragraphs 46–54, *per* Dickson C.J. and Wilson and Lamer JJ.

118. *R. v. Morgentaler*, [1988] 1 S.C.R. 30, paragraphs 32–33.

119. Knopff and Morton, *Charter Politics*, p. 131; Morton and Knopff, *The Charter Revolution and the Court Party*, p. 50.

120. Peter H. Russell, "Canada's Charter of Rights and Freedoms: A Political Report," *Public Law* (Autumn 1988), p. 395.

121. Manfredi, *Judicial Power*, pp. 33–35.

122. Robert E. Hawkins and Robert Martin, "Democracy, Judging and Bertha Wilson," *McGill Law Journal* 41 (1995–96), p. 36.

123. Russell, "Canada's Charter of Rights and Freedoms," p. 394.

124. Manfredi, *Judicial Power*, p. 153.

125. See, e.g., Morton and Knopff, *The Charter Revolution and the Court Party*, Chapter 2; Michael Mandel, *The Charter of Rights & the Legalization of Politics in Canada*, rev. ed. (Toronto: Thompson, 1994), Chapter 2.

126. Manfredi, *Judicial Power*, Chapter 6.

127. Morton and Knopff, *The Charter Revolution and the Court Party*, p. 38.

128. Bertha Wilson, "We Didn't Volunteer," in Paul Howe and Peter H. Russell, eds., *Judicial Power and Canadian Democracy* (Montreal and Kingston: McGill-Queen's University Press/Institute for Research in Public Policy, 2001), p. 75.

129. Manfredi, *Judicial Power*, p. 156. See also Donald L. Horowitz, *The Courts and Social Policy* (Washington, DC: Brookings Institution, 1977), especially Chapters 2 and 7.

130. See *Skapinker* and *Hunter v. Southam*.

131. *R. v. Edwards Books and Art Ltd.*, [1986] 2 S.C.R. 713, paragraphs 101–02.

132. *MacKay v. Manitoba*, [1989] 2 S.C.R. 357, paragraphs 8–9.

133. Manfredi, *Judicial Power*, p. 25. On "originalism," see Peter W. Hogg, "Legislative History in Constitutional Cases," in Robert J. Sharpe, ed., *Charter Litigation* (Toronto: Butterworths, 1987), p. 151. See also John Hart Ely, *Democracy and Distrust: A Theory of Judicial Review* (Cambridge, MA: Harvard University Press, 1980), Chapter 1.

134. Robert H. Bork, *The Tempting of America: The Political Seduction of the Law* (New York: Free Press, 1990), pp. 153 and 176.

135. See the survey of various noninterpretivist theories in Terri Jennings Peretti, *In Defense of a Political Court* (Princeton: Princeton University Press, 1999), pp. 20–24 and 30–32.

136. Manfredi, *Judicial Power*, pp. 28–30. See also Robert H. Bork, "Neutral Principles," pp. 1–35; Robert H. Bork, "Styles in Constitutional Theory," *South Texas Law Journal* 26 (1985), pp. 383–95.

137. Wilson, "The Making of a Constitution," pp. 375–377.

138. Morton and Knopff, *The Charter Revolution and the Court Party*, pp. 45–47.

139. Wilson, "The Making of a Constitution," p. 380.

140. Hogg, "Legislative History in Constitutional Cases," pp. 152–54.

141. *Reference re Upper Churchill Water Rights Reversion Act,* [1984] 1 S.C.R. 297, *per* McIntyre J., p. 319; reproduced in *B.C. Motor Vehicle,* paragraph 48, *per* Lamer J.

142. See, e.g., Lorraine Weinrib, "The Activist Constitution," in Howe and Russell, *Judicial Power,* pp. 80–86; Beverley McLachlin, "Courts, Legislatures and Executives in the Post-Charter Era," in Howe and Russell, *Judicial Power,* pp. 63–72; Patrick Monahan, "Judicial Review and Democracy" (1985, unpublished), cited in Hogg, "Legislative History in Constitutional Cases," p. 156.

143. See, e.g., Patrick J. Monahan, *Politics and the Constitution: The Charter, Federalism and the Supreme Court of Canada* (Toronto: Carswell, 1987), pp. 78–79.

144. Roach, *The Supreme Court on Trial,* p. 219.

145. Morton and Knopff, *The Charter Revolution and the Court Party,* pp. 42–44.

146. Hogg, "Legislative History in Constitutional Cases," pp. 145–47.

147. Ibid., pp. 146–47.

148. Ibid., pp. 131–32.

149. F.L. Morton and Ian Brodie, "The Use of Extrinsic Evidence in Charter Litigation before the Supreme Court of Canada," *National Journal of Constitutional Law* 3 (1993), p. 13, Table 1.

150. Debra M. McAllister, *Taking the Charter to Court: A Practitioner's Analysis* (Victoria: Trafford, 2001), volume 2, 17.4(c)(ii) (pp. 17–24).

151. Janet L. Hiebert, *Charter Conflicts: What Is Parliament's Role?* (Montreal and Kingston: McGill-Queen's University Press, 2002),

Chapter 3. See also Chapters 4 and 5 in this volume.

152. On the use of preambles to preempt the Supreme Court, see Kent Roach, *Due Process and Victims' Rights: The New Law and Politics of Criminal Justice* (Toronto: University of Toronto Press, 1999), pp. 174, 179, and 186–87.

153. *RJR-MacDonald Inc. v. Canada (Attorney General),* [1995] 3 S.C.R. 199, paragraph 160.

154. *Morgentaler,* paragraphs 234, 255, and 258.

155. Justice Bastarache, in his majority ruling in *Thomson Newspapers* (1998), struck down a section of the Canada Elections Act that banned the publication of new polling results in the last 72 hours before an election. He noted that the Royal Commission on Electoral Reform and Party Financing had recommended a 24-hour ban coupled with the mandatory disclosure of methodological information, and implied that the federal government should have followed this advice (paragraph 119). After the *Thomson* ruling, it did so.

156. Morton and Knopff regard judicial reliance on law journals as proof that "post-materialists" and "elitists" have hijacked the Charter for their own purposes. They argue that "the advocacy scholarship of Court Party academics" is designed to encourage and legitimize activist rulings from appellate judges. See *The Charter Revolution and the Court Party,* Chapters 2 and 6.

157. See, e.g., Brian G. Morgan, "Proof of Facts in Charter Litigation," in Sharpe, *Charter Litigation,* pp. 163–64; Manfredi, *Judicial Power,* pp. 156–57.

158. Morton and Brodie, "The Use of Extrinsic Evidence," p. 5; Wilson, "Decision-Making in the Supreme Court," p. 244.

159. Peter H. Russell, "The Effect of a Charter of Rights," pp. 1–33.

160. Morton and Brodie, "The Use of Extrinsic Evidence," pp. 5–6; Katherine Swinton, "What Do the Courts Want from the Social Sciences?" in Sharpe, *Charter Litigation*, pp. 187–89.

161. Rosemary J. Erickson and Rita J. Simon, *The Use of Social Science Data in Supreme Court Decisions* (Chicago: University of Illinois Press, 1998), pp. 12–13.

162. "The Effects of Segregation and the Consequences of Desegregation: A Social Science Statement," Appendix to Appellants' Briefs in *Brown v. Board of Education of Topeka*, 347 U.S. 483 (1954), excerpt reproduced in John Monahan and Laurens Walker, eds., *Social Science in Law*, 5th ed. (New York: Foundation Press, 2002), pp. 194–97. See also Erickson and Simon, *The Use of Social Science Data*, pp. 15–16.

163. Erickson and Simon, *The Use of Social Science Data*, p. 151.

164. Swinton, "What Do the Courts Want," p. 203. The study in question was "Racial Identification and Preference in Negro Children," by Kenneth B. Clark and Mamie P. Clark. The authors asked a sample of 253 Black children whether they would rather play with "Negro" dolls or white dolls. The choice of doll was interpreted as an indicator of racial self-esteem: a higher preference for the white doll indicated feelings of low self-esteem. They found that children in Southern segregated schools had more positive feelings toward the "Negro" doll than those in Northern integrated schools, where Black and white children mixed. Although this finding suggested that Black children in Black-only schools felt better about themselves than those who were education with whites—which would tend to support the "separate but equal" doctrine—the Clarks testified in court that "segregation inflicts injuries upon the Negro." See an excerpt from the Clark study, and a discussion of its failings, in Monahan and Walker, *Social Science in Law*, pp. 189–94, and the methodological critiques by Swinton (at p. 203) and Horowitz (*The Courts and Social Policy*, p. 278).

165. The academic literature on *Brown* is too voluminous to cite here. A good place to start is the recent debate between Earl Maltz and Walter F. Murphy over the sources of the Court's opinion. See Maltz, "*Brown v. Board of Education* and 'Originalism,'" in Robert P. George, ed., *Great Cases in Constitutional Law* (Princeton: Princeton University Press, 2000), pp. 136–53, and Murphy, "Originalism—The Deceptive Evil: *Brown v. Board of Education*," in George, *Great Cases*, pp. 154–74. For a useful review of recent books on the case, see Cass R. Sunstein, "Did Brown Matter?" *The New Yorker*, May 3, 2004.

166. See, e.g., Manfredi, *Judicial Power*, pp. 156–60; Morton and Knopff, *The Charter Revolution and the Court Party*, pp. 142–42; Swinton, "What Do the Courts Want," pp. 203–10; Morgan, "Proof of Facts," p. 161; Morton and Brodie, "The Use of Extrinsic Evidence," p. 4.

167. Horowitz, *The Courts and Social Policy*, p. 45.

168. *Harrison v. Carswell*, [1976] 2 S.C.R. 200.

169. Brian Dickson, "The Development of a Distinctively Canadian Jurisprudence," Faculty of Law, Dalhousie University, Halifax, October 29, 1983, quoted in Sharpe in Roach, *Brian Dickson*, p. 310.

170. Brian Dickson, "The Public Responsibilities of Lawyers," *Manitoba Law Journal* 13 (1983), p. 186, quoted in Sharpe and Roach, *Brian Dickson*, p. 310.

171. *Irwin Toy*, paragraph 78, *per* Dickson C.J. and Lamer and Wilson JJ.

172. Ibid., paragraph 79.

173. *B.C. Motor Vehicle*, paragraph 31, *per* Lamer J.

174. *McKinney v. University of Guelph*, [1990] 3 S.C.R. 229, paragraph 105. La Forest's majority judgment illustrated this principle

well: it included an extensive historical discussion of policies concerning mandatory retirement.

175. *RJR-MacDonald*, paragraphs 68 and 70.

176. Ibid., paragraphs 79–80.

177. Ibid., paragraph 136.

178. Ibid., paragraph 141.

179. Brandeis's success was noteworthy not merely for his innovatory use of evidence, but because he had persuaded a notoriously *laissez-faire* Court to endorse a progressive law aimed at improving the lives of workers. See the discussion of *Error Muller v. Oregon*, 208 U.S. 412 (1908), in Monahan and Walker, *Social Science in Law*, pp. 4–11.

180. Morgan, "Proof of Facts," pp. 177–78.

181. See ibid., pp. 174–79.

182. Horowitz, *The Courts and Social Policy*, p. 50.

183. Clause 90 of the Supreme Court Rules permits any party to an appeal, with the permission of a judge or the court registrar, to cross-examine the author of an affidavit submitted in evidence by another party. The cross-examination must take place before a person designated by the Court, and the transcript must be filed with the registrar within ten days. Refusal to submit to cross-examination, where a request has been made, results in the automatic removal of the affidavit from the record of the case. It is not known how often this procedure is invoked.

184. Morgan, "Proof of Facts," p. 171.

185. Horowitz, *The Courts and Social Policy*, pp. 49–50.

186. Morgan, "Proof of Facts," pp. 172–73.

187. Susan Delacourt, "The Media and the Supreme Court of Canada," in Mellon and Westmacott, *Political Dispute*, p. 32.

188. James W. O'Reilly, "The Supreme Court of Canada and the Media," *St. Louis University Law Journal* 42 (1997–98), p. 1191.

189. O'Reilly, "The Supreme Court," p. 1195.

190. The much-anticipated ruling in the *Patriation Reference* was broadcast live. "Unaccustomed to having so many wires underfoot, one of the judges accidentally kicked a connecting cable, cutting off the sound in the middle of a crucial point." Robert Sheppard and Michael Valpy, *The National Deal: The Fight for a Canadian Constitution* (Toronto: Macmillan, 1982), p. 241.

191. O'Reilly, "The Supreme Court," p. 1190.

192. Delacourt, "The Media and the Supreme Court," p. 34.

193. Stephen Bindman, "Judicial Independence and Accountability," *University of New Brunswick Law Journal* 45 (1996), p. 62, quoted in Delacourt, "The Media and the Supreme Court," p. 35. Bindman has since left journalism and now serves as a special advisor to the federal Department of Justice.

194. Sharpe and Roach, *Brian Dickson*, pp. 353–54.

195. Kirk Makin, "Lamer Worries about Public Backlash," *The Globe and Mail*, February 6, 1999, p. A1, quoted in Delacourt, "The Media and the Supreme Court," p. 38.

196. See Roach, *Due Process and Victims' Rights*, especially Chapters 2, 3, and 5.

197. William Halton, *Reporting on the Courts: How the Mass Media Cover Judicial Actions* (Chicago: Nelson-Hall, 1998), p. 106.

198. O'Reilly, "The Supreme Court," p. 1189.

199. Joseph F. Fletcher and Paul Howe, "Supreme Court Cases and Court Support: The State of Canadian Public Opinion" (Montreal: Institute for Research on Public Policy, May 2000), p. 39.

200. The terms "citizens' constitution" and "governments' constitution" are taken from Alan C. Cairns, "Citizens (Outsiders) and Governments (Insiders) in Constitution-Making: The Case of Meech Lake," in Douglas E. Williams, ed., *Disruptions: Constitutional Struggles, from the Charter to Meech Lake* (Toronto: McClelland and Stewart, 1991), pp. 108–38.

201. Snell and Vaughan, *The Supreme Court of Canada*, p. 154.

202. Ibid., p. 231.

203. Julien Chouinard, Clark's only Court appointee, had run for the Conservatives in the 1968 federal election. Clark, obviously convinced that Chouinard supported his party, asked him to serve in his cabinet before appointing him to the Supreme Court. Peter McCormick, *Supreme at Last*, p. 85.

204. There is one recent exception to this rule: Wishart Spence of Ontario was succeeded in 1979 by William McIntyre from Alberta. Three years later, the conventional distribution of Justices was restored. (McCormick, *Supreme at Last*, p. 85).

205. Joseph F. Fletcher and Paul Howe, "Canadian Attitudes toward the Charter and the Courts in Comparative Perspective" (Montreal: Institute for Research on Public Policy, May 2000), pp. 22–23.

206. Irwin Cotler, testimony before the House of Commons Standing Committee on Justice, Human Rights, Public Safety and Emergency Preparedness, March 30, 2004.

207. See, e.g., Jacob S. Ziegel, "Merit Selection and Democratization of Appointments to the Supreme Court of Canada," in Howe and Russell, *Judicial Power*, pp. 131–64; Manfredi, *Judicial Power*, pp. 171–74. The survey by Fletcher and Howe found that fewer than one in ten Canadians approved of the current process; almost half believed that the provinces should be involved, and over one-third thought

that Parliament should be involved (pp. 23–25).

208. Canada, House of Commons Standing Committee on Justice, Human Rights, Public Safety and Emergency Preparedness, "Improving the Supreme Court of Canada Appointments Process" (Ottawa: House of Commons, May 2004), p. 2.

209. The minutes of the public hearings can be found at www.parl.gc.ca, under "Committee Business." The relevant dates are March 23, 25, and 30, and April 1 and 20, 2004.

210. Most provinces and territories have one committee; Ontario has three and Quebec two, to reflect geographic divisions within those provinces. Andre S. Millar, "The 'New' Federal Judicial Appointments Process: The First Ten Years," *Alberta Law Review* 38 (2000–01), pp. 619–20.

211. Millar, "The 'New' Federal Judicial Appointments Process," p. 622. The specific criteria on which the committees are required to base their evaluations are intriguing: they include "ability to exercise role conferred by Charter" (without elaboration), "sensitivity to gender and racial equality," and "writing and communication skills." See Millar, Appendix 5, p. 653.

212. Although the justice minister is not bound by law to follow the advisory committees' recommendations, none has appointed a judge who had not previously been approved by this process. (Millar, "The 'New' Federal Judicial Appointments Process," p. 620) It is interesting to note the discrepancies among the various committees: in the first ten years of the program, some recommended more than half of all applicants, while others rejected a majority of those seeking judicial appointments. See Millar, Appendix 1, p. 623.

213. Canada, "Improving the Supreme Court of Canada Appointments Process," p. 5.

214. Ibid., pp. 15–16.

215. Ibid., pp. 17–20.

216. Ibid., pp. 21–22 (emphasis in original).

217. Tonda MacCharles, "Harper: Judge Veto Needed," *The Toronto Star*, June 23, 2004, accessed online at www.thestar.com; Kirk Makin, "Tories Would Act Fast to Fill Court Vacancies, Toews Says," *The Globe and Mail*, June 16, 2004, accessed online at www.globeandmail.com.

218. "The Conservatives and the Judges," *The Globe and Mail*, June 21, 2004, accessed online at www.globeandmail.com.

219. Kim Lunman and Brian Laghi, "Commons Panel to Accept Judges," *The Globe and Mail*, August 26, 2004, accessed online at www.globeandmail.com.

220. For an excellent survey of the literature on judicial impact, with a focus on the Canadian context, see W.A. Bogart, *Courts and Country: The Limits of Litigation and the Social and Political Life of Canada* (Toronto: Oxford University Press, 1994), Chapter 2.

221. Bradley C. Canon and Charles A. Johnson, *Judicial Policies: Implementation and Impact*, 2nd ed. (Washington, DC: CQ Press, 1999).

222. Rod Mickleburgh and Erin Conway-Smith, "Elections Canada Won't Enforce Results Blackout on Polling Day," *The Globe and Mail*, June 11, 2004; see also Gerry Nicholls, "Will Elections Canada Never Learn?" *The Globe and Mail*, June 14, 2004; both accessed online at www.globeandmail.com. There is scattered anecdotal evidence that lifting the blackout may have encouraged some strategic voting, but no significant effect was apparent; see Canadian Press, "Chance to Vote Strategically Gets Mixed Reviews," June 28, 2004, accessed online at www.thestar.com.

223. See the discussion of the *Libman* ruling, and its evasion by courts in Alberta and British Columbia, in Chapter 9, pages 290–91.

224. Canon and Johnson, *Judicial Policies*, pp. 52–53; Gerald N. Rosenberg, *The Hollow Hope: Can Courts Bring about Social Change?* (Chicago: University of Chicago Press, 1991), p. 52.

225. Knopff and Morton, *Charter Politics*, pp. 22–24; Bogart, *Courts and Country*, pp. 259–60.

226. Lauren Bowen, "Do Court Decisions Matter?" in Lee Epstein, ed., *Contemplating Courts* (Washington, DC: CQ Press, 1995), pp. 376–89.

227. On the numbers of same-sex couples who wed in Ontario and British Columbia by the end of 2003, see Kathleen A. Lahey and Kevin Alderson, *Same-Sex Marriage: The Personal and the Political* (Toronto: Insomniac Press, 2004), pp. 86 and 92.

228. A particularly good example is the attempt by some provincial governments to block access to abortion services after the 1988 *Morgentaler* ruling. See Janine Brodie, Shelley A.M. Gavigan, and Jane Jenson, *The Politics of Abortion* (Toronto: Oxford University Press, 1992).

229. Iacobucci, "The Charter: Twenty Years Later," pp. 411–14.

230. Gerald Owen, "Disclosure after *Stinchcombe*," in Anthony A. Peacock, ed., *Rethinking the Constitution: Perspectives on Canadian Constitutional Reform, Interpretation, and Theory* (Toronto: Oxford University Press, 1996), pp. 177–85.

231. Horowitz, *The Courts and Social Policy*, pp. 232–33.

232. Rosenberg, *The Hollow Hope*, p. 322.

233. John Arnold Epp, "Penetrating Police Investigative Procedure Post-*Morin*," *University of British Columbia Law Review* 31 (1997), p. 99.

234. Canon and Johnson, *Judicial Policies*, pp. 83–84.

235. Richard A. Leo, "Miranda's Revenge: Police Interrogation as a Confidence Game," *Law and Society Review* 30 (1996), pp. 259–88.

236. Canon and Johnson, *Judicial Policies*, pp. 104–05; Rosenberg, *The Hollow Hope*, pp. 326–30.

237. See Kent Roach, "Twenty Years of the Charter and Criminal Justice: A Dialogue between a Charter Optimist, A Charter Realist and a Charter Sceptic," in Magnet et al., *The Canadian Charter*, pp. 49–50.

238. See, e.g., Sopinka J.'s comments on the *Askov* fallout in *Morin*, paragraphs 22, 24, and 48–52, and the Court's "clarification" of the

first *Marshall* ruling on the Aboriginal fishery in *R. v. Marshall*, [1999] 3 S.C.R. 533.

239. Canon and Johnson, *Judicial Policies*, p. 37.

240. Fletcher and Howe, "Canadian Attitudes toward the Charter and the Courts," p. 11.

241. Ibid., p. 16, Figure 11.

242. Ibid., pp. 19–22.

243. Fletcher and Howe, "Supreme Court Cases and Court Support," pp. 31 and 52.

244. *R. v. Collins*, [1987] 1 S.C.R. 265, paragraph 32.

245. *B.C. Motor Vehicle*, paragraph 19, *per* Lamer J.

Chapter 4

Parliament and the Courts in the Charter Era

Prime Minister Paul Martin listens to Governor General Adrienne Clarkson read the Speech from the Throne in the Senate chamber in February 2004.

CP PHOTO/Tom Hanson

While the courts are guardians of the Constitution and of individuals' rights under it, it is the legislature's responsibility to enact legislation that embodies appropriate safeguards to comply with the Constitution's requirements.[1]

INTRODUCTION

The proclamation of the Charter in 1982 affected all three branches of government, not just the judiciary. Although the Supreme Court has received the lion's share of the attention, the Charter also imposed new obligations on the legislative and executive branches. As we saw in Chapter 1, constitutionalism and the rule of law bind all public actors—MPs, cabinet ministers, bureaucrats—to make policy choices that are consistent with federalism, democracy, and the protection of rights. In the next two chapters, we will examine the ways in which legislators and the political and permanent executives have adapted to the Charter.[2] Although the chapter is devoted primarily to the federal Parliament, many of the developments that have occurred at the national level are parallelled in provincial legislatures.

Our discussion of the parliamentary process will focus on the committee stage, and specifically the examination of government bills by standing committees of the House of Commons. (See Dossier 4.1, pages 147–48 for a description of the various stages.) There are three reasons to emphasize the committee stage. First, committees are subject to a lesser degree of cabinet control than the House of Commons as a whole. It is true that standing committees are usually dominated (and chaired) by government MPs. Nonetheless, committees can play an independent role in the legislative process. A strong committee chair can create a consensus among the members from all parties and put political pressure on the government to accept amendments arising from the hearings.

Second, committee members have the opportunity to study the relevant policy issues in depth, whereas other MPs may have little interest or expertise in a particular field. Committees hold hearings, listen to witnesses, and write reports to Parliament. These hearings and reports give committee members a deep understanding of the issues involved in a particular bill. Third, committee proceedings generate extensive written records, including minutes of proceedings and evidence, as well as reports. These documents are potentially useful to government lawyers when they defend laws against Charter challenges. If they demonstrate that the committee gave the Charter due weight in its deliberations, they may encourage courts to defer to Parliament's chosen balance between protected rights and other social values.

This chapter advances two central arguments. First, Parliament should, and increasingly does, take its Charter responsibilities seriously. It is invited to do so by the wording of s. 1, which allows governments to balance the protected rights and freedoms against competing social values. Such a balancing act is inevitably political, because it requires public officials to decide which interests will be given priority in a given context and how that priority will be expressed. Should the state intervene directly in the workplace by requiring employers to consider personal characteristics—such as gender or ethnicity—in hiring? Should public funds be spent on religious education? Should police be required to obtain a warrant before taking DNA samples from criminal suspects? Many laws, if not most, engage the values protected by the Charter. Ideally, elected legislators will strike an appropriate balance between those values and competing priorities (e.g., fiscal restraint).

When Parliament does its part to ensure that a law conforms to the Charter, the balance of interests reflected in that law should be endorsed by the courts. But if Parliament neglects its Charter duties, judges may conclude that nullification is the only option. Moreover, relatively few laws are subject to Charter challenge in the courts. As they review proposed legislation, parliamentarians cannot ignore protected rights and leave them for the judges to sort out. Nor should Parliament necessarily substitute "Charter-proofing"(see Chapter 5) for its own reasoned judgment about the proper balance between protected rights and other social values. After all, a law that is technically consistent with the Charter may not always promote the public good.[3]

The second argument is that, contrary to the arguments of some Charter critics, Parliament is not helpless in the face of court rulings with which a majority of its members disagree. In the Charter era, Parliament is no longer supreme. As some judges have pointed out, perhaps self-servingly, the decision to entrench rights and freedoms was made by elected legislators themselves.[4] But it is a mistake to equate the end of parliamentary supremacy with the beginning of parliamentary impotence. As we saw in Chapter 3, judicial decisions are rarely self-enforcing. While Parliament has a duty to interpret and implement judge-made policies, it also has the power to reinterpret or repudiate court rulings that do not fit with the government's political priorities. Three of the case studies in this chapter reflect the conflict between the legislative and judicial branches over the relative importance of due-process rights and the need to protect the public from violent offenders.[5] In these cases (Case Studies 1, 2, and 5, pages 157–64 and 168–73), Parliament adopted an interpretation of the Charter that differed from that of the Supreme Court; as Case Study 5 demonstrates, judges often defer to such choices.

In policy fields other than criminal justice, the relationship between the two branches is particularly complicated. For example, the judicial protection of equality rights may force legislators to alter their spending plans. (See the discussion of the *Schachter* and *Eldridge* cases elsewhere in this book.) This intrusion on Parliament's "power of the purse" is problematic. But because Parliament (not the courts) has the final word on public spending, it can minimize the impact of court rulings with which it disagrees. In general, as Chapter 3 points out, the Supreme Court has become increasingly deferential to Parliament since its initial period of activism in the mid-1980s. On balance, therefore, it is inaccurate to claim that parliamentary supremacy has been entirely replaced by "judicial supremacy."[6]

PARLIAMENT AND THE LEGISLATIVE PROCESS

Before it can become law, a bill—whether sponsored by the government of the day or by an individual MP—must go through several stages. These are described in Dossier 4.1.

DOSSIER 4.1

THE LEGISLATIVE PROCESS IN THE FEDERAL PARLIAMENT[1]

At first reading in the House of Commons, the sponsor of a bill (a cabinet minister or a **backbench MP**) moves that it be read a first time and placed on the parliamentary agenda (the order paper). There is no debate at this stage. At some later time, the bill may come up for second reading. Here the House debates the bill and decides whether to approve it in principle. If a majority of the MPs in attendance vote in favour, the bill is sent to a parliamentary committee for clause-by-clause review. Whereas the other stages in the legislative process occur in the Commons chamber, committees meet elsewhere on Parliament Hill.[2]

In most cases, a bill is assigned to the standing (i.e., permanent) committee that specializes in its subject matter. For example, a bill to amend the Criminal Code is reviewed by the Standing Committee on Justice, Human Rights, Public Safety and Emergency Preparedness.[3] Most members of these committees are backbenchers; the exceptions are the parliamentary secretaries assigned to each minister. The number of MPs from each party is in rough proportion to the size of each caucus in the House. When one party holds a majority of the seats in the Commons, it also occupies a majority of the seats on each committee.

Since 1986, committees have enjoyed the power and the resources to hold public hearings, both on Parliament Hill and, where necessary, across the country. They can call witnesses, request documents, and question public officials. After it concludes its hearings, a committee examines the bill in minute detail and debates proposed amendments. Those amendments must not alter the principle of the bill, which has already been endorsed by the House. The results of the committee's investigation and the text of any amendments approved by its members are contained in a report back to the Commons. Amendments that have been approved by a majority of committee members are automatically incorporated into the bill.

At report stage in the House, MPs have an opportunity to propose and debate any further amendments to the bill. After the conclusion of the report stage, the amended bill undergoes one final round of debate at third reading. If it passes there, it leaves the House of Commons and moves up to the Senate (where the various stages are repeated). Once both Houses of Parliament have approved the bill, it goes to the governor general for royal assent. It may come into effect immediately or on a later date specified in the bill. Once it takes effect, the bill officially becomes a law.

Since 1994, the government has had the option of referring a bill to committee before second reading. When that happens (increasingly often), the committee has a freer rein because the principle of the bill has not yet been accepted by the whole House. In most cases, the committee can only propose technical amendments. However, as the examples in this

(continued)

chapter illustrate, even this restricted power of revision can have an important influence on the operation of a future law.

ENDNOTES

1. This summary of the legislative process is based on the "Précis of Procedure" issued by the Table Research Branch in the House of Commons. The document is available on the Parliamentary website (www.parl.gc.ca).

2. The exception is the Committee of the Whole, to which all MPs belong. The House operates in Committee of the Whole when it considers the

government's spending plans for the year and (more rarely) when the government is particularly keen to pass a bill quickly. Although the Committee of the Whole is held in the Commons chamber, the rules are considerably more relaxed than in the usual parliamentary debates.

3. This committee was established in early 2004, as a result of the creation of the new Department of Public Safety and Emergency Preparedness in December 2003. In previous Parliaments, it was known as Justice and Legal Affairs, and then Justice and Human Rights.

One feature of the legislative process is particularly relevant to a discussion of the Charter: the partisanship fostered by adversarial parliamentary debate. The political clash between the governing party and the opposition parties shapes, and sometimes distorts, the process of examining and amending legislation. Partisan divisions among parliamentarians can stall or even kill legislation, especially on issues that carry significant moral or religious freight—many of which are now affected by the Charter. Elected politicians may try to avoid divisive questions such as abortion and euthanasia. Judges have no such latitude: when they are presented with a concrete dispute between two parties, they must reach a decision. Consequently, courts sometimes have the last word on controversial issues where legislators cannot reach a consensus. (See Case Study 3, pages 164–66.)

When they take their Charter duties seriously, as they did in Case Studies 1 and 2, pages 157–64, committees perform the "**first-order**" duties of Parliament in an effective way. (See the discussion of the coordinate model below.) Their deliberations also produce a written record that can be used to sway the courts. When it seeks to defend an impugned law under s. 1, the federal Department of Justice can refer to the committee proceedings as evidence of a "pressing and substantial objective," a "rational connection" between the law and its purpose, and a thorough examination of alternative policy choices. Under those circumstances, a court may be more willing to conclude that the infringement of a Charter right or freedom is justified (see Dossier 1.6, pages 27–30).

THE EVOLVING RELATIONSHIP BETWEEN PARLIAMENT AND THE COURTS IN THE CHARTER ERA

The Coordinate Model

It is clear that the Charter is changing the relationship between the legislative and judicial branches of government. The direction of that change is less obvious. Will one institution—either Parliament or the Supreme Court—gain the upper hand, or will the two branches work together to give effect to the Charter's guarantees of rights and freedoms? While it is still too early answer this question definitively, it is clear that Parliament is no longer supreme. As we saw in Chapter 2, courts played a relatively minor role in Canadian policy-making before 1982. Within the jurisdictions assigned to each level of government, legislators in Ottawa and the provinces enjoyed broad discretion in making policy choices. The most pressing limits on that discretion were practical (e.g., fiscal constraints), not constitutional. The Charter imposes a new set of restrictions on legislators: if they fail in their "first-order" duties, the courts may strike down or modify the resulting laws as part of their "**second-order**" duties.

Nonetheless, reports of the death of parliamentary supremacy are somewhat exaggerated. First, s. 33 of the Charter allows a legislature to immunize laws from judicial review under ss. 2 and 7–15. For the reasons discussed in Chapter 12, pages 379–83, s. 33 is rarely invoked. But its existence allows legislators to defy judicial fiat, if they are willing to do so. Second, the Charter does not apply to every aspect of public policy. Outside the "Charter zone," governments are free to act as they wish. Third, court rulings are not self-enforcing. As discussed earlier, judges have few tools to force their interpretations of the Constitution on reluctant legislators. Indeed, the Supreme Court has sometimes endorsed parliamentary interpretations of the Charter that are directly at variance with its own (see Case Study 5, pages 168–73). Fourth, the existence of s. 1 allows a government to balance entrenched rights and freedoms against competing social and political goals. Fifth and finally, if all else fails, federal and provincial legislators can overturn judicial interpretations of the Charter by amending the text. Given the failure of the Meech Lake and Charlottetown Accords in the early 1990s, the practicality of this last option should not be overstated. But it is useful to remember that the other two branches of government could amend the Charter to close off avenues of judicial policy-making, if they had the political will to do so.

If neither Parliament nor the judiciary is entirely supreme, as the preceding discussion suggests, it follows that their evolving relationship can best be described as involving a "coordinate model." From this perspective, both Parliament and the Supreme Court (together with the executive branch) are responsible for ensuring that laws conform to the Charter. Each institution has a unique set of resources to carry out that task. Parliament can benefit from extensive policy expertise, in the executive branch and elsewhere, while the court is confined to the evidence presented by the contending parties and intervenors. On the other hand, judicial independence from political pressures frees the Court to examine laws impartially. These institutional resources can complement each other, as long as each side respects the other's constitutional mandate and tries to resolve Charter conflicts in a constructive way.

Brian Slattery's formulation of the coordinate model distinguishes between first-order and second-order Charter duties.[7] First-order duties require governments "to assess the reasonableness of *their own* anticipated acts in light of fundamental rights and to act accordingly." In other words, public officials must scrutinize their own actions for conformity to Charter values. The most prominent example of this first-order activity is the "Charter-proofing" carried out by the Human Rights Law Section of the federal Department of Justice (see Chapter 5, page 184). Second-order duties require "certain bodies to review the acts of others for conformity with Charter rights where the latter are bound in a first-order way to take account of the Charter in acting."[8] Most obviously, the courts are authorized to assess the constitutionality of laws and regulations adopted by the other branches of government.

Slattery argues that "the proper functioning of the Charter depends less on the activities of those responsible for policing others than on the activities of those bound in a first-order way by its provisions."[9] Relatively few executive and legislative decisions are reviewed by the courts. If legislators and/or executives were to try to evade their Charter duties, judges would be powerless to intervene unless someone challenged their actions in court. However, Slattery notes that second-order functions are not confined to the judicial branch. In particular, Parliament has both the first-order duty to examine its own laws, and the second-order responsibility for scrutinizing orders-in-council and other regulatory instruments issued by the executive branch. Where possible Charter violations are found, the House of Commons and the Senate should make the government aware of them and ensure that they are properly addressed before the law takes effect.[10]

When Parliament takes its first-order and second-order duties seriously, the second-order function of the courts becomes less important. Conversely, if Parliament were unwilling or unable to perform its Charter duties, the courts might have no choice but to nullify its work (if they were given the opportunity to do so). Ideally, both institutions will carry out these responsibilities to the best of their respective duties. Where good-faith conflicts arise over the implementation of Charter values, these should be resolved through mutual respect and a proper understanding of the respective institutional duties of each institution (see Case Study 5, pages 168–73).

For Slattery, the coordinate model offers both a persuasive empirical account of the Charter's impact and a powerful normative demand for institutional cooperation.

> ... the Charter allows for a continuing dialogue between the courts and legislatures as to the true nature of Charter rights and the reasonableness of limits on them. But this dialogue can occur only if it is accepted that the roles of the executive, legislative, and judicial branches under the Charter are reciprocal and not confrontational, and that their attitudes to one another should be flexible and founded on mutual respect.[11]

Over the past two decades, the Supreme Court has become more deferential to the first-order efforts of the other two branches—although, as previously discussed, that deference varies across policy fields. At the same time, most legislators and executives have grown accustomed to the Charter, and tried to ensure that the laws conform to its requirements. Confrontations still occur, especially over hot-button issues like same-sex rights. On the whole, however, the relationships among the three branches are characterized by the flexibility and mutual respect that Slattery prescribes.

Is There a "Democratic Dialogue" between Parliament and the Courts?

The idea of a Charter "dialogue" between Parliament and the Supreme Court has great normative appeal for advocates of judicial supremacy, as well as judges themselves.[12] An influential 1997 article by Peter Hogg and Allison Bushell argued that the Charter "isn't such a bad thing after all," because it generates a constructive dialogue between legislators and judges.[13] Whereas true judicial supremacy would give judges the last word in every instance, Hogg and Bushell claim that Parliament can respond to court rulings on the Charter by amending or reenacting impugned laws. "The legislative body is in a position to devise a response that is properly respectful of the Charter values that have been identified by the Court,

but which accomplishes the social or economic objectives that the judicial decision has impeded."[14]

Hogg and Bushell observe that the Supreme Court rarely rejects the objective of a law; instead, it usually invalidates a law on the ground that it fails the "minimal impairment" stage of the *Oakes* test. When this happens, the "legislative sequel" represents an attempt by Parliament to achieve its policy ends by choosing means that infringe the Charter to a lesser degree than those that have been found unconstitutional. Such means are often suggested by the Court itself. For example, the majority in the *RJR-Macdonald* case invalidated a blanket prohibition on tobacco advertising as an unjustifiable limit on freedom of expression (s. 2(b)). However, it endorsed a ban on "lifestyle" advertising, such as visual images associating tobacco use with healthy outdoor pursuits.[15] According to Hogg and Bushell, the subsequent enactment of a revised Tobacco Act by Parliament illustrates both the value of Charter dialogue and its congruency with the democratic process: "the invalidity of the law could be corrected by the enactment of a new law that was more respectful of the Charter right while still substantially accomplishing the important purpose... it is hard to claim that an unelected court is thwarting the wishes of the people."[16]

Although Hogg and Bushell present this dialogue as a coordinate relationship between the two institutions, critics see it as an example of judicial supremacy. Because Hogg and Bushell "[equate] judicial interpretation of the Charter with the document itself."[17] they overlook the fact that the "legislative sequels" do not necessarily reflect Parliament's own priorities. Rather, these laws represent an abdication of Parliament's first-order duties and a triumph of judicial supremacy. Ted Morton argues that this conception of "dialogue" is more accurately portrayed as a "monologue," in which the Court gives orders and Parliament obeys.[18]

Manfredi and Kelly criticize Hogg and Bushell for failing to distinguish among different types of "legislative sequel." They argue that few such laws emerge from a positive dialogue between equals.[19] Most are "negative" responses to Court rulings, which "border on Charter ventriloquism":[20] either Parliament declines to reenact or amend the invalidated law, or it amends the law in a way that reflects the Court's interpretation of the Charter rather than its own. The exceptions are those instances in which Parliament reacts to a Court ruling by crafting a new law that does not slavishly adhere to judicial priorities. Manfredi and Kelly cite the legislative response to the *Daviault* ruling (Case Study 1, pages 157–61) as an example of genuine dialogue. However, Manfredi cautions against assuming that a law that deviates from a majority ruling is free from judicial "monologue." For example, Parliament chose to enact a law regulating the disclosure of counselling records in sexual-assault cases that differed in key respects from the majority ruling in *O'Connor* (Case Study 5, pages 168–73). But this law was not entirely reflective of Parliament's own view of the Charter, because it was based on Justice L'Heureux-Dubé's dissenting opinion. In other words, Parliament simply chose between two competing Court interpretations instead of crafting its own.[21] Manfredi and Kelly conclude that "Genuine dialogue only exists when legislatures are recognized as legitimate interpreters of the constitution and have an *effective* means to assert that interpretation."[22]

Against these critics, Kent Roach asserts that the dialogue metaphor is both empirically sound and normatively compelling. His conception of the proper relationship between the Supreme Court and Parliament is "a respectful conversation among those who have different abilities, concerns, and perspectives." Such a conversation is permitted, indeed required, by s. 1 of the Charter, which "promotes a constructive and respectful dialogue in which courts and legislature can each do what they do best without competing over who is the best interpreter of the Charter or who has the most popular support."[23] Roach uses the legislative sequel to the *Seaboyer* case (Dossier 4.2), in which Parliament replaced the invalidated "rape shield," to illustrate the virtues of "constructive" dialogue. In that instance, "Parliament used its institutional advantage over the Court by comprehensively reforming the law of sexual assault"[24] instead of merely reenacting the old law with a few cosmetic changes.

DOSSIER 4.2

THE "RAPE SHIELD"

In 1991, the Supreme Court struck down a section of the Criminal Code that was intended to protect the privacy of complainants in sexual-assault trials. The "rape shield" barred the defence from introducing evidence about the sexual history of the complainant, in an effort to diminish her credibility or to imply that the accused might reasonably have believed that she consented to the sexual act at issue in the case. The majority ruled that the "rape shield" violated the due-process rights of the accused (ss. 7 and 11(d) of the Charter) because it automatically excluded evidence that might have probative value in some cases. They left the question of admissibility to the discretion of the trial judge, subject to four common-law principles:

- First, evidence of the prior sexual history of the complainant could not be used "solely to support the inference that the complainant is by reason of such conduct: (a) more likely to have consented to the sexual conduct at issue in the trial; (b) less worthy of belief as a witness."

- Second, evidence of the complainant's consensual sexual activity with the accused (or anyone else) is only admissible when "it possesses probative value on an issue in the trial and where that probative value is not substantially outweighed by the danger of unfair prejudice flowing from the evidence." Examples include proof that the alleged sexual assault was committed by someone other than the accused, or facts that would tend to support the accused's claim of a reasonable belief in consent.

- Third, evidence that would have been excluded under the "rape shield" could be introduced only after a hearing to determine its validity and probative value.

(continued)

- Fourth, "Where evidence that the complainant has engaged in sexual conduct on other occasions is admitted on a jury trial, the judge should warn the jury against inferring from the evidence of the conduct itself, either that the complainant might have consented to the act alleged, or that the complainant is less worthy of credit."[1]

Women's groups reacted angrily to the nullification of the "rape shield."[2] They pressured Justice Minister Kim Campbell to create a replacement law, in consultation with their members.[3] The Court's implicit acceptance of the "honest but mistaken belief in consent" defence was widely viewed as a defeat for women and a threat to their security.[4] In response, the groups that Campbell consulted demanded that consent be defined explicitly, to prevent defendants from invoking this defence. Bill C-49 (passed in 1992) turned the common-law rules in *Seaboyer* into statute law, with some exceptions. It added two restrictions on judicial discretion: (1) it required judges to balance the interests of society (especially the reporting of sexual crimes) and the privacy rights of the complainant against the due-process rights of the defendant; and (2) any decision to admit evidence of prior sexual activity must be accompanied by written reasons identifying the probative value of the evidence.[5] In addition, the new law required an accused to demonstrate that he had taken "reasonable steps" to ascertain consent, instead of merely assuming it. This provision was intended to counteract the "honest but mistaken belief" defence.[6]

Although Bill C-49 struck a balance between the rights of the complainant and the accused that differed in some respects from the *Seaboyer* doctrine, it preserved the essence of the majority ruling. The Court recognized this fact in the 2000 *Darrach* ruling, which unanimously upheld the new "rape shield." Justice Gonthier declared that "The current version of s. 276 of the Criminal Code is in essence a codification by Parliament of the Court's guidelines in *Seaboyer*.... In view of *Seaboyer*, the constitutionality of both the rule and the procedure has already been established at a general level."[7] It also accepted Parliament's decision to modify the due-process rights of defendants by requiring judges to take other interests into account. Gonthier acknowledged that "The fair trial protected by s. 11(d) is one that does justice to all the parties." In this instance, Parliament and the minister respected the Court's prerogative to devise common-law rules of criminal procedure; the Justices, in turn, respected the decision by the other branches of government to protect the wider interests of society and the rights of alleged victims.

ENDNOTES

1. *R. v. Seaboyer; R. v. Gayme*, [1991] 2 S.C.R. 577, paragraph 96, *per* McLachlin J.

2. See, e.g., Adelyn L. Bowland, "Sexual Assault Trials and the Protection of 'Bad Girls': The Battle between the Courts and Parliament," in Julian V. Roberts and Renate M. Mohr, eds., *Confronting Sexual Assault: A Decade of Legal and Social Change* (Toronto: University of Toronto Press, 1994), pp. 241–67, and Diana Majury, "*Seaboyer* and *Gayme*: A Study in InEquality," in Roberts and Mohr, *Confronting Sexual Assault*, pp. 268–92.

3. This process is described in Sheila McIntyre, "Redefining Reformism: The Consultations That Shaped Bill C-49," in Roberts and Mohr, *Confronting Sexual Assault*, pp. 293–326.

4. The Court accepted the "honest but mistaken belief" defence in the notorious *Pappajohn* case (1980). Under *Pappajohn*, the question of consent to sexual activity was addressed from the perspective of the accused, not the alleged victim. See Christine Boyle, "The Judicial Construction of Sexual Assault Offences," in Roberts and Mohr, *Confronting Sexual Assault*, pp. 147–48.

5. The "rape shield" provisions are located in s. 276 of the Criminal Code.

6. This effort appears to have failed. In 1993, a five-judge majority on the Supreme Court ruled that the "honest but mistaken belief" defence may be put to a jury in a sexual-assault trial, as long as there is sufficient evidence to give that

defence "an air of reality." See *R. v. Osolin*, [1993] 4 S.C.R. 595, *per* Cory J.

7. *R. v. Darrach*, [2000] 2 S.C.R. 443, paragraph 1.

In practice, constructive dialogue is sometimes displaced by in-your-face confrontation between the two institutions. For Roach, Parliament takes an in-your-face position when it "rejects or reverses the Court's decisions on the basis that the Court has wrongly interpreted the Charter or that its decision is simply unacceptable."[25] He cites the legislative sequels to *Daviault* and *O'Connor* as examples of inappropriate parliamentary disregard for the legitimate role of the courts (Case Studies 1 and 5, pages 157–61 and 168–73).

> Parliament's right to tell the Court that it was wrong in this way can only be supported on the basis that Parliament is entitled to act on its own interpretation of the constitution, even when it is at odds with that of the Court, or to override Charter decisions that it determines are unacceptable to the majority of Canadians.[26]

For Roach, the only legitimate way for Parliament to defy the Court is to invoke the notwithstanding clause, which would encourage public debate over the proper meaning of the Charter and set a time limit on any majoritarian infringements of protected rights.[27]

Roach argues that to allow Parliament to "judge ... its own majoritarian causes"[28] places the rights of unpopular individuals and groups at risk. The coordinate model is dangerous because it "diminishes respect for the Court as an institution, trivializes the Court's precedents, and allows the rights of the most unpopular people to be defined by elected politicians."[29] Roach's skepticism about the claim that "Parliament is entitled to act on its own interpretation of the constitution" reveals a preference for judicial supremacy and undermines his discussion of democratic dialogue between the two institutions. If "constructive" dialogue simply means that Parliament adopts the Supreme Court's interpretation of the Charter, and legislative insistence on a different—though perhaps

equally valid—interpretation is characterized as illegitimate, then there is no true equality between the legislative and judicial branches of government. Roach implies that the Court is both competent and entitled to interpret the Charter and to dictate its proper implementation in public policy; Parliament is not. As discussed in Chapter 3, however, courts do not possess the institutional capacity to craft and implement public policy; while they often produce good laws, their competence to do so in all cases cannot be taken for granted. Nor is it correct to suggest that the courts should monopolize Charter interpretation. It is more plausible to argue that judges should set the broad outlines of constitutionality and leave Parliament to fill them in.

The claim that the Charter promotes a democratic dialogue between the two branches of government has an obvious appeal for judges, especially those who are uncomfortable with public attacks on the legitimacy of judicial review. In the 1998 *Vriend* ruling, Justice Iacobucci sought to deflect criticism of the Court's decision to amend Alberta's human rights law by "reading in" sexual orientation as a prohibited ground of discrimination (recall Dossier 1.8, pages 36–37). Iacobucci argued that the Charter required courts and legislators to "respond" to each other's decisions.

> To my mind, a great value of judicial review and this dialogue among the branches is that each of the branches is made somewhat accountable to the other. The work of the legislature is reviewed by the courts and the work of the court in its decisions can be reacted to by the legislature in the passing of new legislation (or even overarching laws under s. 33 of the *Charter*). This dialogue between and accountability of each of the branches have the effect of enhancing the democratic process, not denying it.[30]

One might question the claim that Parliament should be "accountable" to judges, who are themselves immune from accountability to the electorate—or to anyone else. Indeed, the above passage implies that the Court should always dictate to Parliament, while MPs are accorded only the limited function of "reacting" to judicial rulings. Nonetheless, in the context of the *Vriend* case, the assertion of judicial power may have been justified. The Supreme Court—and many provincial courts—had made it clear that the Charter forbade discrimination against gay men and lesbians.

By refusing to incorporate sexual orientation in the Individuals' Rights Protection Act (IRPA), the Alberta legislature had arguably neglected its first-order duties. Under those circumstances, the Supreme Court was only doing its second-order job when it brought the IRPA into conformity with the supreme law of Canada. Dossier 4.3 describes another instance where Parliament may have failed in its Charter duties, prompting a spirited debate on the Supreme Court about the relationship between dialogue and deference.

DOSSIER 4.3

THE 2002 *SAUVÉ* RULING

Richard Sauvé, a convicted murderer and former Hell's Angel, has twice challenged the constitutionality of laws that prohibit voting by prison inmates. In 1993, the Supreme Court struck down s. 51(e) of the Canada Elections Act, which denied all prisoners the right to vote in federal elections.[1] On behalf of a unanimous Court, Justice Iacobucci delivered a brief oral judgment. After noting that the government had conceded a violation of s. 3 of the Charter and argued that it was justified under s. 1, Iacobucci said, "We do not agree. In our view, s. 51(e) is drawn too broadly and fails to meet the proportionality test, particularly the minimal impairment component of the test, as expressed in the s. 1 jurisprudence of the Court." There was no analysis of the relationship between s. 3 and s. 1, and the Court offered no guidelines for reenactment.

The federal government replaced the invalidated section with a slightly less restrictive version, which allowed prisoners serving sentences of less than two years to vote by special ballot. All other incarcerated citizens were still denied the franchise.[2] The law reflected the preexisting distinction between those sentenced to serve less than two years, who are held in provincial jails, and federal prisoners sentenced to longer terms. In effect, all federal prisoners lost their voting rights when they entered the penitentiary. Sauvé won his

second round in November 2002 when the new law was struck down by a 5-4 majority. (By that time, he had been released from prison.)

In his dissent, Justice Gonthier enunciated a version of the dialogue metaphor consistent with the coordinate model. After noting that the impugned law was Parliament's reasoned response to an earlier Supreme Court ruling, he argued that it would be inappropriate for the Court to reject the balance struck by the legislature.

> In my view, especially in the context of the case at bar, the heart of the dialogue metaphor is that neither the courts nor Parliament hold a monopoly on the determination of values. Importantly, the dialogue metaphor *does not signal a lowering of the s. 1 justification standard*. It simply suggests that when, after a full and rigorous s. 1 analysis, Parliament has satisfied the court that it has established a reasonable limit to a right that is demonstrably justified in a free and democratic society, the dialogue ends; the court lets Parliament have the last word and does not substitute Parliament's reasonable choices with its own.[3]

Writing for the majority, Chief Justice McLachlin rejected this model of dialogue. First, she argued that the fundamental importance of voting rights in a free and democratic society made deference to Parliament inappropriate in this instance. "This is not a matter of substituting the Court's philosophical preference for that of the legislature, but of ensuring that the legislature's proffered justification is supported by logic and common sense."[4] Second, the mere fact that the law at issue was Parliament's second attempt to restrict the voting rights of prisoners could not justify the infringement of democratic rights.

> ... the fact that the challenged denial of the right to vote followed judicial rejection of an even more comprehensive denial, does not mean that the Court should defer to Parliament as part of a "dialogue." Parliament must ensure that whatever law it passes, at whatever stage of the process, conforms to the Constitution. The healthy and important promotion of a dialogue between the legislature and the courts should not be debased to a rule of "if at first you don't succeed, try, try again."[5]

This exchange reveals the flaws in the Court-centric version of the dialogue model (i.e., the approach of Hogg, Bushell, and Roach). Gonthier argued that Parliament is entitled to strike its own balance between Charter values and other priorities, and that any reasonable legislative choice should be respected by the Court. McLachlin countered by refusing to defer to Parliament unless a law "conforms to the Constitution," without acknowledging the difference between the Constitution itself and the Court's interpretation of it. In effect, McLachlin rejected the idea that Parliament can and should follow its own understanding of the Charter, an understanding that the Court should respect whenever possible, and argued instead that the Court's opinion should prevail when the two institutions disagree.

ENDNOTES

1. *Sauvé v. Canada (Attorney General)*, [1993] 2 S.C.R. 438.

2. The new provision was contained in s. 23 of Bill C-114, which was passed in June 1993. It was subsequently incorporated in the 2000 version of the Canada Elections Act as s. 4(c).

3. *Sauvé v. Canada (Chief Electoral Officer)*, [2002] 3 S.C.R. 418, paragraph 104 (emphasis in original).

4. Ibid., paragraph 9.

5. Ibid., paragraph 17.

While Gonthier's approach may have been more satisfactory in principle, it was based on an inaccurate characterization of the *Sauvé* case. In the first place, there was little real dialogue between the two branches of government. When Parliament enacted the revised prisoner-voting law, it did so without any judicial guidance beyond a cursory reference to the "minimal impairment" branch of the *Oakes* test. It is difficult to engage in dialogue when one of the partners is silent. Second, the legislative record reveals that Parliament failed to take its Charter duties seriously. There was no attempt, by the minister or by MPs, to find a reasonable balance between the voting rights of prisoners and other social objectives. The Royal Commission on Electoral Reform and Party Financing had recommended that all prisoners be allowed to vote, except for those convicted of "an offence punishable by a maximum of life imprisonment and sentenced for ten years or more."[31] The House of Commons Special Committee on Electoral Reform accepted that recommendation. But the minister responsible for electoral matters rejected the extension of voting rights to a majority of prisoners, arguing that citizens "whose crime is sufficient to require them to pay the penalty in a federal penitentiary" should lose the right to vote while incarcerated.[32] Although the committee was concerned about the Charter implications of the two-year cutoff, the minister (and, by extension, the government) refused to take their arguments seriously:

> There's no question that if we allowed everybody the right to vote, we wouldn't get a Charter challenge. The thing that bothers me is that I just don't believe that criminals should be voting. I don't think Clifford Olson should have a vote.... I find it incredible that such is our feeling about

the act they have committed that we would throw them into prison, but yet say that we don't want to deny them the right to vote. That, to me, just isn't common sense.[33]

The government members of the committee defeated several attempts to broaden the franchise for inmates. In the absence of a legislative objective more pressing than the minister's "common sense," and in light of the importance of voting rights, McLachlin's refusal to accept the ban as a "reasonable limit" may be more appropriate than Gonthier's deferential approach.

The coordinate model of the relationship between Parliament and the courts acknowledges that each institution has a legitimate role in making public policy. Each is responsible for striking a balance between protected rights and freedoms, on the one hand, and competing goals—e.g., fiscal prudence or public security—on the other. Where Parliament strikes a different balance from that endorsed by a majority on the Supreme Court, the latter should not automatically declare it to be inconsistent with the Charter. After all, there is a difference between the Charter itself and its interpretation by the courts. To overlook that difference is to deny Parliament an independent role in policy-making wherever legislative objectives touch on protected rights *as defined by the Court*. If, as Slattery argues, constitutionalism and the rule of law impose first-order and second-order duties on Parliament, these would be rendered meaningless by a Court that regarded its own second-order duties as the only safeguard against unjustified violations of the Charter. None of the three levels of government, by itself, can fully protect entrenched rights and freedoms.

The "Relational" Approach

A recent example of the coordinate approach is Hiebert's "relational" model. Rejecting the "dialogue" concept, which implicitly requires that both parties reach an agreement on the meaning of the Charter in a particular context, Hiebert suggests that Parliament and the Court should sometimes agree to disagree.

The normative goal is not that Parliament aspire to ensure that legislation addresses all judicial concerns or, alternatively, that the judiciary defer

to Parliament's judgment. Rather, it is that each body satisfy itself that its judgment respects Charter values, particularly when faced with the other's contrary judgment. Thus, a relational approach is informed by the assumption that parliamentary and judicial judgments be guided by a degree of modesty about the superiority of their conclusions and by respect for the other's contrary interpretation.[34]

This mutual respect rests on the distinction between the institutional responsibilities and resources of legislators and judges. In theory, Parliament takes all relevant interests into account when it assesses the bills proposed by the executive branch. Public policies must be carefully designed to achieve their particular goals, without imposing excessive fiscal burdens on the state. The expertise required to design and evaluate policies is often technical, and always specialized. While Charter values should play an important role in Parliament's deliberations, they are only one factor in a broader process of decision-making.[35] Judges have a different responsibility: to determine whether a law, once passed, violates the Charter rights of those whom it affects. To this task, judges bring a wealth of legal knowledge and a "relative insulation from public and political pressures."[36]

In effect, each institution has to answer a different question. For Parliament, the question is whether a proposed law would effectively address a public problem without undue cost. The question for judges to answer is whether the law, once it takes effect, infringes Charter values to a degree that cannot be justified under s. 1. Although both institutions are obliged to ensure that laws conform to the Charter, neither has the resources required for a complete and satisfactory answer to either question. Contrary to the conventional stereotype, a majority of MPs are not lawyers.[37] Parliamentarians may avail themselves of legal advice from the Department of Justice, the law clerks of the Commons and Senate, the researchers at the Library of Parliament, witnesses at committee hearings, and any outside experts whom they choose to consult. But they cannot match the legal expertise embodied in the Supreme Court and its provincial counterparts. And because Parliament is primarily a partisan and political institution, Charter considerations are not always at the forefront. The Reform

Party (subsequently the Canadian Alliance, and now the Conservative Party of Canada) has been harshly critical of judicial power and the protection of certain rights under the Charter (especially those of criminal suspects). Consequently, Charter discussions can degenerate into partisan posturing that produces more heat than light.[38]

For their part, the courts cannot rely on objective policy advice when they assess the constitutionality of a law under the *Oakes* test. As we saw in Chapter 3, the Court is at the mercy of the evidentiary record. Much of that record is supplied by lawyers and intervenors, whose approach to the policy issues arising from a particular dispute may be neither comprehensive nor objective. If he or she wishes, a member of the Court can take judicial notice of extrinsic evidence. However, the *Askov* ruling (Dossier 3.4, pages 120–21) is a sobering reminder of the danger inherent in the judicial misuse of social-science data.

As the Supreme Court itself has acknowledged on several occasions, it lacks the institutional competence to accurately assess the impact of much public policy.[39] Therefore, deference to Parliament at the various stages of the *Oakes* test is often warranted. However, excessive judicial deference under s. 1 might lead the Court to neglect its second-order duties. If these are to be performed adequately, as Chapter 3 argues, the Supreme Court may need to be reformed in order to enhance its capacity to evaluate policy on non-Charter grounds. Otherwise, Canadian policy-makers may not achieve a reasonable balance between their respective institutional responsibilities under the Charter.

THE EVOLVING RELATIONSHIP BETWEEN PARLIAMENT AND THE COURTS IN THE CHARTER ERA: CASE STUDIES

The case studies in this section have been chosen to illustrate the theoretical perspectives discussed in the preceding pages. The first two describe in-your-face parliamentary replies to Supreme Court rulings. To date, neither has been the subject of a Charter challenge to the top court; the dialogue is therefore incomplete. The third case study examines the failed attempt to enact a replacement law on abortion after the 1988 *Morgentaler* decision (Dossier 2.12, pages 77–79). The fourth discusses the reaction of a provincial legislature to a Supreme Court ruling on equality rights. The fifth and final case study is devoted to the dialogue between Parliament and the Court over the use of confidential records in sexual-assault trials. The case studies were chosen on the basis of two criteria: (1) their relevance to the themes of the chapter and (2) the volume of written material, both primary and secondary, on each case.[40] We begin with two controversial rulings on the due-process rights of criminal suspects.

INTOXICATION AS A CRIMINAL DEFENCE

Every criminal offence has two elements: the prohibited act (*actus reus*) and the mental element of the crime (*mens rea*). (See Chapter 10, pages 308–11.) To obtain a conviction, the Crown prosecutor must prove beyond a reasonable doubt that the suspect committed the offence and that he or she did so with the requisite degree of foreknowledge and intent. The "moral blameworthiness" attaching to a crime is usually determined by the mental element. For example, a person who deliberately kills another person is guilty of first- or second-degree murder (depending on the circumstances), but someone who kills through negligence or foreseeable accident may be found guilty of manslaughter.

As discussed in Chapter 10, pages 308–11, proving the mental element of an offence is often the most difficult challenge for a prosecutor. A suspect who can prove that he was mentally ill when he committed the prohibited act, to such an extent that he did not understand the likely consequences of his decisions, cannot be held responsible in law. However, the common law usually exempted one particular form of "mental defect"—severe intoxication—from being used as a defence.[41] Unlike a "disease of the mind" such as schizophrenia, intoxication was generally regarded as a moral choice. A person who willfully got drunk and then committed a violent offence could not escape the consequences, unless other mitigating factors were present. In effect, the intent to become dangerously intoxicated made up for any lack of intent to commit the crime. This rule applied to sexual assault and other crimes of violence.

In 1994, the Supreme Court overturned this common-law rule in cases where the accused was so drunk as to be in a state of "automatism." In legal terms, "automatism" describes a condition in which the person has no control over his or her actions, or in which he or she is unable to appreciate the nature and quality of his or her deeds. By a majority of six to three, the Court quashed the conviction of a man who sexually assaulted a woman while he was acutely intoxicated.[42] The majority argued that "the substituted *mens rea* of an intention to become drunk cannot establish the *mens rea* to commit the assault."

> Moreover, the presumption of innocence requires that the Crown bear the burden of establishing all elements of a crime, including the mental element of voluntariness. Assuming that voluntary intoxication is reprehensible, it does not follow that its consequences in any given situation are either voluntary or predictable.... To deny that even a very minimal mental element is required for sexual assault offends the Charter in a manner that is so drastic and so contrary to the principles of fundamental justice that it cannot be justified under s. 1 of the Charter.[43]

Although the *Daviault* decision did not provide a "get out of jail free" card to all violent alcoholics, it did require judges and juries to consider evidence of extreme intoxication as a defence to a criminal charge.

The public reaction was immediate and hostile.[44] Women's groups were horrified by what they perceived as "open season" on women and children.

> ... this new defence will have an impact on the filtering of offences of violence against women. It will affect women's ability to identify and report violence against them, because the message from the Supreme Court is that this behaviour is not criminal if the man is extremely intoxicated. It will affect police decisions as to whether they file charges, and it will affect crown attorneys' decisions about the pursuit of charges.[45]

Daviault's alleged victim was sixty-five years old and confined to a wheelchair. Her obvious vulnerability caught public attention and increased the political pressure on the federal government to close the loophole created by the Court. Making matters worse, the new defence to a charge of sexual assault—which the majority predicted would be used very rarely—immediately became popular with defence lawyers. Within six months of the ruling, five men accused of either assault or sexual assault were acquitted using the *Daviault* defence.[46] The media reported these acquittals, heightening public outrage at the Court's ruling. The failure of the *Daviault* defence in other trials, and the overturning of two of the acquittals on appeal, received less attention,[47] as did the fact that the Court had ordered a new trial for Mr. Daviault. (In the event, however, the victim died before a new trial could be held, and the charges were dropped.[48])

The Department of Justice was unsure how to proceed. It eventually decided, after sustained lobbying by women's groups, to "focus on the issue of violence against women and the impact of that violence on women's struggle for equality."[49] Less than six months after the Court issued its ruling, and shortly before a national day of protest against *Daviault*, Bill C-72 was introduced in the House of Commons. Highlights of the bill are reproduced in Dossier 4.4, page 159.

Bill C-72 differed from the majority ruling in *Daviault* in at least two respects. First, it accepted Justice Sopinka's dissenting opinion that there was no need for a new defence of extreme intoxication in the criminal law. In effect, Parliament chose to eliminate the defence created by the *Daviault* majority. In the absence of legislation, the majority's ruling would have governed all future trials in which a defence of intoxication was advanced. But when Parliament acted by adopting Bill C-72, that provision took priority over all judge-made law on the issue. It meant that an accused could no longer be acquitted on the ground that he was too drunk to form the requisite *mens rea*.

Second, the bill's analysis of the Charter went far beyond that of the majority on the Court. Whereas the only rights mentioned in *Daviault* were the s. 7 and s. 11(d) rights of the defendant, the Preamble to Bill C-72 referred explicitly to the security and

DOSSIER 4.4

THE LEGISLATIVE SEQUEL TO *DAVIAULT*

Background: The Preamble to Bill C-72 sets out Parliament's understanding of the Charter as it applies to the link between self-induced intoxication and criminal acts. The Preamble, which is almost twice as long as the text of the bill itself, has no binding effect and does not appear in the amended Criminal Code. Nonetheless, its inclusion was intended to persuade courts that the law is justified under s. 1 of the Charter, despite its possible infringement of the legal rights of criminal suspects (ss. 7 and 11(d)). The italicized sections in the excerpts below were amended by the Standing Committee on Justice and Legal Affairs.

Whereas the Parliament of Canada is gravely concerned about the incidence of violence in Canadian society;

Whereas the Parliament of Canada recognizes that violence has a particularly disadvantaging impact on the equal participation of women and children in society and on the rights of women and children to security of the person and to the equal protection and benefit of the law as guaranteed by sections 7, 15 and 28 of the Canadian Charter of Rights and Freedoms;

Whereas the Parliament of Canada recognizes that there is a close association between violence and intoxication and is concerned that self-induced intoxication may be used socially and legally to excuse violence, particularly violence against women and children;

Whereas the Parliament of Canada recognizes that the potential effects of alcohol and certain drugs on human behaviour are well known to Canadians and is aware of scientific evidence that *most* intoxicants, including alcohol, *by themselves, will* not cause a person to act involuntarily;

Whereas the Parliament of Canada shares with Canadians the moral view that people who, while in a state of self-induced intoxication, violate the physical integrity of others are blameworthy in relation to their harmful conduct and should be held criminally accountable for it;

Whereas the Parliament of Canada desires to promote and help to ensure the full protection of the rights guaranteed under sections 7, 11, 15 and 28 of the Canadian Charter of Rights and Freedoms for all Canadians, including those who are or may be victims of violence....

The Criminal Code is amended by adding the following after section 33:

33.1 (1) It is not a defence to an offence referred to in subsection (3) that the accused, by reason of self-induced intoxication, lacked the general intent or the voluntariness required to commit the offence, where the accused departed markedly from the standard of care as described in subsection (2).

(2) For the purposes of this section, a person departs markedly from the standard of reasonable care generally recognized in Canadian society and is thereby criminally at fault where the person, while in a state of self-induced intoxication that renders the person unaware of, or incapable of consciously controlling, their behaviour, voluntarily or involuntarily interferes or threatens to interfere with the bodily integrity of another person.

(3) This section applies in respect of an offence under this Act or any other Act of Parliament that includes as an element an assault or any other interference or threat of interference by a person with the bodily integrity of another person.

equality rights of women and children under ss. 7 and 15(1).[50] Although the Supreme Court has, on occasion, interpreted the "principles of fundamental justice" in light of other Charter values—in particular, the protection of vulnerable individuals and groups—it did not do so in *Daviault*.[51] By framing the issue of violence against women and children as a question of equality, Parliament rejected the narrow due-process approach of the Court and sought to balance the rights of the accused against other social interests (including the rights of alleged victims).

Because of the perceived urgency of the bill, some MPs suggested that it be reviewed in Committee of the Whole instead of referring it to the Standing Committee on Justice and Legal Affairs. The latter was tied up with amendments to the gun-control law (Bill C-68), and there was some concern that the committee's workload would delay the passage of Bill C-72. In the end, the government decided that the standing committee would be the best forum for detailed review. The strongest argument was that the committee would be able to hold hearings and call expert witnesses who would provide "a track record for why this bill is needed and why it does what we want it to do."[52] That record might help the government to win a future Charter challenge, by demonstrating that Parliament had struck a reasonable balance between the rights of the accused and competing social values.

At the committee stage, the MPs and most witnesses supported the bill. One of the few controversial issues was whether the proposed law would survive a Charter challenge. Several MPs questioned the legal experts about the discrepancies between the bill and the *Daviault* decision. They were reassured that the Court would probably uphold the bill, even though it might be found to violate ss. 7 and 11(d) of the Charter. In the first place, the majority had pointed out that "it is always open to Parliament to fashion a remedy which would make it a crime to commit a prohibited act while drunk."[53] Second, the *Daviault* ruling concerned a judge-made common law. The common law receives a lower degree of deference than that which would be accorded to a legislated statute.[54] There is little, if any, need to conduct a s. 1 analysis

in such an instance. Most witnesses predicted that Bill C-72 would pass the *Oakes* test because it reflected a thoughtful balance between the due-process rights of the accused and the equality rights of women and other vulnerable groups.[55]

Third, the Preamble and the legislative record would provide proof that Parliament had taken its first-order Charter duties seriously. Indeed, the Preamble drew almost as much attention as the text of the bill. The National Association of Women and the Law (NAWL) argued that the principles stated in the Preamble should be contained within the bill itself, in a separate statement of purpose. Otherwise, the courts might not feel obliged to take the Preamble into consideration when assessing the proportionality of the law under s. 1 of the Charter. However, the Preamble itself drew praise from most witnesses. On behalf of NAWL, law professor Elizabeth Sheehy explained the importance of the Preamble in the following terms:

> I think it does serve an important purpose. It flags for the courts the specific problems this bill is intended to address. It identifies the public policy concerns behind the bill. It identifies the constitutional rights that are at issue in this bill, which is also very important. It gives an indication that Parliament has considered all of the conflicting interests and rights here and this is its considered response to those conflicts.[56]

More broadly, the Preamble served an educative purpose by clarifying Parliament's intent when it passed the law. This would benefit both Canadians at large, by explaining the issues involved in Bill C-72, and the legal profession in particular.[57]

Another important feature of the committee hearings was the presentation of evidence that refuted the Court's factual assumptions about intoxication and automatism. Dr. John Bradford, then head of forensic psychiatry at the Royal Ottawa Hospital, told the committee that "the mere fact an accused person was intoxicated on a voluntary basis should not support a finding of automatism under any circumstances, regardless of the level of intoxication."[58] Bradford pointed out that while a large quantity of alcohol may produce retrospective amnesia—the condition that the Court called "blackout"—it does not necessarily create a condition of automatism at the moment when an offence was committed. In other words, a man who can't remember killing someone in a bar fight may well have known what he was doing when he stabbed the victim.

Dr. Bradford's argument was supported by other experts on the relationship between alcohol and violence. Dr. Harold Kalant, former director of the Addiction Research Foundation (ARF), stated that the *Daviault* defence of alcoholic automatism arose from the judicial misuse of scientific evidence. He asked Parliament, through the committee, to correct "the error I believe was made, that is, a scientific error made by the *Daviault* decision."[59] Another ARF official was equally blunt: "alcohol in and of itself cannot induce a state akin to automatism. The so-called *Daviault* decision would *de facto* seem to have created the legal defence of alcohol-induced intoxication akin to automatism, which is indefensible in scientific terms."[60] One MP suggested that "if the people in the *Daviault* decision [i.e., the Justices] had that testimony before them, maybe we wouldn't be here today."[61] The committee took these views into consideration and amended the bill accordingly. It reworded the Preamble to reflect Dr. Bradford's argument that alcohol does not, by itself, cause automatism. (See the italicized sections in Dossier 4.4, page 159.) Although an amendment to the Preamble does not affect the content of the bill, it may have an impact on future judicial review.

In the end, the *Daviault* saga may have been much ado about relatively little. It did not deter the Supreme Court from creating an intoxication defence to murder charges.[62] The intoxication defence is rarely supported by credible evidence, so Bill C-72 affected few sexual-assault trials.[63] The real importance of Bill C-72 lies in Parliament's rejection of a due-process ruling that appeared to threaten the security or equality of vulnerable groups in Canadian society. In addition, the Commons justice committee showed that legislative policy-making based on sound empirical evidence can produce better law than judges working with questionable "expert" testimony.

CASE STUDY 2

SEARCH WARRANTS

In May 1997, the Supreme Court handed down a ruling that infuriated police officers and prosecutors. It overturned the murder conviction of Michael Feeney, on the grounds that his Charter rights had been violated in his investigation and trial, and ordered a new trial at which tainted evidence would be excluded. The investigating officer, having discovered the battered body of 85-year-old Frank Boyle at his home in northern British Columbia, was told by two local women that they had recently seen Feeney near the scene of an accident involving Boyle's truck. The officer spoke to Feeney's sister and her partner, who informed him that Michael had come home a few hours earlier from a night of drinking. The officer went to the windowless equipment trailer where Feeney was living, knocked on the door, and identified himself as a police officer. Receiving no response, he entered the trailer and awoke Feeney by touching him on the leg. The officer noticed blood on Feeney's clothing, and immediately arrested him for the murder. Without benefit of legal counsel, Feeney eventually confessed to killing Boyle and stealing his truck, money, and cigarettes. Acting on this information, the RCMP obtained a search warrant for the trailer; the search produced evidence that corroborated Feeney's confession.

At trial, the judge ruled that the officer's initial entry into the trailer did not violate the s. 8 rights of the suspect. Had the officer waited for a search warrant before going in, Feeney might have taken the opportunity to destroy incriminating evidence (recall that the trailer had no windows, which made it impossible for police waiting outside for a warrant to know what was going on inside). The warrantless arrest was justified by the violent nature of the crime and by the reasonable and probable grounds arising from the bloody clothing. Feeney was convicted of second-degree murder. The British Columbia Court of Appeal unanimously upheld the conviction. The case was appealed to the Supreme Court of Canada.

In a 5-4 decision, the Court quashed the conviction and ruled that the evidence taken from the trailer should not have been admitted at trial. Writing for the majority, Justice Sopinka rejected the common-law rules authorizing warrantless entry into a dwelling place for the purpose of arrest. Under the Charter, he wrote, "the privacy interest outweighs the interest of the police and warrantless arrests in dwelling houses are prohibited."[64] An arrest warrant alone could not authorize the limitation of privacy rights under s. 8. The only exceptions were in cases of hot pursuit, e.g., where an officer chased a suspect into a private home, although Sopinka suggested that other, unspecified "exigent circumstances" might justify a warrantless entry. The effect of the majority ruling was to require an officer to secure two separate judicial authorizations before entering a dwelling place to detain a suspect: an arrest warrant and a "*Feeney* warrant" for entry into the home. Because Sopinka found that the officer had violated Feeney's rights by entering his trailer without prior authorization, none of the evidence secured as a result of that entry was admissible under s. 24(2) of the Charter.

Police, victims' rights advocates, and prosecutors condemned the decision, arguing that the Court had gone too far in protecting the due-process rights of criminals while ignoring public safety and tying the hands of police officers.[65] They pointed out that, in some provinces, an arrest warrant may only be issued after a Crown prosecutor has signed off on the proposed charges; in those jurisdictions, the *Feeney* decision could impose unmanageable delays on law enforcement personnel.[67]

The decision was handed down during a general election, when Parliament was dissolved. Federal and provincial attorneys general quickly sought a six-month stay, which would allow Parliament to reconvene and consider a legislative response.[67] The *Feeney* ruling had not been anticipated by the Department of Justice; it is routinely notified of challenges to federal statutes, but Feeney dealt with a challenge to common law. Consequently, the federal government had not considered its options in the event that the common-law rules were overturned.[68] The Department of Justice consulted provincial governments and other interested parties, seeking guidance on possible legislation.

In late October 1997, the minister of justice tabled Bill C-16,[69] which provided for the new warrants required under *Feeney*. It also forbade officers to execute a warrant in a dwelling-house unless they had good reason to believe that the suspect was in the house at the time of entry. In other words, they could not use a "*Feeney* warrant" to stake out the interior of a private home and wait for the suspect to return. However, the bill did not reflect the balance that Sopinka had struck between privacy rights and law enforcement. Instead, the minister and Parliament followed Justice L'Heureux-Dubé's dissenting opinion. She argued that there was no abuse of police discretion in the *Feeney* investigation and that the Court should not impose unnecessary due-process constraints on police officers. For excerpts from the Preamble to the bill, see Dossier 4.5.

The actual text of the law differed from the *Feeney* decision in two ways. First, it modified the require-

---

DOSSIER 4.5

EXCERPTS FROM THE PREAMBLE TO BILL C-16

Whereas the Parliament of Canada recognizes that there is a societal interest in the proper administration of justice including effective law enforcement, and that to achieve effective law enforcement, peace officers must be granted the power to enter a dwelling-house to arrest or apprehend persons who they believe have committed a criminal offence....

Whereas the Parliament of Canada recognizes that while it is necessary for peace officers to obtain prior judicial authorization to enter a dwelling-house in order to arrest or apprehend a person, circumstances may nonetheless exist that justify entry into a dwelling-house for such a purpose in the absence of prior judicial authorization;

Whereas the Parliament of Canada recognizes the societal importance of providing peace officers with the ability to effectively respond to urgent calls for assistance....

Whereas the Parliament of Canada declares that nothing in this Act is intended to limit or restrict the circumstances under which peace officers may be justified in entering a dwelling-house for the purposes of arrest or apprehen-

sion in the absence of prior judicial authorization, under this or any other Act or law, including the common law;

And Whereas the Parliament of Canada declares that nothing in this Act is intended to limit or restrict the ability of peace officers to enter a dwelling-house for purposes other than arrest or apprehension, under this or any other Act or law, including the common law....

ment for police officers to identify themselves before executing a warrant in a private home. Whereas Justice Sopinka had implied that a proper announcement was required in all circumstances short of "hot pursuit" and argued that a warrantless entry could not be justified in order to protect possible evidence, Bill C-16 suspended the requirement of announcement where the officer has "reasonable grounds to believe" that it "would result in the imminent loss or imminent destruction of evidence relating to the commission of an indictable offence" (s. 529.4(2) and (3)). Second, the bill exempted police officers from the obligation to obtain a warrant where "exigent circumstances" made it "impracticable" to do so. It defined "exigent circumstances" as those in which a person inside the house is in danger of "imminent bodily harm or death," or in which a delayed entry might permit someone inside the house to destroy evidence. This definition is considerably broader than the "hot pursuit" exemption allowed by Sopinka.

The bill was rushed through the Commons and Senate because of the tight deadline imposed by the Supreme Court.[70] Members of the Commons Standing Committee on Justice and Human Rights were so incensed by this perceived insult to Parliament that they issued a separate report condemning the process.[71] The committee had time for only four witnesses on Bill C-16, apart from the minister of justice and her officials: the Canadian Police Association, the Canadian Resource Centre for Victims of Crime, the Canadian Association of Chiefs of Police, and the Criminal Lawyers' Association of Ontario. The first three were highly critical of the Supreme Court—and not only in the context of the *Feeney* ruling itself. They supported the bill while arguing that the exemptions

should be even broader. On behalf of the Criminal Lawyers' Association, Irwin Koziebrocki took the opposite view: the bill gave too much discretion to the police and would likely fail a Charter challenge.

Reform MP Jack Ramsay shared that concern, asking repeatedly whether the section that permitted a warrantless entry into a dwelling-house for the purpose of preserving evidence contradicted the *Feeney* ruling and was therefore doomed to be struck down. Justice Minister Anne McLellan replied that while one could never guarantee that a particular law would be upheld by the courts, "we believe the Supreme Court will agree with us and uphold this legislation because we have struck the right balance between important values."[72] Yvan Roy, senior general counsel at the Department of Justice, pointed out the difference between rewriting a common-law rule and invalidating a legislated statute. In the former case, the Supreme Court is simply changing the law that it, or another court, has made in previous cases. It need not defer to the Charter interpretations of another branch of government.[73] But in the latter instance, "when Parliament speaks—and this has been said by the Supreme Court on numerous occasions—a measure of deference is owed to Parliament in those circumstances."[74]

The nub of the issue, the extent to which Parliament should defer to the Supreme Court in drafting legislation, was addressed by Scott Newark of the Canadian Police Association:

I guess, Mr. Ramsay, with respect, the point is who's driving the train here? That is the approach that, frankly, many people take. You end up virtually inserting yourself into the position of guessing what a Supreme Court Justice would do, given a set of circumstances.... Rather than attempting to anticipate what the Supreme Court might or might not do, the person driving the train should be Parliament and Parliament should express that this is what it intends exigent circumstances to be.[75]

Because it lacked the time to consider changes to the law, the committee reported the bill to the House of Commons without amendment.[76]

Roach portrays *Feeney* and its legislative sequel as a classic case of dialogue, in which the Supreme Court defended the Charter and Parliament responded by readjusting the balance between due-process rights and competing social values.[77] Hiebert's assessment is more negative. She points out that the Court's failure to notify Parliament of an impending decision with serious implications for the criminal-law power "was premised on the faulty assumption that Parliament does not have a valid interest in changes to common law rules."[78] Moreover, the Court's initial refusal to suspend the effect of the majority ruling created administrative chaos; even the subsequent extensions left Parliament little time to consider the important issues raised by the *Feeney* case. Although the committee engaged in a serious debate over the Charter and Parliament's role in relation to it, the looming deadline forced its members to accept a bill that caused them grave concern.

The most positive aspect of the *Feeney* "dialogue" is Parliament's assertiveness in the face of a Court ruling that, in the view of many observers, struck the wrong balance between due-process rights and public safety: "This willingness to develop a warrant regime that differs from the court's revised rule suggests that Parliament does not accept a judicial-centric view of constitutional judgment."[79] On the downside, the legislative process was constrained by an unrealistic Court-imposed deadline. The Justices' apparent failure to appreciate the logistical difficulties arising from the election campaign, and their insistence that their interpretation of the Charter should take effect immediately (without giving the other two branches sufficient time to respond), did not demonstrate a proper respect for the legitimate policy-making role of the other branches of government.

ABORTION

The dialogue metaphor implies that both parties are free to speak on any issue. But as we noted earlier in this chapter, some issues are too hot for legislators to handle. While it might be preferable for laws on sensitive moral questions to be made by our elected representatives, policy-making on such issues can shift to the courts by default. This is particularly true in the Charter era. Dossier 2.12, pages 77–79, contrasts the Supreme Court's two rulings on abortion: the first, under the Bill of Rights, left the restrictive law intact, while the second invalidated it as an unjustified infringement of Charter rights. The 1988 *Morgentaler* ruling caused problems for the Mulroney government. Its own caucus was bitterly polarized over abortion, and the government would greatly have preferred to keep it off the legislative agenda. The failure of Bill C-43, the government's attempt to strike an acceptable compromise between the "pro-choice" and "pro-life" positions, illustrated the difficulty of dialogue when both the legislature and the public are deeply divided.

The 1988 *Morgentaler* decision also revealed divisions on the Court.[80] Each of the three concurring decisions in the majority hinted that Parliament should adopt a new abortion law that struck a reasonable balance between the state's interest in protecting the fetus and the rights of pregnant women to "life, liberty and security of the person" under s. 7 of the Charter. The strongest hint came from Justice Beetz: "This does not preclude, in my view, Parliament from adopting another system, free of the failings of s. 251(4), in order to ascertain that the life or health of the pregnant woman is in danger, by way of a reliable, independent and medically sound opinion."[81] Justice Wilson proposed that Parliament adopt a "gestational" approach, which would make abortion more difficult to obtain as the pregnancy progressed.[82]

While pro-choice groups celebrated the second *Morgentaler* ruling, the pro-life forces rallied for a counterattack. The Progressive Conservative government came under intense pressure to recriminalize abortion, especially from some of its own backbench MPs. The socially conservative "Family Caucus" was particularly vocal in its demand that the government act to fill the legislative vacuum left by the Court decision. In the summer of 1988, Mulroney announced a free vote in the Commons on a range of policy options. One of the five motions would have returned the law to the restrictive regime that the Court had just struck down; three adopted the gestational approach; and the fifth would have left the decision to the woman and her doctor at any stage of pregnancy.[83] In addition, the government proposed to recriminalize abortion except under certain conditions; those conditions became more onerous in the latter stages of gestation.[84] Female MPs from all three parties (Progressive Conservative, Liberal, and New Democratic Party) voted as a block. They supported the motions that imposed few conditions on access to abortion and voted against the more restrictive proposals. All five private members' motions were defeated, as was the government proposal. Parliament was in a stalemate.

Over the next several months, the pressure on the government intensified. Two men sought and won court injunctions preventing their ex-girlfriends from obtaining abortions. Although the Supreme Court subsequently overturned one of the injunctions,[85] pro-choice groups realized that they may have won the battle only to lose the war. In November 1989, the government introduced Bill C-43, which would have criminalized abortion except when performed "by or under the direction of a medical practitioner who is of the opinion that, if the abortion were not induced, the health or life of the female person would be likely to be threatened."[86] "Health" was defined broadly, to include psychological as well as physical factors. Justice Minister Doug Lewis told the legislative committee on the bill that the word "psychological" should be interpreted as including environmental reasons for terminating a pregnancy, such as economic constraints.[87] Despite the permissiveness of the bill, pro-choice activists opposed the recriminalization of abortion and fought against the law. So, for more obvious reasons, did groups opposed to abortion.

At second and third readings, the government allowed PC backbenchers to vote according to their consciences; the cabinet, however, had to vote in support of the bill. It passed at second reading by a margin of 164 to 114. Several members of the "Family Caucus" voted in favour because they hoped that the legislative committee would amend the bill to make it more restrictive.[88] However, the government refused to accept any amendments. Justice Minister Lewis told the committee that the bill was a carefully crafted compromise not only between Charter rights and other social values, but between the two levels of government. He argued that provincial governments, which are responsible for the delivery of health care services, could block the implementation of the bill if the balance tipped too far toward the pro-choice side. The unamended bill passed narrowly, with 140 in favour and 131 against.

The bill was delayed in the Senate for several months, largely because of the political furor surrounding the introduction of the Goods and Services Tax. In the meantime, several doctors stopped performing abortions because they were afraid of criminal prosecution under the new law.[89] The fight for access shifted to the provincial level, where some governments cut funding for abortions and tried to block the creation of free-standing clinics.[90] The Mulroney government appears to have lost the heart to defend Bill C-43. It did not force PC Senators to vote in favour of the legislation, although it did warn advocates of recriminalization that there would be no new law if C-43 failed.[91] When the bill finally reached third reading in the Senate in January 1991, the vote was tied 43-43. Under Senate rules, a tied vote is deemed to be negative. For the first time that anyone could remember, the Senate had defeated a government bill originating in the House of Commons.

Critics of the Charter attribute the demise of C-43 to "the climate of polarized intransigence promoted by the black-and-white, rights-based quality of Charter litigation."[92] This claim is questionable, if only because the "polarized intransigence" on the abortion issue dates back to the adoption of the abortion law in 1969—well before the advent of the Charter. Parliament's failure to adopt a new abortion law should not be taken as proof of judicial hegemony. Rather, it demonstrates that Parliament can play its role in the dialogue only when government legislation is supported by a majority in both Houses. If interest groups, the electorate, and party caucuses are too divided to reach a consensus on an issue, judges will have the last word in the discussion by default. Whatever one thinks of the judicial balance between

Charter rights and competing social values on the abortion issue, it will remain in force until such time as Parliament is prepared to replace it.

CASE STUDY 4

EXTENDING COMMON-LAW STATUS TO SAME-SEX COUPLES IN ONTARIO

As discussed in Chapter 11, Canada's courts have repeatedly told its elected governments that discrimination on the basis of sexual orientation violates the Charter. Although it was deliberately omitted from the list of prohibited grounds in s. 15(1), sexual orientation was "read in" to the Charter in 1995.[93] Once an "analogous ground" of discrimination—e.g., marital status[94]—has been identified, it must be treated in the same way as an "enumerated ground" (e.g., sex or age). It cannot be assumed that sexual orientation or marital status is a prohibited ground of discrimination in one context but not in others.[95] In effect, the recognition of an analogous ground amends s. 15(1) by limiting legislative and executive power in relation to a particular group. When the recognition issues from the Supreme Court of Canada, it applies to both federal and provincial governments.

Family law in Canada is divided between federal and provincial jurisdictions. Parliament legislates on marriage and divorce; the provinces legislate on the religious dimensions of the marriage contract, the division of assets and child custody issues attendant on divorce, and the recognition and regulation of common-law unions. The latter are generally defined as intimate relationships of some duration, involving cohabitation and the sharing of assets and responsibilities, but without a formal marriage ceremony. Whereas the rights and obligations of legal marriage are fairly clear, common-law unions have only recently received formal recognition by governments. By the 1990s, some provincial laws had been amended to extend some legal protection to the partners in common-law unions. For example, employers in some jurisdictions were required to extend benefit and pension coverage to the common-law "spouses" of their employees. The incremental extension of "spousal" status to unmarried couples was quickened by the Supreme Court's 1995 ruling in *Miron v. Trudel*, which held that marital status is an "analogous ground" under s. 15(1) of the Charter. In other

words, legislators could not discriminate against common-law "spouses" by denying them benefits that would flow automatically to legally married couples.[96]

By the late 1990s, gay and lesbian groups were using the courts to advance their fight for same-sex marriage. As a first step, they decided to challenge laws that defined common-law couples in exclusively heterosexual terms. While a victory on this front would not allow gay and lesbian couples to get married, it would give their relationships some legal recognition. It would also protect individual gays and lesbians from being left destitute after a breakup, by allowing them to sue for spousal support.

In 1999, the Supreme Court ruled on the case of *M. v. H.* (see Dossier 11.4, pages 359–62). The majority refused to defer to the Ontario legislature, which was opposed to amending the Family Law Act (FLA) to accord common-law status to same-sex relationships. Justice Cory rejected the provincial government's request for deference, which was based on the promise of incremental legislative reform: "there is no evidence of any progress with respect to [gay men and lesbians] since the inception of the spousal support regime. If the legislature refuses to act so as to evolve towards *Charter* compliance then deference as to the timing of reforms loses its *raison d'être*."[97] The Court gave the Ontario government six months to amend the FLA by incorporating same-sex couples into the definition of common-law unions.

Although the ruling in *M. v. H.* dealt only with the FLA, the majority noted that its decision would likely affect other provincial laws dealing with spousal benefits.

> The legislature may wish to address the validity of these statutes in light of the unconstitutionality of s. 29 of the *FLA*. On this point, I agree with the majority of the Court of Appeal which noted that if left up to the courts, these issues could only be resolved on a case-by-case basis at great cost to private litigants and the public purse. Thus, I believe the legislature ought to be given some latitude in order to address these issues in a more comprehensive fashion.[98]

The Conservative government of Premier Mike Harris did not want to extend the benefits of common-law status to same-sex couples. The issue had long divided Ontario politicians. In 1994, the provincial legislature had defeated a bill proposed by the then–NDP government that would have extended the benefits available to heterosexual common-law couples to Ontarians in homosexual relationships. The motion was defeated when the opposition Liberals, who had publicly supported the measure, changed their position and voted against it. After the 1995 provincial election that brought Harris to power, there was little political will to recognize the rights of same-sex couples. Indeed, the Tory government had intervened in the ongoing litigation between M. and H., arguing that the impugned section of the FLA was justified under s. 1 of the Charter. Instead of accepting the 1996 judgment of the Ontario Court of Appeal, which found s. 29 unconstitutional, the Harris government appealed to the Supreme Court of Canada. Meanwhile, M. and H. had settled their dispute. The Ontario NDP, now in opposition, accused the Tories of forcing the two women to undergo three years of needless litigation, instead of accepting the appellate decision and amending the law accordingly.[99] The Supreme Court of Canada seems to have shared this concern: it granted Ontario's attorney general leave to appeal, on the condition that M. would not have to pay the costs of the proceeding.

Predictably, the Harris government greeted the Supreme Court ruling in *M. v. H.* with dismay. Although he sponsored a bill that complied with the ruling (at least in part), Attorney General Jim Flaherty distanced himself from the issue of same-sex equality as best he could. Bill 5 was titled the "Amendments Because of the Supreme Court of Canada Decision in *M. v. H.* Act, 1999." (One Liberal MPP, recognizing the political symbolism of the title, called it the "Devil made me do it" Bill.[100]) It amended sixty-seven provincial statutes by adding a new category of "same-sex partner." As mandated by the Court, the law extended the definition of common-law marriage to include gay and lesbian couples. However, the definition of "spouse" remained exclusively heterosexual. In other words, same-sex couples would be entitled to the benefits flowing from common-law status, but Ontario law would continue to distinguish between common-law relationships (whether heterosexual or homosexual) and legal marriages (heterosexual). This "separate but equal"[101] approach appears to conflict

not only with the ruling in *M. v. H.*, but with the *Miron* decision as well (Dossier 11.1, pages 346–48). Nonetheless, the Supreme Court dismissed M.'s challenge to the constitutionality of Bill 5. M. argued that the new category of "same-sex partner" discriminated against gays and lesbians by treating them differently from other "spouses."[102] The Court gave no reason for its dismissal.

During the brief debate on Bill 5, Flaherty acknowledged that the government would not have made these legislative changes without an explicit directive from the Supreme Court of Canada:

> This bill responds to the Supreme Court of Canada decision while preserving the traditional values of the family by protecting the definition of "spouse" in Ontario law. This legislation is not part of our Blueprint agenda. We are introducing this bill because of the Supreme Court of Canada decision.... It is important for members to be aware of that fundamental in this debate, that marriage is not affected by this bill. Marriage, as members know, involves a man and a woman in Ontario.[103]

Liberal and NDP members who spoke at second reading—no Conservatives participated in the debate, apart from Flaherty—criticized the government for its attacks on the Supreme Court. They defended "judicial activism" as a necessary remedy for legislative prejudice and political timidity.[104] New Democrat MPP Peter Kormos was the most outspoken:

> This should be a cautionary note to all of us. When we're confronted with legislation, more often than not presented by the government, we, as legislators, had better make darn sure that it passes fundamental tests of constitutionality and gives effect to those fundamental principles of rights and freedoms, or else, once again, the courts will be stepping in, as they should.... Thank God for an independent judiciary that won't be constrained or directed by political considerations, but rather will do what they're entrusted to do and that's to enforce the law and to make sure that parliaments follow the law.[105]

Less than three years after Bill 5 took effect, Ontario's Divisional Court struck down the common-law definition of legal "marriage" as the "lawful and voluntary union of one man and one woman."[106] (See Dossier 11.4, pages 359–62.) That ruling was upheld by the Court of Appeal in June 2003. Although the definition of marriage is a federal responsibility, which gave the provincial government few legal options, the province could have tried to block same-sex couples from obtaining marriage licences in Ontario. Instead, the Conservative government (then led by Ernie Eves) decided to implement the Court of Appeal ruling immediately. It instructed registrars across the province to issue licences for gay and lesbian couples. This apparent change of heart may be attributed to a shift in public opinion: by 2003, a majority of Canadians accepted the idea of same-sex marriage.[107]

CASE STUDY 5

THE DISCLOSURE OF PERSONAL RECORDS TO THE DEFENCE IN SEXUAL-ASSAULT CASES

Our last case study exemplifies the constructive institutional relationship portrayed in the coordinate model. The Supreme Court rewrote the common law, Parliament responded by effectively overruling the majority opinion, and the Justices subsequently accepted Parliament's interpretation of the Charter. Unlike in the *Seaboyer* case, discussed earlier, Parliament did not "codify" the majority ruling in the Criminal Code; instead, it issued a "point-by-point repudiation" of the Court's decision.[108] To the surprise of some observers, the Court deferred to Parliament, acknowledging that "The courts do not hold a monopoly on the protection and promotion of rights and freedoms."[109]

The issue was whether, and under what circumstances, the accused in a sexual-assault case should be granted access to confidential records pertaining to the alleged victim. It arose in the prosecution of Hubert O'Connor, a former Catholic bishop accused of numerous sexual offences against Aboriginal children in a residential school in the 1960s. Lawyers for O'Connor petitioned the trial judge for access to the medical and school records of the four complainants. After the judge granted the order, without consulting the alleged victims, the Crown reluctantly turned over some, but not all, of the requested records. The trial

judge issued repeated requests for the outstanding materials, and eventually stayed the charges against O'Connor on the ground that the Crown's refusal to comply with the production order had irreparably tainted the fairness of the proceedings.

When it ruled on the case in 1995, a 5-4 majority of the Supreme Court held that the right of the accused to full answer and defence—a right that the Court had previously "read in" to s. 7 of the Charter as a "principle of fundamental justice"[110]—trumped any privacy interest attaching to medical records, notes of counselling sessions, and other personal materials relating to the complainant. The ruling distinguished between two classes of records: those that were already in the possession of the Crown, and those that were still in the hands of "third parties"(e.g., medical professionals, therapists, or sexual-assault crisis workers). Any personal records held by the Crown must be turned over to the defence as quickly as possible, under the broad disclosure rules laid down in *Stinchcombe*. (See Chapter 10, page 312.)

When the defence requested records held by "third parties," it would trigger a two-stage process. At the first stage, the judge would have to determine whether the requested information was "logically probative to *an issue at trial or the competence of a witness to testify.*"[111] If the judge determined, without having seen the records, that they met this test, he or she would issue an order for production. At the second stage, the judge would examine the records to determine their relevance to the case, any probative value they might have, and their admissibility under the common-law criteria flowing from s. 24(2) of the Charter. In making these decisions, the judge would be required to balance the privacy interest of the complainant against the due-process rights of the accused. Any records deemed to be relevant and admissible would then be turned over to the Crown.

Women's groups, victims' advocates and prosecutors were appalled by the ruling. The media overlooked the fact that a 6-3 majority had overturned the stay of proceedings and ordered a new trial. Instead, they emphasized the possible impact of the ruling on sexual-assault victims.[112] Justice L'Heureux-Dubé's vigorous dissent was applauded. She argued that the majority ruling would deter women from reporting sexual assaults, and that victims should not be further

humiliated by the disclosure of confidential information. In her view, counselling records are rarely relevant to the question of the guilt or innocence of the
accused; they would be employed by defence counsel
only as a tool for undermining the credibility of complainants and reinforcing societal stereotypes about
women who claim to have been raped. Finally, she
argued that the rights of the complainant—equality,
security, and privacy—are as deserving of protection
as the due-process rights of the accused.

Sexual-assault crisis centres worried about the
majority's comments concerning the possible relevance of their counselling records. Chief Justice Lamer
and Justice Sopinka gave three illustrations of the probative value of notes taken during therapy sessions.[113]
First, "they may contain information concerning the
unfolding of events underlying the criminal com-
plaint." The two Justices referred specifically to a case
in which the complainant told a therapist that she felt
"guilty" about having been sexually assaulted. The
trial judge in that case had forbidden the defence
attorney to cross-examine the complainant about that
statement. While acknowledging that guilt is a
common reaction to sexual violation, the majority
nonetheless found that the trial judge should have
permitted the cross-examination. They speculated
that the cross-examination might have revealed "a possible motive of the complainant to allege that she was
the victim of sexual assault" or some aspect of her
behaviour "which might have led the appellant to
believe that she was consenting to sexual advances."[114]
In other words, they suggested that either the woman
was lying about being raped or she had brought it on
herself by her own actions. Crisis workers were horrified at the suggestion that their counselling notes
might be used in court to attack the women they were
trying to help.

Second, the *O'Connor* majority suggested that private therapeutic records might "reveal the use of a
therapy that influenced the complainant's memory of
the alleged events." This appears to have been a reference to "recovered memory therapy," which can create
false "memories" of sexual violation in the minds of
vulnerable patients. While there is little doubt that
such cases have occurred in the United States and
Canada, most have involved allegations of childhood
incest and the "Satanic ritual cult" abuse of infants—

not the recent sexual assault of adult women.[115] The
implicit portrayal of overzealous crisis counsellors
brainwashing women into false accusations of rape
was bitterly resented by volunteers who had devoted
themselves to helping genuine victims of sexual violence. Third, counselling records may "contain information that bears on the complainant's credibility."
The majority concluded, "we disagree with
L'Heureux-Dubé J.'s assertion that therapeutic records
will only be relevant to the defence in rare cases."[116]
This seemed to indicate that any defence lawyer who
wanted to use the private records of alleged rape victims should be allowed to do so, no matter how great
the emotional cost to the woman (or man) involved.

The Liberal government began to consult with
affected groups, seeking guidance on a legislative
response to *O'Connor*. It introduced Bill C-46 in
February 1997. Two days later, the Supreme Court
handed down the *Carosella* ruling. *Carosella* began in
1992, when a Windsor woman went to the local
sexual assault crisis centre to report that she had been
sexually abused by a teacher almost thirty years earlier.
She was interviewed by a social worker at the centre
for almost two hours. The complainant subsequently
signed a release form, authorizing the disclosure of the
notes of that interview to the Crown and defence. In
October 1994, the defence applied to the judge for
access to the centre's records on the case. It turned out
that the centre had shredded the social worker's notes
in April 1994, as part of its efforts to protect the complainant's confidentiality in cases with police involvement. The trial judge ruled that the destroyed material
would likely have assisted the accused, and that its
absence breached his right to make full answer and
defence. He stayed the charges.

When the *Carosella* case reached the Supreme
Court, the five Justices in the *O'Connor* majority
upheld the trial judge's decision. They ruled that if the
notes had been produced in court, they could have
"assisted the defence in the preparation of cross-
examination questions."

They may have revealed the state of the complainant's perception and memory. They might
have revealed that some of the complainant's
statements resulted from suggestions made by
the interviewer. They could have pointed the

appellant in the direction of other witnesses. The notes may have demonstrated, in addition to the rest of the evidence disclosed to the accused, that he would not have had to testify at the trial, or that he would have had to mount a defence.[117]

Based on this speculative reasoning, the majority found that the breach of Mr. Carosella's right to make a full answer and defence was sufficiently serious to warrant a stay of proceedings. They also condemned the centre's decision to shred documents in order to prevent their disclosure in court.

> The justice system functions best and instils public confidence in its decisions when its processes are able to make available all relevant evidence which is not excluded by some overriding public policy. Confidence in the system would be undermined if the administration of justice condoned conduct designed to defeat the processes of the court. The agency made a decision to obstruct the course of justice by systematically destroying evidence which the practices of the court might require to be produced. This decision is not one for the agency to make. Under our system, which is governed by the rule of law, decisions as to which evidence is to be produced or admitted is for the courts.[118]

The four *O'Connor* dissenters reunited in their opposition to the *Carosella* majority. On their behalf, Justice L'Heureux-Dubé argued that the relevance of the destroyed records was likely tangential at best. Even if they had been relevant to the guilt or innocence of the accused, their destruction did not, in and of itself, justify a stay of proceedings: "While the production of every relevant piece of evidence might be an ideal goal from the accused's point of view, it is inaccurate to elevate this objective to a right, the non-performance of which leads instantaneously to an unfair trial."[119] Speculations as to the nature of the missing evidence are no substitute for proof of genuine prejudice to the defence. Referring to her ruling in *O'Connor*, she described the request for the counselling notes as "a fishing expedition in the hopes of uncovering a prior inconsistent statement."[120] She concluded with an expression of concern about the growing frequency of such "fishing expeditions":

> Finally, I must comment upon the fact that these agencies have even felt it necessary to go to such lengths. From a quick perusal of lower court judgments, it would appear as if a request for therapeutic records in cases of sexual assault is becoming virtually automatic, with little regard to the actual relevancy of the documents. We have now come to a situation where people trying to help victims have resorted to foregoing the taking of notes or destroying them *en masse* in order to prevent what they see as a grave injustice. It is extremely likely that the therapeutical process for which these notes are actually created is being harmed in their absence.[121]

Carosella increased the political pressure on the federal government to overturn the majority ruling in *O'Connor*. Bill C-46 was referred to the House of Commons Standing Committee on Justice and Legal Affairs before second reading, an unusual procedure that allows the committee greater latitude in amending draft legislation (see Dossier 4.1, pages 147–48). Like the legislative sequels to *Feeney* and *Daviault*, the bill followed the dissenting judgment and rejected the approach taken by the Court majority. L'Heureux-Dubé's emphasis on the rights of the complainant and her concerns about dissuading victims from reporting sexual offences are clearly reflected in the Preamble (see Dossier 4.6, page 171). That section of the bill followed the now-established practice of setting out Parliament's distinct approach to the Charter issues raised by the legislation.

The text of the Bill defined a "record" as anything containing "personal information for which there is a reasonable expectation of privacy." Examples included medical and counselling notes, employment records, and personal diaries. Police files relating to the alleged sexual assault were excluded. The bill modified the *Stinchcombe* disclosure rule—that all relevant evidence in the hands of the Crown must be turned over to the defence in a timely fashion—in cases of sexual assault. The Crown would be required to inform the defence of any personal records in its possession without disclosing the actual contents of that material. All records, whether in the hands of the Crown or of a third party (e.g., a sexual assault crisis centre), were covered by the same production rules. The defence

---

DOSSIER 4.6

THE PREAMBLE TO BILL C-46

Whereas the Parliament of Canada recognizes that violence has a particularly disadvantageous impact on the equal participation of women and children in society and on the rights of women and children to security of the person, privacy and equal benefit of the law as guaranteed by sections 7, 8, 15 and 28 of the Canadian Charter of Rights and Freedoms;

Whereas the Parliament of Canada intends to promote and help to ensure the full protection of the rights guaranteed by the Canadian Charter of Rights and Freedoms for all, including those who are accused of, and those who are or may be victims of, sexual violence or abuse;

Whereas the rights guaranteed by the Canadian Charter of Rights and Freedoms are guaranteed equally to all and, in the event of a conflict, those rights are to be accommodated and reconciled to the greatest extent possible;

Whereas the Parliament of Canada wishes to encourage the reporting of incidents of sexual violence and abuse and to provide for the prosecution of offences within a framework of laws that are consistent with the principles of fundamental justice and that are fair to complainants as well as to accused persons;

Whereas the Parliament of Canada recognizes that the compelled production of personal information may deter complainants of sexual offences from reporting the offence to the police and may deter complainants from seeking necessary treatment, counselling or advice....

And whereas the Parliament of Canada recognizes that, while production to the court and to the accused of personal information regarding any person may be necessary in order for an accused to make a full answer and defence, that production may breach the person's right to privacy and equality and therefore the determination as to whether to order production should be subject to careful scrutiny....

---

must apply to the trial judge for a production order, without having seen the actual record sought. Written applications must specifically identify the record, the name of the person holding it, and "the grounds on which the accused relies to establish that the record is likely relevant to an issue at trial or to the competence of a witness to testify." This section was clearly designed to prevent "fishing expeditions" of the type deplored by Justice L'Heureux-Dubé in her dissenting judgments.

The bill limits the grounds on which the judge may rely when deciding whether or not to issue the production order sought by the defence. For example, the judge may not grant an order based solely on the assertion that the record exists, that it relates to the complainant's psychiatric treatment, that it "may disclose a prior inconsistent statement" or affect the credibility of the complainant (or a witness), that it may relate to other sexual acts by the complainant (volun-

tary or otherwise), or that it contains information about the "sexual reputation" of the complainant. If the judge considers the production of the record to be "necessary in the interests of justice," she may compel a third party named in the application to produce the records at a closed hearing. The third party in question may testify at the hearing, although he or she is not compelled to do so. When the judge reviews the records, she must "consider the salutary and deleterious effects of the determination on the accused's right to make a full answer and defence and on the right to privacy and equality of the complainant." Should she determine that the records have probative value to the case at bar, she may take any necessary steps to protect the privacy of the complainant (e.g., editing the contents or imposing publication bans). All in all, Bill C-46 set a higher threshold for the production of personal records than the "likely relevance" test adopted by the *O'Connor* majority.

Most of the witnesses who appeared before the committee supported the legislation. These included women's groups, representatives from sexual assault centres, and the Canadian Mental Health Association. The strongest opponents of the law were representatives of the criminal defence bar. The Canadian Council of Criminal Defence Lawyers told the committee that the law would not withstand Charter scrutiny. Whereas a majority of the Supreme Court had found in favour of disclosure, the bill was designed to prevent the production of "potentially exculpatory evidence." The resulting infringement of the due-process rights of the accused doomed the law to judicial invalidation.[122] Moreover, denying access to therapeutic records could cause a miscarriage of justice in cases where allegations of sexual abuse were based on "recovered memories," not on actual crimes. The defence lawyers refuted L'Heureux-Dubé's claim that the enforced production of personal records would deter women from reporting sexual assaults, and argued that the bill inappropriately restricted the discretion of trial judges. Finally, they challenged Parliament's attempt to impose its own definition of the Charter on the criminal justice process where that definition differed from that of the Supreme Court:

> ... this preamble supposes to interpret the Charter of Rights to indicate that certain Charter rights have applicability and should be treated in a certain fashion, that they should be equated to other Charter rights. With respect, I would have thought that this is something that should be left to the Charter itself and to those who interpret the Charter as opposed to this piece of evidentiary-type legislation telling us how the Charter ought to be interpreted. Effectively, this portion of the bill tends to be a piece of Charter legislation without the type of solemnity to which Charter legislation should be addressed. There is a process, as I understand it, for passing Charter legislation, and this isn't it.[123]

The belief that the bill would fail a Charter challenge extended to lower-court judges, who had to choose between competing interpretations of the Charter.[124] After an Alberta judge found the new rules

unconstitutional, on the ground that they infringed the legal rights of the accused, the Supreme Court had the opportunity to pass judgment on Parliament's in-your-face reply to *O'Connor* and *Carosella*.[125] In the 1999 *Mills* ruling,[126] to the surprise of many observers, seven Justices voted to uphold the law. This reversal has been attributed to two primary factors. First, the composition of the Court had changed in the two years between *O'Connor* and *Mills*.[127] Justice Sopinka, the strongest due-process advocate among the Justices, had died prematurely. His replacement, Ian Binnie, voted with the majority in *Mills*, as did newly appointed Justice Bastarache (replacing former dissenter La Forest). They joined the three remaining dissenters from *O'Connor* and *Carosella*, guaranteeing at least a five-Justice majority in favour of the new law. The second factor was the decision of Justices Major and Iacobucci to switch sides. Whereas both had voted against the impugned common-law rule in *O'Connor*, they now deferred to Parliament and upheld the statute.[128] The lone dissenter was Chief Justice Lamer, who stuck to his earlier position that the right to make full answer and defence should trump the privacy interest of complainants and witnesses. (The ninth Justice, Cory, who had joined the majority in *O'Connor* and *Carosella*, took no part in the *Mills* ruling.)

The *Mills* majority made it clear that, when Parliament strove to find a reasonable balance among competing Charter rights, and between the Charter and competing social values, the courts should defer to the judgment of the elected legislature.

> Although the procedure governing the production of private records of complainants in sexual assault proceedings set out in Bill C-46 differs significantly from the *O'Connor* regime, it does not follow that Bill C-46 is unconstitutional. Parliament may build on the Court's decision, and develop a different scheme as long as it meets the required constitutional standards. A posture of respect towards Parliament has been adopted by the courts.... While it is the role of the courts to specify constitutional standards, there may be a range of permissible regimes that can meet these standards. In adopting Bill C-46, Parliament sought to recognize the prevalence of sexual violence against women and children and

its disadvantageous impact on their rights, to encourage the reporting of incidents of sexual violence, to recognize the impact of the production of personal information on the efficacy of treatment, and to reconcile fairness to complainants with the rights of the accused.[129]

In reviewing the new legislation, the majority repeatedly stressed the careful balance that the Parliament had struck between the Charter rights of the accused—in particular, the right to make full answer and defence—and those pertaining to the complainant (the "reasonable expectation of privacy" under s. 8 and the right to equality under s. 15). The Court held that "The rights of full answer and defence, and privacy, must be defined in light of each other, and both must be defined in light of the equality provisions of s. 15."[130] This statement implies that the Court had modified its single-minded emphasis on due-process rights and endorsed Parliament's efforts to balance them against other sections of the Charter.

"TAKING RIGHTS SERIOUSLY"? THE CHARTER'S IMPACT ON LAWMAKING IN THE HOUSE OF COMMONS

The case studies in this chapter trace the evolving relationship between Parliament and the courts in the Charter era. Legislators have become more sophisticated, and more assertive, in response to Court rulings. In particular, most members of the justice committee took their first-order and second-order Charter duties to heart. They reviewed government bills carefully, looking for possible Charter violations. When they discussed amendments, MPs from all parties were anxious to ensure that their proposed changes would stand up to judicial scrutiny. The evidence presented here suggests that legislators are maturing in their approach to rights and freedoms. As time goes on, and federal and provincial legislators become increasingly comfortable in their new relationship with the courts, the assertive approach embodied in Bills C-72, C-16, and C-46 should become more common.

The case studies also suggest that allegations of judicial supremacy are somewhat overstated. Governing parties can find ways to satisfy their political constituencies, where these are opposed to particular rights, without resorting to the notwithstanding clause. However, as Chief Justice McLachlin pointed out in the 2002 *Sauvé* ruling (Dossier 4.3, pages 154–55), laws that do not reflect an honest effort to respect the Charter may not be entitled to the judicial deference shown in *Mills*. We may conclude that judges are prepared to respect the policy-making prerogatives of legislators, but only so long as the latter perform their first-order duties conscientiously. Otherwise, the courts are more likely to use their second-order power to remedy laws that infringe protected rights and freedoms.

Parliament's growing acceptance of its first-order Charter duties appears to be motivated by two primary pressures: public support for protected rights and freedoms—which may or may not be accurately reflected in interest-group outrage at perceived violations—and the Supreme Court's willingness to strike down laws that do not reflect an appropriate balance between rights and other values. Both are potentially problematic in a democratic state. The former may tend to produce narrow and self-serving interpretations of the Charter, while the latter opens the possibility of judicial supremacy by giving the Court the last word on what an "appropriate balance" might be. But as long as Parliament tries to forge its own interpretations, steering a middle path between opposing interest groups and standing up to the Court where circumstances permit, neither danger will be fully realized. Although the days of parliamentary supremacy are over, the legislative and executive branches of government retain the power to make public policy. The question is whether they will continue to do so with a proper emphasis on their Charter duties. (See Chapter 13.)

In the end, while the Charter and its supporters have imposed new constraints on Parliament, the greatest constraint on the legislative branch is not the judicial branch or nongovernmental organizations. It is the executive branch, whose control over legislators has not been affected by the constitutional settlement of 1982. In the next chapter, we will explore the role of the cabinet and the federal public service under the Charter and examine their roles in the lawmaking process.

GLOSSARY OF KEY TERMS

backbench MP (also called a backbencher) A member of the House of Commons (or a provincial legislature) who is not a member of the cabinet. Most MPs in the governing party and all of the MPs in the opposition parties are backbenchers.

first-order and **second-order** Charter duties Each of the three branches of government is bound by the Charter to perform particular duties. The first-order duties are those that pertain to the actions of an institution itself. For example, the Department of Justice must ensure that the legislation sponsored by the federal government is consistent with the Charter. Second-order duties involve the review of one institution by another. The judicial review of statutes passed by Parliament, on Charter grounds, is a second-order duty.

DISCUSSION AND REVIEW QUESTIONS

1. Parliament and the Supreme Court do not always agree about the proper balance among Charter rights, or the relative importance of Charter values and competing priorities. In your view, which institution should prevail when the two differ? Explain your answer.

2. Briefly summarize the coordinate model of the relationship between the Supreme Court and Parliament. How does it differ, if at all, from the dialogue model advanced by Hogg, Bushell, and Roach?

3. Briefly summarize at least one argument in favour of parliamentary supremacy and one argument against it. Which do you find more persuasive, and why?

4. Choose one of the five case studies in this chapter. What does it tell us about the evolving relationship between Parliament and the courts under the Charter?

SUGGESTED READINGS

Brodie, Janine, Shelley A.M. Gavigan, and Jane Jenson. *The Politics of Abortion.* Toronto: Oxford University Press, 1992.

Hiebert, Janet L. *Charter Conflicts: What Is Parliament's Role?* Montreal and Kingston: McGill-Queen's University Press, 2002.

Hogg, Peter W., and Allison A. Bushell. "The Charter Dialogue between Courts and Legislatures (Or Perhaps the Charter of Rights Isn't Such a Bad Thing After All." *Osgoode Hall Law Journal* 35 (1997), pp. 75–123.

Manfredi, Christopher P., and James B. Kelly. "Six Degrees of Dialogue: A Response to Hogg and Bushell." *Osgoode Hall Law Journal* 37 (1999), pp. 513–27.

Morton, F.L. *Morgentaler v. Borowski: Abortion, the Charter, and the Courts.* Toronto: McClelland and Stewart, 1992.

Roach, Kent. *Due Process and Victims' Rights: The New Law and Politics of Criminal Justice.* Toronto: University of Toronto Press, 1999.

———. *The Supreme Court on Trial: Judicial Activism or Democratic Dialogue.* Toronto: Irwin Law, 2001.

ENDNOTES

1. *Hunter v. Southam Inc.,* [1984] 2 S.C.R. 145, p. 169, *per* Dickson J. (as he then was).

2. Admittedly, the division of the policy-making process into separate legislative and executive responsibilities is somewhat artificial, at least in Canada. Our federal cabinet dominates the House of Commons and, to a lesser degree, the Senate. With a few exceptions, laws must be approved by both the political executive—the prime minister and cabinet—and the permanent executive (the federal public service) before they can be introduced into Parliament.

3. Kent Roach, "The Dangers of a Charter-Proof and Crime-Based Response to Terrorism," in Ronald J. Daniels, Patrick Macklem, and Kent Roach, eds., *The Security of Freedom: Essays on Canada's Anti-Terrorism Bill* (Toronto: University of Toronto Press, 2002), p. 132.

4. See, e.g., Bertha Wilson, "We Didn't Volunteer," in Paul Howe and Peter H. Russell, eds., *Judicial Power and Canadian Democracy* (Montreal and Kingston: McGill-Queen's University Press/Institute for Research in Public Policy, 2001), p. 75. This point is discussed in more detail in Chapter 3.

5. For a general discussion of this conflict, see Kent Roach, *Due Process and Victims' Rights: The New Law and Politics of Criminal Justice* (Toronto: University of Toronto Press, 1999).

6. See, e.g., F.L. Morton and Rainer Knopff, *The Charter Revolution and the Court Party* (Peterborough: Broadview Press, 2000), Chapter 1; Christopher P. Manfredi, *Judicial Power and the Charter: Canada and the Paradox of Liberal Constitutionalism*, 2nd ed. (Toronto: Oxford University Press, 2001), Introduction and Chapter 7.

7. Brian Slattery, "A Theory of the Charter," *Osgoode Hall Law Journal* 25 (1987), pp. 701–47.

8. Slattery, "A Theory of the Charter," p. 707.

9. Ibid., p. 708.

10. The parliamentary debate over the 2001 Anti-Terrorism Act illustrates the importance of parliamentary and public scrutiny when the cabinet seeks to limit rights and freedoms. See Kent Roach, *September 11: Consequences for Canada* (Montreal and Kingston: McGill-Queen's University Press, 2003), Chapter 3.

11. Slattery, "A Theory of the Charter," p. 710.

12. See *Vriend v. Alberta*, [1998] 1 S.C.R. 493, paragraphs 137–39, *per* Iacobucci J.; *R. v. Mills*, [1999] 3 S.C.R. 668, paragraphs 57 and 125, *per* McLachlin and Iacobucci JJ.; and the debate over "dialogue and deference" between McLachlin C.J.C. and Gonthier J. in *Sauvé v. Canada (Chief Electoral Officer)*, [2002] 3 S.C.R. 418.

13. Peter W. Hogg and Allison A. Bushell, "The Charter Dialogue between Courts and Legislatures (Or Perhaps the Charter of Rights Isn't Such a Bad Thing After All," *Osgoode Hall Law Journal* 35 (1997), pp. 75–123.

14. Hogg and Bushell, "The Charter Dialogue," pp. 79–80.

15. *RJR-MacDonald Inc. v. Canada (Attorney General)*, [1995] 3 S.C.R. 199, paragraphs 164–66, *per* McLachlin J. (as she then was).

16. Hogg and Bushell, "The Charter Dialogue," pp. 86–87.

17. Manfredi, *Judicial Power*, p. 179.

18. F.L. Morton, "Dialogue or Monologue?" in Howe and Russell, *Judicial Power*, p. 111.

19. Christopher P. Manfredi and James B. Kelly, "Six Degrees of Dialogue: A Response to Hogg and Bushell," *Osgoode Hall Law Journal* 37 (1999), pp. 513–27.

20. Manfredi and Kelly, "Six Degrees of Dialogue," p. 521.

21. Manfredi, *Judicial Power*, 180; see also Janet L. Hiebert, *Charter Conflicts: What Is Parliament's Role?* (Montreal and Kingston: McGill-Queen's University Press, 2002), p. 111. Manfredi overlooks the fact that his characterization of the legislative sequel to *O'Connor* might just as easily apply to the *Daviault* "dialogue," inasmuch as Parliament enacted the minority opinion into law in both instances.

22. Manfredi and Kelly, "Six Degrees of Dialogue," p. 524.

23. Kent Roach, *The Supreme Court on Trial: Judicial Activism or Democratic Dialogue* (Toronto: Irwin Law, 2001), p. 13.

24. Roach, *The Supreme Court on Trial*, p. 273.

25. Ibid., p. 274.

26. Ibid., p. 276.

27. Ibid., pp. 13, 67, and 265.

28. Ibid., p. 243.

29. Ibid., pp. 276–77.

30. *Vriend v. Alberta*, paragraph 139.

31. Royal Commission on Electoral Reform and Party Financing, *Reforming Electoral Democracy*, vol. 1 (Ottawa: Minister of Supply and Services Canada, 1991), p. 45.

32. Harvie Andre, Minister of State and Leader of the Government in the House of Commons, testimony to the House of Commons Special Committee on Electoral Reform, February 23, 1993, p. 10:14.

33. Harvie Andre, testimony to the House of Commons Special Committee on Electoral Reform, March 15, 1993, p. 16:13.

34. Hiebert, *Charter Conflicts*, p. 52.

35. Ibid., p. 53.

36. Ibid., p. 53.

37. According to the Library of Parliament, lawyers accounted for a majority of MPs until recently. In the 37th Parliament, which ended in May 2004, just over one-tenth of all members of the House of Commons were practising lawyers.

38. During the 2004 federal election campaign, for example, Conservative leader Stephen Harper insisted that sexual orientation was not a prohibited ground of discrimination in the Charter. While this is technically true, Harper's statement overlooks the fact that the courts have "read in" sexual orientation as an "analogous ground" in s. 15(1). See Chapter 11, pages 346–48.

39. See, e.g., *RJR-MacDonald*, paragraphs 68–70, *per* La Forest J. (dissenting); see also *Irwin Toy Ltd. v. Quebec (Attorney General)*, [1989] 1 S.C.R. 927 and *McKinney v. University of Guelph*, [1990] 3 S.C.R. 229.

40. It could be argued that the choice of case studies is arbitrary, and that the episodes chosen for analysis do not accurately reflect the overall relationship between courts and legislatures in the Charter era. For example, two of the cases—*Morgentaler* and *M. v. H.*—involve the judicial nullification of statutes. As Manfredi and Kelly point out ("Six Degrees of Dialogue," p. 516), an overemphasis on this particular judicial remedy may lead us to overlook the implications of "reading in" and other remedial devices. Moreover, the other three cases concern changes to the common law, which are generally confined to criminal appeals. They are therefore unrepresentative of the broader spectrum of Charter cases. These are valid concerns. On the other hand, the cases discussed here have generated a great deal of debate among policy-makers, academics, and the media. They have been discussed in books, journal articles, and parliamentary deliberations. This volume of source material, in contrast to the thin evidentiary record pertaining to other cases, makes it possible to reconstruct events that would otherwise remain obscure. In addition, the focus of this chapter limits the choice of cases to those in which legislators attempted to respond to a court ruling. It is hoped that the case studies present a reasonably accurate, if somewhat limited, picture of the evolving relationship between courts and legislatures.

41. See, for example, the Court's majority ruling in *R. v. Bernard*, [1988] 2 S.C.R. 833, which held that "Drunkenness in a general sense is not a true defence to a criminal act."

42. *R. v. Daviault*, [1994] 3 S.C.R. 63.

43. Ibid., headnotes.

44. See Isabel Grant, "Second Chances: Bill C-72 and the Charter," *Osgoode Hall Law Journal* 33 (1995), pp. 383, footnote 12, for a survey of Canadian and American press coverage. See also the testimony of the women's groups that appeared before the House of Commons Standing Committee on Justice and Legal Affairs during its deliberations on Bill C-72 (June 6, 7, 13, and 15, 1995).

45. Professor Elizabeth Sheehy, National Association of Women and the Law, testimony before the House of Commons Standing Committee on Justice and Legal Affairs, June 6, 1995, available online at www.parl.gc.ca.

46. Professor Elizabeth Sheehy, "A Brief on Bill C-72, An Act to Amend the Criminal Code," presented to the House of Commons Standing Committee on Justice and Legal Affairs, June 6, 1995, referenced in Hiebert, *Charter Conflicts*, p. 101. Under questioning by committee members, Professor Sheehy subsequently referred to ten acquittals on the grounds of extreme drunkenness since *Daviault*, eight of which involved alleged crimes against women.

47. Roach, *Due Process and Victims' Rights*, p. 178.

48. Hiebert, *Charter Conflicts*, p.99

49. Grant, "Second Chances," p. 385.

50. Ibid., p. 388.

51. Ibid., p. 391.

52. Russell MacLellan, Parliamentary Secretary to the Minister of Justice, Proceedings of the House of Commons Standing Committee on Justice and Legal Affairs, June 15, 1995.

53. *Daviault*, paragraph 62, *per* Cory J.

54. *R. v. Swain*, [1991] 1 S.C.R. 933, *per* Lamer C.J.; *Hill v. Church of Scientology of Toronto*, [1995] 2 S.C.R. 1130, paragraphs 97–98, *per* Cory J.

55. Michelle Fuerst, Chair of the National Criminal Justice Section, Canadian Bar Association, testimony before the House of Commons Standing Committee on Justice and Legal Affairs, June 6, 1995. See also the testimony of Professor Elizabeth Sheehy, on behalf of the National Association of Women and the Law. However, the representatives from the Barreau du Québec were sufficiently concerned about the constitutionality of the bill to call for an immediate reference to the Supreme Court; see the Committee Proceedings for June 7, 1995.

56. Testimony before the House of Commons Standing Committee on Justice and Legal Affairs, June 6, 1995.

57. Sheldon E. Pinx, Vice-Chair, National Criminal Justice Section, Canadian Bar Association, and Michelle Fuerst, testimony before the House of Commons Standing Committee on Justice and Legal Affairs, June 6, 1995.

58. Testimony before the House of Commons Standing Committee on Justice and Legal Affairs, June 13, 1995.

59. Testimony before the House of Commons Standing Committee on Justice and Legal Affairs, June 13, 1995.

60. Dr. Perry Kendall, President and Chief Executive Officer, Addiction Research Foundation, testimony before the House of Commons Standing Committee on Justice and Legal Affairs, June 13, 1995.

61. Sue Barnes, Liberal MP for London West, Proceedings, June 13, 1995.

62. *R. v. Robinson*, [1996] 1 S.C.R. 683.

63. Roach, *Due Process and Victims' Rights*, p. 181.

64. *R. v. Feeney*, [1997] 2 S.C.R. 13, paragraph 44, *per* Sopinka J.

65. Roach, *Due Process and Victims' Rights*, p. 83.

66. Hiebert, *Charter Conflicts*, 152; Anne McLellan, then–minister of justice, testimony before the House of Commons Standing Committee on Justice and Human Rights, November 4, 1997, available online at www.parl.gc.ca.

67. On June 27, 1997, the Court granted a motion by the federal Department of Justice to suspend the effect of the ruling for six months. However, the stay was deemed to have begun on May 22, when the ruling was issued. The day before the deadline, November 21, the Court granted a further extension until December 19. See *R. v. Feeney*, [1997] 2 S.C.R. 117, and *R. v. Feeney*, [1997] 3 S.C.R. 1008.

68. Canada, House of Commons, Standing Committee on Justice and Human Rights, "Second Report," November 1997, p. 2.

69. Bill C-16, An Act to Amend the Criminal Code and the Interpretation Act (Powers to Arrest and Enter Dwellings, 36th Parliament, 1st Session, 1997, royal assent, December 1997.

70. A second stay was eventually granted, but only for one month. The bill received royal assent on the day before the deadline; see Hiebert, *Charter Conflicts*, pp. 153–54.

71. Canada, House of Commons, Standing Committee on Justice and Human Rights, "Second Report," November 1997.

72. Anne McLellan, then–minister of justice, testimony before the House of Commons Standing Committee on Justice and Human Rights, November 4, 1997, available online at www.parl.gc.ca.

73. See *R. v. Swain, per* Lamer C.J.

74. Testimony before the House of Commons Standing Committee on Justice and Human Rights, November 4, 1997, available online at www.parl.gc.ca.

75. Scott Newark, Executive Officer of the Canadian Police Association, testimony before the House of Commons Standing Committee on Justice and Human Rights, November 4, 1997, available online at www.parl.gc.ca.

76. The committee accepted a technical amendment from the justice department, but it made no changes of its own. See Canada, House of Commons, Standing Committee on Justice and Human Rights, "First Report," November 1997.

77. Roach, *The Supreme Court on Trial*, pp. 178–79.

78. Hiebert, *Charter Conflicts*, p. 160.

79. Ibid., p. 160.

80. *R. v. Morgentaler*, [1988] 1 S.C.R. 30.

81. Ibid., paragraph 130.

82. Ibid., paragraphs 256–57.

83. Janine Brodie, "Choice and No Choice in the House," in Janine Brodie, Shelley A.M. Gavigan, and Jane Jenson, *The Politics of Abortion* (Toronto: Oxford University Press, 1992), pp. 86–87.

84. Ibid., pp. 67–68.

85. *Tremblay v. Daigle*, [1989] 2 S.C.R. 530. See the discussion of this case in Chapter 3, pages 101–2.

86. Bill C-43, s. 1, 34th Parliament, 2nd Session, 1989–90.

87. Doug Lewis, Minister of Justice, reported in *Minutes of Proceedings and Evidence of the Legislative Committee on Bill C-43*, December 5, 1989, pp. 1:38, 1:45, and 1:49.

88. Brodie, "Choice and No Choice," p. 99.

89. Ibid., pp. 111–13.

90. For a discussion of the Nova Scotia government's failed attempt to prohibit abortions in the province, see *R. v. Morgentaler*, [1993] 3 S.C.R. 463.

91. Brodie, "Choice and No Choice," pp. 108 and 115.

92. F.L. Morton, *Morgentaler v. Borowski: Abortion, the Charter, and the Courts* (Toronto: McClelland and Stewart, 1992), p. 292.

93. *Egan v. Canada*, [1995] 2 S.C.R. 513, paragraph 5, *per* La Forest J., and paragraphs 171–78, *per* Cory J.

94. *Miron v. Trudel*, [1995] 2 S.C.R. 418, paragraphs 150–54, *per* McLachlin J. (as she then was).

95. *Corbiere v. Canada (Minister of Indian and Northern Affairs)*, [1999] 2 S.C.R. 203, paragraphs 8–9, *per* McLachlin and Bastarache JJ.

96. *Miron v. Trudel*, [1995] 2 S.C.R. 418.

97. *M. v. H.*, [1999] 2 S.C.R. 3, paragraph 129, *per* Iacobucci J.

98. Ibid., paragraph 147, *per* Iacobucci J.

99. Peter Kormos, NDP MPP for Niagara Centre, speech to the Legislative Assembly of Ontario, October 27, 1999, reported in *Hansard*, at pp. 164–65.

100. George Smitherman, Liberal MPP for Toronto Centre-Rosedale; speech to the Legislative Assembly of Ontario, October 27, 1999, reported in *Hansard*, at p. 162.

101. Mary C. Hurley, "Sexual Orientation and Legal Rights" (Ottawa: Library of Parliament Research Branch, October 2001).

102. Roach, *The Supreme Court on Trial*, p. 198.

103. Jim Flaherty, Attorney General of Ontario, speech to the Legislative Assembly of Ontario,

October 27, 1999, reported in *Hansard*, at p. 159.

104. See., e.g., the remarks of Liberal MPP Michael Bryant (St. Paul's) at p. 167 of *Hansard*, and NDP MPP Rosario Marchese's (Trinity-Spadina) remarks at p. 170.

105. Ontario *Hansard*, October 27, 1999, at p. 165.

106. *Halpern v. Canada (Attorney General)*, Ontario Superior Court of Justice (Divisional Court), July 12, 2002.

107. An Environics poll of 2001 Canadians conducted in the fall of 2003 found that 56 percent favoured allowing same-sex couples to marry. Source: Environics, "A Majority of Canadians Continue to Support Gay Marriage," accessed online at www.environics.ca (posted October 21, 2003).

108. Bruce Feldthusen, "Access to the Private Therapeutic Records of Sexual Assault Complainants," *Canadian Bar Review* 75 (1996), p. 562, quoted in Roach, *The Supreme Court on Trial*, p. 278.

109. *R. v. Mills*, [1999] 3 S.C.R. 668, paragraph 58, *per* McLachlin and Iacobucci JJ.

110. *R. v. Stinchcombe*, [1991] 3 S.C.R. 326, paragraph 17, *per* Sopinka J. (for a unanimous Court).

111. *R. v. O'Connor*, [1995] 4 S.C.R. 411, paragraph 22, *per* Lamer C.J. and Sopinka J. (emphasis in original).

112. Roach, *Due Process and Victims' Rights*, p. 185.

113. *R. v. O'Connor*, paragraph 29.

114. *R. v. Osolin*, [1993] 4 S.C.R. 595, headnotes.

115. See, e.g., Jeffrey S. Victor, *Satanic Panic: The Creation of a Contemporary Legend* (Chicago: Open Court, 1993); Richard Ofshe and Ethan Watters, *Making Monsters: False Memories,*

Psychotherapy, and Sexual Hysteria (Berkeley: University of California Press, 1994); and Elizabeth Loftus and Katherine Ketcham, *The Myth of Repressed Memory: False Memories and the Allegations of Sexual Abuse* (New York: St. Martin's Press, 1994).

116. *R. v. O'Connor*, paragraph 29.

117. *R. v. Carosella*, [1997] 1 S.C.R. 80, paragraph 46, *per* Sopinka J.

118. Ibid., paragraph 56, *per* Sopinka J.

119. Ibid., paragraph 72.

120. Ibid., paragraph 114.

121. Ibid., paragraph 147.

122. Mr. Marvin R. Bloos, Chair, Canadian Council of Criminal Defence Lawyers, testimony before the House of Commons Standing Committee on Justice and Legal Affairs, March 13, 1997.

123. Mr. Irwin Koziebrocki, Treasurer, Criminal Lawyers' Association, testimony before the House of Commons Standing Committee on Justice and Legal Affairs, March 13, 1997. Note: The assertion that legislation with Charter implications must be passed by a special process is incorrect.

124. Hiebert, *Charter Conflicts*, p. 115.

125. Roach, *The Supreme Court on Trial*, pp. 277–81.

126. *R. v. Mills*, [1999] 3 S.C.R. 668.

127. Hiebert, *Charter Conflicts*, p. 115.

128. Roach, *The Supreme Court on Trial*, pp. 278–79.

129. *R. v. Mills* (1999), headnotes.

130. Ibid., paragraph 21, *per* McLachlin and Iacobucci JJ.

Chapter 5

The Executive Branch

The Supreme Court of Canada building (right) and Parliament are reflected in the calm waters of the Ottawa River.
CP PICTURE ARCHIVE/Andy Clark

32. (1) *This Charter applies*

    (a) *to the Parliament and government of Canada in respect of all matters within the authority of Parliament including all matters relating to the Yukon Territory and Northwest Territories; and*

    (b) *to the legislatures and governments of each province in respect of all matters within the authority of the legislature of each province.*

INTRODUCTION

In the two previous chapters, we have reviewed the new duties imposed on the courts and Parliament by the Charter of Rights. To complete the analysis of the Charter's impact on Canadian policy-making, we now turn to the executive branch. (This chapter will focus almost exclusively on the national government.) The executive contains three elements: the Crown (person-ified by the governor general), the political executive (the prime minister and cabinet), and the permanent execu-tive (public servants). Senior public servants in the **central agencies** and **line departments** work with the political executive to craft laws and public policies; more junior public servants—e.g., front-line workers and police officers—deliver programs and enforce the law.

In a parliamentary system of government, the executive branch performs three primary functions:

1. Initiating and developing policy. The vast majority of the laws passed by Parliament originate with the permanent executive. They are drafted by bureaucrats with technical expertise in both the subject matter of the law and the mechanics of policy implementation.
2. Issuing executive orders (orders-in-council), which are not ratified by Parliament but which carry the force of law. The cabinet is authorized by parliamentary statutes (known as **enabling legislation**) to make the detailed regulations necessary to implement laws (**delegated legislation**). The executive branch is also responsible for negotiating and implementing treaties with foreign governments, usually without the participation of Parliament.
3. Administering and enforcing the laws. Once a law is passed by Parliament, or a regulation issued by the cabinet, it must be put into effect. Tens of thousands of public servants across Canada carry out the policies ordained by the cabinet and Parliament. The majority are engaged in front-line tasks: service delivery, law enforcement, and compliance monitoring.

Each of these executive functions has been affected by the Canadian Charter of Rights and Freedoms. Policy-making is a complicated and often lengthy exercise in which fiscal and practical considerations must be balanced against political and social demands. The proclamation of the Charter in 1982 forced the executive branch (both federal and provincial) to protect rights and freedoms in the substance of law and policy. Regulations and orders-in-council are also subject to Charter review by the courts, as are the ways in which public officials administer and enforce the law. Procedural violations of the Charter cannot be shielded under s. 1 unless they are explicitly "prescribed by law." Since 1982, the traditional norms of professionalism and public service that have always guided the administrative arm of government have been reinforced by the threat of Charter litigation. Together with the rule of law principle (Chapter 1, pages 5–10), these factors require the executive branch

to balance its first-order Charter duties against the other imperatives of policy-making and enforcement.

This chapter describes and analyzes the Charter's effects on the operation of Canada's federal executive branch. It is relatively brief not because the subject matter is unimportant, but because much of the activity within the executive branch is hidden from public view. Despite this secrecy, we do have some evidence of the executive response to the Charter. The key player is the federal Department of Justice, whose power within the federal government has grown substantially since 1982. The 1980s were often disorienting for federal lawmakers and bureaucrats: the Supreme Court repeatedly struck down or amended laws that did not conform to Charter standards and rewrote the rules under which public servants—including police officers and Crown prosecutors—operated. In effect, the Supreme Court's early and enthusiastic embrace of its second-order Charter duties forced the political and permanent executives to take their own first-order duties more seriously than they might otherwise have done.

THE FEDERAL DEPARTMENT OF JUSTICE: THE NEWEST CENTRAL AGENCY

As we saw in Chapter 2, page 60, the 1960 Bill of Rights required the federal minister of justice to scrutinize draft laws for potential violations and to report any such violations to Parliament. That requirement was replaced in 1985 by s. 4.1 of the Department of Justice Act, reproduced in Dossier 5.1, page 183.

The Charter duties of the minister of justice and his or her department are more extensive than Dossier 5.1 suggests. Indeed, if the Department of Justice (DOJ) confined itself to the review of bills that had already reached the stage of parliamentary debate, its impact on the executive branch would be relatively minor. Instead, the DOJ conducts a Charter analysis of new laws and policies at every stage of development, from the initiation phase within the line department to the drafting of bills for legislative amendment and ratification.

DOSSIER 5.1

SECTION 4.1 OF THE DEPARTMENT OF JUSTICE ACT

4.1 (1) Subject to subsection (2), the Minister shall, in accordance with such regulations as may be prescribed by the Governor in Council, examine every regulation transmitted to the Clerk of the Privy Council for registration pursuant to the *Statutory Instruments Act* and every Bill introduced in or presented to the House of Commons by a minister of the Crown, in order to ascertain whether any of the provisions thereof are inconsistent with the purposes and provisions of the *Canadian Charter of Rights and Freedoms* and the Minister shall report any such inconsis-

tency to the House of Commons at the first convenient opportunity.

Exception

(2) A regulation need not be examined in accordance with subsection (1) if prior to being made it was examined as a proposed regulation in accordance with section 3 of the Statutory *Instruments Act* to ensure that it was not inconsistent with the purposes and provisions of the *Canadian Charter of Rights and Freedoms*.

R.S., 1985, c. 31 (1st Supp.), s. 93; 1992, c. 1, s. 144(F).

There are at least two reasons for the uniquely powerful role of the DOJ in the Charter era:

- First, the DOJ monopolizes the provision of legal expertise within the federal executive branch.
- Second, the DOJ provides and trains the staff of the legal services unit (LSU) within each line department of the federal government.[1]

The DOJ Monopoly

Whereas other federal departments (e.g., the Department of Finance) can, and often do, consult experts in the private sector, confidentiality rules and other institutional norms prevent federal policy-makers from seeking advice on Charter issues from anyone outside the DOJ (except in the Department of Foreign Affairs, which has its own legal staff).[2] The growing importance of legal analysis since 1982 has given the justice department unprecedented influence in the policy process. In effect, the DOJ has been transformed from an ordinary line department—albeit one with a special responsibilities across the range of policy, particularly the drafting of all federal laws—into a new central agency.[3] It coordinates the

Charter-compliance activities of the entire executive branch, in much the same way as the Treasury Board Secretariat (TBS) coordinates the spending of the federal government.

The Charter scrutiny and reporting duties of the minister, together with the department's monopoly of Charter expertise, have also given federal and provincial justice ministers "additional leverage in dealing with Cabinet colleagues that may be useful in resolving occasional differences of opinion."[4] In the competitive arenas of the political and permanent executives, where the contest for power is often perceived as a zero-sum game, this power shift has provoked some resentment and resistance.[5]

To overcome any lingering opposition to the DOJ's new role, two long-established central agencies have encouraged policy-makers to take their Charter concerns seriously. The Privy Council Office (PCO), the agency that coordinates the policy activities of the executive branch, has long recognized the importance of Charter compliance. In 1991, the then-clerk of the Privy Council, Paul Tellier, sent a memo to all deputy ministers (the senior officials in each department) that ordered them to conduct a Charter "risk analysis" at each stage of policy development.[6] Before a new law or policy may be presented to the cabinet, the sponsoring department must assess "the risk of successful challenge in the courts, the impact of an adverse decision, and possible litigation costs."[7] That assessment is incorporated into the memorandum to cabinet, the document that presents the new policy for consideration by the political executive, so that ministers can determine whether or not to proceed. In its *Guide to Making Federal Acts and Regulations*, the PCO warns policy-makers that "Acts and regulations are ineffective to the extent that they are inconsistent with the Charter."[8] In other words, cooperation with the DOJ is mandatory, not optional. However, the *Guide* points out that the Charter does not restrict "the matters that may be dealt with," but only "how legislative objectives may be achieved."[9]

The PCO's emphasis on Charter compliance is reinforced by the TBS, the central agency responsible for government spending. When a federal law is challenged in the courts, the TBS and the sponsoring department are jointly responsible for paying the government's legal costs. Anxious to avoid incurring unnecessary expenditures, the TBS "disciplines line departments to the seriousness of a Charter review under the direction of the Department of Justice."[10] By stressing the importance of collaboration with the DOJ, the more senior central agencies have helped convince reluctant departments to take Charter concerns seriously from the very beginnings of the policy-making process.

The Legal Services Units

The LSU staff lawyers are responsible for providing legal advice and analysis to the policy branch within their particular department. The LSU evaluates policy proposals, using a detailed "Charter checklist" prepared by the Human Rights Law Section in the DOJ.[11] If it identifies a possible Charter conflict, the LSU alerts the policy experts. The legal and policy teams then work together to achieve the department's goals without compromising Charter values.

Since 1994, the senior general counsel, the head of the LSU in each department, has met weekly with senior policy officials. James Kelly interprets this change as proof that "the initial resistance to a Charter review has been overcome" and "departments recognize how important it is that policy conform to the Charter."[12] While this is probably the case, anecdotal evidence suggests that receptivity to Charter advice varies from department to department.[13] So the influence of a particular LSU may depend on departmental willingness to take Charter concerns seriously. Where the LSU lawyers are regarded as "outsiders" seeking to impose the will of the DOJ, not as key players in the policy process, conflicts between Charter concerns and competing policy goals may have to be resolved outside the department—for example, at a cabinet committee meeting attended by the minister of justice.[14]

The Evolving First-Order Duties of the DOJ

Although the central agency status of the DOJ may seem inevitable in retrospect, few could have foreseen the department's transformation when the Charter was proclaimed in 1982. The post-Charter evolution of the DOJ has occurred in two distinct phases. In the first phase, from 1982 until the late 1980s, few federal policy-makers understood the full implications of the entrenched rights and freedoms. The DOJ itself, under the leadership of Deputy Minister Roger Tassé, tried to make the other line departments aware of their new responsibilities and policy constraints. As early as November 1981, shortly after the First Ministers' Meeting that produced the new Charter, Tassé and his officials held workshops and seminars to prepare policy-makers for the impending constitutional change.[15] At the same time, Tassé—who had played a key role in the drafting of the Charter—set up a committee within the DOJ to establish a coherent approach to the issues and lay the groundwork for an expanded departmental role within federal government.[16]

Neither initiative had an immediate effect. Official opinion inside the DOJ was divided between liberals, who expected the department to play "a substantive policy role ... under the Charter," and conservatives, who saw no need to move beyond their traditional drafting and litigation functions.[17] Policy-makers outside the DOJ resented efforts to establish formal mechanisms for Charter assessment as "an attempt by Justice to use the Charter to enlarge its own jurisdiction."[18] This aversion to a perceived "power-grab," coupled with a broader incomprehension of the Charter's possible effects on policy-making, stymied Tassé's efforts to sustain the greater sensitivity toward rights and freedoms that had emerged during the 1980–82 constitutional round.[19]

Despite these obstacles, the DOJ undertook two important initiatives in response to the Charter. The first was the creation of the Human Rights Law Section (HRLS) within the department. The second was a detailed review of all existing federal legislation, which was intended to forestall litigation by identifying and removing provisions that might violate the Charter. This review, which was conducted by the new HRLS, produced two omnibus bills: the 1985 Statute Law (Canadian Charter of Rights and Freedoms) Amendment Act and a 1988 law designed to bring federal statutes into line with s. 15. During this first phase, the DOJ assumed responsibility for ensuring that the substance of laws respected the entrenched rights and freedoms; however, this responsibility "was confined to existing legislation and did not have an impact on the development of new policy within the administrative state."[20]

The inadequacy of the DOJ's limited and reactive role under the Charter was revealed in April 1985, when the Supreme Court issued its ruling in *Singh v. Minister of Employment and Immigration.*[21] The Court struck down Canada's procedure for adjudicating refugee claims, on the ground that it violated the guarantees of "fundamental justice" in s. 7 of the Charter and s. 2(e) of the 1960 Bill of Rights. (See Dossier 1.5, page 25). The Department of Employment and Immigration had not foreseen significant financial costs and administrative difficulties created by the ruling.[22] There was no budget allocation for setting up a new refugee-determination process, and no planning had been undertaken in the event that the existing process was nullified. The fallout from *Singh* and other early Charter rulings—

including *Hunter v. Southam* (Chapter 10, pages 312–15), which forced the federal government to reexamine all of its legislation concerning search warrants—persuaded federal policy-makers to take rights seriously, if only to avoid another costly surprise from the Supreme Court.[23] So the Supreme Court's initial Charter activism benefited the DOJ, and especially the HRLS, by forcing other departments to recognize the potential impact of judicial nullification on their policy agendas and fiscal frameworks.[24]

The second phase of the DOJ's post-Charter evolution brought a shift away from purely reactive and technical functions to a proactive and substantive role in policy-making. If the prospect of hanging concentrates a man's mind wonderfully,[25] so does the prospect that a cherished policy goal will be thwarted because the means chosen to achieve it failed a second-order Charter review. After 1988, the DOJ branches found it easier to persuade other line departments to conduct thorough first-order reviews of proposed legislation. The HRLS assumed a new responsibility for "Charter-proofing" policy proposals, both directly and through the guidelines that it prepared for the various LSUs. Part of that responsibility lay in convincing policy-makers that the Charter does not constitute a barrier to creativity; it merely imposes a duty to weigh alternative policy instruments against the constitutional standards set by the courts. Line departments are encouraged to incorporate the Charter into their analyses of alternative mechanisms, partly because a failure to do so can make a policy more vulnerable at the s. 1 stage of judicial review. Because the DOJ is responsible for defending federal laws in court, it has a strong incentive to eliminate obvious Charter violations. (Note, however, that the lawyers in the HRLS are not responsible for defending statutes in court; that duty falls to separate litigation branches across the country.)

Once the means to achieve a particular goal have been chosen, the HRLS must determine the likelihood that the proposed law—if found to violate the Charter, despite its best efforts—would pass the "rational connection" and "minimal impairment" prongs of the *Oakes* test.[26] This "Charter risk analysis" is based on previous court rulings, especially those from the Supreme Court of Canada. The difficulty of predicting judicial decisions was particularly daunting in the early years of Charter jurisprudence, when there were few precedents on which to rely.[27] With the passage of time, and the accumulation of a sizable body of case law, less uncertainty attaches to the process of risk assessment.

The "Charter-proofers" at the DOJ have become increasingly adept at protecting federal laws from judicial nullification. Most of the statutes that have been struck down by the Supreme Court on Charter grounds were passed before the DOJ assumed its current proactive role in policy-making.[28] Only two federal statutes adopted since 1988 have been subjected to judicial remedy on Charter grounds. As we saw in Chapter 4 (Dossier 4.3, pages 154–55), a 1993 amendment to the Canada Elections Act was struck down in the 2002 *Sauvé* ruling. (The 2003 *Figueroa* ruling struck down a key element of the same act, which was first adopted in 1970; see Chapter 9, pages 290–92 for details.) The other impugned provision was a section of the 1993 child pornography law that was deemed to be overbroad because it criminalized visual and written material the creation of which did not involve victimization and which was intended for the sole use of the creator. It was "read down" to exclude those two categories of pornographic material.[29] With those exceptions, the substance of federal laws that have undergone a proactive Charter review within the executive branch has been upheld by the courts.

The problem with this "Charter-proofing" exercise, as critics rightly point out, is that it effectively subordinates the executive branch to the courts. To undertake a "risk assessment" based entirely on speculation about what judges will do is to substitute judicial interpretation of the Charter for the document itself. Such an assessment also has the effect of conceding a monopoly over rights and freedoms to the courts, instead of asserting the legitimate role of the federal government to protect rights and freedoms as it sees fit. As discussed in Chapter 3, courts lack the institutional capacity to make and enforce good public policy. Consequently, the apparent practice of

"Charter ventriloquism" by the DOJ raises troubling questions about the policy process in the Charter era.[30] Those questions go beyond the proper division of powers among the three branches of government to engage the quality of public policy itself. As noted in Chapter 4, even a bad law can be made completely "Charter-proof."

In practice, as we saw in Chapter 1, the courts are increasingly willing to suspend the nullification of impugned statutes in order to allow the legislative and executive branches an opportunity to bring the law within the requirements of the Charter. Note, however, that this type of remedy can throw a wrench into the policy-making agenda of the affected department; bureaucrats are not always prepared to make new laws within the short time frame allowed by the courts, as the *Feeney* saga illustrates (Chapter 4, pages 161–64). Courts are also increasingly deferential to the policy choices of Parliament—which are (in most cases) simply a ratification of the choices made within the federal executive—even where these differ from judicial preferences. (See Chapter 4.) Despite these developments, the HRLS seems content to base its Charter analyses on court rulings.[31] This may reflect a realistic assessment of judicial power in the Charter era and the harsh lessons learned in the 1980s.

Alternatively, it might be interpreted as a failure of political will. In rare cases, such as the 2001 Anti-Terrorism Act, the federal government has gambled that legislation that appears to infringe protected rights and freedoms would be upheld by the courts. The first Supreme Court ruling on the act, in June 2004, proved that the Justices were more than willing to construe the law in a way that would allow them to uphold it—despite several acknowledged infringements on basic legal rights.[32] That outcome could be perceived as the result of careful "Charter-proofing" by the DOJ.[33] On the other hand, it could reflect the willingness of judges to defer to the executive in a policy field—national security—that has been traditionally the prerogative of that branch of government. Either way, the refusal to nullify such a controversial law may, and perhaps should, embolden the executive branch to challenge the courts more frequently.

JUDICIAL REVIEW OF EXECUTIVE ORDERS AND REGULATIONS

Section 32(1) of the Charter (reproduced at the beginning of the chapter) defines the scope of Charter application. On the surface, it appears to restrict that scope to the statutes made by Parliament and the provincial legislatures. The phrase "all matters within the authority of" the legislative branch suggests that the Charter does not apply to purely executive matters, such as treaties, although it indicates that executive decisions taken under legislative authority (e.g., regulations issued under enabling legislation) fall within the scope of Charter review. Indeed, the federal government has argued that the royal prerogative—the power of the Crown to make binding decisions without Parliamentary sanction, e.g., international agreements and policies concerning national security—is exempt from s. 32(1), and that decisions made under the prerogative power are thus immune from judicial scrutiny for violations of rights and freedoms.[34]

This narrow reading of s. 32 has been decisively rejected by the Supreme Court of Canada. As Dossier 5.2 explains, any cabinet decision that engages a genuine constitutional issue may be subject to judicial review.

DOSSIER 5.2

OPERATION DISMANTLE V. THE QUEEN (1985)

In 1983, a coalition of peace movements and labour unions, led by Operation Dismantle Inc., challenged the constitutionality of the federal cabinet's decision to permit the testing of American cruise missiles on Canadian territory.[1] The coalition argued that the tests increased the risk of nuclear war and exposed Canada's population to nuclear reprisals from the Soviet bloc. Consequently, the cabinet's decision violated the right to "security of the person" under s. 7 of the Charter.

In 1985, the Supreme Court dismissed the claim, on the grounds that the plaintiffs had no factual basis for their claims of suffering.[2] Justice Wilson[3] rejected the Crown's argument that the courts should have refused to hear the case at all—in technical terms, that the agreement between the Canadian and American governments was "non-justiciable." In the first place, the Crown had argued that cabinet's decision to permit the missile testing was an exercise of the royal prerogative pertaining to matters of national security and defence. It further argued that the royal prerogative lay outside the scope of Charter review, which was confined by s. 32 of the Constitution Act, 1982 to the legislative power. Wilson dismissed both arguments. In the first place, she held that the phrase "within the authority of Parliament" in s. 32(1) was not intended to insulate the executive branch from the reach of the Charter. Instead, it referred to the division of powers between the national and provincial governments in ss. 91–95 of the Constitution Act, 1867.[4] Secondly, she pointed out that "however unsuited courts may be for the task, they are called upon all the time to decide questions of principle and policy."[5]

The question of justiciability really turned on the third issue: whether the testing of cruise missiles was a "political question" with which the judicial branch ought not to concern itself. In American jurisprudence, the political questions doctrine restrains judges from making final determinations on matters that properly belong to the legislative or executive branch. Wilson declined to import the political questions doctrine into Canadian jurisprudence: "the courts should not be too eager to relinquish their judicial review function simply because they are called upon to exercise it in relation to weighty matters of state."[6] She was careful not to claim unfettered judicial discretion over public policy: if the plaintiffs had simply asked the Court to

(continued)

"substitute its opinion for that of the executive to whom the decision-making power is given by the Constitution," then the case would indeed be nonjusticiable. But because the question before the Court concerned the interpretation and application of the Charter, the Justices were entitled to answer it: "if what we are being asked to do is to decide whether any particular act of the executive violates the rights of the citizens, then it is not only appropriate that we answer the question; it is our obligation under the *Charter* to do so."[7]

Chief Justice Dickson agreed that "cabinet decisions fall under s. 32(1)(a) of the Charter and are therefore reviewable in the courts and subject to judicial scrutiny for compatibility with the Constitution." In general terms, "the executive branch of the Canadian government is duty bound to act in accordance with the dictates of the Charter."[8] Justice McIntyre built on this interpretation in the 1986 *Dolphin Delivery* ruling. Because the word "government" in s. 32(1) is used in a way that distinguishes it from "legislature," he concluded that it must refer to "the executive or administrative branch of government" (either federal or provincial).[9]

ENDNOTES

1. For a brief account of the case by a participant, see Michael Mandel, *The Charter of Rights and the Legalization of Politics in Canada*, 1st ed. (Toronto: Wall and Thompson, 1989), pp. 64–70.

2. *Operation Dismantle v. The Queen*, [1985] 1 S.C.R. 441.

3. Wilson wrote a separate concurring judgment. However, her ruling on the justiciability of the plaintiffs' claim was endorsed by the majority.

4. *Operation Dismantle*, paragraph 50.

5. Ibid., paragraph 52. As discussed in Chapter 3, the issue of the Court's institutional capacity is not quite so easily dismissed.

6. Ibid., paragraph 62.

7. Ibid., paragraph 64.

8. Ibid., paragraph 28.

9. *RWDSU v. Dolphin Delivery Ltd.*, [1986] 2 S.C.R. 573, paragraph 33.

The effect of *Operation Dismantle* and *Dolphin Delivery* was to open all executive and administrative decisions to second-order Charter review. This means that the three elements of the executive branch—Crown, cabinet, and public service—must exercise their exclusive powers in accordance with the protected rights and freedoms as interpreted by the courts. If they do not do so, and their decisions are challenged in the courts, they risk the imposition of judicial remedies. Decisions taken under the Crown prerogative or enabling legislation, which are not subject to second-order review by Parliament, are now subject to review by the courts.

In response, the executive branch has altered its procedures for drafting regulations under enabling legislation. As noted earlier, the official PCO guide for policy-makers in the executive branch requires that all regulations fall within the proper scope of government activity as defined by the Charter. Moreover, the minister of justice and his or her officials in the DOJ are responsible for ensuring the constitutionality of all draft regulations before they can be issued (recall Dossier 5.1, page 183). Although evidence is scarce, it is reasonable to conclude that the cumulative effect of these new responsibilities on the executive branch has been significant.

JUDICIAL REVIEW OF ADMINISTRATIVE ACTS

As we have seen, the broad remedial powers conferred on the courts by s. 24(1) go beyond reviewing the substance of legislation. The actions of public officials are also subject to judicial review, most commonly under s. 7. According to Roger Tassé, "The Charter applies to all the administrative decisions of government even if these decisions are not taken pursuant to a statute or to subordinate legislation and do not represent the exercise of a statutory power. Decisions which have legislative authorization are doubly bound,"[35] because they flow from both the legislative and executive branches of government. Consequently, the acts of officials responsible for implementing and enforcing the law—including cabinet ministers, police officers, and prison guards—are subject to judicial review.

The procedural legal rights in sections 7–14 of the Charter are most often invoked against executive and administrative actors. The majority of Charter challenges in this area arise from criminal investigations and prosecutions, which we will discuss in Chapter 10. Others originate in the application of the Immigration Act and the Extradition Act, which we will discuss in this section. Recently, the Supreme Court has faulted customs officials for failing to respect the guarantee of "equal benefit of the law" in s. 15(1). In most of these cases, the legislation that authorized executive decision-making was upheld, but the ways in which certain public servants implemented those laws were found to infringe the Charter. Such infringements receive no protection from the limitation clause; as the Supreme Court recently observed, "Violative conduct by government officials that is not authorized by statute is not 'prescribed by law' and cannot therefore be justified under s. 1."[36]

As noted in the earlier discussion of the *Singh* case, the Supreme Court has held the federal government to strict procedural standards in its handling of refugee cases. While acknowledging that national security is an important consideration, the Court has consistently required the minister of citizenship and immigration to exercise his or her discretionary powers under the Immigration Act in a manner that conforms to the "principles of fundamental justice." This is particularly important when deportation to the home country may result in torture or other mistreatment of the applicant. Where the evidentiary record reveals serious procedural shortcomings—e.g., the denial of the opportunity to make a full answer or defence against the government's case, or the minister's failure to provide written reasons for his or her decision—an unsuccessful applicant may be granted a new hearing.[37] In the absence of such procedural failings, judges should defer to the minister's decision to deny refugee status and/or to deport,[38] notwithstanding the Supreme Court's assertion that "generally to deport a refugee, where there are grounds to believe that this would subject the refugee to a substantial risk of torture, would unconstitutionally violate the Charter's s. 7 guarantee of life, liberty and security of the person."[39]

The minister of citizenship and immigration is not the only member of the political executive who must decide whether or not to deport individuals to potentially risky situations. Under s. 25 of the Extradition Act, the minister of justice has the discretion to accept or reject requests from other countries for the return of criminal suspects who have fled to Canada. He or she is also bound by the terms of extradition treaties between Canada and specific countries, where these exist. Article 6 of the extradition treaty between Canada and the United States reads as follows:

> When the offense for which extradition is requested is punishable by death under the laws of the requesting State and the laws of the requested State do not permit such punishment for that offense, extradition may be refused unless the requesting State provides such assurances as the requested State considers sufficient that the death penalty shall not be imposed, or, if imposed, shall not be executed.[40]

In other words, the minister of justice may request a written assurance that a person extradited to the United States will not face the death penalty before issuing the extradition order; but he or she is not required to do so.

Section 7 of the Charter prohibits government officials from depriving anyone—citizen or noncitizen—of life, liberty, or security of the person "except in accordance with the principles of fundamental justice." The Supreme Court has found that s. 7 applies both to legal procedures and to the substance of laws.[41] Therefore, a minister confronted with an extradition request from another country must follow basic norms of due process (e.g., the opportunity for a full answer and defence) and the written rules set out in Canadian law and foreign treaties (the latter, as we saw earlier, are also subject to Charter review). Consequently, a challenge to a ministerial decision to extradite may focus on either the procedure by which the decision was taken or the laws that authorized it, or both. Dossier 5.3 summarizes two high-profile cases dealing with ministerial discretion to extradite suspected or convicted criminals to jurisdictions where they could face capital punishment. (In this instance, "high-profile" is an understatement: the American TV series *Law & Order* devoted an entire episode to the issues raised by the second ruling.) Between 1991 and 2001, the Supreme Court changed its position on this issue—though without explicitly acknowledging the reversal.

DOSSIER 5.3

KINDLER AND *BURNS*[1]

Joseph Kindler was convicted of first-degree murder and other serious offences in a Philadelphia court in 1983. The jury unanimously recommended the death penalty. Before the judge could pronounce sentence, Kindler escaped from custody and fled to Canada. He was recaptured in Quebec in 1985. Shortly thereafter, the American government made a formal request for his extradition under article 6 of the Extradition Treaty between Canada and the U.S. Section 25 of Canada's Extradition Act gives the federal minister of justice the discretion to extradite criminal suspects either with or without conditions. In particular, the minister may decide to seek formal assurances from the requesting state that the suspect will not face the death penalty. In Kindler's case, Justice Minister John Crosbie decided not to seek such assurances. Kindler fought extradition, arguing that the minister's decision to extradite without assurances violated ss. 7 and 12 of the Charter. Because Canadian law has no application in the United States, the issue before the courts was not the constitutionality of capital punishment per se. Rather, the questions were whether (1) the Extradition Act violated the Charter, and (2) the minister had acted improperly when he agreed to the extradition request without conditions.

At the Supreme Court, a seven-judge panel split four ways. Four of the Justices—La Forest, L'Heureux-Dubé, Gonthier, and McLachlin—upheld the minister's decision. They found that the Extradition Act did not violate the Charter,

and that the minister had exercised his discretion properly. In dissent, Chief Justice Lamer and Justice Cory held that capital punishment constituted "cruel and unusual" punishment under s. 12, although they based their decision on the finding that the minister's decision had violated Kindler's s. 7 rights to liberty and security of the person. Justice Sopinka did not address s. 12 in his dissenting judgment.

Justice Cory provided a lengthy and often passionate critique of the death penalty. He argued that public attitudes had changed over the centuries, and that capital punishment was no longer acceptable to a majority of Canadians. He also noted that Canada was bound by both the Charter and international law to respect human dignity, whereas state-sponsored execution is the ultimate desecration of human dignity. Finally, referring to Chief Justice Lamer's comments in the 1987 *Smith* ruling, Justice Cory inferred from s. 12 that "punishments must not in themselves be unacceptable no matter what the crime, no matter what the offender.... when a punishment becomes so demeaning that all human dignity is lost, then the punishment must be considered cruel and unusual."[2]

Both the majority ruling by Justice La Forest and the concurring judgment of Justice McLachlin rejected Kindler's s. 12 argument, on the ground that the imposition of the death penalty by a foreign court fell outside the scope of the Charter; however, they agreed that the values protected by s. 12 helped define "fundamental justice." They found that neither the Canadian legislation nor the minister's decision violated the "principles of fundamental justice." In the first place, they argued, most Western countries had retained the death penalty despite the post-1945 international trend toward abolition. Second, the federal government had a duty to prevent Canada, with its long and porous border, from becoming a "safe haven" for American fugitives. Third, the American justice system was similar to that in Canada; it provided strong procedural safeguards for those accused of capital crimes. There was no compelling reason to disrupt Canada's extradition regime, which was founded on mutual respect between sovereign states. Although the Justices in the majority expressed some discomfort with the death penalty, they did not believe that extraditing Kindler without assurances violated the Charter.

Ten years later, the Court revisited the issue of ministerial discretion and reached an entirely different conclusion. The case of *U.S. v. Burns* (also known as *Burns and Rafay*) dealt with two young Canadian men who were wanted in Washington state for the 1994 murders of three members of the Rafay family at their home in Bellingham. Shortly after the murders, Sebastian Burns and Atif Rafay returned to British Columbia; they were arrested there and held in custody pending the outcome of an extradition request from the state of Washington. They each faced three charges of aggravated first-degree murder. If convicted, they could have faced the death penalty. Justice Minister Allan Rock decided to extradite without assurances, prompting an appeal to the Federal Court of Canada and ultimately to the Supreme Court.

When the Court issued its ruling in 2001, the divisions prompted by the *Kindler* case were nowhere in evidence. All nine Justices voted to overturn the minister's decision and ordered him to seek assurances against the death penalty before extraditing Burns and Rafay. Whereas the *Kindler* majority had held that

extradition without assurances was acceptable in most cases, the Court now ruled that "assurances are constitutionally required in all but exceptional cases.... A balance which tilted in favour of extradition without assurances in *Kindler* ... now tilts against the constitutionality of such an outcome."[3]

The Court refused to acknowledge the obvious fact that it was overruling its own precedent, which would have been tantamount to admitting that the *Kindler* majority had been wrong.[4] Instead, it claimed that *Kindler* had established a test for balancing the factors favouring extradition without assurances against those that militated against such extradition. That balance had shifted, said that Court, because of legal and international developments in the years since *Kindler* was issued. These developments included a growing public awareness of wrongful convictions, new research into the horrors of life on death row, and the abolition of the death penalty in a majority of United Nations member states. The Court also rejected two arguments in favour of extradition without assurances that three of its members had found persuasive in 1991: the claim that Canada would become a "safe haven" for criminals if it insisted on assurances, and the obligation to respect the sovereignty of the United States notwithstanding the fact that it engaged in penal practices that would be unconstitutional in Canada.

Although the outcome of *Burns* rested on s. 7, the Court implied that its understanding of the values in s. 12 had changed since the earlier ruling. Whereas Justice McLachlin (as she then was) had argued in *Kindler* that "the effect of any Canadian law or government act is too remote from the possible imposition of the penalty complained of to attract the attention of s. 12,"[5] the Court now concluded that "The Minister's decision is a prior and essential step in a process that may lead to death by execution."[6] Without explicitly repudiating its earlier finding that s. 12 did not apply in the extradition context, the *Burns* Court effectively adopted a

(continued)

new view of the relationship between s. 12 and the "principles of fundamental justice." The possibility of executing an innocent person and the psychological trauma of the "death row phenomenon"—both of which had been well known in 1991[7]—now constituted "cruel and unusual" violations of fundamental justice. Although Minister Rock had acted in good faith when he agreed to extradite the two suspects without conditions, the Court voided his exercise of ministerial discretion and ordered him to seek assurances against the death penalty before proceeding.[8]

ENDNOTES

1. *Kindler v. Canada (Minister of Justice)*, [1991] 2 S.C.R. 779; *United States v. Burns*, [2001] 1 S.C.R. 283.

2. *Kindler*, paragraph 83, *per* Cory J.

3. *Burns*, headnotes, *per curiam*.

4. Richard Haigh, "A Kindler, Gentler Supreme Court? The Case of Burns and the Need for a Principled Approach to Overruling," *Supreme Court Law Review* 14 (2d) (2001), pp. 139–51.

5. *Kindler*, paragraph 68.

6. *Burns*, paragraph 29.

7. Haigh, "A Kindler, Gentler Supreme Court," pp. 153–55.

8. The two suspects were eventually extradited to Washington state on the condition that they would not be executed if found guilty. In the spring of 2004, Burns and Rafay were convicted of the murders and sentenced to life in prison without parole.

While the procedural rights in ss. 7–14 offer the most explicit protection against arbitrary or unfair administrative decisions, s. 15(1) has recently been invoked against customs officials who allegedly targeted gay and lesbian bookstores in their examination of "obscene" materials crossing the Canada–U.S. border. Section 114 of the Customs Tariff prohibits the importation into Canada of written materials that, in the opinion of customs inspectors, violate the obscenity provisions in the Criminal Code, although the Customs Act provides for a process of administrative appeal and, ultimately, judicial review of any such prohibition. In the 2000 *Little Sisters* case,[42] the Supreme Court ruled that these legal provisions infringed freedom of expression, but were justified under s. 1. The exception was the "reverse onus" provision, which required the importer to prove that the questionable materials were not "obscene" within the meaning of the Criminal Code. That section of the Customs Act failed the *Oakes* test; it was read down, to exclude cases of alleged obscenity.

Having established that most of the impugned statute did not violate the Charter, the Court turned to the question of its application. The majority concluded as follows:

there is nothing on the face of the Customs legislation, or in its necessary effects, which contemplates or encourages differential treatment based on sexual orientation. The definition of obscenity, as already discussed, operates without distinction between homosexual and heterosexual erotica. The differentiation was made here at the administrative level in the implementation of the Customs legislation.[43]

The appellants, the co-owners of a Vancouver bookstore specializing in gay and lesbian literature, argued that customs officials targeted their shipments for particular scrutiny and applied different standards in determining whether the imported materials were "obscene." They pointed out that Little Sisters often sought to import written materials that, when shipped to "mainstream" bookstores, entered the country without incident.[44] The appellants alleged that Canada Customs officers in Vancouver deliberately targeted shipments that they believed to contain homosexual erotica. Heterosexual erotica was far less likely to be deemed "obscene" and confiscated, despite a written memorandum from the DOJ instructing customs officers to treat all forms of erotica—

including depictions of particular sexual acts associated with gay men—equally.[45] Writing for the majority, Justice Binnie concluded that "the appellants suffered differential treatment when compared to importers of heterosexually explicit material, let alone more general bookstores that carried at least some of the same titles as Little Sisters."[46]

As we will see in Chapter 11, s. 15(1) of the Charter does not prohibit differential treatment by the state unless that treatment is clearly discriminatory. In this case, the Court found that the targeting of gay bookstores by customs officers discriminated on the "analogous ground" of sexual orientation: "The appellants were entitled to the equal benefit of a fair and open Customs procedure, and because they imported gay and lesbian erotica, which was and is perfectly lawful, they were adversely affected in comparison to other individuals importing comparable publications of a heterosexual nature."[47] However, Binnie declined to impose a specific remedy under s. 24(1). He noted that the impugned administrative acts had occurred at least six years earlier. Canada Customs claimed that it had corrected its procedures in the interim, and the appellants had provided no contrary evidence. In the absence of a specific judicial remedy, Binnie hoped that the Court's findings in the case would both establish clear guidelines for future administrative conduct and provide the appellants with grounds for future litigation should the need arise.

In the Charter era, the Supreme Court has had relatively few opportunities to evaluate the exercise of executive discretion. Perhaps because such cases are rare, the Justices have used them to set broad standards for public administrators. As the *Singh* and *Little Sisters* rulings demonstrate, the Court has gone beyond the imposition of retrospective remedies for specific violations. It has tried to preempt future violations by establishing clear incentives for Charter compliance. By establishing clear procedural criteria for executive decision-making, the Court has narrowed the range of administrative discretion. While this might be viewed as an instance of "judicial activism," it is perhaps more accurately interpreted as an effort to enforce the first-order duties on the powerful executive branch of government.

CONCLUSION

The evidence presented in this chapter shows that the courts hold the executive branch to a high standard of Charter compliance in every field of activity. When new policies are proposed, laws drafted, regulations issued, treaties enforced, and laws put into effect, the responsible public servants at all levels are subject to Charter review on procedural (and often substantive) grounds.

For Kelly, the apparent success of the DOJ's "risk assessments" proves that the executive branch—and, by extension, the legislative branch, which passes its laws—has reclaimed the upper hand in its relationship with the judiciary.[48] Whereas the early years of the Charter era witnessed repeated, unexpected nullifications that threw the policy agenda into chaos, the new proactive role of the DOJ as a central agency has allowed the executive branch to regain control of the policy agenda and thus reassert its primacy over the courts. But as we saw in Chapter 4, the evidence that the other two branches of government have adjusted to the new powers of judicial review granted by the Charter can be interpreted in different ways. One could argue that because the HRLS bases its risk-assessments not on the Charter itself but on the interpretations that it has received from the courts, the latter continue to dominate the policy-making process—at least in areas that directly affect protected rights and freedoms. Therefore, one might well question Kelly's conclusion that "bureaucratic activism" has now offset "judicial activism" and thus "contained the threat of jurocracy."[49]

It is more illuminating to describe the shifting balance of power since 1982 in terms of Charter "duties," rather than Charter "activism." As Slattery argues, the second-order duties of the courts assume greater importance where the first-order duties of the other branches of government have been neglected. The full potential of the entrenched rights and freedoms to reshape Canadian public policy can be realized only if the incentives for compliance are strong enough to overcome political resistance and bureaucratic inertia. This preemptive approach is particularly important, given the rarity of Charter challenges to executive activity. The willingness of the Supreme Court of

Canada to impose judicial remedies for laws and official acts that conflict with its interpretation of the Charter has forced legislators and public servants to take rights and freedoms more seriously than they might have done otherwise.

GLOSSARY OF KEY TERMS

central agencies   Departments of the federal government responsible for coordinating public policy across a range of fields. These include the Privy Council Office (PCO), which monitors and guides policy development across the federal executive; the Treasury Board Secretariat (TBS), which sets and enforces the annual spending estimates for every government department and program; and the Department of Finance, which makes and coordinates budgetary policies for the federal government.

delegated legislation   Regulations made by the executive branch, which have been previously authorized by Parliament (**enabling legislation**) but which do not require parliamentary ratification. When Parliament passes a law, it empowers the executive to make any regulations necessary for its effective implementation. Under the Department of Justice Act and the Statutory Instruments Act, proposed regulations must be scrutinized for conformity to the Charter.

line departments   Departments of the federal government responsible for making and enforcing policy in a particular field, e.g., the Department of Agriculture and Agri-Food or the Department of Transport.

DISCUSSION AND REVIEW QUESTIONS

1. Describe the process of "Charter-proofing" by the Human Rights Law Section of the Department of Justice. In your opinion, should the "Charter-proofers" base their work on court rulings? Why or why not?

2. Explain the significance of the *Operation Dismantle* ruling for Canada's executive branch of government.

3. Identify two ways in which the Supreme Court has used the Charter to narrow the scope of administrative discretion in Canada. In your opinion, is it legitimate for courts to do this?

SUGGESTED READINGS

Dawson, Mary. "The Impact of the Charter on the Public Policy Process and the Department of Justice." *Osgoode Hall Law Journal* 30 (1992), pp. 595–605.

Kelly, James B. "Bureaucratic Activism and the Charter of Rights and Freedoms: The Department of Justice and Its Entry into the Centre of Government." *Canadian Public Administration* 42, no. 4 (Winter 1999), pp. 476–511.

Monahan, Patrick J., and Marie Finkelstein. "The Charter of Rights and Public Policy in Canada." *Osgoode Hall Law Journal* 30 (1992), pp. 501–47.

ENDNOTES

1. James B. Kelly, "Bureaucratic Activism and the Charter of Rights and Freedoms: The Department of Justice and Its Entry into the Centre of Government," *Canadian Public Administration* 42, no. 4 (Winter 1999), p. 480.

2. Ibid., p. 481.

3. Mary Dawson, "The Impact of the Charter on the Public Policy Process and the Department of Justice," *Osgoode Hall Law Journal* 30 (1992), p. 597.

4. Ian G. Scott, "The Role of the Attorney General and the Charter of Rights," *Criminal Law Quarterly* 29, no. 2 (March 1987), pp. 195–96.

5. See, e.g., Patrick J. Monahan and Marie Finkelstein, "The Charter of Rights and Public Policy in Canada," *Osgoode Hall Law Journal* 30 (1992), p. 518; Kelly, "Bureaucratic Activism," p. 493.

6. Kelly, "Bureaucratic Activism," pp. 496–98; Dawson, "The Impact of the Charter," p. 597.

7. Dawson, "The Impact of the Charter," p. 597.

8. Canada, Privy Council Office, *Guide to Making Federal Acts and Regulations* (2003), p. 34, available online at www.pco-bcp.gc.ca.

9. Ibid., p. 34.

10. Kelly, "Bureaucratic Activism," p. 498.

11. Ibid., p. 496.

12. Ibid., p. 500.

13. Monahan and Finkelstein, "The Charter of Rights and Public Policy," pp. 506 and 513.

14. Kelly, "Bureaucratic Activism," p. 499.

15. Ibid., pp. 493–94.

16. Roger Tassé, interview with the author, June 17, 2003.

17. Kelly, "Bureaucratic Activism," p. 494.

18. Ibid., p. 493.

19. Roger Tassé interview.

20. Kelly, "Bureaucratic Activism," p. 493.

21. [1985] 1 S.C.R. 177.

22. Rainer Knopff and F.L. Morton, *Charter Politics* (Scarborough: Nelson Canada, 1992), pp. 22–24.

23. Roger Tassé interview.

24. Kelly, "Bureaucratic Activism," p. 494.

25. Aphorism attributed to Dr. Samuel Johnson (1709–84).

26. Janet L. Hiebert, *Charter Conflicts: What Is Parliament's Role?* (Montreal and Kingston: McGill-Queen's University Press, 2002), p. 9.

27. Dawson, "The Impact of the Charter," p. 601.

28. Kelly, "Bureaucratic Activism," pp. 504–6.

29. *R. v. Sharpe* [2001] 1 S.C.R. 45.

30. The phrase "Charter ventriloquism" is taken from Christopher P. Manfredi and James B. Kelly, "Six Degrees of Dialogue: A Response to Hogg and Bushell," *Osgoode Hall Law Journal* 37 (1999), at p. 521. See the discussion of "dialogue" between courts and legislators in Chapter 4, pages 150–56.

31. In 2003, the HRLS reviewed its Charter evaluation procedures. No information about any reforms to the process was available at the time of writing.

32. *Application under s. 83.28 of the Criminal Code (Re)*, 2004 SCC 42.

33. Although DOJ staff rarely comment publicly about the work of the HRLS, two senior DOJ officials spoke to a conference on the Anti-Terrorism Act while the bill was still before Parliament. See the comments of Rick Mosley, an assistant deputy minister, and Stan Cohen, general counsel to the HRLS, in Ronald J. Daniels, Patrick Macklem, and Kent Roach, eds., *The Security of Freedom: Essays on Canada's Anti-Terrorism Bill* (Toronto: University of Toronto Press, 2001), pp. 435–45.

34. *Operation Dismantle v. The Queen*, [1985] 1 S.C.R. 441, paragraph 50, summarized by Wilson J.

35. Roger Tassé, "Application of the Canadian Charter of Rights and Freedoms," in Gérald-A. Beaudoin and Ed Ratushny, eds., *The Canadian Charter of Rights and Freedoms,*

2nd ed. (Toronto: Carswell, 1989), p. 87; see also pp. 72–73.

36. *Little Sisters Book and Art Emporium v. Canada (Minister of Justice)*, [2000] 2 S.C.R. 1120, paragraph 141.

37. See, e.g., *Suresh v. Canada (Minister of Citizenship and Immigration)*, [2002] 1 S.C.R. 3; *Ahani v. Canada (M.C.I.)*, [2002] 1 S.C.R. 72.

38. *Ahani v. Canada*, paragraph 17.

39. *Suresh v. Canada*, paragraph 129, *per curiam*.

40. Reproduced in *Kindler v. Canada (Minister of Justice)*, [1991] 2 S.C.R. 779, paragraph 18.

41. *Re B.C. Motor Vehicle Act*, [1985] 2 S.C.R. 486, paragraph 124, *per* Lamer J.

42. *Little Sisters Book and Art Emporium v. Canada (Minister of Justice)*, [2000] 2 S.C.R. 1120.

43. Ibid., paragraph 125.

44. Ibid., paragraph 112.

45. Ibid., paragraph 114.

46. Ibid., paragraph 116.

47. Ibid., paragraph 120.

48. Kelly, "Bureaucratic Activism," pp. 507–8.

49. Ibid., p. 508.

Chapter 6

Interest Groups and the Charter

Saskatchewan farmer Percy Schmeiser is surrounded by microphones as he addresses the media at the Supreme Court in January 2004. Schmeiser lost his case against biotech company Monsanto, which had accused him of deliberately growing its genetically modified seeds without permission.
CP PHOTO/Jonathan Hayward

INTRODUCTION

Since 1982, and especially since section 15 took effect in 1985, the Charter has given Canada's **interest groups** a new way to influence public policy-making. In addition to their traditional activities—e.g., lobbying legislators, cabinet ministers, and public servants—interest groups can now seek to change the law through the courts. Over the past two decades, a variety of groups have participated in Charter litigation via two separate routes:

1. by applying for **standing** to initiate their own court challenges (or to sponsor a case brought by another plaintiff); or
2. by applying to intervene in cases already before the courts.

The former strategy has one great advantage: it allows the group to define the issues in the case. If the group wins, the judicial remedies will likely be tailored to the priorities of the group. However, the cost of pursuing a Charter challenge from the trial level to the Supreme Court of Canada is prohibitive for all but the wealthiest groups. When a government decides to defend an impugned law, it may adopt the litigation style of "any long-pursed, cut-throat corporation hoping to bankrupt the opposition before the case ever gets to trial."[1] So most **advocacy groups** choose instead to intervene in existing cases. That approach also has considerable disadvantages: a group must "expend resources to ensure its right to intervene"; the time allowed to prepare submissions is limited; the issues at bar are framed by the direct parties, and do not necessarily reflect the goals of intervenors; and the judges are under no obligation to take third-party arguments into account in their rulings.[2]

For some critics of the Charter, interest-group influence in the courts is both excessive and inherently undemocratic. Morton and Knopff argue that the "Court Party"—a "well-organized group" of left-wing organizations[3]—has encouraged and exploited judicial activism as a tool to impose its policy priorities on a reluctant majority. Feminists, equality-seekers, **postmaterialists**, and other "special interests" use the Charter to hijack the agendas of elected governments. In the process, they distort Canada's political system by shifting power away from accountable legislators to unaccountable judges and nongovernmental groups.

These claims are controversial.[4] Roach points out that the various elements in the "Court Party"— "national unity advocates, civil libertarians, equality-seekers, **social engineers**, and postmaterialists"[5]— often take opposing sides in particular cases. For example, both the Women's Legal Education and Action Fund (LEAF) and the Canadian Civil Liberties Association (CCLA) intervened in the *Butler* case before the Supreme Court of Canada (Dossier 3.3, pages 113–15). LEAF argued that the law against obscenity should be upheld because pornography harms women and children; the CCLA asked the Court to strike down the law as an unjustified restriction on free speech. Morton and Knopff acknowledge that "Court Party interest groups are sometimes policy enemies rather than allies," but they maintain that "The Court Party coalition is not so fragmented ... that its coherence or identity exists mainly in the mind of the analyst; when galvanized into action, it can pull together as a self-conscious and highly effective political force."[6]

The force that binds the coalition together is "a vested interest in judicial power."[7] While the "Court Party" groups also engage in political lobbying, their primary tool is Charter-based **public-interest litigation**. They have turned to the courts because they cannot reliably command the support of a majority, either inside or outside Parliament. For Morton and Knopff, this concerted campaign to enhance the power of judges constitutes a threat to democracy. They argue that "Shifting power from the legislative to the judicial arena ... is a way of substituting coercion for government by discussion."[8]

The "Court Party" thesis offers two important insights. First, entrenched guarantees of rights and freedoms require a "support structure for legal mobilization" if they are to shape public policy. After examining various hypotheses to explain the changes in judicial policy since 1982, Charles Epp identified public-interest litigation by Charter advocacy groups as the most important variable.[9] In the absence of groups (and individuals) with the will and resources to bring cases before the courts, judges are powerless to act. They cannot make policy outside the context of an actual case (except when they receive reference questions from one or more governments). Intervenors also play a role, by advancing Charter arguments distinct from those raised by the parties. Epp concludes that "constitutional reform alone, in the absence of resources in civil society for legal mobilization, is likely to produce only empty promises."[10]

Second, Morton and Knopff have correctly identified some of the key interests involved in public-interest litigation. Civil libertarians and equality-seekers have been particularly active, as have "national unity" groups (Morton and Knopff's term for advocates of minority language rights—see Chapters 7 and 12, pages 224–27 and 375–77). However, there is little evidence to demonstrate a distinct "postmaterialist" agenda. It is probably more accurate to describe most public-interest litigators as postmaterialist in orientation (the exceptions are those who try—so far unsuccessfully—to use the Charter to redistribute wealth).[11]

Despite these contributions, the "Court Party" thesis is inaccurate in at least four respects. First, it implies that "left-wing" interests monopolize Charter litigation. In reality, business organizations and corporations also use the Charter when it suits their purposes. Between 1985 and 1999, almost one-quarter (23.8 percent) of applications for leave to intervene at the Supreme Court came from business organizations, professional organizations, and corporations. Well over 80 percent of these applications were granted.[12] The statistics on intervenors actually understate the participation of business interests in Charter litigation. Unlike advocacy groups, corporate interests often possess the resources to launch their own Charter challenges. Consequently, they rarely have to rely on the uncertain strategy of intervention. From the very beginning of the Charter era, corporations have successfully challenged laws and administrative decisions that constrained their activities or reduced their profits. Examples include *Hunter v. Southam* (1984), *Big M Drug Mart* (1985), and *RJR-Macdonald* (1995).[13]

Moreover, it is misleading to suggest that left-wing advocacy groups are the only ones to take advantage of the new opportunities afforded by the Charter. The National Citizens' Coalition, a right-wing lobby group, has successfully challenged the Canada Elections Act under ss. 2(b) and 3 on several occasions.[14] In three major cases on sexual orientation, the Supreme Court granted intervenor status to groups opposed to the recognition of same-sex relationships, not just those—such as LEAF and Equality for Gays and Lesbians Everywhere (EGALE)—that supported the appellants.[15] Cases on Aboriginal rights follow a similar pattern. In the 1990 *Sparrow* case, which recognized the constitutional status of Aboriginal fishing rights, the Court admitted twenty-two intervenors—only one of whom supported the appellant. The rest were governments and fishermen's associations opposed to the recognition of an Aboriginal right to fish. Three of the six named intervenors in the landmark *Delgamuukw* case on Aboriginal land title were opposed to the claim of the Gitksan and Wet'suwet'en First Nations. Taken as a whole, the rights cases heard by the Supreme Court demonstrate that "public interest standing, like intervenor status, is open to all comers and not restricted to the politically correct and left-leaning elites."[16]

Second, the "Court Party" thesis is flawed insofar as it implies that the Charter itself transformed the activities of Canada's interest groups. The truth is more complicated. While it is certainly true that the entrenchment of rights and freedoms encouraged organized interests to pursue public-interest litigation, the use of the courts to further policy agendas was already on the rise before 1982.[17] As we saw in Chapter 2, the cultural changes that inspired the movement for an entrenched Charter began shortly after World War II. By the 1970s, the "support structure for legal mobilization" had already taken shape. It united advocacy groups, human rights commissions,

law schools, and law-reform agencies.[18] While most interest groups lacked the will and the means to litigate, some saw court challenges as a way to seek policy change and mobilize their constituencies.[19] So the Charter did not, in itself, start a "revolution"; it simply reinforced trends that were already in evidence.

Third, Morton and Knopff imply that "Court Party" groups exert too much influence over the courts, and thereby over public policy. In practice, it is impossible to determine the extent of their power to shape Charter rulings. In the absence of empirical proof, which judges rarely provide, we cannot demonstrate a causal connection between the argument submitted by a particular interest group and the outcome of the case at bar. Similarities certainly exist. As Dossier 6.2, pages 208–9 demonstrates, some of the arguments submitted by LEAF in the landmark *Andrews* case bear a *prima facie* resemblance to the majority opinion. Moreover, Justices often extol the benefits of third-party intervention in Charter appeals; as former Justice Iacobucci said in 2002, they "frequently provide the Court with a richer understanding of the context in which the impugned legislation must be assessed."[20] This implies that intervenors play a key role in judicial review.

Nonetheless, we cannot know for sure whether, or to what extent, groups such as LEAF have succeeded in using the courts to shape public policy in their preferred directions. The claim, by both LEAF's critics and its champions,[21] that the group has strongly influenced the Court's approach to the Charter is unproven and possibly misleading. LEAF, the most frequent "Court Party" intervenor, has lost several high-profile battles at the Court. According to a lawyer who has represented intervenors in several Charter cases, "the evidence does not support extravagant claims about intervenor influence."[22]

Fourth and finally, Morton and Knopff appear to allow their doubts about the Charter itself to colour their description of interest-group influence since 1982. The claim that Charter litigation by organized interests is inherently "undemocratic" is open to question on at least three grounds:

1. Prime Minister Trudeau *intended* the Charter to empower private individuals and groups, especially those groups that transcended provincial

boundaries. To deny "Charter groups" (e.g., official-language minorities) access to the remedies in ss. 24(1) and 52(1) would defeat the purpose of the entrenched guarantees. After all, if popular or legislative majorities could always be trusted to protect minority rights and individual freedoms, the Charter would serve no useful function.

2. The remedies in the Charter are not self-enforcing. Courts are powerless to act in the absence of concrete disputes. If judges are to perform their second-order duties, someone has to challenge the laws and administrative actions that allegedly infringe their guaranteed rights and freedoms. Recognizing that few advocacy groups can afford to go to court to protect or advance their interests, the federal government established the Court Challenges Program (CCP) to fund litigation under ss. 15–23 of the Charter (equality and minority language rights). As we will see, the CCP has had some impact on judicial policies—though probably not to the extent that its detractors claim.

3. If Charter litigation always and inevitably thwarted the will of the majority, we would expect the courts to suffer a loss of public legitimacy. But as we saw in Chapter 3, most Canadians place greater trust in the courts than in Parliament despite widespread disagreement with particular rulings. The arguments of Knopff, Morton, and other Charter critics do not appear to resonate with the wider public.

The rest of this chapter elaborates on the arguments just presented. It argues that the spectre of an almighty "Court Party" using the Charter to trample majority opinion is overstated. We begin by examining the processes by which interest groups gain access to the courts.

INTEREST GROUPS AND THE COURTS

Interest Groups as Litigators: The Evolution of "Standing"

Before the 1970s, the Supreme Court rarely granted standing to groups or individuals who wished to challenge a particular law on public-interest grounds.

Standing was reserved for those who were directly embroiled in an active dispute, e.g., a person who had been convicted of a criminal offence or a party to a lawsuit. In a 1986 ruling, former Justice Le Dain explained the restrictive approach to standing:

> The traditional judicial concerns about the expansion of public interest standing may be summarized as follows: the concern about the allocation of scarce judicial resources and the need to screen out the mere busybody; the concern that in the determination of issues the courts should have the benefit of the contending points of view of those most directly affected by them; and the concern about the proper role of the courts and their constitutional relationship to the other branches of government.[23]

The Court began to modify this restrictive approach in the 1970s. Three cases—*Thorson, McNeil,* and *Borowski*[24]—relaxed the rules of standing to permit a wider range of public-interest litigants. Now an individual (acting for himself, or for a group) who was not directly engaged in a concrete dispute could challenge the constitutionality of a statute or administrative act, as long as he could show that "he is affected by it directly or that he has a genuine interest as a citizen in the validity of the legislation and there is no other reasonable and effective manner in which the issue may be brought before the Court."[25] The implications of this change were significant: "No longer would the courts strike out cases simply because they did not meet traditional rules of standing. Every law could be subject to a constitutional challenge, and thus subject to being rewritten by the Supreme Court."[26]

In *Canadian Council of Churches* (1992), Justice Cory (for a unanimous court) described standing rules as a compromise between "the need to balance the access of public interest groups to the Courts" and "the need to conserve scarce judicial resources."[27] The appellant council, on behalf of several churches dedicated to helping refugee claimants, had applied for standing to challenge the constitutionality of amendments to the federal Immigration Act. It argued that the changes violated the rights of refugee claimants by making it more difficult to qualify for refugee status in Canada. The Court rejected the application.

Noting that the Justices had already opened up the process in the pre-1982 "standing trilogy," Justice Cory argued that the language of the Charter required the courts to take "a generous and liberal approach" to groups and individuals who sought to challenge the constitutionality of laws and administrative decisions. Otherwise, "Charter rights might be unenforced and Charter freedoms shackled."[28] Therefore, courts must use their discretion to grant standing "in those situations where it is necessary to ensure that legislation conforms to the Constitution and the Charter."[29]

On the other hand, the courts must be mindful of their own scarce resources. They cannot allow themselves to be overwhelmed by frivolous or unnecessary Charter challenges. Justice Cory identified three criteria for courts to use when deciding whether or not to hear a case brought by an individual or group acting in the "public interest":

> First, is there a serious issue raised as to the invalidity of legislation in question? Second, has it been established that the plaintiff is directly affected by the legislation or if not does the plaintiff have a genuine interest in its validity? Third, is there another reasonable and effective way to bring the issue before the court?[30]

The third criterion refers to the likelihood that a private litigant—i.e., a party directly affected by the impugned law or policy—will bring a separate appeal based on a "clear concrete factual background."[31] Where such a likelihood can be established on a balance of probabilities, the courts should wait for a concrete dispute instead of preempting it by hearing a hypothetical challenge from an outside party. In the case at bar, Justice Cory held that the constitutionality of the impugned provisions could be challenged by individual refugee claimants in the course of appealing adverse decisions. Therefore, there was no need to grant public-interest standing to the Canadian Council of Churches.[32]

The rules of standing are only one barrier to interest groups that wish to pursue their goals through Charter litigation. Another, more potent obstacle is the cost of sponsoring a case through years of court battles, from the lower court all the way up to the Supreme Court of Canada.[33] For criminal suspects wishing to appeal on Charter grounds, provincial legal aid programs may provide some financial support. But there is no legal aid for public-interest litigants filing challenges under other Charter sections. While the CCP subsidizes selected cases, its mandate is restricted to challenges involving equality rights and official-language minority rights.[34] Between 1984 and 1993, it funded fifteen public-interest litigants, most of whom represented official-language minorities.[35] Although Morton and Knopff suggest that the CCP has helped to turn the Supreme Court into the captives of the "Court Party,"[36] these figures hardly support that hypothesis. Nor does CCP funding imply that the recipient enjoys the favour of the federal government. What the CCP gives, litigators in the Department of Justice often take away by following a "deep pockets" defence strategy.[37]

Public-Interest Intervention at the Supreme Court of Canada

Public-interest intervention is "the participation by non-parties in litigation in order to influence the judicial lawmaking process in a way the intervenor considers to be in the public interest."[38] The rules for groups or individuals who wish to intervene in court cases are set out in Dossier 6.1.

DOSSIER 6.1

THE RULES FOR INTERVENORS AT THE SUPREME COURT OF CANADA (EXCERPTS)[1]

PART 8—APPEALS AND CROSS-APPEALS

37. Within eight weeks of the order granting leave to intervene ... an intervener shall

(a) serve on all other parties a copy of the intervener's factum and book of authorities; and

(b) file with the Registrar the original and 23 copies of the factum and 14 copies of the book of authorities.

(continued)

42. (4) Parts I to V of the factum[2] of any appellant or respondent, and of that of an attorney general who files a notice of intervention ... shall not exceed 40 pages, unless a judge or the Registrar, on motion, otherwise orders.

(5) Parts I to V of the factum of an intervener other than an attorney general ... shall not exceed 20 pages unless a judge or the Registrar, on motion, otherwise orders.

PART 11—PARTICULAR MOTIONS
Motion for Intervention.

55. Any person interested in an application for leave to appeal, an appeal or a reference may make a motion for intervention to a judge.

57. (2) A motion for intervention shall
(1) identify the position the person interested in the proceeding intends to take in the proceeding; and
(2) set out the submissions to be advanced by the person interested in the proceeding, their relevance to the proceeding and the reasons for believing that the submissions will be useful to the Court and different from those of the other parties.

59. (2) After all of the memoranda of argument on an application for leave to appeal or the *facta* on an appeal or reference have been filed and served, a judge may, in his or her discretion, authorize an intervener to present oral argument at the hearing of the application for leave to appeal, if any, the appeal or the reference, and determine the time allotted for oral argument.

61. (4) Within four weeks of the service of a notice of constitutional question, an attorney general who intends to participate in the appeal, whether or not the attorney general intends to present oral argument, shall serve on all other parties and file with the Registrar a notice of intervention ... without being required to obtain leave to intervene.

PART 13—SCHEDULING AND APPEARANCES

71. (1) Unless the Court or a judge otherwise orders,
(a) no more than two counsel for each appellant or respondent and one counsel for each intervener shall present oral argument on an appeal; and
(b) no more than one counsel for each appellant shall have the right of a reply.

(2) Respondents and interveners do not have the right of reply unless the Court or a judge otherwise orders.

(3) A respondent or intervener who fails to file their factum within the [required] time ... shall not present oral argument on the appeal unless a judge, on motion, otherwise orders.

ENDNOTES

1. Rules of the Supreme Court of Canada, as amended April 2002, available on the Supreme Court of Canada website (www.scc-csc.gc.ca).

2. Parts I to V of an intervenor's factum to the Supreme Court contain, respectively: the response to the appellant's statement of the facts in issue; a brief summary of the argument; the argument itself; and the requested remedy.

Under these rules, government intervenors are treated more generously than nongovernmental intervenors. Attorneys general from other jurisdictions enjoy an automatic right to intervene. In contrast, a private intervenor must prove that its factum will assist the Court in resolving the issues at bar without duplicating the arguments advanced by one of the parties or by another prospective intervenor. Moreover, a government factum may be twice as long as a factum submitted by a private group or individual. This gives government intervenors a significant advantage, because few intervenors are granted permission to present an oral argument before the Court.[39] The preferential treatment of attorneys general magnifies their preexisting resource advantage: unlike most advocacy groups, federal and provincial attorneys general have staffs of full-time lawyers who can be assigned to work on interventions as soon as the constitutional questions are issued.[40] Other public-interest litigants must rely on *pro bono* work by volunteers; the other expenses of litigation, especially court costs, can be too high for groups that have to do their own grassroots fundraising.[41] Under these circumstances, it makes sense that the government of Canada is the most frequent intervenor at the Supreme Court; five provincial governments also appear on the top-ten list.[42]

The relative frequency of interventions is a recent phenomenon. Since its founding in 1875, the rules of the Supreme Court allowed third parties to apply for intervenor status in appeals and references. Few applications were granted, because the Court was reluctant to allow third parties—i.e., anyone other than the two sides involved in a dispute—to present arguments in appeals. This reluctance is grounded in the adversarial system of English law, in which one side (the appellant) challenged a particular law or governmental action (e.g., a trial conviction) and the other side (the respondent) defended the impugned law or action. It also appears to have arisen from judicial distaste for "extrinsic evidence" (see the discussion in Chapter 3, pages 108–22). Adjudicative facts and arguments were considered appropriate for judges to consider; "legislative" or policy-based arguments, of the sort likely to be raised by intervenors, were not.

American courts began to move away from the strict adversarial system early in the twentieth century.

As we saw in Chapter 3, they have long allowed *amici curiae* ("friends of the court") to present written briefs on the policy issues raised by the case at bar. In the English tradition, an *amicus curiae* is supposed to take a neutral position in the dispute between the two parties. He serves the court as "an advisor on a point of law and as a guardian to assist and protect the rights of those unrepresented in litigation."[43] In practice, American "friends of the court" have evolved from neutral advisors into partisan combatants. For most of the twentieth century, and particularly in the past fifty years, most have "play[ed] an active advocacy role by persuading the court to resolve one or more of the issues raised in the litigation in a manner that they consider desirable."[44] As discussed in Chapter 3, *amicus* briefs have been an important (though often flawed) source of extrinsic evidence in policy-related cases. These briefs allowed the Court to consider a wider range of issues and interests than those presented by the two parties immediately involved in the dispute. By the 1970s, intervenors appeared in a majority of constitutional cases before the U.S. Supreme Court.[45]

The tension between the English and American attitudes to "third parties" helps explain their erratic treatment by Canadian courts.[46] The English distaste for public-interest advocacy prevailed until the 1970s: the Supreme Court entertained few interventions in "private" (i.e., nonreference) cases, even those that raised significant constitutional issues.[47] The 1960 Bill of Rights prompted a modest change in approach, although "the mere fact that the case involved important questions of general public interest" was insufficient to overcome the traditional attitude toward interventions.[48] When former Chief Justice Laskin allowed several intervenors to participate in the *Lavell* (1974) and *Morgentaler* (1975) appeals,[49] law-reform advocates were heartened by this unprecedented move toward the American model of *amicus curiae*.

In January 1983, as new and established groups prepared to embark on Charter litigation, the Court changed its rules on intervention for the first time since 1905. It gave the federal and provincial attorneys general the right to intervene in cases in which they were not directly involved. It also adopted rule 18(2), which granted automatic intervenor status to groups that had already intervened in that particular case before a lower court.[50] With these amendments, the Justices opened the door to public-interest litigation by both governmental and nongovernmental lawyers.

Less than a year later, the door suddenly slammed shut. In November 1983, the Court announced that it would not allow nongovernment intervenors in criminal appeals.[51] In late December, the Court revoked rule 18(2). Public-interest groups that had intervened before the lower courts lost their automatic status before the Court. They would have to rely on judicial discretion for permission to intervene. For the next several months, such permission was rarely granted.

The Court's fluctuating rules reflected the Justices' uncertainty about their expanded policy-making role under the Charter. They also demonstrated the depth of the internal disagreement over the usefulness of intervenors. Justice Wilson was an outspoken advocate of public-interest intervention in Charter cases. In a 1986 article, she argued that the Court should reform its procedures in order to enhance its institutional policy-making capacity. The most important reform, according to Wilson, "is to alter the traditional two-party structure of public-law litigation by giving a generous interpretation to the Court's rules governing interventions."

> If constitutional decisions have ramifications for a broad range of interests and involve distinct choices between conflicting social policies, then we must devise some way of bringing these interests before the Court.... [Liberalized intervention] would [also] assist in legitimizing the Court's new role through a more open and accessible court process.[52]

Acknowledging that some of her colleagues were loath to spend time listening to intervenors, Wilson pointed out that the problem could be addressed "by a more rigid control on the oral presentations of intervenors by the presiding judge or by limiting the participation of intervenors to submissions in writing."[53] Although it is true that some Justices were reluctant to entertain oral arguments from intervenors,[54] their concerns went further than the merely logistical. The more conservative members of the Court—including Beetz, Estey, McIntyre, and even Chief Justice Dickson—"insisted that cases had to be decided on purely legal principles."[55] This principle applied with particular force to criminal appeals, "where the liberty of the subject is involved."[56] These Justices were comfortable with the traditional adversarial model of adjudication, and did not believe that the Court should entertain policy arguments from groups or individuals with no direct stake in the resolution of the dispute.

Like their brethren in other Canadian courts, the Justices also worried about the effects of intervention on the parties to the case. If they admitted third parties who opposed the interests of one side or the other, those arguments could prejudice the outcome and create an injustice. Moreover, if intervenors were allowed to "expand the range of issues before the court," or to lengthen the time required to hear the case, they would increase the costs to be borne by one or both parties.[57] For most Justices in the mid-1980s, these considerations outweighed the potential benefits of interventions. Critics decried the Court for ruling on Charter issues "in a social vacuum" and questioned the exclusion of viewpoints other than those of the direct parties to the dispute.[58] There were exceptions to the tacit rule against intervenors: individual Justices rule on applications for leave to intervene, so the lack of consensus on the Court produced some inconsistent rulings.[59] However, the overall pattern was clear: nongovernmental intervenors were unwelcome.

The vacillations on the Court are reflected in the statistics. Three of the four Charter cases decided in 1984 featured third-party intervenors, most of which were governments.[60] The Court received eleven applications for leave in 1985, roughly one-quarter of the number submitted the previous year, and accepted only two (18 percent).[61] Groups that had mobilized for Charter litigation protested furiously, and sometimes publicly. After being denied leave to intervene in *Oakes*, Alan Borovoy of the CCLA submitted a brief calling for a more liberal approach. He argued that public-interest groups could give the Court not only a broader perspective on policy issues, but a more moderate perspective than they were likely to hear from the adversaries in a dispute. Borovoy asked the Court to consider accepting written submissions from interest groups and permitting oral arguments when appropriate. He also recommended that the same rules be applied to attorneys general, so that governments would not have "a special advantage over every other interest in the community."[62]

The Court did not respond to Borovoy's brief. That silence prompted a lobbying campaign by interest groups wishing to engage in public-interest litigation. In March 1986, an article appeared in *The Globe and Mail*, citing complaints by the CCLA. The public criticism persuaded Dickson to reassess his conservative position on intervenors. He referred the issue to the Liaison Committee of the Supreme Court and the Canadian Bar Association, which recommended a new policy in October 1986. Public-interest intervenors would be allowed to submit factums, as long as they did not duplicate the arguments of the parties; oral argument would be permitted only in exceptional cases. Wilson argued that the proposed policy was too restrictive, reiterating her argument (quoted earlier) that intervenors would enhance the Court's policy-making capacity under the Charter.[63] Borovoy was equally disappointed. He wrote to the minister of justice, urging him to amend the Supreme Court Act in order to override the Justices' own rules.[64] Despite these arguments, the rules that took effect in May 1987 were based on the liaison committee's proposal. They remain essentially unchanged today.

On their face, the 1987 amendments gave public-interest litigators little reason for optimism. But they heralded a marked change of attitude: the Court was decided to use its discretion to admit intervenors, instead of excluding them. The percentage of successful leave applications jumped from 18 percent in 1985 to 96 percent in 1987, and has remained at roughly 90 percent since then.[65] Because the Justices rarely issue written reasons for granting or denying leave to intervene, it is difficult to explain their change of heart. The exception is the late Justice Sopinka, who made a point of explaining his reasons in some leave applications.[66] In a 1989 ruling, Sopinka summarized his position on intervenors.[67] He identified two criteria that the Justices used in evaluating potential intervenors: (1) whether or not the applicant has a sufficient interest in the case at bar to warrant the Court's attention, and (2) the likely usefulness of the submission, relative to the arguments advanced by the two contending parties.[68]

Sopinka did not explain the precise degree of "interest" required to satisfy the Court, although he suggested that the need to balance the contending sides in the dispute would sometimes be sufficient. An "imbalance of representation" on one side of a particular issue would create "an aura of unfairness," which could be dispelled only by granting leave to an intervenor on the other side. "Ganging up" is to be avoided whenever possible, especially in criminal cases where a preponderance of interventions against the position of the accused could interfere with her due-process rights.[69]

Sopinka was more explicit about the criterion of usefulness: "[It] is easily satisfied by an applicant who has a history of involvement in the issue giving the applicant an expertise which can shed fresh light or provide new information on the matter." This suggests that an established advocacy group with a track record of interventions that specializes in a particular subject area will have an advantage over other applicants. In fact, the Justices do appear to favour "more mainstream, higher profile groups which [have] already established a credible reputation before the Court."[70]

In addition to the factors identified by Sopinka, the Justices also appear to be influenced by the receptiveness of the parties to the dispute. If the lawyer for one of the parties expresses a strong and reasoned objection to a particular application, the Justice involved may reject it unless there are strong countervailing reasons.[71] The overriding concern is to ensure a fair hearing for both the appellant and respondent. The interests of intervenors, especially nongovernmental intervenors, are secondary. This is entirely appropriate, given the adjudicative role of courts and the high stakes for the direct participants in a lawsuit. It is also legitimate to allow governments, which are responsible for upholding the rule of law, to play a role in determining the constitutionality of particular statutes or programs. What has changed in recent years is the willingness of judges to accommodate other participants, where it is appropriate to do so.

It is not known whether the Court's more positive attitude toward intervenors was prompted by membership turnover or by a recognition that intervenors could help produce better and more legitimate policy. Whatever its cause, aspiring intervenors were quick to respond to the Court's new generosity. The number of applications rose from 14 in 1986 to 23 in 1987, reaching a high of 139 in 1996.[72] There is no clear trend; application figures fluctuate from year to year, based on the types of cases on the Court's docket and the resources available for public-interest litigation. For example, the number of applications fell from 115 in 1991 to 29 in 1992. The Mulroney government eliminated the Court Challenges Program in its 1992 budget, cutting off an important funding source for minority language and equality-rights organizations.[73] From 1984 to 1993, the CCP funded 13 percent of nongovernmental intervenors in Supreme Court Charter cases (30 out of 230).[74] It may be assumed, therefore, that the number of would-be intervenors dropped when the CCP funding dried up. The drought was temporary; Liberal Prime Minister Jean Chrétien reinstated the CCP in 1994, in response to protests from inside and outside the federal government.[75] By 1996, the number of applications had risen to 139, although the increase cannot be attributed solely to the restoration of public funding for public-interest litigation.

The statistics on interest-group intervention do not support the "Court Party" thesis. Governments—attorneys general, federal and provincial agencies, and municipalities—are by far the most frequent intervenors in Charter cases. This is largely attributable to the factors discussed earlier, especially the automatic right to intervene and the access to substantial legal resources. In total, governments accounted for 59 percent of all interventions between 1984 and 1999.[76] Between 1985 and 1999, eight of the ten most frequent intervenors were attorneys general; the federal justice department alone filed 126 interventions.[77] Two "Court Party" groups, LEAF and the CCLA rounded out the top ten, with 19 and 18 interventions respectively.

Altogether, public-interest groups intervened in 21 percent of Charter cases between 1984 and 1999.[78] Most of these interventions have occurred in noncriminal cases, particularly those concerned with equality and Aboriginal rights; while much has changed since 1987, the Court still appears reluctant to allow nongovernmental interventions in criminal appeals. The statistics cast doubt on Morton and Knopff's claim that the Court favours left-wing interests. The Justices have accepted 89 percent of applications from business groups and 83 percent

from corporations, compared to 72 percent from labour unions. Business organizations and corporations intervened in 40 and 24 cases, respectively, while unions participated in 21.[79] In general, advocacy groups (including unions) enjoy fewer resources than corporate and professional interests. They must choose their cases carefully, to avoid wasting money and effort on hopeless causes. We will discuss other barriers to public-interest litigation in the next section.

Varieties of Public-Interest Litigators: Resources and Motivations

The various categories of public-interest litigators differ from each other in important ways. Gregory Hein argues that groups with certain stable characteristics—access to legal resources, "identities bolstered by rights," and a positive attitude toward the courts—are the most likely to pursue Charter litigation as a deliberate strategy.[80] Where legal expertise (or the money to purchase it) is lacking, "rights" fail to mobilize a group's constituency, or judges are viewed with suspicion, litigation becomes a last resort. Hein points out, however, that even those interests that do not regard legal action as a core strategy may go to court to "take advantage of interpretive opportunities, counter immediate threats, and move policy battles into the courtroom when their political resources wane."[81] For example, a group that eschews Charter litigation for ideological reasons may be forced to intervene in defence of a law that protects the interests of its members, or as a rearguard action against a hostile legislative majority.

Morton and Allen categorize Charter litigation as either "offensive" or "defensive." An offensive suit or intervention is intended to change the "policy status quo" (PSQ) in a direction favoured by the sponsoring group, whereas a defensive intervention seeks to preserve the PSQ against a less favoured alternative.[82] Since 1982, some advocacy groups that hoped to pursue offensive Charter litigation have been forced to retreat to a defensive position. When LEAF was founded in 1985, its members planned to launch test cases, "breaking new ground [or] challenging a discriminatory law."[83]

This proactive vision was severely tested by early equality cases that often involved male litigants who sought to undermine benefits achieved by feminist law reform.... In these and other cases, LEAF participated simply to ensure that existing positive schemes for women were not dismantled. This participation was different from what LEAF originally envisioned. Instead of initiating a challenge on behalf of a woman or women adversely affected by existing laws, LEAF's role was as an intervenor.[84]

As one senior member of LEAF put it, "section 15 is getting a far more vigorous workout as a shield than as a sword."[85]

The success or failure of a particular case, from the perspective of the interest group(s) involved, can be measured on three dimensions: "dispute, law and policy."[86] The "dispute" dimension refers to the actual disposition of the appeal: does the Court find in favour of the appellant or the respondent? As Morton and Allen point out, "While winning the dispute is the priority of the actual litigant, often it is secondary for interest group intervenors."[87] The latter may focus instead on the law—the *ratio decidendi*, which sets the precedent for future cases—and/or the final policy outcome of the litigation. A "win" in a particular case can turn into a hollow victory if the *ratio* fails to produce the desired policy result. For example, the 1988 *Morgentaler* ruling[88] struck down the existing abortion law; but four of the five Justices in the majority based their decisions on procedural issues unrelated to feminist arguments for "choice." Conversely, a lost dispute can produce a long-term victory in law and policy. James Egan failed in his claim for same-sex pension benefits in 1995, despite winning the unanimous recognition that sexual orientation constitutes an "analogous ground" under s. 15. The *Egan* ruling set a precedent that has transformed Canadian law relating to same-sex couples and individuals (see Dossier 11.4, pages 359–62).[89]

In isolation, a particular judgment may tell us little about policy change. To gauge the real impact of a Charter ruling, we must look at the response by the other two branches of government. The real-world impact of a judicial "win" can be blunted by resistance from reluctant implementers (see Chapter 3). On the other hand, a "loss" in court may be reversed by polit-

ical pressure on Parliament and the political executive. As we saw in Chapter 4, the Supreme Court rulings in *Seaboyer*, *Daviault*, and *O'Connor* provoked widespread condemnation from women's and victims' rights groups. Parliament responded in each instance by amending the Criminal Code to undo the effect of the Court decisions—though to a greater extent in the latter two cases than in *Seaboyer*. These examples remind us that litigation is only one part of a successful interest-group strategy to influence public policy.

For a public-interest litigator, the consequences of success or failure vary with the purpose of the suit or intervention. Morton and Allen distinguish four categories of outcomes: an offensive win, a defensive win, an offensive loss, and a defensive loss. The ideal result is an offensive win based on a favourable *ratio*, generating a judicial remedy that is fully implemented by the relevant public and private agencies. The two *Sauvé* rulings,[90] which struck down federal laws restricting the voting rights of prison inmates, are good examples. As soon as the laws were invalidated, Elections Canada set up procedures to enumerate and enfranchise federal inmates. A defensive win on the legal and policy dimensions is somewhat less valuable: it leaves the PSQ intact but does not secure any new benefits for the particular group. However, it may justify the cost of litigation if it generates a favourable *ratio* or preserves an important public benefit from attack on Charter grounds. The *Keegstra* case, in which the "hate speech" section of the Criminal Code survived a challenge from a convicted Holocaust denier, was a defensive win for the Canadian Jewish Congress and the League for Human Rights of B'nai B'rith Canada (but a loss for the CCLA).[91] LEAF intervened in the case, arguing that the protection of vulnerable groups from harmful speech was a valid legislative objective. The majority *ratio* reflected this perspective, laying the groundwork for a subsequent defence of the laws against pornography.[92]

The third best (or second worst) outcome for a public-interest litigator is an offensive loss, which wastes the group's resources but does not alter the PSQ for the worse. The *Symes* case was an offensive loss for LEAF, one of whose founders unsuccessfully challenged the Income Tax Act.[93] Finally, the worst outcome is a defensive loss, which thwarts the group's efforts to preserve the PSQ. In the *Seaboyer* case, for example, LEAF intervened to defend the "rape shield" in the Criminal Code against two men who sought to strike down the law on the ground that it violated their right to a fair trial (s. 11(d) of the Charter).[94] Similarly, the group intervened in *O'Connor* to oppose the disclosure of counselling records to the defence in sexual-assault cases.[95] In both instances, a majority of the Court rejected LEAF's arguments in favour of a strict due-process approach. As noted above, however, it is misleading to categorize either case as an outright defeat for feminism (as Morton and Allen do with *Seaboyer*). Parliament reacted to these unpopular rulings by imposing its own balance between the due-process rights of the accused and the interests of actual and potential victims. In lobbying terms, these "legislative replies" were clear victories for LEAF and other women's groups (see Chapter 4).

Morton and Allen conclude that the Charter success rate of feminist litigators is 44 percent in offensive cases and 83 percent in defensive cases—higher than that of unions and governments, but lower than that of official-language minorities.[96] This conclusion rests on an unprovable assumption: that a court ruling that furthers the interests of a particular group was influenced by an intervenor representing that group. We cannot know whether or not a particular argument played the decisive role in a Court ruling. Dossier 6.2 argues that LEAF's intervention in the *Andrews* case, which has been cited as proof that advocacy groups funded by the CCP have enjoyed undue influence in the Charter era,[97] may have had little if anything to do with the Supreme Court's analysis of equality rights.

Supreme Court Justices do not give interviews to explain their reasoning in particular cases; nor, for the

---

DOSSIER 6.2

LEAF AND *ANDREWS*

As we have seen, both critics and supporters of LEAF claim that the group's interventions in some Charter cases have been decisive. Among other accomplishments, LEAF is credited (or blamed) for persuading the Supreme Court to take a purposive approach to s. 15 of the Charter.[1] Such claims can never be definitively proved or disproved, unless and until the Justices involved tell us what was really going on in their minds when they drafted their opinions (which rarely happens).

The best evidence we can muster is a comparison between LEAF's written submissions and the majority opinion in *Andrews*. The main points in LEAF's factum to the Court are as follows:

1. the Court should repudiate the "similarly situated" test for equality that it had adopted in *Bliss* (see Chapters 2 and 11, pages 67 and 105);
2. the Court should use s. 15 to examine the substance of laws, not just their procedural aspects;

3. the court should interpret s. 15 "purposively," as it did other Charter sections (see Chapter 3, page 105);
4. s. 15 should be used to assist historically disadvantaged groups, not to roll back their recent legislative gains;
5. the Court should consider both overt and "adverse effects" discrimination in applying s. 15; and
6. the prohibited grounds of discrimination in s. 15 should not be treated as an exhaustive list—the Court should "read in" others, but only where these can be shown to be "proxies for enumerated grounds or akin to enumerated grounds."[2]

The majority opinion by Justice McIntyre conforms closely to LEAF's analysis.[3] McIntyre explicitly overruled *Bliss*, adopted a purposive approach to equality rights, endorsed an "adverse effects" analysis, and treated citizenship (the basis of the appeal) as an "analogous ground." He also, though less explicitly, applied s. 15 to the substance of the impugned law; in emphasizing its "remedial" intent, McIntyre effectively endorsed the view that it was designed to assist historically disadvantaged groups. One might conclude, from this superficial comparison, that the majority ruling was based on LEAF's analysis.

A deeper reading of the judgment raises doubts about this conclusion. In the first place, the Court established its "purposive" and substantive approach to Charter analysis in 1984 and 1985. By the time *Andrews* was issued in 1989, a narrow procedural approach could not have gained the support of a majority of Justices. McIntyre was the most conservative member of the Court; his endorsement of these broad rules of interpretation shows how firmly they had been established. Second, the text of s. 15 had been deliberately crafted to overturn *Bliss*. The formal equality analysis embodied in the "similarly situated" test was no longer an option. Third, the Court had previously endorsed the "adverse effects" and "historic disadvantage" principles in its jurisprudence on human rights.[4] The common-law rule of *stare decisis*, in which McIntyre believed strongly, would have required him to endorse these doctrines with or without LEAF's intervention.

McIntyre's sources are equally suggestive. He did not cite the evidentiary materials submitted by LEAF, nor did he refer to most of the precedents cited in its factum. Without proof

that McIntyre deliberately and dishonestly concealed his intellectual debt to LEAF, it may reasonably be concluded that the group's intervention made little or no difference to the outcome of the case. This conclusion has one further advantage over the competing account: it is consistent with McIntyre's negative attitude toward public-interest litigation.[5]

ENDNOTES

1. The "purposive approach" is explained in Chapter 3, page 105.

2. LEAF's factum is reproduced in Women's Legal Education and Action Fund, *Equality and the Charter: Ten Years of Feminist Advocacy Before the Supreme Court of Canada* (Toronto: Emond Montgomery, 1996), at pp. 6–22.

3. *Andrews v. Law Society of British Columbia*, [1989] 1 S.C.R. 143.

4. *Ontario Human Rights Commission and O'Malley v. Simpsons-Sears Ltd.*, [1985] 2 S.C.R. 536; *Canadian National Railway Co. v. Canada (Canadian Human Rights Commission)* ["*Action Travail des Femmes*"], [1987] 1 S.C.R. 1114.

5. Robert J. Sharpe and Kent Roach, *Brian Dickson: A Judge's Journey* (Toronto: University of Toronto Press/Osgoode Society for Canadian Legal History, 2003), p. 385.

most part, do they cite interest-group factums in their opinions.[98] It is possible, given the similarities between the LEAF factum in the *Butler* case and the opinion of Justice Sopinka, that the group helped shape his thinking on the topic of pornography. (See Dossier 3.3, pages 113–15.) But the weight given to the LEAF arguments, relative to the other evidence in the case and a myriad of other possible influences, cannot be proven with any certainty.

If we accept the proposition that public-interest intervention cannot be proven to affect judicial reasoning, then it might be tempting to conclude that it serves no useful purpose. That conclusion overlooks

two important points. In the first place, an intervenor can improve the quality of judicial policy-making without ghostwriting the majority opinion. By giving judges the opportunity to consider the impact of a particular law on persons other than the direct parties to the case, public-interest groups can shape the Court's perspective in ways that are not always obvious from the written *ratio*. Second, the legitimacy of the disposition is enhanced when some or all of the affected interests have had the opportunity to participate in the process.[99] That increased legitimacy benefits not only the Court itself, but the entire political system.[100]

Before we leave the topic of public-interest litigation, it is important to note the risks for advocacy groups that employ the Charter. We cannot assume that LEAF, or any other advocacy group, speaks for its entire constituency of interest. For some feminists, LEAF's arguments in *Butler* marked the rejection of a truly woman-centred legal discourse and obscured the important differences among women.[101] More broadly, the feminist movement has long been divided over the value and legitimacy of LEAF's litigation strategy: some feminists take a pragmatic approach to the Charter, perceiving it as a potentially useful tool (whether offensive or defensive), whereas others are deeply suspicious of the male-dominated legal system.[102] A LEAF litigator has summed up the anti-Charter arguments:

(1) that litigation itself is a man's game, played by men's rules in which women cannot be heard; (2) that litigation is inefficient as a tool for social change because it drains money, energies, and resources that could be better deployed on other strategies; and (3) that litigation is reactionary because it fosters the illusion that real change is possible within existing social power relations and political structures.[103]

In the end, a victory for LEAF may be a defeat for feminists (and nonfeminist women) who do not share the experiences and approaches of white, heterosexual female lawyers.

That ambivalence toward Charter litigation divides other "social movements," including organizations that promote gay and lesbian rights. After a slow start, EGALE's litigation strategy appears to have scored some notable successes. The group received a grant from the CCP to intervene in *Egan*, which established sexual orientation as an analogous ground of discrimination under s. 15.[104] It also intervened in *M. v. H.* and *Halpern* (although not, curiously, in *Vriend*), and was a party to *Barbeau*.[105] These apparent victories came at a considerable cost to the gay and lesbian movement. First, EGALE's reliance on government funding "privileged lawyers and case development rather than organizing or grass-roots efforts."[106] Second, the group's perceived success in Court cases led the media to treat it as the official "face" of the gay and lesbian rights movement. This

public prominence angered other groups, many of which were already suspicious of EGALE's engagement with the legal system and its lack of accountability to gays and lesbians generally. EGALE's isolation and its failure to reach out and build legitimacy within the movement weakened its organizational and funding base; this in turn made it harder for the group to secure government funding for its litigation strategy.[107]

The experiences of LEAF and EGALE demonstrate four risks of public-interest litigation.[108] First, movements whose ultimate goal is to transform power structures in Canadian society are often suspicious of the legal system. Charter litigation is bitterly resisted by many grassroots activists, splitting the movement and weakening its organizational resources. Second, litigation is a zero-sum game in which the odds favour the government.[109] A former president of the British Columbia Civil Liberties Association argues that "If the primary purpose of the Charter is to give Canadians a vehicle for asserting rights against government, it seems strange that governments that were not initially parties to the litigation should be provided with an automatic vehicle for conveying their message to the courts, while those interested in presenting a non-governmental perspective must depend on the willingness of the courts to let their voices be heard."[110]

Third, the procedural and financial barriers are too high for groups that lack political and economic resources. Admission is controlled by judges; there is no guarantee that any particular group will be allowed into the game. Even if a public-interest group manages to secure standing to bring a Charter challenge, and can afford to spend up to a million dollars to pursue its case all the way up to the Supreme Court of Canada,[111] its odds of success are less than even. As we saw in Chapter 3, the success rate for Charter challenges has fallen over the past twenty years. Interventions are less expensive, but (as Dossier 6.2, pages 208–9 suggests) their impact on judicial policy may be less than meets the eye.

Fourth and finally, a loss in the Supreme Court can be particularly demoralizing for an advocacy group. Lobbying policy-makers in the legislative and executive branches of government is a long-term process with few visible gains; however, the incrementalism of legislative policy-making means that few options are ever completely foreclosed. On the other hand, a decisive defeat at the hands of the Justices can derail a policy change, perhaps permanently, unless Parliament decides to overrule the Court in response to political pressure. That contingency highlights a point made in Chapters 3 and 4: the Justices do not always have the last word on public policy. The legislative and executive branches have retained much of their control over the substance of laws. Consequently, as the next section demonstrates, advocacy groups cannot afford to ignore traditional channels of influence.

CHARTER ADVOCACY GROUPS AND THE OTHER TWO BRANCHES OF GOVERNMENT

The courts are not the only institutional forum for "Charter groups." When Parliament evaluates a bill, most of the detailed scrutiny occurs in committee. Groups and individuals who wish to state a position on pending legislation can submit written briefs; where possible, they appear in person to give oral testimony. Indeed, committees often seem more receptive to interest groups than does the Court.

As suggested earlier, a group that loses a court battle can still win the policy war. The *Seaboyer* case, discussed in Dossier 4.2, pages 151–53, illustrates the point.[112] LEAF intervened, unsuccessfully, to defend the "rape shield" law in the Criminal Code against a due-process challenge. The majority ruling infuriated women's groups, which used the media to convey their anger at the Court's decision. Justice Minister Kim Campbell reacted quickly. After consulting feminist organizations, she introduced a new law that codified the *Seaboyer* ruling while strengthening the statutory requirement of consent to sexual activity. LEAF's arguments found a more receptive audience at the justice committee than they had in court. Indeed, the new bill seemed to be influenced at least as strongly by Justice L'Heureux-Dubé's dissent—which, in turn, resembled LEAF's arguments—as by Justice McLachlin's majority ruling. The net result was a win for LEAF. The same can be said for *Daviault* (where

LEAF did not intervene) and *O'Connor*. Where the relatively new technique of public-interest intervention fails, advocacy groups can fall back on their traditional avenues of public persuasion: the news media, lobbying, and participation in parliamentary review. The costs are lower, the barriers to access are easier to surmount, and implementation is less hit-and-miss.

This does not mean, however, that advocacy groups always prevail. Members of Parliament are no less likely than judges to turn a deaf ear to arguments with which they disagree. Leslie Pal's 1993 study of "Charter lobbying" concluded that the influence of advocacy groups on parliamentary committees is limited and uneven.[113] In the first place, "Charter advocacy groups" tend to concentrate their efforts on a handful of bills—probably because of resource constraints.[114] Second, advocacy groups on opposite sides of a particular issue may effectively cancel each other out. Third, few of the groups studied (most of them members of the "Court Party") relied on the Charter in their arguments before the committees. Where they did mention the Charter, it was usually in the context of a reference to "Charter values" or to previous Court rulings that the particular group interpreted as supportive of its position. In other words, the Charter was treated as a political resource, not as "the supreme law of Canada" to which public policy must conform.

Pal identified one exception: Bill C-43, the abortion law introduced by the federal government in response to the 1988 *Morgentaler* ruling. Feminist groups, which endorsed the ruling and feared that the bill would restrict access to abortion services, based their critique on the perceived contradictions between C-43 and the Court's interpretation of legal and equality rights.[115] The bill passed in the Commons, despite this concerted effort, but was defeated in the Senate in early 1991. Pal concluded that "advocacy lobbying, grounded in the Charter, had changed the balance of power in the legislative process" and defeated the bill. In all of the other cases studied, where the advocacy groups were scattered or divided and their Charter analyses were superficial, "the activities of advocacy organizations and Charter arguments made little difference to legislative outcomes."[116]

If, as Chapter 4 suggests, the legislative branch has learned to take its first-order Charter duties more seriously, then advocacy groups appearing before parliamentary committees would be well advised to do the same. Vague assertions of Charter values do not help lawmakers in the difficult task of balancing protected rights and freedoms against competing social goals. Specific Charter-based arguments will not overcome countervailing political pressures in all cases; but they are likely to have more impact in the long term.

CONCLUSION

This chapter has argued that the "Court Party" is more mythical than real. Not all interest groups have embraced Charter litigation as a tool of policy change. For those who have, the record of success is mixed at best. The courts have not been overly receptive to public-interest litigators, either as parties to Charter challenges or as intervenors. It is reasonable to assume that groups such as LEAF and EGALE have had some influence on the development of Charter jurisprudence, but it is not reasonable to conclude that the entrenchment of rights and freedoms has transformed interest groups into a powerful and unified "Court Party." Even Morton and Knopff concede that the alleged "social engineering" agenda of Charter advocacy groups has not been fully realized.[117]

On balance, the Charter's impact on interest groups has been more limited than it appears at first blush. For every victory in court or before a parliamentary committee, there are damaging and costly defeats. Divisions between pro- and anti-litigation activists damage organizational networks and weaken the legitimacy of groups that claim to speak for unified constituencies. The Charter is only one tool of policy influence, and not necessarily the most effective.

GLOSSARY OF KEY TERMS

advocacy groups   See *interest groups*.

interest groups   Organizations that seek to influence public policy in order to advance the shared interests of their members. Examples include the Canadian Chamber of Commerce, the Assembly of First Nations, and Greenpeace. Interest groups that work on behalf of the disadvantaged, or that hope to challenge the existing distribution of power in society, are often called **advocacy groups** (e.g., the National Anti-Poverty Organization or the Women's Legal Education and Action Fund).

postmaterialists   A catch-all term for groups and individuals whose policy goals emphasize quality-of-life issues over the production and distribution of wealth. It has often been argued that North Americans and West Europeans born after 1945 valued rights, freedoms, cultural identity, and social justice more highly than previous generations.[118]

public-interest litigation   See *standing*.

social engineers   According to Morton and Knopff, "social engineers" believe that the institutions and values endorsed by the majority should be dismantled and replaced by "democratic elites." The goal is social transformation, which is to be achieved through top-down decision-making by unelected judges.[119]

standing   The right to bring a case before a court. Either party in an active dispute will automatically receive standing. The situation is more complex in **public-interest litigation**, which is focused on the broad policy outcome of a case. A public-interest litigator may not be directly involved in a live dispute; she must ask the court for permission to act as the appellant or respondent, on behalf of a larger group whose interests are engaged by the legal issues at bar.

DISCUSSION AND REVIEW QUESTIONS

1. Explain the differences between applying for standing in a Charter challenge and applying to intervene. Identify at least one advantage and disadvantage of each litigation strategy.

2. In *Canadian Council of Churches*, former Justice Cory identified three criteria for evaluating applications for intervenor status. What are they? Based on the evidence in this chapter, do you believe that these criteria are always applied consistently? Why or why not?

3. Which category of intervenors is represented most frequently in Charter challenges at the Supreme Court? How do the rules favour that particular group?

4. Morton and Allen distinguish among four categories of outcomes for public-interest litigants: offensive wins, offensive losses, defensive wins, and defensive losses. Briefly define all four categories. Using the cases discussed in this book, identify at least one example of each.

5. In your opinion, do interest groups have too much influence over public policy in the Charter era? Why or why not?

SUGGESTED READINGS

Brodie, Ian. *Friends of the Court: The Privileging of Interest-Group Litigants in Canada.* Albany: State University of New York Press, 2002.

———. "Interest Group Litigation and the Embedded State: Canada's Court Challenges Program." *Canadian Journal of Political Science* 34, no. 2 (June 2001), pp. 357–76.

Gotell, Lise. "Towards a Democratic Practice of Feminist Litigation? LEAF's Changing Approach to Charter Equality." In Radha Jhappan, ed., *Women's Legal Strategies in Canada.* Toronto: University of Toronto Press, 2002, pp. 135–74.

Hein, Gregory. "Interest Group Litigation and Canadian Democracy." In Paul Howe and Peter H. Russell, eds., *Judicial Power and Canadian Democracy.* Montreal and Kingston: McGill-Queen's University Press/Institute for Research on Public Policy, 2001, pp. 221–22.

Koch, John. "Making Room: New Directions in Third Party Intervention." *University of Toronto Faculty Law Review* 48 (1990), pp. 151–67.

Lavine, Sharon. "Advocating Values: Public Interest Intervention in Charter Litigation," *National Journal of Constitutional Law* 2 (1992), pp. 27–62.

Morton, F.L., and Avril Allen. "Feminists and the Courts: Measuring Success in Interest Group Litigation in Canada." *Canadian Journal of Political Science* 34, no. 1 (March 2001), pp. 55–84.

Razack, Sherene. *Canadian Feminism and the Law: The Women's Legal Education and Action Fund and the Pursuit of Equality.* Toronto: Second Story Press, 1991.

Seidle, F. Leslie, ed. *Equity and Community: The Charter, Interest Advocacy and Representation.* Montreal: Institute for Research on Public Policy, 1993.

Shilton, Elizabeth J. "Charter Litigation and the Policy Process of Government: A Public Interest Perspective." *Osgoode Hall Law Journal* 30 (1992), pp. 653–60.

Smith, Miriam. *Lesbian and Gay Rights in Canada: Social Movements and Equality-Seeking, 1971–1995.* Toronto: University of Toronto Press, 1995.

Welch, Jillian. "No Room at the Top: Interest Group Intervenors and Charter Litigation in the Supreme Court of Canada." *University of Toronto Faculty Law Review* 43 (1985), pp. 204–32.

Women's Legal Education and Action Fund. *Equality and the Charter: Ten Years of Feminist Advocacy before the Supreme Court of Canada.* Toronto: Emond Montgomery, 1996.

ENDNOTES

1. Elizabeth J. Shilton, "Charter Litigation and the Policy Process of Government: A Public Interest Perspective." *Osgoode Hall Law Journal* 30 (1992), p. 656.

2. Carissima Mathen, "Introduction," in Women's Legal Education and Action Fund, *Equality and the Charter: Ten Years of Feminist Advocacy Before the Supreme Court of Canada* (Toronto: Emond Montgomery, 1996), p. xxiii.

3. F.L. Morton and Rainer Knopff, *The Charter Revolution and the Court Party* (Peterborough: Broadview Press, 2000), p. 27.

4. For critiques of the "Court Party" thesis, see Kent Roach, *The Supreme Court on Trial: Judicial Activism or Democratic Dialogue?* (Toronto: Irwin Law, 2001), pp. 75–77; Miriam Smith, "Ghosts of the Judicial Committee of the Privy Council: Groups, Politics and Charter Litigation in Canadian Political Science," *Canadian Journal of Political Science* 35 (2002), pp. 3–29.

5. Morton and Knopff, *The Charter Revolution and the Court Party*, p. 31.

6. Ibid., p. 27.

7. Ibid., p. 28.

8. Ibid., p. 157.

9. Charles R. Epp, "Do Bills of Rights Matter? The Canadian Charter of Rights and Freedoms," *American Political Science Review* 90, no. 4 (December 1996), p. 775.

10. Epp, "Do Bills of Rights Matter?" p. 777.

11. The definition of "social engineering," which portrays Canada's judges as the modern equivalent of Lenin's "vanguard of the proletariat," requires little comment.

12. Ian Brodie, *Friends of the Court: The Privileging of Interest Group Litigants in Canada* (Albany: State University of New York Press, 2002), p. 39, Table 2.3.

13. In *Hunter v. Southam Inc.*, [1984] 2 S.C.R. 145, the Southam newspaper chain successfully challenged a provision of the Combines Investigation Act under which federal agents had entered and searched its premises in Edmonton. In *R. v. Big M Drug Mart Ltd.*, [1985] 1 S.C.R. 295, a chain of stores succeeded in its bid to strike down the federal Lord's Day Act, which prohibited it from transacting business on Sundays. The issue in *RJR-MacDonald Inc. v. Canada (Attorney General)*, [1995] 3 S.C.R. 199 was whether federal restrictions on tobacco advertising violated the guarantee of free expression; a majority held that it did and invalidated several sections of the Tobacco Products Control Act.

14. *National Citizens' Coalition v. Canada (A.G.)* (1984), 11 D.L.R. (4th) 481 (Alberta Court of Queen's Bench); *Somerville v. Canada* (1996), 136 D.L.R. (4th) 205 (Alberta Court of Appeal); *Harper v. Canada (A.G.)*, 2002 Alberta Court of Appeal 301. The NCC also sponsored, though with less success, a challenge to the use of union dues for political purposes as a violation of s. 2(d). See the discussion of *Lavigne v. Ontario Public Service Employees Union*, [1991] 2 S.C.R. 211 in Chapter 8, page 277.

15. In the 1995 *Egan* case, the Court heard from the Inter-Faith Coalition on Marriage and the Family, which sought to defend the traditional definition of "marriage." *M. v. H.* (1999) drew interventions from the Evangelical Fellowship of Canada, the Ontario Council of Sikhs, the Islamic Society of North America, Focus on the Family, and REAL Women of Canada. The largest number of intervenors participated in the 1998 *Vriend* case, including the Christian Legal Fellowship, the Alberta Federation of Women United for Families, the Evangelical Fellowship of Canada, and Focus on the Family (Canada) Association. The issues and outcomes of these cases are discussed in Chapter 11, particularly Dossier 11.4, pages 359–62.

16. Roach, *The Supreme Court on Trial*, p. 144.

17. Gregory Hein, "Interest Group Litigation and Canadian Democracy," in Paul Howe and Peter H. Russell, eds., *Judicial Power and Canadian Democracy* (Montreal and Kingston: McGill-Queen's University Press/Institute for Research on Public Policy, 2001), pp. 221–22; Kent Roach, "The Role of Litigation and the Charter in Interest Advocacy," in F. Leslie Seidle, ed., *Equity and Community: The Charter, Interest Advocacy and Representation* (Montreal: Institute

for Research on Public Policy, 1993), pp. 159–65.

18. Epp, "Do Bills of Rights Matter?" pp. 769–71.

19. Miriam Smith, *Lesbian and Gay Rights in Canada: Social Movements and Equality-Seeking, 1971–1995* (Toronto: University of Toronto Press, 1995), Chapter 3.

20. Frank Iacobucci, "The Charter: Twenty Years Later," in Joseph Eliot Magnet, Gérald-A. Beaudoin, Gerald Gall, and Christopher Manfredi, eds., *The Canadian Charter of Rights and Freedoms: Reflections on the Charter after Twenty Years* (Toronto: Butterworths, 2003), p. 385 (see also p. 401).

21. Morton and Knopff, *The Charter Revolution and the Court Party*, p. 68; Ian Brodie, "Interest Group Litigation and the Embedded State: Canada's Court Challenges Program," *Canadian Journal of Political Science* 34, no. 2 (June 2001), pp. 372–73; Sherene Razack, *Canadian Feminism and the Law: The Women's Legal Education and Action Fund and the Pursuit of Equality* (Toronto: Second Story Press, 1991), pp. 105–7.

22. Roach, *The Supreme Court on Trial*, p. 147. Roach points out that the Court was most willing to accept Charter claims during the very same years (1985–87) when it turned away most would-be intervenors.

23. *Finlay v. Canada (Minister of Finance)*, [1986] 2 S.C.R. 607, paragraph 32, *per* Le Dain J.

24. *Thorson v. Canada (A.G.)*, [1975] 1 S.C.R. 138; *Nova Scotia Board of Censors v. McNeil*, [1976] 2 S.C.R. 265; *Borowski v. Canada (Minister of Justice)*, [1981] 2 S.C.R. 575.

25. *Borowski, per* Martland J., p. 598.

26. Brodie, *Friends of the Court*, p. 55.

27. *Canadian Council of Churches v. Canada (Minister of Employment and Immigration)*, [1992] 1 S.C.R. 236, paragraphs 12 and 28–30.

28. Ibid., paragraph 31.

29. Ibid., paragraph 32. Surprisingly, Cory's judgment does not refer to s. 24(1) of the Charter: "Anyone whose rights or freedoms, as guaranteed by this Charter, have been infringed or denied may apply to a court of competent jurisdiction to obtain such remedy as the court considers appropriate and just in the circumstances." The word "anyone" implies that the courts should accept, if not welcome, public-interest litigants who can demonstrate even an indirect infringement of Charter values. See Kenneth Swan, "Intervention and Amicus Curiae Status in Charter Litigation," in Robert J. Sharpe, ed., *Charter Litigation* (Toronto: Butterworths, 1987), pp. 27–28.

30. *Canadian Council of Churches*, paragraph 37.

31. Ibid., paragraph 40.

32. Critics of the ruling argue that it "forced individual refugee applicants, who often did not have funds and found themselves in urgent and dire circumstances, to litigate complex Charter issues through confusing and complicated levels of administrative and judicial review." Roach, *The Supreme Court on Trial*, p. 145.

33. Roach, *The Supreme Court on Trial*, p. 143.

34. On the history of the CCP, see Brodie, "Interest Group Litigation and the Embedded State," pp. 357–76.

35. Ibid., p. 373, Table 2.

36. Morton and Knopff, *The Charter Revolution and the Court Party*, pp. 95–99.

37. Shilton, "Charter Litigation and the Policy Process of Government," p. 657.

38. Philip Bryden, "Public Interest Intervention in the Courts," *Canadian Bar Review* 66 (1987), p. 490.

39. Alan Borovoy, general counsel to the Canadian Civil Liberties Association (CCLA), criticized the rules for nongovernment intervenors in a 1987 letter to the federal minister of justice: "A restriction of this kind might be workable for a party who will have the opportunity to make oral argument in court, although even this seems questionable in light of the new rule limiting time for oral argument. But it could make intervention an empty ritual for those who have to rely exclusively on the written word." Quoted in John Koch, "Making Room: New Directions in Third Party Intervention," *University of Toronto Faculty Law Review* 48 (1990), p. 164.

40. Roach, "The Role of Litigation and the Charter in Interest Advocacy," pp. 174–75.

41. On the founding and operation of LEAF, see Mathen, "Introduction"; Roach, *The Supreme Court on Trial*, pp. 145–46.

42. Brodie, *Friends of the Court*, p. 38, Table 2.2.

43. Sharon Lavine, "Advocating Values: Public Interest Intervention in Charter Litigation," *National Journal of Constitutional Law* 2 (1992), p. 38.

44. Bryden, "Public Interest Intervention in the Courts," p. 494.

45. Swan, "Intervention and Amicus Curiae Status," pp. 39–40.

46. Lavine, "Advocating Values," pp. 39–40; Bryden, "Public Interest Intervention in the Courts," pp. 496–97 and 500.

47. Koch, "Making Room," pp. 155–58.

48. Swan, "Intervention and Amicus Curiae Status," p. 31.

49. Brodie, *Friends of the Court*, p. 26; Robert J. Sharpe and Kent Roach, *Brian Dickson: A Judge's Journey* (Toronto: University of Toronto Press/Osgoode Society for Canadian Legal History, 2003), p. 383.

50. Brodie, *Friends of the Court*, pp. 32–33; Jillian Welch, "No Room at the Top: Interest Group Intervenors and Charter Litigation in the Supreme Court of Canada," *University of Toronto Faculty Law Review* 43 (1985), p. 216.

51. Welch, "No Room at the Top," pp. 218–19.

52. Bertha Wilson, "Decision-Making in the Supreme Court," *University of Toronto Law Journal* 36 (1986), pp. 242–43.

53. Ibid., p. 242.

54. Justice Estey is reported to have said, "The Court no longer has the time to fritter away sitting and listening to repetition, irrelevancies, axe-grinding, cause advancement, and all the rest of the output of the typical intervenor." Quoted in Sharpe and Roach, *Brian Dickson*, p. 385. Swan suggests that the Court's growing backlog of appeals, combined with the high incidence of illness on the Court in the early to-mid-1980s, may have prompted the Court to pull in the welcome mat for intervenors ("Intervention and Amicus Curiae Status," p. 34).

55. Sharpe and Roach, *Brian Dickson*, p. 384. For a critique of this view, see Swan, "Intervention and Amicus Curiae Status," p. 33.

56. Former Chief Justice Howland of the Ontario Court of Appeal, in *R. v. Zundel* (1986), 16 O.A.C. 244 (C.A.) at p. 245, quoted in Lavine, "Advocating Values," p. 45.

57. Bryden, "Public Interest Intervention in the Courts," p. 514.

58. Welch, "No Room at the Top," p. 222. One example is the decision to exclude the Ontario Association for the Mentally Retarded from intervening in a case where a group-home worker convicted of assaulting a resident had been granted an absolute discharge. *R. v. Ogg-Moss*, [1984] 2 S.C.R. 173; see Welch, No Room at the Top," p. 222.

59. Sharpe and Roach, *Brian Dickson*, pp. 385–86; Bryden, "Public Interest Intervention in the Courts," pp. 503–4.

60. The numerical data are taken from Brodie, *Friends of the Court*, p. 43, Table 2.6. Both nongovernmental intervenors were involved in *Law Society of Upper Canada v. Skapinker*, [1984] 1 S.C.R. 358. See the discussion of the case in Chapter 7, pages 227–29. The Court permitted interventions by the Federation of Law Societies of Canada and John Calvin Richardson (as an individual). It appears that Richardson was granted intervenor standing because the original plaintiff, Mr. Skapinker, had been granted citizenship before the case reached the top court; the case would have been moot without the participation of another individual whose current situation fit the facts of the appeal. See Welch, "No Room at the Top," p. 217.

61. Brodie, *Friends of the Court*, Table 2.1, p. 37.

62. A. Alan Borovoy, "Submission of the Canadian Civil Liberties Association to Supreme Court of Canada," July 17, 1984, pp. 1–2, quoted in Koch, "Making Room," p. 161. See also Sharpe and Roach, *Brian Dickson*, p. 386. The 1987 *Alberta Labour Reference* (heard in 1985, when the Court was shutting out most nongovernmental intervenors) appears to illustrate Borovoy's concerns. The Court entertained interventions from the federal government and eight provincial governments, but denied leave to the Canadian Labour Congress. See Sharpe and Roach, *Brian Dickson*, p. 387.

63. Sharpe and Roach, *Brian Dickson*, pp. 386–89.

64. Koch, "Making Room," p. 162.

65. Brodie, *Friends of the Court*, Table 2.1, p. 37.

66. Lavine, "Advocating Values," pp. 43 and 52. Justice Sopinka's willingness to defy the Court's secretive handling of leave applications seems consistent with his openness toward journalists, as discussed in Chapter 3, page 122.

67. *Reference re Workers' Compensation Act, 1983 (Nfld.)*, [1989] 2 S.C.R. 335.

68. Ibid.

69. Swan, "Intervention and Amicus Curiae Status," p. 43. See also Lavine, "Advocating Values," p. 53; Bryden, "Public Interest Intervention in the Courts," pp. 515–16.

70. Lavine, "Advocating Values," p. 53.

71. Lavine ("Advocating Values," pp. 44–45) refers to the *Zundel* case, in which defence counsel Doug Christie objected to applications from five groups (four of which were prepared to argue against his case). Justice L'Heureux-Dubé, who was assigned to hear motions on that particular day, accepted his arguments with regard to two of the applicants.

72. Brodie, *Friends of the Court*, Table 2.1, p. 37.

73. On the death and resurrection of the program, see Brodie, "Interest Group Litigation and the Embedded State," pp. 368–70.

74. Brodie, "Interest Group Litigation and the Embedded State," p. 372, Table 1.

75. Brodie, *Friends of the Court*, pp. 112–14.

76. Ibid., Table 2.8, p. 45.

77. Ibid., Table 2.7, p. 44.

78. Ibid., Tables 2.7 and 2.8.

79. Ibid., Tables 2.3 and 2.8.

80. Hein, "Interest Group Litigation," pp. 232–33.

81. Ibid., p. 233.

82. F.L. Morton and Avril Allen, "Feminists and the Courts: Measuring Success in Interest Group Litigation in Canada," *Canadian Journal of Political Science* 34, no. 1 (March 2001), p. 67.

83. Mathen, "Introduction," p. xviii.

84. Ibid., p. xxiii.

85. Shilton, "Charter Litigation and the Policy Process of Government," p. 658.

86. Morton and Allen, "Feminists and the Courts," p. 65.

87. Ibid., p. 65.

88. *R. v. Morgentaler*, [1988] 1 S.C.R. 30. Only Justice Wilson adopted an explicitly feminist analysis of the issues raised by abortion; see, e.g., paragraphs 218, 238–40, and 242.

89. *Egan v. Canada*, [1995] 2 S.C.R. 513. Dossier 11.4, pages 359–62 describes the significance of recognizing sexual orientation as an "analogous ground."

90. *Sauvé v. Canada (Attorney General)*, [1993] 2 S.C.R. 438, and *Sauvé v. Canada (Chief Electoral Officer)*, [2002] 3 S.C.R. 418; see Chapter 9, pages 288–89 for details.

91. *R. v. Keegstra*, [1990] 3 S.C.R. 697; see Dossier 8.10, pages 271–72.

92. *R. v. Butler*, [1992] 1 S.C.R. 452, discussed in Dossier 3.3, pages 113–15; see also Morton and Allen, "Feminists and the Courts," p. 66.

93. *Symes v. Canada*, [1993] 4 S.C.R. 695.

94. *R. v. Seaboyer; R. v. Gayme*, [1991] 2 S.C.R. 577.

95. *R. v. O'Connor*, [1995] 4 S.C.R. 411.

96. Morton and Allen, "Feminists and the Courts," pp. 72–73.

97. Morton and Knopff, *The Charter Revolution and the Court Party*, p. 97; Knopff and Morton, *Charter Politics*, p. 29.

98. One notable exception is the majority opinion of then–Chief Justice Dickson in the 1990 *Keegstra* ruling. At paragraph 75, he quoted LEAF's factum and expressed his agreement with the group's argument. However, this was in the context of a case that had nothing to do with gender equality.

99. Bryden, "Public Interest Intervention in the Courts," pp. 508–10.

100. Iacobucci, "The Charter," p. 401.

101. Lise Gotell, "Towards a Democratic Practice of Feminist Litigation? LEAF's Changing Approach to Charter Equality," in Radha Jhappan, ed., *Women's Legal Strategies in Canada* (Toronto: University of Toronto Press, 2002), pp. 135–74.

102. Mathen, "Introduction," pp. xiii–xv.

103. Shilton, "Charter Litigation and the Policy Process of Government," p. 654.

104. Smith, *Lesbian and Gay Rights*, p. 87.

105. *Egan*, *M. v. H.*, and *Vriend* are discussed in Dossier 11.4, pages 359–62. The first two cases challenged laws that discriminated against same-sex couples, while the third concerned the exclusion of sexual orientation from Alberta's human rights legislation. *Halpern* and *Barbeau* are the Ontario and British Columbia cases (respectively) that granted same-sex couples the right to marry.

106. Smith, "Charter Litigation and the Policy Process of Government," p. 87.

107. Ibid., pp. 87–97.

108. For a general discussion of these risks, see Roach, "The Role of Litigation and the Charter in Interest Advocacy," pp. 172–75.

109. On governmental resistance to Charter challenges, see Shilton, "Charter Litigation and the Policy Process of Government," especially pp. 656–57.

110. Bryden, "Public Interest Intervention in the Courts," p. 511.

111. The cost estimate is taken from Shilton, "Charter Litigation and the Policy Process of Government," p. 657.

112. The *Seaboyer* saga, and LEAF's role in it, are described in Kent Roach, *Due Process and Victims' Rights: The New Law and Politics of Criminal Justice* (Toronto: University of Toronto Press, 1999), pp. 167–74. Sheila McIntyre represented LEAF in the consultations with the justice department; her account of that experience is described in "Redefining Reformism: The Consultations That Shaped Bill C-49," in Julian V. Roberts and Renate M. Mohr, eds., *Confronting Sexual Assault: A Decade of Legal and Social Change* (Toronto: University of Toronto Press, 1994), pp. 293–326.

113. Leslie A. Pal, "Advocacy Organizations and Legislative Politics: The Effects of the Charter of Rights and Freedoms on Interest Lobbying of Federal Legislation, 1989–91," in Seidle, *Equity and Community*, pp. 119–57.

114. Ibid., p. 138.

115. Ibid., pp. 139–40.

116. Ibid., pp. 152–53.

117. Morton and Knopff, *The Charter Revolution and the Court Party*, pp. 85–86.

118. See, e.g., Ronald Inglehart, *The Silent Revolution: Changing Values and Political Styles among Western Publics* (Princeton: Princeton University Press, 1977), and *Culture Shift in Advanced Industrial Society* (Princeton: Princeton University Press, 1990).

119. Morton and Knopff, *The Charter Revolution and the Court Party*, pp. 74–77.

Chapter 7

The Charter and Canadian Federalism

Canada reached a historic milestone when, on November 5, 1981, all provinces except Quebec agreed on a way to give the country an independent Constitution with a charter of rights and an amending formula. In the front row, from left to right, are Prime Minister Trudeau, Minister of Finance Allan MacEachen, and Quebec Premier René Lévesque.
CP PHOTO

Mobility Rights

6. (1) *Every citizen of Canada has the right to enter, remain in, and leave Canada.*

(2) *Every citizen of Canada and every person who has the status of a permanent resident of Canada has the right*

(a) *to move to and take up residence in any province; and*

(b) *to pursue the gaining of a livelihood in any province.*

(3) *The rights specified in subsection (2) are subject to*

(a) *any laws or practices of general application in force in a province other than those that discriminate among persons primarily on the basis of province of present or previous residence; and*

(b) *any laws providing for reasonable residency requirements as a qualification for the receipt of publicly provided social services.*

(4) *Subsections (2) and (3) do not preclude any law, program or activity that has as its object the amelioration in a province of conditions of individuals in that province who are socially or economically disadvantaged if the rate of employment in that province is below the rate of employment in Canada.*

Minority Language Educational Rights

23. (1) Citizens of Canada

  (a) whose first language learned and still understood is that of the English or French linguistic minority population of the province in which they reside, or

  (b) who have received their primary school instruction in Canada in English or French and reside in a province where the language in which they received that instruction is the language of the English or French linguistic minority population of the province, have the right to have their children receive primary and secondary school instruction in that language in that province.

 (2) Citizens of Canada of whom any child has received or is receiving primary or secondary school instruction in English or French in Canada, have the right to have all their children receive primary and secondary school instruction in the same language.

 (3) The right of citizens of Canada under subsections (1) and (2) to have their children receive primary and secondary school instruction in the language of the English or French linguistic minority population of a province

  (a) applies wherever in the province the number of children of citizens who have such a right is sufficient to warrant the provision to them out of public funds of minority language instruction; and

  (b) includes, where the number of those children so warrants, the right to have them receive that instruction in minority language educational facilities provided out of public funds.

29. Nothing in this Charter abrogates or derogates from any rights or privileges guaranteed by or under the Constitution of Canada in respect of denominational, separate or dissentient schools.

31. Nothing in this Charter extends the legislative powers of any body or authority.

59. (1) Paragraph 23(1)(a) shall come into force in respect of Quebec on a day to be fixed by proclamation issued by the Queen or the Governor General under the Great Seal of Canada.

 (2) A proclamation under subsection (1) shall be issued only when authorized by the legislative assembly or government of Quebec.

INTRODUCTION

It is often argued that the Charter has strengthened the national government in Ottawa at the expense of the provincial governments. In the words of constitutional scholar Peter Hogg, "The Charter of Rights is a centralizing force in Canada."[1] This "centralizing force" is alleged to operate in two ways. First, Prime Minister Trudeau intended the Charter to "offset, if not reverse, the **centrifugal** forces" of **regionalism** and **province-building**.[2] In the 1960s and 1970s, Canadians appeared to have become more attached to their regions and provinces than to Canada as a whole. This was partly the result of deliberate efforts by some provincial governments, notably in Alberta and Quebec, to strengthen their political resources vis-à-vis the federal government.[3] Trudeau believed that a Charter would give all Canadians a unifying symbol

of their shared citizenship. It would create a new sense of national pride and enhance the perceived value of "Canadianness" relative to competing regional loyalties. In the process, it would reinforce the legitimacy of the federal government at the expense of the provinces. Trudeau claimed that "The Charter was not intended to subordinate the provinces to the federal government through judicial interpretation of the document, but to act as an instrument of national unity by highlighting what Canadians have in common, not by limiting how the provinces could act."[4]

Whether or not Trudeau intended it, some experts argue that the Charter has indeed subordinated the provinces. The second claim, which will be evaluated in this chapter, is that the entrenchment of rights and freedoms has shifted policy-making power from the provinces to Ottawa. The Charter's impact on the division of powers arises from the unique structure of the Canadian judicial system. Whereas the national executive cannot tell the provincial executives what to do, and the federal Parliament is equally powerless vis-à-vis its provincial counterparts, the Supreme Court of Canada sits at the top of the judicial hierarchy. This means that provincial appellate courts can be overturned by the Supreme Court. It also means that the legal interpretations issued by the nine Justices in Ottawa must be followed by all lower courts (see the discussions of *stare decisis* in Chapters 1 and 3, pages 10 and 103–4). Therefore, critics argue that despite the explicit disclaimer in s. 31—"Nothing in this Charter extends the legislative powers of any body or authority"—the enforcement of entrenched rights by the Supreme Court empowers the judicial branch of the national government at the expense of provincial legislators and executives.

Before and during the 1980–82 constitutional round, most provincial governments opposed the entrenchment of rights. They feared that a Charter would restrict their freedom to enact laws reflecting local needs and preferences. Their fears seemed to be well founded. By the fall of 1980, when Trudeau announced that his government would seek unilateral patriation, the Charter was part of a national legislative agenda with a decidedly pro-Ottawa bent.[5] Whereas the federal government perceived the centrifugal forces within Confederation as a direct threat to national unity, most premiers regarded them as a powerful source of leverage in their battles for greater provincial autonomy. As discussed in Chapter 2, pages 69–77, eight provincial governments fought Trudeau's patriation plan all the way to the Supreme Court of Canada. In the end, they reluctantly accepted the Charter—but only after the insertion of the notwithstanding clause (s. 33), which would allow them to override court rulings on particular rights and freedoms.

Trudeau managed to exempt the two overtly centralizing sections of the Charter, ss. 6 and 23, from the notwithstanding clause. However, the guarantees that are subject to s. 33—the fundamental freedoms, legal rights, and equality rights—also have the potential to limit provincial jurisdiction. Under the Constitution Act, 1867, responsibility for criminal justice is divided between the federal and provincial governments (see the Appendix to this chapter, pages

240–43, especially ss. 91(27), 92(6), 92(14), 92(15), and 96). The Criminal Code is a federal statute. It defines criminal offences and defences, and it regulates the conduct of police investigations and criminal trials. Examples include the procedure for obtaining a valid search warrant, the rules for gathering and admitting evidence, and the length of sentences. The federal government also appoints senior provincial judges. Provincial governments administer their own courts, write and enforce laws concerning their own jurisdictions (e.g., highway safety), and establish whatever legal-aid programs they deem necessary. So while the content of the criminal law is largely a matter for the federal Parliament, much of the responsibility for investigation and enforcement lies with the provinces. Therefore, the legal rights in the Charter are binding on provincial officials. When the Supreme Court uses the Charter to impose higher standards of due process, whether in police practice or the administration of justice, it asserts the power to make policy in areas that had previously lain within the exclusive control of the provinces.

Similarly, the equality rights in s. 15 raised the spectre of "national standards" in many areas of provincial jurisdiction. Recall that s. 15(1) guarantees equality "before and under the law" and "the equal protection and equal benefit of the law." Provinces worried that if the Supreme Court decided that a particular provincial program denied the equal protection or benefit of the law to a "discrete and insular minority," it could nullify or amend that program as it saw fit. Such a ruling would apply to all provinces, not just the single province in which the case arose. If the Justices were unprepared to accept varying local priorities and conditions as a justification for differential provincial laws, section 92 of the 1867 Constitution would lose much of its force. The only way for a provincial government to safeguard its legislative autonomy would be to invoke the notwithstanding clause.

In response to these concerns, Trudeau repeatedly denied that the Charter was intended to centralize power in Ottawa. In October 1980, he told Canadians that "The charter ... will not transfer power from the provincial governments to the Canadian government. To the contrary, it will confer power on the people of Canada, power to protect themselves from abuse by public authorities."[6] This statement is not quite accurate, as Trudeau himself must have known. In the first place, the Charter does not directly empower the people. Rather, it gives the courts an explicit mandate to identify and remedy violations of protected rights and freedoms. Second, the remedies imposed by the Supreme Court of Canada are equally binding on both levels of government. In practice, the Charter has transferred policy-making power both horizontally—from the other two branches of the federal government to the Supreme Court—and vertically, from provincial governments to the judicial branch of the national government. Hence, "every time the Supreme Court exercises its Charter powers, it symbolically reinforces national unity over provincial diversity."[7]

In practice, however, the Charter's effect on Canadian federalism should not be overstated. As we saw in Chapters 4 and 5, the second-order duties of judges are exercised less vigorously when other policy-makers take their first-order duties seriously. Provincial legislators and ministers must ensure that their laws respect Charter values; public servants must avoid infringing protected rights and freedoms as they conduct their official duties. Laws and actions that infringe the entrenched guarantees, and that cannot be justified by the pursuit of other social goods, should be subject to judicial remedy. In general, the Supreme Court has tried to avoid unwarranted intrusion into provincial jurisdictions. Such intrusions cannot always be avoided in cases dealing with mobility rights or minority language education. Those guarantees were expressly designed to override provincial governments. Other sections of the Charter, such as legal rights, affect the division of powers in a less direct way. Whenever possible, the Court respects the policy diversity inherent in a federal system.

THE SUPREME COURT AND FEDERALISM: BEFORE AND AFTER 1982

The distribution of legislative responsibilities between the federal and provincial governments is spelled out in Part VI of the Constitution Act, 1867 (see the Appendix to this chapter, pages 240–43). The Preamble to s. 91 assigns the **residual power** to the national Parliament. Any policy field that is not explicitly assigned to the provincial governments in ss. 92 and 93 or shared under s. 95 belongs automatically to the federal government. Provincial jurisdictions include primary and secondary education, health care, and social welfare. The assignment of the residual power to Ottawa reflects the unusually high degree of centralization in our federal system. But since 1867, and especially since the 1960s, the pendulum has swung away from the national government toward the provinces. By the time the first ministers met to discuss the Constitution in September 1980, Canada had become one of the most decentralized federations on earth.

In the years immediately before the Charter, the Supreme Court had drawn the ire of provincial governments for its perceived pro-Ottawa bias. The Judicial Committee of the Privy Council (JCPC), the British court empowered to hear appeals from the former colonies, had been consistently favourable to the provinces. The Law Lords interpreted s. 92(13), "Property and Civil Rights in the Province," as generously as they could, in an effort to rebalance a federal system that they perceived as overly centralized.[8] After 1949, when appeals to the JCPC were abolished, the Supreme Court favoured the national government in some prominent division-of-powers cases.[9] By the time of the 1980–82 constitutional negotiations, many of the premiers (especially those in the Western provinces) were convinced that a court appointed by the prime minister could not be trusted to shape the division of powers through judicial review.[10] If one believed that the Justices favoured Ottawa, one would expect them to use the Charter to strike down more provincial laws, and to intervene more actively in provincial jurisdictions, while leaving the national government relatively unaffected.

In the early years of the Charter era, some observers argued that the Supreme Court was fulfilling the worst fears of the dissident premiers. Between 1982 and 1992, according to Morton, Russell, and Riddell, the Supreme Court struck down 23 of 75 impugned federal statutes (30.7 percent) and 18 of 26 provincial statutes (69.2 percent) on Charter grounds.[11] These numbers suggest a worrisome judicial disregard for the legitimate prerogatives of provincial legislators. Six of the invalidated provincial laws were found to violate minority language rights, while a seventh infringed the mobility rights of lawyers.[12] On the surface, it looked as though the Charter had indeed centralized policy-making power, by allowing a pro-Ottawa Court to substitute its priorities in provincial jurisdictions for those of the elected governments.

Unfortunately for the Court's critics, their figures provide a misleading picture of the Charter's impact on the division of powers. Of the six cases involving minority language rights, only two were actually decided on Charter grounds.[13] The other four rulings were based on earlier constitutional documents: the Constitution Act, 1867 and the acts under which Manitoba and Saskatchewan joined Confederation. A similar caveat applies to many of the other 18 cases where the Charter supposedly allowed the Supreme Court to intervene in provincial jurisdiction. In total, only 10 of the 18 nullifications were actually based on the Charter. This lowers the nullification rate from 69 percent to 38.5 percent—still higher than the federal average, but not by much. Moreover, the s. 6 case did not invalidate a substantive provincial statute, as Morton, Russell, and Riddell claim; instead, it struck down two internal regulations of a self-governing independent body (the Law Society of Alberta). Therefore, the real percentage of provincial laws invalidated on Charter grounds between 1982 and 1992 is 34.6 percent (9 out of 26)—less than half the proportion erroneously claimed by the Court's critics. Overall, the data do not support the authors' claim that "The greater impact of the Charter on provincial law-making ... supports earlier predictions about the potential of the Charter to act as a force for policy uniformity across Canada."[14]

Over the past decade, the Court has become increasingly respectful of provincial jurisdiction. Whereas provincial laws were slightly more likely to suffer invalidation than federal laws in the mid-1980s, that trend was reversed after 1989.[15] By 1997, federal statutes had overtaken provincial laws as the most vulnerable targets of Charter challenge.[16] Kelly suggests two reasons for the change. First, the number of cases arising from the "centralizing rights"—mobility and language—fell off steeply in the 1990s. Second, "The Supreme Court demonstrated a renewed sensitivity to

federalism in the 1993–1997 period and a greater appreciation of policy variation among the provinces." Overall, "the Charter has not had the enduring effect on federalism that is claimed by Charter critics."[17] Nor has it had "a disproportionate impact on provincial policy."[18]

Kelly's empirical analysis reveals the Court's effort to balance protected rights and freedoms against the realities of federalism—specifically, the legitimate diversity of provincial policies demanded by unique local conditions.[19] At both stages of Charter analysis, the Justices have interpreted Charter guarantees in a flexible way that accommodates differing provincial priorities and policy mechanisms. Despite their appointment by the federal government, which makes them suspect in the eyes of some provincial politicians, the Justices have usually been sensitive to provincial priorities that did not infringe a reasonable interpretation of the entrenched rights and freedoms. Although one can argue that the Court should have been more respectful of provincial autonomy in some cases—such as the 1998 *Vriend* decision[20]—these are the exception rather than the rule. In most instances (e.g., Dossier 7.1, page 230), the Court has considered the legitimate interests of provincial governments at the first stage of Charter review, and concluded that there was no infringement. If this were not possible, the Justices could incorporate federalism into their analysis of competing social values under s. 1, and find infringements of Charter guarantees to be justified on that basis.[21] So despite the institutional changes wrought by the Charter, its impact on the day-to-day policy-making of provincial governments has been less than anticipated.

THE "CENTRALIZING RIGHTS": SECTIONS 6 AND 23 OF THE CHARTER

Official Language Minority Education Rights

Quebec nationalists perceive their province as the homeland of the French language in North America. They believe that its government has a duty to protect francophone culture in all areas of life. The survival of that culture became a matter of urgent concern in the 1970s, as the birthrate of francophone Quebeckers fell to one of the lowest levels in the world. The only way to prevent Quebec's share of the national population from falling below twenty percent was to accept a large number of immigrants.

Because most immigrants send their children to public schools, the education system is a crucial agency of socialization. If nonfrancophone children were allowed to attend English schools, they could find it difficult to assimilate into a French-speaking society. Over time, Quebec's leaders feared, the province would lose its distinct francophone character. In 1976, the separatist Parti Québécois won a provincial election. One of its first laws was Bill 101, the "Charter of the French Language." It provided— with some narrow exceptions—that all public education in the province would be delivered in French. The exceptions included: (1) the children of parents who had themselves attended anglophone schools in Quebec; (2) the children of parents who had lived in Quebec before the law came into force, and who had been educated in English outside Quebec; and (3) children who had been educated in English in the province before the law took effect, together with their younger siblings. The effect of the law was to deny English schooling to the children of later immigrants, whether from inside or outside Canada. Over time, the number of children entitled to attend anglophone public schools would diminish, to the point where it would no longer be necessary to maintain such facilities. English-speaking parents would have three options: educate their children in French, send them to anglophone private schools (if they could afford the tuition), or leave the province.

Pierre Trudeau rejected the idea of Quebec as the unique homeland of French Canada. He was determined to promote his vision of a bilingual Canada. One element of his strategy was the protection of official-language minorities, both inside and outside Quebec. By the late 1960s, when he became prime minister, the francophone minorities in most of the English-speaking provinces were losing their mother tongue and assimilating into the linguistic majority. Many francophones married anglophones and sent their children to English schools (especially where

there was no French alternative). Trudeau believed that if the French language were to survive outside Quebec, provincial governments across Canada would have to establish and maintain francophone schools. Such schools were a low priority in most English-speaking provinces. So Trudeau concluded that the only way to ensure the survival of official-language minorities across the country was to force provincial governments to accommodate them in the school system.

Trudeau had two goals in mind when he crafted s. 23: (1) to extend English schooling to all anglophone children in Quebec, regardless of their parents' situation or their date of arrival in the province, and (2) to ensure that French-speaking children in the rest of Canada would be able to attend francophone schools, as long as they were sufficiently numerous in a particular area to justify the expense. The section has one significant limitation: it applies only to Canadian citizens. Therefore, it does not guarantee an anglophone education to children who have recently arrived in Quebec from another country.

As a gesture of propitiation, Trudeau delayed the full implementation of s. 23 in any province until such time as the provincial government explicitly accepted it (s. 59 of the Constitution Act, 1982). Although the Parti Québécois government did not ratify s. 23(1)(a), the Supreme Court wasted no time in nullifying the provisions of Bill 101 that conflicted with the rest of the section.[22] In *Quebec Protestant School Boards* (1984), a unanimous Court ruled that the restrictions on English education in Bill 101 were inconsistent with ss. 23(1)(b) and 23(2). The Charter guarantees minority language education to all Canadian citizens, regardless of where their parents were educated or how long they have lived in a particular province; Bill 101 denies minority language education to children whose parents moved to Quebec after August 1977. The Court ruled that the infringement of s. 23 could not be justified under s. 1. In the first place, the Justices pointed out that the section had been deliberately designed to override the impugned sections of Bill 101. They concluded that the framers of the Charter could not possibly have considered the restrictions in the Quebec law to be "reasonable limitations" on the s. 23 guarantee. Second, the Court reasoned that s. 1 might justify a law that *limits* a Charter right, but it cannot be used to uphold a law that *denies* a Charter right.

The Quebec government was predictably incensed by the ruling. Relations between the Parti Québécois government and Ottawa, already strained by the outcome of the 1980–82 constitutional negotiations, grew even worse. Nonetheless, it cannot plausibly be argued that the Court treated Bill 101 unfairly.[23] Since 1984, the Court has ordered governments and school boards in Alberta, Manitoba, Prince Edward Island, and Nova Scotia to provide French-language education in communities with substantial francophone populations.[24] Most of these rulings, like the *Quebec Protestant School Boards* decision, have been unanimous. (The exception is the 2003 *Doucet-Boudreau* ruling, discussed in Dossier 1.2, pages 15–17.)

That unanimity is easily explained: the wording of s. 23 leaves judges with few options. If Canadian citizens in a given area demand that their children be educated in the minority official language, and if their numbers are large enough to warrant the expenditure of public funds, the province and/or the local trustees must provide them with a separate school. The test for applying the "where numbers warrant" standard was set out in the 1990 *Mahé* ruling. A court must determine the number of children in the district who are currently entitled to minority language education, as well as the approximate percentage of those who would likely take advantage of it. The court must also attempt to predict the future demand for such a school. The projected number of students must be sufficient to ensure access to a reasonable quality of education and to justify the cost of providing that education.

The precise administrative arrangements for each minority language school will depend on the size of the projected student population. A large group may be entitled to set up its own school board. At a minimum, the trustees who have jurisdiction over the minority language school must include a proportionate number of minority language parents. Otherwise, the purpose of setting up the school—the preservation and promotion of the minority official language in the province—might be jeopardized. Where a minority language board has been established, its management decisions must be respected by the provincial government; a minister of education cannot overrule a board decision to offer French-language schooling in a particular area of an anglophone province if the number of francophone students meets the criteria.[25]

These rulings carry significant fiscal consequences for provincial governments and local school boards. They also raise questions about the Charter's impact on the division of powers in the Constitution Act, 1867. Under ss. 23 and 52 of the Constitution Act, 1982, a federally appointed Court can claim the power to overrule the spending decisions and the educational policies of a provincial legislature and/or an elected school board. While the Supreme Court has repeatedly stated that one section of the written Constitution cannot be used to nullify another (see the general discussion of education, below), the operation of s. 23 appears to be an exception to that rule. It seems to modify the effect of s. 93, which declares that primary and secondary education are exclusive provincial responsibilities.

On the other hand, it should be remembered that s. 23 is concerned not with education in general, but with the provision of educational services in a specific language. It does not require a province to set up a separate school in every village and hamlet, but only where numbers warrant. The Court has been careful not to exceed its constitutional mandate. It does not order that specific subjects be taught or particular facilities provided. Instead, the Justices instruct the appropriate public body to establish a minority language school where it is reasonable to do so, and leave the details to the appropriate decision-makers. Finally, s. 23 has an explicitly remedial purpose. It is designed to protect official-language minorities against the pressure to assimilate. Consequently, s. 23 expressly requires judges to overrule the spending choices of provincial governments and school boards where these conflict with the preservation of minority language communities. In combination with the broad remedial powers in s. 24(1), it may even authorize judges to supervise the execution of an order. While this suggestion is highly controversial, as Dossier 1.2, pages 15–17 explains, it could be seen as the logical extension of the values protected by s. 23.

Recent statistics suggest that the Supreme Court's jurisprudence on s. 23 has had less impact than the

Prime Minister Trudeau might have hoped. In 2000, French-language students in three English-speaking provinces (Ontario, Manitoba, and Nova Scotia) enjoyed fewer instructional resources and less support from their teachers than their counterparts in majority language schools. The availability of minority language education varied from province to province: 84 percent of francophone children attended French-language schools in Manitoba, compared to 67 percent in Nova Scotia, while 70 percent of anglophones in Quebec attended English-language schools. Finally, 40 percent of students in French-language schools in Ontario, Manitoba, and Nova Scotia reported that they usually spoke English at home.[26] Taken together, these figures suggest that the overriding purpose of s. 23—the preservation and promotion of minority language communities—has not been fulfilled. Education in the minority language is not always available; when it is, the quality is often lower than in comparable majority language schools. While the courts are right to respect the constitutional autonomy of provincial governments and school boards, most of which operate under tight fiscal constraints, they may do so at the cost of watering down the guarantee in s. 23.

Mobility Rights

Section 6 of the Charter was intended to prevent provinces from balkanizing the national economy, by making it difficult for people to live and work wherever they chose. The distinction between the purpose and the effect of an impugned law is particularly important here. Deliberate efforts to shield the local labour market from out-of-province competition infringe the guarantee of mobility rights, unless they fall under the "affirmative action" exemption in clause (4). On the other hand, laws and regulations that unintentionally restrict access to the workplace on the basis of provincial origin or residence are protected under s. 6(3).

Section 6, like section 23, was tested in the courts almost as soon as the Charter took effect. The second major Charter case at the Supreme Court, *Skapinker*,[27] dealt with the meaning and application of mobility rights. A second leading case was decided in 1989, and a third in 1998. Since then, no challenge under s. 6 has reached the top court. The scarcity of jurisprudence on mobility rights is surprising, in light of the controversy that swirled around s. 6 during the 1980–82 negotiations.[28] It may be that the *Skapinker* ruling dampened the enthusiasm of potential litigants by taking a fairly narrow view of the mobility guarantee.

Skapinker challenged the exclusion of noncitizens from the practice of law in Ontario. In accordance with the provincial Law Society Act, which regulates the legal profession, the Law Society of Upper Canada refused Joel Skapinker's application on the ground that he was a citizen of South Africa. He argued that the exclusionary rule violated his mobility rights under s. 6(2)(b) of the Charter.[29] The Supreme Court unanimously disagreed. Justice Estey ruled that the Charter guaranteed the right to work in any province, but not the right to pursue a particular occupation. In other words, s. 6 does not confer a "right to work" that overrides the residency rules of provincial professional associations. It simply allows citizens and permanent residents a right to live where they choose.

Five years later, the Court narrowly overturned its decision in *Skapinker*. The 1989 case of *Black v. Law Society of Alberta* gave lawyers the right to pursue their profession in any province.[30] In September 1981, the Toronto law firm McCarthy and McCarthy established Black & Co. in Calgary. Although all of the lawyers in the satellite Calgary firm were members of Alberta's Law Society, some lived in Toronto; its partners were also partners in McCarthy. Alberta lawyers objected strongly. The Alberta Law Society adopted two new rules: the first to prohibit Alberta lawyers from working in partnership with lawyers who were not ordinarily resident in the province, and the second to ban lawyers from being partners in more than one firm at a time. Black & Co. challenged the constitutionality of the new rules on several grounds, one of which was the brand-new guarantee of mobility rights in the Charter.

The case was heard by a seven-judge panel of the Supreme Court, although only five of the original members remained when the decision was issued. Three of the five Justices found that the impugned Alberta Law Society rules infringed mobility rights and were not saved under s. 1; the other two disagreed. Justice La Forest, writing for the majority, noted that s. 6 "is not expressed in terms of the structural elements of federalism, but in terms of the rights of the citizen and permanent residents of Canada." Citizenship and permanent residency imply "the right to reside wherever one wishes in the country and to pursue the gaining of a livelihood without regard for provincial boundaries."[31] He cited Justice Estey's decision in *Skapinker* as authority for the proposition that one need not live in a particular province in order to enjoy a right to work therein. Moreover, "Section 6(2)(a), in my view, guarantees not simply the right to pursue a livelihood, but more specifically, the right to pursue the livelihood of choice to the extent and subject to the same conditions as residents."[32] Wherever a province interfered with the right of an individual to work in his or her chosen profession, that interference violated s. 6 of the Charter. Provincial governments are free to regulate employment, but not on the basis of residency.

La Forest found that the violation of s. 6(2)(b) was not justified, either by the internal limitation in s. 6(3)(a) or by s. 1. The former section insulates provincial laws from the effect of the mobility rights guarantee, but only so long as they do not "discriminate among persons primarily on the basis of province of present or previous residence." As for s. 1, La Forest rejected the arguments proffered by the law society to justify its infringement of mobility rights. The rules were not minimally impairing of s. 6, nor did the value of their objectives outweigh their harmful effects.[33]

It was perhaps predictable that early mobility-rights litigation would be launched by lawyers. At the provincial level, doctors have also used the guarantee of mobility rights to challenge provincial attempts to encourage them to practise in underserviced regions.[34] In 1999, the British Columbia Court of Appeal struck down a provincial regulation that paid new physicians on a sliding scale. A doctor who set up a new practice in an overserved area of the province would receive half of the standard payment for each service performed, for approximately the first five years. Only those doctors who established practices in areas with fewer doctors than the provincial average would be entitled to

full payment immediately. Similar measures had been adopted by other provinces. The Court of Appeal ruled that the regulations discriminated against doctors who moved to British Columbia after completing their training in another province; the sliding scale only applied to "new billers," and there was a partial exemption for graduates of the University of British Columbia. Such discrimination on the basis of "present or previous residence" infringed s. 6, and could not be justified under s. 1. The use of differential payment scales per se was not affected.

In 1998, the Supreme Court heard the first major s. 6 challenge brought by a plaintiff who was not a member of a provincially regulated profession. The *Richardson* case dealt with the constitutionality of the Canadian egg marketing system, which prohibited the sale of eggs across provincial boundaries without a federal quota and licence. The quotas and licences were not available to producers in the two (now three) territories. Consequently, the Canadian Egg Marketing Agency (CEMA) effectively prohibited egg producers in the territories from selling their products elsewhere in Canada. The Court was asked whether the federal regulations governing the CEMA violated the mobility rights of egg producers operating in the North, by denying them access to the larger national market.

For the seven-judge majority, Justices Iacobucci and Bastarache noted that the interpretation of s. 6 "has significant implications for the exercise of the federal and provincial powers enumerated in ss. 91 and 92 of the *Constitution Act, 1867*, respectively. This context makes it necessary to consider carefully the purpose and role of the mobility section, and of the Charter itself in our constitutional order."[35] The Justices argued that the breadth of the language in s. 6(2) is limited by s. 6(3), which protects most "laws of general application." Contrary to the majority in *Black*, Iacobucci and Bastarache insisted that the "right to work" provision in s. 6(2) was internally limited by s. 6(3); the two clauses should be read together, not in isolation. The *Black* approach, they argued, extends the scope of mobility rights well beyond the clear intent of the framers. However, mobility rights must not be given too narrow a construction; "Section 6 is rooted in a concern with human rights, not the conditions or operation of the federal structure of Canada."[36] The chief problem, then, is to balance the legitimate interest of the provinces in regulating their own economies against the right of Canadian citizens to live and work where they choose, without discrimination on the basis of residence.

To locate that balance, the Justices returned to the *Skapinker* doctrine. They held that the rights in s. 6 "[are] not violated by legislation regulating any particular *type* of economic activity, but rather by the *effect* of such legislation on the fundamental right to pursue a livelihood on an equal basis with others."[37] They pointed out that in the 1980–82 constitutional round, the eleven senior governments had considered and rejected an amendment to s. 121 of the 1867 Constitution that would have explicitly entrenched a right to pursue any livelihood in any province. In this light, "The objective of s. 6 should not be interpreted in terms of a right to engage in any specific type of economic activity."[38] Nor does it justify court-enforced "uniformity of legislative treatment as between different provinces,"[39] which would clearly violate the division of powers. Rather, s. 6 is intended to protect Canadians who live in one province and who wish to earn their living in a different province (e.g., people in Western Quebec who cross the border to work in Ontario). "In this case, residents of an origin province (the Northwest Territories), seek to market something of value—eggs—in other destination provinces. This is clearly an attempt to 'pursue the gaining of a livelihood' in another province and engages the mobility right guaranteed by s. 6."[40]

Whereas the majority in *Black* had defined mobility rights broadly, and left the issue of balance to the s. 1 analysis, Iacobucci and Bastarache insisted that the interpretation of s. 6(2) in the context of a particular case must involve a consideration of whether the impugned law discriminates "*primarily* on the basis of residence" (s. 6(3)(a)). In other words, a court must determine if the law arbitrarily or unfairly distinguishes between residents and nonresidents of a particular province. The two Justices ruled that the CEMA did not discriminate primarily on the basis of residence; instead, it discriminated against *any* egg producer who did not hold a production and marketing quota at the time when the case was initiated.

Therefore, the regulations did not violate the guarantee of mobility rights.

With the exception of *Black*, the Supreme Court has interpreted s. 6 narrowly. The centralizing intent of clauses (1) and (2) was modified during the constitutional negotiations by the insertion of the two latter exemptions. As a result, the Court has resisted most attempts to use the Charter to weaken the power of provincial governments to regulate and protect their own labour markets.

THE CHARTER'S INDIRECT EFFECTS ON THE DIVISION OF POWERS

Federalism and Equality Rights

As Chapter 11 explains, one of the central problems in equality jurisprudence is to draw a clear line between neutral distinctions and harmful discrimination. A law that treats two groups of people differently will infringe s. 15 only if that differential treatment is based on stereotype instead of reality, and if its effect is to undermine human dignity. In the 1989 *Turpin* case, the Supreme Court's second major ruling on equality rights, the Justices unanimously rejected a claim of discrimination on the basis of provincial residence. (See the case summary in Chapter 11, pages 344–45.) Justice Wilson found that the difference between criminal procedures in Alberta and the rest of Canada infringed the appellant's right to "equality before the law," but it did not discriminate within the meaning of s. 15(1). Wilson explicitly overturned several lower-court rulings that had interpreted s. 15(1) as requiring uniform criminal laws throughout Canada.[41] However, she suggested that some legislative distinctions based on provincial residency might engage the protection of s. 15(1).

The latter issue was clarified in the 1990 case of *R. v. S. (S.)*, in which a young offender in Ontario argued that his equality rights were infringed (Dossier 7.1, page 230).

DOSSIER 7.1

R. V. S. (S.) (1990)

The Young Offenders Act (since repealed and replaced) permitted provinces to adopt alternative measures (e.g., counselling or restitution) for defendants. However, it did not require provincial governments to establish alternative programs in cases where a criminal trial would be inappropriate; the matter was left to provincial discretion. All of the provinces except Ontario set up programs to administer alternatives to criminal punishment. Young offenders in Ontario were the only ones who did not have access to nonjudicial resolution of their cases.

A young Ontario man named Sheldon S., who had been arrested for shoplifting, argued that his right to equal treatment before and under the law was infringed by the absence of noncriminal programs in the province. The Supreme Court, led by Chief Justice Dickson, unanimously rejected his argument. In the first place, it found that Ontario's failure to create a discretionary program of alternative measures "cannot be constitutionally attacked simply because it creates differences between provinces. To find otherwise would potentially open to Charter scrutiny every jurisdictionally permissible exercise of power by a province, solely on the basis that it creates a distinction in how individuals are treated in different provinces."[1] Second, Dickson concluded that discrepancies among the provinces in the administration of federal laws are not inherently discriminatory.

> Obviously, the federal system of government itself demands that the values underlying s. 15(1) cannot be given unlimited scope. The division of powers not only permits differential treatment based upon province of residence, it mandates and encourages geographical distinction. There can be no question, then, that unequal treatment which stems solely from the exercise, by provincial legislators, of their legitimate jurisdictional powers cannot be

the subject of a s. 15(1) challenge on the basis only that it creates distinctions based upon province of residence.[2]

Dickson agreed with Justice Wilson's comment in *Turpin* that discrimination on the basis of province must be determined on a case-by-case basis, although he went on to suggest some guidelines for that determination. He explicitly rejected the claim that federal laws must be applied identically across the country. Citing the constitutional division of powers between the two senior levels of government in the field of criminal law, he found that "diversity in the criminal law, in terms of provincial application, has been recognized consistently as a means of furthering the values of federalism. Differential application arises from a recognition that different approaches to the administration of the criminal law are appropriate in different territorially based communities."[3] He concluded that "province of residence" was not a "personal characteristic," and that legislative distinctions on that basis were not discriminatory within the meaning of s. 15.

The implications of *Turpin* and *S. (S.)* should reassure those who feared that the courts would use the Charter to shift administrative authority from the provinces to Ottawa. Provincial governments are free to tailor their own laws and programs, and apply federal laws, in ways that reflect the unique priorities and concerns of their residents—so long as they do so in conformity with the requirements of the Constitution.

ENDNOTES

1. *R. v. S. (S.)*, [1990] 2 S.C.R. 254, paragraph 42, *per* Dickson C.J.C.

2. Ibid., paragraph 45.

3. Ibid., paragraph 47.

Education

Apart from ss. 23 and 29, the Charter does not mention education. However, several Charter guarantees—e.g., freedom of religion (2(b)), equality (15(1)) and multiculturalism (27)—could be used to challenge provincial or local school board policies. If, as some experts had predicted, the Supreme Court chose to use these guarantees to impose "national standards applicable to all the provinces,"[42] provincial autonomy in a key policy field would be compromised.

Contrary to these expectations, the Supreme Court has given wide latitude to provincial ministries of education. In the 1986 *Jones* case, for example, the Court took a hands-off attitude toward an Alberta law that allegedly infringed religious freedom. The case (discussed in Chapter 8, page 254) concerned a Christian preacher who ran a private religious school in his church. He refused to apply for a provincial licence, or an exemption from the School Act, claiming that government control of education violated his religious beliefs. Jones's argument that his freedom of religion outweighed the province's power to regulate education failed. The Court concluded, in the words of Justice La Forest, that "The provinces must be given room to make choices regarding the type of administrative structure that will suit their needs unless the use of such structure is in itself so manifestly unfair, having regard to the decisions it is called upon to make, as to violate the principles of fundamental justice."[43] He also observed that "Those who administer the province's educational requirements may not do so in a manner that unreasonably infringes on the right of parents to teach their children in accordance with their religious convictions. The interference must be demonstrably justified."[44] Within these broad parameters, the Court was not prepared to meddle with the details of school administration; these were matters properly left to each province or school board.

Two subsequent cases also engaged the relationship between religion and schooling. In 1987, the Court issued a reference opinion on the constitutionality of Ontario's Bill 30 (also called An Act to Amend the Education Act). The bill extended full public funding to Catholic high schools in the province, a benefit that had previously been restricted to primary schools. The Ontario government asked the courts whether Bill 30 was consistent with s. 93 of the Constitution Act, 1867, and whether it violated any part of the Charter. Groups and individuals opposed to the bill argued that the diversion of tax dollars to Catholic schools violated both the equality rights and the religious freedom of non-Catholics. The attorney general replied that s. 29 insulates denominational schools from other sections of the Charter, including ss. 2 and 15.

For the majority, Justice Wilson made two crucial points. First, she declared that Bill 30 was a valid exercise of provincial power under s. 93 of the 1867 Constitution. Second, she exempted legislation arising from s. 93 from Charter review. To argue that the Charter could be used to review Bill 30 was tantamount to saying that one part of the Constitution could be used to invalidate another, which was clearly contrary to the intentions of the drafters.[45] Her argument was strongly supported by Justice Estey:

> The role of the Charter is not envisaged in our jurisprudence as providing for the automatic repeal of any provisions of the Constitution of Canada which includes all of the documents enumerated in s. 52 of the *Constitution Act, 1982*. Action taken under the *Constitution Act, 1867* is of course subject to Charter review. That is a far different thing from saying that a specific power to legislate as existing prior to April 1982 has been entirely removed by the simple advent of the Charter.... Although the Charter is intended to constrain the exercise of legislative power conferred under the *Constitution Act, 1867* where the delineated rights of individual members of the community are adversely affected, it cannot be interpreted as rendering unconstitutional distinctions that are expressly permitted by the *Constitution Act, 1867*.[46]

This line of interpretation should have comforted those who feared the Charter's impact on the division of powers. The Court expressly insulated the terms of Confederation—more specifically, the maintenance of Catholic schools in Ontario—from Charter review. It did the same in the 1996 *Adler* ruling, which also concerned the extension of public funding to Catholic schools.[47] The Court dismissed the claims of Jewish parents and members of various Christian sects that their schools were equally entitled to public funds. The Justices concluded that s. 93 of the Constitution Act, 1867 protected the denominational school system in place at the time of Confederation. It cannot now be amended to provide for new denominations, even assuming that their exclusion from the public funding regime violated the Charter. "Given that the appellants cannot bring themselves within the terms of s. 93's guarantees, they have no claim to public funding for their schools.... To decide otherwise by accepting the appellants' claim that s. 2(a) requires public funding of their religious schools would be to hold one section of the Constitution violative of another."[48] The Justices confirmed the principle that the Charter cannot and will not be used to cancel or modify the division of powers in the Constitution Act, 1867.

The Administration of Justice in the Provinces

We have already seen that the Court accepts different provincial applications of national laws—including the Criminal Code—as a necessary element of our federal system. Following *R. v. S. (S.)*, a province that chooses not to establish a discretionary program cannot be found guilty of discrimination on that basis. Had the Supreme Court upheld Sheldon S.'s appeal, it would implicitly have ordered Ontario to establish an alternative measures program for young offenders. Such an outcome would have constituted a judicial intrusion into both provincial jurisdiction (s. 92(14)) and the legislative "power of the purse." The Justices are understandably reluctant to flout either the written division of powers or the separation between the three branches of government.

This reluctance was clearly evident in a trio of cases concerning the right to counsel, which had serious implications for provincial legal aid programs. Section 10(b) of the Charter guarantees two separate rights to anyone who has been detained or imprisoned. The first is the right "to retain and instruct counsel without delay"; the second is "to be informed of that right." In other words, a person who has been detained by the police must be informed as soon as possible that he or she may consult a lawyer before making a statement or undergoing an interview (see Chapter 10, pages 318–20). Since the advent of the Charter, police officers have been issued with preprinted "caution cards" that must be read to a suspect before any interrogation can begin. Dossier 7.2 provides an example of the standard police caution to criminal suspects.

DOSSIER 7.2

THE S. 10(B) CAUTION CARD

You have the right to retain and instruct counsel without delay.

You have the right to telephone any lawyer that you wish.

You also have the right to free advice from a Legal Aid lawyer.

If you are charged with an offence, you may apply to the Ontario Legal Aid Plan for legal assistance.[1]

ENDNOTES

1. Reproduced in *R. v. Bartle*, [1994] 3 S.C.R. 173, paragraph 2.

The Supreme Court has held that s. 10(b) imposes three specific duties on the police:

1. to inform the detainee of his or her right to retain and instruct counsel, and of the existence and availability of legal aid and duty counsel, without delay;[49]
2. if a detainee has indicated a desire to exercise this right, to provide the detainee with a reasonable opportunity to exercise the right (except in urgent and dangerous circumstances); and
3. to refrain from eliciting evidence from the detainee until he or she has had that reasonable opportunity (again, except in cases of urgency or danger).[50]

If any or all of these duties are overlooked, a confession or other evidence gathered subsequent to the

Charter violation may be ruled inadmissible at trial under s. 24(2).

The first of the three duties just listed, like the third and fourth lines on the caution card in Dossier 7.2, page 232, raise an important question: does s. 10(b) require governments to establish or maintain "duty counsel" programs? All ten provinces have some form of legal aid, which assists poor defendants at the trial stage. However, poorer provinces may not be able to afford 24-hour "duty counsel" to handle requests from people who have just been taken into police custody. While most lawyers, including those employed by legal aid services, keep regular business hours, many arrests take place at night and on weekends. This gap may be filled by "duty counsel," who are available around the clock for initial consultations as required by s. 10(b) but who may not represent accused in subsequent legal proceedings. One way to provide such consultations is to set up a 24-hour call centre, staffed with lawyers, with a 1-800 number that is given to all criminal suspects immediately upon being cautioned by a police officer. The question is whether or not s. 10(b) requires provincial governments to establish such services. Is the right to counsel "without delay" meaningful for a suspect who cannot afford a private lawyer and who lives in a province where legal aid lawyers are unavailable after-hours and on weekends?

In answering this question, the Supreme Court faces a dilemma. On the one hand, it stated clearly in the 1990 *Brydges* ruling that the Charter requires governments to provide publicly funded legal services:

> ... the right to retain and instruct counsel, in modern Canadian society, has come to mean more than the right to retain a lawyer privately. It now also means the right to have access to counsel free of charge where the accused meets certain financial criteria set up by the provincial Legal Aid plan, and the right to have access to immediate, although temporary, advice from duty counsel irrespective of financial status.[51]

On the other hand, the Court is loath to interfere in the spending decisions of provincial governments. While it has instructed the police "to inform detainees about Legal Aid and duty counsel services which are in existence and available in the jurisdiction at the time of detention,"[52] it has stopped short of requiring the provinces to provide 24-hour "*Brydges* counsel." In the 1994 *Prosper* ruling, Chief Justice Lamer noted that the 1980–81 Special Joint Committee had considered, and rejected, an amendment to s. 10(b) that would have constitutionalized a right to legal aid.[53] More important, in Lamer's view, were the far-reaching implications of forcing provinces to set up 24-hour duty counsel services. "In effect, this Court would be saying that in order to have the power of arrest and detention, a province must have a duty counsel system in place. In provinces and territories where no duty counsel system exists, the logical implication would be that all arrests and detentions are *prima facie* unconstitutional."[54] The constitutional implications of ordering a provincial government to create a new program, the difficulty of devising a system for provinces to implement, and the prospect of inadvertently invalidating hundreds of criminal cases deterred the Court from imposing "duty counsel" on the provinces.

Justice McLachlin endorsed this conclusion, although for different reasons. She held that the sole constitutionally mandated remedy for a violation of s. 10(b) of the Charter was the exclusion of tainted evidence under s. 24(2). To go beyond this remedy, and impose a new spending obligation on provincial governments, would be illegitimate. Moreover, she suggested that the existing remedy should be sufficient to persuade the provinces of the wisdom of setting up "*Brydges* counsel":

> The state may choose to take measures to prevent Charter breaches, knowing that as a consequence evidence obtained will be receivable against the accused, provided it meets general criteria of admissibility. On the other hand, if the state fails to take such measures and permits Charter breaches, it faces the prospect that the evidence obtained in violation of the Charter may be ruled inadmissible under s. 24(2). Only in this sense does the Charter impose "requirements" on the state. Since the prospect of being unable to adduce evidence against an accused often means that the prosecution cannot proceed, the net effect of the scheme which Parliament has set up in the Charter is substantial compliance.[55]

Indeed, in the wake of *Brydges*, "Most provinces set up toll-free numbers to ensure that all detainees could speak to duty counsel at all hours of the day."[56] But police in poorer provinces, which would not provide "*Brydges* counsel" unless forced to do so by the Court, had to hope that lawyers would answer calls at home (sometimes late at night). If their suspect tried repeatedly, but unsuccessfully, to obtain legal advice, some types of evidence (e.g., breathalyzer readings) would be lost forever. This example suggests that judicial respect for the principles of federalism and the separation of powers may weaken the practical impact of a Charter guarantee.

The judicial self-restraint evident in the legal aid cases is not absolute. While provincial governments cannot be forced to exercise their discretion in particular ways, they can be required to perform their explicit duties according to Charter standards. One of those duties, imposed by s. 11(b) of the Charter, is to try criminal suspects "within a reasonable time" after the charge has been laid. In the 1990 *Askov* ruling (Dossier 3.4, pages 120–21), the Supreme Court stayed conspiracy charges against four men whose trials in the Peel Region of Ontario had dragged on for almost three years. While Justice Cory acknowledged that local conditions would inevitably affect the administration of justice, he condemned the Ontario government for failing to provide its courts with the resources needed to ensure speedy trials.

> Section 11(b) applies to all Canadians in every part of our land. In a country as vast and diverse as ours, the institutional problems are bound to differ greatly from province to province and from district to district within each province. Differences of climate, terrain, population and financial resources will require different solutions for the problem of providing adequate facilities and personnel.... Wise political decisions will be required with regard to the allocation of scarce funds. Due deference will have to be given to those political decisions as the provisions of courtroom facilities and Crown Attorneys must, for example, be balanced against the provision of health care and high-

ways. Yet solutions must be found as indeed they have been in many jurisdictions outside Ontario.

> The right guaranteed by s. 11(b) is of such fundamental importance to the individual and of such significance to the community as a whole that the lack of institutional resources cannot be employed to justify a continuing unreasonable postponement of trials.... Where inordinate delays do occur, it is those who are responsible for the lack of facilities who should bear the public criticism that is bound to arise as a result of the staying of proceedings which must be the inevitable consequence of unreasonable delays. Members of the community will not and should not condone or accept a situation where those alleged to have committed serious crimes are never brought to trial solely as a result of unduly long delays. It is a serious consequence with potentially dangerous overtones for the community. It is right and proper that there be criticism of the situation when it occurs.[57]

As discussed in Chapter 3, Justice Cory imposed a six- to eight-month deadline on criminal trials in heavily populated judicial districts such as Peel Region. In effect, he stayed the criminal charges against the defendants to indicate judicial displeasure with the spending priorities of successive Ontario governments. The political fallout from *Askov* prompted the Court to modify its position in a subsequent ruling (Dossier 3.4, pages 120–21).

The legal aid and trial delay rulings illustrate two general points. First, as noted in Chapter 3, the Supreme Court takes a more hands-on approach to criminal law than to social policy. The degree to which the Court will defer to legislators, whether federal or provincial, varies across different policy fields. Second, the Court is more reluctant to intervene in exclusive provincial jurisdictions (e.g., education) than in concurrent jurisdictions (such as the administration of criminal justice). Critics who decry the Charter's impact on the division of powers would do well to distinguish among the various policy areas affected by the Charter.

CONCLUSION: FEDERALISM AND THE CHARTER

In the 1998 *Secession Reference*, the Supreme Court identified four principles underlying Canada's constitutional order: "federalism, democracy, constitutionalism and the rule of law, and respect for minority rights."[58] None of these principles, in isolation, trumps any of the others. The Justices made it clear that all four must be interpreted in consonance with each other. Consequently, the federal principle modifies the strict application of minority rights:

> The principle of federalism recognizes the diversity of the component parts of Confederation, and the autonomy of provincial governments to develop their societies within their respective spheres of jurisdiction. The federal structure of our country also facilitates democratic participation by distributing power to the government thought to be most suited to achieving the particular societal objective having regard to this diversity.... A federal system of government enables different provinces to pursue policies responsive to the particular concerns and interests of people in that province.[59]

This desire to balance federalism against the protection of rights is reflected in the decisions discussed in this chapter. Despite the transfer of decision-making from provincial legislatures and executives to the federal judiciary, the Charter's impact on the division of powers has been relatively minor. Any lingering suspicions about a pro-Ottawa bias on the Supreme Court may be addressed in the near future, as the appointment process for Justices is reformed (see Chapter 3, pages 123–26). But even under the current system, where the prime minister chooses the members of the Court, these suspicions are not well-founded. The "centralizing force" of the Charter has been muted by judicial sensitivity to federalism. If Pierre Trudeau intended the 1982 Constitution to centralize our federal system, as the Gang of Eight premiers suspected, his wishes have not been fulfilled.[60]

GLOSSARY OF KEY TERMS

centrifugal force   A force that pushes outward, rather than inward. If, for example, you put a small weight on the end of a piece of string and then whirl it in a circle, the centrifugal force of the weight as it moves through the air will pull the string taut. In Canadian political jargon, the term "centrifugal force" refers to any phenomenon that tends to shift power from Ottawa to the provinces, e.g., the pro-province rulings from the Judicial Committee of the Privy Council.

province-building   A deliberate effort by a provincial government to increase its autonomy from the central government, by building up its own political expertise and resources. Province-building often involves a campaign to convince voters that their provincial government can do a better job of achieving their collective goals than the national government.

regionalism   A sentiment or a set of political attitudes that emphasizes the value and distinctiveness of a particular area within a country. A province with a strong sense of regionalism—e.g., Alberta, or Newfoundland and Labrador—may be more aggressive in its demands for autonomy from the national government; its citizens are often (but not always) more likely to vote for political parties that express the grievances of the particular province (e.g., the old Reform Party, which originated in Alberta and whose first campaign slogan was "The West Wants In").

residual power   The residual power in a federal constitution is the power to make laws in policy fields that are not explicitly assigned to one level of government or the other.

DISCUSSION AND REVIEW QUESTIONS

1. Explain the significance of the following statement by former Chief Justice Dickson: "The

division of powers not only permits differential treatment based upon province of residence, it mandates and encourages geographical distinction." What are the implications for Charter jurisprudence?

2. Distinguish between the explicitly centralizing sections of the Charter and the rest of the guaranteed rights and freedoms. Has the Supreme Court used the former sections to rewrite the division of powers? Why or why not?

3. Has the entrenchment of minority language education rights worked as well as the framers hoped? Why or why not?

4. In your opinion, should a provincial government have the right to reserve particular jobs for people who live in that particular province? Or should any qualified person be allowed to earn a living as he or she chooses, regardless of provincial boundaries?

SUGGESTED READINGS

Fletcher, Joseph F., and Paul Howe. "Canadian Attitudes toward the Charter and the Courts in Comparative Perspective." Montreal: Institute for Research on Public Policy, May 2000.

Hogg, Peter W. "Federalism Fights the Charter of Rights." In David P. Shugarman and Reg Whitaker, eds., *Federalism and Political Community: Essays in Honour of Donald Smiley.* Peterborough: Broadview Press, 1989, pp. 249–66.

Kelly, James B. "The Charter of Rights and Freedoms and the Rebalancing of Liberal Constitutionalism in Canada, 1982–1997." *Osgoode Hall Law Journal* 37 (1999), pp. 625–91.

———. "Reconciling Rights and Federalism during Review of the Charter of Rights and Freedoms: The Supreme Court of Canada and the Centralization Thesis, 1982 to 1999." *Canadian Journal of Political Science* 34, no. 2 (June 2001), pp. 321–55.

Knopff, Rainer, and F.L. Morton. "Nation-Building and the Canadian Charter of Rights and Freedoms." In Alan C. Cairns and Cynthia Williams, eds., *Constitutionalism, Citizenship and Society in Canada*, vol. 33 of the collected research studies for the Royal Commission on the Economic Union and Development Prospects for Canada. Toronto: University of Toronto Press, 1985, pp. 133–82.

Morton, F.L., Peter H. Russell, and Troy Riddell. "The Canadian Charter of Rights and Freedoms: A Descriptive Analysis of the First Decade, 1982–1992." *National Journal of Constitutional Law* 5 (1995), pp. 1–60.

———, Peter H. Russell, and Michael J. Withey. "The Supreme Court's First One Hundred Charter of Rights Decisions: A Statistical Analysis." *Osgoode Hall Law Journal* 30 (1992), pp. 1–56.

Smithey, Shannon Ishiyama. "The Effects of the Canadian Supreme Court's Charter Interpretation on Regional and Intergovernmental Tensions in Canada." *Publius: The Journal of Federalism* 26, no. 2 (Spring 1996), pp. 83–100.

ENDNOTES

1. Peter W. Hogg, "Federalism Fights the Charter of Rights," in David P. Shugarman and Reg Whitaker, eds., *Federalism and Political Community: Essays in Honour of Donald Smiley* (Peterborough: Broadview Press, 1989), p. 249.

2. Peter H. Russell, "The Political Purpose of the Canadian Charter of Rights and Freedoms," *Canadian Bar Review* 61, no. 1 (March 1983), p. 31. See also, e.g., Rainer Knopff and F.L. Morton, "Nation-Building and the Canadian Charter of Rights and Freedoms," in Alan C. Cairns and Cynthia Williams, eds., *Constitutionalism, Citizenship and Society in Canada*, vol. 33 of the collected research studies

for the Royal Commission on the Economic Union and Development Prospects for Canada (Toronto: University of Toronto Press, 1985), pp. 133–82; Alan C. Cairns, "Recent Federalist Constitutional Proposals," in Douglas E. Williams, ed., *Disruptions: Constitutional Struggles from the Charter to Meech Lake* (Toronto: McClelland and Stewart, 1991), pp. 43–44; Alan C. Cairns, *Charter versus Federalism: The Dilemmas of Constitutional Reform* (Montreal and Kingston: McGill-Queen's University Press, 1992), pp. 76–77.

3. Alan C. Cairns, "The Governments and Societies of Canadian Federalism," in Douglas E. Williams, ed., *Constitution, Government, and Society in Canada: Selected Essays by Alan C. Cairns* (Toronto: McClelland and Stewart, 1988), pp. 139–70.

4. Interview with Pierre Elliott Trudeau, September 1997, reported in James B. Kelly, "Reconciling Rights and Federalism during Review of the Charter of Rights and Freedoms: The Supreme Court of Canada and the Centralization Thesis, 1982 to 1999," *Canadian Journal of Political Science* 34, no. 2 (June 2001), pp. 321–55.

5. It included a National Energy Program, in defiance of Alberta's insistence on provincial management of oil and gas. The NEP soured the already tense relationship between the Western provinces and the Trudeau government, making the constitutional negotiations even more difficult. See Roy Romanow, John Whyte, and Howard Leeson, *Canada ... Notwithstanding: The Making of the Constitution, 1976–1982* (Toronto: Carswell/Methuen, 1984), pp. 114–16.

6. "Statement by the Prime Minister, Ottawa, October 2, 1980," reprinted in *McGill Law Journal* 30 (1984–85), p. 648.

7. Shannon Ishiyama Smithey, "The Effects of the Canadian Supreme Court's Charter Interpretation on Regional and Intergovernmental Tensions in Canada," *Publius: The Journal of Federalism* 26, no. 2 (Spring 1996), p. 86.

8. Donald V. Smiley, *The Federal Condition in Canada* (Toronto: McGraw-Hill Ryerson, 1987), pp. 48–49; Alan C. Cairns, "The Judicial Committee and Its Critics," in Douglas E. Williams, ed., *Constitution, Government and Society in Canada: Selected Essays by Alan C. Cairns* (Toronto: McClelland and Stewart, 1988), pp. 43–85.

9. See, e.g., *Caloil Inc. v. Attorney General of Canada*, [1971] S.C.R. 543; *Attorney General of Manitoba v. Manitoba Egg and Poultry Association et al.*, [1971] S.C.R. 689; *Canadian Industrial Gas and Oil Ltd. v. Government of Saskatchewan*, [1978] 2 S.C.R. 545.

10. Romanow, Whyte, and Leeson, *Canada ... Notwithstanding*, pp. 12–16; Robert Sheppard and Michael Valpy, *The National Deal: The Fight for a Canadian Constitution* (Toronto: Macmillan, 1982), p. 236.

11. F.L. Morton, Peter H. Russell, and Troy Riddell, "The Canadian Charter of Rights and Freedoms: A Descriptive Analysis of the First Decade, 1982–1992," *National Journal of Constitutional Law* 5 (1995), pp. 1–60; Table 7, p. 19.

12. The six minority language cases listed by Morton, Russell, and Riddell were: *Attorney General of Quebec v. Greater Hull School Board*, [1984] 2 S.C.R. 575; *Greater Montreal Protestant School Board v. Quebec (Attorney General)*, [1989] 1 S.C.R. 377; *R. v. Mercure*, [1988] 1 S.C.R. 234; *Re Manitoba Language Rights*, [1985] 1 S.C.R. 721; *Bilodeau v. A.G. (Man.)*, [1986] 1 S.C.R. 449; and *Mahé v. Alberta*, [1990] 1 S.C.R. 342. The mobility-rights case was *Black v. Law Society of Alberta*, [1989] 1 S.C.R. 591.

13. These were *Greater Montreal Protestant School Board* and *Mahé v. Alberta*.

14. Morton, Russell, and Riddell, "The Canadian Charter of Rights and Freedoms," p. 28. In a separate study, Shannon Ishiyama Smithey analyzed the impact of Supreme Court Charter rulings on federalism; she found that the Court had actually favoured the provincial governments. See Smithey, "The Effects of the Canadian Supreme Court's Charter Interpretation," pp. 87–88.

15. F.L. Morton, Peter H. Russell, and Michael J. Withey, "The Supreme Court's First One Hundred Charter of Rights Decisions: A Statistical Analysis," *Osgoode Hall Law Journal* 30 (1992), Table 7, p. 25; Morton, Russell, and Riddell, "The Canadian Charter of Rights and Freedoms," p. 20.

16. James B. Kelly, "The Charter of Rights and Freedoms and the Rebalancing of Liberal Constitutionalism in Canada, 1982–1997," *Osgoode Hall Law Journal* 37 (1999), pp. 625–95.

17. Kelly, "The Charter of Rights and Freedoms," pp. 646–47.

18. Knopff and Morton, "Nation-Building," p. 148.

19. Janet L. Hiebert, *Limiting Rights: The Dilemma of Judicial Review* (Montreal and Kingston: McGill-Queen's University Press, 1996), p.132.

20. *Vriend v. Alberta*, [1998] 1 S.C.R. 493; see the discussions in Chapters 1, 4, and 11, pages 36–37, 153, and 350.

21. Hiebert, *Limiting Rights*, pp. 137–38.

22. *Attorney General of Quebec v. Quebec Association of Protestant School Boards*, [1984] 2 S.C.R. 66.

23. Smithey, "The Effects of the Canadian Supreme Court's Charter Interpretation," p. 91.

24. In *Mahé v. Alberta*, the Court ordered the Alberta government to amend the School Act to guarantee the maintenance of a French-language school in Edmonton. Because the number of students was too small to warrant the establishment of a separate French-language school board, the existing francophone school would remain under the auspices of the Edmonton Roman Catholic trustees; however, the act would have to be amended to ensure that francophone parents were represented on the Catholic school board. The Justices applied the *Mahé* doctrine in *Reference re Public Schools Act (Man.)*, s. 79(3), (4), and (7), [1993] 1 S.C.R. 839, *Arsenault-Cameron v. Prince Edward Island*, [2000] 1 S.C.R. 3, and *Doucet-Boudreau v. Nova Scotia (Minister of Education)*, [2003] 3 S.C.R. 3.

25. *Arsenault*, paragraph 51, *per* Major and Bastarache JJ.

26. Statistics Canada, "Study: Student Reading Performance in Minority-Language Schools," *The Daily*, March 22, 2004, available online at www.statcan.ca.

27. *Law Society of Upper Canada v. Skapinker*, [1984] 1 S.C.R. 357.

28. Robert Sheppard and Michael Valpy, *The National Deal: The Fight for a Canadian Constitution* (Toronto: Macmillan, 1982), pp. 150–51; Romanow, Whyte, and Leeson, *Canada ... Notwithstanding*, pp. 13, 71, and 197.

29. After initiating his lawsuit, Skapinker was granted Canadian citizenship and subsequently became a member of the Law Society. He was replaced as the plaintiff by an American lawyer in the same situation.

30. [1989] 1 S.C.R. 591.

31. *Black v. Law Society of Alberta*, [1989] 1 S.C.R. 591, paragraph 40.

32. Ibid., paragraph 54.

33. In dissent, Justice McIntyre argued that the impugned rules violated freedom of association

(s. 2(d) of the Charter) but not mobility rights. In his view, neither rule prohibited anyone from entering, or practising law in, the province of Alberta. Their only effect was to forbid Alberta lawyers from forming partnerships with nonresident lawyers and with multiple firms; the mobility interest of Alberta lawyers was unaffected. McIntyre seems not to have considered the impact of the rules on the non-Albertan lawyers, whose ability to pursue a career in the province was seriously impaired by their inability to enter into partnerships. While the practice of law does not require the establishment of multi-lawyer firms, or of partnerships, a solo practitioner cannot call on the wide range of resources and expertise available to a large legal team. The type of case that he or she can competently undertake is thus restricted to relatively simple matters, such as residential real estate and wills. This restriction violates the right to pursue the livelihood of one's choice, which *Skapinker* established as a core element of s. 6.

34. See, e.g., *Wilson v. Medical Services Commission of British Columbia* (1987), 9 B.C.L.R. (2d) 350; *Mia v. British Columbia Medical Services Commission* (1985), 17 D.L.R. (4th) 385. However, a more recent challenge to such policies failed; see *Waldman et al. v. The Medical Services of British Columbia et al.*, 1999 BCCA 0508 (available online at www.canlii.org/bc/cas/bcca/1999/1999bcca508.html).

35. *Canadian Egg Marketing Agency v. Richardson*, [1998] 3 S.C.R. 157, paragraph 49.

36. Ibid., paragraph 59.

37. Ibid., paragraph 61 (emphasis in original).

38. Ibid., paragraph 66.

39. Ibid., paragraph 75.

40. Ibid., paragraph 72.

41. *R. v. Turpin*, [1989] 1 S.C.R. 1296, paragraphs 46–47, *per* Wilson J. (for a unanimous Court).

42. Peter H. Russell, "The First Three Years in Charterland," *Canadian Public Administration* 28 (1985), p. 380.

43. *The Queen v. Jones*, [1986] 2 S.C.R. 284, paragraph 41.

44. Ibid., paragraph 25.

45. *Reference re Bill 30, An Act to Amend the Education Act (Ont.)*, [1987] 1 S.C.R. 1148, paragraph 62.

46. Ibid., paragraph 80.

47. *Adler v. Ontario*, [1996] 3 S.C.R. 609.

48. Ibid., paragraph 35, *per* Iacobucci J.

49. This element of the "informational component" of s. 10(b) was added by *R. v. Brydges*, [1990] 1 S.C.R. 190.

50. *R. v. Bartle*, [1994] 3 S.C.R. 173, paragraph 17, *per* Lamer C.J.C. (as he then was).

51. *R. v. Brydges*, paragraph 23, *per* Lamer J. (as he then was).

52. *R. v. Bartle*, paragraph 28, *per* Lamer C.J.C. (for the majority).

53. *R. v. Prosper*, [1994] 3 S.C.R. 236, paragraphs 30–31, *per* Lamer C.J.C. (for the majority on this issue).

54. Ibid., paragraph 32.

55. Ibid., paragraph 96, *per* McLachlin J. (concurring on this issue).

56. Roach, *Due Process and Victims' Rights*, p. 58.

57. *R. v. Askov*, [1990] 2 S.C.R. 1199, paragraphs 54–56 and 59.

58. *Reference re Secession of Quebec*, [1998] 2 S.C.R. 217, paragraph 49.

59. Ibid., paragraphs 58 and 66.

60. Trudeau's stated goal, to offset regionalism by giving Canadians a unifying national symbol, has been more fully realized. A majority of Canadians in all provinces applaud the Charter and approve of its application by the courts. Even in Quebec, where political reaction to rulings on minority language rights has been strongly negative, a majority of survey respondents express a positive view of the Charter. See Joseph F. Fletcher and Paul Howe, "Canadian Attitudes toward the Charter and the Courts in Comparative Perspective" (Montreal: Institute for Research on Public Policy, May 2000), pp. 7–8 and Figure 3.

Appendix

Sections 91–93 and 95–96 of the Constitution Act, 1867

VI. DISTRIBUTION OF LEGISLATIVE POWERS
Powers of the Parliament

91. It shall be lawful for the Queen, by and with the Advice and Consent of the Senate and House of Commons, to make Laws for the Peace, Order, and good Government of Canada, in relation to all Matters not coming within the Classes of Subjects by this Act assigned exclusively to the Legislatures of the Provinces; and for greater Certainty, but not so as to restrict the Generality of the foregoing Terms of this Section, it is hereby declared that (notwithstanding anything in this Act) the exclusive Legislative Authority of the Parliament of Canada extends to all Matters coming within the Classes of Subjects next hereinafter enumerated; that is to say,

1. Repealed.
1A. The Public Debt and Property.
2. The Regulation of Trade and Commerce.
2A. Unemployment insurance.
3. The raising of Money by any Mode or System of Taxation.
4. The borrowing of Money on the Public Credit.
5. Postal Service.
6. The Census and Statistics.
7. Militia, Military and Naval Service, and Defence.
8. The fixing of and providing for the Salaries and Allowances of Civil and other Officers of the Government of Canada.
9. Beacons, Buoys, Lighthouses, and Sable Island.
10. Navigation and Shipping.
11. Quarantine and the Establishment and Maintenance of Marine Hospitals.
12. Sea Coast and Inland Fisheries.
13. Ferries between a Province and any British or Foreign Country or between Two Provinces.
14. Currency and Coinage.
15. Banking, Incorporation of Banks, and the Issue of Paper Money.
16. Savings Banks.
17. Weights and Measures.
18. Bills of Exchange and Promissory Notes.
19. Interest.
20. Legal Tender.
21. Bankruptcy and Insolvency.
22. Patents of Invention and Discovery.
23. Copyrights.
24. Indians, and Lands reserved for the Indians.
25. Naturalization and Aliens.

26. Marriage and Divorce.
27. The Criminal Law, except the Constitution of Courts of Criminal Jurisdiction, but including the Procedure in Criminal Matters.
28. The Establishment, Maintenance, and Management of Penitentiaries.
29. Such Classes of Subjects as are expressly excepted in the Enumeration of the Classes of Subjects by this Act assigned exclusively to the Legislatures of the Provinces.

And any Matter coming within any of the Classes of Subjects enumerated in this Section shall not be deemed to come within the Class of Matters of a local or private Nature comprised in the Enumeration of the Classes of Subjects by this Act assigned exclusively to the Legislatures of the Provinces.

Exclusive Powers of Provincial Legislatures

92. In each Province the Legislature may exclusively make Laws in relation to Matters coming within the Classes of Subjects next hereinafter enumerated; that is to say,

1. Repealed.
2. Direct Taxation within the Province in order to the raising of a Revenue for Provincial Purposes.
3. The borrowing of Money on the sole Credit of the Province.
4. The Establishment and Tenure of Provincial Offices and the Appointment and Payment of Provincial Officers.
5. The Management and Sale of the Public Lands belonging to the Province and of the Timber and Wood thereon.
6. The Establishment, Maintenance, and Management of Public and Reformatory Prisons in and for the Province.
7. The Establishment, Maintenance, and Management of Hospitals, Asylums, Charities, and Eleemosynary Institutions in and for the Province, other than Marine Hospitals.
8. Municipal Institutions in the Province.
9. Shop, Saloon, Tavern, Auctioneer, and other Licences in order to the raising of a Revenue for Provincial, Local, or Municipal Purposes.

10. Local Works and Undertakings other than such as are of the following Classes:
    (a) Lines of Steam or other Ships, Railways, Canals, Telegraphs, and other Works and Undertakings connecting the Province with any other or others of the Provinces, or extending beyond the Limits of the Province:
    (b) Lines of Steam Ships between the Province and any British or Foreign Country:
    (c) Such Works as, although wholly situate within the Province, are before or after their Execution declared by the Parliament of Canada to be for the general Advantage of Canada or for the Advantage of Two or more of the Provinces.
11. The Incorporation of Companies with Provincial Objects.
12. The Solemnization of Marriage in the Province.
13. Property and Civil Rights in the Province.
14. The Administration of Justice in the Province, including the Constitution, Maintenance, and Organization of Provincial Courts, both of Civil and of Criminal Jurisdiction, and including Procedure in Civil Matters in those Courts.
15. The Imposition of Punishment by Fine, Penalty, or Imprisonment for enforcing any Law of the Province made in relation to any Matter coming within any of the Classes of Subjects enumerated in this Section.
16. Generally all Matters of a merely local or private Nature in the Province.

Non-Renewable Natural Resources, Forestry Resources and Electrical Energy

92A. (1) In each province, the legislature may exclusively make laws in relation to
    (a) exploration for non-renewable natural resources in the province;
    (b) development, conservation and management of non-renewable natural resources and forestry resources in the province, including laws in relation to the rate of primary production therefrom; and

(c) development, conservation and management of sites and facilities in the province for the generation and production of electrical energy.

(2) In each province, the legislature may make laws in relation to the export from the province to another part of Canada of the primary production from non-renewable natural resources and forestry resources in the province and the production from facilities in the province for the generation of electrical energy, but such laws may not authorize or provide for discrimination in prices or in supplies exported to another part of Canada.

(3) Nothing in subsection (2) derogates from the authority of Parliament to enact laws in relation to the matters referred to in that subsection and, where such a law of Parliament and a law of a province conflict, the law of Parliament prevails to the extent of the conflict.

(4) In each province, the legislature may make laws in relation to the raising of money by any mode or system of taxation in respect of

(a) non-renewable natural resources and forestry resources in the province and the primary production therefrom, and

(b) sites and facilities in the province for the generation of electrical energy and the production therefrom,

whether or not such production is exported in whole or in part from the province, but such laws may not authorize or provide for taxation that differentiates between production exported to another part of Canada and production not exported from the province.

(5) The expression "primary production" has the meaning assigned by the Sixth Schedule.

(6) Nothing in subsections (1) to (5) derogates from any powers or rights that a legislature or government of a province had immediately before the coming into force of this section.

Education

93. In and for each Province the Legislature may exclusively make Laws in relation to Education, subject and according to the following Provisions:

(1) Nothing in any such Law shall prejudicially affect any Right or Privilege with respect to Denominational Schools which any Class of Persons have by Law in the Province at the Union:

(2) All the Powers, Privileges and Duties at the Union by Law conferred and imposed in Upper Canada on the Separate Schools and School Trustees of the Queen's Roman Catholic Subjects shall be and the same are hereby extended to the Dissentient Schools of the Queen's Protestant and Roman Catholic Subjects in Quebec:

(3) Where in any Province a System of Separate or Dissentient Schools exists by Law at the Union or is thereafter established by the Legislature of the Province, an Appeal shall lie to the Governor General in Council from any Act or Decision of any Provincial Authority affecting any Right or Privilege of the Protestant or Roman Catholic Minority of the Queen's Subjects in relation to Education:

(4) In case any such Provincial Law as from Time to Time seems to the Governor General in Council requisite for the due Execution of the Provisions of this Section is not made, or in case any Decision of the Governor General in Council on any Appeal under this Section is not duly executed by the proper Provincial Authority in that Behalf, then and in every such Case, and as far only as the Circumstances of each Case require, the Parliament of Canada may make remedial Laws for the due Execution of the Provisions of this Section and of any Decision of the Governor General in Council under this Section.

93A. Paragraphs (1) to (4) of section 93 do not apply to Quebec.

Agriculture and Immigration

95. In each Province the Legislature may make Laws in relation to Agriculture in the Province, and to Immigration into the Province; and it is hereby declared that the Parliament of Canada may from Time to Time make Laws in relation to Agriculture in all or any of the Provinces, and to Immigration into all or any of the Provinces; and any Law of the Legislature of a Province relative to Agriculture or to Immigration shall have effect in and for the Province as long and as far only as it is not repugnant to any Act of the Parliament of Canada.

VII. JUDICATURE

96. The Governor General shall appoint the Judges of the Superior, District, and County Courts in each Province, except those of the Courts of Probate in Nova Scotia and New Brunswick.

The Impact of the Charter on Public Policy

3

Chapter 8

Fundamental Freedoms

British Columbia ferry workers' union spokesman Tom McNeilage holds a portable radio as striking workers listen to news reports at the Horseshoe Bay Ferry Terminal in West Vancouver in December 2003. The courts have yet to recognize a right to strike in the Charter.

CP PHOTO/Chuck Stoody

Fundamental Freedoms

2. *Everyone has the following fundamental freedoms:*

   (a) freedom of conscience and religion;

   (b) freedom of thought, belief, opinion and expression, including freedom of the press and other means of communication;

   (c) freedom of peaceful assembly; and

   (d) freedom of association.

INTRODUCTION

As discussed in Chapter 1, the central question in a Charter case is whether, and under what circumstances, the state can do a particular thing. In cases concerning s. 2, the issue is whether or not the state can limit the "fundamental freedoms" of any indi-

vidual. These freedoms are "fundamental" in more than name. For at least three centuries, they have been recognized as core guarantees of freedom and, latterly, of democracy. Freedom of conscience, religion, and expression have long been enshrined in Anglo-American common law; more recently, they have been given pride of place in constitutional and international guarantees of human rights. The First Amendment in the American Bill of Rights is an obvious example. It declares that "Congress shall make no law respecting an **establishment** of religion, or prohibiting the free exercise thereof; or abridging the freedom of speech, or of the press; or the right of the people peaceably to assemble, and to petition the Government for a redress of grievances."

Canadians, like their American neighbours, have long enjoyed the freedom to believe and to speak as their consciences dictated. But as long as these freedoms were left to the protection of the common law, to an "implied bill of rights" (see Dossier 2.3, pages 52–54), or to statutory guarantees (Dossier 2.5, pages 58–60), their exercise was not always guaranteed. While Parliament was supreme, governments retained the power to restrict religious activities and political expression that attracted the hostility of the majority (or a well-organized minority). Although this power was used sparingly, usually in times of actual or perceived crisis, the freedoms claimed by adherents of marginalized religious and political groups were not always respected by legislators or enforced by courts. Their vulnerability to arbitrary state power is illustrated by the persecution Communists and Jehovah's Witnesses in Quebec under Premier Duplessis (Dossier 2.4, pages 54–60).

Section 2 of the Charter differs from the common-law protections in two ways. First, it gives judges the remedial power to strike down or modify laws that unduly restrict individual freedoms. Although the success rate for plaintiffs in s. 2 cases at the Supreme Court has fallen in recent years—from 28.6 percent in 1982–92[1] to 24 percent in 1993–97[2]—that drop is consistent with the overall trend for Charter cases (discussed in Chapter 3). Most of the successful plaintiffs have alleged violations of expressive freedom, which the Supreme Court has been particularly keen to address. Plaintiffs seeking a remedy for infringements of religious or associative freedom have not been as fortunate, as we will see in subsequent sections of this chapter. (Because s. 2(c) has not yet been subject to review by the Supreme Court, it will not be discussed in this chapter.)

Second, the Charter requires all three branches of government to respect the guarantee of fundamental freedoms. The common-law freedoms were binding only on the courts; legislators could override them by statute as they saw fit. Moreover, the Charter applies to both federal and provincial governments. Although the federal government could boast a good record of protecting individual liberties before the Charter—with a few notable exceptions, such as the 1919 "Red Laws"[3]—some provincial governments had committed egregious violations of religious and expressive freedom in the nineteenth and early twentieth centuries. (For examples, see Dossiers 2.3 and 2.4.) Such violations had all but ceased in the 1960s and 1970s. Even so, the extension of entrenched guarantees to the provinces was significant. Provincial governments are responsible for primary and secondary education, as well as labour relations and business regulation within their boundaries. These policy fields often engage the values protected by s. 2 of the Charter.

Unlike the American Bill of Rights, the Charter contains an external limitation clause (s. 1). Its presence encourages judges to define the freedoms in s. 2 very broadly, without "reading in" specific limitations. The exception is s. 2(d), which—until recently—was interpreted narrowly. Courts defined the freedom to associate as a purely *individual* right. It did not protect inherently collective activities such as collective bargaining or going out on strike, partly because judges were reluctant to apply the Charter to economic disputes. Since 2001, the Supreme Court has redefined s. 2(d) as a guarantee of *collective* rights. It has moved away from the American practice of limiting rights within the meaning of the actual guarantee and adopted the "two-step" approach that it applies to other protected rights and freedoms (Dossier 1.6, pages 27–30).

As we saw in Chapter 1, the distinction between the "freedoms" in s. 2 and the "rights" guaranteed elsewhere in the Charter is more apparent than real. Former Chief Justice Dickson questioned its usefulness in Charter interpretation.

Section 2 of the *Charter* protects fundamental "freedoms" as opposed to "rights." Although these two terms are sometimes used interchangeably, a conceptual distinction between the two is often drawn. "Rights" are said to impose a corresponding duty or obligation on another party to ensure the protection of the right in question whereas "freedoms" are said to involve simply an absence of interference or constraint. This conceptual approach to the nature of "freedoms" may be too narrow since it fails to acknowledge situations where the absence of government intervention may in effect substantially impede the enjoyment of fundamental freedoms (e.g., regulations limiting the monopolization of the press may be required to ensure freedom of expression and freedom of the press).[4]

For example, the Court ruled against a man who claimed that the denial of his right to vote in the 1992 Charlottetown Accord referendum also violated his expressive freedom. The majority held that "s. 2(b) of the Charter does not impose upon a government, whether provincial or federal, any positive obligation to consult its citizens through the particular mechanism of a referendum. Nor does it confer upon all citizens the right to express their opinions in a referendum. A government is under no constitutional obligation to extend this platform of expression to *anyone*, let alone to *everyone*." In more colloquial terms, "the freedom of expression contained in s. 2(b) prohibits gags, but does not compel the distribution of megaphones."[5] So far the distinction between rights and freedoms is clear. However, the majority added that "While s. 2(b) of the *Charter* does not include the right to any particular means of expression, where a government chooses to provide one, it must do so in a fashion that is consistent with the Constitution."[6] In other words, where a government assumes a positive obligation to facilitate free expression, it creates a *right* of equal access to that expression.

So despite the theoretical differences between rights and freedoms, the process of judicial review is the same for both. First, the plaintiff must demonstrate that his or her freedom has been infringed by the state; second, the relevant government must try to justify the infringement under s. 1. While the procedure is consistent, the jurisprudence on s. 2 has not been so. There have been important differences and reversals of opinion, especially over the constitutional protection of commercial speech and collective bargaining. These conflicts reveal the difficulty of reconciling individual liberties with competing social goals. The courts have searched for a middle ground between unlimited freedom and the collective good.

The inescapable subjectivity of this process, combined with the abstractness of the freedoms guaranteed in s. 2, has shaped the meaning of the fundamental freedoms in unpredictable ways.

Section 2(a): Freedom of Conscience and Religion

Freedom of Conscience

The phrase "freedom of conscience" does not appear in the 1960 Bill of Rights. Its inclusion in then–justice minister Trudeau's 1968 draft Charter was intended to broaden the guarantee of religious freedom, in order to protect nonreligious beliefs from state interference. In practice, the guarantee of freedom of conscience has been interpreted in three ways. First, as Trudeau intended, it protects "the person who chooses to have no religion."[7] Former Chief Justice Dickson ruled that the first part of s. 2(a) protects "the freedom to manifest religious non-belief, as well as the freedom to refuse to participate in religious practice."[8] Among other things, it guarantees freedom *from* religion. "Freedom of conscience" also requires the state to respect "views based on strongly held moral ideas of right and wrong, not necessarily founded on any organized religious principles.... For example, a secular conscientious objection to service in the military might well fall within the ambit of freedom of conscience, though not religion."[9]

Second, the guarantee recognizes "the centrality of individual conscience and the inappropriateness of governmental intervention to compel or to constrain its manifestation."[10] These values are reflected in other Charter sections as well, although the Supreme Court has been divided over the extent to which s. 2(a) should determine the meaning of the word "liberty" in s. 7 (Dossier 8.1, page 250). Freedom of conscience was one of the less controversial elements in the Charter,[11] perhaps because it already seemed secure from legislated restrictions. The freedom to *speak*, which has always been more difficult for governments to tolerate, is distinguished in s. 2 from the freedom to *think* or to *believe*. Democratic governments are not in the habit of forcing their citizens to think in particular ways. Therefore, entrenched protection against state-imposed **orthodoxy** of opinion does not alter the legal status quo as significantly as other sections of the Charter.

DOSSIER 8.1

"FREEDOM OF CONSCIENCE" AND THE RIGHT TO "LIBERTY" IN SECTION 7

In 1988, the Supreme Court of Canada struck down section 251 of the Criminal Code.[1] That section had declared abortion to be a criminal offence, unless it was performed under certain conditions. (For a more detailed discussion of the case, see Dossier 2.12, pages 77–79.) In her concurring judgment, Justice Wilson held that the law violated women's freedom of conscience. She argued that the word "liberty" in s. 7 incorporated the individual's moral freedom to act according to his or her conscience.

> I believe that the decision whether or not to terminate a pregnancy is essentially a moral decision, a matter of conscience. I do not think there is or can be any dispute about that. The question is: whose conscience? Is the conscience of the woman to be paramount or the conscience of the state? I believe... that in a free and democratic society it must be the conscience of the individual. Indeed, s. 2(a) makes it clear that this freedom belongs to "everyone," i.e., to each of us individually.[2]

Justice Wilson then distinguished between religious beliefs, which are protected by the second part of s. 2(a), and "conscientious beliefs which are not religiously motivated."[3]

The latter are protected from state interference by the guarantee of "freedom of conscience."

> Accordingly, for the state to take sides on the issue of abortion, as it does in the impugned legislation by making it a criminal offence for the pregnant woman to exercise one of her options, is not only to endorse but also to enforce, on pain of a further loss of liberty through actual imprisonment, one conscientiously-held view at the expense of another. It is to deny freedom of conscience to some, to treat them as means to an end, to deprive them ... of their "essential humanity."[4]

She concluded that "Legislation which violates freedom of conscience in this manner cannot, in my view, be in accordance with the principles of fundamental justice within the meaning of s. 7."

ENDNOTES

1. *R. v. Morgentaler*, [1988] 1 S.C.R.

2. Ibid., paragraph 246, *per* Wilson J.

3. Ibid., paragraph 248, *per* Wilson J.

4. Ibid., paragraph 250, *per* Wilson J.; citation omitted.

Justice Wilson's argument for a connection between ss. 2(a) and 7 drew strong criticism from some of her fellow Justices. In his dissenting judgment in *B. (R.) v. Children's Aid Society of Metropolitan Toronto*,[12] then–Chief Justice Lamer argued that the freedoms in s. 2 and the rights in s. 7 are conceptually distinct. Moreover, he denied Wilson's claim that the word "liberty" in s. 7 must be interpreted as a reference to the "fundamental freedoms"; instead, Lamer argued, the word "liberty" in the context of s. 7 refers only to physical freedom—the absence of state-

imposed incarceration or other forms of detention.[13] Lamer's interpretation of s. 7 as a purely legal provision was rejected by the other judges in that case, as in others,[14] and Wilson's broader approach appears to have prevailed.

Third, if the guarantee of freedom of conscience has any practical meaning, it must (as Justice Wilson argued) protect the liberty to act in the manner dictated by one's inner convictions. That liberty is necessarily limited by the rights of others, and by the need to preserve social order. For Dickson, its purpose is to ensure that "every individual [is] free to hold and to manifest whatever beliefs and opinions his or her conscience dictates, provided *inter alia* only that such manifestations do not injure his or her neighbours or their parallel rights to hold and manifest beliefs and opinions of their own."[15] For example, an Ontario court rejected a constitutional challenge against an injunction that prohibited picketing in front of a Toronto abortion clinic. The judge found that "'action' motivated by conscience [was not] intended to be protected by the Charter," whereas "'protection against invasion' of a sphere of individual intellect and spirit" is fundamental to the Charter's purpose.[16] In other words, the state must not actively interfere with my moral *beliefs* (by enforcing a particular orthodoxy), but it does not have to condone whatever *actions* those beliefs might direct me to commit.

Freedom of Religion

Freedom to worship as one pleases, without undue interference by the state, is a central tenet in liberal thought. The separation of Church and state forbids governments to enforce or prohibit a particular religious dogma or ritual. In Canada, where the proportion of Roman Catholics and mainstream Protestants is shrinking,[17] freedom of religion is both a practical necessity and a question of principle. When religious faiths conflict with each other, or with secular values, the Charter requires federal and provincial governments to tread carefully and to avoid privileging one set of beliefs over another.

Long before the Charter, religious freedom was recognized as a fundamental value in Canadian law. Because the French-speaking population was overwhelmingly Catholic and the English-speaking population largely Protestant, the very existence of Canada depended on mutual tolerance and accommodation between people of different faiths. In 1953, Justice Rand summarized our history of religious freedom:

> From 1760 ... to the present moment religious freedom has, in our legal system, been recognized as a principle of fundamental character; and although we have nothing in the nature of an established church, that the untrammelled affirmation of religious belief and its propagation,

personal or institutional, remain as of the greatest constitutional significance throughout the Dominion is unquestionable.[18]

The text of the Charter contains five references to religion. First, the Preamble states that "Canada is founded upon the principles that recognize the supremacy of God and the rule of law," a holdover from the Preamble to the 1960 Bill of Rights. (The latter also declared that "men and institutions remain free only when freedom is founded upon respect for moral and spiritual values," a sentiment that has no equivalent in the Charter.) Second, both documents explicitly guarantee "freedom of religion," although without elaboration. Third, s. 15(1) of the Charter protects against discrimination on the basis of religion, as did s. 1 of the Bill. Fourth, s. 29 exempts existing Catholic and Protestant schools from Charter challenge; this section reinforces the guarantee of denominational schools in s. 93 of the Constitution Act, 1867. Finally, s. 27 implicitly protects the rights of religious minorities by requiring courts to interpret the Charter "in a manner consistent with the preservation and enhancement of the multicultural heritage of Canadians." Collectively, these guarantees of religious freedom have yielded two key principles of jurisprudence:

1. laws whose *purpose* is to enforce or denigrate a particular religious faith are generally nullified, whereas secular laws that impose unintended negative *effects* on adherents of minority religions are generally upheld; and
2. the Charter protects the individual against state coercion based on religion, but it does not require the state to privilege one person's faith over another person's rights or the collective good.

The guarantee of religious freedom in the Bill of Rights received short shrift from the Supreme Court (see Dossier 2.6, pages 61–62). When the Charter took effect in 1982, it was not immediately clear whether the Supreme Court would exercise its new remedial powers to strike down the federal Lord's Day Act, which had been upheld under the "frozen rights" approach to the Bill. Those questions were addressed in one of the very first, and most important, Charter rulings: *Big M Drug Mart* (see Dossier 8.2, pages 252–53).

DOSSIER 8.2

THE CONSTITUTIONALITY OF SUNDAY-CLOSING LAWS UNDER THE CHARTER

Six weeks after the proclamation of the Charter, Calgary police raided a drugstore that was open for business on a Sunday. The company, Big M Drug Mart, was charged with violating the federal Lord's Day Act. That law, originally adopted in 1906, designated the Christian Sabbath as a compulsory day of rest. Big M challenged the constitutionality of the act, as a violation of the religious freedom guaranteed by s. 2(a). The trial judge agreed and dismissed the charges. The Alberta Court of Appeal narrowly upheld the ruling. The Supreme Court of Canada heard the case in March 1984, although it did not issue its decision until April 1985. It had to answer three important questions. First, was the Court bound by the 1963 *Robertson and Rosetanni* precedent (Dossier 2.6, pages 61–62)? Second, did the Sunday-closing law infringe s. 2(a) of the Charter? Third, was any such infringement justified under s. 1?[1]

Writing for the majority, Justice Dickson (as he then was) answered the first question in the negative. As discussed in Chapter 3, page 105, he rejected the assertion of former Justice Ritchie that the purpose of the impugned law was irrelevant.[2] He also dismissed the "frozen rights" approach in *Robertson*. Unlike the Bill of Rights, which merely "declared" the existence of certain rights and freedoms, "the language of the *Charter* is imperative." It binds all current and future governments, and its provisions must be interpreted by the courts to keep pace with evolving social conditions. Third, Dickson distinguished between the statutory Bill of Rights and the entrenched Charter. He pointed out that "[since] the entrenchment of the *Charter* the definition of freedom of conscience and religion is no longer vulnerable to legislative incursion."[3]

The answer to the second question depended on the purpose of the Lord's Day Act. As Dickson noted, such a law could serve either of two objectives: "securing public obser-

vance of the Christian institution of the Sabbath" or "providing a uniform day of rest from labour." If the true purpose of the law was religious, as Big M argued, then s. 2(a) of the Charter was engaged; if it was secular, as the federal government contended, the constitutional guarantee of religious freedom was irrelevant. After summarizing the history of the act, Dickson concluded that its primary purpose was "the compulsion of sabbatical observance."[4] He criticized the Crown's argument that a law, originally religious in intent, could evolve over time into a purely secular statute. This "shifting purposes" doctrine, Dickson declared, was untenable both in practical terms and as a principled approach to judicial review (Dossier 3.2, pages 110–12).

Having determined the purpose of the Lord's Day Act, Dickson went on to discuss the meaning of religious freedom. As summarized in Chapter 3, page 105, he found that the purpose of the guarantee is to protect the individual against state coercion on behalf of any religion, even if practised by the majority of citizens. Consequently, a law that prohibits the transaction of business on a Sunday for religious reasons must infringe religious freedom.

> To the extent that it binds all to a sectarian Christian ideal, the *Lord's Day Act* works a form of coercion inimical to the spirit of the Charter and the dignity of all non-Christians. In proclaiming the standards of the Christian faith, the Act creates a climate hostile to, and gives the appearance of discrimination against, non-Christian Canadians. It takes religious values rooted in Christian morality and, using the force of the state, translates them into a positive law binding on believers and non-believers alike. The theological content of the legislation remains as a subtle and constant reminder to religious minorities within the country of their differences with, and alienation from, the dominant religious culture.

Non-Christians are prohibited for religious reasons from carrying out activities which are otherwise lawful, moral and normal. The arm of the state requires all to remember the Lord's day of the Christians and to keep it holy. The protection of one religion and the concomitant non-protection of others imports disparate impact destructive of the religious freedom of the collectivity.[5]

So the answer to the second question was affirmative.

The answer to the third question—whether the infringement of s. 2(a) could be justified under s. 1—was brief and cursory. The *Big M* ruling was issued before the *Oakes* ruling; there was, as yet, no uniform approach to s. 1, although Dickson hinted at the elements of a test (discussed in Chapter 3, page 105). Using this embryonic form of the *Oakes* test, Dickson found the Lord's Day Act unconstitutional and declared it invalid under s. 52. He hinted, however, that a law that mandated a weekly day of rest for purely secular reasons might be acceptable.

That hint was fleshed out in December 1986, when the Court upheld Ontario's Retail Business Holidays Act.[6] *Edwards Books and Art* differed from *Big M* in at least two ways. First, the Ontario law was clearly secular in intent, if not in effect. Six of the seven Justices found that Sunday closing infringed the religious freedom of store owners whose Sabbath fell on Saturday. Nonetheless, the law was found to be valid because it was designed to ensure a weekly day of rest—not to enforce the Christian faith—and because it allowed some exemptions for non-Christian merchants. Second, and more importantly, *Edwards Books* was written after the *Oakes* test took effect. The s. 1 analysis was considerably longer and more detailed than that in *Big M*. Most important, it relied on empirical evidence about the effects of Sunday opening on store clerks and their families. After noting that retail workers were among the most powerless and low-paid groups in the workforce, Dickson (now Chief Justice) cautioned courts to ensure that the Charter "does not simply become an instrument of better situated individuals to roll back legislation which has as its object the improvement of the condition of less advantaged persons."[7] In the end, the incidental infringement of s. 2(a) was proportional to the benefits flowing from the law.

ENDNOTES

1 There were also two threshold issues to resolve before the Court could proceed: whether a corporation could apply for a remedy under s. 24 of the Charter (yes), and whether a successful challenge to the impugned law would require dismissal of the criminal charges. The Supreme Court determined that resort to s. 24 was not necessary where the central issue was the constitutionality of a law under s. 52 of the Constitution Act, 1982. As Justice Dickson put it, "no one can be convicted of an offence under an unconstitutional law." *R. v. Big M Drug Mart Ltd.*, [1985] 1 S.C.R. 295, paragraph 38. The significance of this ruling is twofold: it allows any criminal defendant—whether an individual or a corporation—to challenge the constitutionality of the law under which that defendant is charged; and it clarifies the remedial effect of s. 52 in relation to s. 24.

2. *Big M Drug Mart*, paragraphs 80–81 and 85.

3. Ibid., paragraph 128.

4. Ibid., paragraph 85.

5. Ibid., paragraphs 97–98.

6. *R. v. Edwards Books and Art Ltd.*, [1986] 2 S.C.R. 713.

7. Ibid., paragraph 141.

Where Sunday closing is required by law, a business owner who worships on Friday or Saturday must either close her premises on two days per week or sacrifice the observance of her faith. This is true even where, as in the *Edwards Books* case, the purpose of the law is entirely secular. The cases in Dossier 8.2, pages 252–53 illustrate the first general trend in Charter jurisprudence: laws that explicitly privilege the majority Christian faith are struck down, because their *purpose* is to restrict religious freedom; such a purpose cannot be justified under s. 1. For example, the Ontario Court of Appeal has struck down two school board policies, one requiring Christian prayer in the classroom and the other mandating "religious instruction" with a heavily Christian emphasis, even though both policies allowed students to seek exemptions.[19] The Court held that the exemption provisions did not save the policies from violating s. 2(a), because they drew attention to the differences between non-Christian students themselves and their Christian peers. In effect, the former were forced to publicly "stigmatize" themselves.[20] These rulings reflect an egalitarian approach to minority faiths, at least where explicitly religious statutes are impugned.[21] Any law that is designed to enforce a particular religion is in serious jeopardy under s. 2(b).

However, secular laws with incidental negative *effects* for religious minorities—whether Christian or non-Christian—are generally upheld as justified limitations on s. 2(a). One example is the Alberta School Act, which the Supreme Court upheld in 1986. The case was brought by Thomas Larry Jones, a fundamentalist pastor in Alberta who educated his children and those of other congregants in the church basement. Reverend Jones refused to send the children to a public school or to ask the provincial government to certify his religious school as a valid alternative to public education. He was charged with truancy.

Jones challenged the Alberta School Act on the ground that it violated his religious freedom. He argued that "his authority over his children and his duty to attend to their education comes from God, and that it would be sinful for him to request the state to permit him to do God's will."[22] While the Court was prepared to accept the sincerity of Jones's beliefs, it found that the objective of the law—namely, to provide a high-quality public education for all Alberta children—outweighed any incidental infringement of his religious freedom. Given the secular *purpose* of the law, and the fact that it permitted exemptions for private religious schools that met provincial standards, it could not be invalidated under s. 2(a) despite its impact on Jones's congregants.

The second principle in the jurisprudence on religious freedom holds that faith cannot be used to justify acts that break the law or violate the rights of others. No matter how sincerely held, the religious beliefs of an individual do not permit him or her to do or say harmful things. While the state may not restrict religious *beliefs*, "the same cannot be said of religious *practices*, notably when they impact on the fundamental rights and freedoms of others."[23] This principle was clearly enunciated in a case that pitted the religious freedom of a teacher against the equality rights of Jewish students. Moncton educator Malcolm Ross was well known for his public denunciations of Jews and his denial of the Holocaust. He claimed that his religious beliefs required him to publicize these opinions in speeches and letters to newspapers.

Unlike in the case of James Keegstra (see Dossier 8.10, pages 271–72), there was no evidence that Ross taught these beliefs to his students. Nonetheless, a Jewish parent complained to the New Brunswick Human Rights Commission, citing both Ross and the local school board. The commission found that the board had implicitly endorsed Ross's anti-Semitic views by continuing his employment, and ordered it to suspend him without pay until a nonteaching position could be found for him. If he had not accepted such a position by the time his current contract expired, he would be fired. Ross challenged the order as a violation of his religious and expressive freedoms. Although the New Brunswick Court of Queen's Bench upheld most of the commission's order, its ruling was subsequently overturned by the Court of Appeal. The appellate judges accepted Ross's claim that the order violated ss. 2(a) and (b) of the Charter.

The Supreme Court of Canada overturned the Court of Appeal ruling. In a unanimous judgment, the Justices held that religious freedom is "restricted by the right of others to hold and to manifest beliefs and opinions of their own, and to be free from injury from the exercise of the freedom of religion of others." Moreover, it is "subject to such limitations as are necessary to protect public safety, order, health or morals and the fundamental rights and freedoms of others."[24] Although the order of the Human Rights Commission was found to constitute a *prima facie* infringement of s. 2(a) (and 2(b)), the violation was justified under s. 1. Justice La Forest argued that Ross's public campaign against Jews had poisoned the educational atmosphere in his school, persuading non-Jewish children to adopt anti-Semitic beliefs and making Jewish students feel threatened. Ross's anti-

Jewish comments were not protected by s. 2(a); indeed, they eroded "the very basis of the guarantee in s. 2(a)" by demeaning a particular faith. La Forest had no difficulty in justifying the order under s. 1 of the Charter.

A more dramatic clash between religious freedom and protected rights is described in Dossier 8.3. In this case, as in *Ross*, the Court rejected the claim that the faith of one person outweighs the interests of others.

DOSSIER 8.3

MEDICAL TREATMENT VERSUS RELIGIOUS FREEDOM

A premature baby born in Toronto, known to the law as Sheena B., required constant medical attention for a variety of physical ailments. Her parents were Jehovah's Witnesses; their faith forbids blood transfusions. When Sheena's doctors determined that she needed an operation to save her life, they asked the Children's Aid Society (CAS) of Metropolitan Toronto to seek temporary custody of the child. If the order were granted, the CAS would have the power to authorize the necessary transfusions. The CAS obtained the custody order and approved the transfusions. The operation saved Sheena's life. After recuperating for three weeks, she was returned to the custody of her parents. They sued the Children's Aid Society, claiming that their religious freedom had been infringed. Both the District Court and the Ontario Court of Appeal dismissed their claims.

The parents appealed to the Supreme Court, which heard their case in 1994.[1] The appeal turned on three questions. First, did the statute under which the order was granted violate parents' freedom to choose their children's medical treatment, and thus infringe s. 7 of the Charter? Second, did the statute violate their freedom of

religion under s. 2(a)? Finally, if either section of the Charter had been infringed, was the violation justified under s. 1?

Five Justices determined that the custody order, and the legislation under which it had been granted, infringed the parents' religious freedom by denying them the opportunity to make decisions for their child on the basis of their faith. However, the infringement was justified under s. 1 because the purpose of the law—the protection of vulnerable children—was pressing and substantial, and the wardship order had been handled in a fair and reasonable way. The other four Justices saw no infringement of s. 2(a). They argued that little Sheena "never expressed any agreement with the Jehovah's Witness faith or any religion," and that her freedom of conscience—not to mention her right to life and security of the person under s. 7—far outweighed her parents' freedom to express their religious beliefs.[2]

ENDNOTES

1. *B. (R.) v. Children's Aid Society of Metropolitan Toronto*, [1995] 1 S.C.R. 315.

2. *B. (R.) v. Children's Aid Society*, headnotes.

Two further characteristics of Canadian jurisprudence on religious freedom deserve mention. First, the Courts have read an "anti-establishment" clause into s. 2(a). Unlike the American Bill of Rights, the Charter does not explicitly prohibit a government from favouring one religion over another. But ever since *Big M Drug Mart*, the courts have ruled that state coercion violates religious freedom. As we have seen, s. 2(a) protects both the freedom *to* worship and freedom *from* worship. Second, rulings on religious freedom have relied almost exclusively on s. 2(a), despite the references to religion elsewhere in the Charter. In *Big M Drug Mart*, former Chief Justice Dickson suggested that a free and democratic society, by definition, grants all citizens the equal enjoyment of their fundamental freedoms without reference to s. 15. Subsequent rulings have taken a similar approach, bypassing ss. 15 and 27. While this may not be a problem in cases like *Big M*, where the impugned law is explicitly religious in intent, it does militate against religious minorities seeking relief from the unintended effects of secular laws. Most legislated infringements on religious freedom fall into the latter category because Canadian governments are no longer in the business of enforcing a particular faith. "Thus, in the hands of judges, the Charter has not provided as much protection for religion or religious multiculturalism as it might imply."[25]

Section 2(a): Summary and Conclusions

To date, the broad and unqualified guarantees in s. 2(a) have made little difference in Canadian law. While the courts have been uncompromising in their rejection of deliberate state-sponsored restrictions of conscience and religion, few such restrictions survived into the Charter era. Judges have been considerably more lenient toward secular laws that inadvertently infringe individual beliefs, even though such inadvertent violations are common in Canada's diverse society. Finally, s. 2(a) does not give individuals a blank cheque to act on their personal convictions—whether religious or secular in origin—without regard for the rights of others or the collective good. The state can no longer tell us what to believe (assuming that it has any interest in doing so), but it can still tell us what we can and cannot say or do about our beliefs.

Every individual retains the freedom to follow the dictates of her conscience or her deity, but she must be prepared to face the legal consequences of her choices.

Section 2(b): Freedom of Expression

Human beings are expressive creatures. We feel compelled to share our opinions and discuss our problems. We use sounds, images, and words to communicate our feelings. When we are prevented from expressing ourselves, by enforced isolation or other unfortunate circumstances, our well-being suffers. Usually, the people with whom we communicate share our views and appreciate our creative efforts. But the situation is more complicated when others reject our opinions or seek to suppress our creativity—especially when those others occupy positions of power.

Consequently, the greatest practical effect of s. 2(b) of the Charter is to protect unpopular or unorthodox opinions.[26] The freedom to dissent is a central value in liberal thought. In his essay "On Liberty," the Victorian philosopher John Stuart Mill defended the value of free expression for both the speaker and the audience:

> If all mankind minus one, were of one opinion, and only one person were of the contrary opinion, mankind would be no more justified in silencing that one person, than he, if he had the power, would be justified in silencing mankind. Were an opinion a personal possession of no value except to the owner; if to be obstructed in the enjoyment of it were simply a private injury, it would make some difference whether the injury was inflicted only on a few persons or on many. But the peculiar evil of silencing the expression of an opinion is, that it is robbing the human race; posterity as well as the existing generation; those who dissent from the opinion, still more than those who hold it. If the opinion is right, they are deprived of the opportunity of exchanging error for truth: if wrong, they lose, what is almost as great a benefit, the clearer perception and livelier impression of truth, produced by its collision with error.[27]

This famous passage has been cited by the Supreme Court, to elucidate the meaning and purpose of s. 2(b).[28] Its significance is twofold. First, it defends the freedom of the individual to express unpopular ideas. No such defence of mainstream ideas is required; the crunch comes when the majority finds an opinion offensive or misguided. Second, it argues that the search for truth demands the unrestricted exchange of ideas and information. An erroneous opinion cannot be proved wrong until it has been expressed; nor can a legitimate opinion be accepted as such until it has prevailed over contrary arguments. In either case, society as a whole—the audience as well as the speaker—reaps the benefit of expressive freedom.

Nowhere is a collective search for "truth" more important than in politics, which deals with issues of general concern. Long before Mill and other liberals championed freedom of speech, the ancient Greeks celebrated the freedom to exchange political opinions as the great virtue of Athenian democracy.[29] Aristotle famously described human beings as "political animals," because of their unique gifts of reason and speech. The latter "is intended to set forth the expedient and inexpedient, and therefore likewise the just and the unjust."[30] Only through the free exchange of political ideas and information can man reach his *telos*, or ultimate fulfilment: individual and collective self-government. The liberty to express political opinions without restriction by the state is the foundation of both individual freedom and democratic institutions.

This principle has long been recognized in Canadian law. As we saw in Dossier 2.3, pages 52–54,

Bill C-250 extended Canada's hate speech laws to prohibit expressions of homophobia. To some people, this was an unfair restriction on free speech.

Graham Harrop/artizans.com

Chief Justice Duff identified freedom of expression as a vital principle of our parliamentary Constitution in the 1938 *Alberta Press* case. But because the "implied bill of rights" never commanded majority support on the Supreme Court, governments have been free to restrict speech if they so chose. The purpose of s. 2(b), according to former Chief Justice Dickson, is to ensure that such restrictions are never reenacted—regardless of the form or content of expression at issue—unless the sponsoring government meets a strict test of justification under s. 1 (see Dossier 8.4).

DOSSIER 8.4

THE MEANING AND SCOPE OF SECTION 2(B)

In 1989, the Supreme Court issued its ruling in *Irwin Toy Ltd. v. Quebec (Attorney General)*. At issue was the constitutionality of a Quebec law that prohibited commercial advertisements aimed at children under thirteen years of age. Three of the five judges on the panel voted to uphold the law, despite the clear infringement of free expression, because they found that the infringement was justified under s. 1.

The significance of the *Irwin Toy* ruling lies in the majority's approach to s. 2(b). Chief Justice Dickson, together with Justices Wilson and Lamer, set out what has become the authoritative interpretation of "expression" under the

(continued)

Charter. When a plaintiff seeks to argue that a particular law violates his or her freedom of expression, the court must first determine whether or not the restricted activity lies within the scope of the 2(b) guarantee. That scope is defined so broadly as to be all but limitless:

> "Expression" has both a content and a form, and the two can be inextricably connected. Activity is expressive if it attempts to convey meaning. That meaning is its content. Freedom of expression was entrenched in our Constitution ... so as to ensure that everyone can manifest their thoughts, opinions, beliefs, indeed all expressions of the heart and mind, however unpopular, distasteful or contrary to the mainstream. Such protection is, in the words of both the Canadian and Quebec Charters, "fundamental" because in a free, pluralistic and democratic society we prize a diversity of ideas and opinions for their inherent value both to the community and to the individual....
>
> We cannot, then, exclude human activity from the scope of guaranteed free expression on the basis of the content or meaning being conveyed. Indeed, if the activity conveys or attempts to convey a meaning, it has expressive content and *prima facie* falls within the scope of the guarantee. Of course, while most human activity combines expressive and physical elements, some human activity is purely physical and does not convey or attempt to convey meaning. It might be difficult to characterize certain day-to-day tasks, like parking a car, as having expressive content. To bring such activity within the protected sphere, the plaintiff would have to show that it was performed to convey a meaning. For example, an unmarried person might, as part of a public protest, park in a zone reserved for spouses of government employees in order to express dissatisfaction or outrage at the chosen method of allocating a limited resource. If that person could demonstrate that his activity did in fact have expressive content, he would, at this stage, be within the protected sphere and the s. 2(b) challenge would proceed.

> The content of expression can be conveyed through an infinite variety of forms of expression: for example, the written or spoken word, the arts, and even physical gestures or acts. While the guarantee of free expression protects all content of expression, certainly violence as a form of expression receives no such protection. It is not necessary here to delineate precisely when and on what basis a *form* of expression chosen to convey a meaning falls outside the sphere of the guarantee. But it is clear, for example, that a murderer or rapist cannot invoke freedom of expression in justification of the form of expression he has chosen.[1]

Once a court has determined that the restricted activity merits protection, it must then proceed to the second stage of analysis under s. 2(b): "whether the purpose or effect of the impugned governmental action was to control attempts to convey meaning through that activity."[2] In some cases, the purpose of the law can be attained only by restricting expression (e.g., a law restricting the sale of pornography). In other instances, where a law is designed for some other purpose and incidentally restricts expression—for example, a municipal bylaw that bans postering on public property[3]—the incidental effects may be sufficient to violate s. 2(b)if the restricted activity engages the values that it protects:

(1) "seeking and attaining the truth is an inherently good activity"
(2) "participation in social and political decision-making is to be fostered and encouraged"; and
(3) "the diversity in forms of individual self-fulfillment and human flourishing ought to be cultivated in an essentially tolerant, indeed welcoming, environment not only for the sake of those who convey a meaning, but also for the sake of those to whom it is conveyed."[4]

If the plaintiff can demonstrate that the impugned law restricts a nonviolent expressive activity, he or she will discharge the burden of proof at the first stage of Charter analysis.

ENDNOTES

1. *Irwin Toy Ltd. v. Quebec (Attorney General)*, [1989] 1 S.C.R. 927, paragraphs 40–42.

2. *Irwin Toy*, paragraph 46.

3. See *Ramsden v. Peterborough (City)*, [1993] 2 S.C.R. 1084, in which the Court struck down such a bylaw on the grounds that it prevented citizens from advertising political and cultural events.

4. *Irwin Toy*, paragraph 52; see also *Ford v. Quebec (A. G.)*, [1988] 2 S.C.R. 712, paragraph 56, *per curiam*.

The constitutional protection of unpopular forms of speech is often controversial. As we will see, the claim that the Charter protects the rights of hate-mongers and child pornographers is rejected by many Canadians. The terrorist attacks of September 11, 2001, generated a new controversy: whether expression that allegedly furthers or endorses the aims of terrorist organizations should be exempt from the Charter guarantee. Under the 2001 Anti-Terrorism Act, an individual may be found guilty of participating in a terrorist group if he "uses a name, word, symbol or other representation that identifies, or is associated with" that particular organization.[31] The implicit substitution of nonviolent verbal or visual expression for a finding of intent to commit terrorism infringes both freedom of speech and the "principles of fundamental justice in s. 7 of the Charter. But in a ruling issued shortly after the attacks on New York and Washington, the Supreme Court signalled that such restrictions on expressive freedom would be upheld under s. 1: "expression taking the form of violence or terror, or directed towards violence or terror, is unlikely to find shelter in the guarantees of the Charter."[32] Indeed, a law that effectively criminalizes nonviolent expression in a terrorist context may not violate s. 2(b) at all. So the Court may be willing to exempt this class of speech from the ambit of the guarantee, either because it is analogous to violence—an approach that the majority of Justices rejected in an earlier ruling[33]—or because it constitutes a potential threat to other Charter values (e.g., security of the person).

The Content of Expression: "Core" and "Periphery"

Once the plaintiff has demonstrated an infringement of expressive freedom, the sponsoring government has to justify the infringement under s. 1. That task will be more difficult where the content in question engages one or more of the three values protected by the guarantee. Although the language of s. 2(b) implies that all forms and sources of communication should receive equal protection, the Supreme Court distinguishes among various types of content at the s. 1 stage of analysis.[34] As noted in Dossier 8.4, pages 257–59, the *Irwin Toy* ruling identified three "values" or "principles" that s. 2(b) is intended to protect. Content that advances scientific truth, political debate,[35] or artistic self-fulfilment is considered to be "core" expression, which merits the highest degree of protection. More "peripheral" content—some commercial advertising,[36] pornography,[37] hate propaganda,[38] or soliciting for the purpose of prostitution[39]—deserves less protection because it does not directly engage the purpose of the s. 2(b) guarantee. Consequently, a lower standard of justification under s. 1 is required for laws restricting "peripheral" expression than for those affecting "core" content.

The distinction between "core" and "peripheral" content arises from the "contextual approach" to s. 2(b) (see Chapter 3, page 106). When a court has to define the purpose of a particular Charter section, it should do so in the context of a particular set of facts. In particular, the purpose of the guarantee in s. 2(b) varies according to the type of expression at issue. The court should also consider the characteristics of the intended audience—e.g., its vulnerability to manipulation—and the potential impact of the expression. The context is relevant at both the initial stage of Charter scrutiny—determining the purpose of the allegedly infringed right or freedom—and again at the "balancing" stage under s. 1.

Perhaps the clearest example of the contextual approach, and its relationship to the content of speech, is the issue of commercial expression (i.e., advertising). This type of expression includes "speech of any kind that advertises a product or service for profit or for some business purpose."[40] The degree to which s. 2(b) protects commercial speech—in effect, whether business advertising should be considered "core" or "peripheral"—is disputed. As a general rule, the courts have refused to apply the Charter to the private economy. In other words, there are no "economic rights" in the Constitution.[41] For this reason, commercial advertisements are not entitled to the full protection of s. 2(b). On the other hand, an advertisement that imparts useful information to consumers, even while soliciting them to purchase a specific product, could promote the interests of the listener along with the profits of the sponsor.[42] The relative weight of these factors and the potential vulnerability of the audience can be only assessed in the context of a specific case.

Under *Irwin Toy*, s. 2(b) protects all nonviolent forms of expression. Therefore, commercial speech cannot be excluded from the protection of the guarantee altogether. The real issue is the stringency of the s. 1 justification for limitations on commercial advertising. As Dossier 8.5 points out, the stringency depends on both the content of the advertisement and the nature of the product being marketed.

DOSSIER 8.5

THE PROTECTION OF COMMERCIAL SPEECH

In 1990, the Supreme Court heard the case of two Ontario dentists who had advertised their services to the public. In so doing, they violated the rules of the Royal College of Dental Surgeons of Ontario. The dentists challenged the constitutionality of the advertising ban, arguing that it infringed their freedom of expression. The Supreme Court unanimously agreed, for the reasons given by Justice McLachlin (as she then was). She began by asserting that restrictions on purely commercial speech were easier to justify than those affecting political or artistic expression; lower profits were not as serious a matter as "loss of opportunity to participate in the political process or the 'marketplace of ideas,' or to realize one's spiritual or artistic self-fulfilment."[1] However, she noted that the advertising prohibited by the impugned regulation was not purely economic in effect:

> ... expression of this kind does serve an important public interest by enhancing the ability of patients to make informed choices. Furthermore, the choice of a dentist must be counted as a relatively important consumer decision. To the extent, then, that this regulation denies or restricts access of consumers to information that is necessary or relevant to their choice of dentist, the infringement of s. 2(b) cannot be lightly dismissed.[2]

McLachlin acknowledged that these two factors—the profit motive and consumer education—are present in every advertisement, although the balance between them varies with the type of ad and the nature of the product being marketed. Therefore, she refused to set out a general test for the constitutionality of commercial speech. Instead, she argued, judicial assessments should be case-specific and contextual, taking into account both the audience's vulnerability to manipulation and the nature of the product being advertised.

> Consumers of dental services would be highly vulnerable to unregulated advertising. As non-specialists, they would lack the ability to evaluate competing claims as

to the quality of different dentists. Indeed, the practice of dentistry, like other professions, calls for so much exercise of subjective personal judgment that claims about the quality of different dentists may be inherently incapable of verification. Furthermore, the choice of a dentist is, as noted above, a relatively important one. The consuming public would thus be far more vulnerable to unregulated advertising from dental professionals than it would be to unregulated advertising from manufacturers or suppliers of many other, more standardized, goods or services.[3]

McLachlin concluded that the particular regulations governing Ontario dentists were too broadly drawn to meet the "minimal impairment" test.

ENDNOTES

1. *Rocket v. Royal College of Dental Surgeons of Ontario*, [1990] 2 S.C.R. 232, paragraph 29, *per* McLachlin J.

2. Ibid., paragraph 30.

3. Ibid., paragraph 33.

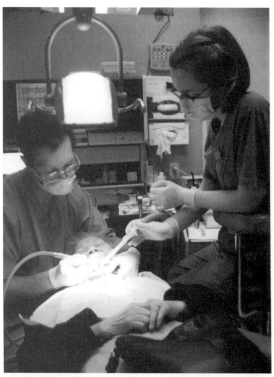

Some commercial advertising, such as this ad for dental services, receives the highest degree of protection under s. 2(b).

Photo by Neal Chan, www.netpac.com of Dr. D. Bays, Victoria, BC, in 2002.

The most controversial Court ruling on commercial speech concerned the 1988 Tobacco Products Control Act. The law prohibited tobacco advertising,

including the sponsorship of sporting and cultural events by cigarette companies. The act also required manufacturers to display unattributed health warnings on cigarette packages. RJR-MacDonald, one of Canada's largest tobacco companies, challenged the act as an infringement on free expression. In its 1995 ruling,[43] the Court agreed unanimously that the law infringed s. 2(b) of the Charter. However, five Justices found that the infringement was not justified under s. 1, while the other four took the opposite view. In the result, much of the act was struck down.

The majority, led by Justice McLachlin, took a dim view of "lifestyle advertising" that portrays tobacco use as a normal and healthy practice. McLachlin argued that a partial ban on cigarette ads, which targeted "lifestyle" campaigns and appeals aimed at teenagers, was justified by the proven health risks of smoking. But because the act prohibited *all* forms of tobacco advertising, including those—such as the placement of brand names and trademarks in public places—that were not shown to increase cigarette use, it failed the rational connection and minimal impairment prongs of the *Oakes* test. Whereas the dissenting Justices were willing to defer to Parliament's judgment that only an absolute ban could meet the legislative objective of discouraging tobacco use, the Justices in the majority refused to do so. As McLachlin put it, s. 1 requires that Charter infringements be "*demonstrably* justified." If the courts are too eager to accept Parliament's judgment, they risk "reliev[ing] the state of the burden the Charter imposes of demonstrating that the limits imposed on our constitutional rights and freedoms are reasonable and justifiable in a free and democratic society."[44]

Both sides took a contextual approach to the Charter issues in the case. The dissenters argued that the harmful effects of tobacco use mandated a low level of constitutional protection for advertisements that encouraged people to start smoking or discouraged them from quitting.[45] While the majority shared this concern about the health risks of cigarettes, it was not prepared to uphold an absolute restriction on tobacco advertising or the placement of unattributed health warnings on packaging. In his concurring judgment, Justice Iacobucci suggested that a "tailored" ban on tobacco ads, and the identification of Health Canada as the source of the health warnings on cigarette packs, would pass Charter scrutiny.[46] In

summary, the majority found that even potentially harmful commercial speech merited some degree of constitutional protection—at least in the absence of proof that "informational" or "brand name" advertising made vulnerable people more likely to smoke.

While the Court has been divided over the proper degree of Charter protection for commercial speech, political speech is universally regarded as "core" expression under s. 2(b). Canadian law has long recognized that democracy depends on the freedom of the speaker to express political views. Democracy also requires that voters be given the timely and accurate information they need to make an informed choice. Consequently, as Dossier 8.6 illustrates, the Supreme Court requires strong justification for laws restricting the free exchange of political opinions and information.

DOSSIER 8.6

THE IMPORTANCE OF POLITICAL EXPRESSION

In the 1998 *Thomson Newspapers* case, the Supreme Court struck down an election law without reference to the democratic rights in s. 3. The impugned law was s. 322.1 of the Canada Elections Act, which prohibited media companies from publishing new survey results in the 72 hours immediately before voting day. Section 322 was intended to protect the public from false or misleading opinion data as they made up their minds at the end of the campaign. The Royal Commission on Electoral Reform and Party Financing heard from several witnesses who expressed concerns about the bandwagon effect, the underdog effect, and other potential distortions of the voting process arising from survey results.[1] In its 1991 report, the commission recommended a publication blackout on election day itself and requiring media organizations to publish complete methodological information when they reported survey results.[2] When the act was amended in 1993, Parliament extended the blackout to 72 hours and omitted the methodology requirement.

In 1995, the Ontario Court (General Division) heard a motion from the Thomson newspaper

chain to declare the blackout unconstitutional. The Court dismissed the motion, finding that the law infringed freedom of expression but was justified under s. 1. The Ontario Court of Appeal upheld the ruling.[3] It found that the objective of the blackout, "to respond to widespread perceptions that opinion surveys can be distorting," was pressing and substantial; that it was rationally connected to the three-day ban; and that it constituted a minimal impairment of s. 2(b).

Thomson appealed to the Supreme Court of Canada, which overturned the Ontario Court of Appeal. Five Justices, led by Justice Bastarache, ruled that the infringement on freedom of expression was not justified under s. 1. Following the practice laid down in *Irwin Toy*, Bastarache began by identifying the publication of survey data as a protected activity under s. 2(b). He then observed that both the purpose and the effect of the impugned law restricted freedom of expression.[4] The real question was whether it could be justified under s. 1.

Justice Bastarache, citing the precedents discussed in this chapter, noted that "The degree of constitutional protection may vary depending on the nature of the expression at issue."[5] As we have already seen, some types of expression—such as pornography or hate speech—may be "more easily outweighed by the government objective" than those which reflect the core values of the Charter.

> In this case, the speech infringed is political information. While opinion polls may not be the same as political ideas, they are nevertheless an important part of the political discourse, as manifested by the attention such polls receive in the media and in the public at large, and by the fact that political parties themselves purchase and use such information. Indeed, the government argues that opinion polls have an excessive impact on the electoral choices made by voters. As a genre of speech, unlike hate speech or pornography, this expression is not intrinsically harmful or demeaning to certain members of society because of its direct impact, or its impact on others. It is without moral content, and yet it is widely perceived as a valuable and important part of the discourse of elections in this country....
>
> The government argues that there is the potential that *some* inaccurate poll might undermine the freedom of choice of the Canadian voter, or that *some* voters might be excessively influenced by polls. Leaving those exceptional or potential cases aside, polls are not generally inimical to the interests of Canadian voters. They are sought after and widely valued which, independently of their value to any one voter or specific content, places this type of speech at the core of the political process.... I would conclude that the nature of the expression in issue here does not *prima facie* suggest that a deferential approach is appropriate in this case.[6]

In other words, the government would have to demonstrate a genuine social harm arising from the unrestricted publication of survey data.

The majority concluded that no such likelihood had been proven. Unlike the lower courts, the Supreme Court rejected the claim that a "reasonable apprehension" of harm—without compelling evidence to substantiate it—could justify a law whose clear purpose was to restrict political expression. The government failed to prove, on a balance of probabilities, that the publication of misleading survey results in the last three days of an election campaign would distort the vote or damage the integrity of the democratic system. Justice Bastarache argued that Canadian voters were not dupes or simpletons, ready to jump on a political bandwagon just because they read some polling data.

> Canadian voters must be presumed to have a certain degree of maturity and intelligence. They have the right to consider the results of polls as part of a strategic exercise of their vote. It cannot be assumed that in so doing they will be so naïve as to forget the issues and interests which motivate them to vote for a particular candidate. Nor can Canadians be presumed to assume that polls are absolutely accurate in predicting outcomes of elections and that they thus will overvalue poll results.... I cannot accept, without gravely insulting the Canadian voter, that there is any likelihood that an individual would be so enthralled by a particular poll result as to allow his or her electoral judgment to be ruled by it.[7]

The law failed the rational connection and minimal impairment tests, and it was accordingly struck down. Echoing the Royal Commission on Electoral Reform and Party Financing, Justice Bastarache suggested that a shorter blackout period, coupled with the mandatory disclosure of survey methodology would be more consistent with the Charter.[8] Parliament duly amended the Canada Elections Act in 2000, prohibiting the publication of new survey results on the day of an election and requiring media outlets to accompany stories about polling data with the appropriate methodological information.[9] The law appears to have had little effect: "any improvement [in survey reporting] between 1997 and 2000 is so small that the act might as well never have been passed.... The media outlets responsible for the

(continued)

polls clearly did not ensure that the pollsters provided the required information, nor did they reply to formal requests to provide the missing information."[10] If Bastarache is correct in assuming that voters pay little attention to survey results, failure to comply with the reporting requirements may be of little consequence. But in light of the fact that one-quarter of voters wait until the end of a campaign to make up their minds,[11] and the evidence that some Canadians vote strategically—abandoning their first choice because of a perception that it cannot win, and opting instead for the best alternative[12]—Bastarache's assumption is open to question.

ENDNOTES

1. Guy Lachapelle, *Polls and the Media in Canadian Elections: Taking the Pulse*, vol. 16 of the collected research studies for the Royal Commission on Electoral Reform and Party Financing (Toronto: Dundurn, 1991), Chapter 2.

2. Royal Commission on Electoral Reform and Party Financing, *Reforming Electoral Democracy*, vol. 1 (Ottawa: Minister of Supply and Services Canada, 1991), pp. 460–66.

3. *Thomson Newspapers Co. v. Canada (Attorney General)*, Ontario Court of Appeal (1996), 30 O.R. (3d) 350, 92 O.A.C. 290, 138 D.L.R. (4th) 1, 37 C.R.R. (2d) 225, p. 359, quoted in *Thomson Newspapers Co. v. Canada (Attorney General)*, [1998] 1 S.C.R. 877, paragraph 75, *per* Bastarache J. (for the majority).

4. *Thomson Newspapers* [1998], paragraph 85.

5. Ibid., paragraph 91. The cited precedents included the *Edmonton Journal* case, *Rocket v. Royal College of Dental Surgeons of Ontario*, *Keegstra*, and *RJR-MacDonald* (all discussed in this chapter), as well as *Libman* (see Chapter 9, pages 290–91).

6. *Thomson Newspapers* [1998], paragraphs 91, 93, and 95.

7. Ibid., paragraph 101.

8. Ibid., paragraph 119.

9. Section 326 of the amended act requires all news organizations to provide the following data: the name of the survey sponsor, the company that conducted the survey, the date(s) on which respondents were questioned, the target population, the number of people contacted—although not, surprisingly the number of actual respondents—and the margin of error. Print journalists also had to provide the wording of the question or questions that generated the results reported in the particular story, as well as a source from which readers could obtain additional information if they so desired. Section 327 banned the news media from reporting unscientific polls (e.g., the "hamburger polls" run by some restaurants) as though they were reliable measures of public opinion. Finally, s. 328 contained the new, shorter blackout provision.

10. Claire Durand, "The 2000 Canadian Elections and Poll Reporting under the New Elections Act," *Canadian Public Policy* 28, no. 4 (2002), p. 545.

11. Jon H. Pammett, "The People's Verdict," in Jon H. Pammett and Christopher Dornan, eds., *The Canadian General Election of 2000* (Ottawa: Carleton University Press, 2001), Table 7, p. 306.

12. See, e.g., André Blais, Elisabeth Gidengil, Richard Nadeau, and Neil Nevitte, *Anatomy of a Liberal Victory: Making Sense of the Vote in the 2000 Canadian Election* (Peterborough: Broadview Press, 2002), Chapter 13

Despite the intrinsic importance of political expression in a "free and democratic society," the Supreme Court has upheld restrictions on certain forms of political speech. In particular, it has endorsed spending limits on "issue advertising" by interest groups during election campaigns.[47] As Chapter 9 explains, a majority of Justices believe that such restrictions are justified by the need to ensure equality between richer and poorer interests. In this instance, the *form* of the expression—paid advertising through the print and broadcast media—allows governments to restrict "core" *content*, albeit only during election campaigns. Less costly forms of political expression, such as postering[48] or handing out leaflets[49] may not be restricted by the state.

Freedom of the Press

Section 2(b) explicitly protects the freedom of the press. The courts have held that the right of the news media to convey information—and the corresponding right of Canadians to receive that information—should be given the widest possible scope.[50] But that scope is not unlimited, especially when press freedom conflicts with competing social values. One thorny issue is the relationship between press freedom and the needs of law enforcement—e.g., whether a journalist can legitimately refuse to turn over evidence that the police need to prosecute a criminal suspect. According to the Supreme Court, the answer depends on two factors: whether the evidence at issue can be obtained elsewhere, and whether the media outlet in question has already aired or published the relevant information. In general, a warrant to search the premises of a news organization demands a higher degree of proof than an ordinary warrant, because of the potential "chilling" effect of police searches on reporters and their sources. As former Justice La Forest put it, "the freedom to disseminate information would be of little value if the freedom under s. 2(b) did not also encompass the right to gather news and other information without undue governmental interference.... The press should not be turned into an investigative arm of the police."[51]

A second issue is the proper balance between press freedom and personal privacy. Trial judges often impose publication bans to protect the privacy of crime victims. News organizations sometimes challenge the bans, arguing that the public has a right to know as much as possible about a particular trial. The Supreme Court does not necessarily share this view, for the reasons explained in Dossier 8.7.

DOSSIER 8.7

PROTECTING THE IDENTITY OF SEXUAL-ASSAULT VICTIMS

In 1988, the Supreme Court issued its first major ruling on press freedom. The central issue was the constitutionality of s. 442(3) of the Criminal Code, which protects the identity of sexual-assault complainants by allowing the judge to impose a publication ban. The ban does not cover the details of the alleged crime, the name of the accused, or any other facts relating to the trial. The purpose of the law is to encourage victims of sexual assault to report the crimes against them and to pursue the charges to trial. If women who had already suffered the pain and humiliation of sexual assault knew that their names and the details of their ordeal would be made public, even fewer might come forward.

In the mid-1980s, an Ontario man was on trial for sexually assaulting his wife. She applied for, and was granted, a publication ban under s. 442(3). The Canadian Newspapers Company challenged the ban, and the statute under which it was granted, as a violation of press freedom under s. 2(b). The trial judge dismissed the Charter claim. The Ontario Court of Appeal reversed the decision, finding that the law violated press freedom and could not be saved under s. 1. Because publication bans were mandatory under the impugned law—in

(continued)

other words, the trial judge had to issue a ban to any plaintiff who requested it, without discretion—the provision failed the "minimal impairment" prong of the *Oakes* test.

The Supreme Court of Canada disagreed. In a unanimous decision authored by Justice Lamer (as he then was), the Court acknowledged the importance of press freedom in "a free and democratic society." Nonetheless, it found that the infringement of that freedom by a publication ban under s. 442(3) was justified. In the first place, the objective of the law—to encourage the reporting and prosecution of sexual crime—was pressing and substantial. Second, the mandatory ban was justified because it was the only effective way to achieve that objective.

> Obviously, since fear of publication is one of the factors that influences the reporting of sexual assault, certainty with respect to non-publication *at the time of deciding*

whether to report plays a vital role in that decision. Therefore, a discretionary provision under which the judge retains the power to decide whether to grant or refuse the ban on publication would be counterproductive, since it would deprive the victim of that certainty. Assuming that there would be a lesser impairment of freedom of the press if the impugned provision were limited to a discretionary power, it is clear, in my view, that such a measure would not, however, achieve Parliament's objective, but rather defeats it.[1]

So if a sexual-assault complainant wants a publication ban, her desire for privacy constitutes a justifiable limit on freedom of the press.

ENDNOTES

1. *Canadian Newspaper Co. v. Canada (A. G.),* [1988] 2 S.C.R. 122, paragraph 18 (emphasis in original).

While the Supreme Court is prepared to accept publication bans to protect the privacy of crime victims, it is less concerned about the participants in civil trials. In *Edmonton Journal* (1989), a majority struck down sections of Alberta's Judicature Act, which restricted news coverage of divorce cases. The impugned sections prohibited the publication of potentially embarrassing details (e.g., financial difficulties or alleged infidelities), even after they had been disclosed in open court. The Court ruled that the prohibition was too sweeping to be justified under s. 1 of the Charter. More broadly, it found that news coverage of court proceedings was a "core" form of expression: "It is ... essential to a democracy and crucial to the rule of law that the courts are seen to function openly. The press must be free to comment upon court proceedings to ensure that the courts are, in fact, seen by all to operate openly in the penetrating light of public scrutiny."[52] Although the majority acknowledged the importance of personal privacy and reputation, the protection of these values could not outweigh the infringement created by the absolute ban on publication.

Libel and Defamation under the Charter

Notwithstanding the outcome in *Edmonton Journal,* the Court has generally upheld laws restricting free expression where these are necessary to protect individual reputations. **Libel** denotes a statement or other form of expression that damages the reputation of its target. The law of libel originated as a self-protective measure on the part of the Crown; it now applies to both public figures and private citizens. To prohibit someone from expressing a negative opinion about another person is clearly an infringement of free speech. The question is whether that infringement can be justified, either by society's interest in accurate information or by the individual's desire to maintain a good name. In general, the courts have upheld the statutory and common-law rules against libelling and defaming individuals.[53] As Dossier 8.8, page 267 explains, statements injurious to the dignity and reputation of any person are "peripheral" expression, and merit little protection from the Charter.

DOSSIER 8.8

HILL V. CHURCH OF SCIENTOLOGY (1995)

The common law of defamation forbids one person to publicly attack the competence or integrity of another person without solid evidence and/or for purely malicious reasons. There is a partial exception to this principle: lawyers and legislators, in their official capacities, may make "privileged" statements regarding the character or conduct of an individual. But that privilege is qualified by the requirement that the defamatory statements be proven, that they further the cause of justice or the public good, and that they are uttered in furtherance of the speaker's public duties.

In 1984, Toronto lawyer Morris Manning stood on the front steps of the Toronto courthouse and told a crowd of reporters that a particular Crown prosecutor was both unprincipled and incompetent. Manning represented the Church of Scientology of Toronto, which believed that the prosecutor in question was persecuting them for their religious beliefs. Officers of the church, which had earlier labelled the prosecutor an "Enemy Canada," also participated in the press conference. The prosecutor sued for damages under the common law of defamation. At trial, the jury decided that Manning's statements had not been privileged; those comments, together with documents distributed to the media by Scientology, had caused serious and malicious damage to the prosecutor's reputation. They awarded the plaintiff more than a million dollars in damages, most of which would be paid by the Church of Scientology. The Ontario Court of Appeal upheld the verdict and the damages.

The Supreme Court of Canada agreed. The majority began by identifying defamation as a "peripheral" form of expression. In the words of Justice Cory, "False and injurious statements cannot enhance self-development. Nor can it ever be said that they lead to healthy participation in the affairs of the community. Indeed, they are detrimental to the advancement of these values and harmful to the interests of a free and democratic society."[1] Consequently, the suppression of such statements would require little in the way of justification. While the common law is not fully subject to the Charter, including the formal application of the *Oakes* test, Justice Cory ruled that it must conform to Charter principles. Therefore, the law of defamation must strike a proper balance between freedom of expression and competing social values.

The competing social value in this case is the protection of individual reputation. Justice Cory noted that "A good reputation is closely related to the innate worthiness and dignity of the individual";[2] these are Charter values of equivalent weight to free expression. "It follows that the protection of the good reputation of an individual is of fundamental importance to our democratic society."[3] Moreover, the law of defamation engages the constitutional right to privacy. Cory concluded that the common law of defamation struck an appropriate balance between free expression and the privacy and dignity of the individual. The damage award was reaffirmed.

ENDNOTES

1. *Hill v. Church of Scientology of Toronto*, [1995] 2 S.C.R. 1130, paragraph 106.

2. Ibid., paragraph 107.

3. Ibid., paragraph 120.

In 1998, the statutory law of libel faced a similar challenge. John and Joanna Lucas had been convicted of libel against a Saskatchewan police officer. They had picketed the courthouse where the officer worked, carrying signs that accused him of sexually abusing children. There was no evidence to support these allegations. They challenged the constitutionality of the Criminal Code provisions against defamatory libel, arguing that the law was an unjustified infringement of s. 2(b) of the Charter. The trial judge dismissed the argument and found both defendants guilty. The Saskatchewan Court of Appeal affirmed the verdict.

The Supreme Court of Canada unanimously agreed that the law was constitutional, with one exception. Section 299(c) of the Criminal Code, under which a person could be convicted of libel if the only person aware of the defamatory statement was the target him- or herself, was declared overbroad and severed from the rest of the section. The Court held that the nature of the expression—false and defamatory statements injurious to the reputation of another person—was protected by s. 2(b), but the law restricting it was easy to justify under s. 1. The minimal impairment prong of the *Oakes* test depended on the issue of *mens rea*. Specifically, did a libel conviction require proof that the accused intended to

The *Sharpe* case provoked public debate about the proper limits of free expression.

Bruce MacKinnon/artizans.com

defame the target—in other words, that the accused knew the libellous statements were both false and injurious? Justice Cory concluded that it did, and that the requirement on the Crown to demonstrate a guilty intent saved the law from violating the Charter. Because the evidence showed that Mr. and Mrs. Lucas were aware that the accusations on their placards were unfounded, Justice Cory upheld both the impugned law and the criminal convictions.

Child Pornography and Hate Propaganda: The Most "Peripheral" Forms of Expression

Few Canadians would publicly endorse the right of any person to produce, use, or distribute sexual images of children. The creation of photographic or video images entails the traumatic exploitation of innocent victims. Although there is no conclusive scientific proof, most people find it reasonable to assume that the consumption of such materials may encourage others to commit similar violations. Similarly, most of us are shocked and revolted by hate propaganda against vulnerable religious or racial minorities. In particular, it is difficult for many people to accept the claim that a Holocaust denier deserves any constitutional protection for his writings and speeches.

But despite the worthlessness of such material, both moral and historical, the broad definition of expressive freedom in *Irwin Toy* extends the protection of s. 2(b) to all nonviolent forms of expression. The real question is whether an infringement of the freedom to distribute child pornography or hate propaganda could be found to be *un*justified. Given the intrinsic importance of free expression, however, the constitutionality of laws that restrict even the most "peripheral" types of content cannot simply be assumed.

In 1993, Parliament amended the Criminal Code to prohibit the production, possession, and distribution of child pornography. Bill C-128 defined "child pornography" as any visual material that shows "a person who is or is depicted as being under the age of eighteen years and is engaged or is depicted as engaged in explicit sexual activity" or that depicts the body of a child with undue emphasis on the genital or anal regions.[54] The definition also covered written or visual material that promotes sexual activity with children. However, it excluded material that has "artistic merit or an educational, scientific or medical purpose." The law was intended to strike a balance between the Charter guarantee of free expression on the one hand and the need to protect children from sexual exploitation on the other. It goes without saying that the objective was politically popular. The question was whether the proper balance had been struck. If the law went too far in restricting self-expression, it would be nullified by the courts. Dossier 8.9 describes the Supreme Court's answer.

DOSSIER 8.9

R. V. SHARPE (2002)

John Robin Sharpe was arrested in 1998, after police searched his home. He was charged with simple possession of child pornography and with possession for the purpose of distribution. One of the simple possession charges related to written materials seized from Mr. Sharpe's home, which he claimed he had created purely for his own enjoyment. They did not contain images of real children; they were works of fiction that did not appear to be inspired by actual victimization. Sharpe's lawyer challenged the constitutionality of the simple possession charge, arguing that it violated s. 2(b) of the Charter and could not be saved under s. 1. The Crown acknowledged the Charter infringement, but defended the law as a necessary measure to protect children. Both the trial judge and the British Columbia Court of Appeal found for Mr. Sharpe, ruling that the simple possession charge was neither rationally connected to the law's objective nor "minimally impairing" of free expression.

The core issue for the Supreme Court was whether, and to what degree, the Charter protected Mr. Sharpe's freedom to craft pornographic fictions for his own enjoyment. Chief Justice McLachlin began her majority ruling by noting that child pornography did not fit two of the three principles that underlie the guarantee in s. 2(b), namely the search for truth and the engagement of the citizenry in politics. However, it did engage the third principle: the search for self-fulfilment, albeit of a sort that most Canadians find repugnant.[1] Next,

McLachlin ruled that the simple possession of expressive materials fell under the protection of s. 2(b); communication with another party was not required for "free expression."[2] Nonetheless, she noted that fictional materials that are never shared with others pose considerably less risk of harm to children than, say, sexually explicit photographs posted on the Web.[3] Moreover, "self-created works of the imagination, written or visual, intended solely for private use by the creator" engage values central to the Charter:

> The intensely private, expressive nature of these materials deeply implicates s. 2(b) freedoms, engaging the values of self-fulfilment and self-actualization and engaging the inherent dignity of the individual... Personal journals and writings, drawings and other forms of visual expression may well be of importance to self-fulfilment. Indeed, for young people grappling with issues of sexual identity and self-awareness, private expression of a sexual nature may be crucial to personal growth and sexual maturation. The fact that many might not favour such forms of expression does not lessen the need to insist on strict justification for their prohibition.[4]

In the end, McLachlin upheld the prohibition of simple possession with two exceptions: "private works of the imagination" that did not involve actual victimization, and self-depictions for personal use. She wrote that "The inclusion of these peripheral materials in the law's prohibition

(continued)

trenches heavily on freedom of expression while adding little to the protection the law provides children. To this extent, the law cannot be considered proportionate in its effects, and the infringement of s. 2(b) contemplated by the legislation is not demonstrably justifiable under s. 1."[5] She "read in" exceptions for those two categories of material and left the remainder of the law unchanged.

ENDNOTES

1. *R. v. Sharpe*, [2001] 1 S.C.R. 45, paragraph 24.

2. Ibid., paragraph 25.

3. Ibid., paragraphs 59, 76–77, and 100.

4. Ibid., paragraph 107.

5. Ibid., paragraph 110.

The Court's decision to uphold the child pornography law surprised many observers. Charter skeptics expected the Supreme Court to affirm the British Columbia Court of Appeal, thereby endorsing its preference for free expression over the goal of child protection. Although the law was upheld in its entirety, with only two limited exceptions added, the decision was greeted with dismay by some police officers and child advocates. Under pressure from victims' rights groups and others, Parliament moved to close the new loopholes when it introduced Bill C-20 in December 2002. The defences to a charge of simple possession were narrowed, and the offences broadened to include much of the material that Chief Justice McLachlin had "read out" of the law. At the time of writing, the bill had yet to receive parliamentary approval.[55]

Like child pornography, hate propaganda is widely perceived as a threat to the self-esteem and security of vulnerable groups in Canadian society. Under the "large and liberal" approach, as set out in *Irwin Toy*, the courts are required to extend Charter protection to all forms of nonviolent expression. Some critics argue that speech that promotes hatred against identifiable groups should be excluded, both because it is untrue and because it is analogous to violence. Moreover, anti-Semitism and other forms of racist propaganda conflict with Charter values of equality and multiculturalism. On the other side of the issue, civil libertarians argue that hatred cannot be eradicated unless it comes out into the open. Nor can we hope to offer persuasive arguments against hate propaganda without confronting it directly, instead of driving it underground by prosecuting its distributors.

At the extreme, laws against hate speech may be caricatured as political correctness run amok—as the illegitimate censorship of ideas that may be offensive to some people but that cause no real harm.[56]

The Supreme Court's approach to hate speech has not been entirely consistent. In general, the Court has considered expression that demeans the human dignity of a particular group to be unworthy of strict constitutional protection. But the Court has been deeply split over the proper balance between free speech and the protection of vulnerable groups from public expressions of hatred and contempt. In the two best-known cases on the issue, *Keegstra* (1990)[57] and *Zundel* (1992),[58] seven-judge panels reached opposite conclusions by 4-3 margins. While it is tempting to conclude that the outcomes were determined by the composition of the judicial panels that heard the two cases, the differences between the impugned laws were at least as significant. Keegstra challenged the law against hate speech, which was sufficiently well-crafted to pass the *Oakes* test. Zundel impugned the law against spreading "false news," an outdated provision ripe for nullification. The two cases are discussed in Dossier 8.10, pages 271–72.

Keegstra and *Zundel* left many questions unanswered. How, if at all, can we distinguish between permissible and impermissible expression about religious and ethnic minorities? Is it necessary to prove that a particular statement causes tangible harm (e.g., by provoking the listener to commit violence against a vulnerable person), or is the damage caused by hate propaganda to the human dignity of the targets sufficient to justify infringing s. 2(b)? Finally, which causes the greater harm to expressive freedom:

DOSSIER 8.10

HATE SPEECH AND THE CHARTER

The *Keegstra* case arose from the conviction of an Alberta high school teacher under s. 319(2) of the Criminal Code. That section provides that "Every one who, by communicating statements, other than in private conversation, wilfully promotes hatred against any identifiable group" is guilty of an offence. Section 319(3) provides four separate defences, including proof that the offending statements are true and attempt to counter hate speech by exposing errors. James Keegstra was found guilty of uttering anti-Semitic statements in his classroom. He tried to convince his history students that the Holocaust never happened, and he expected them to parrot his beliefs in their written work for his class. He was convicted at trial, after the judge dismissed his claim that the law violated his freedom of expression. The Alberta Court of Appeal overturned the conviction. It ruled that s. 319(2) of the Code was not justified under s. 1 of the Charter because there was no demonstrable connection between the harm caused by actual hatred and the effects of hearing hate speech. The law was overbroad because it permitted the conviction of a person who honestly (but mistakenly) believed in the truth of his statements or whose efforts to incite hatred were ineffective. The federal government appealed to the Supreme Court.

The Justices were deeply divided. Chief Justice Dickson wrote for the majority, joined by Justices Wilson, L'Heureux-Dubé, and Gonthier. He ruled that the hate speech law infringed s. 2(b), but it was justified by the importance of protecting vulnerable groups in society. He also found that ss. 15 and 27 of the Charter should be taken into account at the s. 1 stage of analysis, although they could not be used at the first stage to limit the scope of the protection offered by s. 2(b). Justice McLachlin wrote the dissent, which was supported by Justices La Forest and Sopinka. She agreed with the Alberta Court of Appeal that s. 319(2) of the

Code was too broad. She also speculated that the prohibition of unpopular expression could backfire on the government, by publicizing hate groups and turning their leaders into political martyrs. Finally, McLachlin suggested that the "chilling" effect of s. 319(2) could stifle political and social debate, without making life any easier for vulnerable groups. In the end, the law was upheld and Keegstra was sent to prison.

The division on the Court was predictable. Justice McLachlin has always insisted on the primacy of free expression, while Justice Sopinka was reluctant to accept laws that could permit the conviction of a morally innocent person. On the other side, Justices Dickson, Wilson, and L'Heureux-Dubé consistently upheld equality rights and the protection of vulnerable groups. Two years after *Keegstra*, when the Court issued its ruling in *Zundel*, the membership of the Court had changed. Justices Dickson and Wilson had retired; their places on the new seven-judge panel were taken by Justices Cory and Iacobucci. Among the remaining members of the *Keegstra* panel, McLachlin, Sopinka, and La Forest were consistent: they voted to uphold a law restricting hate speech. Justice Gonthier remained firmly on the opposite side, where he was joined by the two newer members of the panel. The swing vote belonged to Justice L'Heureux-Dubé, who abandoned her earlier position and voted to uphold the law at issue in the *Zundel* case.

The *Zundel* majority, led by Justice McLachlin, held that s. 2(b) protects the dissemination of deliberate falsehoods; consequently, s. 181 infringed the guarantee of expressive freedom. The infringement was unjustified, partly because the original objective of the law—to protect the powerful against slanderous attack—was no longer "pressing and substantial." Nor did it really apply to the offences committed by Mr. Zundel. He ran a

(continued)

small publishing house in Toronto, devoted to producing and distributing books and pamphlets denying the Holocaust.[1] He was not attacking "the nobles of the realm"; instead, he appears to have been attempting to remove the stain of Nazism and the "final solution" from German history. Therefore, unlike the law upheld in *Keegstra*, the "false news" provision was neither "rationally connected" to the purpose of protecting the vulnerable nor "minimally impairing" of free expression.

ENDNOTES

1. For an account and analysis of Zundel's career as a Holocaust denier, see Michael Shermer and Alex Grobman, *Denying History: Who Says the Holocaust Never Happened and Why Do They Say It?* (Berkeley: University of California Press, 2002). See also D.D. Gutttenplan, *The Holocaust on Trial* (New York: Norton, 2001), pp. 52–54.

restricting certain forms of speech, or stifling the voices of those who seek to undermine the "values central to freedom of expression"?[59]

The debates over child pornography and hate speech reveal the difficulty of balancing expressive freedom against competing social values. For those who believe that some types of nonviolent expression can be harmful in and of themselves, the need to restrict that expression is self-evident. Others argue that expressive freedom is too important to be restricted on hypothetical grounds. The courts have attempted to resolve the controversies over s. 2(b) on a case-by-case basis, weighing the various interests at stake in the context of each dispute. While this may be the most helpful approach from a judicial perspective, it can leave legislators and other policy-makers in the dark when they attempt to craft new laws trenching on freedom of expression.

SECTION 2(D): FREEDOM OF ASSOCIATION

According to former Chief Justice Dickson, the purpose of s. 2(d) is twofold: "protecting individuals from the vulnerability of isolation and ensuring the potential of effective participation in society."[60] The late Justice Sopinka offered a more detailed definition of associative freedom:

[F]irst, that s. 2(d) protects the freedom to establish, belong to and maintain an association;

second, that s. 2(d) does not protect an activity solely on the ground that the activity is a foundational or essential purpose of an association; third, that s. 2(d) protects the exercise in association of the constitutional rights and freedoms of individuals; and fourth, that s. 2(d) protects the exercise in association of the lawful rights of individuals.[61]

In other words, s. 2(d) protects lawful collective activities. Whatever an individual may lawfully do alone, he may do in concert with one or more additional persons. However, an activity does not automatically merit Charter protection merely because it is performed in association. For example, a religious group that seeks to deter women from entering an abortion clinic cannot use s. 2(d) to defend itself against criminal charges by arguing that this activity is an essential purpose of its organization.

Under this narrow reading of associative freedom, s. 2(d) serves no real purpose in the Charter. It is surely unnecessary to reiterate that one may exercise one's freedom of expression in a group, inasmuch as talking to oneself cannot be regarded as the focus of s. 2(b). Nor are the freedom of conscience and religion in s. 2(a) explicitly restricted to solitary individuals; they obviously protect group activities (e.g., religious ceremonies). If, as the Supreme Court insisted, s. 2(d) conferred no protection for specifically *collective* freedoms, then the guarantee was meaningless and redundant.

In recent years, the Court has adopted a more expansive approach to s. 2(d)—one more in keeping with the "large and liberal" interpretation of other protected rights and freedoms. Many of the internal limitations that it had imposed on associative freedom were abandoned in the 2001 *Dunmore* ruling (Dossier 8.12, pages 276–77). At present, legislated limits on collective action must be justified under s. 1; they are not automatically upheld because they fall outside the narrow scope of the guarantee.

Most of the jurisprudence on s. 2(d) has arisen in the context of labour relations. When the Charter was first proclaimed, some observers regarded s. 2(d) as a boon to the labour movement. They predicted that the courts would use the guarantee of associative freedom to protect and extend the statutory privileges of unions, including strikes and collective bargaining. These expectations were dashed in 1986 and 1987. In contrast to the "large and liberal" approach to the other fundamental freedoms, the Supreme Court narrowed associative freedom by excluding labour relations from Charter protection.[62] Because it defined the freedom to associate in purely noneconomic terms, the Court permitted governments to restrict the activities of organized labour without having to justify those restrictions under s. 1.

The Supreme Court first signalled its unwillingness to extend full Charter protection to organized labour in the 1986 *Dolphin Delivery* case (discussed in Dossier 1.4, pages 22–24). On April 9, 1987, the Court issued three rulings that are collectively called the "labour trilogy."[63] The most important was the *Alberta Labour Reference*, which determined the outcome of the other two cases. Justice McIntyre's majority opinion, and the dissenting judgment of former Chief Justice Dickson, are summarized in Dossier 8.11. The majority ruling restricted the scope of s. 2(d) in two ways: (1) it excluded economic interests from Charter protection; (2) it claimed that the Charter guaranteed only individual rights, not collective rights. In other words, individuals could choose to exercise their constitutional rights in a group; but the group per se could not claim special Charter rights under s. 2(d).

McIntyre's approach was consistent with the liberal view of rights. From this perspective, human beings are free individuals who enjoy certain "inalienable rights" by virtue of their reason. The state cannot interfere with the free exercise of those rights, unless it somehow threatens the greater good. Nor can it intervene in the free market for goods, services, and labour. Private property and individual liberty are sacred concepts in the liberal tradition. On this view, the Charter—itself a strongly liberal document—does not and should not protect specifically collective and/or economic rights.

DOSSIER 8.11

THE "OLD LABOUR TRILOGY"

In 1983, the lieutenant governor of Alberta, at the request of the Conservative government, exercised his reference powers under the provincial Judicature Act. He asked the Court of Appeal to determine the constitutionality of three new labour laws. The laws removed the right to strike from various public-sector unions and imposed compulsory arbitration to resolve disputes between labour and management. The Alberta Court of Appeal advised the lieutenant governor that the laws did not violate the Charter, because s. 2(d) did not protect the collective rights of union members. Four of the seven Supreme Court Justices who heard the case agreed with the lower court's decision. One Justice did not issue an opinion, and the other two—then–Chief Justice Dickson and Justice Wilson—dissented.

On behalf of the majority, Justice McIntyre ruled that the Charter did not protect either the right to strike or the right to bargain collectively in the workplace. Although he acknowledged that the protected rights and freedoms were to be given a broad and generous construction, McIntyre took a different approach to s. 2(d). He declared that freedom of association belongs to the individual members of a group, not to the group as a discrete entity.

(continued)

Collective bargaining is a group concern, a group activity, but the group can exercise only the constitutional rights of its individual members on behalf of those members. If the right asserted is not found in the Charter for the individual, it cannot be implied for the group merely by the fact of association. It follows as well that the rights of the individual members of the group cannot be enlarged merely by the fact of association.[1]

Because there is no individual right to withdraw one's labour in order to apply economic pressure to the employer, there can be no Charter right to strike.[2]

Second, McIntyre argued that the Charter does not protect peculiarly economic rights, such as the right to strike or to bargain collectively. "Since trade unions are not one of the groups specifically mentioned by the Charter, and are overwhelmingly, though not exclusively, concerned with the economic interests of their members, it would run counter to the overall structure and approach of the Charter to accord by implication special constitutional rights to trade unions."[3] McIntyre also noted that the Special Joint Committee that examined the draft Charter in 1980–81 had considered and rejected an amendment that would have specifically protected the right to strike. "This affords strong support for the proposition that the inclusion of a right to strike was not intended."[4]

Third, while the right of individuals to form political and social groups to further their interests is well established in the common law, the rights of labour unions are protected only by provincial and federal statutes. McIntyre argued that the constitutionalization of labour relations would be premature, and would involve the courts in disputes that they could not competently resolve. Finally, he applied the claim that the right to strike merited no Charter protection because it had not been deemed worthy of such protection before 1982. While McIntyre did not completely rule out the possibility of Charter protection for collective bargaining,[5] he

concluded that the laws at issue were not protected by the guarantee of associative freedom.

The dissent written by then–Chief Justice Dickson rejected much, but not all, of McIntyre's interpretation of s. 2(d). Dickson agreed that the freedom to associate is primarily an individual freedom.[6] But he did not accept the conclusion that McIntyre had drawn from this premise—that the absence of an *individual* right to strike precluded a *collective* right to strike under s. 2(d). According to Dickson, labour unions exist precisely because individual employees lack the power to force an employer to the table. In this context, the absence of an individual right to strike is meaningless. "The capacity to bargain collectively has long been recognized as one of the integral and primary functions of associations of working people"[7]— a function that the Charter should protect.

Nor did Dickson share McIntyre's view that economic rights had no place in the Charter: "If by this it is meant that something as fundamental as a person's livelihood or dignity in the workplace is beyond the scope of constitutional protection, I cannot agree."

Work is one of the most fundamental aspects in a person's life, providing the individual with a means of financial support and, as importantly, a contributory role in society. A person's employment is an essential component of his or her sense of identity, self-worth and emotional well-being. Accordingly, the conditions in which a person works are highly significant in shaping the whole compendium of psychological, emotional and physical elements of a person's dignity and self respect.[8]

Dickson also dismissed McIntyre's "frozen rights" approach: "The Constitution is supreme law. Its provisions are not to be circumscribed by what the Legislature has done in the past, but, rather, the activities of the Legislature— past, present and future—must be consistent with the principles set down in the Constitution."[9]

Most fundamentally, Dickson argued that the freedom to associate has always been a vital weapon in the hands of the powerless in their struggle against the powerful:

> Freedom of association is most essential in those circumstances where the individual is liable to be prejudiced by the actions of some larger and more powerful entity, like the government or an employer. Association has always been the means through which political, cultural and racial minorities, religious groups and workers have sought to attain their purposes and fulfil their aspirations; it has enabled those who would otherwise be vulnerable and ineffective to meet on more equal terms the power and strength of those with whom their interests interact and, perhaps, conflict.[10]

He concluded that, "Under our existing system of industrial relations, effective constitutional protection of the associational interests of employees in the collective bargaining process requires concomitant protection of their freedom to withdraw collectively their services, subject to s. 1 of the Charter."[11]

In the companion *PSAC* case, Dickson went even further: "I believe that freedom of association in the labour relations context includes the freedom to participate in determining conditions of work through collective bargaining and the right to strike."[12] While other aspects of his dissenting judgments have recently been endorsed by a majority of the Court (see Dossier 8.12, pages 276–77), this particular statement has not.

ENDNOTES

1. *Reference Re Public Service Employee Relations Act (Alta.)*, [1987] 1 S.C.R. 313, paragraph 157.

2. Ibid., paragraph 177.

3. Ibid., paragraph 178.

4. Ibid., paragraph 179.

5. *PSAC v. Canada*, [1987] 1 S.C.R. 424, paragraph 54.

6. *Reference Re Public Service Employee Relations Act (Alta.)*, paragraph 88.

7. Ibid., paragraph 92.

8. Ibid., paragraphs 90–91.

9. Ibid., paragraph 75.

10. Ibid., paragraph 87.

11. Ibid., paragraph 97.

12. *PSAC v. Canada*, paragraph 23.

There are good reasons to question this view of the Charter. In the first place, s. 6 guarantees the right to work in any province. Second, the language rights in ss. 16–23 obviously pertain to communities, not just to individuals. Third, Pierre Trudeau had hoped to incorporate economic rights into the Charter, following the model of the 1966 International Covenant on Economic, Social and Cultural Rights, although he recognized the difficulty of reaching agreement on these issues.[64] His proposal to protect property rights was deleted at the insistence of provincial governments, who feared the dilution of their power over "Property and Civil Rights" (s. 92(13) of the Constitution Act, 1867). So the omission of economic rights from the Charter is best understood not as a deliberate choice by the federal framers, but as a reluctant concession to gain the support of the provinces.

However flawed the Court's approach to s. 2(d) may have been, it remained intact for almost fifteen years.[65] In 1999, a new set of Justices began to signal a change in attitude. Over the next few years, the Court issued what may be called the "new labour trilogy." Labour unions have been recognized as a key social and political institutions, and not merely as economic organizations. Section 2 of the Charter now protects some, though not all, of their collective activities. In effect, the Court has repudiated key elements of McIntyre's majority ruling in the *Alberta Labour Reference*, in favour of Dickson's dissent.

The first chapter of the trilogy is the 1999 ruling in *U.F.C.W., Local 1518 v. Kmart Canada*.[66] The United Food and Commercial Workers at two Kmart stores in British Columbia were on strike. Some members of the local undertook secondary picketing at other Kmart stores, where they distributed leaflets urging shoppers to boycott the company until the labour dispute was resolved. The province's Labour Relations Board ordered the local to stop the secondary picketing. That order was subsequently appealed all the way to the Supreme Court of Canada, which unanimously declared that the definition of "secondary picketing" in the British Columbia Labour Relations Code violated the Charter guarantee of free expression. Justice Cory explicitly based his ruling on the dissent of former Chief Justice Dickson in the *Alberta Labour Reference*:

The importance of work for individuals has been consistently recognized and stressed. A person's employment is an essential component of his or her sense of identity, self-worth and emotional well-being. As well, the vulnerability of individual employees, particularly retail workers, and their inherent inequality in their relationship with management has been recognized. It follows that workers, particularly those who are vulnerable, must be able to speak freely on matters that relate to their working conditions.[67]

In the 2002 *Pepsi* ruling, the Court unanimously reiterated this positive attitude toward organized labour: "Workers have the right to be represented by a union, and when a union supported by a majority of the workers is in place, employers are obliged to negotiate in good faith with the union."[68] The Court's new approach to labour relations is clearly evident in the remaining case in the trilogy, which deals more explicitly with s. 2(d); it is discussed in Dossier 8.12.

The impact of the "new labour trilogy" should not be overstated. While the Court's new approach to expressive and associative freedom recognizes the social and political importance of organized labour,

---

DOSSIER 8.12

DUNMORE V. ONTARIO (2001)

The central issue in *Dunmore*[1] was the constitutionality of an Ontario law forbidding agricultural workers from forming unions. Eight of the nine Justices supported the opinion of Justice Bastarache, which laid the McIntyre doctrine to rest. Bastarache declared that the rights and freedoms of unions, which McIntyre had dismissed as purely economic and thereby excluded from constitutional protection, actually "lie at the core of the Charter."[2] Although Bastarache refused to recognize a constitutional right to strike or to bargain collectively, he argued forcefully that s. 2(d) protects the lawful activities of organizations per se. In other words, he defined the freedom to associate as a *collective* right, not merely the collective exercise of an *individual* right.

In some cases s. 2(d) should be extended to protect activities that are inherently collective in nature, in that they cannot be performed by individuals acting alone. Trade unions develop needs and priorities that are distinct from those of their members individually and cannot function if the law protects exclusively the lawful activities of individuals. The law must thus recognize that certain union activities may be central to freedom of association even though they are inconceivable on the individual level.[3]

Moreover, Bastarache argued that s. 2(d) may impose a positive duty on the state; this is a repudiation of McIntyre's liberal approach. In the context of labour relations, "it must be asked whether, in order to make the freedom to organize meaningful, s. 2(d) of the Charter imposes a positive obligation on the state to extend protective legislation to unprotected groups."[4] The Court ruled that by denying agricultural workers the opportunity to form unions, the Ontario law violated the guarantee of associative freedom. The violation was not justified under s. 1.

ENDNOTES

1. *Dunmore v. Ontario (Attorney General)*, [2001] 3 S.C.R. 1016.

2. Ibid., paragraph 37.

3. Ibid., headnotes and paragraph 17.

4. Ibid., paragraph 20.

Charter protection has not been extended to strikes and collective bargaining. Nonetheless, a more positive attitude toward unions may reflect a willingness to consider such an extension in the future.

The Court's jurisprudence on organized labour has raised a separate issue: does s. 2(d) protect the freedom *not* to associate? This question arose in the 1991 case of Mervin Lavigne, an Ontario community college instructor who claimed that the rules of his union were unconstitutional.[69] Lavigne argued that the compulsory payment of dues to the Ontario Public Service Employees' Union (OPSEU), together with OPSEU's decision to give some of those dues to causes that he did not support, violated his freedoms of expression and association. The seven-judge panel unanimously ruled that there was no infringement of s. 2(b), but it was divided over the s. 2(d) issues. Three Justices ruled that the "mandatory check-off" rules for the payment of union dues infringed freedom of association, but the Charter violation was justified by the vital role of unions in Canadian society and politics. The other four found no infringement of s. 2(d).

The most contentious aspect of the ruling was the claim by four of the Justices—La Forest, Sopinka, Gonthier and McLachlin—that s. 2(d) guarantees the freedom *not* to associate. La Forest argued that a law that forces individuals to join particular groups is just as pernicious as a law forbidding them to associate with others:

Forced association will stifle the individual's potential for self-fulfillment and realization as surely as voluntary association will develop it.... One need only think of the history of social stag-

nation in Eastern Europe and of the role played in its development and preservation by officially established "free" trade unions, peace movements and cultural organizations to appreciate the destructive effect forced association can have upon the body politic. Recognition of the freedom of the individual to refrain from association is a necessary counterpart of meaningful association in keeping with democratic ideals.[70]

Justice McLachlin (as she then was) added another dimension to this "freedom from association": "the interest in freedom from coerced ideological conformity."[71]

On the other side of the issue, Justice Wilson (on behalf of herself and Justice L'Heureux-Dubé) argued that to recognize a freedom not to associate would necessarily involve the courts in disputes which they could not properly resolve:

to include a negative freedom of association within the compass of s. 2(d) would set the scene for contests between the positive associational rights of union members and the negative associational rights of non-members. To construe the section in this way would place the Court in the impossible position of having to choose whose s. 2(d) rights should prevail.... an interpretation leading to such a result should be avoided if at all possible.[72]

This dispute over the meaning of s. 2(d) came back to haunt the Court in 1999. In *Advance Cutting and Coring*, the Court was asked whether Quebec's labour laws—specifically, the requirement that construction workers join one of five unions in order to be legally employed in the province—violated the freedom not to associate. The Justices split four ways. Three of them, led by Justice LeBel, followed Justice McLachlin's ruling in *Lavigne*, and found that the law violated s. 2(d) because it enforced ideological conformity. Nonetheless, they upheld the law because it was found to be justified under s. 1. Justice L'Heureux-Dubé agreed with LeBel that the law was constitutional, but adhered to her earlier view that s. 2(d) did not protect freedom from association. Also concurring, Justice Iacobucci opined that the Charter did protect the freedom not to associate, but that the test should be broader than the "ideological conformity" standard adopted by Justice LeBel. The four dissenting Justices, led by Justice Bastarache, shared Iacobucci's view on s. 2(d) but did not consider the violation of s. 2(d) to be justified. While the recent retirement of Justice L'Heureux-Dubé might allow the Court to reach a consensus on this question, the other issues raised by the *Lavigne* ruling could take a long time to resolve.

CONCLUSION: FUNDAMENTAL FREEDOMS IN THE CHARTER ERA

In most respects, the entrenchment of the fundamental freedoms has made little difference in Canadian law and policy. One reason is that our governments rarely try to interfere with individual thought and belief. While inadvertent infringements occur frequently in a diverse society like Canada, these rarely trigger a judicial remedy. The state is more likely to restrict overt acts, including speech and association, than to concern itself with the ideas that motivate those acts—although the current "war on terror" may prove the exception to this rule. The 2001 anti-terrorism law defines terrorist offences in terms of the beliefs held by those who commit them. A violent crime "committed in whole or in part for a political, religious or ideological purpose, objective or cause"[73] may be subject to harsher penalties than an identical crime committed for other reasons; moreover, it may be investigated and prosecuted with minimal regard for the due-process rights of the accused.[74] At the time

of writing, few of these provisions had been subject to Charter review by the Supreme Court (see Chapter 13).

The heightened emphasis on national security has prompted the federal government to restrict the expressive and associative freedoms as well. As we have seen, the Anti-Terrorism Act restricts freedom of expression by treating the use of particular words or symbols as an indicator of involvement in terrorist organizations. The freedom to associate is more obviously infringed,[75] in at least two ways. First, an individual may be found guilty of participating in terrorist activity if he "frequently associates with any of the persons who constitute the terrorist group."[76] The law does not distinguish between a morally innocent person who happens to be related to a terrorist or whose friends are (unbeknownst to him) plotting to commit an offence under the act, and a person who knowingly participates in the planning and execution of a terrorist crime. Nor does it require that the accused knew or approved of any particular terrorist act committed by the organization. In effect, the government has substituted guilt by association for part of the *mens rea* element of the crime. Second, the Anti-Terrorism Act imposes a mandatory sentence of life imprisonment for any indictable offence committed "in association with a terrorist group."[77] Because the law lacks a clear definition of "association," it could permit a court to convict an innocent person and send him to jail for twenty-five years.

These infringements of s. 2 appear to be intentional, not inadvertent. The federal government believed, perhaps reasonably, that they would help to safeguard Canadians against the possibility of terrorist attacks. While the accuracy of this assessment is open to question, the real issue is whether the courts will defer to the executive and legislative branches. When judges are asked to balance limits on fundamental freedoms against the objectives of the Anti-Terrorism Act, national security will weigh heavily in favour of the latter. It is probable that they will find terrorist expression and association to be unworthy of strict Charter protection, and justify the restrictions under s. 1. But if they uphold the legislated infringements on conscience and religion, they will, for the first time, accept deliberate violations of the individual liberty to think and believe. Such an outcome should cause us to question whether any freedom is truly fundamental.

GLOSSARY OF KEY TERMS

establishment In the context of bills of rights, the term refers to an official religion. An established church is part of, or at least supported by, the political structure of a state. For example, the Church of England is the official church of the United Kingdom; its bishops sit in the House of Lords, and the monarch is its titular head (for nontheological purposes).

inter alia Latin for "among others."

libel A statement or other form of expression that damages the reputation of its target.

orthodoxy An opinion or belief that is required and enforced by the state or by a religious authority. Unlike "conventional wisdom," orthodoxy usually implies some kind of punishment for those who deviate.

DISCUSSION AND REVIEW QUESTIONS

1. How does "freedom of conscience" differ from "freedom of religion"? Briefly summarize the Supreme Court's jurisprudence on both guarantees.

2. Identify and briefly explain three ways in which "core" expression differs from "peripheral" expression. What is the relationship between these categories of expression and the justification analysis under s. 1?

3. Contrast the Court's approach to s. 2(d) in the "old labour trilogy" and the "new labour trilogy." Identify at least two differences.

4. In your opinion, has the entrenchment of the fundamental freedoms changed Canadian law in any significant way? Why or why not?

SUGGESTED READINGS

Durand, Claire. "The 2000 Canadian Elections and Poll Reporting under the New Elections Act." *Canadian Public Policy* 28, no. 4 (2002), pp. 539–45.

Moon, Richard. *The Constitutional Protection of Freedom of Expression.* Toronto: University of Toronto Press, 2000.

Smithey, Shannon Ishiyama. "Religious Freedom and Equality Concerns under the Canadian Charter of Rights and Freedoms." *Canadian Journal of Political Science* 34, no. 1 (March 2001), pp. 85–107.

ENDNOTES

1. F.L. Morton, Peter H. Russell, and Troy Riddell, "The Canadian Charter of Rights and Freedoms: A Descriptive Analysis of the First Decade, 1982–1992," *National Journal of Constitutional Law* 5 (1995), Table 5, p. 12.

2. James B. Kelly, "The Charter of Rights and Freedoms and the Rebalancing of Liberal Constitutionalism in Canada, 1982–1997," *Osgoode Hall Law Journal* 37 (1999) Table 5, p. 648.

3. The "Red Laws" criminalized membership and participation in Communist organizations. See F.R. Scott, "The Trial of the Toronto Communists" and "Freedom of Speech in Canada," in F.R. Scott, *Essays on the Constitution: Aspects of Canadian Law and Politics* (Toronto: University of Toronto Press, 1977), pp. 49–75.

4. *Reference Re Public Service Employee Relations Act (Alta.)*, [1987] 1 S.C.R. 313, paragraph 77, *per* Dickson C.J.C. (dissenting).

5. *Haig v. Canada; Haig v. Canada (Chief Electoral Officer)*, [1993] 2 S.C.R. 995.

6. Ibid., [1993] 2 S.C.R. 995, paragraphs 79–80, *per* L'Heureux-Dubé J. (emphasis in original).

7. Pierre Elliott Trudeau, "A Canadian Charter of Human Rights," January 1968, reprinted in Anne F. Bayefsky, ed., *Canada's Constitution Act, 1982 and Amendments: A Documentary History* (Toronto: McGraw-Hill Ryerson, 1989), vol. 1, p. 55.

8. Irwin Cotler, "Freedom of Conscience and Religion," in Gérald-A. Beaudoin and Ed Ratushny, eds., *The Canadian Charter of Rights and Freedoms*, 2nd ed. (Toronto: Carswell, 1989), p. 174.

9. *Roach v. Canada*, [1994] 2 F.C. 406 (F.C.A.).

10. *R. v. Big M Drug Mart Ltd.*, [1985] 1 S.C.R. 295, paragraph 121, *per* Dickson J.

11. The word "conscience" was deleted by the premiers in their draft Charter of August 28, 1980, for reasons that are unclear in the documentary record. See "The Charter of Rights and Freedoms, Provincial Proposal (In the Event that There Is Going to be Entrenchment)," reprinted in Bayefsky, *Canada's Constitution Act*, vol. 2, p. 678. Given their general concern about the breadth of the Charter's language and the transfer of power to the courts, it is reasonable to suppose that the premiers made this change in order to narrow the impact of entrenchment. The federal government made no consequential change to its own draft Charter, and there appears to have been no further objection.

12. *B. (R.) v. Children's Aid Society of Metropolitan Toronto*, [1995] 1 S.C.R. 315, paragraph 14, *per* Lamer C.J.

13. Ibid., paragraph 33, *per* Lamer C.J.

14. *New Brunswick (Minister of Health and Community Services) v. G. (J.)* [1999], 3 S.C.R., paragraph 58, *per* Lamer C.J.; *R. v. O'Connor*, [1995] 4 S.C.R. 411, *per* L'Heureux-Dubé J.

15. *Big M Drug Mart*, paragraph 123, *per* Dickson J.

16. *Ontario (Attorney General) v. Dieleman* (1994), 117 D.L.R. (4th) 449 (Ont. Gen. Div.).

17. Statistics Canada, "2001 Census: Religions in Canada," catalogue number 96F0030XIE2001015, pp. 5–9 and Table 1, accessed online at www.statcan.ca, September 17, 2003.

18. *Saumur v. Quebec (City)*, [1953] 2 S.C.R. 299, p. 329. Rand's claim that Canada has never had "an established church"—i.e., an organized religion openly affiliated with the state—is open to question. In the 1940s and 1950s, Quebec Premier Maurice Duplessis was determined to use the power of his office to defend the Roman Catholic Church. In the nineteenth century, the Church of England was similarly influential in the colony that later became Ontario.

19. *Zylberberg v. Sudbury Board of Education (Director)* (1988), 52 D.L.R. (4th) 577; *Canadian Civil Liberties Association v. Ontario (Minister of Education)* (1990), 65 D.L.R. (4th) 1.

20. *Zylberberg*, p. 592.

21. Shannon Ishiyama Smithey, "Religious Freedom and Equality Concerns under the Canadian Charter of Rights and Freedoms," *Canadian Journal of Political Science* 34, no. 1 (March 2001), pp. 85–107.

22. *The Queen v. Jones*, [1986] 2 S.C.R. 284, paragraph 3, *per* La Forest J.

23. *B. (R.) v. Children's Aid Society of Metropolitan Toronto*, paragraph 107 (emphasis added).

24. *Ross v. New Brunswick School District No. 15*, [1996] 1 S.C.R. 825, paragraph 72, *per* La Forest J.

25. Smithey, "Religious Freedom and Equality Concerns," p. 104.

26. As Chief Justice McLachlin put it in the 2001 *Sharpe* ruling, "Among the most fundamental rights possessed by Canadians is freedom of expression. It makes possible our liberty, our creativity and our democracy. It does this by protecting not only 'good' and popular expression, but also unpopular or even offensive expression.... If we do not like an idea or an image, we are free to argue against it or simply turn away. But, absent some constitutionally adequate justification, we cannot forbid a

person from expressing it." (*R. v. Sharpe*, [2001] 1 S.C.R. 45, paragraph 21).

27. John Stuart Mill, "On Liberty," in John Stuart Mill, *On Liberty and Other Essays*, ed. John Gray (Oxford: Oxford University Press, 1991 [1859]), p. 21.

28. See *RWDSU v. Dolphin Delivery Ltd.*, [1986] 2 S.C.R. 573, paragraph 13, *per* McIntyre J.; *Edmonton Journal v. Alberta (Attorney General)*, [1989] 2 S.C.R. 1326, paragraph 4, *per* Cory J.

29. See Thucydides's account of Pericles's funeral oration in *The History of the Peloponnesian War* (Harmondworth: Penguin, 1972), pp. 143–51.

30. Aristotle, *Politics*, trans. Benjamin Jowett (New York: Carlton Books, n.d.), p. 54.

31. Anti-Terrorism Act, 2001, c. 41, s. 83.18(4)(a).

32. *Suresh v. Canada (Minister of Citizenship and Immigration)*, [2002] 1 S.C.R. 3, paragraph 107, *per curiam*.

33. *R. v. Keegstra*, [1990] 3 S.C.R. 697, paragraphs 34–38, *per* Dickson C.J.

34. See the comment of former Chief Justice Dickson: "the s. 1 analysis of a limit upon s. 2(b) cannot ignore the nature of the expressive activity which the state seeks to restrict. While we must guard carefully against judging expression according to its popularity, it is equally destructive of free expression values, as well as the other values which underlie a free and democratic society, to treat all expression as equally crucial to those principles at the core of s. 2(b)." *Keegstra*, paragraph 82.

35. *Committee for the Commonwealth of Canada v. Canada*, [1991] 1 S.C.R. 139; *Ramsden v. Peterborough (City)*, [1993] 2 S.C.R. 1084.

36. See *Irwin Toy Ltd. v. Quebec (Attorney General)*, [1989] 1 S.C.R. 927; see also *RJR-MacDonald Inc. v. Canada (Attorney General)*, [1995] 3 S.C.R. 199.

37. *R. v. Butler*, [1992] 1 S.C.R. 452; *R. v. Sharpe*.

38. *Keegstra*; *R. v. Zundel*, [1992] 2 S.C.R. 731.

39. *Reference re ss. 193 and 195.1(1)(c) of the Criminal Code (Man.)*, [1990] 1 S.C.R. 1123.

40. Clare Beckton, "Freedom of Expression," in Gérald-A. Beaudoin and Ed Ratushny, eds., *The Canadian Charter of Rights and Freedoms*, 2nd ed. (Toronto: Carswell, 1989), p. 203.

41. See, e.g., *Reference Re Public Service Employee Relations Act (Alta.)*, paragraph 178, *per* McIntyre J. (for the majority).

42. *Ford v. Quebec (A. G.)*, [1988] 2 S.C.R. 712, paragraph 59, *per curiam*.

43. *RJR-MacDonald*.

44. Ibid., paragraph 138.

45. Ibid., paragraphs 75–77, *per* La Forest J.

46. Ibid., paragraph 191.

47. *Libman v. Quebec (Attorney General)*, [1997] 3 S.C.R. 569, *per curiam*; *Harper v. Canada (Attorney General)*, 2004 SCC 33, *per* Bastarache J.

48. *Ramsden v. Peterborough*.

49. *Committee for the Commonwealth of Canada v. Canada*, [1991] 1 S.C.R. 139; *U.F.C.W., Local 1518 v. Kmart Canada*, [1999] 2 S.C.R. 1083.

50. See the dissenting judgment of McLachlin J. (as she then was) in *Canadian Broadcasting Corp. v. Lessard*, [1991] 3 S.C.R. 421. See also the Court's unanimous ruling in *Canadian Newspaper Co. v. Canada (A. G.)*, [1988] 2 S.C.R. 122, especially paragraph 14 (*per* Lamer J., as he then was).

51. *Canadian Broadcasting Corp. v. Lessard*, paragraphs 2 and 7.

52. *Edmonton Journal v. Alberta*, paragraph 9, *per* Cory J.

53. The courts are less assiduous in protecting corporate reputations. In 2002, a Supreme Court endorsed the right of an individual to put up a sign claiming that he had received poor service from a particular insurance company: *R. v. Guignard*, [2002] 1 S.C.R. 472.

54. Bill C-128, An Act to Amend the Criminal Code and the Customs Tariff (Child Pornography and Corrupting Morals), s. 2, 34th Parliament, 3rd Session, royal assent in June 1993.

55. Bill C-20 died on the order paper when Parliament was prorogued in November 2003. It was revived in February 2004 as Bill C-12. The bill was passed by the House of Commons a few days before Parliament was dissolved for the 2004 general election; it reached first reading in the Senate before time ran out. See the legislative summary of Bill C-12 prepared by the Library of Parliament Research Branch (available online at www.parl.gc.ca).

56. The debate over hate speech is well summarized by Richard Moon in *The Constitutional Protection of Freedom of Expression* (Toronto: University of Toronto Press, 2000), Chapter 5.

57. *R. v. Keegstra*, [1990] 3 S.C.R. 697.

58. *R. v. Zundel*, [1992] 2 S.C.R. 731.

59. *Keegstra*, paragraph 89, *per* Dickson C.J.

60. *Reference Re Public Service Employee Relations Act (Alta.)*, paragraph 22.

61. *Professional Institute of the Public Service of Canada v. Northwest Territories (Commissioner)*, [1990] 2 S.C.R. 367, paragraph 74.

62. *Irwin Toy*, paragraph 40, *per* Dickson C.J.C. and Wilson and Lamer JJ.

63. *Reference Re Public Service Employee Relations Act (Alta.)*; *PSAC v. Canada*, [1987] 1 S.C.R. 424; *RWDSU Locals 544, 496, 635, 955 v. Saskatchewan*, [1987] 1 S.C.R. 460.

64. Anne F. Bayefsky, ed., *Canada's Constitution Act*, vol. 1, p. 60.

65. See, e.g., *Professional Institute of the Public Service of Canada v. Northwest Territories*; *Canadian Egg Marketing Agency v. Richardson*, [1998] 3 S.C.R. 157.

66. [1999] 2 S.C.R. 1083 (hereinafter cited as "*Kmart*").

67. *Kmart*, headnotes and paragraph 25.

68. *RWDSU Local 558 v. Pepsi-Cola Beverages (West) Ltd.*, [2002] 1 S.C.R. 158, *per* McLachlin C.J.C. and LeBel J., paragraph 24.

69. *Lavigne v. Ontario Public Service Employees Union*, [1991] 2 S.C.R. 211.

70. Ibid., paragraph 221.

71. Ibid., paragraph 280.

72. Ibid., paragraph 83.

73. Anti-Terrorism Act, s. 83.01(1)(b)(A)(i).

74. See Kent Roach, "The Dangers of a Charter-Proof and Crime-Based Response to Terrorism" and "The New Terrorism Offences and the Criminal Law," in Ronald J. Daniels, Patrick Macklem, and Kent Roach, eds., *The Security of Freedom: Essays on Canada's Anti-Terrorism Bill* (Toronto: University of Toronto Press, 2001), pp. 131–72. See also the chapters by Don Stuart and Gary Trotter.

75. See David Schneiderman and Brenda Cossman, "Political Association and the Anti-Terrorism Bill," in Daniels, Macklem, and Roach, *The Security of Freedom*, pp. 173–94.

76. Anti-Terrorism Act, s. 83.18(4)(b).

77. Ibid., s. 83.20.

Chapter 9

Democratic Rights

The right to vote in s. 3 is the foundation of a "free and democratic society."
CP PHOTO/Aaron Harris

Democratic Rights

3. *Every citizen of Canada has the right to vote in an election of members of the House of Commons or of a legislative assembly and to be qualified for membership therein.*

4. *(1) No House of Commons and no legislative assembly shall continue for longer than five years from the date fixed for the return of the writs of a general election of its members.*

    (2) In time of real or apprehended war, invasion or insurrection, a House of Commons may be continued by Parliament and a legislative assembly may be continued by the legislature beyond five years if such continuation is not opposed by the votes of more than one-third of the members of the House of Commons or the legislative assembly, as the case may be.

5. *There shall be a sitting of Parliament and of each legislature at least once every twelve months.*

INTRODUCTION: THE UNIQUE IMPORTANCE OF DEMOCRATIC RIGHTS

The "democratic rights" guaranteed by sections 3–5 of the Charter were the least controversial elements of the Constitution Act, 1982. Sections 4 and 5 merely consolidate the existing rules for Parliament—sections 50 and 20 of the Constitution Act, 1867, respectively—and extend them to the provinces and territories. Section 3 was more innovative: it entrenched voting rights previously enshrined in ordinary statutes, which could be repealed or amended at any time.

Another difference between s. 3 and the two subsequent sections is the nature of the rights contained therein. Whereas ss. 4 and 5 protect the political rights and freedoms of the electorate as a whole, whether national or provincial/territorial, s. 3 applies to individual citizens. In consequence, s. 3 has generated a fairly large body of litigation; the other rights in this section have not yet been invoked in court. Therefore, the remainder of this chapter will focus on the rights to vote and run for public office.

Section 3 differs from other Charter guarantees in several ways. First, unlike many of the legal rights, it does not contain an internal limitation clause. Consequently, there is no explicit instruction to judges to weigh the democratic rights against competing social values. The October 1980 draft of the Charter was more cautious; it guaranteed the rights in s. 3 "without unreasonable distinction or limitation."[1] This phrase was deleted in November 1981. The effect of the change was to strengthen the guarantee of political

rights, while forcing governments to rely solely on s. 1 of the Charter to justify infringements.

Second, electoral rights are central to the "free and democratic society" that the Charter reflects and defends.[2] In 1964, the then–Chief Justice of the U.S. Supreme Court identified the right to vote as the foundation of all other rights:

> Undoubtedly, the right of **suffrage** is a fundamental matter in a free and democratic society. Especially since the right to exercise the **franchise** in a free and unimpaired manner is preservative of other basic civil and political rights, any alleged infringement of the right of citizens to vote must be carefully and meticulously scrutinized.[3]

According to former Chief Justice Dickson, "the values and principles essential to a free and democratic society" include "faith in social and political institutions which enhance the participation of individuals and groups in society."[4] Canada's current Chief Justice is equally emphatic: "Charter rights are not a matter of privilege or merit, but a function of membership in the Canadian polity that cannot lightly be cast aside. This is manifestly true of the right to vote, the cornerstone of democracy."[5] Consequently, limits on democratic rights must meet a particularly stringent test of justification under s. 1.[6]

Third, the democratic rights—unlike legal rights—lie outside the "inherent domain of the judiciary."[7] Indeed, they seem to fall exclusively within the inherent domain of Parliament. Consequently, the proposition that judges should use the Charter to police the electoral process is particularly controversial (see Dossier 9.1).[8]

DOSSIER 9.1

SHOULD COURTS ANSWER "POLITICAL QUESTIONS"?

The arguments against judicial involvement in ~e electoral process are both practical and the-~al. On the practical side, legislators and ~ministers run for office; judges do not.[1] ~the latter cannot be expected to ~ne understanding of election laws

as those who are directly bound to follow them. Nor does there seem to be any need for the courts to "clean up" the democratic system: Parliament and the provincial legislatures removed most legislative barriers to suffrage and candidacy well before the Charter took effect. Most Canadian women received the federal franchise in 1920.[2] Race-based distinctions were more persistent. Many Asian Canadians were denied federal suffrage until 1947, while Aboriginal Canadians living on reserves could not vote, without giving up their tax-free status, until 1960.[3] As attitudes changed over the years, legislators responded by repealing outdated laws. No court order was necessary; indeed, as we saw in Dossiers 2.1 and 2.2, pages 50–51, courts were either unwilling or unable to force governments to broaden the franchise. From a theoretical standpoint, it has been argued that a country in which the rules of the electoral game are set by unelected judges is not fully democratic.[4] When the courts deal with "political questions," they violate the separation of powers and undermine democratic self-government.

The counter-arguments are mostly practical in nature. The central claim is that legislators cannot always be trusted to write the rules of their own game. The self-interest of ambitious politicians creates an incentive to rig the rules for their own benefit—e.g., by **gerrymandering** electoral districts or making it difficult for smaller and newer parties to compete. Therefore, unelected judges must defend democracy from the self-seeking excesses of elected officials.[5] Ely argues that "Courts must police inhibitions on expression and other political activity because we cannot trust elected officials to do so; ins have a way of wanting to make sure the outs stay out."[6] Laws regulating the right to vote require particular judicial scrutiny because "they involve rights (1) that are essential to the democratic process and (2) whose dimensions cannot safely be left to our elected representatives, who have an obvious vested interest in the status quo."[7] From this perspective, judges have a legitimate and necessary role to play in reinforcing representative democracy and ensuring electoral fairness to all parties. In a more theoretical vein, some judges have rejected the distinction between "political" and "nonpolitical" questions. They argue that if a plaintiff makes a plausible claim that his or her rights have been violated, the courts have a duty to consider that claim regardless of its subject matter.[8]

ENDNOTES

1. Senators are the exception: they are appointed by the prime minister. At the time of writing, only one senator had been elected by the voters in his province: the late Stan Waters won an Alberta-wide election to fill a vacant Senate seat and was appointed by Prime Minister Mulroney. Alberta elected another two senators subsequently, neither of whom has yet been appointed by the federal government.

2. Some Canadian women—those with sons or husbands fighting overseas—were allowed to vote in the 1917 "khaki election." White women with Canadian citizenship received the franchise in 1920. But many Asian women, even those born in Canada, could not vote federally until 1947, while Aboriginal women living on-reserve could not vote until 1960.

3. For an account of the evolving Canadian franchise, see Elections Canada, *A History of the Vote in Canada* (Ottawa: Public Works and Government Services, 1997).

4. This argument is made explicitly by Rainer Knopff and F.L. Morton in *Charter Politics* (Scarborough: Nelson, 1992), p. 367, and implicitly by Christopher Manfredi in *Judicial Power and the Charter: Canada and the Paradox of Liberal Constitutionalism*, 2nd ed. (Toronto: Oxford University Press, 2001), Chapter 6. See also Frederick Schauer, "Judicial Review of the Devices of Democracy," *Columbia Law Review* 94 (1994), p. 1336.

5. John Hart Ely, *Democracy and Distrust: A Theory of Judicial Review* (Cambridge, MA: Harvard University Press, 1980), especially Chapters 4 and 5. See also Terri Jennings Peretti, *In Defense of a Political Court* (Princeton: Princeton University Press, 1999), Chapter 1.

6. Ely, *Democracy and Distrust*, p. 106.

(continued)

7. Ibid., p. 117.

8. The leading opinion in Canadian law is the judgment of Wilson J. in *Operation Dismantle v. The Queen*, [1985] 1 S.C.R. 441, especially paragraph 64. See Chapter 5, pages 187–88 for a fuller discussion of the case.

Despite the arguments against their involvement, judges are now key players in the electoral process in both Canada and the United States. Until the 1960s, the U.S. Supreme Court refused to answer "political questions," on the ground that such questions properly belonged to the elected branches of government. In the words of the late Justice Frankfurter, "It is hostile to a democratic system to involve the judiciary in the politics of the people.... Courts ought not to enter this political thicket."[9] This doctrine was modified (if not abandoned altogether) in 1962: "The courts cannot reject as 'no law suit' a *bona fide* controversy as to whether some action denominated 'political' exceeds constitutional authority."[10] Since then, the highest American court has heard an average of six "political" cases per year, compared to one per year before 1960.[11]

Similarly, Canadian courts have been drawn into the political thicket with growing frequency in the Charter era. Although court cases over political rights were all but unknown before 1982—with a few exceptions (see Dossiers 2.1 and 2.2, pages 50–51)—the first successful Charter challenge to a federal law involved the Canada Elections Act.[12] The Supreme Court of Canada heard its first election-law case in 1989; in May 2004, it issued its fourteenth major ruling on the electoral process.[13] The cases are listed in Table 9.1.

Table 9.1 Supreme Court Rulings on Democratic Rights

Case	Charter Section	Issue	Disposition
MacKay v. Manitoba, [1989] 2 S.C.R. 357	2(b)	Do public subsidies to political parties infringe the expressive freedom of voters who do not support a particular party?	Case dismissed for lack of evidence; Manitoba law upheld
Committee for the Commonwealth of Canada v. Canada, [1991] 1 S.C.R. 139	2(b)	Can a federal facility (e.g., an airport) prohibit the distribution of political literature to the public?	No; federal regulation struck down
Osborne v. Canada (Treasury Board), [1991] 2 S.C.R. 69	2(b)	Can a government forbid its employees to engage in political activity?	Yes; provincial law upheld
Reference re Prov. Electoral Boundaries (Sask.), [1991] 2 S.C.R. 158	3	Can a government create an electoral map with unequal numbers of voters in rural and urban districts?	Yes; Saskatchewan electoral map upheld
Lavigne v. Ontario Public Service Employees Union, [1991] 2 S.C.R. 211	2(d)	Can a portion of union dues be used to support political causes which its members do not support?	Yes; collective agreement upheld
Sauvé v. Canada (Attorney General), [1993] 2 S.C.R. 438	3	Can a government deny prisoners the right to vote?	No; federal law struck down

Case	Charter Section	Issue	Disposition
Haig v. Canada; Haig v. Canada (Chief Electoral Officer), [1993] 2 S.C.R. 995	3	Can a government deny a citizen the right to vote in a referendum for administrative reasons?	Yes; Quebec and federal laws upheld
Ramsden v. Peterborough (City), [1993] 2 S.C.R. 1084	2(b)	Can a government prohibit postering on utility poles?	No; municipal bylaw struck down
Harvey v. New Brunswick (Attorney General), [1996] 2 S.C.R. 876	3	Can a government prohibit a person convicted of electoral violations from running for office again?	Yes; New Brunswick law upheld
Libman v. Quebec (Attorney General), [1997] 3 S.C.R. 569	2(b)	Can a government impose spending limits in referendum campaigns?	Yes, but the limits at issue were too low; Quebec law struck down
Thomson Newspapers Co. v. Canada (Attorney General), [1998] 1 S.C.R. 877	2(b)	Can a government prohibit the publication of new polling data during the last three days before the vote?	No; federal law struck down
Sauvé v. Canada (Chief Electoral Officer), [2002] 3 S.C.R. 519	3	Can a government deny prisoners the right to vote?	No; federal law struck down
Figueroa v. Canada (Attorney General), [2003] 1 S.C.R. 912	3	Can a government require a political party to nominate at least fifty candidates in order to qualify for public benefits?	No; federal law struck down
Harper v. Canada (Attorney General), 2004 SCC 33	2(b) and 3	Can a government restrict the amount of "third-party" advertising during an election campaign?	Yes; federal law upheld

In half the cases in the table, the impugned law, regulation, or practice was upheld. This does not suggest a wholesale judicial determination to overrule legislative choices about the democratic process. In three cases—*Saskatchewan*, *Haig*, and *Harper*—the Court found little or no infringement of s. 3; in *Harvey*, it deferred to the sponsoring legislature despite finding a significant violation of the right to run for public office. Two of the three cases in which the Court struck down the impugned law—the *Sauvé* rulings—concerned laws that deliberately deprived particular Canadians of the right to vote. The Court held that these were serious and intentional infringements of s. 3, with no countervailing benefits to society. In *Figueroa*, the federal government failed to justify a law that made it difficult for smaller parties to participate in the electoral process. Taken as a whole, these cases show that the Court is willing to defer to legislative choices that restrict democratic rights—but only

when Charter infringements are clearly outweighed by competing social values (e.g., the integrity of the electoral process). So while the Justices have shown a willingness to referee the democratic game, they have not completely usurped legislators' power to make and enforce the rules.

Fourth, s. 3—unlike the fundamental freedoms, legal rights, and equality rights—is not subject to the s. 33 override clause. Canadian courts have interpreted this fact as an indicator of its importance, especially at the s. 1 stage of analysis.[14] As Justice Bastarache commented in 1998, "Even though the override power is rarely invoked, the fact that s. 3 is immune from such power clearly places it at the heart of our constitutional democracy."[15] While there is no official hierarchy of Charter values, and s. 3 does not automatically "trump" competing rights,[16] its exemption from s. 33 may give it a special status.

If the framers assumed that entrenching democratic rights would make little or no difference in Canadian law, they were not entirely correct. While the Supreme Court's jurisprudence on election rights has been far from revolutionary, it has wrought some significant changes in the Canada Elections Act. The Court has broadened the scope of s. 3, using it to protect the interests of smaller political parties and extending the right to vote beyond the simple act of casting a ballot. It has tried to level the playing field in electoral contests, and to create new political opportunities for voters and activists. In the field of election law, however, the power of the Court is limited. The real-world impact of the Court's efforts to reinvigorate Canadian democracy will depend on political factors beyond the Court's control.[17]

THE RIGHT TO VOTE

The Purpose of the Right to Vote

As we have seen elsewhere in this book, the Supreme Court of Canada has adopted a "purposive" approach to Charter rights. The purpose of the right to vote is clear on its face: to protect Canadian citizens from losing their franchise without a very good reason. At a deeper level, a universal right to vote reflects a broad and generous conception of citizenship, founded on a recognition of equal human worth and dignity. In practical terms, the denial of voting rights to a particular group within the population prevents its members from obtaining political power. One obvious example is the Black majority population of South Africa, whose members were barred from voting under the apartheid regime, which finally ended in the 1990s. No country that denies suffrage to adult citizens on the basis of race or sex can claim democratic status in today's world.

This does not mean that the right to vote cannot be restricted on pragmatic or administrative grounds. In the words of former Justice La Forest, "It must be remembered that the business of government is a practical one. The Constitution must be applied on a realistic basis having regard to the nature of the particular area sought to be regulated and not on an abstract theoretical plane."[18] Courts have upheld laws requiring a specified period of residency in a particular jurisdiction in order to qualify for inclusion on the electoral list.[19] Certain public officials, such as the chief electoral officer, are denied the franchise in order to safeguard their political neutrality. Moreover, the Charter does not guarantee the right to vote in referendums or in municipal elections.[20] With these exceptions, the right of Canadian citizens to vote is sacrosanct.

Even after voting rights were extended to all citizens, regardless of sex or race, some individuals and groups were denied the franchise. Federally appointed judges were barred from participating in politics, to avoid a public perception of partisan bias. People with mental disabilities were also excluded from the franchise, as were most prison inmates. Since the introduction of the Charter, court rulings under s. 3 have extended the right to vote to all of these groups.[21] By far the most controversial rulings are those that have enfranchised prisoners.[22] The Supreme Court of Canada has twice upheld the right of prisoners who are not otherwise barred from voting (e.g., by reason of citizenship, to cast ballots in federal elections.[23] Similar rulings have been handed down by lower courts, affecting the administration of provincial elections.

As we saw in Dossier 4.3, pages 154–55, the blanket denial of federal voting rights to prisoners was struck down by the Supreme Court in 1993. Parliament responded by amending the Canada Elections Act to prohibit federal prisoners—those serving sentences of two years or longer—from voting. Richard Sauvé, who had successfully challenged the earlier provision, took the federal government to court again. In November 2002, by a 5-4 margin, the Supreme Court ruled that the law violated s. 3 and could not be saved under s. 1.

The second *Sauvé* ruling drew harsh criticism, especially from the *National Post* and the Canadian Alliance. Opponents argued that convicted criminals should forfeit their democratic rights, and that they are not "morally worthy" to participate as full citizens.[24] Canadian Alliance justice critic Vic Toews, a former Manitoba attorney general, tabled a private member's bill calling for an amendment to the Charter. The proposed amendment, which the Liberal government refused to support, would have removed the voting rights of "anyone who is imprisoned."[25] In May 2003, the House of Commons debated an Alliance motion calling on the government to "protect and reassert the will of Parliament against certain court decisions,"[26] including *Sauvé*. In an emotional attack on the Supreme Court and the Charter, Toews declared that a man "who recently was convicted of stabbing his wife to death while their children watched" should not be allowed to vote in an impending federal **by-election**. Another Alliance MP charged—without substantiation—that "the Liberal government is hoping that granting prisoners the right to vote may improve their chances in the next election," and alleged that Canada's most notorious murderers "can hardly wait to vote for the Liberal Party."[27] The motion polarized the House: it was criticized by the Liberals, the Bloc Québécois, and the NDP, and hotly defended by several Alliance and Progressive Conservative MPs.

The deep divisions on the Court, evident in the second *Sauvé* ruling, have not yet been resolved. In June 2003, the Justices split 6-3 over the meaning of s. 3. The majority opinion in the *Figueroa* case (see Dossier 9.3, pages 296–97), defined the right to vote as "the right of each citizen to play a meaningful role in the electoral process."[28] Justice Iacobucci emphasized the individual aspects of voting, even while acknowledging that most Canadians participate in politics by joining or voting for political parties. The three concurring Justices, led by Justice LeBel, rejected this individualistic approach to democratic rights. LeBel argued that "s. 3 is also inherently concerned with the representation of communities, both the various communities that make up Canadian society and the broader community of all Canadians."[29]

Whereas Iacobucci had adopted an individualistic approach to s. 3, LeBel insisted that its true meaning and purpose could be discerned only by looking at the historical and political context. He proposed a form of internal balancing test, analogous to the internal limitations contained in ss. 7, 8, and 9 of the Charter. At the first stage of analysis, a court should weigh all of the values protected by s. 3—including regional representation, community interests, and individual participation—before determining whether democratic rights have been infringed. An overemphasis on individual rights could lead the courts to undervalue the communitarian aspects of Canadian politics. In effect, LeBel attempted to shift the process of balancing rights against competing social values from s. 1 to s. 3. Indeed, he suggested that a violation of s. 3 could never be justified under s. 1: "my finding that the legislation infringes s. 3 essentially amounts to a conclusion that it is inconsistent with the values of Canadian democracy. It is hard to see how it could nevertheless be shown to be 'justified in a free and democratic society.'"[30]

The Court was divided again in the May 2004 *Harper* ruling, which upheld the regulatory regime for "third parties"—i.e., anyone other than a registered party or candidate—who wanted to participate in federal election campaigns through paid advertisements.[31] All nine Justices agreed that the spending limits on campaign advertising infringed the freedom to express political views. Nonetheless, six Justices voted to uphold the law. For the majority, Justice Bastarache ruled that the spending limits promoted a "pressing and substantial" objective: to ensure that the wealthiest groups and individuals could not drown out other interests (including parties and candidates) by monopolizing the airwaves and print media during a campaign. By giving third parties with fewer resources the opportunity to express their views, the limits promoted electoral fairness and "informed voting." In so doing, they "enhance[d] the right to vote under s. 3."[32]

The dissenters, led by Justice Major and Chief Justice McLachlin, found that the limits were too low to permit the effective dissemination of ideas that were not espoused by registered parties or candidates. Moreover, the violation of s. 2(b) was compounded by an unjustified infringement of s. 3, by restricting the right of each citizen to play a meaningful role in the political process.[33] The *Harper* ruling revealed the persistent disagreements on the Court over the meaning and purpose of democratic rights. It also highlighted the importance of the relationship between ss. 2(b) and 3, to which we now turn.

The Relationship between Sections 2(b) and 3: Informed Voting and Political Equality

As we saw in Chapter 8, political expression lies at the core of the values protected by s. 2(b). Consequently, it is difficult for a government to justify restrictions on the *content* of political speech. On the other hand, some *forms* of political speech—such as campaign advertising on television—are too costly for all but the wealthiest citizens and groups. As noted in the preceding discussion of *Harper*, some observers argue that the rich would monopolize campaign speech in the absence of legislated spending limits. Others believe that restrictions on freedom of political expression are never constitutional. What should the courts do when freedom of expression conflicts with democratic rights?

The Supreme Court has repeatedly declared that when two protected rights conflict, judges must not automatically privilege one over the other. Instead, they must find a balance that "fully respects the importance of both sets of rights."[34] In a series of cases dealing with democratic speech, the Court has reconciled ss. 2(b) and 3 by recognizing a right that overlaps the two sections: the right to cast an *informed* vote, based on adequate and reliable data about the various options on the ballot. Before the voter goes to the polls, she must have the opportunity to hear a wide variety of political opinions. If she is denied access to one or more potentially persuasive viewpoints, both her expressive freedom (as a listener) and her right to meaningful participation in politics are infringed. A majority on the Court has ruled that the right to cast an informed vote requires the state to intervene in the political marketplace, in order to "prevent the most affluent members of society from exerting a disproportionate influence by dominating the [election] debate through access to greater resources."[35] Therefore, the state may justifiably limit the *quantity* of political expression by the wealthy, where such limits are needed to protect both the right to an informed vote and the democratic rights of those who support or represent political parties with fewer resources. The right to receive political information also implies that the state must treat all political parties fairly, regardless of their respective sizes; if it

discriminates against smaller parties, only the large and well-established parties will have the means to communicate their platforms to the voters.[36]

This approach to the relationship between free expression and democratic rights is termed the "egalitarian model."[37] The Supreme Court of Canada first endorsed this model in the 1997 *Libman* ruling. The central issue in the case was the constitutionality of Quebec's referendum law, which required individuals and groups to affiliate themselves with the official "Yes" and "No" committees. Campaign spending by unaffiliated participants was severely restricted. Although the Court found that the limits on unaffiliated spending were too low to pass the "minimal impairment" prong of the *Oakes* test, its support for the principle of spending limits was unanimous and unequivocal.

> [First], what is sought is in a sense an equality of participation and influence between the proponents of each option. Second, from the voters' point of view, the system is designed to permit an informed choice to be made by ensuring that some positions are not buried by others. Finally, as a related point, the system is designed to preserve the confidence of the electorate in a democratic process that it knows will not be dominated by the power of money.... In our view, the pursuit of an objective intended to ensure the fairness of an eminently democratic process, namely a referendum on a question of public interest, is a highly laudable one.[38]

The *Harper* ruling is even more explicit. Justice Bastarache approvingly described the federal spending limits on third-party campaign advertising as an example of Canada's egalitarian approach to electoral regulation, which "promotes an electoral process that requires the wealthy to be prevented from controlling the electoral process to the detriment of others with less economic power."[39]

Critics of the *Harper* ruling—including the dissenting Justices—point out that the impugned spending limits are considerably lower than those imposed on the registered parties and candidates. The national ceiling in the 2004 federal election was $168 000, roughly one percent of the cap on spending by national parties. At the constituency level, the limit on advertising by interest groups and individuals was $3378, approximately eleven percent of the maximum spending by a candidate. It is misleading to describe this disparate treatment of registered parties and third parties as egalitarian.[40]

On the other hand, political parties and candidates face significant campaign expenses that are unrelated to advertising. For example, candidates have to rent office space and equipment, install telephone and fax lines, feed their volunteers, and pay their auditors. Parties hire temporary employees (sometimes numbering in the dozens) at their national headquarters. They also rent airplanes and buses for the leader's tour, at considerable cost (although this is partly offset by the fees charged to reporters who accompany the leaders). An established interest group does not have to shoulder these extraordinary costs. It already has an office, with equipment and staff, and its officers do not have to travel the country. So it is reasonable to allow the people who actually run for office to spend more than third parties. The real question, as the *Harper* dissenters pointed out, is whether the third-party limits are high enough to permit effective participation in campaign discourse.

In contrast to the egalitarian approach, the "libertarian model" opposes any restriction on political speech. It is consistent with the Court's treatment of political speech as a core form of expression, any restriction of which requires strong justification (see Chapter 8, pages 256–59). The problem with the libertarian model is that it overlooks the expense associated with many forms of political speech—especially television advertising. If all forms of political speech were available at low cost, the libertarian position would be unassailable. But because they are not, libertarians would effectively "permit those with greater resources or abilities to express themselves disproportionately in the so-called 'marketplace of ideas.'"[41]

The libertarian approach has been adopted by the U.S. Supreme Court and by the provincial courts in both British Columbia and Alberta. In *Buckley v. Valeo* (1976), the U.S. Court struck down campaign spending limits as a violation of the First Amendment.[42] That section of the Bill of Rights states that "Congress shall make no law ... abridging freedom of speech." The majority found that campaign spending was a form of speech, because "virtu-

ally every means of communicating ideas in today's mass society requires the expenditure of money."[43] Once the First Amendment was engaged, the outcome of the case was all but predetermined, partly because the U.S. Bill of Rights contains no explicit limitation clause analogous to s. 1 of the Charter.

> It is argued ... that the ancillary governmental interest in equalizing the relative ability of individuals and groups to influence the outcome of elections serves to justify the limitation on express advocacy of the election or defeat of candidates imposed by [the] expenditure ceiling. But the concept that government may restrict the speech of some elements of our society in order to enhance the relative voice of others is wholly foreign to the First Amendment.[44]

The Alberta Court of Queen's Bench has relied on *Buckley* to argue that restrictions on campaign spending by interest groups (so-called third parties) infringe the guarantee of political expression and cannot be justified under s. 1. That Court has repeatedly signalled its reluctance to countenance limits on any form of campaign spending: "It is indeed difficult to imagine a time when the guarantee to engage in free political expression would be more important than during an election."[45] Citing a lack of evidence that unregulated campaign spending damages Canadian democracy, Alberta judges consistently conclude that the objective of spending limits—"to prevent those with greater access to financial resources from dominating the electoral discourse"[46]—is neither pressing nor substantial.

Despite the Supreme Court's explicit repudiation of the libertarian approach in *Libman*,[47] courts in Alberta and British Columbia have declined to limit free speech on egalitarian grounds.[48] Judges in both provinces have distinguished *Libman* on the ground that the social-science evidence cited by the Supreme Court of Canada was unreliable.[49] In the 2004 *Harper* ruling, which overturned the Alberta judgments, the majority at the Supreme Court of Canada stated that the lower courts had "erred"; their deviation from *Libman* was simply "wrong."[50] The explicitness of this remonstrance from the top court reveals the stark division between egalitarian and libertarian judges.

The consequences of the libertarian approach are clearly evident in American politics.[51] Unrestricted campaign spending allows wealthy individuals and groups to dominate electoral contests, forcing politicians to engage in dubious fundraising practices and raising voter cynicism about politics. In effect, "a system of unregulated expenditures [is] a regulatory decision to allow disparities in resources to be turned into disparities in political influence."[52] Two current members of the U.S. Supreme Court have repeatedly urged their colleagues to overturn *Buckley*, both for practical reasons and as an erroneous application of the First Amendment.[53] By endorsing the egalitarian model, the Supreme Court of Canada has sought to preserve the integrity and the openness of our electoral system.

Drawing Electoral Boundaries: *Reference re Provincial Electoral Boundaries (Saskatchewan)* (1991)

Few issues provoke more heated debate among elected politicians than the boundaries of the districts that they represent. Given the chance, legislators will try to manipulate the electoral map to serve their own self-

interest.[54] For example, governing parties with strong support in rural areas will create as many nonurban districts as they can, even though the smaller population outside the cities means that these rural seats will have far fewer voters than the average. Conversely, city-based parties may try to minimize the impact of the rural vote by reducing the number of nonurban constituencies, thus producing enormous and sparsely populated districts that pose serious representational challenges. These practical problems, combined with the appearance of corruption, have prompted the federal and provincial legislatures to delegate their responsibility for drawing electoral boundaries to nonpartisan riding commissions.[55] In 1991, the Supreme Court of Canada ruled on the Charter's application to electoral districting. Dossier 9.2 discusses the Court's approach to riding boundaries under s. 3.

The impact of the Saskatchewan case on subsequent electoral redistributions has varied across jurisdictions. According to John Courtney, "if it served a government's purpose it was invoked; if it did not, it was not."[56] In general, the ruling seems to have encouraged boundary commissioners to issue more precise and detailed reasons for recommended changes to electoral districts, but it does not seem to have produced a more equitable division of voters among constituencies.

DOSSIER 9.2

REFERENCE RE PROVINCIAL ELECTORAL BOUNDARIES (SASKATCHEWAN) (1991)

In 1991, the Supreme Court of Canada ruled on the constitutionality of Saskatchewan's provincial electoral districts.[1] The province of Saskatchewan, like many Canadian provinces, is densely populated in the south and sparsely settled in the north. The resulting disparity in voter populations, coupled with the vast size of the northern region, makes it impossible to divide the electorate evenly among the various ridings. Huge constituencies pose a representational challenge to legislators and generate high campaign costs for candidates. To complicate matters further, Saskatchewan is politi-

cally divided between the rural constituencies, which historically favoured the Conservatives,[2] and urban ridings in Regina and Saskatoon, which often returned New Democrats to the legislature.

Between 1905 (when Saskatchewan achieved provincial status) and the late 1980s, boundary commissions had managed to produce districts whose voting populations deviated from the provincial quotient by no more than fifteen percent. But the Electoral Boundaries Commission Act (EBCA), adopted by the Conservative government in 1988, imposed three new conditions on the commission responsible for the province's electoral map. First, the numbers of rural and urban ridings were fixed by law: there would be 29 seats for the cities, 35 for the rural areas in the south of the province, and two northern seats.[3] Rural voters, who made up about fifty percent of the population in 1989, were guaranteed more than half the seats in the legislature—even though the rapid urbanization of the province would soon reduce them to a minority of the electorate. Second, the boundaries of urban ridings had to follow the existing city limits. Third, the northern part of the province would be divided into two huge districts.

The EBCA was troubling for at least three reasons. First, it ensured that the ruling Conservatives would win more seats in the legislature by carving out more constituencies in their rural strongholds. Second, it gerrymandered the urban ridings to limit the number of seats in which the NDP had a realistic chance to elect legislators. Third, and most important in Charter terms, the EBCA forced the commission to draw an electoral map with wide disparities among the voting populations in different constituencies. The northern riding of Athabasca had 6309 eligible voters, roughly half the number in Saskatoon Greystone.[4] The electorate in the most populous rural riding was two-thirds the size of the electorate in the smallest rural riding; the same discrepancy existed between Saskatoon Greystone, the largest urban constituency, and the neighbouring district of Saskatoon Sutherland-University.[5]

After considerable public criticism, the government of Saskatchewan asked the province's Court of Appeal to rule on the constitutionality of the new electoral map, and specifically on whether the disparities among voting populations violated the right to vote in s. 3 of the Charter. The Court upheld the section of the EBCA establishing the two northern ridings, but found that the quota of rural southern seats caused unjustifiable deviations from the principle of voter parity.[6] The Saskatchewan government appealed to the Supreme Court of Canada. Because a provincial election was in the offing, Saskatchewan asked the Justices to rule on the issue as quickly as possible. The Supreme Court heard arguments at the end of April 1991 and issued its decision on June 6.

Six of the Justices, led by Justice McLachlin (as she then was), overturned the Court of Appeal. They found that the impugned electoral distribution did not violate s. 3 of the Charter, because the right to vote did not guarantee "absolute voter parity." Instead, the purpose of s. 3 was to ensure "effective representation" in legislative bodies:

> Ours is a representative democracy. Each citizen is entitled to be *represented* in government. Representation comprehends the idea of having a voice in the deliberations of government as well as the idea of the right to bring one's grievances and concerns to the attention of one's government representative.[7]

McLachlin concluded that the proper approach to electoral districting under the Charter was to balance the guarantee of "relative voter parity" against "countervailing factors"—such as "geography, community history, community interests and minority representation"—which may justify deviations from the average population size in a given constituency.[8] On this interpretation of s. 3, the disparities in the Saskatchewan electoral map were legitimate. Despite the implicit political interference in the process of districting, McLachlin insisted that "the courts ought not to interfere with the legislature's electoral map under s. 3 of the Charter unless it appears that reasonable persons applying the appropriate principles ... could not have set the electoral boundaries as they exist."[9]

The majority ruling has been criticized on three primary grounds. First, McLachlin effectively read an internal limitation into s. 3, by requiring courts to balance the right to vote against competing social values. Instead of taking the usual approach to a Charter right—

(continued)

interpreting the guarantee broadly and then requiring the Saskatchewan government to justify any infringement under s. 1—McLachlin defined s. 3 in a way that made the second step of Charter interpretation all but obsolete.[10] Second, the ruling put a judicial stamp of approval on any redistribution scheme in which deviations from voter parity could be framed as a response to geographic or community considerations. Consequently, "legislation that provides some latitude to the drawers of the electoral boundaries is virtually unassailable," regardless of its underlying purpose or the political considerations involved.[11]

Third, and most broadly, McLachlin's narrow reading of s. 3 weakened the judicial protection of democratic rights in subsequent cases. For example, the Ontario Court of Appeal ruled in 2000 that smaller political parties cannot provide "effective representation," because they have little chance of electing MPs and even less of forming governments. It is therefore legitimate for the federal government to discriminate against such parties in the Canada Elections Act.[12] By restricting the import of s. 3 to the *outcome* of an election, while ignoring the electoral *process*, McLachlin inadvertently legitimized the "two-tier" approach to political parties.

McLachlin's limited interpretation of s. 3 contradicts her 1989 ruling in the *Dixon* case, written when she was Chief Justice of the British Columbia Supreme Court. In *Dixon*, McLachlin offered a broader and more comprehensive definition of the right to vote. She identified ten "core rights or values" protected by s. 3, including "the right to be presented with a choice of candidates or parties," "the right to sufficient information about public policies to permit an informed decision," "the right to be represented by a candidate with at least a plurality of votes in a district," and—last but not least—"the right to cast one's vote in an electoral district which has not been 'gerrymandered'—that is, deliberately engineered so as to

favour one political party over another."[13] Had McLachlin followed the same interpretation of s. 3 when she moved to the Supreme Court of Canada, the outcome and impact of the *Saskatchewan Boundary Reference* might have been different.

ENDNOTES

1. *Reference re Prov. Electoral Boundaries (Sask.)*, [1991] 2 S.C.R. 158.

2. After a series of damaging scandals in the 1990s, the Saskatchewan Conservative Party virtually disappeared. Its place has been taken by the Saskatchewan Party, an alliance of Liberals, federal Reform Party (then Canadian Alliance, and now Conservative) members, and former Conservatives.

3. Robert E. Charney, "Saskatchewan Election Boundary Reference: 'One Person—Half a Vote,'" *National Journal of Constitutional Law* 1 (1991), p. 225.

4. Ibid., p. 225.

5. Ibid., p. 226.

6. *Reference re Provincial Election Boundaries*, (1991), 78 D.L.R. (4th) (Sask. C.A.).

7. *Reference re Prov. Electoral Boundaries*, paragraph 49, per McLachlin J. (emphasis in original).

8. Ibid., per McLachlin J.

9. Ibid., paragraph 64, quoting her earlier ruling as Chief Justice of the British Columbia Supreme Court in *Dixon v. B.C. (A.G.)*, 35 B.C.L.R. (2d), 273.

10. Charney, "Saskatchewan Election Boundary Reference," p. 231.

11. Ronald E. Fritz, "Drawing Electoral Boundaries in Compliance with the Charter: The Alberta Experience," *National Journal of Constitutional Law* 6 (1996), p. 360.

12. *Figueroa v. Canada (Attorney General)*, Ontario Court of Appeal, August 16, 2000, accessed online at the Court's website (www.ontariocourts.on.ca).

13. *Dixon v. B.C.*, pp. 285–86. Why did she change her mind? The most likely reason is that she wrote the Dixon ruling alone, as a one-judge panel, whereas the Supreme Court heard the Saskatchewan Reference as a nine-judge panel. In order for her opinion to prevail, at least four other Justices had to support McLachlin's interpretation of the Charter. Perhaps she had to water down her earlier approach to democratic rights in order to build a majority consensus on the Court.

THE RIGHT TO RUN FOR PUBLIC OFFICE

As we have seen, the text of s. 3 contains no internal limitations. This implies that the right to run for office is unrestricted. On the other hand, legislatures have historically had the privilege of policing their own members, including the power to expel those who violate either the rules of the House or the laws under which they were elected. This conflict raises two important issues about the relationship between the Charter and the judiciary, on the one hand, and the legislative branch of government on the other. First, does the Charter override the historic privileges and immunities of Parliament where the two conflict? Second, is the practice of expelling miscreant members consistent with s. 3?

These issues were addressed in two rulings from the Supreme Court: the 1993 *New Brunswick Broadcasting*[57] case and the 1996 *Harvey* case.[58] In the former, the Speaker of the Nova Scotia legislature sought to ban television cameras from the House. He was taken to court by a broadcasting company that wanted to tape the proceedings from the gallery with hand-held cameras. The Speaker argued that the House enjoyed a traditional privilege of determining who should be admitted to its premises, a privilege that was not affected by the Charter. A majority on the Supreme Court of Canada agreed, ruling that "The privilege of the legislative assembly to exclude strangers enjoys constitutional status as part of the Constitution of Canada, and hence cannot be abrogated by another part of the Constitution."[59] In other words, the establishment of a Westminster-style parliamentary system in Canada was entrenched in the Constitution Act, 1867, and could not be overridden by the Charter. As discussed in Chapter 7, page 231, one part of the Constitution of Canada cannot be used to invalidate another.[60]

Having insulated parliamentary privilege from Charter review, the Court faced a dilemma when it ruled on the *Harvey* case. Fred Harvey had been elected to the New Brunswick legislature in 1991. Shortly thereafter, he was convicted of violating the provincial Election Act by persuading a sixteen-year-old girl (who was too young to cast a legal ballot) to vote for him. The law provided that a sitting member who had been found guilty of such an offence would be forced to vacate his legislative seat, and a by-election would be called to fill it. In addition, the law forbade Harvey from voting or running in a provincial election for a period of five years. He challenged the constitutionality of these provisions, on the grounds that they violated his s. 3 rights to vote and run for office. A lower court ruled that the five-year ban on voting was unconstitutional, a finding that was not appealed to the Supreme Court.

Seven members of the Supreme Court found that the Charter applied in this instance, because the case involved a provincial statute rather than the constitutional convention of parliamentary privilege. The two remaining Justices insisted that the Charter was inapplicable, inasmuch as the central issue was the power of the legislature to police its own members. Having resolved this preliminary question, the court moved on to the second issue. Six Justices ruled that the infringement of Harvey's right to seek office violated s. 3, but was saved under s. 1. For the majority, Justice La Forest wrote that the rights in s. 3 must be interpreted broadly, both because of the language of the section and because of their inherent importance. Without an express limitation on the right to seek office, any infringement could be justified only under s. 1.[61] He described the objective of the impugned law—"to maintain and enhance the integrity of the electoral process"—as "pressing and substantial," and concluded that the five-year exclusion from the legislature was both "rationally connected" to the objective and minimally impairing of the Charter right. Whereas a permanent ban would have been excessive, the five-year rule struck an appropriate balance between democratic rights and the need to deter and punish election fraud.

THE CONSTITUTIONAL STATUS OF POLITICAL PARTIES AND CANDIDATES

The right to vote implies the presence of someone (or something) to vote *for*. In Canada, political parties provide the candidates and the campaign organization that make competitive elections possible. While the wording of s. 3 does not refer specifically to political parties, the rights to vote and to seek office cannot be exercised in a vacuum. Most voters are influenced by the party leader and the party as a whole, not by the individual candidates in their ridings.[62] Parties all but monopolize the nomination of successful candidates in legislative elections.[63] The most successful party elects more of its candidates than any other and forms the government. So in practice, the rights guaranteed in s. 3 are exercised in the context of a competitive party system.

The Charter's applicability to political parties is a hotly contested issue. In 1994, the Quebec Court of Appeal skirted the question by confining its analysis to the treatment of individual candidates under the Canada Elections Act.[64] Two years later, a majority on the Alberta Court of Appeal found that the rights in s. 3 do not pertain to parties per se: "It is the rights of individuals that are constitutionally enshrined. Political parties do not have similar constitutional protection; rather they emerge as an expression of the people. Having said that, I recognize that the party system constitutes the framework of our democratic process."[65] Consequently, courts have generally refused to allow political parties full standing in constitutional litigation. Parties are usually represented by their leaders[66] or by individual candidates.[67] The major exception is the *Reform Party* case in Alberta.[68]

Despite their supposed irrelevance to the democratic rights in s. 3, political parties have attracted considerable judicial attention under the Charter. Two contending approaches to parties have emerged in provincial courts: "party equality" and "two-tier."[69] Judges who follow the party equality approach will strike down laws that discriminate against smaller or newer parties, on the grounds that they violate democratic rights and cannot be justified under s. 1.[70] Their two-tier colleagues uphold discriminatory laws because they benefit the larger and well-established parties that can provide "effective representation."[71] Dossier 9.3 describes a seminal 2003 ruling from the Supreme Court of Canada, which established the party equality model as the predominant judicial approach to national political parties.

DOSSIER 9.3

THE *FIGUEROA* CASE (2003)

The debate over the constitutional status of parties was resolved, to some degree, by the June 2003 Supreme Court ruling in *Figueroa v. Canada (Attorney General)*. All nine Justices voted to strike down sections of the Canada Elections Act that discriminated against parties with fewer than fifty candidates in a federal election. The act established a regime for the registration of federal parties and provided public benefits to those that met the registration criteria. Those benefits included the power to issue tax receipts for donations and the right to identify their candidates by placing party labels on the ballot.[1] The most difficult criterion for registered status was the fifty-candidate threshold. Before a party could be placed on the register at Elections Canada, it had to run at least fifty candidates in a general election; if it failed to nominate that many candidates at a subsequent election, it would be stricken from the register and lose its benefits.

The Court found that the threshold violated the rights of voters because it deprived smaller parties of the resources they needed to participate effectively in the electoral process. Consequently, the law silenced parties whose ideas, while not mainstream, might appeal to voters who would otherwise find no echo of their own political opinions in the party system.[2] Justice Iacobucci explicitly rejected the two-tier approach to parties in favour of party equality:

> It is my conclusion that the ability of a political party to make a valuable contribution to the electoral process is not dependent upon its capacity to offer the electorate a genuine "government option." Rather, political parties enhance the meaningfulness of individual participation in the electoral process for reasons that transcend their capacity (or lack thereof) to participate in the governance of the country subsequent to an election. Irrespective of their capacity to influence the outcome of an election, political parties act as both a vehicle and outlet for the meaningful participation of individual citizens in the electoral process.
>
> It likely is true that a large party will be able to play a larger role in the open discourse of the electoral process, but it does not thereby follow that the capacity of a political party to represent the ideas and opinions of its members and supporters in the electoral process is dependent upon its

capacity to offer the electorate a "government option." Large or small, all political parties are capable of introducing unique interests and concerns into the political discourse. Consequently, all political parties, whether large or small, are capable of acting as a vehicle for the participation of individual citizens in the public discourse that animates the determination of social policy.[3]

Iacobucci's endorsement of party equality was not absolute. He made it clear that his ruling "does not stand for the proposition that the differential treatment of political parties will always constitute a violation of s. 3," or for "the proposition that an infringement of s. 3 arising from the differential treatment of political parties could never be justified."[4] Nonetheless, the egalitarian tenor of the ruling suggests that a two-tier law would face the strictest scrutiny under s. 1, and that statutory discrimination against smaller parties on illegitimate grounds will no longer be tolerated by the courts.

ENDNOTES

1. By the time the Supreme Court of Canada ruled on the *Figueroa* case, the Canada Elections Act had been amended to reduce the number of candidates required for ballot labels from fifty to twelve. This amendment was in response to the 1999 ruling of Justice Molloy in the same case.

2. *Figueroa v. Canada (A.G.)*. paragraph 42, *per* Iacobucci J.

3. Ibid., paragraphs 39 and 41.

4. Ibid., paragraph 91.

THE OTHER DEMOCRATIC RIGHTS

Unlike section 3, sections 4 and 5 have not been interpreted by the courts. Their principal function is to apply the preexisting rules for the federal Parliament to the provincial and territorial legislatures, and in so doing to standardize the democratic rights of

Canadians vis-à-vis both levels of government. If a cabinet decided to flout the rules—either by abusing the emergency extension power in s. 4(2), or by refusing to meet the legislature within the time limits set by s. 5—the citizens in that jurisdiction might be able to challenge that decision under s. 24(1). However, the courts could not directly order the political executive to abide by the terms of the Charter. Any effective remedy would lie not with the judicial branch, but with the Crown. The governor general or lieutenant governor "would have the power to dismiss the Prime Minister and call upon someone else to form a government," or to dissolve a legislature that had outlived its constitutional limits.[72]

CONCLUSION

Section 1 of the Charter requires all branches of government to weigh rights infringements against the protection of "a free and democratic society." Respect for the democratic rights in ss. 3–5 is the foundation of such a society. This does not mean that the rights to vote and seek office will always trump competing values; the Supreme Court has upheld laws that limit those rights when the limitations are justified by countervailing political and social factors. Perhaps the most problematic aspect of the jurisprudence on s. 3 is the fact that the balance is being struck by the courts, not by elected legislators themselves. On the other hand, the existence of "two-tier" laws and the temptation to gerrymander electoral boundaries suggest that the political branches cannot always be trusted to craft election laws that reflect Charter values of fairness and equality. Under those circumstances, nonpartisan judges armed with entrenched democratic rights may be the best safeguard of self-government, not a threat to it.

GLOSSARY OF KEY TERMS

by-election An election held to fill a single vacant seat in Parliament. Unlike during a general election, the House of Commons remains in operation during a by-election.

franchise The right to vote in elections for public officials.

gerrymandering The process of manipulating electoral boundaries to favour the election of candidates from one particular party (usually the governing party).

suffrage See *franchise*.

DISCUSSION AND REVIEW QUESTIONS

1. Briefly explain the relationship between ss. 2(b) and 3 of the Charter. How has the Supreme Court reconciled the two sections?

2. The Supreme Court has defined the purpose of s. 3 in two ways. In your own words, explain both definitions. Give an example of each, referring to a specific case discussed in this chapter.

3. In your opinion, should prisoners be allowed to vote? Why or why not?

4. Should interest groups and other third parties be allowed to advertise their opinions during election campaigns? If so, should they be allowed to spend as much as the political parties and candidates? Why or why not?

SUGGESTED READINGS

Elections Canada. *A History of the Vote in Canada*. Ottawa: Public Works and Government Services, 1997.

Ely, John Hart. *Democracy and Distrust: A Theory of Judicial Review*. Cambridge, MA: Harvard University Press, 1980.

Feasby, Colin. "Libman v. Quebec (A.G.) and the Administration of the Process of Democracy under the Charter: The Emerging Egalitarian Model." *McGill Law Journal* 44 (1999), pp. 5–38.

MacIvor, Heather. "The Charter of Rights and Party Politics: The Impact of the Supreme Court Ruling in *Figueroa v. Canada (Attorney General)*." Montreal: Institute for Research on Public Policy, May 2004.

———. "Judicial Review and Electoral Democracy: The Contested Status of Political Parties under the Charter." *Windsor Yearbook of Access to Justice* 21 (2002), pp. 479–504.

Schauer, Frederick. "Judicial Review of the Devices of Democracy." *Columbia Law Review* 94 (1994), pp. 1326–47.

ENDNOTES

1. Reprinted in Anne F. Bayefsky, ed., *Canada's Constitution Act, 1982 and Amendments: A Documentary History*, vol. 2 (Toronto: McGraw-Hill Ryerson, 1989), p. 746.

2. *Reference re Prov. Electoral Boundaries (Sask.)*, [1991] 2 S.C.R. 158, paragraphs 1–2, *per* Cory J.

3. *Reynolds v. Sims*, 377 U.S. 533 (1964), *per* Warren C.J., pp. 561–62.

4. *R. v. Oakes*, [1986] 1 S.C.R. 103, paragraph 64.

5. *Sauvé v. Canada (Chief Electoral Officer)*, [2002] 3. S.C.R. 418, paragraph 14, *per* McLachlin C.J. (hereinafter cited as "*Sauvé* 2002").

6. *Sauvé* 2002, paragraph 9, *per* McLachlin C.J.

7. The phrase is taken from *Re B.C. Motor Vehicle Act*, [1985] 2 S.C.R. 486, paragraph 31, *per* Lamer J. (as he then was).

8. Heather MacIvor, "The Charter of Rights and Party Politics: The Impact of the Supreme Court Ruling in *Figueroa v. Canada (Attorney General)*" (Montreal: Institute for Research on Public Policy, May 2004), pp. 3–4.

9. *Colegrove v. Green*, 328 U.S. 549 (1946), pp. 553–54 and 555, *per* Frankfurter J.

10. *Baker v. Carr*, 369 U.S. 186 (1962), p. 217, *per* Brennan J. See also David K. Ryden, "The U.S. Supreme Court, the Electoral Process, and the Quest for Representation: An Overview," in David K. Ryden, ed., *The U.S. Supreme Court and the Electoral Process*, 2nd ed. (Washington, DC: Georgetown University Press, 2002), pp. 1–14; Richard L. Hasen, *The Supreme Court and Election Law: Judging Equality from Baker v. Carr to Bush v. Gore* (New York: New York University Press, 2003), pp. 50–53.

11. Hasen, *The Supreme Court and Election Law*, p. 3, Figure 1.1.

12. *National Citizens' Coalition et al. v. Canada (Attorney General)*, Alberta Court of Queen's Bench, 1984, 11 D.L.R. (4th), pp. 481–96. See also Peter H. Russell, "The First Three Years in Charterland," *Canadian Public Administration* 28, no. 3 (Fall 1985), p. 377.

13. For a complete list of cases on electoral rights, see James R. Robertson, "Electoral Rights: Charter of Rights and Freedoms" (Ottawa: Library of Parliament Research Branch). Updated versions of this paper are available online at www.parl.gc.ca.

14. *Thomson Newspapers*, paragraph 79, *per* Bastarache J.; *Sauvé* 2002, paragraphs 14 and 44, *per* McLachlin C.J. Note that the dissenting minority in *Sauvé* 2002 argued that the exemption of s. 3 had no bearing whatsoever on the standard for justification under s. 1; see paragraphs 95–96, *per* Gonthier J.

15. *Thomson Newspapers Co. v. Canada (Attorney General)*, [1998] 1 S.C.R. 877, paragraph 79.

16. *Harvey v. New Brunswick (Attorney General)*, [1996] 2 S.C.R. 876, paragraphs 29–30, *per* La Forest J. However, some observers argue that the Supreme Court has imported the "balancing" process under s. 1 into its application of s. 3; see Robert E. Charney, "*Saskatchewan Election Boundary Reference*: 'One Person—Half a Vote,'" *National Journal of Constitutional Law* 1 (1991), pp. 225 and 229.

17. See MacIvor, "The Charter and Party Politics," pp. 18–19.

18. *R. v. Edwards Books and Art Ltd.*, [1986] 2 S.C.R. 713, paragraph 163.

19. *Storey v. Zazelenchuk* (1982), 5 C.R.R. 99 (Sask. Q.B.); appeal dismissed (1984), 12 C.R.R. 261 (Sask. C.A.); *Arnold v. A.G. Ont.* (1987), 61 O.R. (2d) 481 (Ont. S.C.).; *Reference Re Yukon Election Residency Requirements* (1986), 27 D.L.R. (4th) 146 (Y.T.C.A.). See also *Scott v. A.G.B.C. et al.* (1986), 29 D.L.R. (4th) 544 (B.C.S.C.) and

Weremchuk v. Jacobsen (1986), 35 D.L.R. (4th) 278 (B.C.C.A.).

20. In the 1992 referendum, the province of Quebec held a separate vote while Elections Canada was responsible for administering the referendum in the rest of Canada. The appellant had lost his right to vote in the federal referendum by moving to Quebec, but he had not lived there long enough to qualify as a voter in that province. The Supreme Court rejected his appeal, on the ground that there was no Charter right to vote in a referendum. See *Haig v. Canada; Haig v. Canada (Chief Electoral Officer)*, [1993] 2 S.C.R. 995, especially paragraphs 62–64, *per* L'Heureux-Dubé J.

21. The mentally disabled won the right to vote in a court case; see *Canadian Disability Rights Council v. Canada* (1988), 21 F.T.R. 268 (T.D.). Parliament granted judges the right to vote shortly before the 1988 federal election. See Gérald-A. Beaudoin, "Democratic Rights," in Gérald-A. Beaudoin and Ed Ratushny, eds., *The Canadian Charter of Rights and Freedoms*, 2nd ed. (Toronto: Carswell, 1989), p. 276.

22. See, e.g., *Maltby et al. v. A.G. Saskatchewan et al.* (1982), 2 C.C.C. (3d) 153 (Sask. Q.B.); appeal dismissed (1984), 10 D.L.R. (4th) 745 (Sask. C.A.).; *Reynolds v. A.G.B.C.* (1983), 143 D.L.R. (3d) 365 (B.C.S.C.); affirmed (1984), 11 D.L.R. (4th) 380 (B.C.C.A.); *Jolivet and Barker v. The Queen et al.* (1983), 7 C.C.C. (3d) 431 (B.C.S.C.); *Badger et al. v. A.G. Manitoba* (1986), 27 C.C.C. (3d) 158 (Man. Q.B.); appeal dismissed on other grounds (1986), 29 C.C.C. (3d) 92 (Man. C.A.); *Paul et al. v. Chief Electoral Officer* (1990), 72 D.L.R. (4th) 396 (Man. Q.B.); *Grondin v. A.G. Ont. et al.* (1988), 65 O.R. (2d) 427 (Ont. S.C.); *Belczowski v. The Queen*, [1991] 3 F.C. 151 (F.C.T.D.); appeal dismissed (1992), 90 D.L.R. (4th) 330 (F.C.A.); appeal dismissed, [1993] 2 S.C.R. 438.

23. *Sauvé v. Canada (Attorney General)*, [1993] 2 S.C.R. 438; *Sauvé* 2002.

24. "They Are Not Worthy," *National Post*, November 4, 2002, accessed online at www.nationalpost.com; F.L. Morton, "Once Again: Court-Made Law," *National Post*, November 2, 2002, accessed online at www.nationalpost.com.

25. The text of the proposed amendment was accessed online at www.canadianalliance.ca. The amendment is a purely symbolic gesture, given the impossibility of securing unanimous consent to amend the Charter.

26. House of Commons Debates, May 8, 2003, available online at www.parl.gc.ca.

27. Kevin Sorenson (Crowfoot), House of Commons Debates, May 8, 2003.

28. *Figueroa v. Canada (Attorney General)*, [2003] 1 S.C.R. 912, paragraph 25, *per* Iacobucci J. This definition was based on the majority opinion in *Haig v. Canada; Haig v. Canada*, authored by L'Heureux-Dubé J. (at paragraph 61).

29. *Figueroa v. Canada (A.G.)*, paragraph 101.

30. Ibid., paragraph 178.

31. *Harper v. Canada (Attorney General)*, 2004 SCC 33 (hereinafter cited as "Harper 2004").

32. Ibid., paragraph 140, *per* Bastarache J.

33. Ibid., paragraphs 13–15, *per* McLachlin C.J. and Major J.

34. *Dagenais v. Canadian Broadcasting Corp.*, [1994] 3 S.C.R. 835, paragraph 72, *per* Lamer C.J.C. (as he then was).

35. *Libman v. Quebec (Attorney General)*, [1997] 3 S.C.R. 569, paragraph 41, *per curiam*.

36. *Figueroa v. Canada (A.G.)*, paragraph 54, *per* Iacobucci J.

37. Colin Feasby, "*Libman v. Quebec (A.G.)* and the Administration of the Process of Democracy

under the Charter: The Emerging Egalitarian Model," *McGill Law Journal* 44 (1998–99), pp. 5–38.

38. *Libman v. Quebec (A.G.)*, paragraphs 41–42, *per curiam*.

39. *Harper* 2004, paragraph 62, *per* Bastarache J.

40. See "The Courts Seals Off a Charter Freedom," *The Globe and Mail*, Wednesday, May 19, 2004, accessed online at www.globeandmail.com.

41. Feasby, "*Libman v. Quebec*," p. 8.

42. *Buckley v. Valeo*, 424 U.S. 1 (1976).

43. Ibid., p. 19.

44. Ibid., pp. 48–49. The U.S. Supreme Court has modified the *Buckley* doctrine in several recent decisions, culminating in *McConnell v. Federal Election Commission* (124 S.Ct. 619 (2003)). However, it has not repudiated the idea that political contributions are a form of speech. See Richard L. Hasen, "*Buckley* Is Dead, Long Live *Buckley*: The New Campaign Finance Incoherence of *McConnell v. Federal Election Commission*," Loyola Law School Research Paper No. 2004-1, January 2004, available online at www.electionlawblog.org.

45. *Harper v. Canada (A.G.)*, 2001 ABQB 558, paragraph 222, *per* Cairns J.

46. Ibid., paragraph 249.

47. In the 1996 *Somerville* ruling, the Alberta Court of Appeal held that spending limits on third parties violate the guarantee of free expression and cannot be saved under s. 1. Conrad J.A. suggested that the real objective of the limits was to privilege political parties over interest groups in the electoral process. In *Libman* the Supreme Court of Canada expressly repudiated *Somerville*: "we cannot accept the Alberta Court of Appeal's point of view because we disagree with its conclusion regarding the legitimacy of the objective of the provisions."

48. In the words of Justice Paperny of the Alberta Court of Appeal, "I do not understand *Libman* to support the argument that political equality, is, by definition, a pressing and substantial objective such that any and all measures which purport to promote political equality can be presumed to outweigh any restriction on constitutionally guaranteed rights and freedoms." *Harper v. Canada (A.G.)*, 2002 ABCA 301, paragraph 164.

49. The evidence in question was a study of the impact of third-party advertising in the 1988 federal election. It was conducted by political scientist Richard Johnston for the Royal Commission on Electoral Reform and Party Financing. Johnston's preliminary findings indicated that the intensive pro–free trade ad campaign by business groups swayed some voters toward the Progressive Conservative government, which had negotiated the deal. The commission relied on these preliminary findings when it recommended spending limits on third-party advertising in its 1991 report. But by the time the report was issued, Johnston had changed his mind. After reviewing his data, he found no net effect on voter choice from the pro–free trade campaign. He informed a member of the commission's research staff that his preliminary findings were inaccurate. That staff member, who was responsible for writing the commission's primary research study on third-party spending, suppressed this information; she did not amend her own work, which was based on the preliminary findings, and did not tell the research director that Johnston had disavowed his earlier conclusions. Consequently, the royal commission's report and recommendations—on which the Supreme Court of Canada relied in *Libman*—were based on invalid social-science data. For the Alberta and British Columbia courts, this was sufficient grounds to rule that *Libman* was not a binding precedent. See the 2001 and 2002 *Harper* rulings from the Alberta Court of Queen's Bench and the Court of Appeal, respectively, and the 2000 *Pacific Press* ruling from the Supreme Court of British Columbia.

50. *Harper* 2004, paragraphs 64 and 99.

51. See, e.g., E. Joshua Rosenkrantz, ed., *If Buckley Fell: A First Amendment Blueprint for Regulating Money in Politics* (New York: Century Foundation Press, 1999); Cass Sunstein, *Democracy and the Problem of Free Speech*, rev. ed. (New York: Free Press, 1995), especially Chapter 4; Ronald Dworkin, *Sovereign Virtue: The Theory and Practice of Equality* (Cambridge, MA: Harvard University Press, 2000), Chapter 10; John Rawls, *Political Liberalism* (Cambridge, MA: Harvard University Press, 1993), pp. 362–63, and "Basic Liberties and Their Priority," in Sterling McMurrin, ed., *Selected Tanner Lectures on Moral Philosophy* (Salt Lake City: University of Utah Press, 1987).

52. Sunstein, *Democracy and the Problem of Free Speech*, p. 98.

53. See the judgments of Kennedy and Thomas JJ. in, e.g., *Colorado Republican Federal Campaign Committee and Douglas Jones, Treasurer, Petitioners v. Federal Election Commission* (1996) and *Nixon, Attorney General of Missouri, et al. v. Shrink Missouri Government PAC et al.* (2000).

54. John C. Courtney, *Commissioned Ridings: Designing Canada's Electoral Districts* (Montreal and Kingston: McGill-Queen's University Press, 2001), p. 11.

55. Roughly once every ten years, following the release of the latest census data, independent commissions in each province and territory are assigned the task of adjusting the national electoral map to reflect changes in population. The process begins with the chief electoral officer, who announces the new seat totals for each province. In early 2003, he determined that the total number of seats in the House of Commons would rise from 301 to 308. Ontario would receive three new seats, while Alberta and British Columbia would gain two seats apiece. The riding commissions then set to work, consulting with the public and eventu- ally producing a draft election map. The time- line was tight because the last federal election had been held in November 2000. If the new boundaries were to be in place before the next election, as the two westernmost provinces demanded, there would be little time for parlia- mentary review. Nonetheless, the new bound- aries were subjected to intense scrutiny by MPs, which slowed down the process. The revised electoral map was originally scheduled to take effect in August 2004. This posed a problem for aspiring Liberal leader (and prime minister) Paul Martin, who let it be known that he wanted to dissolve Parliament in spring 2004 shortly after winning the party leadership. Elections Canada was already working on two tracks: preparing for an election under the old boundaries, while getting ready for a vote under the new boundaries. In September 2003, the federal government introduced Bill C-49, which moved back the deadline from August to the first dissolution of Parliament after April 1, 2004. The bill was passed in March 2004. Bill C-49, An Act Respecting the Effective Date of the Representation Order of 2003, 37th Parliament, 2nd Session, 2002–03.

56. Courtney, *Commissioned Ridings*, p. 203.

57. *New Brunswick Broadcasting Co. v. Nova Scotia (Speaker of the House of Assembly)*, [1993] 1 S.C.R. 319.

58. *Harvey v. New Brunswick (Attorney General)*, [1996] 2 S.C.R. 876.

59. *New Brunswick Broadcasting*, headnotes, *per* McLachlin J. (as she then was).

60. *Reference re Bill 30, An Act to Amend the Education Act (Ont.)*, [1987] 1 S.C.R. 1148.

61. *Harvey v. New Brunswick*, paragraphs 29–30.

62. Between 1974 and 2000, the percentage of respondents to national surveys who cited their local candidates as the most important factor in their voting choice ranged from 20 to 27 percent, compared to 40–58 percent for "party

as a whole" and 20–37 percent for the party leaders. Jon H. Pammett, "The People's Verdict," in Jon H. Pammett and Christopher Dornan, eds., *The Canadian General Election of 2000* (Ottawa: Carleton University Press, 2001), Table 3, p. 298.

63. On rare occasions, an independent candidate will win a seat; but for all practical purposes, parties monopolize the electoral process.

64. *Barrette v. Canada (Attorney General)*, Quebec Court of Appeal, March 18, 1994, 113 D.L.R. (4th), pp. 623–33.

65. *Somerville v. Canada (Attorney General)*, Alberta Court of Appeal, 1996, 136 D.L.R. (4th) 205, p. 234, *per* Conrad J.A.

66. In *Figueroa v. Canada (Attorney General)*, the Communist Party of Canada is represented by its former leader, Miguel Figueroa.

67. In the *Barrette* case, the two respondents were a former NDP candidate and his official agent.

68. *Reform Party of Canada et al. v. Canada (Attorney General)*, Alberta Court of Appeal, March 10, 1995, 123 D.L.R. (4th), pp. 366–445.

69. For a fuller discussion of these two approaches, see Heather MacIvor, "Judicial Review and Electoral Democracy: The Contested Status of Political Parties under the Charter," *Windsor Yearbook of Access to Justice* 21 (2002), pp. 479–504.

70. The two key examples are the dissenting judgment in the *Reform Party* case and the solo ruling of Justice Molloy in *Figueroa v. Canada (Attorney General)*, Ontario Court (General Division), March 10, 1999, 170 D.L.R. (4th), pp. 647–731.

71. See the *Barrette* case, the majority ruling in *Reform Party v. Canada*, and *Figueroa v. Canada (Attorney General)*, Ontario Court of Appeal, August 16, 2000, accessed online at the Court's website (www.ontariocourts.on.ca).

72. Beaudoin, "Democratic Rights," pp. 298–99.

Chapter 10

Legal Rights

Under the Charter, police must exercise their powers to search, seize evidence, and arrest suspects in accordance with strict norms of due process.

CP PHOTO/Jeffrey Racette

Legal Rights

7. *Everyone has the right to life, liberty and security of the person and the right not to be deprived thereof except in accordance with the principles of fundamental justice.*

8. *Everyone has the right to be secure against unreasonable search or seizure.*

9. *Everyone has the right not to be arbitrarily detained or imprisoned.*

10. *Everyone has the right on arrest or detention*

    (a) to be informed promptly of the reasons therefor;

    (b) to retain and instruct counsel without delay and to be informed of that right; and

    (c) to have the validity of the detention determined by way of habeas corpus and to be released if the detention is not lawful.

11. *Any person charged with an offence has the right*

    (a) to be informed without unreasonable delay of the specific offence;

    (b) to be tried within a reasonable time;

    (c) not to be compelled to be a witness in proceedings against that person in respect of the offence;

(d) to be presumed innocent until proven guilty according to law in a fair and public hearing by an independent and impartial tribunal;

(e) not to be denied reasonable bail without just cause;

(f) except in the case of an offence under military law tried before a military tribunal, to the benefit of trial by jury where the maximum punishment for the offence is imprisonment for five years or a more severe punishment;

(g) not to be found guilty on account of any act or omission unless, at the time of the act or omission, it constituted an offence under Canadian or international law or was criminal according to the general principles of law recognized by the community of nations;

(h) if finally acquitted of the offence, not to be tried for it again and, if finally found guilty and punished for the offence, not to be tried or punished for it again; and

(i) if found guilty of the offence and if the punishment for the offence has been varied between the time of commission and the time of sentencing, to the benefit of the lesser punishment.

12. Everyone has the right not to be subjected to any cruel and unusual treatment or punishment.

13. A witness who testifies in any proceedings has the right not to have any incriminating evidence so given used to incriminate that witness in any other proceedings, except in a prosecution for perjury or for the giving of contradictory evidence.

14. A party or witness in any proceedings who does not understand or speak the language in which the proceedings are conducted or who is deaf has the right to the assistance of an interpreter.

Enforcement

24. (1) Anyone whose rights or freedoms, as guaranteed by this Charter, have been infringed or denied may apply to a court of competent jurisdiction to obtain such remedy as the court considers appropriate and just in the circumstances.

(2) Where, in proceedings under subsection (1), a court concludes that evidence was obtained in a manner that infringed or denied any rights or freedoms guaranteed by this Charter, the evidence shall be excluded if it is established that, having regard to all the circumstances, the admission of it in the proceedings would bring the administration of justice into disrepute.

INTRODUCTION

As we saw in Chapter 2, the legal rights in the Charter attracted intense criticism during the 1980–81 drafting process. Police chiefs and Crown prosecutors warned the Special Joint Committee that the entrenched due-process protections, together with the exclusionary rule in s. 24(2), would make it more difficult for them to do their jobs.[1] Their fears were justified, at least to a degree. Over the past two decades, the Supreme Court and many provincial appellate courts have adopted a fairly strict interpretation of the due-process guarantees in the Charter. Police interrogation techniques, plea-bargaining, the collection of evidence, and the process by which suspects are taken into custody have been evaluated by the courts, and sometimes found wanting. Crown prosecutors have been criticized for failing to disclose evidence to the defence, while court administrators have seen thousands of charges stayed because of lengthy pretrial delays—some arising from motions to exclude evidence under s. 24(2). Several sections of the Criminal Code, and some provincial laws relating to highway offences, have been struck down.

The Supreme Court has used the guarantees of legal rights to evaluate both the substance of laws and the procedures by which they are enforced (see Dossier 3.2, pages 110–12). When statutes are found to infringe one or more legal rights, they are rarely "saved" by s. 1. The standard of justification is particularly high,[2] and deference to Parliament on matters of criminal justice is relatively rare. (For examples, see the case studies in Chapter 4, pages 157–73.) The courts have been more willing to impose constitutional remedies in the field of criminal law than in other policy areas[3] because they consider criminal law to be part of "the inherent domain of the judiciary as guardian of the justice system."[4]

The impact of the Charter on law enforcement and criminal investigation is impossible to measure. We cannot assume that the Supreme Court's due-process rulings have been fully implemented.[5] The flaws in the criminal-justice system that produced the wrongful convictions of Donald Marshall Jr., Guy Paul Morin, David Milgaard, and others have not been miraculously cured by the entrenchment of legal rights.[6] On the other side of the ledger, some critics complain that the Supreme Court is biased toward criminals and overlooks innocent victims and the need to protect society.[7] Whether or not the courts have gone too far in defence of due-process rights is a matter of opinion. But as the cases discussed in this chapter demonstrate, it is never easy to find the proper balance between the rights of the accused and competing social values.

Criminal appeals account for two-thirds of all Charter cases at the Supreme Court.[8] A majority of these cases involve alleged procedural violations of legal rights and requests for relief under s. 24. Challenges to the constitutionality of statutes under s. 52 are less common. The large volume of jurisprudence on legal rights makes it impossible to provide more than a brief overview in this chapter. Instead of attempting to provide a comprehensive account, the chapter focuses on the provisions that have generated the greatest volume of case law, and thus imposed the greatest constraints on the legislative and executive branches of government. We will proceed section by section, summarizing the key common-law principles arising from Charter interpretation. Although the emphasis on court rulings may seem unusual in a political science text, it is appropriate for a chapter on legal rights. (Parliament's role in the criminal-justice system is covered in Chapter 4.)

Section 7: The Right to Life, Liberty, and Security of the Person

Section 7 has been interpreted by the Supreme Court as a broad summary of all the legal rights in the Charter.[9] Unlike the sections which follow it, s. 7 is not restricted to the criminal-justice system.[10] It applies to any law or government action that threatens life, liberty, or physical security, e.g., the process for evaluating refugee claims or the power to place children in the care of the state.[11] Where the law or action in question conforms to the requirements of "fundamental justice," no violation of s. 7 will be found. The phrase "principles of fundamental justice" operates as an internal limitation on the guarantees of life, liberty, and security of the person.[12] In other words, the state may legitimately infringe on any or all of those guaranteed rights as long as it has a compelling reason and follows proper procedures.

The three interests protected by the first part of the section are treated by the courts as distinct and separate guarantees, not as elements of a single right.[13] In other words, a violation of s. 7 does not require a deprivation of life, liberty, *and* security of the person; it occurs when any of the three is infringed in a manner incompatible with fundamental justice. The judicial interpretation of these broad guarantees has evolved over time; the major doctrines are briefly summarized here.

Life

The guarantee of life has received the least judicial attention, perhaps because people in Canada rarely face the threat of death at the hands of the state. The most important case on this point is the 1993 *Rodriguez* appeal,[14] one of the most famous and controversial decisions in the first two decades of the Charter. Sue Rodriguez suffered from amyotrophic lateral sclerosis (ALS), a progressive neuromuscular condition that erodes the brain's ability to control the voluntary and involuntary muscles. Her condition deteriorated to the point where she could barely speak, move, or eat. Rodriguez knew that she would soon lose the ability to swallow, to breathe unassisted, and to communicate. She wanted to secure the assistance of a physician to end her life when she could no longer enjoy living, but she was prohibited from doing so by a section of the Criminal Code banning assisted suicide. Rodriguez challenged the law as a violation of her right to liberty and security of the person.[15]

Although the Court was deeply divided over the disposition of the case, all of the Justices agreed that the protection of human life is a core value in Canadian society. For the five Justices in the majority, Justice Sopinka ruled that to allow Rodriguez to choose the manner and timing of her death would violate the right to life in s. 7. He acknowledged that the impugned law infringed her liberty and security of the person, but held that "a consideration of these interests cannot be divorced from the sanctity of life."[16] However important liberty and security of the person may be, they cannot override the state's interest in protecting life. He further argued that "security of the person, by its nature, cannot encompass a right to take action that will end one's life as security of the person is intrinsically concerned with the well-being of the living person."[17] He upheld the law and refused to grant Rodriguez a constitutional exemption, over the vigorous dissents of Chief Justice Lamer and Justices L'Heureux-Dubé, McLachlin, and Cory. The latter argued that "dying is an integral part of living," and consequently that "it is entitled to the constitutional protection provided by s. 7. It follows that the right to die with dignity should be as well protected as is any other aspect of the right to life."[18] From Sue Rodriguez's perspective, the majority's rejection of that argument left her with no alternative but to break the law. Shortly after the ruling was issued, an anonymous doctor helped her to end her life.

At the time of the Charter's proclamation, there was considerable speculation that the guarantee of life to "everyone" would protect the fetus and require the courts to prohibit abortion.[19] The hopes of anti-abortion groups were dashed by the 1988 *Morgentaler* ruling, in which the Supreme Court refused to declare whether the word "everyone" in s. 7 included the fetus.[20] In a 1989 case involving the Quebec Charter of Human Rights, the Court declared unanimously that the fetus was not a human being in the legal sense.[21] That doctrine was reaffirmed in 1997: "The law of Canada does not recognize the unborn child as a legal person possessing rights. This is a general proposition applicable to all aspects of the law."[22]

Liberty

The liberty protected by s. 7 is not absolute: "Freedom of the individual to do what he or she wishes must, in any organized society, be subjected to numerous constraints for the common good."[23] Therefore, the Charter allows the state to impose reasonable restrictions on liberty. The "liberty interest" in s. 7 is usually understood to refer to physical incarceration: the state cannot imprison or otherwise detain an individual except in accordance with the principles of fundamental justice. However, the guarantee ensures more than "mere freedom from physical restraint"; it also protects the individual's "personal autonomy to live his or her own life and to make decisions that are of fundamental personal importance."[24] That autonomy does not extend to the purely commercial sphere, because the Charter does not protect the "economic liberty" of either individuals or corporations.[25] The liberty guarantee also engages the Charter values of human dignity and privacy, neither of which can be infringed by the state in an arbitrary fashion.[26]

Security of the Person

The guarantee of security of the person protects both the physical and psychological well-being of the individual against unjustified government action.[27] It forbids actual as well as potential threats to personal safety and integrity.[28] An executive action or law will not infringe s. 7 if it imposes mere physical discomfort or emotional stress. It must seriously imperil bodily safety and/or psychological integrity, and it must do so in a way that is incompatible with fundamental justice. Security of the person has generally been interpreted in negative terms, as a personal condition with which the state may not interfere unduly.[29]

To summarize, the guarantees of life, liberty, and security of the person are separate, though related, provisions. They protect the individual against the arbitrary power of the state. Their ambit extends beyond the criminal-justice system (although they do not protect economic rights). These guarantees do not impose positive duties on the state; rather, they represent crucial aspects of individual autonomy with which the state may not interfere except as necessary, and in accordance with the principles of fundamental justice. We now turn to the meaning of that latter phrase.

Section 7: The Principles of Fundamental Justice

The phrase "principles of fundamental justice" describes the long-standing common-law rules that shield individuals against the state. These are "to be found in the basic tenets of our legal system."[30] This does not mean that all common-law rules are covered by s. 7:

> For a rule or principle to constitute a principle of fundamental justice for the purposes of s. 7, it must be a legal principle about which there is significant societal consensus that it is fundamental to the way in which the legal system ought fairly to operate, and it must be identified with sufficient precision to yield a manageable standard against which to measure deprivations of life, liberty or security of the person.[31]

Most of the common-law rules that have been "read into" s. 7 are replicated in subsequent sections of the Charter. These include:

1. the right against self-incrimination;
2. *mens rea*;
3. clarity and precision in legal drafting; and
4. the right of an accused to make a full answer and defence.

The Right against Self-Incrimination

Unlike the written guarantees in ss. 11(c) and 13, this first principle of fundamental justice applies to every stage of the criminal process. It incorporates the common-law right to remain silent before trial, during the investigation of an alleged offence. It also engages

the principle that confessions must be given freely and voluntarily if they are to be used against the accused at trial. Dossier 10.1, pages 309–10 summarizes the application and purpose of these shields against self-incrimination.

Dossier 10.1 implies that any incriminating statement to the police (or their agents) must be completely voluntary; otherwise it will not be admissible at trial. The Supreme Court modified this position in 1994. While in police custody, Douglas James Whittle repeatedly refused legal advice and made numerous incriminating statements about several serious crimes. When he finally agreed to speak to a lawyer, who advised him to cease talking to the police, Mr. Whittle rejected that advice. He told the lawyer that the voices in his head were forcing him to unburden his conscience. Although Whittle was found to be suffering from schizophrenia, the Supreme Court held unanimously that his statements to the police were voluntary—that he had effectively waived his right to silence when he refused legal advice and that he confessed of his own free will. Therefore, the admission of his incriminating statements at trial would not have brought the administration of justice into disrepute.[32] The finding in this case reveals the limits of the "voluntariness" rule at common law.

Mens Rea

A second principle of fundamental justice is the onus on the Crown to demonstrate that the accused possessed a "guilty mind"—in legal Latin, *mens rea*. An accused person cannot be convicted on the basis of the act alone; both the physical and mental elements of the crime must be proven beyond a reasonable doubt. This common-law rule is premised on the belief that legal guilt must be founded on moral guilt—that the heaviness of the punishment for a crime must be proportionate to the degree of moral blameworthiness attaching to the deed. For example, a person who acted knowingly and with "malice aforethought" when he killed someone else deserves a greater punishment than a person who accidentally caused the death of another human being.

The *mens rea* principle applies primarily to the definition of offences and defences, whether statutory or common-law. (Any procedural issues are covered by

DOSSIER 10.1

THE RIGHT TO REMAIN SILENT AND THE "CONFESSIONS RULE"

In 1990, the Supreme Court upheld the acquittal of a robbery suspect, on the ground that the trial judge had properly excluded evidence that was obtained in violation of the right to silence. Neil Gerald Hebert had been arrested and taken to the police station, whereupon he spoke to a lawyer who advised him to invoke his right to silence. After he told the police that he would not make any statement concerning the charges against him, Mr. Hebert was placed in a holding cell with an undercover police officer. The officer, pretending to be a fellow suspect, "engaged the accused in conversation, during which the accused made various incriminating statements implicating him in the robbery."[1] These statements were ruled inadmissible at trial because the police had tricked Mr. Hebert and thus violated the right to silence that he had clearly invoked. The remaining evidence against him was insufficient to discharge the Crown's burden of proof, and he was found not guilty. The Crown appealed the acquittal to the Yukon Court of Appeal, which overturned the acquittal and ordered a new trial. Hebert appealed to the Supreme Court of Canada to restore the original acquittal.

For a unanimous Court, Justice McLachlin began by defining the purpose of s. 7: "The appellant's liberty is at stake. Under section 7 of the Charter, he can only be deprived of that liberty in accordance with the principles of fundamental justice. The question is whether the manner in which the police obtained a statement from him violates that right."[2] She found that s. 7 protected the common-law right to remain silent while in police custody. The key element of that right is "the idea that a person in the power of the state in the course of the criminal process has the right to choose whether to speak to the police or remain silent."[3] By tricking Hebert into making incriminating statements to an officer, the police had deprived him of that choice. Consequently, the admission of those statements into his trial would have "brought the administration of justice into disrepute."

The *Hebert* doctrine was broadened in *R. v. Broyles*, in which the Court granted a new trial to a young offender who had been convicted of murdering his grandmother.[4] Shortly after the murder was discovered, the police arrested Broyles. Their case rested on circumstantial evidence, which might not have been sufficient to secure a conviction. In an attempt to secure an incriminating statement, officers asked a friend of the suspect to visit Broyles in jail while wearing a concealed tape recorder. During their conversation, Broyles did not confess to the murder; however, he made a somewhat incriminating statement that was used against him at trial.

In a unanimous decision, authored by Justice Iacobucci, the Court found that the friend had acted as "an agent of the state" when he elicited and recorded the incriminating statements. The police had attempted to use him to accomplish what they themselves could not—namely, to trick the suspect into incriminating himself. Iacobucci held that the taped conversation would not have violated the right to silence if the police had not instigated it, and if the informer had conducted a normal conversation with the accused. Because the taped conversation took place at the behest of the authorities and resembled an interrogation more than a friendly chat, the incriminating statements could not be regarded as voluntary. Iacobucci acknowledged the seriousness of the alleged offence, but he concluded that the severity of the rights violation and the existence of other (albeit weaker) evidence against the accused made the taped statement inadmissible in court. The Charter violation had tainted the first trial. So the Court granted Broyles a new trial and ordered the exclusion of the incriminating statements elicited by the friend.

(continued)

ENDNOTES

1. *R. v. Hebert*, [1990] 2 S.C.R. 151, headnotes.

2. Ibid., paragraph 13.

3. Ibid., paragraph 20.

4. *R. v. Broyles*, [1991] 3 S.C.R. 595.

s. 11(d) of the Charter.) A law that allows an accused to be found guilty of a serious offence, without definitive proof that he knowingly or intentionally committed that offence, is inconsistent with the principles of fundamental justice, although it may be saved under s. 1. For example, the Supreme Court has held that "absolute liability offends the principles of fundamental justice" if it results in the deprivation of liberty.[33] "Absolute liability" offences permit the conviction of the accused on physical evidence alone, without permitting her to defend herself by arguing that she did not intend to commit the crime. Dossier 10.2 presents a case in which the degree of legal guilt was found to be unrelated to moral guilt.

A crime like murder, which carries a harsh moral stigma and a long prison sentence, requires the Crown to demonstrate that the accused intended to cause either death or severe bodily harm that could be expected to result in death. The offence of manslaughter, which carries a lesser stigma and punishment, does not impose the same burden of proof on the Crown. In 1993, the Court upheld the common-law offence of "unlawful act manslaughter" in a case where the accused did not anticipate that his illegal actions would lead to the death of another person. In *Creighton*, the issue was whether a man had been properly convicted of manslaughter because he had unintentionally injected a woman with a lethal overdose of cocaine. The Court held that "The standard of *mens rea* required for manslaughter is ... appropriately tailored to the seriousness of the offence."[34] The "tailoring" principle also applies to lesser crimes.[35] In general, then, there must be a proportionality between moral and legal guilt; where no such proportionality exists, a conviction and prison term violate the guarantee of liberty in a manner contrary to the principles of fundamental justice.

DOSSIER 10.2

THE "GUILTY MIND"

The 1987 *Vaillancourt* case challenged the constitutionality of the crime of "constructive murder" (also called "felony murder") in the Criminal Code. Under s. 213 of the Code, an accused could be convicted of murder if he caused the death of a human being in the course of committing another crime (e.g., robbery or hijacking), "whether or not the person means to cause death to any human being and whether or not he knows that death is likely to be caused to any human being." The mental element of murder was replaced by the intent to commit the other crime, and (where appropriate) by the possession of a dangerous weapon.

In the early 1980s, Yvan Vaillancourt was convicted of a constructive murder committed while he robbed a pool hall. Vaillancourt's accomplice had shot a customer; because the two men had planned the robbery, both were held to account for the killing. Vaillancourt appealed his conviction for the murder, arguing that s. 213 of the Criminal Code violated the principle of *mens rea* and was thus contrary to the principles of fundamental justice. According to Vaillancourt, the robbery plan was to be carried out with knives and not with firearms. He was shocked when his accomplice showed up with a handgun on the night of the crime. Vaillancourt took the gun, removed three bullets, and handed it back—as he believed—unloaded. This statement, which was supported by physical evidence, was the basis for his claim that he had no intent to kill anyone at the pool hall and his murder conviction was unjust.

The Supreme Court of Canada agreed. It struck down s. 213 as a violation of s. 7. In his opinion, which was endorsed by the majority, Justice Lamer wrote: "it is a principle of fundamental justice that, absent proof beyond a reasonable doubt of at least objective foreseeability, there surely cannot be a murder conviction."[1] Because of "the special nature of the stigma attached to a conviction" for murder, and the severity of the resulting punishment, "the princi-

ples of fundamental justice require a *mens rea* reflecting the particular nature of that crime."[2] The Court vacated Vaillancourt's constructive murder conviction, and remitted him for trial on a charge of manslaughter.

ENDNOTES

1. *R. v. Vaillancourt*, [1987] 2 S.C.R. 636, paragraph 28, *per* Lamer J. In a subsequent case, the Court added the requirement of *subjective* foreseeability of death to the standard set out in *Vaillancourt*. See *R. v. Martineau*, [1990] 2 S.C.R. 633, *per* Lamer J., and the dissenting opinion by Sopinka J.

2. *Vaillancourt*, paragraph 28, *per* Lamer J.

The "Void for Vagueness" Doctrine

Third, fundamental justice requires that laws be drafted clearly and precisely. As Justice Lamer put it in the 1988 *Prostitution Reference*, "if a person is placed at risk of being deprived of his liberty when he has not been given fair notice that his conduct falls within the scope of the offence as defined by Parliament, then surely this would offend the principles of fundamental justice."[36] Moreover, a vaguely worded law imposes few restraints on the arbitrary power of the state; it "permits a 'standardless sweep' allowing law enforcement officials to pursue their personal predilections."[37] When determining whether a law is impermissibly vague, a court must take into account "a) the need for flexibility and the interpretative role of the courts, (b) the impossibility of achieving absolute certainty, a standard of intelligibility being more appropriate and (c) the possibility that many varying judicial interpretations of a given disposition may exist and perhaps coexist."[38] In practice, this usually means that the courts will defer to the legislature unless the language of a statute is so fuzzy that it cannot be given an intelligible interpretation.

One aspect of vagueness is the problem of "overbreadth." In June 2004, the Court summed up its

jurisprudence on this point: "It is a well-established principle of fundamental justice that criminal legislation must not be overbroad."[39] A law will be found to be excessively broad, and thereby in violation of s. 7, when it risks inflicting punishment on the morally guiltless.

> If the State, in pursuing a legitimate objective, uses means which are broader than is necessary to accomplish that objective, the principles of fundamental justice will be violated because the individual's rights will have been limited for no reason. The effect of overbreadth is that in some applications the law is arbitrary or disproportionate.[40]

In 1994, for example, the Court struck down a section of the Criminal Code that made it illegal for persons convicted of sexual offences against children to "loiter in or near a school ground, playground, public park or bathing area." The majority observed that, while the law properly barred such individuals from places where children congregate, it also forbade them from entering a park or a beach where no children were present.[41] The possibility that an innocent hike through a national wilderness reserve could result in imprisonment clearly violated the guarantee of liberty in s. 7, in a way that was not compatible with fundamental justice. Where a law is found to violate s. 7 by reason of overbreadth, it cannot be justified under s. 1 because it will, by definition, fail the "minimal impairment" prong of the *Oakes* test.[42]

Full Answer and Defence

The fourth and final principle of fundamental justice is the right of the accused to make a full answer and defence to criminal charges. In practical terms, this means at least two things. First, a law that prevents the accused from introducing potentially **exculpatory evidence** will violate s. 7 (and the right to a fair trial in s. 11(d)). In the 1991 *Seaboyer* case (Dossier 4.2, pages 151–53), the Supreme Court struck down the "rape shield" in the Criminal Code because it prevented defendants in sexual-assault cases from making a full answer and defence.[43] The majority, led by Justice McLachlin, ruled that a blanket prohibition on introducing evidence of the complainant's prior sexual history risked excluding "evidence which is relevant to the defence and the probative value of which is not substantially outweighed by the potential prejudice to the trial process."[44] (See the Glossary of Key Terms for Chapter 2 on page 80 for a definition of "probative.")

Second, the Crown is required to disclose all relevant information in its possession to the defence. In the absence of such disclosure, the accused cannot make a full answer and defence to the case for the prosecution. "The fruits of the investigation which are in the possession of counsel for the Crown are not the property of the Crown for use in securing a conviction but the property of the public to be used to ensure that justice is done."[45] This broad rule applies even to the confidential therapeutic records of complainants in sexual-assault cases, as long as proper safeguards for confidentiality and probative value are observed.[46] However, the failure to disclose will affect the right to make a full answer and defence only if the accused can demonstrate "a reasonable possibility that the failure to disclose affected the outcome at trial or the overall fairness of the trial,"[47] and if defence counsel demonstrated "due diligence" in seeking the production of all relevant information in the Crown's possession.[48]

The Supreme Court's interpretation of the phrase "principles of fundamental justice" has effectively "read in" the basic common-law protections available to an individual confronted with the awesome power of the state. For the most part, the Court has sought to reinforce these protections while restricting the investigative and prosecutory discretion available to law enforcement. Its general attitude was summarized in *Irwin Toy* (see Dossier 8.4, pages 257–59): in the criminal justice system, "the government is best characterized as the singular antagonist of the individual whose right has been infringed."[49]

Sections 8 and 24(2): Unreasonable Search and Seizure and the Exclusion of Evidence

The wording of s. 8 contains an internal limitation on the freedom from search and seizure. It does not protect the individual against any conceivable intrusion by the state. It protects only "a reasonable expectation of privacy," which must be balanced against "the government's interest in intruding on the individual's privacy in order to advance its goals, notably those of law enforcement."[50] That balance should be struck before a search takes place, not after the fact.

> This can only be accomplished by a requirement of prior authorization. Accordingly, prior authorization, where feasible, is a precondition for a valid search and seizure. It follows that warrantless searches are *prima facie* unreasonable under s. 8. The party seeking to justify a warrantless search bears the onus of rebutting the presumption of unreasonableness.[51]

In general, "A search will be reasonable if it is authorized by law, if the law itself is reasonable and if the manner in which the search was carried out is reasonable."[52] Consequently, s. 8 may be used to review the substance of the authorizing statute, the procedure followed by the police, or both.

The balance between individual privacy and the interests of the state varies with the location and nature of the search. In effect, the expectation of privacy carries more or less legal weight depending on the circumstances. The strongest protection attaches to the home and the body of the person being investigated. At common law, police are forbidden to trespass on the dwelling place of a citizen without express prior authorization based on reasonable grounds. That protection was effectively entrenched in s. 8 of the Charter, and reinforced by the exclusionary rule in s. 24(2).[53] Whenever police enter a home "to secure evidence against the occupant," they are by definition engaged in a search that engages the values enshrined in s. 8.[54] The same degree of protection does not attach to the perimeter of the home, which is less private than the interior; in some cases, police may trespass on the exterior of a property in order to gather evidence that may secure a warrant to search the interior.[55]

The sanctity of the body is founded in the common law, and reinforced by the Charter values of human dignity and security of the person.[56] However, the "expectation of privacy" in one's own body is not absolute. In particular, an individual who crosses an international border should expect to be searched by customs agents, even to the extent of being strip-searched if there are reasonable grounds authorized by law to justify such action. In the 1988 *Simmons* case, the Supreme Court upheld the provisions of the Customs Act that authorize border agents to search individuals as they enter the country for the purpose of detecting contraband or illegal goods.[57] Similarly, prison inmates cannot expect to be free from searches of their bodies and personal effects; their privacy is already compromised by the conditions of their confinement.[58]

The privacy interest in a motor vehicle is significant, but not to the same degree as the home or the body.[59] In rare cases, the fact that a vehicle can be used to escape from legitimate police scrutiny may justify warrantless searches on the grounds of exigency—in other words, to prevent the removal or destruction of evidence.[60] Nonetheless, a police officer cannot use a random stop to conduct a search of a vehicle without reasonable and probable grounds to do so. In *Mellenthin*, a car was stopped at night and the police officer used a flashlight to conduct a visual check of its contents. Spotting an open gym bag on the passenger seat, the officer asked the driver what was in it. When the driver reached into the bag to produce a sandwich, the officer noticed some glass vials that might be used

to store hash oil. He ordered the driver to get out of the car, searched the bag, and found hash oil and joints of marijuana. At trial, the driver was found guilty of possessing narcotics. The Supreme Court overturned the conviction, on the grounds that the search of the car was unreasonable and unauthorized by law.[61]

The lowest expectation of privacy attaches to public areas, such as commercial shops, and to the homes of persons other than the suspect.[62] The 1996 *Edwards* case provides an example of the latter. The appellant had been convicted of trafficking in drugs. He argued that the evidence against him—a large quantity of narcotics—should have been excluded at his trial because its seizure violated s. 8. The Supreme Court rejected this claim, on the ground that the drugs were seized at his girlfriend's apartment. This was not a place where Mr. Edwards could claim a reasonable expectation of privacy, because he spent relatively little time there and did not contribute to the rent.[63] The majority upheld his conviction.

The impact of s. 8 on police conduct is reinforced by the exclusionary rule in s. 24(2). Police officers know that if they conduct warrantless searches, they risk the exclusion of their discoveries at trial. To invoke the protection afforded by the exclusionary rule, a person accused of a criminal offence must prove (1) that the evidence was obtained in consequence of a Charter violation and (2) that the administration of justice would be brought into disrepute by its admission at trial.[64] The standard of proof is the civil standard of a balance of probabilities. In the landmark *Collins* case, the Court set out a test for judges to follow when they assess applications under s. 24(2). That test is briefly summarized in Dossier 10.3, pages 314–15.

The *Collins* test reflects an effort to balance all of the relevant factors, and to provide comprehensive rules for trial judges. Its subsequent history has been contentious. Lamer's emphasis on trial fairness as the determining factor under s. 24(2) has since been rejected by several Justices, including Justice (now Chief Justice) McLachlin and retired Justice L'Heureux-Dubé. In *Stillman*, McLachlin wrote that "The framers of the Charter did not intend s. 24(2) to act as an automatic exclusionary or quasi-exclusionary rule and, accordingly, the view that any

DOSSIER 10.3

THE *COLLINS* TEST

As she sat in a pub in Gibsons, British Columbia, Ruby Collins suddenly found herself "seized by the throat and pulled down to the floor by a man who said to her 'police officer.'"[1] The RCMP Drug Squad officer applied the "throat hold" to keep Ms. Collins, a suspected drug trafficker, from swallowing any drugs that she may have been holding in her mouth. At the time of the arrest, Ms. Collins and her husband had been under surveillance for several hours; he had already been found with heroin in his possession and was in police custody. While she was immobilized on the ground, the officer found a balloon containing heroin clutched in her hand.

This was the dramatic beginning of a case that ultimately established the rules for excluding evidence under the Charter. Ruby Collins was convicted of trafficking in narcotics, even though the judge ruled that the officer did not have sufficient grounds to "take her down" and search her. While he found that the officer's actions had violated s. 8 of the Charter, the judge rejected Ms. Collins's motion to exclude the drugs in the balloon as evidence against her. The British Columbia Court of Appeal upheld her conviction. When the *Collins* case reached the Supreme Court of Canada in 1987, five of the six Justices on the panel voted to overturn the conviction and order a new trial. The sole issue was whether the drug evidence should have been excluded because it arose from a violation of Ms. Collins's rights under s. 8.

For the majority, Justice Lamer identified three sets of factors that must be taken into account when a judge considers a motion to exclude evidence. First, would the admission of the evidence impair the fairness of the trial?

> Misconduct by the police in the investigatory process often has some effect on the repute of the administration of justice, but s. 24(2) is not a remedy for police misconduct, requiring the exclusion of the evidence if, because of this misconduct, the administration of justice was brought into disrepute. Section 24(2) could well have been drafted in that way, but it was not. Rather, the drafters of the *Charter* decided to focus on the admission of the evidence in the proceedings, and the purpose of s. 24(2) is to prevent having the administration of justice brought into *further disrepute* by the admission of the evidence in the proceedings. This further disrepute will result from the admission of evidence that would deprive the accused of a fair hearing, or from judicial condonation of unacceptable conduct by the investigatory and prosecutorial agencies.[2]

The degree of disrepute arising from the admission of tainted evidence depends on "the nature of the evidence obtained as a result of the violation and the nature of the right violated and not so much the manner in which the right was violated." As a general rule, "real" evidence—such as fingerprints, stolen property found in the possession of the accused, or a DNA sample left at the crime scene—exists independently of any Charter breach and would probably have been found anyway. Its admission would not render a trial unfair. However, "conscriptive" evidence—e.g., incriminating statements to the police in the absence of counsel—may have been manufactured or obtained as a direct result of the Charter breach; its admission "will generally go to the very fairness of the trial and should generally be excluded."[3]

The second set of factors "relates to the seriousness of the Charter violation and therefore to the disrepute that will result from judicial acceptance of evidence obtained through that violation."[4] These include:

- "was the Charter violation serious or was it of a merely technical nature?"
- "was it deliberate, willful, or flagrant, or was it inadvertent or committed in good faith?"

- "did it occur in circumstances of urgency or necessity?"
- "were there other investigatory techniques available?"
- "would the evidence have been obtained in any event?"[5]

Third, would the exclusion of the evidence "bring the administration of justice into disrepute"? The relevant factors include the seriousness of the charge, the importance of the impugned evidence to the trier of fact, and the proper balance between public safety and Charter values. Lamer argued that "the administration of justice would be brought into disrepute by the exclusion of evidence essential to substantiate the charge, and thus the acquittal of the accused, because of a trivial breach of the Charter."[6] However, he suggested that a serious criminal charge did not excuse Charter violations by investigators. Instead, judges should be especially careful to safeguard trial fairness—using s. 24(2), if necessary—when dealing with the most heinous crimes.

Lamer concluded, on the basis of the factors just summarized, that the trial judge erred by admitting the drug evidence at Ruby Collins's trial. Even though the balloon of heroin was "real" evidence, and necessary to sustain the charge of drug trafficking, the behaviour of the RCMP officer at the time of arrest was "a flagrant and serious violation of the rights of an individual. Indeed, we cannot accept that police officers take flying tackles at people and seize them by the throat when they do not have reasonable and probable grounds to believe that those people are either dangerous or handlers of drugs."[7]

ENDNOTES

1. *R. v. Collins*, [1987] 1 S.C.R. 265, paragraph 1, *per* Lamer J.

2. Ibid., paragraph 31, *per* Lamer J.

3. Ibid., paragraph 37, *per* Lamer J.

4. Ibid., paragraph 38, *per* Lamer J.

5. Ibid., paragraph 35, *per* Lamer J.

6. Ibid., paragraph 39, *per* Lamer J.

7. Ibid., paragraph 45, *per* Lamer J.

evidence which affects the fairness of the trial must be excluded under s. 24(2) should be rejected."[65] On the other side of the issue, former Justice Arbour recently wrote that "Section 24(2) is not an automatic exclusionary rule; in my view, neither should it become an automatic inclusionary rule when the evidence is non-conscriptive and essential to the Crown's case."[66] *Collins* has become a litmus test for the attitudes of Supreme Court Justices toward legal rights: those who tend to favour the Crown believe that evidence should generally be admitted with some exceptions, while those whose greatest concern lies with the accused take the opposite view.[67] The Court, as a whole, has not been particularly consistent on this issue; this may pose problems for police engaged in criminal investigations.

SECTION 9: ARBITRARY DETENTION AND IMPRISONMENT

Like s. 8, the guarantee in s. 9 is internally limited. The state is not prohibited from detaining or imprisoning individuals under *any* circumstances; it must only avoid doing so arbitrarily. A deprivation of liberty will generally be considered arbitrary "if there are no criteria, express or implied, which govern its exercise."[68] In other words, where agents of the state deprive someone of his or her liberty, they must do so for good reasons, and under statutory authorization. The discretion of a police officer or judge to detain any individual must be subject to clear written criteria; in the absence of such criteria, the detention will generally be found to be arbitrary.[69]

While the meaning of "imprisonment" is clear enough, the meaning of "detention" in ss. 9 and 10 of the Charter requires more comment. The Supreme Court has defined "detention" broadly, to cover a wide range of circumstances in which the state restrains the liberty of an individual. In general, a detention occurs when "a police officer or other agent of the state assumes control over the movement of a person by a demand or direction which may have significant legal consequence."[70] Even a brief encounter with a police officer, such as a traffic stop under a RIDE program, is considered to be a "detention" for the purposes of s. 9.[71] Such detentions are generally legitimate, as long as they are authorized ahead of time (as they are in RIDE programs) and the statutory criteria are applied fairly. (It is perfectly acceptable for an officer to stop a car because the driver is weaving erratically across two lanes; it is not permissible to stop a car just because the driver belongs to a particular racial group.)

The Supreme Court has shown some flexibility in the interpretation of s. 9. It has held, for example, that a criminal suspect may be detained in police custody for several hours without charge, as long as the delay is necessary to complete the precharge investigation of an alleged offence.[72] Even in questionable cases, where an officer's decision to detain an individual might appear to be arbitrary, the Court has generally allowed the police some latitude in pursuing their "reasonable suspicions."[73] The exception is a case in which investigating officers acted without specific statutory authority. That case, which is discussed in Dossier 10.4, is noteworthy for two reasons. First, the majority implicitly endorsed two lower-court rulings that condemned the police in harsh (and perhaps unjustified) terms. Second, it illustrates a deep division between the Justices over the proper balance between due-process rights and the duty of the police to solve crimes.

The sentiments expressed in L'Heureux-Dubé's dissent have never been endorsed by a majority of the Court. Unlike most of her colleagues, she usually defended police discretion to investigate crimes without undue interference or restriction on Charter

---

DOSSIER 10.4

R. V. DUGUAY (1989)[1]

The victims of a burglary told police that they had seen three young men in their neighbour's backyard shortly before the offence was committed. At the request of the police, the neighbour called the three suspects and invited them over; the victims identified two of them as the young men they had seen on the previous evening. A police officer approached the three suspects and asked them to sit in the squad car for a few moments. They complied. While they were in the police car, the officer asked them to tell him where the stolen stereo was. One of the young men gave an incriminating answer. The suspects were then cautioned and formally charged. They were driven to the police station, where they signed written confessions and their fingerprints were taken. None asked to speak to a lawyer. The fingerprints were later matched to prints on the stolen property—which was found

in the home of one of the suspects—and on the window frame through which the burglars had entered the house on the night of the crime.

At trial, the Crown tried to introduce both the "real" evidence (the stolen stereo and fingerprints) and the "conscriptive" evidence (the confessions). The trial judge found that all of the evidence against the accused had been tainted by the "arbitrary detention" in the squad car, and excluded it. He concluded that the suspects were "in effect under arrest" from the moment they voluntarily entered the back of the police car—thus tainting all subsequent evidence—and characterized the actions of the officers as nearly tantamount to "torture."[2] The arrest was an unlawful attempt, made in bad faith, to intimidate the suspects into incriminating themselves. The evidence was excluded under s. 24(2), and the three suspects were acquitted.

That acquittal was upheld by the Ontario Court of Appeal (OCA). While it repudiated some of the trial judge's attacks on the police, the OCA panel criticized the "incipient Star Chamber attitude" of the police officers involved.[3] It implied that the police had improperly jumped to the conclusion that the appellants were guilty, and deliberately disregarded their Charter rights in pursuing evidence against them. The Crown then asked the Supreme Court of Canada to quash the acquittal and order a new trial, on the ground that the lower courts had erred in excluding the evidence. Six of the seven Justices on the panel voted to uphold the acquittals, stating simply that neither the trial judge nor the appellate judges had committed a reversible error of law.

In a strongly worded dissent, Justice L'Heureux-Dubé criticized both the lower courts and the Crown. Her ruling contains the most extensive discussion of s. 9 to date. She found, on the facts of the case, that the officers had acted in good faith. They were anxious to solve a break-and-enter, and they had been fortunate enough to identify promising suspects early in the investigation. She did not believe that the invitation to sit in the police car constituted an arbitrary arrest or detention; consequently, there was no infringement of s. 9. Given this finding, and the impossibility of proving the charges against the accused in the absence of the evidence gathered subsequent to the infraction, L'Heureux-Dubé concluded that the application of s. 24(2) at the trial had itself brought the administration of justice into disrepute. In effect, she scolded her colleagues for distorting the *Collins* test: they improperly held that voluntary statements to police would impair trial fairness if admitted; they failed to acknowledge that the fingerprints and the stolen property were "real" evidence; and they overlooked Lamer's comments about the disrepute that may arise from the automatic exclusion of probative evidence.

ENDNOTES

1. *R. v. Duguay*, [1989] 1 S.C.R. 93.

2. Ibid., paragraph 14, *per* L'Heureux-Dubé J.

3. Ibid., paragraph 17, *per* L'Heureux-Dubé J.

grounds. The effect of the majority ruling in *Duguay* is to forbid police from imposing any form of detention without prior authorization. The problem, from the police perspective, is that such authorization is not always available. As *Duguay* suggests, the use of the Charter to restrict law-enforcement discretion does not necessarily yield just results.

SECTION 10: THE RIGHTS OF AN ACCUSED IN POLICE CUSTODY

Section 10(a): The Right to Be Informed Promptly of a Charge

The purpose of s. 10(a) is to allow a criminal suspect to make a sound judgment about his or her situation vis-à-vis the police, and to act accordingly, as soon as possible after being arrested.[74] The guarantee reflects the common-law principle that "one is not obliged to submit to an arrest if one does not know the reasons for it."[75] Finally, it reinforces the right to counsel in s. 10(b) by ensuring that the suspect can give his or her lawyer accurate information during their initial consultation.[76] The duty of police under s. 10(a) continues throughout the period of detention: if further charges are laid after the initial disclosure to the suspect, he or she must be informed immediately.

When the police exercise their duties under s. 10(a), they must ensure that the suspect actually understands what they are saying. The mere recitation of the technical language of the Criminal Code is insufficient: "The question is whether what the accused was told, viewed reasonably in all the circumstances of the case, was sufficient to permit him to make a reasonable decision to decline to submit to arrest, or alternatively, to undermine his right to counsel under s. 10(b)."[77] As Dossier 10.5 explains, the requirements of s. 10(a) are satisfied if the suspect understands that he or she is in legal trouble, and that anything that he or she says or does could have serious consequences.

In the *Latimer* case, despite the failure of the s. 10(a) argument, the 1997 appeal was granted on other grounds.[78] Mr. Latimer was retried for second-degree murder, convicted, and sentenced to a minimum of ten years in prison. The judge at the second trial granted Robert Latimer a constitutional exemption from the statutory sentence, reducing the punishment to one year in prison and twelve months of house arrest.[79] The Saskatchewan Court of Appeal denied the constitutional exemption and restored the life sentence with parole eligibility after ten years, a judgment that was later upheld by the Supreme Court of Canada.[80]

Section 10(b): The Right to Counsel

Section 10(b) guarantees the right to legal counsel without delay, and the right to be informed of that right. Its purpose is "to ensure that the accused is treated fairly in the criminal process,"[81] even in situations (such as arrest) where "the restraint of liberty might otherwise effectively prevent access to counsel or induce a person to assume that he or she is unable to retain and instruct counsel."[82] The section "imposes at least two duties on the police in addition to the duty to inform the detainee of his rights." First, "the police must provide the detainee with a reasonable opportunity to exercise the right to retain and instruct counsel without delay."[83] This means, in practice, that a suspect in police custody must be given timely access to a telephone to call a lawyer, unless there are urgent circumstances that might reasonably prevent the police from facilitating contact with counsel. Second, "s. 10(b) imposes on the police the duty to cease questioning or otherwise attempting to elicit evidence from the detainee until he has had a reasonable opportunity to retain and instruct counsel."[84] Otherwise the guarantee of counsel would have little practical value because most laypeople do not understand their legal rights and must rely on lawyers to explain them.

Therefore, s. 10(b) both reflects and reinforces the common-law doctrine of the right to silence. Former Chief Justice Lamer explained this relationship in the 1985 *Therens* ruling:

DOSSIER 10.5

THE *LATIMER* CASE (1997)

In October 1993, twelve-year-old Tracy Latimer died in the cab of her father's truck on the family farm in Saskatchewan. Tracy had been born with severe cerebral palsy and other physical problems. She was immobile, incapable of looking after herself, and in constant pain. She had the intellectual capacity of a baby and could not communicate except through facial expressions. At the time of her death, Tracy was scheduled to undergo a third operation to correct severe musculoskeletal problems. Her father, Robert Latimer, had been a devoted and patient caregiver throughout her life. On the day of her death, while the rest of the family was at church, Latimer carried Tracy out to his truck and put her in the cab. He ran a hose from the truck's exhaust pipe into the cab, turned on the engine, and left Tracy to die of carbon monoxide poisoning. Once she was dead, he carried her into her room and laid her on the bed. He called the RCMP to report her death, telling them that his daughter had died in her sleep. When the autopsy results revealed carbon monoxide in her blood, the police began to treat the case as a homicide. Robert Latimer, the only member of the family who was present at the time of death, became the sole suspect.

In early November 1993, two RCMP officers went to the Latimer farm and asked Mr. Latimer if they could speak to him. He agreed to sit with them in an unmarked police car. One of the officers later testified about their conversation:

I said I realize that this is a very trying time for him and his family and *I said what I am about to say has very serious consequences and he should listen very closely. He nodded to me. I said, "You are being detained for investigation into the death of your daughter Tracy."*[1]

The officers did not explicitly inform Mr. Latimer that he was under arrest. He voluntarily accompanied them to the North Battleford RCMP detachment, where he confessed to causing his daughter's death and signed a written statement to that effect. He then returned to the farm with the officers and showed them exactly how he had caused Tracy's death; the demonstration was videotaped by one of the officers.

Mr. Latimer was convicted of second-degree murder. His lawyer argued that neither the confessions nor the videotaped demonstration should have been admissible at trial, because Latimer had not been properly warned of his jeopardy under s. 10(a) or made fully aware of his right to consult a lawyer (s. 10(b)). Both the Saskatchewan Court of Appeal and the Supreme Court of Canada disagreed. Chief Justice Lamer explained the reasoning of the latter court. He acknowledged that "Mr. Latimer was not told that he was under 'arrest'; he was told that he was being 'detained.' Nor was he explicitly told that he could be charged with murder."

However, as with determining whether there has been a *de facto* arrest, when considering whether there has been a violation of s. 10(a), one must look beyond the exact words used.... On the facts of this case, I have no doubt that the trial judge was right in finding that Mr. Latimer understood the basis for his apprehension by the police and hence the extent of his jeopardy. He knew that his daughter had died, and that he was being detained for investigation into that death. Constable Lyons prefaced his comments in the car by saying "what I am about to say has very serious consequences." Mr. Latimer was then informed of his right to counsel and his right to silence, which clearly conveyed that he was being placed under arrest. Finally, he was told that he could not go into his own house by himself to change his clothes. It is clear on these facts that Mr. Latimer knew that he was in an extremely grave situation as regards his daughter's death, and that s. 10(a) cannot be said to have been violated.[2]

ENDNOTES

1. Quoted in *R. v. Latimer*, [1997] 1 S.C.R. 217, paragraph 8, *per* Lamer C.J. (emphasis added by Chief Justice Lamer).

2. Ibid., paragraphs 30–31, *per* Lamer C.J.

In my view, s. 10(b) requires at least that the authorities inform the detainee of his rights, not prevent him in any way from exercising them and, where a detainee is required to provide evidence which may be incriminating and refusal to comply is punishable as a criminal offence ... s. 10(b) also imposes a duty not to call upon the detainee to provide that evidence without first informing him of his s. 10(b) rights and providing him with a reasonable opportunity and time to retain and instruct counsel. Failure to abide by that duty will lead to the obtainment of evidence in a manner which infringes or denies the detainee's s. 10(b) rights. Short of that, s. 10(b) would be a near empty right, as remedies could seldom affect the admissibility of evidence obtained through the accused.[85]

The Supreme Court has identified the right to counsel as a foundation of the other procedural guarantees in ss. 7–14. Consequently, violations of s. 10(b) will often trigger one or both of the remedies in s. 24. As we saw earlier, one of the factors that a judge must consider when assessing an application to exclude evidence is the nature of the Charter violation that allegedly tainted that evidence. A deliberate violation of the right to counsel casts serious doubt on the fairness of all of the suspect's dealings with the criminal justice system, and it may produce conscriptive evidence; these factors will usually trigger the exclusion of evidence under s. 24(2).

The words "without delay" should not be taken too literally. Where the safety of arresting officers is potentially at risk, police can take the necessary time to secure the scene before turning their attention to the s. 10(b) rights of the suspect.[86] Nor is the guarantee of counsel absolutely ironclad. In the first place, a suspect can waive the right to counsel, either explicitly or implicitly; where he or she does so, no violation of s. 10(b) will be found. For such a waiver to be valid, the suspect must be shown to have been fully aware of the consequences and capable of making a reasoned decision.[87] An initial waiver of the right to counsel, even if fully valid, will cease to apply at the moment when police advise the suspect of any new charges; the police duty to inform under s. 10(a) creates a corresponding duty under s. 10(b).[88] Second, the suspect must be "reasonably diligent" in seeking the advice of counsel. If he or she tries to obstruct an investigation by refusing to call a lawyer, the s. 10(b) duties of the police "are suspended and are not a bar to their continuing their investigation."[89]

The extent of the police duty to facilitate communication between suspect and lawyer depends, to a degree, on the availability of legal counsel at the time and place of the arrest. As we saw in Chapter 7, page 233, the Supreme Court has implicitly advised—but not required—provincial governments to establish 24-hour "duty counsel" who would advise criminal suspects by telephone.[90] Where such "duty counsel" are provided under a provincial legal aid program, the police must inform suspects of their availability. Failure to do so may lead a suspect to waive the right to counsel, not for valid reasons, but because of a concern about cost. If the police question the suspect following such a refusal, this constitutes a violation of s. 10(b).[91] In areas where "duty counsel" are not available, the police must refrain from questioning a suspect until such time as he or she has had a reasonable opportunity to contact a legal aid lawyer or private counsel.[92]

Section 10(b) does more than require the police to refrain from questioning a suspect until after he or she has had an opportunity to speak with a lawyer. As the Supreme Court held in *Burlingham*, it also imposes restrictions on plea-bargaining and forbids "dirty tricks" (see Dossier 10.6).

DOSSIER 10.6

R. V. BURLINGHAM (1995)

In late 1984, two women in Cranbrook, British Columbia, were sexually assaulted and murdered. After police had charged Terrence Wayne Burlingham with one of the murders, the similarity between the two crimes led them to charge him with the second. In January 1985, over a period of four days, Cranbrook police subjected Burlingham to "an intensive and often manipulative interrogation,"[1] ignoring his repeated statements that he would not speak to them unless his lawyer was present.

In an apparent attempt to circumvent their duty under s. 10(b) to cease questioning at the moment when the right to counsel is invoked, the police repeatedly suggested to Burlingham that his lawyer was greedy and untrustworthy. On the fourth day, officers decided to offer the suspect a "deal" in the second murder: they would allow him to plead guilty to second-degree murder instead of first-degree murder if he told them where he had hidden the murder weapon and gave them other necessary information. Burlingham initially refused to respond to the plea-bargain without legal advice. The officers continued to press him for an answer, reminding him that his lawyer was "taking the weekend off" and emphasizing that the "one-time offer" would expire on the Sunday evening—i.e., before his lawyer returned to work.

Under the mistaken impression that he would be allowed to plead not guilty to second-degree murder—when in fact the deal allowed him only to plead guilty—Burlingham finally agreed to accept the deal. He made a full confession to the second murder, took police to the crime scene, and helped them recover the gun used in the murders. He was subsequently charged with first-degree murder. At trial, the Crown tried to introduce the evidence that Burlingham had provided under the terms of the invalid "deal" with the police. Although the trial judge excluded some of the evidence arising from the violation of s. 10(b), he admitted enough of the evidence to secure a conviction against Burlingham. The latter's appeal was dismissed by the British Columbia Court of Appeal.

A majority on the Supreme Court of Canada granted Burlingham's request for a new trial on the second murder charge. They found that his rights under s. 10(b) had been violated in several respects, and that any evidence that would not have been found in the absence of the violations should be excluded from the retrial. This meant that the gun, which was at the bottom of the frozen Kootenay River when the accused pointed out its location to the police, could not be admitted into evidence.

The Court identified three separate violations of the right to counsel. First, the police continued to interrogate Burlingham in the absence of his lawyer, after he had repeatedly invoked his right to silence. There was no waiver of the right to counsel, either express or implied. Second, "s. 10(b) specifically prohibits the police, as they did in this case, from belittling an accused's lawyer with the express goal or effect of undermining the accused's confidence in and relationship with defence counsel." As Justice Iacobucci put it, "It makes no sense for s. 10(b) of the Charter to provide for the right to retain and instruct counsel if law enforcement authorities are able to undermine either an accused's confidence in his or her lawyer or the solicitor-client relationship."[2]

Finally, the police resorted to "trickery and subterfuge" when they pressured Burlingham to accept a plea-bargain while they knew that his lawyer was unavailable.[3] Iacobucci concluded that "s. 10(b) mandates the Crown or police, whenever offering a plea-bargain, to tender that offer either to accused's counsel or to the accused while in the presence of his or her counsel, unless the accused has expressly waived the right to counsel."[4]

ENDNOTES

1. *R. v. Burlingham*, [1995] 2 S.C.R. 206, paragraph 3, *per* Iacobucci J.

2. Ibid., paragraph 14.

3. Ibid., paragraph 16.

4. Ibid., paragraph 21.

Section 10(c): *Habeas Corpus*

This section entrenches the traditional common-law protection of *habeas corpus* and subjects any legislated infringements to the test of justification under s. 1 of the Charter.[93] The *habeas corpus* rule applies to anyone who has been jailed without a formal charge. If the person in custody—or, more likely, his or her lawyer—files a *habeas corpus* motion, the Crown is required to bring that person before a judge and explain why the person is being detained. If the Crown cannot justify the detention, the judge must release the prisoner immediately. At the time of writing, there was no jurisprudence on this section from the Supreme Court of Canada.

SECTION 11: THE RIGHT(S) TO A FAIR TRIAL

Section 11 lists eight separate procedural guarantees, which flesh out the principles of fundamental justice in s. 7. Some of these guarantees have had a notable impact on both the substance and the procedure of Canadian criminal law; others have had little measurable effect. We will focus here on four crucial elements of s. 11: the right to trial within a reasonable time (11(b)); the shield against self-incrimination at trial (11(c)); the presumption of innocence and the guarantee of a fair trial (11(d)); and access to bail (11(e)). We begin with a brief discussion of s. 11 as a whole.

The Scope of the Protections in Section 11

The guarantees in s. 11 apply to any person who is "prosecuted by the state for public offences involving punitive sanctions, i.e., criminal, quasi-criminal, and regulatory offences, either federally or provincially enacted."[94] They are engaged wherever the liberty of the accused is at stake. Consequently, they do not reach to purely regulatory or internal proceedings, such as a disciplinary hearing of a professional body (e.g., a provincial law society), although they do apply to military tribunals that have the power to impose custodial sentences.[95] Nor, in general, do they extend beyond the trial phase to any appeals that may flow from either exoneration or conviction,[96] although s. 11(b) does require that the sentencing of convicted offenders be carried out promptly.[97]

Section 11(b): The Right to Be Tried within a Reasonable Time

The purpose of s. 11(b) is to safeguard the liberty and security of a person accused of a criminal offence. The guarantee of an early trial "protects against an over-long subjection to a pending criminal case and aims to relieve against the stress and anxiety which continue until the outcome of the case is final."[98] The Court has also suggested, albeit less consistently,[99] that the guarantee protects the community at large, as well as the witnesses and victims involved in a particular trial:

> That community interest has a dual dimension. First, there is a collective interest in ensuring that those who transgress the law are brought to trial and dealt with according to the law. Second, those individuals on trial must be treated fairly and justly. Speedy trials strengthen both those aspects of the community interest.... There are as

well important practical benefits which flow from a quick resolution of the charges. There can be no doubt that memories fade with time. Witnesses are likely to be more reliable testifying to events in the immediate past as opposed to events that transpired many months or even years before the trial.... It can never be forgotten that the victims may be devastated by criminal acts. They have a special interest and good reason to expect that criminal trials take place within a reasonable time.[100]

The relevant time period begins when a formal charge is laid—the moment when the accused's liberty comes under direct threat from the state—and ends with the trial verdict.[101] The criteria for determining whether a delay is "reasonable" are as follows:

1. the length of the delay;
2. waiver of time periods;
3. the reasons for the delay, including
   (a) inherent time requirements of the case,
   (b) actions of the accused,
   (c) actions of the Crown,
   (d) limits on institutional resources, and
   (e) other reasons for delay; and
4. prejudice to the accused.[102]

The longer the delay, the greater the adverse impact on the liberty and security of the accused. Long delays can also create a presumption of prejudice against the accused and impair the fairness of the eventual trial.[103] The existence of a violation depends on whether the delay was caused by the Crown or the court system, by the accused, or by a combination of the two. A waiver by the accused allows the reviewing court to subtract the resulting delay from the total length of time since the charge, but only if the waiver is "clear, unequivocal and informed."[104] However, deliberate delaying tactics by defence counsel hoping to trigger a stay under s. 11(b) will not be rewarded by the courts.[105]

Under s. 24(1), the only effective remedy for a violation of s. 11(b) is a judicial stay of proceedings imposed by a "court of competent jurisdiction." Generally, this is the court in which the trial was held (or was scheduled to be held), but where the delays are caused by that court itself—for example, where the presiding judge takes eleven months to consider a motion that normally takes a few days[106]—then a higher court may properly intervene to impose a stay.

Section 11(b) prompted one of the most controversial legal-rights decisions ever issued by the Supreme Court: the 1991 *Askov* ruling. As we saw in Dossier 3.4, pages 120–21, *Askov* touched off a legal and political explosion in the province of Ontario. Justice Cory scolded successive Ontario governments for devoting insufficient resources to the court system, especially in the fast-growing Peel Region.[107] Although he had identified limited institutional resources as a factor to be weighed against the interests of the accused under s. 11(b), Cory made it clear that an underfunded justice system that could not handle its case load in an efficient manner was not to be tolerated:

> Where inordinate delays do occur, it is those who are responsible for the lack of facilities who should bear the public criticism that is bound to arise as a result of the staying of proceedings which must be the inevitable consequence of unreasonable delays. Members of the community will not and should not condone or accept a situation where those alleged to have committed serious crimes are never brought to trial solely as a result of unduly long delays. It is a serious consequence with potentially dangerous overtones for the community. It is right and proper that there be criticism of the situation when it occurs.

Although he acknowledged that "there can be no certain standard of a fixed time which will be applicable in every region of the country," Justice Cory went on to propose a "guideline" of six to eight months as a "reasonable" length of time between charge and verdict.[108] The fallout from that decision is explored in Dossier 3.4.

Section 11(c): The Right Not to Testify against Oneself

Section 11(c) covers one aspect of the broader right against self-incrimination (see also the discussion of s. 13, below). It protects the accused in a criminal trial from being forced to incriminate him- or herself on the stand. Its purpose is "to protect the individual against the affront to dignity and privacy inherent in a practice which enables the prosecution to force the person charged to supply the evidence out of his or her own mouth."[109] Section 11(c) enshrines the common-law rule that the Crown must present a "case to meet" without the assistance of the accused. If the Crown cannot prove his or her guilt without self-incrimination, then it deserves to fail.[110]

One question arising from the "right to silence" is whether the trier of fact is entitled to draw an inference of guilt from the accused's decision to invoke his right under s. 11(c). In other words, should a judge or jury assume that an accused who does not take the stand in his own defence is guilty? In the 1997 *Noble* decision, a five-judge majority held that the trial judge erred in law when he inferred that the accused was guilty because he did not take the stand to rebut the Crown's case. Justice Sopinka, writing for the majority, stated that "the use of silence to help establish guilt beyond a reasonable doubt is contrary to the rationale behind the right to silence."[111] Another issue is the compellability of one co-accused against another, where two or more people are charged with the same crime. The Court has ruled that multiple defendants in a single proceeding cannot be forced to testify against each other, but that they can be so compelled where they are tried separately.[112]

Section 11(d): The Presumption of Innocence

Section 11(d) covers a considerable amount of legal territory. It guarantees:

1. that a person charged with a criminal offence will be presumed innocent until proven guilty in a court of law;
2. that the onus of proof lies on the Crown; and
3. that trials will be carried out in a fair and impartial manner, with all of the appropriate procedural safeguards against the conviction of the morally innocent.[113]

The Crown must prove both elements of the alleged crime—the *actus reus* and the *mens rea*—beyond a reasonable doubt. The Crown may not withhold exculpatory evidence from the defence.[114] The defence must be allowed to counter the prosecution's case, by introducing its own evidence and by challenging the evidence of the Crown (e.g., by cross-examining witnesses). The trial judge must not favour the prosecution over the defence, either in procedural rulings or in her instructions to the jury.[115] In the context of the Charter as a whole, s. 11(d) supplies the detailed content of the principles of fundamental justice insofar as these relate to the conduct of court proceedings.

The presumption of innocence means that laws may not be drafted in such a way that an accused has no realistic defence against the charge.[116] It also prohibits the use of "reverse onus" provisions—laws that require the accused to prove his innocence, instead of requiring the Crown to prove his guilt.

> In general one must, I think, conclude that a provision which requires an accused to disprove on a balance of probabilities the existence of a presumed fact, which is an important element of the offence in question, violates the presumption of innocence in s. 11(d). If an accused bears the burden of disproving on a balance of probabilities an essential element of an offence, it would be possible for a conviction to occur despite the existence of a reasonable doubt.[117]

However, a reverse onus may be upheld under s. 1 as a "reasonable limitation" on s. 11(d). There is an important distinction between the definition of the offence itself and the definition of available defences. Where the statutory definition of a crime requires the accused to prove certain facts as part of his defence, this is an acceptable form of reverse onus. It is not an element of the offence, but rather an aspect of the right to make a full answer and defence.[118] For example, in *Keegstra* (Dossier 8.10, pages 271–72), the Court upheld the hate speech provisions in s. 319(3) of the Criminal Code. That section allows an accused to escape conviction for hate speech if she can prove "that the statements communicated were true," even if those statements were demonstrably intended to promote hatred against an identifiable group. The majority ruled that the requirement to prove the truth of the impugned statements was justified under s. 1.[119] In general, a law will violate s. 11(d) only "if it requires the trier of fact to convict in spite of a reasonable doubt."[120]

One thorny issue under s. 11(d) is the Crown's duty to prove that the accused had the requisite *mens rea* for a criminal conviction. Recall that the Crown bears the onus of proving both the physical and mental elements of a crime beyond a reasonable doubt. It is often a simple matter to prove that the accused actually committed a robbery, sexual assault, or murder. Recent advances in forensic sciences—including DNA typing, "geographic profiling," and the analysis of insect and plant samples at crime scenes—have expanded the range of physical evidence available to police and prosecutors. But the biggest difficulty remains: trying to determine the mental state of the accused at the moment when he or she allegedly committed the crime. Judges and legislators have wrestled with this problem for centuries.[121] In the English common law, and the American and Canadian legal systems flowing from it, an accused who could not appreciate "the nature and quality of his acts" because of "a disease of the mind" cannot be held morally culpable—and, therefore, cannot be found criminally responsible.[122] The central question is whether the accused should be required to prove that his or her mind was diseased at the time of the offence or the Crown should bear the onus of proving that it was not.

Section 16(4) of the Criminal Code of Canada imposes the burden of proof on the accused. It states that an accused is presumed to have been sane until proven otherwise. In 1990, a divided Supreme Court found that this provision violated the presumption of innocence: "If an accused cannot discharge the persuasive burden with respect to his insanity, the trier of fact may well be obliged to convict the accused despite the existence of a reasonable doubt as to sanity, and therefore, as to guilt."[123] However, the five-Justice majority upheld the provision as a "reasonable limit" on s. 11(d); they ruled that the requirement that the accused demonstrate his or her insanity according to the civil standard of proof (a balance of probabilities), rather than the criminal standard (proof beyond a reasonable doubt) brought it within the scope of the proportionality test in *Oakes*.

Perhaps the most notorious case concerning criminal responsibility and the presumption of innocence is the 1994 *Daviault* ruling, which was discussed in Chapter 4, pages 157–61. Briefly, a majority on the

Supreme Court found that a man who committed a sexual assault while severely intoxicated could not be found guilty of the crime. The medical evidence demonstrated, on a balance of probabilities, that Henri Daviault was in an "automatistic state" at the time of the assault. His mind was not "operating," in the legal sense: he was incapable of appreciating the difference between right and wrong. Even though he had freely chosen to become drunk enough to suspend the operation of his reason, Daviault could not be held criminally responsible for the assault.[124] The case prompted a public outcry. Parliament quickly overturned the majority ruling, amending the Criminal Code to substitute the intent to become seriously intoxicated for the requisite mental element in certain crimes (including sexual assault).

Daviault illustrates a general, and likely insoluble, difficulty in applying s. 11(d): it is often difficult to strike a reasonable balance between the due-process rights of the accused and the interests of the other parties involved in a case (including the public at large). In some well-known cases, including the murder trial of O.J. Simpson, judges and prosecutors have been criticized for failing to prevent the acquittal of an accused who is widely believed to be guilty. On the other hand, the failure to observe the norms of due process—in particular, the presumption of innocence and the impartiality of the trial—has produced some equally notorious miscarriages of justice (e.g., the Marshall and Milgaard cases mentioned earlier). According to a well-known legal maxim, "it is better that a hundred guilty men should go free than that one innocent man should be convicted." That sentiment is often ignored, perhaps understandably, in the public outrage over unpopular acquittals.

Section 11(e): The Right to Bail during a Trial

Section 7 of the Charter forbids the state to hold an accused in custody—thereby depriving him of his or her liberty—unless such detention is consistent with the principles of fundamental justice. Section 11(e) elaborates on that guarantee, by ensuring that a person accused of a crime shall not be held in prison before or during his or her trial without "just cause." The internal limitation imposed by the latter phrase

entrenches the common-law practice that evolved before the proclamation of the Charter. In most instances, an accused who has not been convicted of (or pled guilty to) a criminal charge is released from prison after being indicted—provided that he or she gives an undertaking to the court to appear at his trial. The presumption of innocence requires the judge to give the accused the benefit of the doubt, unless there are compelling reasons not to do so (e.g., a history of fleeing the jurisdiction to escape justice). However, the Crown can try to keep the accused in custody, by persuading the judge that the accused is unlikely to show up for trial or that his or her detention is necessary to protect the public.[125]

In 1992, the Court heard two cases challenging the validity of s. 515(6)(d) of the Criminal Code. That provision requires a judge to hold a suspected drug dealer in jail before trial unless the accused can demonstrate that such detention is unjustified. In other words, the onus is on the accused to prove that he should be released, and not on the state to prove that he should be detained. While this particular form of "reverse onus" appears to violate s. 11(e), the majority in *Pearson* and *Morales* found otherwise. The Court held that the impugned law denied bail, but only where necessary to protect public safety. The unique nature of drug offences, and particularly the wealth and sophistication of trafficking rings, justified more stringent standards for bail. The reverse onus was carefully tailored to apply to those particular offences and allowed the accused an opportunity to secure a judicial release in appropriate circumstances. There was no violation of s. 11(e).[126]

SECTION 12: CRUEL AND UNUSUAL TREATMENT OR PUNISHMENT

The wording of this section raises two questions: what does "cruel and unusual" mean in practice, and what is the scope of state activity that falls under the phrase "treatment or punishment"? Neither question has yet been answered definitively by the Supreme Court. The Justices have generally interpreted "treatment or punishment" as a purely penal concept,[127] relating to such issues as the length of prison sentences and the conditions of incarceration.[128] However, they have not foreclosed the possibility that "'treatment' within the meaning of s. 12 may include that imposed by the state in contexts other than that of a penal or quasi-penal nature."[129]

The key phrase here is "imposed by the state." The mere absence of a legal requirement to perform a certain act, or the prohibition thereof, does not constitute "treatment"; there must be a direct and active engagement between the state and a particular individual before s. 12 can be invoked. In the case of Sue Rodriguez, discussed earlier in this chapter, her argument that the prohibition of physician-assisted suicide violated the guarantee against "cruel and unusual treatment" failed because she was not under the direct control of the state. Therefore, s. 12 applies only to persons who are in the custody of the state, e.g., as prisoners or as failed refugee claimants awaiting deportation.

In Canadian jurisprudence, the phrase "cruel and unusual" refers to "grossly disproportionate" punishments. Whether a particular punishment fits this standard will depend on both objective factors (e.g., the absolute length of a prison term) and subjective factors (the effect of the punishment on the individual who must bear it).[130]

> In assessing whether a sentence is grossly disproportionate, the court must first consider the gravity of the offence, the personal characteristics of the offender and the particular circumstances of the case in order to determine what range of sentences would have been appropriate to punish, rehabilitate or deter this particular offender or to protect the public from this particular offender. The other purposes which may be pursued by the imposition of punishment, in particular the deterrence of other potential offenders, are thus not relevant at this stage of the inquiry.... If a grossly disproportionate sentence is "prescribed by law," then the purpose which it seeks to attain will fall to be assessed under s. 1.[131]

When a minimum prison sentence is "prescribed by law," it may violate s. 12 if it does not allow judges to tailor sentences to fit the degree of moral guilt. In 1987, the Supreme Court struck down a section of the Narcotic Control Act that imposed a mandatory minimum sentence of seven years for a wide range of offences, some of which were relatively minor. Under that law, "it is inevitable that, in some cases, a verdict of guilt will lead to the imposition of a term of imprisonment which will be grossly disproportionate."[132] In that ruling, Chief Justice Dickson and Justice Lamer added the following comment: "some punishments or treatments will always be grossly disproportionate and will always outrage our standards of decency: for example, the infliction of corporal punishment, such as the lash, irrespective of the number of lashes imposed, or, to give examples of treatment, the lobotomisation of certain dangerous offenders or the castration of sexual offenders."[133]

Early in 2004, the Court upheld s. 43 of the Criminal Code, which allows parents, guardians, and teachers to use "reasonable force" where necessary to discipline children. For the majority, Chief Justice McLachlin concluded that the law did not violate the rights of children to be safe from "cruel and unusual treatment or punishment." In the first place, she noted that s. 43 applies to parents as well as teachers; because it does not apply solely to governmental acts, s. 12 is not engaged. Second, she noted that the section permits only "reasonable" corrective force: "Conduct cannot be at once both reasonable and an outrage to standards of decency. Corrective force that might rise to the level of 'cruel and unusual' remains subject to criminal prosecution."[134]

Similarly, the Court found in 1987 that the **indeterminate sentences** meted out to "dangerous offenders" did not violate s. 12 because the law was carefully tailored to achieve its objectives.[135] The criteria for identifying habitual and incorrigible criminals were sufficiently clear and precise to prevent the misuse of judicial discretion; the procedure for designating "dangerous offenders" ensured proper safeguards for their rights and interests, including periodic reviews to determine whether an offender should be paroled. The indeterminate sentences were not "grossly disproportionate" because "the group to whom the legislation applies has been functionally defined so as to ensure that persons within the group evince the very characteristics that render such detention necessary."[136]

Overall, the Court has taken a fairly narrow approach to s. 12. It has upheld sentences that are somewhat disproportionate to the seriousness of the offence, as long as the sentencing judge retains some flexibility. It has accepted the infliction of reasonable corporal punishment on children, where necessary and reasonable. It has excluded the question of capital punishment from the ambit of s. 12, leaving that issue to be decided under s. 7 (Dossier 5.3, pages 190–92). The Court's s. 12 jurisprudence could be regarded as a tribute to Canadian moderation and civility, as manifested in the absence of state-sanctioned torture or capital punishment. It is worth asking, however, whether this judicial self-restraint necessarily serves the interests of the most vulnerable persons in our society.

SECTION 13: SELF-INCRIMINATION

The meaning and purpose of s. 13 were first established in the 1985 *Dubois* ruling.[137] The accused had been convicted at his first trial for second-degree murder. That conviction was subsequently overturned by the Alberta Court of Appeal on procedural grounds. At his second trial, the Crown prosecutor used Dubois's testimony from the first trial to impeach his credibility. He identified several contradictions between the stories Dubois told in the two proceedings. Following his second conviction, Dubois appealed unsuccessfully on the ground that his first testimony should have been excluded from the second trial. The technical question for the Supreme Court was whether or not a second trial constituted "any other proceeding" for the purposes of s. 13. More broadly, the Court was asked to determine the scope of the Charter guarantee against self-incrimination, which is divided between ss. 7, 11(c), 11(d), and 13.

The majority, led by Justice Lamer, concluded that s. 13 prohibited the admission of evidence from a first trial into a retrial. Before 1982, such evidence had been admissible. Under the Charter, which both entrenched and reinforced the common-law protections against self-incrimination, it was no longer acceptable. In particular, the rule against compelling an accused to testify against himself (s. 11(c)) required the Court to interpret s. 13 in the strongest terms.

To allow the prosecution to use, as part of its case, the accused's previous testimony would, in effect, allow the Crown to do indirectly what it is **estopped** from doing directly by s. 11(c), i.e. to compel the accused to testify.... To hold that a new trial is not "any other proceedings" within the meaning of s. 13 would in fact authorize an interpretation of a Charter right which would imply a violation of another Charter right. Such a result should be avoided.[138]

In dissent, Justice McIntyre argued that a retrial was not a separate legal proceeding, but rather a continuation or resumption of the first trial.[139] Therefore, he concluded that s. 13 did not apply. But in a case the following year, McIntyre—now bound by *stare decisis*—authored a unanimous ruling that applied the *Dubois* doctrine to a similar fact pattern.[140] The Court's refusal to admit testimony from a first trial to impeach or incriminate the accused in a second trial was now established law.

In 1990, however, the Court backed away from this strict interpretation of s. 13. In *Kuldip*,[141] four of seven Justices weakened the protection against self-incrimination. They ruled that testimony from a previous trial *could* be used by the Crown to establish contradictions in the testimony of the accused at a second trial, although it could not be used to directly incriminate him or her before the trier of fact. In *Dubois*, the majority had ruled that any and all evidence introduced by the Crown at trial should be considered incriminating, including the testimonial record of a previous trial, and without reference to the purpose for which it was adduced.[142] The *Kuldip* majority took a different view, distinguishing between "a cross-examination made for the purpose of impeaching credibility [which was now considered to be nonincriminating] and one made to 'incriminate' the accused, that is, to establish guilt."[143] In the former case, the prior testimony is used only "for the purpose of unveiling a contradiction between what the accused is saying now and what he or she has said on a previous occasion."[144] In effect, the Court was now authorizing prosecutors to take advantage of changes in testimony over time—whether arising from deliberate lies or fading memories—to portray the accused as a dishonest person before a judge and/or jury. The possibility that such a portrayal might in itself incriminate the accused does not appear to have occurred to Lamer, then Chief Justice.

Whereas the *Dubois* majority had applied the protection of s. 13 to every accused, regardless of whether he or she had originally testified voluntarily or under duress, Lamer now took a harder line:

> An accused has the right to remain silent during his or her trial. However, if an accused chooses to take the stand, that accused is implicitly vouching for his or her credibility. Such an accused, like any other witness, has therefore opened the door to having the trustworthiness of his/her evidence challenged. An interpretation of s. 13 which insulates such an accused from having previous inconsistent statements put to him/her on cross-examination where the only purpose of doing so is to challenge that accused's credibility, would, in my view, "stack the deck" too highly in favour of the accused.[145]

No one can be compelled to testify at his or her own trial. But what about the witness or co-accused who is compelled to testify against another person? Can that testimony be used at a subsequent trial to convict him or her? The Supreme Court considered that issue in the 2002 *Noël* case. Eight of the nine Justices ruled that the appellant, who had been convicted of murder, had been improperly incriminated by the admission of his testimony at the trial of his co-accused (who happened to be his brother). The majority appeared to retreat, at least to some degree, from the *Kuldip* doctrine and return to the stronger interpretation of s. 13 in *Dubois* and *Mannion*:

> If there is any indication that the Crown is using the prior evidence to incriminate the accused directly, as in *Dubois*, or indirectly as in *Mannion*, or that the prior evidence was such that it contained, subjectively or objectively, an element of self-incrimination, s. 13 is activated and all reference to the testimony is prohibited, even for the sole purpose of challenging the credibility of the accused. In my view, *Kuldip* is limited to cases where the reference to the prior evidence is exclusively for impeachment purposes and carries no other risk of incrimination. In other words, the cross-examination would be

permitted when there is no possibility that the jury could use the content of the prior testimony to draw an inference of guilt, except to the limited extent that a finding that the accused has been untruthful under oath could be damaging to his defence.[146]

The Court interpreted s. 13 as an explicit guarantee of a *quid pro quo* between compelled witnesses and the state: "when a witness who is compelled to give evidence in a court proceeding is exposed to the risk of self-incrimination, the state offers protection against the subsequent use of that evidence against the witness in exchange for his or her full and frank testimony."[147]

SECTION 14: THE RIGHT TO AN INTERPRETER IN COURT

The Supreme Court of Canada has issued one major ruling on Section 14. The accused in the 1994 *Tran* case was a Vietnamese man with a poor command of English. At his trial for sexual assault, his interpreter testified in English in rebuttal to a Crown identification witness. He failed to provide Mr. Tran with a full translation of his remarks. The interpreter also took part in an exchange with the judge, the contents of which were not conveyed to the accused. Tran was convicted. He appealed on the grounds that "deficiencies in the translation of the evidence deprived him of the right to be actually present at his trial."[148] The Nova Scotia Court of Appeal upheld the conviction. On appeal to the Supreme Court, Mr. Tran succeeded in quashing the conviction and securing a new trial.

In a unanimous ruling, the Justices explored the meaning and purpose of s. 14. In the first place, it "ensures that a person charged with a criminal offence hears the case against him or her and is given a full opportunity to answer it."[149] Therefore, s. 14 engages the basic "principles of fundamental justice" in s. 7. Second, "the right to interpreter assistance touches on the very integrity of the administration of criminal justice in this country";[150] in effect, an accused who understands neither English nor French can receive a fair trial only if he or she receives complete, accurate, and contemporaneous interpretation so that he or she can understand the legal process. Third, the Court ruled that s. 14 must be interpreted in light of the guarantee of multicultural sensitivity in s. 27. In summary, the right to an interpreter in court is grounded in fundamental Charter values and cannot be disregarded.

The Court concluded that Mr. Tran had not received the full protection of the Charter. He had been prevented from participating effectively in his own trial. The Justices declared that any accused who can establish that he or she needs an interpreter is entitled to such assistance. Moreover, the Court set a high standard for interpretation services: they must be characterized by "continuity, precision, impartiality, competency and contemporaneousness."[151] Finally, a violation of s. 14 will arise only where "a vital interest of the accused [is] involved";[152] if the standard of interpretation should fail at an incidental moment of the trial, there will be no infringement of the rights of the accused.

CONCLUSION

The cases in this chapter show that the Charter's most direct impact on policy has come in the field of criminal law. The emphasis on case law, which might seem misplaced in a political science text, reflects the continuity and importance of common law in this particular policy area. Although Parliament still determines the content of the Criminal Code (as we saw in Chapter 4), the courts have been particularly assertive in their interpretations of legal rights. The sheer volume of Charter challenges arising from criminal convictions ensured that the courts would have plenty of opportunity to apply ss. 7–14. Both the substance of the criminal law (e.g., the definition of offences) and the procedures by which crimes are investigated and prosecuted have changed as a result.

The magnitude of those changes, in day-to-day terms, is undetermined. (See the discussion of implementation in Chapter 3, pages 126–28.) However, it is reasonable to conclude that all participants in the justice system have become more aware of the common-law rights entrenched in the Charter, and that this awareness has created new incentives for behaviour. Police officers know that their investigations may be fruitless unless they respect Charter values; Crown prosecutors and judges know that a violation of the right to a fair trial may result in the voiding of a conviction. Perhaps most important, defence lawyers have significantly greater procedural leverage than they would have enjoyed in the pre-Charter era. American studies have found that the best guarantee of due-process rights is a defence lawyer who is willing and able to use those rights on behalf of his or her client.[153] Although aggressive lawyers are sometimes accused of trying to free the guilty on technicalities, the reality is more nuanced. Where abuses of due process occur, everyone benefits from their exposure and correction.

In this context, the legal-rights jurisprudence of the Supreme Court should be viewed as an attempt to protect "the principles of fundamental justice" against the countervailing forces of administrative expediency, public pressure to "put away" alleged criminals (with or without a fair trial), and government under-funding. Some of the individual cases discussed here, and in other chapters, have provoked heated controversy over the proper balance between the rights of the accused and competing social values. Taken as a whole, they reveal a sustained effort to ensure that justice will be done, regardless of the severity of the alleged crime or the identity of the suspect. That effort is well worth making.

GLOSSARY OF KEY TERMS

estopped A technical legal term meaning "prevented" or "prohibited."

exculpatory evidence A piece of evidence that tends to prove the innocence of a criminal accused.

indeterminate sentences Indeterminate sentences are not subject to a fixed length (e.g., ten years in prison). Instead, the convicted offender is detained in custody "at her Majesty's pleasure." In practice, this means that the detention must be reviewed periodically to determine whether the offender can safely be released or paroled.

DISCUSSION AND REVIEW QUESTIONS

1. Identify three principles of fundamental justice that the Supreme Court has read into s. 7. Briefly explain how each principle operates to protect a criminal suspect.

2. Is your "reasonable expectation of privacy" higher in your car or in your home? Explain your answer.

3. Identify one key difference between an arrest or detention that violates s. 9 and one that does not. Give an example of each.

4. Imagine that you have just been placed under arrest and taken to your local police station. What are your rights in that situation? What must the police say or do in order to comply with the Charter, and why?

5. Explain the purpose of the right against self-incrimination in ss. 7, 11(c), and 13 of the Charter. Identify two limitations on that right.

6. Identify two specific punishments that would infringe s. 12.

7. In your opinion, should the due-process guarantees in ss. 7–10 of the Charter take priority over police discretion in the conduct of criminal investigations? Why or why not?

8. In your opinion, should the due-process guarantees in ss. 7, 11, and 13 of the Charter receive greater emphasis than the need to convict criminals who appear to be guilty? Why or why not?

SUGGESTED READINGS

Cameron, Jamie, ed. *The Charter's Impact on the Criminal Justice System.* Toronto: Carswell, 1996.

Huff, C. Ronald, Arye Rattner, and Edward Sagarin. *Convicted but Innocent: Wrongful Conviction and Public Policy.* Thousand Oaks: Sage, 1996.

Paciocco, David M. *Getting Away with Murder: The Canadian Criminal Justice System.* Toronto: Irwin Law, 1999.

Roach, Kent. *Due Process and Victims' Rights: The New Law and Politics of Criminal Justice.* Toronto: University of Toronto Press, 1999.

Westervelt, Saundra D., and John A Humphrey, eds. *Wrongly Convicted: Perspectives on Failed Justice.* New Brunswick, NJ: Rutgers University Press, 2001.

ENDNOTES

1. See Kent Roach, *Due Process and Victims' Rights: The New Law and Politics of Criminal Justice* (Toronto: University of Toronto Press, 1999), pp. 47–48. The most relevant testimony, in a joint presentation by the Canadian Association of Chiefs of Police and the Canadian Association of Crown Counsels, is available in the *Minutes of Proceedings and Evidence* of the Special Joint Committee on the Constitution (pp. 14:6–29).

2. See the statement of Justice Lamer in *Re B.C. Motor Vehicle Act*, [1985] 2 S.C.R. 486, at paragraph 119: "In my view a law which interferes with the liberty of the citizen in violation of the principles of fundamental justice cannot be saved by s. 1 as being either reasonable or justified. The concepts are mutually exclusive." The only exception occurs when the country faces a national emergency, which would shift the balance between legal rights and competing social goods.

3. *Irwin Toy Ltd. v. Quebec (Attorney General)*, [1989] 1 S.C.R. 927, paragraph 79, *per* Dickson C.J. and Lamer and Wilson JJ.; *RJR-MacDonald Inc. v. Canada (Attorney General)*, [1995] 3 S.C.R. 199, paragraph 68, *per* La Forest J.

4. *Re B.C. Motor Vehicle Act*, paragraph 31, *per* Lamer J.

5. See the discussion of implementation in Chapter 3, pages 126–28.

6. On the causes of wrongful convictions, see Saundra D. Westervelt and John A. Humphrey, eds., *Wrongly Convicted: Perspectives on Failed Justice* (New Brunswick, NJ: Rutgers University Press, 2001); C. Ronald Huff, Arye Rattner, and Edward Sagarin, *Convicted but Innocent: Wrongful Conviction and Public Policy* (Thousand Oaks: Sage, 1996). The post-Charter cases of Thomas Sophonow and Gregory Parsons, among others, suggest that

wrongful convictions are still a fact of life in the Charter era.

7. See, e.g., Alex Macdonald, *Outrage: Canada's Justice System on Trial* (Vancouver: Raincoast Books, 1999); Christie Blatchford, "Why the Wheels of Justice Moved Slowly for Farah Khan," *The Globe and Mail*, April 24, 2004, pp. F4–F5.

8. James B. Kelly, "The Charter of Rights and Freedoms and the Rebalancing of Liberal Constitutionalism in Canada, 1982–1997," *Osgoode Hall Law Journal* 37 (1999), p. 648, Table 5.

9. *Re B.C. Motor Vehicle Act*, paragraphs 27–30, *per* Lamer J.

10. *New Brunswick (Minister of Health and Community Services) v. G. (J.)*, [1999] 3 S.C.R. 46, paragraph 65, *per* Lamer C.J.

11. *Singh v. Minister of Employment and Immigration*, [1985] 1 S.C.R. 177, paragraph 47, *per* Wilson J.; *New Brunswick (Minister of Health and Community Services) v. G. (J.)*, paragraph 66, *per* Lamer C.J.

12. *Re B.C. Motor Vehicle Act*, paragraph 24, *per* Lamer J.

13. *Singh*, paragraph 43, *per* Wilson J.; see also *Re B.C. Motor Vehicle*, paragraph 23, *per* Lamer J.

14. *Rodriguez v. British Columbia (Attorney General)*, [1993] 3 S.C.R. 519.

15. Sue Rodriguez also argued that the law constituted cruel and unusual treatment, and thus violated s. 12 of the Charter, and that it discriminated against disabled persons who were physically incapable of committing suicide unassisted (s. 15). Neither argument was given much weight by the Supreme Court.

16. *Rodriguez*, paragraph 125.

17. Ibid., paragraph 129.

18. Ibid., paragraph 231.

19. F.L. Morton, *Morgentaler v. Borowski: Abortion, The Charter, and the Courts* (Toronto: McClelland and Stewart, 1992), pp. 111–16.

20. *R. v. Morgentaler*, [1988] 1 S.C.R. 30, paragraph 170, *per* Beetz J.

21. *Tremblay v. Daigle*, [1989] 2 S.C.R. 530.

22. *Winnipeg Child and Family Services (Northwest Area) v. G. (D.F.)*, [1997] 3 S.C.R. 925, headnotes, *per* McLachlin J.

23. *B. (R.) v. Children's Aid Society of Metropolitan Toronto*, [1995] 1 S.C.R. 315, paragraph 80, *per* La Forest J. (approved by four other Justices).

24. Ibid., paragraph 80, *per* La Forest J.

25. *R. v. Edwards Books and Art Ltd.*, [1986] 2 S.C.R. 713, paragraph 155, *per* Dickson C.J.; *Irwin Toy*, paragraphs 93–93, *per* Dickson C.J. and Lamer and Wilson JJ.

26. *B. (R.) v. Children's Aid Society of Metropolitan Toronto*, paragraph 80, *per* La Forest J.; *R. v. O'Connor*, [1995] 4 S.C.R. 411, paragraphs 110 and 118, *per* L'Heureux-Dubé J.

27. *Morgentaler*, paragraph 20, *per* Dickson C.J.; *New Brunswick (Minister of Health and Community Services) v. G. (J.)*, paragraph 60, *per* Lamer C.J.; *Rodriguez*, paragraph 136, *per* Sopinka J.

28. *Singh*, paragraph 52, *per* Wilson J.

29. In the 2002 *Gosselin* case, Justice Arbour argued forcefully that s. 7 imposed a positive duty on the state to guarantee "security of the person" by providing the necessities of life to its most vulnerable citizens. This argument was rejected by the majority, although the possibility that it might be accepted in the future was not foreclosed. *Gosselin v. Quebec (Attorney General)*, [2002] 4 S.C.R. 429, paragraphs 308–29, *per*

Arbour J.; for the majority ruling by McLachlin C.J., see paragraphs 76–83.

30. *Re B.C. Motor Vehicle Act*, paragraph 31, *per* Lamer J.

31. *R. v. Malmo-Levine; R. v. Caine*, [2003] 3 S.C.R. 571, paragraph 113, *per* Gonthier and Binnie JJ.

32. *R. v. Whittle*, [1994] 2 S.C.R. 914.

33. *Re B.C. Motor Vehicle Act*, paragraph 74, *per* Lamer J.

34. *R. v. Creighton*, [1993] 3 S.C.R. 3, headnotes.

35. See the discussion of "unlawful bodily harm" in *R. v. DeSousa*, [1992] 2 S.C.R. 944.

36. *Reference re ss. 193 and 195.1(1)(c) of the Criminal Code (Man.)*, [1990] 1 S.C.R. 1123, paragraph 38, *per* Lamer J.

37. Ibid., paragraph 41.

38. *R. v. Nova Scotia Pharmaceutical Society*, [1992] 2 S.C.R. 606, paragraph 27, *per* Gonthier J.

39. *R. v. Demers*, 2004 SCC 46, paragraph 37, *per* Iacobucci and Bastarache JJ.

40. *R. v. Heywood*, [1994] 3 S.C.R. 761, paragraph 49, *per* Cory J.

41. Ibid., paragraph 55, *per* Cory J.

42. *Demers*, paragraph 46.

43. *R. v. Seaboyer; R. v. Gayme*, [1991] 2 S.C.R. 577.

44. *Seaboyer*, paragraph 43, *per* McLachlin J. (as she then was).

45. *R. v. Stinchcombe*, [1991] 3 S.C.R. 326, paragraph 12, *per* Sopinka J.

46. *R. v. O'Connor; R. v. Carosella*, [1997] 1 S.C.R. 80. See the Case Study 5 in Chapter 4, pages 168–73.

47. *R. v. Taillefer; R. v. Duguay*, [2003] 3 S.C.R. 307 paragraph 71, *per* LeBel J.

48. *R. v. Dixon*, [1998] 1 S.C.R. 244.

49. *Irwin Toy*, paragraph 79, *per* Dickson C.J. and Lamer and Wilson JJ.

50. *Hunter v. Southam Inc.*, [1984] 2 S.C.R. 145, *per* Dickson J., at pp. 159–60.

51. *Hunter v. Southam*, at p. 148.

52. *R. v. Collins*, [1987] 1 S.C.R. 265, paragraph 23, *per* Lamer J.

53. See, e.g., *R. v. Kokesch*, [1990] 3 S.C.R. 3; *R. v. Feeney*, [1997] 2 S.C.R. 13.

54. *R. v. Evans*, [1996] 1 S.C.R. 8, headnotes, *per* Sopinka J.

55. *R. v. Tessling*, 2004 SCC 67

56. *R. v. Colarusso*, [1994] 1 S.C.R. 20; *R. v. Stillman*, [1997] 1 S.C.R. 607; *R. v. S.A.B.*, [2003] 2 S.C.R. 678.

57. *R. v. Simmons*, [1988] 2 S.C.R. 495, paragraphs 49–52, *per* Dickson C.J.

58. *Conway v. Canada (Attorney General)*, [1993] 2 S.C.R. 872.

59. *R. v. Hufsky*, [1988] 1 S.C.R 621, paragraph 23, *per* Le Dain J.; *R. v. Wise*, [1992] 1 S.C.R. 527, paragraphs 4–6, *per* Cory J.; *R. v. Caslake*, [1998] 1 S.C.R. 51, paragraph 15, *per* Lamer C.J.

60. *R. v. Grant*, [1993] 3 S.C.R. 223.

61. *R. v. Mellenthin*, [1992] 3 S.C.R. 615.

62. *R. v. Fitt* (1995), 96 C.C.C. (3d) 341 (N.S.C.A.); *R. v. Edwards*, [1996] 1 S.C.R. 128.

63. *R. v. Edwards*, [1996] 1 S.C.R. 128, paragraphs 46–50, *per* Cory J.

64. *R. v. Collins*, paragraphs 21 and 30, *per* Lamer J.

65. *R. v. Stillman*, headnotes.

66. *R. v. Buhay*, [2003] 1 S.C.R. 631, paragraph 71, *per* Arbour J.

67. See, for example, the debate between Justices Sopinka and L'Heureux-Dubé over the proper interpretation of Collins in *R. v. Burlingham*, [1995] 2 S.C.R. 206.

68. *R. v. Hufsky*, headnotes, *per* Le Dain J.

69. *R. v. Swain*, [1991] 1 S.C.R. 933.

70. *R. v. Therens*, [1985] 1 S.C.R. 613, paragraph 53, *per* Le Dain J.

71. *R. v. Hufsky*, paragraph 12, *per* Le Dain J.

72. *R. v. Storrey*, [1990] 1 S.C.R. 241.

73. *R. v. Jacques*, [1996] 3 S.C.R. 312.

74. *R. v. Evans*, [1991] 1 S.C.R. 869, paragraph 2, *per* Sopinka J (hereinafter cited as "*Evans* 1991").

75. Ibid., paragraph 29, *per* McLachlin J. (as she then was).

76. Ibid., paragraph 29, *per* McLachlin J.; see also *R. v. Smith*, [1991] 1 S.C.R. 714, *per* McLachlin J.

77. *Evans* 1991, paragraph 33, *per* McLachlin J.

78. The Crown in the *Latimer* case had contaminated the jury pool by administering a questionnaire concerning religious beliefs, euthanasia, and other issues raised by the case. Of the thirty prospective jurors who took the questionnaire, five later served on the trial jury. Neither the Crown nor the RCMP, both of which had been involved with the questionnaire, disclosed their pretrial's contacts with jurors to the trial judge. Chief Justice Lamer characterized these actions as "a flagrant abuse of process and interference with the administra-

tion of justice" [paragraph 43] and ordered a new trial.

79. David M. Paciocco, *Getting Away with Murder: The Canadian Criminal Justice System* (Toronto: Irwin Law, 1999), p. 56.

80. *R. v. Latimer*, [2001] 1 S.C.R. 3 (hereinafter cited as "*Latimer* 2001").

81. *Clarkson v. The Queen*, [1986] 1 S.C.R. 383, paragraph 20, *per* Wilson J.

82. *R. v. Therens*, paragraph 52, *per* Le Dain J. (dissenting, but not on this point).

83. *R. v. Manninen*, [1987] 1 S.C.R. 1233, paragraph 21, *per* Lamer J.

84. Ibid., paragraph 23, *per* Lamer J.

85. *Therens*, paragraph 21, *per* Lamer J. (as he then was).

86. *R. v. Strachan*, [1988] 2 S.C.R. 980, paragraph 34, *per* Dickson C.J.

87. See *Clarkson*, paragraphs 18–20, *per* Wilson J.; *R. v. Whittle*; *R. v. Smith*.

88. *Evans* 1991.

89. *R. v. Tremblay*, [1987] 2 S.C.R. 435, paragraph 9, *per* Lamer J.; *R. v. Smith (Joey Leonard)*, [1989] 2 S.C.R. 368, *per* Lamer and L'Heureux-Dubé JJ.

90. *R. v. Brydges*, [1990] 1 S.C.R. 190; *R. v. Prosper*, [1994] 3 S.C.R. 236, paragraphs 21–27, *per curiam* (on this point).

91. *R. v. Brydges*, paragraphs 15–16, *per* Lamer J.

92. *Prosper*, paragraphs 33–48, *per* Lamer C.J.

93. Robert J. Sharpe, Katherine E. Swinton, and Kent Roach, *The Charter of Rights and Freedoms*, 2nd ed. (Toronto: Irwin Law, 2002), p. 226.

94. *Wigglesworth v. R.*, [1987] 2 S.C.R. 541.

95. *R. v. Généreux*, [1992] 1 S.C.R. 259.

96. *R. v. Potvin*, [1993] 2 S.C.R. 880.

97. *R. v. MacDougall*, [1998] 3 S.C.R. 45.

98. *R. v. Rahey*, [1987] 1 S.C.R. 588, paragraph 40, *per* Lamer J.

99. The claim that s. 11(b) protects collective rights is controversial. In a 1986 dissent, Dickson C.J. and Lamer J. declared that the right to trial within a reasonable time is a purely individual right, designed to minimize the state's infringement of liberty and security of the person (s. 7). See *Mills v. The Queen*, [1986] 1 S.C.R. 863, paragraphs 139–40. Since *Askov*, the Court has backed away from Cory J.'s "societal interests" analysis, although it has not been completely abandoned. See *R. v. Morin*, [1992] 1 S.C.R. 771, paragraphs 26–30, *per* Sopinka J.

100. *R. v. Askov*, [1990] 2 S.C.R. 1199, paragraphs 44–46, *per* Cory J.

101. *Mills*, headnotes; *Rahey*, paragraph 31, *per* Lamer J. (supported by the majority on this point).

102. *Morin*, paragraph 31, *per* Sopinka J.

103. *Askov*, paragraph 67, *per* Cory J.; *R. v. Smith*, [1989] 2 S.C.R. 1120, *per* Sopinka J.

104. *Rahey*, paragraph 45, *per* Lamer J.

105. *Askov*, paragraph 62, *per* Cory J.

106. *Rahey*, paragraph 45, *per* Lamer J.

107. *Askov*, paragraphs 76–83.

108. Ibid., paragraphs 60 and 89.

109. *R. v. Amway Corp.*, [1989] 1 S.C.R. 21, paragraph 35, *per* Sopinka J.

110. *R. v. S. (R.J.)*, [1995] 1 S.C.R. 451, *per* Iacobucci J.; *R. v. Noble*, [1997] 1 S.C.R. 874, *per* Sopinka J.

111. *Noble*, paragraph 75, *per* Sopinka J. In dissent, Chief Justice Lamer pointed out that one of his own earlier rulings—which commanded the support of a majority—had established precisely the opposite: "once there is a 'case to meet' which, if believed, would result in conviction, the accused can no longer remain a passive participant in the prosecutorial process and becomes—in a broad sense—compellable. That is, the accused must answer the case against him or her, or face the possibility of conviction." See *R. v. P. (M.B.)*, [1994] 1 S.C.R. 555, *per* Lamer C.J.

112. *R. v. Clunas*, [1992] 1 S.C.R. 595; *R. v. S. (R.J.)*.

113. *Dubois v. The Queen*, [1985] 2 S.C.R. 350, paragraphs 10–11, *per* Lamer J.; *R. v. Oakes*, [1986] 1 S.C.R. 103, paragraph 32, *per* Dickson C.J.

114. *Stinchcombe*.

115. *R. v. Lifchus*, [1997] 3 S.C.R. 320.

116. *Morgentaler*, paragraph 46, *per* Dickson C.J. and Lamer J.

117. *Oakes*, paragraph 57, *per* Dickson C.J.

118. *R. v. Holmes*, [1988] 1 S.C.R. 914, *per* McIntyre J.; see also *R. v. Schwartz*, [1988] 2 S.C.R. 443, *per* McIntyre J.

119. *R. v. Keegstra*, [1990] 3 S.C.R. 697, *per* Dickson C.J.; *R. v. Whyte*, [1988] 2 S.C.R. 3, *per* Dickson C.J.

120. *Whyte*, paragraph 32, *per* Dickson C.J.; see also *R. v. Downey*, [1992] 2 S.C.R. 10, *per* Cory J.

121. See, e.g., Daniel N. Robinson, *Wild Beasts and Idle Humours: The Insanity Defense from Antiquity to the Present* (Cambridge, MA: Harvard University Press, 1998); Eugene J. Chesney, "The Concept of Mens Rea in the Criminal Law," *Journal of the American Institute for Criminal Law and Criminology* 29 (1938–39), pp. 627–44.

122. This principle, the "M'Naghten Rule," was set down by English Law Lords in *M'Naghten's Case* (1843), 10 Cl. & Fin. 200, 8 E.R. 718. See Robinson, *Wild Beasts*, Chapter 5.

123. *R. v. Chaulk*, [1990] 3 S.C.R. 1303, paragraph 41, *per* Lamer C.J.

124. *R. v. Daviault*, [1994] 3 S.C.R. 63, *per* Cory J.

125. *R. v. Pearson*, [1992] 3 S.C.R. 665, paragraph 51, *per* Lamer C.J. and Sopinka and Iacobucci JJ.

126. Ibid., *per* Lamer C.J. and Sopinka and Iacobucci JJ.; *R. v. Morales*, [1992] 3 S.C.R. 71, *per* Lamer C.J.

127. For a useful summary of this issue, see *Rodriguez*, paragraphs 178–82, *per* Sopinka J.

128. See, e.g., *R. v. Smith*, [1987] 1 S.C.R. 1045 (hereinafter cited as "*Smith* 1987"); *R. v. Lyons*, [1987] 2 S.C.R. 309; *R. v. Goltz*, [1991] 3 S.C.R. 485; *Latimer* 2001.

129. *Rodriguez*, paragraph 182.

130. *Smith* 1987, paragraphs 54–55, *per* Dickson C.J. and Lamer J. .

131. Ibid., paragraph 56, *per* Dickson C.J. and Lamer J.

132. Ibid., paragraph 66, *per* Dickson C.J. and Lamer J.

133. Ibid., paragraph 57, *per* Dickson C.J. and Lamer J.

134. *Canadian Foundation for Children, Youth and the Law v. Canada (Attorney General)*, 2004 SCC 4, paragraph 49.

135. *Lyons, per* La Forest J.

136. *Lyons*, paragraph 45, *per* La Forest J.

137. *Dubois v. The Queen*, [1985] 2 S.C.R. 350.

138. Ibid., paragraph 43, *per* Lamer J.

139. Ibid., paragraphs 72–74, *per* McIntyre J.

140. *R. v. Mannion*, [1986] 2 S.C.R. 272.

141. *R. v. Kuldip*, [1990] 3 S.C.R. 618.

142. *Dubois*, paragraph 40, *per* Lamer J.

143. *Kuldip*, paragraph 28, *per* Lamer C.J.

144. Ibid., paragraph 28.

145. Ibid., paragraph 30.

146. *R. v. Noël*, [2002] 3 S.C.R. 433, paragraph 54, *per* Arbour J.

147. Ibid., paragraph 21.

148. *R. v. Tran*, [1994] 2 S.C.R. 951, paragraph 6, *per* Lamer C.J.

149. Ibid., paragraph 38.

150. Ibid., paragraph 38.

151. Ibid., paragraph 43.

152. Ibid., paragraph 44.

153. See, e.g., Neal A. Milner, *The Court and Local Law Enforcement: The Impact of Miranda* (Beverly Hills, CA: Sage, 1971), especially pp. 135–38.

Chapter 11

Equality Rights

In 2003, same-sex couples in Ontario and British Columbia won the legal right to get married.

CP PHOTO/Kevin Frayer

Equality Rights

15. (1) *Every individual is equal before and under the law and has the right to the equal protection and equal benefit of the law without discrimination and, in particular, without discrimination based on race, national or ethnic origin, colour, religion, sex, age or mental or physical disability.*

    (2) *Subsection (1) does not preclude any law, program or activity that has as its object the amelioration of conditions of disadvantaged individuals or groups including those that are disadvantaged because of race, national or ethnic origin, colour, religion, sex, age or mental or physical disability.*

INTRODUCTION

Section 15 of the Charter took effect in April 1985, three years after the proclamation of the Charter. The delay was intended to allow the federal and provincial governments to review their existing legislation for conformity to s. 15 and to make any necessary amendments. Those governments that undertook such reviews—and not all did so—did not always anticipate the ways in which the courts would interpret equality rights.[1] However, the delay reflected the general expectation that this section, perhaps more than any other, would have a significant impact on public policy.[2] As this chapter demonstrates, those predictions were not entirely correct. The judicial interpretation of s. 15(1) has reshaped some social policies—particularly those relating to gay men and lesbians and to common-law heterosexual couples—while leaving other laws untouched. For example, mandatory-retirement laws have been upheld, despite claims that they discriminate on the basis of age. Feminist groups have twice failed to modify sections of the Income Tax Act that inadvertently deny benefits to some women. Persons with mental and/or physical disabilities have won judicial recognition of their need for special accommodation, but the failure to provide those accommodations may not be found to be discriminatory unless it undermines the dignity or perceived worthiness of those individuals.[3]

While most people agree that everyone should be treated equally, there is no clear consensus about the practical meaning of "equality." The debate has raged for more than two thousand years.[4] What does it mean for a state to treat its citizens "equally"? There are two principal answers to this question, one formal and the other substantive.

- The concept of "formal equality" allows the state to favour one group of people over another, so long as each member of a particular group receives the same treatment. For example, a law that forbids the employment of women as firefighters is justified, as long as all women are denied the opportunity to apply. To determine whether or not the law treats a particular woman unequally, a court would compare her situation to that of other women seeking to become firefighters. It would not compare her to a man who wished to join his local fire department, since men and women belong to different categories.
- The principle of "substantive equality" requires a broader, more contextual approach. It asks whether this particular woman is treated unfairly by the law—not in comparison to all other women, but in relation to all aspiring firefighters. If the law distinguishes between men and women on reasonable factual grounds, there is no violation of equality. But if an individual woman can prove that she is qualified for the job, and is denied the chance to apply on stereotypical or arbitrary grounds, she will establish a violation of substantive equality.

In Canadian law, "formal equality" gave rise to the "similarly situated" principle. In practice, the "similarly situated" test means that "people who are alike should be treated alike and people who are unalike should be treated unalike."[5] On its face, this approach

makes sense. After all, each individual has unique strengths and weaknesses. To treat everyone as though they were exactly the same would make little sense as a principle of public policy. Although such an approach is fair on its face, its effects would privilege some and hurt others. But when a government distinguishes among individuals or groups in a way that does not reflect their actual situations and abilities, that **distinction** is usually called **discrimination**.

Whereas reasonable distinctions may be both necessary and just, unfounded discrimination is not. For example, persons who aspire to become firefighters must meet certain entry criteria that are clearly relevant to the job. They must be physically strong, calm under pressure, and quick to react. There is no discrimination in rejecting applicants who cannot carry a heavy hose up a ladder or who panic at the sight of flames. On the other hand, a fire department whose recruitment policy forbids women to apply is guilty of discrimination. It is true that many, even most, women lack the upper-body strength to fight fires effectively. But there are numerous exceptions. Moreover, there are plenty of men who lack the qualifications to join a fire department. From the standpoint of substantive equality, the blanket exclusion of women not only discriminates against those individuals with the physical and mental strength to become firefighters; it also deprives the community of their talents.

Unfortunately, the difference between distinction and discrimination is not always clear in practice. Nor is it always easy to determine whether a particular instance of discrimination is deliberate or unintentional. It is no easy matter to apply general laws to diverse populations. A law that fails to distinguish among persons with different needs or characteristics may discriminate just as surely as one that distinguishes on illegitimate grounds. Does "adverse effects" discrimination—e.g., failing to require sign-language interpreters in hospitals—violate the Charter? How do we decide whether a particular law violates the government's duty to treat everyone "equally"? When the state tries to justify infringements of equality under s. 1, how stringently should the *Oakes* test be applied? Once a violation has been established by a court, how should it be remedied? These are among the most difficult issues confronting Canadian judges since 1985.

In Canadian jurisprudence on equality rights, the older emphasis on formal equality has been superseded by the substantive approach. The latter requires a contextual analysis, which is better suited to evaluating claims of "adverse effects" discrimination. Incorporating substantive and contextual factors into the legal analysis of equality raises some thorny issues.

- Where is the proper balance between subjective and objective perceptions of discrimination? Is it sufficient to evaluate a claim of discrimination from the standpoint of the hypothetical "reasonable person," or should judges try to put themselves in the plaintiff's shoes?
- Can a contextual, case-by-case approach yield a stable and coherent body of jurisprudence on s. 15? If not, the other two branches of government will find it difficult to make and implement public policy.
- When courts deal with concrete evidence of discrimination, such as lower public benefits, both the disposition and the remedy are relatively straightforward. But when plaintiffs base their cases on such intangible claims as an affront to their human dignity, how are courts to evaluate these claims? What are the appropriate remedies?

These questions have divided Canada's courts. At various times, the Supreme Court has split into three or four contending factions. Building a judicial consensus on the complex and inherently subjective concepts contained in s. 15 has proven difficult, if not impossible. Three issues have been particularly contentious:

- First, what is the purpose of s. 15? Is it intended to shield individuals from state-sponsored violations of their human dignity, or to impose positive duties on governments? Is it a constitutional mandate for judges to amend public policy in order to produce equality of result?
- Second, should the courts recognize additional grounds of discrimination that are not enumerated in s. 15? Which personal characteristics are "analogous" to those listed in the text of the Charter, and what is their legal status?
- Third and finally, what is the proper relationship between ss. 15 and 1? Should judges construe the

guarantees in s. 15 narrowly, separating permissible distinctions from unconstitutional discrimination at the first stage of analysis? Or should they treat all legislated distinctions as *prima facie* infringements of s. 15 and leave the task of balancing to the s. 1 stage?

These debates engage the most fundamental issues in the Charter era. To claim that the courts can use s. 15 to impose new spending responsibilities on governments, or that they can "read in" new grounds of discrimination, is to expand the policy-making powers of judges well beyond their traditional adjudicative duties. The courts have claimed the power to force executives and legislators to extend social programs to new recipients. They have effectively amended the Charter by adding new "**analogous grounds**." Although the Supreme Court's jurisprudence on equality rights is complex, and often confusing, one thing is clear: its interpretation of s. 15 gives the judicial branch a wide latitude to make policy, if it chooses to do so.

THE SOURCES AND EVOLUTION OF SECTION 15

When then–justice minister Trudeau first proposed his Charter of Rights in 1968, he wanted to replace the **nondiscrimination clause** in the 1960 Bill of Rights with a stronger guarantee of equality. Trudeau suggested that Canada adopt the broader language of the Fourteenth Amendment to the U.S. Constitution, thus replacing "equality before the law" with "the equal protection of the laws."[6] These nondiscrimination rights were lumped together with legal rights. Trudeau also proposed a separate section entitled "Egalitarian Rights." It would provide "guarantees against governmental action which would tend to distinguish certain persons or groups of persons for different treatment on the basis of their race, national origin, or other factors unrelated to the purpose for which the distinction is made."[7] He noted that most existing human rights codes were aimed at private conduct, whereas "A constitutional bill of rights would serve to limit discriminatory activities on the part of governments as well."[8] At this early stage in the

Charter's evolution, Trudeau was prepared to reproduce the language in s. 1 of the Bill of Rights, with the addition of further prohibited grounds if appropriate. Like then–prime minister Pearson, he also intended the nondiscrimination clause to apply "both to private conduct and to actions of the state, whether federal or provincial."[9]

The draft Charter that Trudeau presented to the premiers in February 1969 stated that "every individual in Canada is entitled not to be discriminated against by reason of race, colour, national or ethnic origin, religion, or sex," but only in relation to employment, housing and property, and dealings with public authorities.[10] Even this restrained approach to equality rights was too much for most premiers, who were alarmed by the implications for their legislative jurisdictions. The 1971 Victoria Charter did not contain a nondiscrimination clause. After its collapse, the McGuigan-Molgat Committee recommended that any future bill of rights "prohibit discrimination by reason of sex, race, ethnic origin, colour or religion by proclaiming the right of the individual to equal treatment by law."[11]

Bill C-60, tabled in 1978, replaced equality rights with a nondiscrimination clause. It guaranteed the enjoyment of the rights contained elsewhere in the document "without discrimination because of race, national or ethnic origin, language, colour, religion, age, or sex."[12] In the accompanying policy document, Trudeau explained his change of heart since 1968. He argued that precise guarantees of equality rights— particularly those pertaining to the private sphere— were too complex to be entrenched in the Constitution; they were more properly spelled out in federal and provincial human rights codes, which could be amended as necessary.[13] Apart from the inclusion of language and age as prohibited grounds, the proposed section 9 was essentially the same as s. 1 of the Bill of Rights. The Special Joint Committee that reviewed Bill C-60 reported that several witnesses had requested a more comprehensive list of prohibited grounds, but with one exception—marital status—it rejected these proposals on the ground that they were irrelevant to the rights and freedoms covered by the proposed section.[14] The committee suggested that s. 9 be amended by adding an exemption for "special programs on behalf of disadvantaged groups or

New Canadians take the citizenship oath.
CP PHOTO/Aaron Harris

persons."[15] This recommendation was ultimately reflected in s. 15(2) of the Charter.

The failure of the Victoria Charter and the controversy aroused by Bill C-60 appears to have chastened Trudeau. He became convinced that the provinces would accept only a limited version of nondiscrimination rights, and not a full-blown guarantee of "equality." In January 1979, he proposed the following clause, which is narrower than the guarantees found in the Universal Declaration of Human Rights and other international documents:

11. (1) Everyone has the right to equality before the law and to equal protection of the law without distinction or restriction other than any distinction or restriction provided by law that is fair and reasonable having regard to the object of the law.

(2) Nothing in this section shall be interpreted as precluding the enactment of or rendering invalid any affirmative action program on behalf of disadvantaged persons or groups.[16]

This language would have allowed any government to adopt discriminatory laws, so long as it could argue that the discrimination was "fair and reasonable" in relation to the purpose of the law—a purpose that, in and of itself, could not be condemned as discriminatory. Moreover, the insertion of an internal limitation into a clause protecting equality rights would have allowed judges to uphold legislated distinctions that

October 1980	January 1981
Everyone has the right to equality before the law and to the equal protection of the law without discrimination because of race, national or ethnic origin, colour, religion, age or sex.	Every individual is equal before and under the law and has the right to the equal protection and equal benefit of the law without discrimination and, in particular, without discrimination based on race, national or ethnic origin, colour, religion, sex, age, or mental or physical disability.

might otherwise have been found to be discriminatory. This is not to say that Canadian governments were routinely discriminating against particular groups; by the 1970s, deliberate attempts to exclude certain segments of society from legislated benefits were rare. Nonetheless, the persistence of statutes from less egalitarian times posed problems for some Canadians (as witnessed in *Bliss*), as did inadvertent "adverse effects" discrimination. The 1979 version of equality rights might have shielded such laws from judicial scrutiny. In the event, the final wording of s. 15 contains no internal limitations; legislated discrimination may be justified only, if at all, under s. 1.

The practical difference between the January 1979 version and the wording adopted in 1981 can be illustrated with reference to an actual law: the definition of marriage adopted by the House of Commons in 1999, which explicitly excluded same-sex couples. By July 2003, courts in three provinces had declared an exclusively heterosexual definition of marriage to be illegal, for reasons that we will explore later in this chapter. Had the 1979 provision been entrenched instead, the law would probably have been upheld by the courts. While the purpose of the law is to exclude same-sex couples from public benefits, the restrictive definition of marriage is clearly "fair and reasonable" in the context of that purpose. (The second clause, following the McGuigan-Molgat recommendations, remained substantially unchanged throughout the remainder of the constitutional process.)

Throughout the 1980–82 constitutional negotiations, the provinces—not just the Gang of Eight, but Ontario and New Brunswick as well—rejected the proposed entrenchment of equality rights.[17] Ottawa offered several compromises—a short list of enumerated grounds, the narrow language discussed earlier, a delay in implementing equality rights—without success. After Trudeau decided to pursue unilateral patriation, what is now s. 15 (1) started to take shape. The Special Joint Committee heard from several witnesses who wanted stronger guarantees of equality rights. Many represented feminist groups, still angered by the *Lavell/Bedard* and *Bliss* rulings. They demanded that s. 15(1) guarantee equality under the law and equal benefit of the law, to prevent any future court rulings sanctioning discrimination.[18] They also lobbied for an **illustrative**, as opposed to **exhaustive**, list of prohibited grounds.[19] The table above compares the final wording to the version tabled in October 1980 (the January 1981 amendments are italicized).

After the provincial governments had rejected the narrow version proposed in 1979, it was difficult to see how they could accept the strong guarantee of equality rights that emerged from the Special Joint Committee. The deadlock was finally broken at the November 1981 First Ministers' Meeting, when the federal government agreed to insert the notwithstanding clause (s. 33) and to make it applicable to the equality rights. The federal government also agreed to a three-year delay in implementing s. 15.

Even before s. 15 took effect on April 17, 1985, its impact on Canadian law was expected to exceed that of the other Charter sections.[20] Some of the feminist lawyers who had lobbied for stronger equality rights prepared for the implementation of s. 15 by establishing the Women's Legal Education and Action Fund (LEAF).[21] (LEAF is discussed at greater length in Chapter 6.) Groups like LEAF and EGALE (Equality for Gays and Lesbians Everywhere) were determined not only to benefit from rulings under s. 15, but to shape equality jurisprudence as it evolved.

THE SCOPE OF SECTION 15

One of the first questions to be answered was whether or not the section would apply to the private sector. Trudeau had hoped, at least initially, that the Charter would prohibit discrimination in areas of daily life—e.g., rental housing and employment—in which governments rarely intervene directly. Some experts predicted that s. 15 would fulfil these hopes. They assumed that any and all forms of discriminatory action, public and private, would now be subject to challenge in the courts.[22] If they were proved right, the courts would be embroiled in every aspect of daily life: rental agreements, personal employment contracts, collective bargaining, even clashes between neighbours from different cultural traditions. Other observers were more cautious. They noted that s. 32(1) of the Charter restricted its scope to the acts of governments and their agencies, and that the explicit references to "law" in the language of s. 15 seemed to immunize private acts of discrimination from judicial review.[23]

As described in Chapter 1, pages 22–24, the Supreme Court soon made it clear that the Charter would not apply to the economic sphere, and certainly not to private contracts. The majority in *Dolphin Delivery* (1986) held that private disputes in which the government was not directly involved could not be settled on Charter grounds.[24] In the 1990 *McKinney* decision (discussed in Dossier 1.4, pages 22–24), the court had to determine whether a para-public body—i.e., an institution that straddles the line between the public and private sectors, such as a hospital or a university—was subject to s. 15. University professors and librarians challenged the mandatory-retirement provisions in their collective agreements. They argued that people who wanted to keep working after their sixty-fifth birthdays should be allowed to do so, and that a university policy that forced them to retire violated the Charter guarantee against discrimination on the basis of age. Writing for the majority on this issue, Justice La Forest warned that "To open up all private and public action to judicial review could strangle the operation of society" and paralyze the courts.[25] The impugned collective agreements fell within the private sphere and were thereby immunized from Charter review. The Justices were unanimous in their conclusion that if the Charter had applied, they would have found mandatory retirement to be discriminatory on the basis of age. However, most of the seven-judge panel would have justified the violation of s. 15(1) under s. 1.

More recently, the Supreme Court has modified its approach to para-public agencies. It held that universities and hospitals are immune from Charter scrutiny in their internal operations (e.g., human resource management), but not in matters related to the delivery of the public services for which they were established. In the 1997 *Eldridge* ruling, a unanimous nine-judge panel found that the failure to provide sign-language interpreters for hospital patients who were deaf violated s. 15(1), even though there was no specific statute law prohibiting such services. Writing for the Court, Justice La Forest identified two ways in which provincial laws could violate the Charter:

> First, legislation may be found to be unconstitutional on its face because it violates a Charter right and is not saved by s. 1. In such cases, the legislation will be invalid and the Court compelled to declare it of no force or effect pursuant to s. 52(1) of the *Constitution Act, 1982*. Secondly, the Charter may be infringed, not by the legislation itself, but by the actions of a delegated decision-maker in applying it. In such cases, the legislation remains valid, but a remedy for the unconstitutional action may be sought pursuant to s. 24(1) of the Charter.[26]

The Court held that a British Columbia hospital had denied deaf patients the "equal benefit of the law" as mandated by s. 15(1).[27] That failure constituted "adverse effects" discrimination, a clear violation of equality rights. "A legal distinction need not be motivated by a desire to disadvantage an individual or group in order to violate s. 15(1). It is sufficient if the *effect* of the legislation is to deny someone the equal protection or benefit of the law."[28] In this instance, the impugned effect was incidental to the impugned laws; neither the Hospital Insurance Act nor the Medical and Health Care Services Act referred explicitly to sign-language interpretation. Nonetheless, the Court held that the hospital should have taken extra measures to ensure the same level of health-care services to all patients, regardless of mental or physical disability. Justice La Forest ordered the government of

British Columbia to administer the relevant laws "in a manner consistent with the requirements of s. 15(1) as I have described them"[29]—i.e., to make "reasonable accommodation" for the special needs of patients with disabilities.

In summary, the guarantee of equality rights does not apply to private matters in which the government plays no active part. The values that it enshrines may be used to evaluate the common law in litigation between two private parties, but s. 15 itself has no role to play where the state is not directly engaged. Note, however, that an individual who is denied private-sector employment because of a personal characteristic, or who cannot rent an apartment because the landlord is prejudiced against people of a particular race or religion, can seek redress via provincial human rights legislation. Section 15 is part of a broader legal structure designed to combat the arbitrary mistreatment of individuals and groups.

THE EARLY JURISPRUDENCE ON SECTION 15(1)

In 1989, the Supreme Court issued its first major ruling on equality rights. Mark Andrews, a British lawyer living in British Columbia, wished to practise law in that province. Unfortunately for Mr. Andrews, the provincial Barristers and Solicitors Act denied licences to noncitizens. He challenged the law, arguing that it violated his equality rights under s. 15(1), even though citizenship is not among the prohibited grounds listed in the section. The trial judge found that the law violated s. 15(1), but that it was saved by s. 1 because it was reasonable to require persons with the responsibility for the legal system to hold Canadian citizenship. The British Columbia Court of Appeal overturned that ruling, on the ground that the discrimination against noncitizens served no clear purpose and could not be justified under s. 1. The Supreme Court of Canada upheld the Court of Appeal ruling in its outcome and disposition, although a majority of the Justices rejected the reasoning on which it was based. The six Justices who participated in the decision agreed that the law infringed the equality rights of the plaintiff. Two of

the six held that the violation of s. 15(1) was justified under s. 1, while the other four disagreed.

The *Andrews* decision set the course for subsequent jurisprudence on equality rights, in at least three ways:

- First, it showed that the Court would treat the enumerated list of prohibited grounds as illustrative, not exhaustive. It would recognize analogous grounds of discrimination on a case-by-case basis.
- Second, *Andrews* gave the Court an opportunity to define such crucial concepts as "equality," "distinction," and "discrimination." In so doing, it would give lower courts and policy-makers crucial guidance for the future.
- Third, the Court addressed the relationship between s. 15 and s. 1 of the Charter. The key issue was whether the courts should interpret s. 15(1) as a blanket prohibition of legislative distinction in any form (leaving limitations to the s. 1 stage), or distinguish between acceptable and unacceptable legislated distinctions at the initial stage of analysis (thus making s. 1 unnecessary in many cases).

The third issue was particularly important for policy-makers as they undertook their first-order Charter duties and for the courts with the second-order responsibility to evaluate the policy-makers' work. If a court took the first approach, leaving the entire issue of justification to the s. 1 stage of analysis, it risked trivializing the guarantees in s. 15(1) by lumping permissible distinctions together with impermissible discrimination. The British Columbia Court of Appeal (led by then–provincial Chief Justice Beverley McLachlin) preferred the second approach, under which a court would determine the harmless or **invidious** nature of the legislative distinction at the s. 15(1) stage of Charter analysis. That left two questions: "what degree of evaluation of the legislation should be done under s. 15(1), and what role, if any, remained for s. 1 when legislation is attacked under s. 15(1)?"[30]

McLachlin reasoned that "the question to be answered under s. 15 should be whether the impugned distinction is reasonable or fair, having regard to the purposes and aims and its effect on persons adversely affected."[31] This wording is reminiscent of the January 1979 version of the nondiscrimination clause, reproduced earlier in this chapter. By adopting this internally limited approach to s. 15(1), McLachlin left little for s. 1 to do. At most, she suggested that it might permit a government to justify extraordinary acts of discrimination, such as the internment of the Japanese Canadians during World War II.

The lead opinion for the Supreme Court of Canada was written by Justice McIntyre. He observed that, of all the concepts contained in the Charter, equality was the most difficult to define with precision. McIntyre adopted a substantive and contextual approach. He argued that in the context of a particular case, a violation of s. 15(1) could be determined only by comparing the condition of the plaintiff to "the condition of others in the social and political setting in which the question arises."[32] Without such a comparison, judges might make erroneous assumptions—as they did when they endorsed the "similarly situated" test. For McIntyre, the central issue in any equality-rights case is the actual impact of the impugned law on the plaintiff(s) at bar. That impact need not be deliberate; laws that inadvertently impose a disproportionate burden on some particular individual or group will infringe the guarantee of equality.

> Recognizing that there will always be an infinite variety of personal characteristics, capacities, entitlements and merits among those subject to a law, there must be accorded, as nearly as may be possible, an equality of benefit and protection and no more of the restrictions, penalties or burdens imposed upon one than another. In other words, the admittedly unattainable ideal should be that a law expressed to bind all should not because of irrelevant personal differences have a more burdensome or less beneficial impact on one than another.[33]

By emphasizing the substantive impact of the law on the plaintiff(s) instead of the formal idea that likes should be treated alike, McIntyre repudiated the "similarly situated" test that had guided the Court in *Lavell* and *Bliss*. His critique of the "similarly situated" approach was withering: "If it were to be applied literally, it could be used to justify the Nuremberg laws of Adolf Hitler. Similar treatment was contemplated

for all Jews."[34] McIntyre pointedly rejected the *Bliss* ruling, remarking that "This case, of course, was decided before the advent of the Charter."[35] Indeed, he pointed out that "the language of s. 15 was deliberately chosen in order to remedy some of the perceived defects under the Canadian Bill of Rights."[36]

McIntyre separated legislated distinctions—which appear in most statutes—from legislated discrimination, which is explicitly condemned in the Charter. He identified the purpose of s. 15(1) as "the promotion of a society in which all are secure in the knowledge that they are recognized at law as human beings equally deserving of concern, respect and consideration."[37] Inherent in this formulation of equality rights is "a large remedial component." The Charter requires governments not only to refrain from imposing further disadvantages, but to redress existing disadvantages wherever it is reasonable to do so—hence the exception provided in s. 15(2). In general, however, s. 15(1) will be used by those who claim to have suffered discrimination at the hands of government and who seek a remedy. McIntyre defined "discrimination" as

> a distinction, whether intentional or not but based on grounds relating to personal characteristics of the individual or group, which has the effect of imposing burdens, obligations, or disadvantages on such individual or group not imposed upon others, or which withholds or limits access to opportunities, benefits, and advantages available to other members of society.

He added that "Distinctions based on personal characteristics attributed to an individual solely on the basis of association with a group will rarely escape the charge of discrimination, while those based on an individual's merits and capacities will rarely be so classed."[38] To return to the example of female firefighters; a woman who cannot meet the entry requirements because she lacks the requisite upper-body strength will not be considered a victim of discrimination, but a woman who is fully capable of performing the job and prevented from applying solely on the ground of her sex may be entitled to a remedy under s. 15(1).[39]

McIntyre rejected McLachlin's conception of the relationship between ss. 15(1) and 1 as "a radical departure from the analytical approach to the Charter which has been approved by this Court."[40] The protected right must be interpreted in a broad and purposive manner at the first stage of analysis; the question of justification must be left to the s. 1 stage. Recall that McLachlin would have taken a relatively narrow view of s. 15(1), allowing a government to justify legislative distinctions with reference to the purpose of the impugned law before the s. 1 stage was even reached. McIntyre proposed a different approach to equality rights, which focuses on the enumerated and analogous grounds. While he did not propose a specific test for the identification of analogous grounds, McIntyre used the phrase "a discrete and insular minority" to denote the sort of group whose members might claim the protection of s. 15.[41] He deliberately left open the possibility that courts could "read in" additional prohibited criteria for discrimination if they saw fit: "The enumerated grounds in s. 15(1) are not exclusive and the limits, if any, on grounds for discrimination which may be established in future cases await definition."[42]

Under the *Andrews* doctrine, a plaintiff must prove three claims:

- that the impugned law distinguished him or her (whether as an individual or as a member of a particular group) from other Canadians;
- that the criterion on which the distinction rests is an enumerated ground (e.g., sex or race) or a personal characteristic that is analogous to the enumerated grounds; and
- that the effect of the law is discriminatory, even if it is neutral in intent.

Once he or she had met this evidentiary burden, the onus would shift to the sponsoring government to justify the impugned distinction under s. 1. It could do so only by persuading the court that the law did not discriminate, either in its purpose or in its effect. In the case at bar, Mr. Andrews succeeded in persuading the Court that citizenship is an analogous ground under s. 15(1), that his exclusion from the practice of law in British Columbia violated his equality rights, and that the violation was not justified under s. 1.

The *Andrews* decision was immediately recognized as a milestone in Charter jurisprudence, both because it was the first major ruling on s. 15(1) from the top court and because the Justices had reached unanimity on some of the issues that had divided lower courts.[43] These included the application of the Charter to both intentional and unintentional discrimination; the relationship between ss. 15(1) and 1; the endorsement of the substantive and contextual approach, coupled with an uncompromising rejection of formal equality; and the addition of analogous grounds of discrimination.

Some commentators took issue with the analogous grounds approach. They wondered whether the Court had gone too far in assuming the power to rewrite s. 15(1) as it saw fit.[44] After all, the drafters of the Charter had received, and rejected, a number of suggestions for additional prohibited grounds of discrimination. Why should judges be able to overrule the choices made by the framers? And how far would they go in devising additional grounds?

The Supreme Court provided a partial answer a few months later, in the *Turpin* ruling. The central issue was the constitutionality of s. 430 of the Criminal Code, which made jury trials mandatory in all murder cases—except those held in Alberta, where an accused could elect a murder trial by judge alone. In 1983, an Ontario woman was charged, along with two alleged co-conspirators, in the first-degree murder of her husband. In 1985, the trial judge ruled that the law violated ss. 11(f) and 15(1) of the Charter because it required trial by jury. He accordingly proceeded to try the three accused without a jury, according to their wishes. The female defendant, Sharon Turpin, was acquitted; the other two were convicted. The Crown appealed her acquittal, partly on the ground that the trial judge had erred in finding s. 430 unconstitutional and invalid. The Ontario Court of Appeal overturned the acquittal on the ground that the law did not violate s. 15(1). The Supreme Court followed suit in May 1989, although for reasons that differed from those of the appellate judges.

Writing for a unanimous court, Justice Wilson dismissed Turpin's claim that her equality rights had been violated because she was denied the option of a trial by judge alone. She acknowledged that the now-defunct s. 430 treated murder suspects outside Alberta more harshly than those inside the province, by depriving them of a potentially helpful alternative to trial by jury, and that this deprivation constituted a breach of "equality before the law." However, this breach did not amount to discrimination within the meaning set out by Justice McIntyre in *Andrews*, because it neither reflected nor perpetuated a preexisting "social, political and legal disadvantage in our society." There was no evidence of "stereotyping, historical disadvantage or vulnerability to political and social prejudice"[45] attaching to persons who happened to be charged with murder outside the boundaries of Alberta. Nor could such persons be collectively described as "a discrete and insular minority." None of the characteristics that denote an analogous ground under s. 15(1)—immutability, preexisting prejudice, and centrality to the dignity of the individual—was present. Section 430 was upheld,[46] and Turpin's appeal was dismissed.

By the end of 1989, the Court had resolved some of the interpretive problems arising from s. 15(1). It had drawn a relatively clear line between distinction and discrimination; extended its usual approach to the Charter—a "broad and purposive" reading of protected rights, followed by a balancing process at the s. 1 stage of analysis—to the application of equality rights; and suggested a test for the recognition of analogous grounds. The *Turpin* ruling signalled that the highest court was unanimous in its agreement on these points.

In the early 1990s, that consensus fell apart. The Court was divided, especially over the relationship between ss. 15(1) and 1.[47] Four Justices favoured the "internal limits" approach to equality rights that Justice McLachlin had advanced in the British Columbia Court of Appeal ruling on *Andrews*. An equal number preferred Justice McIntyre's doctrine, which countenanced limits only at the s. 1 stage. The remaining Justice, Claire L'Heureux-Dubé, struck out on her own path.

The 1990 *Hess/Nguyen* ruling[48] was the first signal that the Court might back away from the strong guarantee of equality rights that it had enunciated in *Andrews*. The decision dealt with two separate appeals that the Court had decided to address in a single ruling since they raised similar issues. Both appellants had been convicted under s. 146(1) of the Criminal Code, which forbade men to engage in sexual intercourse with girls under the age of fourteen. There was

no equivalent offence pertaining to female offenders and young males. The seven Justices agreed unanimously that the law violated s. 7 of the Charter; five determined that the violation could not be justified under s. 1. The more divisive issue was whether the law discriminated on the basis of sex, and thus infringed s. 15(1). Four Justices found no violation of equality rights; the remaining three concluded that the law did constitute sex discrimination but was saved by s. 1.

The crux of the disagreement was twofold: the legitimacy of the legislative distinction between men and women (both as offenders and as victims) and the relationship between ss. 15(1) and 1. Writing for the majority, Justice Wilson argued that the offence defined by s. 146(1) of the Code reflected biological reality, not mere social prejudice. Thus the distinction on the basis of sex was legitimate, not discriminatory. The issue could be settled under s. 15(1), with no need for a "balancing test" under s. 1. Wilson left it to Parliament to consider whether males under fourteen merited the same degree of protection as their female contemporaries. The suggestion that a distinction based on "biological reality" could not be considered discriminatory is uncomfortably reminiscent of *Bliss*. It would reappear in Justice La Forest's opinion in the *Egan* case.

In dissent, Justice McLachlin—now elevated to the Supreme Court of Canada—reversed her earlier position in the *Andrews* appeal. She found that the law violated the guarantee of sexual equality in s. 15(1): "It makes distinctions on the enumerated ground of sex. It burdens men as it does not burden women. It offers protection to young females which it does not offer to young males. It is discriminatory."[49] McLachlin and Wilson agreed that the key variables in determining the constitutionality of the law were the need to protect young girls against sexual exploitation and the risk of early pregnancy. But while Wilson had applied these factors at the first stage of analysis, McLachlin applied them under s. 1. Although both Justices upheld the law, the different way in which they reached that conclusion was an ominous sign for the future. So was Wilson's willingness to justify a distinction on the basis of sex within the text of s. 15 and without reference to s. 1.[50]

THE 1995 "EQUALITY TRILOGY": DIVISION AND RETREAT

Between 1989 and 1995, the Court was able to reach unanimity in some equality-rights cases.[51] In general, the Justices found it easier to deal with claims based on enumerated grounds (especially age) than with requests to recognize new analogous grounds. In *Tétreault-Gadoury v. Canada (Employment and Immigration Commission)*, for example, the plaintiff challenged a provision of the Unemployment Insurance Act that made persons over the age of sixty-five ineligible for UI benefits even if they wished to continue working and were not covered by a mandatory-retirement policy. All nine Justices agreed that the law discriminated on the basis of age. It "stigmatized [the plaintiff], regardless of her personal skills and situation, as belonging to the group of persons no longer part of the active population and perpetuated the insidious stereotype that a person who is 65 years of age or older cannot be retrained for the labour market."[52] The violation of equality was not justified under s. 1.

Consensus on other enumerated grounds, particularly sex, was more elusive. The male and female Justices split over a challenge to a section of the Income Tax Act that did not permit working women to deduct child-care costs as business expenses. In that instance, the seven male Justices found no sex discrimination; the two female Justices, L'Heureux-Dubé and McLachlin, dissented vigorously, arguing that a contextual approach to the case would have produced the opposite (and, in their view, correct) result.[53] Wherever possible, the Court avoided s. 15 issues—either by resolving cases under other Charter sections or by dismissing claims for analogous status.[54]

The real crunch came with the 1995 "equality trilogy"—*Egan*, *Miron*, and *Thibaudeau*[55]—that raised s. 15(1) issues that the Court could not avoid. These cases revealed the depth of the Court's disagreement, particularly over the relationship of s. 15(1) to s. 1 and the criteria for identifying analogous grounds. (See Dossier 11.1 for an analysis of the *Miron* ruling.)

When it was issued, the *Egan* case appeared to be a defeat for gay-rights groups. The plaintiffs, two men who had lived together for decades, lost their fight for spousal benefits under the Canada Pension Plan. But in the process, they won a significant legal victory (see Dossier 11.4, pages 359–62). All nine Justices recognized sexual orientation as an analogous ground of discrimination. Despite this finding, four Justices (Chief Justice Lamer and Justices La Forest, Gonthier, and Major) found that a law that denied spousal benefits to same-sex partners did not violate s. 15(1). Justice La Forest reasoned that the distinction between heterosexual and homosexual couples was "relevant" to the object of the legislation, which was to promote and support the social institution of marriage. Pointing to "the biological and social realities that underlie the traditional marriage," La Forest declared that "marriage is by nature heterosexual."[56] A law that excluded same-sex couples from the benefits of marriage was not discriminatory because it was based on a valid distinction. The dissenters (Justices L'Heureux-Dubé, Cory, McLachlin, and Iacobucci) found that the law violated s. 15(1) and could not be justified under s. 1. The swing vote was Justice Sopinka, who agreed with the minority that the law violated s. 15(1) but considered it to be justified under s. 1. So while all nine Justices recognized sexual orientation as an analogous ground, five determined that the impugned law did not violate the Charter.

DOSSIER 11.1

MIRON V. TRUDEL

Miron v. Trudel dealt with the fairness of a legislated distinction between married and common-law heterosexual couples. Mr. Miron had been injured in a car accident, which left

him unable to work. He applied for accident benefits from the insurance policy held by his long-time common-law partner. His claim was denied: such benefits were only available to the "spouses" of policy-holders. Under the Ontario Insurance Act, the term "spouse" was restricted to legally married couples. Miron and his partner tried to sue the insurance company, but their suit failed when the judge determined that they were not "spouses" within the meaning of the law. The Ontario Court of Appeal agreed with the trial judge. The appellants took their case to the Supreme Court of Canada. They argued that the definition of "spouse" in the Insurance Act violated s. 15(1) by discriminating on the basis of marital status, which they asked the Court to recognize as an "analogous ground."

The Supreme Court recognized marital status as an analogous ground (a belated victory for the women's groups that lobbied the drafters in 1980–82), albeit by the narrowest possible margin (5-4). Four of the Justices in the majority—Justices Sopinka, Cory, McLachlin, and Iacobucci—argued that a legislated distinction based on the "stereotypical application of presumed group or personal characteristics" would almost always constitute a violation of s. 15(1) and require justification under s. 1.[1] The person(s) seeking relief from the discriminatory effect of a particular law should not be required "to prove that the unequal treatment suffered is irrational or unreasonable or founded on irrelevant considerations." Instead, the onus of proving that the law does not discriminate falls on the sponsoring government.[2] Consequently, the courts should give s. 15(1) a "broad and generous" interpretation. The only internal limitation on s. 15(1) is the requirement that the plaintiff demonstrate a legislated distinction on either an enumerated or an analogous ground: "These grounds serve as a filter to separate trivial inequities from those worthy of constitutional protection."[3]

The four dissenting Justices—all of whom had voted to uphold the impugned law in *Egan*—argued that the legislated distinction between married and common-law couples was valid. Marital status should not be accepted as an analogous ground. There was no violation of s. 15(1). Justice Gonthier ruled

that marriage is a fundamental value in Canadian society, and that laws that protect that institution should be upheld. There was no need for him to consider s. 1; under his interpretation of s. 15(1), the question of constitutionality was resolved at the first stage of analysis. Once again, the Court was split between those who wished to read internal limitations into s. 15(1) and those who did not.

Gonthier did not ask whether distinctions on the basis of marital status might reflect or reinforce social prejudice against cohabiting couples. For Justice L'Heureux-Dubé, this question lay at the heart of the case. She argued that the "discriminatory impact" of an impugned law could not be assessed purely on material grounds, such as the provision or denial of particular benefits. Rather, "a distinction would be discriminatory within the meaning of s. 15 where it is capable of either promoting or perpetuating the view that the individual adversely affected by this distinction is less capable, or less worthy of recognition or value as a human being or as a member of Canadian society, equally deserving of concern, respect, and consideration."[4] L'Heureux-Dubé determined that many, if not all, common-law couples were subject to social disapproval and stigma. She rejected Gonthier's claim that marriage is a contract that individuals choose to undertake, or not to undertake, purely for reasons of personal preference. What about individuals who wish to wed legally but whose long-term partners do not wish to participate in a formal ceremony? Should the state overlook their vulnerability and punish them for a "choice" foisted on them by someone else?[5] L'Heureux-Dubé concluded that the law discriminated on the basis of marital status, which was an analogous ground under s. 15(1), and could not be upheld under s. 1.

ENDNOTES

1. *Miron v. Trudel*, [1995] 2 S.C.R. 418, paragraph 128, *per* McLachlin J.

2. Ibid., paragraph 129, *per* McLachlin J.

(continued)

3. Ibid., paragraph 131, *per* McLachlin J.

4. Ibid., paragraph 90, *per* L'Heureux-Dubé J.

5. However heartfelt this aspect of L'Heureux-Dubé's opinion may have been, it was also a canny tactical move: had she conceded that marriage was purely a matter of individual choice, it would have been more difficult to designate marital status as an "immutable" characteristic meriting analogous status.

The third case in the "trilogy," *Thibaudeau,* split the Court along gender lines. Under the federal Income Tax Act, a divorced parent who paid child support to an ex-spouse could deduct those payments from his or her taxable income. The other parent had to pay income tax on the support payments that he or she received. The effect was to lower the tax burden on the noncustodial parent while increasing the tax burden on the custodial parent, and to deprive the children of part of the money that was supposed to be used for their benefit. Suzanne Thibaudeau took the federal government to court, arguing that the tax law discriminated on the basis of sex. Even though the impugned provisions were facially neutral—there was no explicit reference to mothers or fathers in the law—their effects on men and women were very different in practice. Women make up the vast majority of custodial parents, while most child-support orders are imposed on men. Therefore, Thibaudeau argued, the provisions imposed "adverse effects" on women while benefiting men.

The five male judges who heard the case—Justices Gonthier, La Forest, Sopinka, Cory, and Iacobucci—found no infringement of s. 15(1), although their reasons varied. Justice Gonthier returned to the formal equality approach of *Lavell* and *Bliss*: he treated all divorced parents as a single group and argued that the law equalized the benefits and burdens within that group. His refusal to consider contextual issues, particularly the fact that most custodial parents are women, led him to conclude that "the tax burden of the couple is reduced and this has the result of increasing the available resources that can be used for the benefit of the children."[57] This statement overlooks the whole point of the impugned provisions: if the parents were still "a couple," no court-ordered support payments would be necessary. Although Cory and Iacobucci explicitly disavowed Gonthier's reasoning,[58] they agreed that the act did not discriminate on the basis of sex.

The two female judges, McLachlin and L'Heureux-Dubé, dissented strongly. McLachlin rejected Gonthier's analysis, pointing out that the law imposed unequal burdens on a particular class of divorced parents. She ruled that custodial parents should be treated as an analogous group under s. 15(1), partly because of their history of "disadvantageous treatment" and partly because most of them were women, thus replicating the enumerated ground of sex.[59] The law infringed s. 15(1) and could not be saved under s. 1. For L'Heureux-Dubé, the issue was not whether individuals in the situation of Ms. Thibaudeau constituted either an enumerated or analogous group; rather, the question was whether the impugned law deprived the plaintiff of equality before and under the law or the equal benefit and protection of the law, and if so, whether that deprivation was discriminatory in its effects. She argued, contrary to Gonthier, that "the effects on separated or divorced *custodial* parents must be compared with the effects on separated or divorced *non-custodial* parents."[60] L'Heureux-Dubé identified two key contextual characteristics of custodial parents: their high incidence of poverty, which makes them (as a group) "politically weak, economically vulnerable, and socially disempowered," and the fact that most of them are women.[61] Laws that increased the burdens already borne by custodial parents were inherently discriminatory. As McLachlin had done, L'Heureux-Dubé concluded that the law violated s. 15(1) and was not justified under s. 1.

For many observers of the Court, the "equality trilogy" was both surprising and disappointing.[62]

• Four of the nine Justices had embraced internal limits on s. 15(1). This raised concerns among equality advocates because it reduced the onus on governments to prove that legislated distinctions were not discriminatory.

- The *Thibaudeau* majority had retreated from the position that "adverse effects" discrimination violated the Charter as surely as the deliberate mistreatment of targeted groups. The refusal to consider contextual factors marked a clear deviation from the *Andrews* doctrine.

- By downplaying the importance of historic vulnerability and stereotyping in the analysis of s. 15(1), and by relying on "traditional values" to validate questionable distinctions, the four Justices who dissented in *Miron* and voted against James Egan seemed to reinforce widely held suspicions that rich white male judges were too out of touch with changing social realities to make sound decisions on equality issues.

The good news for groups that preferred an expansive interpretation of s. 15(1) was the recognition of sexual orientation and marital status as analogous grounds. These elements in the "trilogy" provoked grave concern among Court critics, who raised important questions about the legitimacy of judicial amendments to the Charter.[63]

In 1997, the Court issued three unanimous judgments in equality-rights cases: *Eaton, Benner*, and *Eldridge*.[64] While the Justices who wrote the opinions (Sopinka, Iacobucci, and La Forest, respectively) acknowledged the divisions among their colleagues, they insisted that there was sufficient agreement on a "broad analytic framework" to resolve disputes over equality rights.[65] *Eaton* rejected an appeal by the parents of a disabled child who had been placed in a special education class by the local school board (Dossier 11.2).

In *Benner*, the Court struck down a section of the Citizenship Act that granted automatic citizenship to persons born outside Canada if their fathers were Canadian but not to children of Canadian mothers. The Court found that the differential treatment of

---

DOSSIER 11.2

EATON V. BRANT COUNTY BOARD OF EDUCATION

The parents of a twelve-year-old girl with severe cerebral palsy wanted her to attend school in a regular class. The child could not communicate; she was partially blind and confined to a wheelchair. She required a full-time assistant in the classroom. After three years, the school board decided—on the advice of her teachers and assistants—that the girl needed the accommodations available in a special education class. Her parents appealed the decision to a review panel, without success. They pressed their appeals all the way to the Supreme Court of Canada. The parents argued that the board's decision to place their daughter in special education violated s. 15(1).

The Court identified three differences between the enumerated ground of physical and mental disability and the other enumerated grounds of discrimination. First, physical and mental disabilities vary from individual to individual, so claims of discrimination can be assessed only on a case-by-case basis. In contrast, millions of women may share similar experiences of discrimination on the basis of sex. Second, equality issues relating to disability rarely arise from the application of stereotypes; instead, they are the product of actual personal characteristics (e.g., blindness or mental illness). Third, the remedial effect of s. 15(1) is particularly important in relation to disability: "it is the failure to make reasonable accommodation, to fine-tune society so that its structures and assumptions do not result in the relegation and banishment of disabled persons from participation, which results in discrimination against them."[1] In the case at bar, the Court accepted the board's decision. In effect, the girl's equality rights were advanced, not infringed, by her removal from a classroom that could not accommodate her particular needs.

ENDNOTES

1. *Eaton v. Brant County Board of Education*, [1997] 1 S.C.R. 241, paragraph 67, *per* Sopinka J.

persons based on the sex of a parent violated the guarantee of equal benefit of the law. As noted earlier, *Eldridge* dealt with the constitutionality of a hospital's failure to provide sign-language interpreters for deaf patients. All three cases engaged enumerated grounds. The application of s. 1 in *Eldridge* and *Benner* did not divide the Court, as it had done in *Miron* and *Egan*. The Justices had little difficulty in determining that the law challenged in *Benner* was not rationally connected to its objective. The Court refrained from the wide-ranging discussions that had divided its members in the 1995 "trilogy" and confined itself to the issues necessary to resolve each appeal. In effect, the Justices agreed to disagree.

THE SEARCH FOR A NEW CONSENSUS: *VRIEND, LAW V. CANADA*, AND THEIR PROGENY

Shortly after *Eldridge*, the composition of the Court changed. Justice La Forest (the majority author in *Egan*) retired; Justice Sopinka, whose swing vote determined the differing outcomes in *Egan* and *Miron*, died. They were replaced, respectively, by Justices Bastarache and Binnie, who "proved to be more sympathetic to equality claims based on sexual orientation"[66]—and, by extension, to other s. 15(1) claims. The turnover on the Court, together with "an apparent attitudinal shift" by two of the remaining *Miron* dissenters (Chief Justice Lamer and Justice Major) and a sustained campaign of persuasion by Justice L'Heureux-Dubé, produced a new consensus on equality rights.[67]

That consensus was unveiled in the 1998 *Vriend* ruling (see Dossier 1.8, pages 36–37), in which the Court held unanimously[68] that a law that explicitly denied the equal rights of gays and lesbians violated s. 15(1) and could not be saved. The majority was led by Justices Cory, who dealt with the s. 15 issues, and Iacobucci, writing on s. 1 and the remedial options. Justice L'Heureux-Dubé concurred, although she advocated a different approach to equality rights than the one advanced by Justice Cory.[69] Justice Major agreed with the reasoning but dissented on the remedy; he could not accept the decision of the majority to "read in" gays and lesbians to the Alberta Individuals' Rights Protection Act.

Justice Cory began by stressing the connection between the goal of equality and "the recognition of the fundamental importance and the innate dignity of the individual."[70] He argued that a denial of equal treatment to one "enumerated or analogous group" demeans all Canadians. He endorsed the "broad and generous" approach to s. 15(1) that the majority had adopted in *Miron*. Justice Cory found that the law distinguished between heterosexual and homosexual persons and, in so doing, it denied the latter the equal benefit and protection of the law. Relying on *Egan*, Cory found that sexual orientation is an analogous ground of discrimination. He concluded that the omission of gays and lesbians from the Alberta law was discriminatory in its effect; that it legitimated (and perhaps strengthened) anti-homosexual attitudes; and that it implicitly condoned the mistreatment of homosexual persons by private actors (e.g., landlords or employers). The most appropriate remedy, in light of the Alberta legislature's deliberate refusal to include sexual orientation as a prohibited ground in its human rights law, was to "read it in."

The appearance of unanimity in *Vriend* was somewhat misleading. The Court had not yet resolved its differences over the meaning and proper application of s. 15(1); once again, it had avoided the broader issues while it worked its way through individual cases. Lower courts and legislators were still uncertain about which laws or decisions would meet with the Justices' approval and which would not. So in 1999, "members of the Supreme Court made a concerted effort in *Law v. Canada* to reconstruct a cohesive framework for section 15(1)."[71] The case itself, like some other milestone Charter cases, was relatively straightforward. A thirty-year-old woman named Nancy Law was denied Canada Pension Plan survivor benefits after the death of her husband because she was five years too young to qualify. She claimed that the age restriction constituted discrimination under s. 15(1). The Supreme Court had no difficulty in concluding that the denial of benefits to persons under thirty-five was based on a legitimate distinction, and that there was no discrimination on the basis of age. Widows and widowers under the age of thirty-five do not make up a "discrete and insular minority," nor do they typically face social prejudice or economic disadvantage that injures their dignity and conveys an impression of lesser worth. Law lost her appeal.

The real importance of the *Law* case lay in Justice Iacobucci's attempt to synthesize the three divergent strands of equality jurisprudence into one coherent "test" (see Dossier 11.3). He ruled that a legislative distinction that does not violate the purpose of s. 15(1)—"to prevent the violation of essential human dignity and freedom through the imposition of disadvantage, stereotyping, or political or social prejudice, and to promote a society in which all persons enjoy

---

DOSSIER 11.3

THE *LAW* TEST FOR LEGISLATED DISCRIMINATION

When courts are asked to determine whether a law violates s. 15(1), they must begin by answering three questions:

> A. Does the impugned law (a) draw a formal distinction between the claimant and others on the basis of one or more personal characteristics, or (b) fail to take into account the claimant's already disadvantaged position within Canadian society resulting in substantively differential treatment between the claimant and others on the basis of one or more personal characteristics?
>
> B. Is the claimant subject to differential treatment based on one or more enumerated and analogous grounds? and
>
> C. Does the differential treatment discriminate, by imposing a burden upon or withholding a benefit from the claimant in a manner which reflects the stereotypical application of presumed group or personal characteristics, or which otherwise has the effect of perpetuating or promoting the view that the individual is less capable or worthy of recognition or value as a human being or as a member of Canadian society, equally deserving of concern, respect, and consideration?[1]

As it considers these questions, the court must adopt a comparative and contextual approach. In other words, "differential treatment" can be assessed only in relation to a comparable group. The choice of groups for comparison falls to the plaintiff, although the court can substitute a more relevant comparison group if it sees fit. The context of the alleged discrimination must be examined both subjectively—through the eyes of the claimant—and objectively, as would "[a] reasonable person, in circumstances similar to those of the claimant."[2] The claimant may refer to one or more enumerated or analogous grounds "to demonstrate that legislation demeans his or her dignity," although the presence of these grounds is not in itself sufficient proof of discrimination. (As Justice McIntyre pointed out in *Andrews*, not every legislative distinction will be found to violate the Charter.)

In determining whether or not the impugned law violates the purpose of s. 15(1), courts are invited to weigh four additional factors:

> (A) Pre-existing disadvantage, stereotyping, prejudice, or vulnerability experienced by the individual or group at issue. The effects of a law as they relate to the important purpose of s. 15(1) in protecting individuals or groups who are vulnerable, disadvantaged, or members of "discrete and insular minorities" should always be a central consideration. Although the claimant's association with a historically more advantaged or disadvantaged group or groups is not per se determinative of an infringement, the existence of these pre-existing factors will favour a finding that s. 15(1) has been infringed.
>
> (B) The correspondence, or lack thereof, between the ground or grounds on which the claim is based and the actual need, capacity, or circumstances of the claimant or others. Although the mere fact that the

(continued)

impugned legislation takes into account the claimant's traits or circumstances will not necessarily be sufficient to defeat a s. 15(1) claim, it will generally be more difficult to establish discrimination to the extent that the law takes into account the claimant's actual situation in a manner that respects his or her value as a human being or member of Canadian society, and less difficult to do so where the law fails to take into account the claimant's actual situation.

(C) The ameliorative purpose or effects of the impugned law upon a more disadvantaged person or group in society. An ameliorative purpose or effect which accords with the purpose of s. 15(1) of the Charter will likely not violate the human dignity of more advantaged individuals where the exclusion of these more advantaged individuals largely corresponds to the greater need or the different circumstances experienced by the disadvantaged group being

targeted by the legislation. This factor is more relevant where the s. 15(1) claim is brought by a more advantaged member of society.

(D) The nature and scope of the interest affected by the impugned law. The more severe and localized the consequences of the legislation for the affected group, the more likely that the differential treatment responsible for these consequences is discriminatory within the meaning of s. 15(1).[3]

ENDNOTES

1. *Law v. Canada (Minister of Employment and Immigration)*, [1999] 1 S.C.R. 497, paragraph 88.

2. Ibid., paragraph 88.

3. Ibid., paragraph 88.

equal recognition at law as human beings or as members of Canadian society, equally capable and equally deserving of concern, respect and consideration"[72]—cannot be considered discriminatory. His definition of the purpose of equality rights incorporated Justice L'Heureux-Dubé's emphasis on human dignity. *Law* also affirmed Justice McIntyre's opinion in *Andrews*: it focused on the substantive effect of the impugned law, the illegitimacy of differential treatment based on stereotypes, and the remedial intent of the equality guarantee. Finally, Iacobucci tried to bridge the gulf between the La Forest-Gonthier approach in the 1995 "trilogy," which favoured a restricted interpretation of s. 15(1), and the McLachlin-Cory-Iacobucci argument in favour of a broad and generous interpretation (limited only, where justified, by s. 1).

Justice Iacobucci's synthesis was ingenious but incomplete. He did not address the relationship between ss. 15(1) and 1. The Court found no violation of equality rights in the *Law* case, and there was no need to move on to the second stage of Charter analysis. Nor did he provide any additional insight into two other divisive issues: the identification and

status of analogous grounds and the degree to which courts should base their interpretations of s. 15(1) on subjectively perceived violations of human dignity. Those questions would continue to divide the Court in the coming years.

AFTER *LAW*: EQUALITY RIGHTS IN THE SUPREME COURT, 1999–2003

The *Law* consensus began to fall apart almost immediately. Two months after it appeared, the Court divided 5-4 on the issue of analogous grounds—even while both sides claimed to follow the *Law* test to the letter. The *Corbiere* case challenged a section of the Indian Act that restricted voting in band elections to members living on-reserve. All nine Justices agreed that off-reserve band status constituted an analogous ground, and that the law violated s. 15(1) in a way that could not be justified under s. 1. However, their reasons differed. For the majority, Justices McLachlin and Bastarache wrote that an analogous ground, once identified, has the same legal status as an enumerated ground. Legislative distinctions based on personal characteristics analogous to those enumerated in s. 15(1)—i.e., those that "often serve as the basis for stereotypical decisions made not on the basis of merit but on the basis of a personal characteristic that is immutable or changeable only at unacceptable cost to personal identity"[73]—do not vary with the context of the particular case at bar. Like the enumerated grounds, they are "constant markers of suspect decision making or potential discrimination."[74] While neither type of characteristic is determinative of discrimination, one or the other must be present before the second stage of the *Law* test can be met.

On the other side of the issue, Justice L'Heureux-Dubé argued that a personal characteristic need not be recognized as an analogous ground in every context. She advocated a case-by-case approach, "flexible enough to adapt to stereotyping, prejudice, or denials of human dignity and worth that might occur in specific ways for specific groups of people, to recognize that personal characteristics may overlap or intersect (such as race, band membership, and place of residence in this case), and to reflect changing social phenomena or new or different forms of stereotyping or prejudice."[75] The majority's rejection of this approach signals the permanence of analogous grounds. Once the Supreme Court of Canada has designated a particular basis for discrimination as analogous, the text of the Charter has effectively been amended—not through the prescribed process of legislative ratification, but via the common law.

The Court returned to unanimity in the 2000 *Granovsky* case. It rejected the appeal of a man who had been denied a federal disability pension because he had been unable to work, and thus had been unable to make Canada Pension Plan (CPP) contributions, for much of the preceding ten years. He had a recurring back injury, which worsened to the point where he could no longer seek employment. Had he been permanently disabled during that decade, he would have met the criterion for a pension. However, the recurring nature of his back problem had allowed him to work intermittently, which excluded him from eligibility. He argued that the CPP discriminated against the temporarily disabled by failing to reflect

their work-related difficulties. The Court had little difficulty in concluding that the CPP rules did not violate s. 15(1), even though physical disability is an enumerated ground. Although Mr. Granovsky was successful at the first two stages of the *Law* test, he failed to prove discrimination at the third stage. The Justices agreed that the temporarily disabled, unlike the permanently disabled, do not constitute a group suffering from historic prejudice or disadvantage. The human dignity of the plaintiff was not at stake. Parliament was entitled to draw a line between those Canadians who were sufficiently disabled to qualify for the pension and those who were not.[76]

Shortly afterward, the Court issued another unanimous ruling in *Lovelace*. A coalition of Aboriginal groups that were not legally recognized as bands sued the province of Ontario for a share in the proceeds of casinos located on reserves. Under an agreement between the Ontario government and the province's band chiefs, casino profits would be paid into a First Nations Fund, to be used for social and economic development on band territory. Other Aboriginal groups, which were not officially designated as bands because they did not live on their own lands, received no benefit from the fund. The Justices ruled that their claim failed the third stage of the *Law* test: "While the appellants have established pre-existing disadvantage, stereotyping, and vulnerability, they have failed to establish that the First Nations Fund functioned by device of stereotype. Instead, the distinction corresponded to the actual situation of individuals it affects."[77] Without a land base, the nonband groups did not have to bear the expenses and responsibilities carried by the beneficiaries of the First Nations Fund. Consequently, the two situations were not comparable in the context of the case, and there was no discrimination. As in *Granovsky*, the *Law* test made it easier for the Court to reach consensus on the application of s. 15(1).

A more serious challenge to the *Law* consensus arose from the 2002 *Lavoie* case. Under the Public Service Employment Act, Canadian citizens are given preference over noncitizens in job competitions within the federal government. Three women, all noncitizens, challenged the constitutionality of the preference rule. On the surface, this should have been an easy case to resolve. *Andrews* had established that noncitizens in Canada constituted an analogous group and that laws that barred them from particular jobs violated s. 15(1). But *Lavoie* split the Court into four separate factions. Justice Bastarache wrote on behalf of himself and three other judges—Gonthier, Iacobucci, and Major—all of whom had endorsed the *Law* ruling. He ruled that the legislation violated the equality rights of noncitizens but was saved under s. 1. The two Justices appointed after 1999, Arbour and LeBel, concurred in the result, although neither found a violation of s. 15(1). Justice Arbour also expressed strong reservations about Bastarache's interpretation of *Law* and his approach to the criteria for "reasonable limitations" on equality rights. Chief Justice McLachlin and Justice L'Heureux-Dubé dissented from the result, supported by Justice Binnie. While they continued to endorse the *Law* test to which each was a signatory, they found that the violation of s. 15(1) was not justified under s. 1. The overall result was a return to the jurisprudential chaos of the 1995 "trilogy."

Justice Bastarache found that the law discriminated against noncitizens, who constituted an analogous group under *Andrews*. The plaintiffs easily met the first two elements of the three-stage *Law* test. At the third stage, the determination of discrimination, Bastarache emphasized the subjective elements of Iacobucci's contextual approach. In other words, he focused on the way in which the claimant would perceive the discriminatory effects of the impugned law, and not on the perspective of a hypothetical "reasonable person" in the claimant's shoes. Bastarache concluded that the law discriminated against noncitizens because it failed to recognize their individual abilities, because it reinforced their lower status in Canadian society, and because "the nature of the interest in this case—namely, employment—is most definitely one that enjoys constitutional protection."[78] So the plaintiffs succeeded in demonstrating the discriminatory effects of the impugned law, and the onus shifted to the federal government to justify it.

At this stage, Justice Bastarache had to tackle the relationship between ss. 15(1) and 1, which his colleague Justice Iacobucci had been able to avoid in *Law*. He effectively adopted the approach of the *Miron* majority: the text of s. 15(1) contains no internal limitations, and therefore the balancing of equality rights against competing social interests must occur under s. 1.[79] "Reading in" limitations could "create a hierarchy of rights within s. 15(1) itself, whereby public policy considerations may defeat a s. 15(1) claim in certain cases (e.g., citizenship) but not others (e.g., race)."[80] Having established a heavy onus for the state, Justice Bastarache went on to identify two objectives of the impugned law: "first, to enhance the meaning of citizenship as a unifying symbol for Canadians; and second, to encourage permanent residents to naturalize."[81] He found that these objectives were "pressing and substantial" and "rationally connected" to the law. Because the Public Service Employment Act merely imposed a preference for Canadian citizens, not an outright ban on hiring noncitizens, it met the "minimal impairment" test. Bastarache concluded that the beneficial effects of the law outweighed any harm done to noncitizens, and that it was justified under s. 1.

Justice Arbour agreed with her colleague Bastarache, but only up to the second stage of the *Law* test. She argued that the impugned act did not discriminate against noncitizens, and thus the third element of the test was not satisfied. Arbour identified a discrepancy between the contextual analysis required by *Law* and the approach taken by Justice Bastarache in the case at bar. Whereas Justice Iacobucci had stated in *Law* that "the relevant point of view is that of the reasonable person,"[82] Bastarache claimed that discrimination "is to be assessed from the perspective of the claimant."[83] Arbour objected strongly to the latter's emphasis on subjective impressions of discrimination:

> In my view, the latter comments have the effect of reading out the requirement of an objective component in the analysis of claims of discrimination. To do so would be to allow, contrary to the dictum in *Law*, that it is after all sufficient, in order to ground a s. 15(1) claim, for a claimant simply to assert without more that his or her dignity has been adversely affected by a law.[84]

In other words, if the courts are too ready to accept complaints of discrimination at face value, the line between distinction and discrimination disappears.

Any legislative distinction that annoys a particular group or individual, whether based on enumerated or analogous grounds, must be found discriminatory in the courts. For Arbour, s. 15(1) is internally limited by "its differentiation between legislative distinctions and discrimination."[85] Judicial failure to recognize that limitation places an undue burden on s. 1, which would become the only Charter section under which judges could assess whether a law violated equality rights in any substantive way. It would also become the only safeguard for the rights of other individuals and groups, who might not perceive the world in the same way as the plaintiff(s) in a given s. 15(1) case.[86]

Having accused her colleague of trivializing s. 15(1) by "stripping [equality] rights of any meaningful content,"[87] Arbour proposed a revision of its relationship to s. 1. In effect, she suggested that an objectively provable violation of s. 15(1) could rarely be justified as a "reasonable limitation":

> For myself, I cannot accept that the violation of so sacrosanct a right as the guarantee of equality is justified where the government is pursuing an objective as abstract and general as the promotion of naturalization. To find that this objective is sufficiently pressing and substantial to be pursued by discriminatory means would, I believe, leave scarcely any legitimate state objective seriously constrained by the constitutional fetter of equality. Nor can I be persuaded that a law that supposedly undermines the essential human dignity of the complainants, and is therefore considered sufficiently egregious to fail s. 15(1) scrutiny, is also properly characterized for the purposes of a s. 1 analysis as nothing more than an "inconvenience," the price the claimants must "pay for the government's right to define the rights and privileges of its citizens."[88]

Arbour acknowledged that "once the subjective-objective perspective is properly applied as a necessary condition for making a finding of discrimination, it becomes more difficult to establish that one's equality rights have been infringed." She argued, however, that "it also becomes more difficult, having made a finding of discrimination, to establish that the resulting s. 15(1) violation can be justified."[89] She concluded

that the plaintiffs in *Lavoie* were not the victims of *objective* discrimination, and there was no violation of s. 15(1). Had there been such a violation, however, she would have found it impossible to justify under s. 1.

For his part, Justice LeBel issued a brief (two paragraphs) opinion stating that the impugned law did not "affect the essential dignity of non-citizens," most of whom could become naturalized Canadians if they chose to do so. Therefore, any "adverse effects" flowing from the preference for citizens were "largely self-inflicted."[90] He made no explicit criticisms of the *Law* test, although his exclusive focus on the "human dignity" criterion implies a less than ringing endorsement of the remainder of Iacobucci's synthesis.

Justices McLachlin and L'Heureux-Dubé agreed with Bastarache's analysis of s. 15(1) but disagreed with his conclusions under s. 1. In their view, the impugned legislation was not "rationally connected" to the objectives of "enhancing Canadian citizenship" and encouraging permanent residents to seek that status. They argued that a provision that discriminates against noncitizens does not enhance citizenship; rather, discriminatory laws of any stripe impair the value of citizenship for all Canadians.[91] Nor did the government provide any evidence of a causal connection between a law that prefers citizens for certain jobs and the decisions of persons seeking those jobs to apply for citizenship. The dissenting Justices would have struck down the law.

The *Lavoie* ruling reopened issues that *Law* had been intended to resolve and revealed the difficulty of building consensus on the unresolved issues (notably s. 1). Since *Lavoie*, the Court has continued to struggle with the subjectivity element of the contextual analysis. Ironically, the emphasis in *Law* on the violation of human dignity as a criterion of discrimination—which appears to have been adopted in order to placate Justice L'Heureux-Dubé[92]—was no longer sufficient for that purpose. The "Great Dissenter," who retired in 2002, quickly moved beyond her colleagues. Always ambivalent about the emphasis on enumerated and analogous grounds, and an ardent advocate for the claimant's subjective experience of discrimination, L'Heureux-Dubé used one of her last rulings under s. 15(1) to broaden the scope of the "dignity" analysis beyond her earlier statements:

The *only* issue is whether [the impugned law] denies human dignity in purpose or effect. Harm to dignity results from infringements of individual interests including physical and psychological integrity. Such infringements undermine self-respect and self-worth and communicate to the individual that he or she is not a full member of Canadian society. Stereotypes are not needed to find a distinction discriminatory.[93]

The above quotation is taken from L'Heureux-Dubé's dissent in the 2002 *Gosselin* case, which divided the Court as few cases have done in recent years. The origins of the case went back to 1984, when the Quebec government reduced welfare benefits for young recipients as a way to encourage them to enter the workforce. Welfare recipients under thirty years of age who did not participate in a designated training or work experience program would be paid approximately one-third of the amount received by those over thirty. The law was passed under the notwithstanding clause (s. 33 of the Charter); when it expired in 1989, the government replaced it with a new version that did not distinguish among welfare recipients on the basis of age. Some of the welfare recipients who had lost benefits under the 1984 law initiated a class-action suit. They chose one of their number, Louise Gosselin, as the representative plaintiff. She argued that the 1984–89 law violated not only the equality rights of younger welfare recipients, but their "security of the person" under s. 7 of the Charter. (The s. 7 arguments are discussed in Chapter 10, pages 307–8.) The plaintiffs requested damages and financial restitution from the Quebec government.

The complex issues in *Gosselin* preoccupied the Supreme Court for more than a year. When the ruling was finally issued in December 2002, it filled well over 200 pages and contained no fewer than five separate opinions. The s. 15 issues split the Justices into two factions: Chief Justice McLachlin and Justices Gonthier, Iacobucci, Major, and Binnie ruled that the law did not discriminate on the basis of age; Justices L'Heureux-Dubé, Bastarache, Arbour, and LeBel disagreed and found that the violation of equality rights could not be justified under s. 1. Justices Arbour and LeBel endorsed Bastarache's interpretations of ss. 15(1) and 1, while Justice L'Heureux-Dubé wrote a separate opinion on the equality issues.

Once again, the first two stages of the *Law* test generated little controversy: the law obviously distinguished among welfare recipients on the ground of age. The crux of the dispute between Justice Bastarache and Chief Justice McLachlin concerned the law's effect on human dignity. McLachlin determined that none of the four contextual factors in *Law* was present in *Gosselin*. Persons under the age of thirty are not a historically stigmatized or disadvantaged group. The law was based on the actual situation of the young welfare recipients, not on misguided stereotypes; it gave them "precisely the kind of remedial education and skills training they lacked and needed in order eventually to integrate into the work force and become self-sufficient."[94] Instead of wounding the dignity of young people, the revised welfare program was designed to enhance it by encouraging them to become self-reliant. A "reasonable person in the situation of the claimant" (as Iacobucci put it in *Law*) would have "concluded that the program treated young people as more able than older people to benefit from training and education, more able to get and retain a job, and more able to adapt to their situations and become fully participating and contributing members of society."[95] So for McLachlin, the law did not discriminate in any objective way; nor, despite her admission that "A reasonable welfare recipient under

The 2002 *Gosselin* ruling ended any hope of a "free lunch" from the Supreme Court.

Malcolm Mayes/artizans.com

30 might have concluded that the program was harsh, perhaps even misguided," was the Chief Justice willing to concede a subjective perception of indignity. There was no violation of s. 15(1).

Justice Bastarache's opinion devoted considerably more space to the facts of the case, including the dire employment economic situation in Quebec in the early 1980s and the difficult life of Louise Gosselin herself. Whereas the Chief Justice had suggested that distinctions on the basis of age were generally easier to justify within the text of s. 15(1) than those arising from other enumerated grounds,[96] Bastarache implied that a "two-tier" approach to the enumerated grounds was illegitimate. For him, a distinction based on any enumerated ground "reveals a strong suggestion that the provision in question is discriminatory for the purposes of s. 15."[97] He argued that Ms. Gosselin had "a rational foundation for her experience of discrimination." In other words, the 1984 welfare rules violated her dignity both objectively and subjectively.

Bastarache refuted McLachlin's claim that the Court should compare Ms. Gosselin's situation to that of the entire Quebec population under the age of thirty; for him, the only issue was the effect of the law on vulnerable welfare recipients. The line between recipients over and under the age of thirty was arbitrary; it did not reflect the actual situations of younger (or older) people in that group. Contrary to the Chief Justice, Bastarache rejected the argument that the purpose of the 1984 welfare law was to improve the situation of younger recipients: "Groups that are the subject of an inferior differential treatment based on an enumerated or analogous ground are not treated with dignity just because the government claims that the detrimental provisions are 'for their own good.'"[98] Finally, the nature of the appellant's interest in the law—her dependence on the government for the means of physical subsistence—was sufficiently important that any legislated risk to that interest constituted discrimination.

Having found a violation of s. 15(1), Bastarache refused to defer to the Quebec government in his s. 1 analysis. He concluded that the objective of the 1984 welfare law—to "encourag[e] the integration of young people into the workforce"[99]—was pressing and substantial, and that the law was "rationally connected" to this goal. But the law failed the "minimal impairment"

test because the government could not prove that the age discrimination was necessary to achieve the program objectives. Overall, the harmful effects of the reduced benefits to young recipients more than outweighed any positive impact that the law might have had. The violation of equality could not be justified under s. 1.

As noted earlier, Justice L'Heureux-Dubé focused on the subjective perceptions of Ms. Gosselin and the people whom she represented. She concluded that "A reasonable person in the claimant's position, apprised of all the circumstances, would have perceived that her right to dignity had been infringed as a sole consequence of being under 30 years of age, a condition over which she had no control, and that she had been excluded from full participation in Canadian society."[100] The law was discriminatory and could not be saved under s. 1 for the reasons given by Justice Bastarache.

Gosselin is a messy ruling that gives lower courts and legislators little clear guidance. Is the claimant's subjective experience of indignity sufficient to establish a violation of s. 15(1), as L'Heureux-Dubé (and to a lesser degree, Justice Bastarache) implied, or are judges entitled to substitute their own perspectives behind the mask of the "reasonable person"? Are legislative distinctions on the basis of age easier to justify than those based on other enumerated grounds, as McLachlin implied, or is each of the enumerated grounds to be given the same weight? In the wake of *Gosselin*, the only certainty is that the *Law* test has so far failed to provide the clear jurisprudential guidelines that it was meant to establish.

On the same day that *Gosselin* was released, the Court issued its judgment in *Walsh*. Eight of the nine Justices upheld Nova Scotia's Matrimonial Property Act (MPA), even though it denied common-law spouses a benefit that was available to married spouses—an apparent deviation from *Miron*. The benefit in question was "the presumption ... of an equal division of matrimonial property"[101] in the event of a breakup. After her ten-year common-law relationship with Wayne Bona ended, Susan Walsh went to court to secure an equal share of the property that the two had accumulated while they lived together. The definition of "spouse" in the MPA excluded common-law couples; consequently, the provisions that allowed either party to apply to a court for an equal division of matrimonial property after a breakup were not available to Ms. Walsh.

When the case finally reached the Supreme Court, the majority ruled that the act did not violate s. 15(1). As with *Lavoie*, the claimant had no difficulty in meeting the first two elements of the *Law* test: the MPA clearly distinguished between married and unmarried cohabiting couples, and marital status had already been established as an analogous ground in *Miron*. But at the third stage of the test, the majority found that the legislative distinction did not "affect the dignity of unmarried persons who have formed relationships of some permanence"; therefore, it was "not discriminatory within the meaning of s. 15(1)."[102] Justice L'Heureux-Dubé dissented, arguing that the exclusion of common-law spouses from the protection afforded by the presumption of equal division of assets "implies that the needs of heterosexual unmarried cohabitants are not worthy of the same recognition solely because the people in need have not married." Consequently, the law "diminishes their status in their own eyes and in those of society as a whole by suggesting that they are less worthy of respect and consideration. Their dignity is thereby assaulted: they are the victims of discrimination."[103] The case illustrates the difficulty of applying an amorphous concept such as "dignity" to the resolution of concrete disputes.

After L'Heureux-Dubé stepped down from the bench, the Court returned to unanimity. In the 2003 *Trociuk* case, all nine Justices voted to strike down two sections of the British Columbia Vital Statistics Act. The impugned law allowed a new mother to register her baby without acknowledging the name of the father and to choose the child's surname. It also forbade the father to seek amendments to the registration that would acknowledge his paternity or change the name of the child. The case involved Reni Ernst, the mother of triplet boys, whose relationship with their father ended shortly after she gave birth. She registered the boys with her own surname, and wrote "Unacknowledged" in the space provided on the form for the father's name. The father, Darrell Trociuk, made two unsuccessful attempts to insert his name in his sons' records and to change their surname to Ernst-Trociuk. He challenged the law as a violation of his right to sexual equality.

The Supreme Court agreed with Trociuk. Writing for the Court, Justice Deschamps ruled that the law distinguished between mothers and fathers on the enumerated ground of sex, and it injured the dignity of fathers by denying them even the barest acknowledgment of their relationship to their children. While she acknowledged that fathers are not a historically disadvantaged group in Canadian society, Justice Deschamps rejected the respondent's claim that all of the contextual factors in *Law* must be present for the third element of the test to be met. Citing Justice L'Heureux-Dubé's dissent in *Gosselin*, she wrote that "neither the presence nor absence of any of the contextual factors set out in *Law* is dispositive of a s. 15(1) claim."[104] She concluded that "It would be reasonable for [the father] to perceive that the legislature is sending a message that a father's relationship with his children is less worthy of respect than that between a mother and her children. Given the centrality of such relationships to an individual's identity, a reasonable claimant would perceive the message to be a negative judgment of his worth as a human being."[105]

Because it gave fathers no recourse, the law failed the "minimal impairment" test under s. 1. Indeed, the Court noted, the British Columbia legislature itself had admitted that a less drastic alternative existed; before the case reached the Supreme Court of Canada, it had amended the Vital Statistics Act to require the names of fathers who could prove their paternity to be included in their children's records. Moreover, the fact that the mother did not have to justify her decision to "unacknowledge" the father permitted the arbitrary exclusion of men from their children's lives. The Court invalidated the impugned provisions and suspended the invalidity for one year. It did not grant Trociuk's motion to change the surname of his sons, leaving that issue to be resolved by the parents under the amended law.

Shortly after the *Trociuk* ruling was released, judicial interpretations of s. 15(1) became the hottest political issue in the country. While previous judicial interpretations of equality rights had sparked public debate, the reaction to a series of rulings on same-sex marriage was unprecedented in its intensity (see Dossier 11.4, pages 359–62).

The rulings in Ontario, Quebec, and British Columbia provoked intense controversy. The federal cabinet, which had not yet responded to *Barbeau*, now

DOSSIER 11.4

SEXUAL ORIENTATION AS AN ANALOGOUS GROUND

In *Egan*, as we have seen, a divided Supreme Court was able to agree on one key point: sexual orientation constitutes an analogous ground under s. 15(1). This unanimity may have been prompted by the federal government, which conceded that sexual orientation should be considered a prohibited ground of discrimination. Justice La Forest, on behalf of himself, Chief Justice Lamer, and Justices Gonthier and Major, addressed the issue in the following passage:

> I have no difficulty accepting the appellants' contention that whether or not sexual orientation is based on biological or physiological factors, which may be a matter of some controversy, it is a deeply personal characteristic that is either unchangeable or changeable only at unacceptable personal costs, and so falls within the ambit of s. 15 protection as being analogous to the enumerated grounds.[1]

Although Justice Cory (for himself and Justices Iacobucci, L'Heureux-Dubé, and McLachlin, as well as Justice Sopinka on this point) disagreed with La Forest's disposition of the case, he concurred with the approach to sexual orientation. He began by describing the "historic disadvantage suffered by homosexual persons":

> Public harassment and verbal abuse of homosexual individuals is not uncommon. Homosexual women and men have been the victims of crimes of violence directed at them specifically because of their sexual orientation. They have been discriminated against in their employment and their access to services. They have been excluded from some aspects of public life solely because of their sexual orientation. The stigmatization of homosexual persons and the hatred which some members of the public have expressed towards them has forced many homosexuals to conceal their orientation. This imposes its own associated costs in the work place, the community and in private life.[2]

Justice Cory summarized an emerging judicial and governmental consensus that sexual orientation should be recognized as an analogous ground and concluded that this recognition was entirely justified. Unlike Justice La Forest, he argued that s. 15(1) protected same-sex *relationships*—not just to individuals who happened to be homosexual:

> Homosexual couples as well as homosexual individuals have suffered greatly as a result of discrimination. Sexual orientation is more than simply a "status" that an individual possesses. It is something that is demonstrated in an individual's conduct by the choice of a partner. The Charter protects religious beliefs and religious practice as aspects of religious freedom. So, too, should it be recognized that sexual orientation encompasses aspects of "status" and "conduct" and that both should receive protection. Sexual orientation is demonstrated in a person's choice of a life partner, whether heterosexual or homosexual. It follows that a lawful relationship which flows from sexual orientation should also be protected.[3]

Although James Egan and his partner lost their appeal, the case marked a watershed in equality-rights jurisprudence. Its importance became clear in 1998, when eight Justices[4] ruled in favour of Delwyn Vriend. (See Dossier 1.8, pages 36–37). The *Vriend* ruling signalled the Court's future direction in two ways. First, it removed any lingering doubt about the permanence of analogous status for gays and lesbians. For the majority, Justice Cory cited *Egan* as the definitive authority on the application of s. 15(1) to homosexuals.[5]

Second, *Vriend* revealed a growing judicial impatience with legislative "incrementalism" in the area of equality rights. In 1995, the federal government had defended its exclusion of same-sex partners from pension benefits on the ground of fiscal constraint. It also claimed that it

(continued)

intended to move toward an extension of those benefits, on an incremental basis. Step by step, the government claimed, it would redress legislated discrimination against same-sex couples. Justice Sopinka relied on this promise in finding that the exclusion of same-sex couples from pension benefits was justified under s. 1, a finding that tipped the judicial balance against James Egan.[6] By 1998, the Court was less willing to give legislators the benefit of the doubt. Justice Iacobucci's blunt remarks were endorsed by the majority:

> In my opinion, groups that have historically been the target of discrimination cannot be expected to wait patiently for the protection of their human dignity and equal rights while governments move toward reform one step at a time. If the infringement of the rights and freedoms of these groups is permitted to persist while governments fail to pursue equality diligently, then the guarantees of the Charter will be reduced to little more than empty words.[7]

The implications of this statement are twofold. In the first place, the Court made it clear that it was no longer willing to give legislators the benefit of the doubt when they discriminated on the basis of sexual orientation. Second, the Court implicitly told legislators that if they chose not to protect the rights of gay men and lesbians, judges would step in and do it for them. Laws that discriminated against homosexual persons or same-sex relationships would be struck down or judicially amended to remove the discrimination. The Alberta government reacted with outrage, promising to use the notwithstanding clause if necessary to preserve legislated distinctions between heterosexual and homosexual persons. (See Chapter 12, page 382.)

The following year, the Court reaffirmed its determination to overrule legislators on this issue. In *M. v. H.*, it struck down s. 29 of Ontario's Family Law Act (FLA). That section defined a "spouse" as either a legally married person or a partner in a heterosexual common-

law couple. The case arose from the breakup of a long-term relationship between two women. The complainant, M., had cohabited with H. for a decade beginning in 1982. During that time, the couple jointly acquired a business and a residential property. The business ran into difficulties, as did the relationship. When M. left the shared home in 1992, she petitioned the Family Court for an equal share of the value of the joint assets and subsequently for financial support from H. The latter application could be made only under the FLA, which meant that the application would fail unless the definition of "spouse" were broadened to include same-sex couples. M. duly challenged the constitutionality of that definition.

Eight of the nine Justices found that the impugned provision discriminated against same-sex partners. Applying the *Law* test, the majority determined that the exclusively heterosexual definition of "spouse" distinguished between same-sex and opposite-sex couples on the prohibited ground of sexual orientation. It also held that all four of the contextual factors—preexisting social disadvantage, failure to reflect the actual situation of the complainant (in this case, a long-term monogamous relationship similar to marriage), the absence of an "ameliorative effect" in the law, and the fundamental interest involved in the economic survival of a person who had depended on a now-defunct relationship for financial subsistence—were present.[8] Justice Gonthier dissented, arguing that the FLA was designed to protect women against the loss of financial security following a breakup with a (presumably richer) male partner, and that no such imbalance of vulnerability existed between same-sex partners.[9] The Ontario government was given six months to amend the FLA, which it reluctantly did (see Case Study 4 in Chapter 4, pages 166–68).

By the end of 1999, advocates of equal rights for homosexuals had won three significant victories: the "reading in" of sexual orientation in s. 15(1) of the Charter, a more aggressive judicial attitude toward reluctant legislators, and the redefinition of "spouse" to include common-law partners in both heterosexual and same-sex relationships. These developments raised alarm, both among critics of judicial activism and among groups opposed to the legal recognition of gay and lesbian relationships. One major taboo remained: the exclusively heterosexual definition of marriage. Many religious groups, social conservatives, and legislators found the idea of "gay marriage" unthinkable. It was one thing to give same-sex couples legal recognition as common-law partners. It was quite another to allow them to marry, either in civil ceremonies or in churches—and especially the latter. Marriage is viewed by many Canadians as a sacred institution, the fundamental purpose of which is to create and bring up children. In most religious traditions, marriage is divinely ordained as a lifelong commitment between one man and one woman. Any attempt by judges or legislators to extend legal matrimony to same-sex couples would encounter fierce resistance.

In response to *M. v. H.*, the federal Parliament adopted the omnibus Modernization of Benefits Act (MOBA) in 1999. Although the MOBA granted same-sex couples many of the rights accorded to heterosexual common-law couples, it contained an exclusively heterosexual definition of marriage (at the insistence of the Canadian Alliance[10] and several Liberal backbenchers). This statutory definition reflected the existing common-law understanding of marriage, as laid down by a British Law Lord in 1866: "the voluntary union for life of one man and one woman, to the exclusion of all others."[11]

The judicial trend was clear, however, and events moved with surprising speed. In 2002, trial courts in Quebec and Ontario declared that common-law and statutory definitions of marriage that excluded same-sex couples violated s. 15(1) and could not be saved under s. 1.[12] In the *Halpern* case, the Ontario Divisional Court suspended the invalidation of the affected laws

for two years, to allow the federal and provincial governments to craft a proper legislative response. In May 2003, the British Columbia Court of Appeal overturned a lower-court ruling (*Barbeau*) that had upheld the heterosexual definition of marriage. Justice Prowse found that definition to be discriminatory and accordingly "reformulate[d] the common law definition of marriage to mean 'the lawful union of two persons to the exclusion of all others.'"[13] She suspended the force of her declaration until July 12, 2004, the same deadline set by the Ontario Divisional Court in *Halpern*.

Meanwhile, the federal government had appealed *Halpern* to the Ontario Court of Appeal (OCA). In June 2003, a three-judge panel unanimously upheld the lower-court ruling. Significantly, however, it modified the remedy. Instead of allowing the federal and provincial governments a period of time to amend the definition of marriage, the OCA declared that the reformulated common-law rule—"the voluntary union for life of two persons to the exclusion of all others"[14]—would take effect immediately. The judges pointed out that common-law rules are made by the courts, and that the courts alone are responsible for amending them in response to changing circumstances.[15] He also argued that the immediate amendment of the law would not impose the same legislative burden as the voluminous amendments required in the wake of *M. v. H.* "In our view, an immediate declaration will simply ensure that opposite-sex couples and same-sex couples immediately receive equal treatment in law in accordance with s. 15(1) of the Charter."[16] On July 8, the British Columbia Court of Appeal granted a motion to amend its remedy in *Barbeau*: it cancelled the suspension of invalidity and ordered that its ruling would take effect immediately.[17] Same-sex couples could now legally wed in two of Canada's most populous provinces.

(continued)

ENDNOTES

1. *Egan v. Canada*, [1995] 2 S.C.R. 513, paragraph 5.

2. Ibid., paragraph 173 (citations omitted).

3. Ibid., paragraph 175.

4. Justice Sopinka heard the case but took no part in the judgment.

5. *Vriend v. Alberta*, [1998] 1 S.C.R. 493, paragraph 90.

6. *Egan v. Canada*, paragraphs 104–08, *per* Sopinka J.

7. *Vriend v. Alberta*, paragraph 122.

8. *M. v. H.*, [1999] 2 S.C.R. 3, paragraphs 56–74, *per* Cory J.

9. Ibid., paragraph 156, *per* Gonthier J.

10. The Canadian Reform Conservative Alliance was founded in 2000. It was intended to unite the Reform Party (1987–2000) with like-minded conservatives from other parties, especially in Ontario. Its performance in the 2000 general election did not live up to the hopes of its founders. In 2003, the Alliance formally merged with the Progressive Conservative Party of Canada.

11. *Hyde v. Hyde and Woodmansee* (1866), L.R. 1 P. & D. 130 at 133, quoted in *Halpern v. Canada (Attorney General)*, (2003-06-10) Ontario Court of Appeal, paragraph 1, *per curiam* (hereinafter cited as "*Halpern* 2003").

12. *Halpern v. Canada (Attorney General)*, [2002] O.J. No. 2714, (2002) 215 D.L.R. (4th) 223; *Hendricks v. Québec (Attorney General)*, [2002] J.Q. No. 3816.

13. *Barbeau v. British Columbia (Attorney General)*, 2003 British Columbia Court of Appeal, 251, paragraphs 7 and 159, *per* Prowse J.A.

14. *Halpern v. Canada (Attorney General)*, (2003-06-10) ONCA, paragraph 156, *per curiam*.

15. *Halpern* 2003, paragraph 151.

16. Ibid., paragraph 153.

17. *Barbeau v. British Columbia (Attorney General)*, 2003 BCCA 406, paragraph 8, *per* Prowse J.A.

had to decide whether to appeal it and/or *Halpern* to the Supreme Court of Canada. On June 17, 2003, the prime minister and the federal minister of justice announced that the rulings would not be appealed. Instead, Parliament would rewrite the relevant laws to permit same-sex marriage. On July 17, Justice Minister Martin Cauchon published a draft law redefining civil marriage as "the lawful union of two persons to the exclusion of all others" and exempting religious officials from having to perform same-sex weddings.[106] Cauchon immediately submitted the draft law to the Supreme Court for the determination of three constitutional issues.

- The first issue concerned the extent of Parliament's jurisdiction over marriage laws. Under s. 91(26) of the Constitution Act, 1867, marriage and divorce are federal responsibilities, but s. 92(12) gives the provinces control over "the solemnization of marriage."

- The second reference question asked the Court whether the proposed law violated the religious freedom of faiths that refused to perform same-sex marriages. The likely answer to this question is no because the draft law explicitly exempts such faiths from the application of the law.

- Finally, the Court was asked to pronounce on the constitutionality of the draft law under s. 15(1).

The government delayed the introduction of the bill into the House of Commons until after the Court issued its opinion. Prime Minister Chrétien promised that the bill would be subject to a free vote, although cabinet ministers would be required to support it. After Paul Martin became prime minister in December 2003, he decided to modify the reference to the Court. He added a fourth question: "Is the opposite-sex requirement for marriage for civil purposes, as established by the common law and set out for Quebec in s. 5 of the Federal Law—Civil Law

Harmonization Act, No. 1, consistent with the Canadian Charter of Rights and Freedoms? If not, in what particular or particulars and to what extent?"[107]

Before the Court could hear the case, Martin called a general election in May 2004. The draft bill, and the decision to refer it to the Court before a parliamentary vote, became an issue in the campaign. Conservative leader Stephen Harper promised that, if elected prime minister, he would withdraw the reference and put the bill to a free vote in the Commons.[108] Because Harper publicly opposed the legal recognition of same-sex marriage, the prospect of a free vote alarmed advocates of equality for gays and lesbians. Harper predicted that if Parliament rejected same-sex marriage and reaffirmed a strictly heterosexual definition of the institution, the Supreme Court would defer to the legislative branch.[109] (This prediction is almost certainly incorrect, as Dossier 11.4, pages 359–62 explains.[110]) If the Justices refused to defer and permitted same-sex marriage across Canada, Harper said that he might use the notwithstanding clause (s. 33) to reverse their ruling.[111]

Shortly before voting day, a videotaped interview with Conservative MP Randy White was made public. In the interview, which was conducted shortly before the election call, White expressed his frustration with "judicial legislation" and promised that a Conservative government would use s. 33 to bypass any ruling that conflicted with his party's positions on social issues.[112] In response to these comments by Harper, White, and other Conservative MPs, the Liberals and New Democrats painted the Conservatives as a threat to the Charter in general and equality rights in particular.[113] While it is impossible to gauge the impact on the outcome of the election, some observers—including the Conservative campaign co-chair in Ontario—speculated that Liberal "fear-mongering" in the last few days of the campaign turned the tide against the Conservatives in key Ontario ridings.[114] If this is true, it appears that some Canadians voted (in part) to defend the equality guarantee against a perceived threat from Court critics. They may have been motivated not by a particular enthusiasm for same-sex marriage, but by a general desire to protect the Charter.

As *Globe and Mail* columnist Jeffrey Simpson pointed out, there was little the opponents of same-sex marriage—even those in the government—could do in the long run.[115] Almost as soon as the OCA issued the *Halpern* ruling, gay and lesbian couples in Ontario began to obtain marriage licences and hold wedding ceremonies. Given that reality, and the apparently irreversible judicial trends identified in this chapter, it is reasonable to expect that the marriage laws will soon apply to all gays and lesbians in Canada—one way or another.

SECTION 15(2): THE AFFIRMATIVE ACTION CLAUSE

Unlike s. 15(1), s. 15(2) has received little judicial attention. Neither of the leading cases on equality rights (*Andrews* and *Law*) contained more than a passing mention of the affirmative action clause. In *Andrews*, Justice McIntyre referred to the inclusion of s. 15(2) as proof that "identical treatment may frequently produce serious inequality"; he also hinted that the second clause of s. 15 could be used to justify a finding of discrimination under the first clause, without reference to s. 1.[116] Justice Iacobucci echoed the latter sentiment in *Law*, in the course of discussing the "ameliorative effect" of impugned statutes as a contextual factor in determining discrimination.[117]

Section 15(2) finally began to come into its own in the *Lovelace* rulings from the OCA (1997) and the Supreme Court (2000).[118] As discussed earlier, *Lovelace* challenged the constitutionality of the financial arrangements between Ontario Native bands and the provincial agency responsible for on-reserve casinos. The trial judge found that the "ameliorative purpose" of the First Nations Fund did not allow the provincial government to deny gambling profits to nonband groups. In other words, the second clause of s. 15 did not prevent a finding of discrimination under the first clause. The OCA overturned that ruling. It found that the "underinclusiveness" of the Fund was indeed justified by s. 15(2):

> Section 15(2) affirms that the government may target and attempt to remedy specific disadvantage. Governments should, therefore, be able to rely on s. 15(2) to provide benefits to a specific disadvantaged group and should not have to justify excluding other disadvantaged groups even

if those other groups suffer similar disadvantage. To hold that an affirmative government program violates s. 15 because it excludes disadvantaged groups or individuals that were never the object of the program would undermine the effectiveness of s. 15(2) and the ability of governments to redress disadvantage.[119]

The nonband groups appealed to the Supreme Court of Canada, which took the opportunity to clarify the relationship between the two clauses of s. 15. For a unanimous court, Justice Iacobucci rejected the OCA's interpretation of the affirmative action clause on two grounds. First, he held that the *Law* analysis had imported "ameliorative" considerations into s. 15(1); consequently, there was no need to leave these issues to s. 15(2). Second, while Iacobucci reaffirmed the importance of the second clause as an interpretive aid to applying the first clause, he rejected the OCA's finding that s. 15(2) provides "an exemption or a defence to the applicability of the s. 15(1) discrimination analysis."[120] The latter approach wrongly treats programs designed to promote substantive equality as "*prima facie* violations" of equality rights, which belies the "plain meaning" of the two clauses and rules out the possibility of balancing under s. 1.[121] There is no conflict between them, nor is there sufficient overlap to make either clause redundant. Instead, s. 15(2) confirms and defines s. 15(1), and it provides greater certainty regarding the purpose and scope of substantive equality rights. Overall, the effect of the *Lovelace* ruling is to deprive s. 15(2) of a fully independent role in Charter jurisprudence. However, Iacobucci left open the possibility of a more thorough analysis at some point in the future.

THE IMPACT OF SECTION 15 ON CANADIAN PUBLIC POLICY

Like the Charter as a whole, the impact of s. 15 varies across different policy fields. By distinguishing between legitimate distinctions and impermissible discrimination, Canadian courts have adopted a generally moderate approach to equality rights. They have found some legislated distinctions to be necessary and

appropriate, such as the denial of survivor benefits to young people or the provision of special accommodations to disabled children. These distinctions do not engage the dignity interest that courts have recently identified as the core of s. 15. Others, such as the denial of legal recognition to same-sex couples, have been found to be arbitrary and unconstitutional. Their effect on historically vulnerable groups is considered sufficiently damaging to warrant judicial remedy. Although the line between acceptable and unacceptable distinctions is not yet as clear as it might be (as in *Gosselin*), the Supreme Court and its provincial counterparts have made considerable progress in the interpretation of equality rights. However, the complexity of the issues raised by s. 15 make judicial consensus difficult to achieve and maintain. Without clear and coherent guidance from the top court, policy-makers in the legislative and executive branches may struggle to craft defensible legislated distinctions.

Critics argue that judges have overstepped their proper sphere by using s. 15 as a tool to rewrite federal and provincial laws (see the discussion of *Schachter* in Dossier 1.7, pages 33–34).[122] Even worse, the courts have effectively rewritten the section itself by granting permanent constitutional status to "analogous" groups. On the other hand, it could be argued that the language of equality rights invites head-on clashes between the judiciary and the elected branches of government. The guarantees of equality "before and under the law" and "the equal protection and equal benefit of the law" require judges to scrutinize the decisions of legislators and to strike down or amend discriminatory laws in order to bring them into line with the Charter. As the saga of same-sex marriage suggests, legislators occasionally engage in stereotypical discrimination against unpopular minorities. The arbitrary imposition of unequal benefits and burdens signals a failure to conduct a proper first-order review of existing or proposed legislation.

The cases in this chapter demonstrate the problems raised by judicial policy-making, particularly where social policies are concerned. In the first place, the Supreme Court, as it itself has often acknowledged, lacks the institutional capacity to balance competing social goals and priorities.[123] Such decisions are properly left to the other two branches of government. Second, courts should avoid imposing remedies that alter the budgetary plans of legislators and administrators. Former Chief Justice Lamer argued that "reading in" new beneficiaries was often a more appropriate way to correct underinclusive legislation—i.e., legislation that discriminated against a particular group by denying benefits for arbitrary reasons—than waiting for the sponsoring legislature to amend the law: "it immediately reconciles the legislation in question with the requirements of the Charter" instead of forcing victims of discrimination to wait for a remedy.[124]

The practical problems arising from judicial remedies are evident in *Eldridge*: the Court ruled that hospitals had to provide sign-language interpreters for deaf patients, without regard to the cost of such services.[125] The expense may be relatively trivial for a large metropolitan hospital, but small regional facilities could be forced to shift funds away from medical care in order to comply with the ruling. More generally, the costs of ensuring the "equal benefit of the law" to all persons should be weighed against fiscal constraints and competing priorities. Courts are ill equipped to make these decisions, as we saw in Chapter 3.

As a rule, the Supreme Court has tried to avoid excessive "intrusion into budgetary decisions," which could "change the nature of the legislative scheme in question"[126] and hence violate the separation of powers inherent in our constitutional system. Lamer suggested that "reading in" as a remedy for underinclusion is most appropriate when the group to be added is smaller than the existing class of beneficiaries. "Reading in" a large group of new beneficiaries has greater fiscal implications and may alter the legislation in a way that the sponsoring legislature would not have intended or accepted.[127] But even in the absence of budgetary considerations, "reading in" as a remedy for discrimination is highly controversial. The *Vriend* decision overruled an elected legislature that had expressly refused to include sexual orientation in the Alberta human rights code. Although most Canadians appear to agree with the Court's reasoning,[128] the remedy raises important questions about the balance of power between judges and legislators. For some observers, the ends justify the means. If legislators are reluctant to recognize the equality rights of a particular group, the Charter mandates the courts to intervene. Others argue that the choice between equality rights and competing social goals should be made by the elected representatives of the people, especially on divisive issues such as same-sex marriage.

The complexity of the decisions discussed in this chapter makes it impossible to predict the future development of equality jurisprudence. The perspectives of the individual Justices appear to have a greater impact on their approaches to s. 15(1) than their interpretations of other Charter guarantees. Much may depend on the appointments made by future prime ministers. One of the newest Justices, Rosalie Abella, is a well-known expert on (and champion of) equality rights; she may try to resist any trend toward a more deferential approach. The only certainty is that judicial and political consensus on the practical meaning of equality will remain elusive.

GLOSSARY OF KEY TERMS

analogous grounds   Personal characteristics that are sufficiently similar to those listed in s. 15 to warrant constitutional protection against legislated discrimination. In general, an analogous ground is a personal characteristic that is difficult or impossible to change (such as race or sex), that reflects or underlies historic disadvantages relative to the rest of Canadian society (such as disability), and/or that lies at the heart of individual dignity and integrity (such as religion).[129] The Supreme Court has identified several analogous grounds in s. 15, including marital status, sexual orientation, and citizenship.

distinction and **discrimination**   When a law defines a particular category of persons, it distinguishes them from those in different categories. For example, people who earn $20 000 a year pay a lower rate of income tax than those who earn $200 000 a year. Such distinctions do not violate the guarantee of equality rights, unless they are based on false or demeaning criteria. A legislated distinction that reflects traditional stereotypes and prejudices (e.g., the British Columbia law discussed in Dossier 2.1, page 50) or that unfairly benefits one group over another constitutes discrimination. It therefore violates s. 15(1) and must be justified, if at all, under s. 1 of the Charter.

exhaustive and **illustrative**   An exhaustive list cannot be expanded; it contains all of the relevant items or concepts. The items in an illustrative list are examples of a broader category of items or concepts. For example, the list of provincial jurisdictions in s. 92 of the Constitution Act, 1867 is exhaustive (in principle); the list of federal jurisdictions in s. 91 is illustrative. The prohibited grounds of discrimination listed in s. 15(1) of the Charter are illustrative, not exhaustive. The generality of the phrase "without discrimination," followed by the words "and, in particular" signify that the list of personal characteristics that follows is not intended to be exhaustive.

invidious   Harmful or damaging.

nondiscrimination clause   A guarantee that rights and freedoms will be respected regardless of race, sex, or other personal characteristics. A nondiscrimination clause does not protect uniquely egalitarian rights; it simply states that other protected rights will be applied equally. The interpretive clauses in the Charter (ss. 25, 27, and 28) fall into this category (see Chapter 12, pages 377–79). In contrast, a specific guarantee of equality rights (e.g., s. 15(1)) confers a substantive claim to equal treatment from the government, even where the other protected rights and freedoms are not directly engaged.

DISCUSSION AND REVIEW QUESTIONS

1. Identify three criteria that the Supreme Court uses when it decides whether or not to recognize a new analogous ground of discrimination. In your view, should the Court have the power to "read in" to the Charter? Why or why not?

2. Identify one argument for the legal recognition of same-sex marriages and one argument against. Which do you find more persuasive and why?

3. In your own words, summarize the major elements of the *Law* test. If you were a Supreme Court Justice, how would you apply that test to the 2003 reference questions on same-sex marriage?

4. Briefly summarize the arguments for and against a "large and liberal" reading of s. 15(1), which treats all legislated distinctions as suspect unless proven otherwise at the s. 1 stage of analysis. Contrast it to the "internally limited" approach adopted by Chief Justice McLachlin when she was on the British Columbia Court of Appeal. In your view, which approach is preferable?

5. Identify and briefly explain two reasons why the protection of equality rights has divided the Supreme Court. In your view, can these divisions ever be laid to rest? Why or why not?

SUGGESTED READINGS

Black, William, and Lynn Smith. "The Equality Rights." In Gérald-A. Beaudoin and Ed Ratushny, eds., *The Canadian Charter of Rights and Freedoms.* 2nd ed. Toronto: Carswell, 1989, pp. 557–651.

Grabham, Emily. "Law v. Canada: New Directions for Equality under the Canadian Charter?" *Oxford Journal of Legal Studies* 22, no. 4 (2002), pp. 641–61.

Lahey, Kathleen A., and Kevin Alderson. *Same-Sex Marriage: The Personal and the Political.* Toronto: Insomniac Press, 2004.

ENDNOTES

1. Peter H. Russell, "The First Three Years in Charterland," *Canadian Public Administration* 28, no. 3 (Fall 1985), pp. 395–96.

2. Christopher P. Manfredi, *Judicial Power and the Charter: Canada and the Paradox of Liberal Constitutionalism,* 2nd ed. (Toronto: Oxford University Press, 2001), p. 104.

3. *Granovsky v. Canada (Minister of Employment and Immigration),* [2000] 1 S.C.R. 703 paragraphs 50, 54, 60, 62, and 63, *per* Binnie J.

4. For a brief synopsis of the historical background, see William Black and Lynn Smith,

"The Equality Rights," in Gérald-A. Beaudoin and Ed Ratushny, eds., *The Canadian Charter of Rights and Freedoms*, 2nd ed. (Toronto: Carswell, 1989), pp. 558–61. See also Maimon Schwarzchild, "Constitutional Law and Equality," in Dennis Patterson, ed., *A Companion to Philosophy of Law and Legal Theory* (Oxford: Blackwell, 1996), pp. 156–71.

5. Black and Smith, "The Equality Rights," p. 562.

6. Pierre Elliott Trudeau, "A Canadian Charter of Human Rights" (Ottawa, January 1968), reproduced in Anne F. Bayefsky, ed., *Canada's Constitution Act, 1982 and Amendments: A Documentary History* (Toronto: McGraw-Hill Ryerson, 1989), vol. 1, pp. 56–57.

7. Ibid., p. 58.

8. Ibid., p. 59.

9. Lester B. Pearson, "Federalism for the Future: A Statement of Policy by the Government of Canada" (1968), in Bayefsky, *Canada's Constitution Act*, vol. 1, p. 66. See also Pierre Elliott Trudeau, "The Constitution and the People of Canada: An Approach to the Objectives of Confederation, the Rights of People and the Institutions of Government" (1968), in Bayefsky, *Canada's Constitution Act*, vol. 1, p. 83.

10. Trudeau, "The Constitution and the People of Canada," p. 91.

11. The McGuigan-Molgat Committee was a special joint committee of the Commons and Senate that was established to review constitutional issues after the failure of the Victoria Charter. "Final Report of the Special Joint Committee of the Senate and the House of Commons on the Constitution of Canada" (1972), in Bayefsky, *Canada's Constitution Act*, vol. 1, pp. 238 and 241.

12. Bill C-60, in Bayefsky, *Canada's Constitution Act*, vol. 1, p. 349.

13. Pierre Elliott Trudeau, "A Time for Action: Toward the Renewal of the Canadian Federation" (1978), in Bayefsky, *Canada's Constitution Act*, vol. 1, p. 507.

14. "Second Report of the Special Joint Committee of the Senate and of the House of Commons on the Constitution of Canada" (1978), in Bayefsky, *Canada's Constitution Act*, vol. 1, p. 423.

15. Ibid., p. 424.

16. "Canadian Charter of Rights and Freedoms, Federal Draft" (January 1979), in Bayefsky, *Canada's Constitution Act*, vol. 2, p. 539.

17. See, e.g., "Proposed Charter of Rights and Freedoms for Canadians, Ontario Draft" (1979), in Bayefsky, *Canada's Constitution Act*, vol. 2, pp. 549–51, which contains no reference to equality rights; "Report by the Sub-Committee of Officials on a Charter of Rights" (July 1980), in Bayefsky, *Canada's Constitution Act*, vol. 2, p. 662; "Co-Chairman's Summary of Consensus Reached by Ministers on Committee Reports" (July 1980), in Bayefsky, *Canada's Constitution Act*, vol. 2, p. 665; "The Canadian Charter of Rights and Freedoms, Provincial Proposal (In the Event that There Is Going to be Entrenchment)" (August 1980), in Bayefsky, *Canada's Constitution Act*, vol. 2, pp. 678–80, which contains no reference to equality rights; "Charter of Rights, Report to Ministers by Sub-Committee of Officials" (August 1980), in Bayefsky, *Canada's Constitution Act*, vol. 2, p. 686.

18. See, e.g., Peter H. Russell, Rainer Knopff, and Ted Morton, eds., *Federalism and the Charter: Leading Constitutional Decisions* (Ottawa: Carleton University Press, 1989), p. 363; Walter S. Tarnopolsky, "The Equality Rights in the Canadian Charter of Rights and Freedoms," *Canadian Bar Review* 61, no. 1 (March 1983), pp. 248–50; Chaviva Hošek, "Women and the Constitutional Process," in Keith Banting and Richard Simeon, eds., *And No One Cheered: Federalism, Democracy and the*

Constitution Act (Toronto: Methuen, 1983), pp. 287 and 299; Roy Romanow, John Whyte, and Howard Leeson, *Canada ... Notwithstanding: The Making of the Constitution, 1976–1982* (Toronto: Carswell/Methuen, 1984), pp. 253–56; Diana Majury, "Women's (In)Equality before and after the Charter," in Radha Jhappan, ed., *Women's Legal Strategies in Canada* (Toronto: University of Toronto Press, 2002), pp. 101–11.

19. The women's groups did not get everything they wanted. They had hoped to exclude prohibited grounds on which governments can and do legitimately distinguish among persons—specifically, age and disability—because they feared that such "discretionary" grounds would open up the entire section to judicial tampering. Alternatively, they pressed for a "two-tier" approach, under which some grounds of discrimination (including sex) would be absolutely prohibited and others would be subject to the discretion of lawmakers where appropriate. The Ad Hoc Committee of Women on the Constitution also lobbied for the inclusion of marital status, sexual orientation, and political belief in the list of prohibited grounds. See Romanow, Whyte, and Leeson, *Canada ... Notwithstanding*, pp. 254–55; Hošek, "Women and the Constitutional Process," p. 299.

20. See, e.g., Tarnopolsky, "The Equality Rights in the Canadian Charter of Rights and Freedoms," p. 243.

21. See, e.g., Lise Gotell, "Towards a Democratic Practice of Feminist Litigation?: LEAF's Changing Approach to Charter Equality," in Jhappan, *Women's Legal Strategies*, p. 137; Sherene Razack, *Canadian Feminism and the Law: The Women's Legal Education and Action Fund and the Pursuit of Equality* (Toronto: Second Story Press, 1991), Chapter 1.

22. See, e.g., Dale Gibson, "The Charter of Rights and the Private Sector," *Manitoba Law Journal* 12 (1982), pp. 213–19.

23. Walter S. Tarnopolsky, "The Constitution and Human Rights," in Banting and Simeon, *And No One Cheered*, p. 274.

24. *RWDSU v. Dolphin Delivery Ltd.*, [1986] 2 S.C.R. 573, paragraphs 26–35, *per* McIntyre J.

25. *McKinney v. University of Guelph*, [1990] 3 S.C.R. 229, paragraphs 22–23.

26. *Eldridge v. British Columbia (Attorney General)*, [1997] 3 S.C.R. 624, paragraph 20.

27. Ibid., paragraph 57.

28. Ibid., paragraph 59.

29. Ibid., paragraph 92.

30. *Andrews v. Law Society of British Columbia* [1986], 2 B.C.L.R. 305, 27 D.L.R. (4th) 600, *per* McLachlin C.J. (hereinafter cited as "*Andrews* 1986"), as summarized by McIntyre J. in *Andrews v. Law Society of British Columbia*, [1989] 1 S.C.R. 143 (hereinafter cited as "*Andrews* 1989"), at paragraph 22.

31. *Andrews* 1986, p. 609, *per* McLachlin C.J.

32. *Andrews* 1989, paragraph 26.

33. Ibid., paragraph 26.

34. Ibid., paragraph 28. Some legal experts argue that McIntyre did not intend to reject the "similarly situated" test out of hand, but simply to signal that the Court would not treat it as authoritative on equality issues. See A. Wayne MacKay and Dianne Pothier, "Developments in Constitutional Law: The 1988–89 Term," *Supreme Court Law Review* 1 (2d) (1990), pp. 90–92. Note that the Court explicitly disapproved *Bliss* on non-Charter grounds shortly after the *Andrews* decision was issued; see *Brooks v. Canada Safeway Ltd.*, [1989] 1 S.C.R. 1219.

35. *Andrews* 1989, paragraph 29.

36. Ibid., paragraph 33.

37. Ibid., paragraph 34.

38. Ibid., paragraph 37.

39. Fire departments are regulated by municipal and provincial laws. If a discriminatory hiring policy is required or permitted by the enabling statutes, the Charter will apply. However, a discriminatory policy in the private sector would not be subject to Charter review.

40. *Andrews* 1989, paragraph 45.

41. Ibid., paragraph 49; see also the separate opinion of Justice Wilson, at paragraphs 5–7. The phrase is taken from the famous fourth footnote in the *Carolene Products* ruling of the U.S. Supreme Court (304 U.S. 144, pp. 152–153 n. 4 [1938]), in which Justice Stone implied that the overriding purpose of the American Constitution was to protect "discrete and insular minorities" from the prejudices of a hostile majority.

42. *Andrews* 1989, paragraph 38.

43. See, e.g., MacKay and Pothier, "Developments in Constitutional Law," pp. 83–95.

44. See, e.g., Manfredi, *Judicial Power and the Charter*, p. 125.

45. *R. v. Turpin*, [1989] 1 S.C.R. 1296, paragraph 44.

46. A few months after the trial ruling, s. 430 was repealed as part of the omnibus bill designed to bring federal legislation into conformity with s. 15 of the Charter. By the time the Supreme Court ruled on its constitutionality, the issue was moot in practical terms.

47. Robert J. Sharpe, Katherine E. Swinton, and Kent Roach, *The Charter of Rights and Freedoms*, 2nd ed. (Toronto: Irwin Law, 2002), pp. 254–58.

48. *R. v. Hess; R. v. Nguyen*, [1990] 2 S.C.R. 906.

49. *Hess/Nguyen*, paragraph 79, *per* McLachlin J.

50. Sharpe, Swinton, and Roach, *The Charter of Rights and Freedoms*, p. 272.

51. See, e.g., *Stoffman v. Vancouver General Hospital*, [1990] 3 S.C.R. 483; *Tétreault-Gadoury v. Canada (Canada Employment and Immigration Commission)*, [1991] 2 S.C.R. 22.

52. *Tétreault-Gadoury*, headnotes, *per* La Forest J.

53. *Symes v. Canada*, [1993] 4 S.C.R. 695.

54. See, e.g., *R. v. Swain*, [1991] 1 S.C.R. 933; *R. v. Généreux*, [1992] 1 S.C.R. 259; and *Canada (Minister of Employment and Immigration) v. Chiarelli*, [1992] 1 S.C.R. 711.

55. *Egan v. Canada*, [1995] 2 S.C.R. 513; *Miron v. Trudel*, [1995] 2 S.C.R. 418; and *Thibaudeau v. Canada*, [1995] 2 S.C.R. 627 (all released on May 25, 1995).

56. *Egan*, paragraph 21.

57. *Thibaudeau v. Canada*, paragraph 135.

58. Ibid., paragraphs 154–56.

59. Ibid., paragraphs 208 and 211.

60. Ibid., paragraph 11 (emphasis in original).

61. Ibid., paragraph 44.

62. See, e.g., Hester Lessard, Bruce Ryder, David Schneiderman, and Margot Young, "Developments in Constitutional Law: The 1994–95 Term," *Supreme Court Law Review* 7(2d) (1996), pp. 87–99, 105–07, and 110–17; Emily Grabham, "Law v. Canada: New Directions for Equality under the Canadian Charter?" *Oxford Journal of Legal Studies* 22, no. 4 (2002), pp. 645–47; and Dianne Pothier, "M'Aider, Mayday: Section 15 of the Charter in Distress," *National Journal of Constitutional Law* 6 (1996), pp. 295–345.

63. F.L. Morton and Rainer Knopff, *The Charter Revolution and the Court Party* (Peterborough: Broadview Press, 2000), Chapter 1.

64. *Eaton v. Brant County Board of Education,* [1997] 1 S.C.R. 241; *Benner v. Canada (Secretary of State),* [1997] 1 S.C.R. 358; *Eldridge.*

65. See *Eaton,* paragraph 62, *per* Sopinka J.; *Benner,* headnotes; *Eldridge,* paragraph 55.

66. Manfredi, *Judicial Power and the Charter,* p. 132.

67. Ibid., pp. 132–34; see also Graeme G. Mitchell, "Developments in Constitutional Law: The 1997–98 Term—Activism and Accountability," *Supreme Court Law Review* 10 (2d) (1999), p. 139.

68. Eight Justices signed the decision; Justice Sopinka had heard the appeal but died before he could participate in the ruling.

69. She reiterated the position she had taken in the 1995 "trilogy":

    Integral to the inquiry into whether a legislative distinction is in fact discriminatory within the meaning of s. 15(1) is an appreciation of both the social vulnerability of the affected individual or group, and the nature of the interest which is affected in terms of its importance to human dignity and personhood. Given this purpose, every legislative distinction (including, as in this case, a legislative omission) which negatively impacts on an individual or group who has been found to be disadvantaged in our society, the impact of which deprives the individual or group of the law's protection or benefit in a way which negatively affects their human dignity and personhood, does not treat these persons or groups with "equal concern, respect and consideration." Consequently, s. 15(1) of the Charter is engaged. At this point, the burden shifts to the legislature to justify such an infringement of s. 15(1) under s. 1. It is at this stage only that the relevancy of the distinction to the legislative objective, among other factors, may be pertinent.

    See *Vriend v. Alberta,* [1998] 1 S.C.R. 493, paragraph 67.

70. *Vriend,* paragraph 67.

71. Grabham, "Law v. Canada," p. 647.

72. *Law v. Canada (Minister of Employment and Immigration),* [1999] 1 S.C.R. 497, paragraph 51, *per* Iacobucci J. (writing for a unanimous Court).

73. *Corbiere v. Canada (Minister of Indian and Northern Affairs),* [1999] 2 S.C.R. 203, paragraph 13.

74. Ibid., paragraph 8.

75. Ibid., paragraph 61.

76. *Granovsky v. Canada,* paragraph 62, *per* Binnie J.

77. *Lovelace v. Ontario,* [2000] 1 S.C.R. 950, paragraph 73, *per* Iacobucci J. (for a unanimous Court) (hereinafter cited as "*Lovelace* 2000").

78. *Lavoie v. Canada,* [2002] 1 S.C.R. 769, paragraph 45, *per* Bastarache J.

79. Ibid., paragraphs 48–49.

80. Ibid., paragraph 51.

81. Ibid., paragraph 54.

82. *Law v. Canada,* paragraph 60. In fact, Justice Arbour misrepresented Iacobucci's reasoning (probably unintentionally). Immediately after the phrase just quoted, Justice Iacobucci added, "I stress that the inquiry into whether legislation demeans the claimant's dignity must be undertaken from the perspective of the claimant and from no other perspective."

83. *Lavoie v. Canada,* paragraph 38.

84. Ibid., paragraph 80.

85. Ibid., paragraph 92.

86. Ibid., paragraph 88.

87. Ibid., paragraph 86.

88. Ibid., paragraph 85 (quoting Bastarache J. at paragraph 71).

89. Ibid., paragraph 90.

90. Ibid., paragraphs 124–25.

91. Ibid., paragraphs 10–12.

92. Manfredi, *Judicial Power and the Charter*, p. 133.

93. *Gosselin v. Quebec (Attorney General)*, [2002] 4 S.C.R. 429, headnotes, *per* L'Heureux-Dubé J. (emphasis added).

94. Ibid., paragraph 42, *per* McLachlin C.J.C.

95. Ibid., paragraph 69, *per* McLachlin C.J.C.

96. Ibid., paragraphs 31–36, *per* McLachlin C.J.C.

97. Ibid., paragraph 228.

98. Ibid., paragraph 250.

99. Ibid., paragraph 266.

100. Ibid., headnotes, *per* L'Heureux-Dubé J.; see also paragraphs 131–33.

101. *Nova Scotia (A.G.) v. Walsh*, [2002] 4 S.C.R. 325, paragraph 4, *per* Bastarache J.

102. Ibid., paragraph 2, *per* Bastarache J.

103. Ibid., paragraph 118, *per* L'Heureux-Dubé J.

104. *Trociuk v. B.C. (A.G.)*, [2003] 1 S.C.R. 835, paragraph 20; citation to paragraph 126 of *Gosselin*.

105. *Trociuk*, paragraph 21, *per* L'Heureux-Dubé J.

106. Department of Justice website (www.canada.justice.gc.ca), accessed September 24, 2003.

107. It is not clear exactly what the Martin government sought to achieve by referring this highly technical question to the Court. The justice department explained that the new question would address public concerns that the government had prejudged the issue in its original reference questions, and that it would "allow individuals and groups who disagree with the Government's approach to put their case before the Supreme Court." In essence, the government was asking the Court whether it had to allow same-sex couples to marry in the same way as heterosexual couples, or whether a less controversial form of legal recognition—"civil unions"—would be sufficient to conform to the Charter. The revised reference, which was filed on January 28, 2004, was accessed at www.canada.justice.gc.ca/en/news.

108. Allison Dunfield, "Old Issues Continue to Haunt Harper," *The Globe and Mail*, June 3, 2004, accessed online at www.globeandmail.com.

109. Brian Laghi, "Top Court Wouldn't Block Same-Sex Law, Harper Says," *The Globe and Mail*, June 3, 2004, accessed online at www.globeandmail.com.

110. Harper was also mistaken, although perhaps to a lesser extent, when he claimed that the Charter does not protect the rights of homosexual individuals and couples. As we have seen in this chapter, "sexual orientation" does not appear in the enumerated grounds in s. 15(1), but the open-ended wording of the section allows judges to "read in" analogous grounds, which then acquire the force of law. "The Conservatives and the Judges," *The Globe and Mail*, June 21, 2004, accessed online at www.globeandmail.com.

111. Brian Laghi, "Social Issues Hijack Harper's Agenda," *The Globe and Mail*, June 4, 2004, accessed online at www.globeandmail.com.

112. Rod Mickleburgh and Mark Hume, "White Harsh Critic of Justice, Immigration Systems," *The Globe and Mail*, June 26, 2004, accessed online at www.globeandmail.com.

113. Canadian Press, "Martin: Same-Sex Marriage Must Be Allowed," *The Globe and Mail*, June 4, 2004, accessed online at www.globeandmail.com; Brian Laghi, "Tories Accused of Hidden Agenda on Hate Crimes," *The Globe and Mail*, June 9, 2004, accessed online at www.globeandmail.com; Heather Scoffield, "Martin Attacks Harper on Rights," *The Globe and Mail*, June 8, 2004, accessed online at www.globeandmail.com; Darren Yourk, "Minority Rights at Risk under Tories: Martin," *The Globe and Mail*, June 7, 2004, accessed online at www.globeandmail.com. See also the open letter to Stephen Harper from several legal academics entitled "Can We Trust You, Sir, to Defend the Charter?" printed in *The Globe and Mail* on June 5, 2004, and *The Globe*'s editorial for June 4, "How Far Would He Go to Stop Gay Marriage?"

114. Robert Benzie, "Tories Pin Blame on Fear, Rogue Candidates," *The Toronto Star*, June 30, 2004, accessed online at www.thestar.com; Ian Brown, "Earth to Alberta: Blame the Doofus, Not the Voters," *The Globe and Mail*, July 3, 2004, accessed online at www.globeandmail.com.

115. "Forget the Preaching, Gay Marriage Is a Done Deal," *The Globe and Mail*, August 2, 2003, accessed online at www.globeandmail.com.

116. *Andrews* 1989, paragraphs 34 and 47.

117. *Law v. Canada*, paragraph 73.

118. For a more comprehensive analysis of the Supreme Court ruling, see Lori Sterling, "The Impact of *Lovelace v. Ontario* on Section 15 of the Charter," *Supreme Court Law Review* 14(2d) (2001), pp. 53–65.

119. *Lovelace v. Ontario*, [1997] O.J. No. 2313 (Q.L.) (Ont. C.A.).

120. *Lovelace* 2000, paragraph 97.

121. Ibid., paragraphs 101, 105, and 108.

122. See, e.g., Morton and Knopff, *The Charter Revolution and the Court Party*, p. 15; Manfredi, *Judicial Power and the Charter*, Chapter 5.

123. See the discussion of social-science evidence in Chapter 3, pages 115–22.

124. *Schachter v. Canada*, [1992] 2 S.C.R. 679, paragraph 79.

125. Manfredi, *Judicial Power and the Charter*, pp. 155–56.

126. *Schachter v. Canada*, paragraphs 60–61.

127. Ibid., paragraph 67.

128. More than three-quarters of respondents to a 1999 national survey agreed that "a province must provide protection for homosexuals in its human rights legislation." Joseph F. Fletcher and Paul Howe, "Supreme Court Cases and Court Support: The State of Canadian Public Opinion" (Montreal: Institute for Research on Public Policy, May 2000), p. 39, Figure 4.

129. MacKay and Pothier, "Developments in Constitutional Law," p. 92.

Chapter 12

The Remaining Sections of the Charter

The 2003 recipients of the Governor General's Awards in Commemoration of the Persons Case stand in the gallery of the House of Commons in October 2003. From left to right are Nicole Demers of Laval; Jennifer Hustwitt of Waterloo; Joyce Hayden of Whitehorse; Marilou McPhedran of Toronto; Jayanti Negi of Edmonton; and Eira Friesen of Winnipeg.

CP PHOTO/Fred Chartrand

16. (1) *English and French are the official languages of Canada and have equality of status and equal rights and privileges as to their use in all institutions of the Parliament and government of Canada.*

    (2) *English and French are the official languages of New Brunswick and have equality of status and equal rights and privileges as to their use in all institutions of the legislature and government of New Brunswick.*

    (3) *Nothing in this Charter limits the authority of Parliament or a legislature to advance the equality of status or use of English and French.*

16.1. (1) *The English linguistic community and the French linguistic community in New Brunswick have equality of status and equal rights and privileges, including the right to distinct educational institutions and such distinct cultural institutions as are necessary for the preservation and promotion of those communities.*

    (2) *The role of the legislature and government of New Brunswick to preserve and promote the status, rights and privileges referred to in subsection (1) is affirmed.*

17. (1) *Everyone has the right to use English or French in any debates and other proceedings of Parliament.*

    (2) *Everyone has the right to use English or French in any debates and other proceedings of the legislature of New Brunswick.*

18. (1) *The statutes, records and journals of Parliament shall be printed and published in English and French and both language versions are equally authoritative.*

    (2) *The statutes, records and journals of the legislature of New Brunswick shall be printed and published in English and French and both language versions are equally authoritative.*

19. (1) *Either English or French may be used by any person in, or in any pleading in or process issuing from, any court established by Parliament.*

    (2) *Either English or French may be used by any person in, or in any pleading in or process issuing from, any court of New Brunswick.*

20. (1) *Any member of the public in Canada has the right to communicate with, and to receive available services from, any head or central office of an institution of the Parliament or government of Canada in English or French, and has the same right with respect to any other office of any such institution where*

    a) *there is significant demand for communications with and services from that office in such language; or*

    b) *due to the nature of the office, it is reasonable that communications with and services from that office be available in both English and French.*

    (2) *Any member of the public in New Brunswick has the right to communicate with, and to receive available services from, any office of an institution of the legislature or government of New Brunswick in English or French.*

21. *Nothing in sections 16 to 20 abrogates or derogates from any right, privilege or obligation with respect to the English and French languages, or either of them, that exists or is continued by virtue of any other provision of the Constitution of Canada.*

22. *Nothing in sections 16 to 20 abrogates or derogates from any legal or customary right or privilege acquired or enjoyed either before or after the coming into force of this Charter with respect to any language that is not English or French.*

27. *This Charter shall be interpreted in a manner consistent with the preservation and enhancement of the multicultural heritage of Canadians.*

28. *Notwithstanding anything in this Charter, the rights and freedoms referred to in it are guaranteed equally to male and female persons.*

33. (1) *Parliament or the legislature of a province may expressly declare in an Act of Parliament or of the legislature, as the case may be, that the Act or a provision thereof shall operate notwithstanding a provision included in section 2 or sections 7 to 15 of this Charter.*

    (2) *An Act or a provision of an Act in respect of which a declaration made under this section is in effect shall have such operation as it would have but for the provision of this Charter referred to in the declaration.*

    (3) *A declaration made under subsection (1) shall cease to have effect five years after it comes into force or on such earlier date as may be specified in the declaration.*

    (4) *Parliament or the legislature of a province may re-enact a declaration made under subsection (1).*

    (5) *Subsection (3) applies in respect of re-enactment made under subsection (4).*

INTRODUCTION

This chapter provides a brief overview of the Charter sections not discussed in other chapters. These are:

- sections 16–22: official language minority rights (s. 23, on minority language education, is discussed in Chapter 7, pages 224–27);

- sections 27 and 28: interpreting rights and freedoms; and

- section 33 (the notwithstanding clause).

None of these sections has had a particularly significant impact. Many of the rights in ss. 16–22 were already protected, either in the Constitution Act, 1867 or in statute law. The interpretive clauses have not lived up to the initial expectations of the groups who fought for them in 1980–82. Fairly or otherwise, the Charter's popularity has tainted the notwithstanding clause, deterring governments from reasserting parliamentary supremacy in the face of court rulings with which they disagree.

One theme of this book has been the contradiction between expectation and reality. Over the past two decades, those directly involved in crafting the Charter have watched, sometimes with dismay, as its meaning evolved in ways that they could not have anticipated. The sections discussed in this chapter are good examples. Even the language rights—the meaning and purpose of which are unusually clear for constitutional provisions—have produced surprises. A separate theme in this chapter is the distinction between a Charter guarantee based on a widely held principle (e.g., the right to vote) and one that entrenches a political compromise. The sections discussed in this chapter, particularly the notwithstanding clause, have often been characterized as the product of political expediency and horse-trading. The interpretive clauses were inserted at the last minute, in response to public demands by interest groups. The entrenchment of language rights was a central element of Pierre Trudeau's effort to counter Quebec separatism. Trudeau was determined that the provisions of his 1969 Official Languages Act relating to federal institutions should be entrenched in "the supreme law of Canada." This goal was achieved by the inclusion of ss. 16–22 in the Charter.[1] Partly because of their origin in the political battles of the 1980s, the guarantees discussed here have left relatively few traces in Charter jurisprudence and public policy.

SECTIONS 16–22: MINORITY LANGUAGE RIGHTS IN CANADA

With the exception of the rights pertaining to New Brunswick,[2] these sections should be read as a constitutional recognition of the pre-1982 legislative and common-law status quo. The provisions permitting the use of either official language in Parliament and federal courts are substantially similar to s. 133 of the Constitution Act, 1867. Even before the Charter took effect, the Supreme Court had relied on s. 133 to establish the rights guaranteed in ss. 17–19.[3] Those pre-Charter cases established precedents on which later courts relied in resolving post-Charter cases on language rights. Consequently, many were resolved without reference to the Charter itself.[4]

Thus the novelty of the language rights lies not in their content, but in the availability of judicial remedies for their violation. The failure of a government to provide the services mandated by these sections, or by s. 23 (see Chapter 7, pages 224–27), may trigger a remedy under s. 24. Options include a *mandamus* order (forcing public officials to provide the service requested), continuing judicial supervision to ensure compliance (see Dossier 1.2, pages 15–17), or the imposition of monetary damages. Before his elevation to the Supreme Court, Michel Bastarache wrote the following:

> To the extent that the provisions of the Charter create rights to claim public services in both official languages, it is clear that their implementation will not be possible unless the courts accept a more active role. Any right must give rise to a remedy, and the courts are invested with the necessary authority to sanction breaches of constitutional duties. They even have the duty to act in this sense.[5]

In the early years of the Charter, the Supreme Court interpreted the language rights—apart from those in s. 23—cautiously, preferring to leave contentious decisions to the legislatures. In the 1986 *Société des Acadiens* ruling, the majority ruled that the right to address a New Brunswick court in French (s. 19(2)) did not confer a corresponding right to be understood. The wording of s. 20(1)—"the right to communicate with"—differs from the wording of ss. 17 and 19, which guarantees only the right to "use" either official language. Whereas "the right to communicate in either language postulates the right to be heard or understood in either language," the right to "use" a particular language does not guarantee "that the speaker will be heard or understood, or that he has the right to be heard or understood in the language of his choice."[6]

In the case at bar, a francophone group had argued that s. 19(2) required the New Brunswick government to ensure that bilingual judges would hear court cases involving francophones. The majority rejected this claim, for two reasons. The first was the narrow interpretation of the guarantee, as discussed in the preceding paragraph. Second, any such requirement would require the expenditure of resources; the Court left that decision to the provincial legislature.[7] Justice Beetz explicitly limited the scope of judicial remedies arising from infringements of language rights:

> Unlike language rights which are based on political compromise, legal rights tend to be seminal in nature because they are rooted in principle. Some of them, such as the one expressed in s. 7 of the Charter, are so broad as to call for frequent judicial determination. Language rights, on the other hand, although some of them have been enlarged and incorporated into the Charter, remain nonetheless founded on political compromise. This essential difference between the two types of rights dictates a distinct judicial approach with respect to each. More particularly, the courts should pause before they decide to act as instruments of change with respect to language rights. This is not to say that language rights provisions are cast in stone and should remain immune altogether from judicial interpretation. But, in my opinion, the courts should approach them with more restraint than they would in construing legal rights.[8]

This restrictive approach was endorsed in subsequent rulings, although with some qualifications.[9] In the 1990 *Mahé* ruling, Chief Justice Dickson wrote (for the Court) that Justice Beetz's words do not "support the proposition that s. 23 should be given a particularly narrow construction, or that its remedial purpose should be ignored." Instead, according to Dickson, *Société des Acadiens* should be read as a prudent warning to future courts against overstepping their bounds: "Section 23 confers upon a group a right which places positive obligations on government to alter or develop major institutional structures. Careful interpretation of such a section is wise: however, this does not mean that courts should not 'breathe life' into the expressed purpose of the section, or avoid implementing the possibly novel remedies needed to achieve that purpose."[10]

In 1999, a majority of the Justices repudiated Beetz's analysis in explicit terms. Justice Bastarache wrote that "To the extent that *Société des Acadiens* ... stands for a restrictive interpretation of language rights, it is to be rejected."[11] He dismissed the claim that language rights should be interpreted more narrowly than other Charter guarantees because they are based not on principle but on "political compromise." Citing the legislative history of the Charter, he argued that many of its provisions, including ss. 7 and 15, were the product of political negotiations among governmental and nongovernmental actors. "There is no basis in the constitutional history of Canada for holding that any such political compromises require a restrictive interpretation of constitutional guarantees."

Moreover, "language rights that are institutionally based require government action for their implementation and therefore create obligations for the State."[12] Justice Bastarache added that "mere administrative inconvenience is not a relevant factor"; the equal constitutional status of English and French requires governments to "maintain a proper institutional infrastructure and provide services in both official languages on an equal basis" where appropriate.[13] Bastarache's expansive approach to language rights has guided the Court in subsequent cases,[14] as has his assertion of a judicial duty to impose remedies against laggard governments. (See Dossier 1.2, pages 15–17.)

Some provincial courts have used the guarantees of language rights to impose new duties on both federal and provincial governments. For obvious reasons, the New Brunswick courts have been particularly active in this regard. They have held, for example, that all provincial court documents (e.g., a summons to appear to answer a charge) must be delivered in the chosen language of the recipient, and that documentary evidence submitted in court proceedings must be available in both official languages where appropriate.[15] In Nova Scotia, whose southwest coastal region is largely inhabited by francophones, a court ordered the federal Coast Guard to transmit radio messages to fishing boats in both official languages.[16] Otherwise, the entrenched language rights have had little practical effect on the lives of most Canadians and relatively little legal impact. It seems clear, however, that their inclusion in the Charter encouraged members of official-language minority groups to go to court to claim their rights. The fact that most of their claims were settled on other grounds does not negate the Charter's mobilizing impact.

SECTIONS 27 AND 28: HOLLOW VICTORIES

Unlike s. 15(1), which prohibits governments from discriminating on the basis of personal characteristics such as sex and race, ss. 27 and 28 of the Charter do not contain "enforceable guarantees" of multicultural and gender equality.[17] There is no recourse to s. 24(1) for a violation of either section. The interpretive clauses are intended to guide the courts in their definition and application of the substantive rights and freedoms and to "reflect unique Canadian historical, cultural and social realities."[18]

The interpretive clauses were last-minute additions to the Charter. They were not discussed in the pre-1980 negotiations, nor were they included in the draft Charter tabled by the federal government in October 1980. Section 27 first appeared in the package of amendments tabled by the justice minister in January 1981. Multicultural organizations had lobbied the Special Joint Committee for a clause protecting their collective rights from the individual rights and freedoms in the Charter.[19] Their model was article 27 of the 1966 International Covenant on Civil and Political Rights (ICCPR): "In those States in which ethnic, religious or linguistic minorities exist, persons belonging to such minorities shall not be denied the right, in community with the other members of their group, to enjoy their own culture, to profess and practice their own religion, or to use their own language."[20]

Unlike the ICCPR guarantee, s. 27 is both narrow and vague. It does not specify the content of multiculturalism, perhaps because other sections of the Charter expressly guarantee religious freedom, the rights of official-language minorities, and protection against racial and ethnic discrimination. Nor, unlike its counterpart in the ICCPR, does it bind all three branches of government: s. 27 guides judicial interpretation but does not require legislators and executives to remedy infringements.

Section 28 was drafted at a meeting between feminist lawyers and justice department officials in March 1981. It was added to the Charter, by the unanimous agreement of Parliament, in April 1981. The general guarantee of sexual equality was the fruit of a lengthy lobbying effort by the Ad Hoc Committee of Women on the Constitution, the National Association of Women and the Law, the National Action Committee on the Status of Women, and other groups.[21]

The multicultural organizations that mobilized around s. 27 and the feminists who fought for s. 28 expected these interpretive clauses to have a significant impact on Canadian law.[22] The success of the lobby effort that produced s. 28 and then secured its exemption from the notwithstanding clause produced a mood of euphoria among Canadian feminists—or at least those who believed that law could be used to promote social change.[23] In her 1983 book on the fight for gender equality in the Charter, Penney Kome predicted that s. 28 could affect "everything from union negotiations to access to public education."[24] She called the section "an important new tool with which [Canadian women] may be able to force unwilling governments to help them take their rightful places as equal partners in the workforce, the bureaucracy, the professions, and the government."[25] Most observers took a more modest view, predicting that s. 28 would simply reinforce the guarantee of gender equality in s. 15. Unless the courts explicitly read these two sections together and used them to provide "the strongest possible protection" for women's rights, s. 28 would be rendered superfluous and its inclusion in the Charter revealed as "a cruel sham."[26]

Over the past two decades, ss. 27 and 28 have gradually disappeared from Charter jurisprudence. The hopes of their advocates have not been fulfilled. In general, s. 27 appears to have been more influential than s. 28. The different wording of the two sections suggests a possible explanation: whereas s. 28 does not impose specific duties on the courts, s. 27 states that judges "shall" interpret rights and freedoms in a way that "enhances" as well as "preserves" multiculturalism.[27]

At first, the Supreme Court took that mandate seriously. In *Big M Drug Mart* (1985), Chief Justice Dickson observed that "Section 27 makes the multicultural heritage of Canada an interpretive guideline for the Charter."[28] He found that a law intended to compel the observance of the Christian faith, when applied to the guarantee of religious freedom in s. 2(a), "is not consistent with the preservation and enhancement of the multicultural heritage of Canadians."[29] He added: "If I am a Jew or a Sabbatarian or a Muslim, the practice of my religion at least implies my right to work on a Sunday if I wish. It seems to me that any law purely religious in purpose, which denies me that right, must surely infringe my religious freedom."[30] The application of s. 27 does not appear to have determined the outcome of the case. It occurs in a brief discussion of the impugned law's *effects*, whereas Dickson's decision to strike down the law arose from its unconstitutional *purpose*.

In the subsequent *Edwards Books* case, Dickson focused on the effect of a law whose purpose was consistent with the Charter. In his discussion of unconstitutional effects, he referred to "the Court's obligation under s. 27 to preserve and enhance the multicultural heritage of Canadians."[31] This was the only invocation of multicultural rights in the majority opinion; while it seems to have shaped Dickson's thinking, it does not appear to have been determinative. He concluded that Ontario's Sunday-closing law violated s. 2(a) but could be saved under s. 1.

In the 1990 *Keegstra* ruling, the majority upheld the hate speech laws as a justified infringement on freedom of expression (s. 2(b)). In defence of the law, the federal government argued that expressive content that denigrated particular ethnic or religious groups— and thereby violated s. 27—did not merit protection under the Charter. Dickson disagreed. He refused to "attenuate the s. 2(b) freedom on the grounds that a *particular* context requires such," preferring to take s. 27 into account at the s. 1 stage of analysis.[32] There he found that s. 27 highlighted the "pressing and substantial" nature of the government's objective in criminalizing hate speech. He wrote, "This Court has where possible taken account of s. 27 and its recognition that Canada possesses a multicultural society in which the diversity and richness of various cultural groups is a value to be protected and enhanced.... I am of the belief that s. 27 and the commitment to a multicultural vision of our nation bear notice in emphasizing the acute importance of the objective of eradicating hate propaganda from society."[33]

In effect, Dickson ruled out the use of s. 27 to interpret Charter rights and freedoms themselves— and thus to determine whether or not they had been infringed; henceforth, it could be used only to determine whether an infringement was justified. By restricting the effect of s. 27 in this way, Dickson reduced its importance and, arguably, rendered it redundant. The wording of the section does not suggest that multicultural rights are to be relegated to the "balancing" stage of a Charter challenge; it is intended to be applied to the definition of other rights as well.[34]

Since 1985, s. 27 seems to have played an important role in only one case. As discussed in Chapter 10, pages 328–29, s. 14 of the Charter guarantees the accused in a criminal trial the assistance of an interpreter in court. The Court referred to s. 27 when it defined the meaning and purpose of s. 14: "In so far as a multicultural heritage is necessarily a multilingual one, it follows that a multicultural society can only be preserved and fostered if those who speak languages other than English and French are given real and substantive access to the criminal justice system."[35] But in general, the Court does not use s. 27 to define the scope of rights and freedoms whose connection to multiculturalism is less direct. The Justices appear to regard it as a useful way to support a conclusion reached on other grounds, not as a binding requirement to take multiculturalism into account when they do not choose to do so.[36]

Section 28 has received even shorter shrift from the Court. In the mid-1980s, appellants and intervenors routinely invoked s. 28 in their arguments for gender equality—partly because it, unlike s. 15, took effect as soon as the Charter was proclaimed.[37] These arguments are summarized in the following passage from LEAF's intervenor factum in *Butler* (see Dossier 3.3, pages 113–15):

Section 28 of the Charter overrides every other provision therein. It mandates that all rights and freedoms, including freedom of expression, and equality rights, are guaranteed equally to women and men. Therefore, in LEAF's submission, section 28 engages section 2(b) prior to any recourse to section 1 and requires a balancing of speech interests and equality interests. Failure to strike such a balance constitutes a breach of section 28.[38]

These invocations appear to have had little or no effect. In *Morgentaler* (1988), for example, the appellants petitioned the Chief Justice for a constitutional question on the validity of the abortion provisions in the Criminal Code. The question referred to ss. 2(a), 7, 12, 15, 27, and 28.[39] The Justices ignored s. 28, focusing exclusively on s. 7 (apart from Justice Wilson, who also considered s. 2(a)).

Where s. 28 has been taken into account, it has been given little weight. The 1990 *Hess/Nguyen* ruling (discussed in Chapter 11, page 345) is a case in point. Two men had been charged with the crime of sexual intercourse with a girl under the age of fourteen. They argued that a criminal offence that only applied to men violated their right to gender equality under ss. 15 and 28. The majority rejected this argument, although it granted the appeal on other grounds. For the majority, Justice Wilson—who might have been expected to take an expansive approach to s. 28—dismissed the gender argument out of hand: "In my view, [s. 28] does not prevent the legislature from creating an offence that as a matter of biological fact can only be committed by one sex." She added that "The justification for the infringement of a Charter right will have to be linked to considerations other than the sex of the party that has established an infringement of his or her Charter right."[40] In effect, Wilson held that s. 28 should not be determinative at either stage of a Charter analysis. Despite the phrase "Notwithstanding anything in this Charter," which could be taken to mean that s. 1 should never be used to justify unequal treatment for men and women,[41] s. 28 has had no real impact either in defining the scope of rights and freedoms or in determining the standard of justification.

Even in cases where s. 28 should logically have played a role, most Justices have ignored it. Justice McLachlin avoided the issue of gender equality in *Seaboyer* (the constitutionality of the "rape shield" law), over the vigorous protests of Justice L'Heureux-Dubé. The latter dissented again in *Symes*, arguing that s. 28 required the evenhanded application of tax laws to men and women; the seven male justices in the majority took no notice of the provision. (Justice McLachlin also dissented, although she explicitly

refrained from endorsing L'Heureux-Dubé's use of s. 28.) Recent rulings on gender equality have been decided as though the section did not exist.[42]

By the end of the first decade of Charter jurisprudence, LEAF had begun to downplay s. 28 in its submissions to the Court.[43] Its last major s. 28 argument, in *Butler* (see excerpt above), was completely ignored in Justice Sopinka's ruling. The omission is significant, given the pro-feminist tenor of the judgment. A consensus seemed to have emerged: s. 28 is a purely symbolic recognition of sexual equality, with no binding force in law. When gender issues arise, they should be dealt with under s. 15(1) alone. The irrelevance of s. 28 does not indicate a "cruel sham" perpetrated by the framers, but at the very least it must be a disappointment to the women who fought for it.[44]

SECTION 33: IS THE NOTWITHSTANDING CLAUSE A DEAD LETTER?

The notwithstanding clause—also known as the *non obstante* or override clause—is the subject of considerable criticism from Charter advocates. As explained in Chapter 2, pages 69–77, it was added at the November 1981 First Ministers' Meeting as a reluctant concession by the federal government. The idea that a legislature might explicitly override rights and freedoms was already part of Canadian law. Section 2 of the 1960 Bill of Rights allowed Parliament to declare, in the text of a law, that "it shall operate notwithstanding" the rest of the document (refer to Dossier 2.5, pages 58–60). Unlike the Bill of Rights, however, the Charter engages the loyalty and support of a large majority of Canadians. Moreover, a majority believe that the courts, not legislatures, should have the final say on issues pertaining to rights and freedoms—an apparent sea change from the parliamentary supremacy that prevailed under the 1960 Bill.[45] Consequently, the notwithstanding clause in s. 33 is widely unpopular.[46]

Section 33 was a concession to those premiers who feared that the Charter would destroy legislative supremacy and strip the provinces of jurisdiction. The idea of a general *non obstante* clause first surfaced in 1978. By the time of the 1980–82 constitutional round, the negotiators had to choose among three options: "a full charter with a 'soft *non obstante* clause' [i.e., a stronger version of the limitations in s. 1], a limited charter with no *non obstante* clause, or a full charter with a hard *non obstante* clause."[47] The third option eventually prevailed (see Dossier 2.10, pages 73–74).

A general override ("hard *non obstante*") clause began to attract serious attention in July 1980, during the talks that led up to the September First Ministers' Meeting. The Sub-Committee of Officials on a Charter of Rights found considerable support for the idea.[48] In August 1980 the subcommittee proposed "an override clause whereby a legislative body could expressly declare that a law would operate notwithstanding a Charter right." Any such declaration would require the support of sixty percent of the members and would expire after five years.[49] The failure of the September meeting ended provincial participation and, with it, the need to assuage the concerns of Charter critics in the provincial governments. The override was taken off the agenda.

When the eleven senior governments returned to the table in November 1981, it quickly became clear that the "Gang of Eight" could not accept the strong guarantees of rights and freedoms without an escape hatch. The federal government and nine provinces finally agreed to entrench the Charter with an override clause substantially similar to the one proposed in August 1980. The only difference was the deletion of the sixty percent majority rule: the final version of s. 33 permits the insertion of a notwithstanding provision by a simple majority vote. According to one participant, the creation of s. 33 "had more to do with the raw politics of bargaining and chance phone calls late at night than with reasoned debate about what might constitute a rational compromise between democracy and constitutional law."[50]

The text of the First Ministers' Agreement stated that the override would apply to "Fundamental Freedoms, Legal Rights and Equality Rights." The latter phrase worried women's groups and Aboriginal organizations, who feared—with some reason—that the new s. 33 would go beyond s. 15 to cover all of the nondiscrimination clauses in the Charter.[51] The Ad Hoc Committee of Women on the Constitution

and other feminist groups that had participated in the constitutional process mobilized quickly. They lobbied federal and provincial politicians for two intense weeks, demanding that s. 28 be explicitly exempted from the override. Their efforts succeeded: the text of s. 33 refers only to ss. 2 and 7–15.

The initial reaction to s. 33 in other quarters was less intense but generally negative. The federal government sought to reassure Canadians that the notwithstanding clause would make little difference to their newly entrenched rights and freedoms.[52] Those reassurances were belied by the actions of two provincial governments. Shortly after the Charter was proclaimed, the government of Quebec passed Bill 62, An Act Respecting the Constitution Act, 1982—an omnibus statute that retrospectively inserted a s. 33 override clause into every provincial law.[53] This blanket exemption of all provincial laws from the application of ss. 2 and 7–15 of the Charter was a political protest, reflecting Quebec's refusal to endorse the Constitution Act, 1982. (Despite this refusal, the Charter applies in Quebec with the same force as it does in the rest of Canada.) In early 1986, the Saskatchewan legislature passed Bill 144 to force striking public servants back to work. It invoked s. 33 to shield the law from judicial review under s. 2(d). Although, as discussed in Chapter 8, pages 272–78, the Supreme Court subsequently determined that freedom of association did not include a right to strike, the Saskatchewan Court of Appeal had reached the opposite conclusion in an unrelated 1985 ruling. The back-to-work law seemed likely to fail a Charter challenge by the affected union; to forestall that possibility, the government of Saskatchewan preempted judicial review by invoking the override.[54]

Until 1989, no one knew whether, or under what circumstances, a legislature's decision to invoke the override would be subject to review by the courts. If it were, what standards would the courts apply? On the surface, Quebec's Bill 62 did not meet the "manner and form" requirements in s. 33: it did not specify which sections of the affected laws were to be protected from judicial scrutiny, nor did it identify which particular rights and freedoms were overridden in relation to each law.[55] The override clause in Saskatchewan's Bill 144 was a preemptive strike, an attempt to forestall judicial review, not a direct response to judicial nullification of the statute itself. Some observers argue that such prospective uses of s. 33 are illegitimate, both on institutional grounds—they deny the courts an opportunity to pronounce on the constitutionality of legislation, contrary to the well-established practice in Canada—and on legal grounds.

> In order to give the "notwithstanding" declaration any legal effect, the law must be in conflict with the Charter provisions. If the law was not inconsistent with a Charter right or freedom, the notwithstanding declaration would be unnecessary, a meaningless appendage. In other words, when a legislative assembly says that a law operates in spite of a Charter provision, there must be a conflict between the law and the provision if the statement is to have any meaning. The institution charged with rendering an authoritative ruling with respect to incompatibility, before s. 33 is invoked, is the courts. Hence, the override power is contingent on a prior judicial determination that a law violates a Charter right or freedom.[56]

The "manner and form" issue was addressed by the Supreme Court in the 1988 *Ford* ruling on Quebec's sign law. The law, originally enacted in 1977, prohibited the use of English on outdoor commercial signs in the province. Like all provincial laws, it contained a notwithstanding clause inserted by Bill 62. The question before the Court was whether the sign law—which infringed the freedom of expression guaranteed in s. 2(b), and could not be justified under s. 1—was nonetheless immunized from Charter review by the operation of s. 33.

The Court's answer was complex, but its essence can be summarized as follows. First, Bill 62 was a valid exercise of the s. 33 override, even though it did not specify precisely which legal provisions were to be exempted from Charter scrutiny, or which particular rights and freedoms were involved.

> The essential requirement of form laid down by s. 33 is that the override declaration must be an express declaration that an Act or a provision of an Act shall operate notwithstanding a provision included in s. 2 or ss. 7 to 15 of the Charter.

> With great respect for the contrary view, this Court is of the opinion that a s. 33 declaration is sufficiently express if it refers to the number of the section, subsection or paragraph of the Charter which contains the provision or provisions to be overridden. Of course, if it is intended to override only a part of the provision or provisions contained in a section, subsection or paragraph then there would have to be a sufficient reference in words to the part to be overridden.[57]

Second, the Court declared that s. 33 could not be invoked retroactively. Bill 62 purported to cover all provincial laws passed before the Charter took effect on April 17, 1982, even though the act itself was not proclaimed until June of that year. The Court ruled that the s. 33 override did not apply to any Quebec laws until the date when the omnibus law was proclaimed; consequently, it expired in June 1987 and not in April of that year.

The gist of the *Ford* decision is that a validly enacted notwithstanding clause, covering all or part of a particular law, will be respected by the courts for as long as it remains in effect. Unless the party challenging the use of s. 33 can demonstrate that the override is invalid for some technical reason, judges may not overturn the decision of the sponsoring government to shield its legislation from Charter review. The Court's criteria for "valid enactment" are surprisingly weak. In effect, the Court suspended the "manner and form" requirements for invoking s. 33, directly contradicting its own rigorous approach to other sections of the Charter.[58]

It is commonly believed that s. 33 has been used three times: (1) in Quebec's Bill 62; (2) in Saskatchewan's Bill 144; and (3) in Bill 178, the controversial 1988 reenactment of the nullified sign law by former Quebec premier Robert Bourassa.[59] In fact, the notwithstanding clause was invoked on eighteen separate occasions between 1982 and 2000 (including the two omnibus bills in Quebec).[60] Most of these laws went unnoticed, for two reasons. First, they were obscure and relatively uncontroversial. Second, they used s. 33 preemptively. In other words, the sponsoring governments—Quebec, Yukon, and Saskatchewan—sought to avoid Charter review by placing a law off-limits before the courts had spoken; they were not reacting to prior court rulings that nullified that particular law, which might have attracted more public attention.[61] According to a former official who participated in the 1980–82 negotiations, "many who had agreed with the insertion of a *non obstante* clause in 1981 had not anticipated that it would be used to 'bullet-proof' legislation."[62]

The only direct retrospective use of s. 33 was Quebec's Bill 178. Alberta's Bill 202, like the Saskatchewan back-to-work law, was partly "retrospective"; both were enacted in response to court rulings, although the rulings in question did not deal with those specific laws. Bill 202, passed in March 2000, amends Alberta's Marriage Act by explicitly stating that "'marriage' means a marriage between a man and a woman."[63] The use of the override to shield that provision from judicial review under s. 15(1) was a political statement by the Alberta legislature. It reflects the Klein government's opposition to Supreme Court rulings imposing equal treatment for gay and lesbian individuals and couples (see Dossier 11.4, pages 359–62).[64] Perhaps because it was sponsored by a backbencher, not by a Conservative cabinet minister, it passed largely unnoticed. The lack of public attention is particularly striking because the use of s. 33 had recently become a hot political issue for the Klein government. In March 1998, in response to a successful lawsuit by a woman who had been forcibly sterilized under the province's (now defunct) Sexual Sterilization Act, the provincial government tabled a bill limiting the government's financial liability toward other victims. It invoked the notwithstanding clause to shield the legislation from Charter review. Bill 26 triggered a public and media outcry inside and outside Alberta. The day after the bill was tabled, the government announced that it would not proceed with the legislation.[65] It was forced to back down again in April 1998, after threatening to use s. 33 to override the *Vriend* decision from the Supreme Court (see Chapter 11, page 350 and Dossier 1.8, pages 36–37).[66] Premier Klein changed his position after discovering that most of his caucus opposed the use of the notwithstanding clause.[67]

The travails of the Klein government illustrate the political dangers of invoking s. 33. The issue became a flashpoint during the 2004 election campaign, when

Conservative leader Stephen Harper said that he would use s. 33 to strengthen child-pornography laws and (perhaps) to protect legislation denying same-sex couples the right to marry.[68] In theory, legislatures are free to use the notwithstanding clause to reassert parliamentary supremacy against the power of the courts. (This is a favourite argument of those who advocate democratic dialogue, as discussed in Chapter 4, pages 150–56.) In practice, however, recourse to s. 33 is fraught with peril—at least when the public and the media are paying attention. An open declaration that a law will operate notwithstanding the rights and fundamental freedoms of Canadians is out of the question for most governments.

During the 2004 leaders' debates, Liberal leader Paul Martin stated that he "would never use the notwithstanding clause to take away the rights that are enshrined in the Charter."[69] Although this statement is not entirely consistent with Mr. Martin's earlier suggestion that he might use s. 33 to protect churches that refused to perform same-sex marriages,[70] it reflects the general attitude in the federal Liberal Party. When the Anti-Terrorism Act (Bill C-36) was introduced in the wake of the September 11, 2001 attacks on New York and Washington, legal experts and parliamentarians raised serious concerns about its conformity to the Charter.[71] When asked if she would use s. 33 to protect the legislation from Charter review, then–justice minister Anne McLellan made it clear that the notwithstanding clause was simply not an option for a Liberal government. McLellan and her officials insisted that the law had been thoroughly "Charter-proofed" by the Department of Justice (see Chapter 5, pages 184–86), and she predicted that the courts would uphold it under s. 1.[72] This claim illustrates a general trend: governments have learned to rely on first-order Charter review and growing judicial willingness to justify legislation under s. 1 to safeguard their laws, instead of courting the political risks associated with the notwithstanding clause.

A member of the Saskatchewan delegation at the November 1981 First Ministers' Meeting recently observed that "no one could have predicted the lack of enthusiasm shown by Parliament and the provincial legislatures" for a measure designed to preserve their supreme lawmaking power. He suggested that s. 33 is a constitutional "dead letter." It is the Charter equivalent of the federal power to veto provincial laws: "available in theory, but not used in practice."[73] Critics of "judicial activism" condemn this timidity, arguing that the notwithstanding clause is a valuable and often necessary remedy for judicial over-reaching.[74] By refusing to assert their powers under s. 33, the federal and provincial legislatures have effectively told the courts to do whatever they want with the Charter. No matter how misguided a judicial policy may be, it will become the law of the land.

In truth, as we saw in Part 2, legislatures are not powerless in the face of "judicial supremacy." They can, and do, defy court rulings by imposing their own interpretations of rights and freedoms. If s. 33 has indeed become a dead letter, one reason may be the growing willingness of the courts to uphold these leg-islative replies. Equally as important, the Supreme Court rarely nullifies a law without giving the spon-soring legislature a chance to amend it. Judges and leg-islators usually clash over the means chosen to achieve a policy objective, not the objective itself. Under these circumstances, few governments will be tempted to resort to s. 33 and pay the political price.

In an effort to dispel the resistance to s. 33, Manfredi proposes three amendments to its text.[75] The first would prohibit its preemptive use, by lim-iting its application to circumstances in which the Supreme Court has previously nullified the law in question. The second revives the sixty-percent majority first proposed in 1980 and abandoned in November 1981. The third would amend the "sunset clause" by making enactments under s. 33 null and void at the moment when the sponsoring legislature is dissolved for an election. This last proposal would "guarantee that existing notwithstanding clauses would become election issues," thus encouraging public debate about legislated limitations on entrenched rights and freedoms.[76] Given the fact that governments seem more willing to invoke s. 33 prospectively than retrospectively, the first proposal would likely make its use even rarer than it is now. The other two suggestions, while impractical in light of the difficulty of constitutional amendment in Canada, are more promising in theory. Requiring approval by a "super-majority" could legitimize the use of the override, while reassuring the public that it is not being invoked for purely partisan or frivolous

reasons. Forcing governments to defend s. 33 on the campaign trail, while it might further discourage them from using it, would give politicians a clearer sense of the actual political danger of bypassing Charter review. In some instances, that danger could be less than anticipated.

Another reform proposal, from Conservative MP Scott Reid, is also intended to promote public discus-sion. Reid suggests that governments should use s. 33 only when specifically authorized to do so by a refer-endum. At each general election, some or all of the laws that had been struck down by the Supreme Court during the life of the previous legislature would sub-mitted to the voters for their approval; a majority vote in favour of a particular law would bind the new gov-ernment to reenact it with a notwithstanding clause.[77] It is unclear how, or whether, this would work in prac-tice. Holding referendums in conjunction with elec-tions risks contaminating the referendum vote with partisan sentiments; moreover, the public popularity of the Charter might condemn nullified laws to defeat, regardless of their merits. However, Reid's pro-posal has one clear advantage over Manfredi's sugges-tions: it could be achieved without amending the Constitution.

CONCLUSION

For the most part, the sections discussed in this chapter have had less impact than their authors intended. Unlike the substantive rights and freedoms, whose application by the courts has often exceeded expecta-tions, the interpretive clauses and (for the most part) the language rights have been treated cautiously by the courts. On their own, ss. 27 and 28 do not impose new first-order duties on the other branches of govern-ment; the refusal of the courts to enforce them has ren-dered them all but useless in practical terms. Nor has the notwithstanding clause lived up to its early billing, although it has been used more extensively than most people realize. The lesson of this chapter is that a con-stitutional provision born in controversy may, over time, dwindle away into a quiet grave.

The aura of political compromise surrounding these sections seems to have diminished their legiti-macy, both inside and outside government. It may be that entrenched rights and freedoms that enshrine long-standing and widely held principles—e.g., justice, equality, individual liberty—will always have greater impact than those that carry a whiff of political deal-making and compromise, or that—in the case of official-language minority rights—directly affect the lives of few Canadians. While the distinction between principled and "political" guarantees should not be overstated, as Justice Bastarache pointed out, it may help explain why the controversial provisions discussed in this chapter have played such a minor role in the Charter era.

DISCUSSION AND REVIEW QUESTIONS

1. Explain the key difference between preemptive and retrospective applications of the notwithstanding clause. In your opinion, is one preferable to the other? If so, why?

2. During the 2004 election campaign, the Conservatives' former official languages critic suggested that the federal government should not have to provide bilingual services across Canada. Do you agree with this claim? Why or why not?

3. Briefly explain the limited impact of either s. 27 or s. 28 of the Charter. In your opinion, should the courts give either or both sections greater weight in evaluating public policy? Why or why not?

SUGGESTED READINGS

Greschner, Donna, and Ken Norman. "The Courts and Section 33." *Queen's Law Journal* 12 (1987), pp. 155–98.

Hošek, Chaviva. "Women and the Constitutional Process." In Keith Banting and Richard Simeon, eds., *And No One Cheered: Federalism, Democracy and the Constitution Act.* Toronto: Methuen, 1983, pp. 280–300.

Kahana, Tsvi. "The Notwithstanding Mechanism and Public Discussion: Lessons from the Ignored Practice of Section 33 of the Charter." *Canadian Public Administration* 44, no. 3 (Fall 2001), pp. 255–91.

Kome, Penney. *The Taking of Twenty-Eight: Women Challenge the Constitution.* Toronto: Women's Press, 1983.

Leeson, Howard. "The Notwithstanding Clause: A Paper Tiger?" In Paul Howe and Peter H. Russell, eds., *Judicial Power and Canadian Democracy.* Montreal and Kingston: McGill-Queen's University Press/Institute for Research on Public Policy, 2001, pp. 297–327

Russell, Peter H. "Standing Up for Notwithstanding." *Alberta Law Review* 29 (1991), pp. 293–309.

Tremblay, André, and Michel Bastarache. "Language Rights: Sections 16–22." In Gérald-A. Beaudoin and Ed Ratushny, eds., *The Canadian Charter of Rights and Freedoms.* 2nd ed. Toronto: Carswell, 1989, pp. 653–85.

ENDNOTES

1. André Tremblay and Michel Bastarache, "Language Rights: Sections 16–22," in Gérald-A. Beaudoin and Ed Ratushny, eds., *The Canadian Charter of Rights and Freedoms*, 2nd ed. (Toronto: Carswell, 1989), p. 659.

2. The province of New Brunswick is unique in that it is home to a relatively large and well-established francophone minority (roughly one-third of the population). French is the majority language in some areas of the province (e.g., the northwest, close to the Quebec border, and some parts of Moncton). The rights of the *Acadien* minority were a hot political issue in New Brunswick during the 1970s. The premier who participated in the 1980–82 constitutional round, Conservative Richard Hatfield, was determined to woo francophone voters away from the Liberals. He supported Trudeau's patriation project, in exchange for entrenched language rights that would apply to his province.

3. The key ruling is *Attorney General of Quebec v. Blaikie*, [1979] 2 S.C.R. 1016.

4. These include *Re Manitoba Language Rights*, [1985] 1 S.C.R. 721; *R. v. Mercure*, [1988] 1 S.C.R. 234; and *Bilodeau v. A.G. (Man.)*, [1986] 1 S.C.R. 449.

5. Tremblay and Bastarache, "Language Rights," pp. 673–74.

6. *Société des Acadiens v. Association of Parents*, [1986] 1 S.C.R. 549, paragraphs 53–54, per Beetz J.

7. Ibid., paragraph 68, *per* Beetz J. Subsequent to this ruling, the federal government amended the Criminal Code to provide judges and/or juries who understood the official language spoken by the accused (s. 530).

8. Ibid., paragraphs 63–65, *per* Beetz J.

9. *Mahé v. Alberta*, [1990] 1 S.C.R. 342, *per* Dickson C.J.; *Reference re Public Schools Act (Man.), s. 79(3), (4) and (7)*, [1993] 1 S.C.R. 839, *per* Lamer C.J.

10. *Mahé*, paragraph 38. See Chapter 7, page 226 for a more detailed discussion of the case.

11. *R. v. Beaulac*, [1999] 1 S.C.R. 768, paragraph 25, *per* Bastarache J.

12. Ibid., paragraph 24.

13. Ibid., paragraph 39.

14. *Arsenault-Cameron v. Prince Edward Island*, [2000] 1 S.C.R. 3, *per* Major and Bastarache JJ. (unanimous); *Doucet-Boudreau v. Nova Scotia (Minister of Education)*, [2003] 3 S.C.R. 3, *per* Iacobucci and Arbour JJ. (unanimous as to the analysis of language rights).

15. *Gautreau v. R.* (1989), 101 N.B.R. (2d) 1 (N.B.Q.B.); *Boudreau v. R.*, (N.B.C.A., September 5, 1990).

16. *Saulnier v. The Queen* (1989), 90 N.S.R. (2d) 77 (N.S. Cty. Ct.).

17. William F. Pentney, "Interpreting the Charter: General Principles," in Beaudoin and Ratushny, *The Canadian Charter of Rights and Freedoms*, p. 39.

18. Pentney, "Interpreting the Charter," p. 43.

19. Joseph Eliot Magnet, "Multiculturalism and Collective Rights: Approaches to Section 27," in Beaudoin and Ratushny, *The Canadian Charter of Rights and Freedoms*, p. 742.

20. Reproduced in Magnet, "Multiculturalism and Collective Rights," pp. 745–46.

21. That effort also produced the final wording of s. 15, although its other demands were rejected. For a detailed history of the women's lobby, see Penney Kome, *The Taking of Twenty-Eight: Women Challenge the Constitution* (Toronto: Women's Press, 1983). The specific demands of the feminist lobby are set out in Chaviva Hošek, "Women and Constitutional Process," in Keith Banting and Richard Simeon, eds., *And No One Cheered: Federalism, Democracy and the Constitution Act* (Toronto: Methuen, 1983), pp. 280–300.

22. Indeed, the women's groups were concerned that s. 27 would be used to deny sexual equality to minority women; see Hošek, "Women and Constitutional Process," p. 287.

23. Chapter 6, pages 210–11 explains why litigation strategies can be divisive for feminists and other groups working for social change.

24. Kome, *The Taking of Twenty-Eight*, p. 113.

25. Ibid., p. 117.

26. Pentney, "Interpreting the Charter," p. 49.

27. Ibid., pp. 41 and 43; Magnet, "Multiculturalism and Collective Rights," p. 740.

28. *R. v. Big M Drug Mart Ltd.*, [1985] 1 S.C.R. 295, paragraph 11.

29. Ibid., paragraph 99.

30. Ibid., paragraph 100.

31. *R. v. Edwards Books and Art Ltd.*, [1986] 2 S.C.R. 713, paragraph 96, *per* Dickson C.J.

32. *R. v. Keegstra*, [1990] 3 S.C.R. 697, paragraph 39, *per* Dickson C.J. (emphasis in original).

33. Ibid., paragraphs 75–76, *per* Dickson C.J.

34. Pentney, "Interpreting the Charter," pp. 44–47.

35. *R. v. Tran*, [1994] 2 S.C.R. 951, paragraph 37, *per* Lamer C.J.

36. In *Andrews* (1989), Justice McIntyre referred briefly to s. 27 in support of his argument that the equality rights in s. 15 were not designed to eliminate harmless legislative distinctions. *Andrews v. Law Society of British Columbia*, [1989] 1 S.C.R. 143, paragraph 34.

37. Peter W. Hogg, *Constitutional Law of Canada*, 2002 Student Edition (Toronto: Carswell, 2002), p. 1094.

38. Factum submitted in *R. v. Butler* (1992), reproduced in Women's Legal Education and Action Fund, *Equality and the Charter: Ten Years of Feminist Advocacy before the Supreme Court of Canada* (Toronto: Emond Montgomery, 1996), pp. 204–21. The claim that s. 28 overrides the rest of the Charter had been explicitly rejected in the 1986 *Blainey* ruling by the Ontario Court of Appeal ((1986), 21 D.L.R. (4th) 599), which the Supreme Court implicitly affirmed when it denied leave to appeal. As noted earlier, the suggestion that an interpretive clause may be used to qualify the protection afforded by s. 2(b) had been laid to rest in *Keegstra*. LEAF's argument in the passage reproduced was therefore doomed to failure.

39. *R. v. Morgentaler*, [1988] 1 S.C.R. 30.

40. *R. v. Hess; R. v. Nguyen*, [1990] 2 S.C.R. 906, paragraphs 47–48, *per* Wilson J.

41. Pentney, "Interpreting the Charter," p. 51.

42. *Trociuk v. British Columbia (Attorney General)*, [2003] 1 S.C.R 835, dealt with a challenge to a British Columbia law that allowed a mother to delete the name of her child's biological father from all official records. The father's challenge succeeded, on the ground that the law violated the guarantee of sexual equality in s. 15(1); there was no mention of s. 28. The case is discussed in Chapter 11, page 358.

43. For example, in *Seaboyer* (1991), LEAF referred to s. 28 in its factum, but only once and without elaboration. See *Equality and the Charter*, pp. 176–90.

44. It should be noted, however, that s. 28 may yet have an important role to play. Whereas s. 15 is subject to the notwithstanding clause, s. 28 is not. Therefore, it is conceivable that s. 28 could be used to protect gender equality rights even in the face of a s. 33 override.

45. Joseph F. Fletcher and Paul Howe, "Canadian Attitudes toward the Charter and the Courts in Comparative Perspective" (Montreal: Institute for Research on Public Policy, May 2000), p. 7, Figure 2, and p. 11, Figure 7.

46. Howard Leeson, "The Notwithstanding Clause: A Paper Tiger?" in Paul Howe and Peter H. Russell, eds., *Judicial Power and Canadian Democracy* (Montreal and Kingston: McGill-Queen's University Press/Institute for Research on Public Policy, 2001), p. 298. See also the comments of former prime minister Brian Mulroney, reproduced in Leeson, "The Notwithstanding Clause," p. 314.

47. Leeson, "The Notwithstanding Clause," p. 306.

48. "Report by the Sub-Committee of Officials on a Charter of Rights," July 24, 1980, reprinted in Anne F. Bayefsky, ed., *Canada's Constitution Act, 1982 and Amendments: A Documentary*

History (Toronto: McGraw-Hill Ryerson, 1989), vol. 2, p. 664.

49. "Charter of Rights, Report to Ministers by Sub-Committee of Officials," August 29, 1980, reprinted in Bayefsky, *Canada's Constitution Act,* vol. 2, p. 681.

50. Leeson, "The Notwithstanding Clause," p. 298.

51. Kome, *The Taking of Twenty-Eight,* p. 84; Hošek, "Women and Constitutional Process," pp. 291–92.

52. Then–justice minister Jean Chrétien told the House of Commons that s. 33 was "unlikely ever to be used except in non-controversial circumstances." Canada, *Debates of the House of Commons,* November 30, 1981, p. 13042, quoted in Donna Greschner and Ken Norman, "The Courts and Section 33," *Queen's Law Journal* 12 (1987), p. 162, note 21.

53. Leeson, "The Notwithstanding Clause," p. 313.

54. Greschner and Norman, "The Courts and Section 33," pp. 155–59.

55. *Alliance des professeurs de Montréal v. Procureur général du Québec,* [1985] C.A. 376.

56. Greschner and Norman, "The Courts and Section 33," p. 188.

57. *Ford v. Quebec (A. G.),* [1988] 2 S.C.R. 712, paragraph 33, *per curiam.*

58. Peter Russell has suggested that s. 33 be amended to overturn this element of the *Ford* ruling. See his article "Standing Up for Notwithstanding," *Alberta Law Review* 29 (1991), p. 301.

59. The Saskatchewan law was adopted because the Supreme Court of Canada had not yet determined whether s. 2(d) of the Charter protected the right to strike, and the provincial government decided to err on the side of caution. As Chapter 8, pages 272–78 explains, it need not

have bothered. The 1989 sign law was enacted in response to—and, one might argue, in defiance of—the *Ford* ruling. The timing of Quebec's decision to use s. 33 could not have been worse: it helped to turn many English Canadians against the Meech Lake Accord, which made constitutional concessions to Quebec in exchange for its signature on the Constitution Act, 1982. See, e.g., Peter H. Russell, *Constitutional Odyssey: Can Canadians Become a Sovereign People?* 2nd ed. (Toronto: University of Toronto Press, 1993), pp. 145–47; Andrew Cohen, *A Deal Undone: The Making and Breaking of the Meech Lake Accord* (Vancouver: Douglas & McIntyre, 1991), pp. 195–98.

60. Tsvi Kahana, "The Notwithstanding Mechanism and Public Discussion: Lessons from the Ignored Practice of Section 33 of the Charter," *Canadian Public Administration* 44, no. 3 (Fall 2001), p. 256.

61. Ibid., p. 256.

62. Leeson, "The Notwithstanding Clause," p. 315.

63. Marriage Act, R.S.A. 2000, c. M-5, Section 2.

64. Kahana, "The Notwithstanding Mechanism," p. 268.

65. Ibid., pp. 271–72.

66. Ibid., p. 273.

67. Joseph F. Fletcher and Paul Howe, "Supreme Court Cases and Court Support: The State of Canadian Public Opinion" (Montreal: Institute for Research on Public Policy, May 2000), p. 38. Fletcher and Howe point out that a majority of Canadians in all regions, including Alberta, supported the Court's decision in *Vriend*; had Klein given in to the vocal minority opposing the judgment, he would have found himself in serious political trouble (p. 39). See also the discussion of *Vriend* and its political fallout in F.L. Morton and Rainer Knopff, *The Charter Revolution and the Court*

Party (Peterborough: Broadview Press, 2000), pp. 164–65.

68. Heather Scoffield and Drew Fagan, "Debate Exposes Key Differences on Protecting Minority Rights," *The Globe and Mail*, June 16, 2004, accessed online at www.globeandmail.com; Canadian Press, "We'd Use Notwithstanding Clause: Tory MP," *The Toronto Star*, June 25, 2004, accessed online at www.thestar.com.

69. Quoted in Scoffield and Fagan, "Debate Exposes Key Differences."

70. Brian Laghi, "Invoking Charter Clause Scares Pants off Politicians, Harper Notwithstanding," *The Globe and Mail*, June 8, 2004, accessed online at www.globeandmail.com.

71. See Ronald J. Daniels, Patrick Macklem, and Kent Roach, eds., *The Security of Freedom: Essays on Canada's Anti-Terrorism Bill* (Toronto: University of Toronto Press, 2001); Kent Roach, *September 11: Consequences for Canada* (Montreal and Kingston: McGill-Queen's University Press, 2003), Chapter 3.

72. This prediction appears to have been correct; see the discussion of the Anti-Terrorism Act in Chapter 13, pages 392–93.

73. Leeson, "The Notwithstanding Clause," pp. 318 and 322.

74. Christopher P. Manfredi, *Judicial Power and the Charter: Canada and the Paradox of Liberal Constitutionalism*, 2nd ed. (Toronto: Oxford University Press, 2001), Chapters 1 and 7; Morton and Knopff, *The Charter Revolution and the Court Party*, especially Chapter 7; Russell, "Standing Up for Notwithstanding," pp. 293–309.

75. Manfredi, *Judicial Power and the Charter*, pp. 192–93.

76. Ibid., p. 193.

77. Scott Reid, "Penumbras for the People: Placing Judicial Supremacy under Popular Control," in Anthony A. Peacock, ed., *Rethinking the Constitution: Perspectives on Canadian Constitutional Reform, Interpretation, and Theory* (Toronto: Oxford University Press, 1996), p. 204.

Conclusion 4

Chapter 13

The Next Twenty Years of the Charter Era

All Canadians are equal before and under the law, regardless of origin or ethnicity.

CP PHOTO/Kitchener-Waterloo Record

The preceding chapters have traced the history of the Charter, its influence on Canadian law and public policy, and the ways in which our governing institutions have adapted to the entrenchment of rights and freedoms. They describe the evolving relationships among the three branches of government, between federal and provincial governments, and between the state and individual Canadians. On balance, the changes wrought by the Charter—more precisely, by the individuals and agencies that have employed it—are generally positive. Problems arising from the role of courts in the policy process and the uneven quality of judicial policy-making are more than offset by new safeguards against the arbitrary and unfair exercise of state power. The effectiveness of these safeguards should not be taken for granted (especially, as we will

see shortly, in the "war on terrorism"). But their existence, and their enforcement by the courts, is a positive development.

After looking back over more than two decades of the Charter, it is interesting to speculate about the future. This chapter argues that three of the trends identified in this book will persist, at least for the foreseeable future:

1. growing judicial deference to the legislative and executive branches of government, particularly where national security is concerned;
2. the evolving relationship among the three branches of government; and
3. a growing willingness by the Supreme Court to apply the Charter to economic disputes.

NATIONAL SECURITY AND THE CHARTER

Shortly after the terrorist attacks of September 11, 2001, the Supreme Court signalled its willingness to dilute the protections of the Charter in matters relating to national security. In the *Suresh* ruling, it granted the appeal of a failed refugee claimant—whom the Canadian Security and Intelligence Service (CSIS) had identified as a suspected terrorist—who feared that he would be tortured if he were deported to his native Sri Lanka. In the process, however, a unanimous Court made it clear that the "war on terrorism" would weigh heavily against entrenched rights and freedoms in the s. 1 balancing analysis.

First, it removed "expression ... directed towards violence or terror" from the ambit of protected speech under s. 2(b).[1] Second, it quoted approvingly from a recent judgment of England's highest court that explicitly cited September 11 as justification for judicial deference to the executive branch:

> I wrote this speech some three months before the recent events in New York and Washington. They are a reminder that in matters of national security, the cost of failure can be high. *This seems to me to underline the need for the judicial arm of government to respect the decisions of ministers of the Crown on the question of whether support for terrorist activities in a foreign country constitutes a threat to national security.* It is not only that the executive has access to special information and expertise in these matters. It is also that such decisions, with serious potential results for the community, require a legitimacy which can be conferred only by entrusting them to persons responsible to the community through the democratic process. If the people are to accept the consequences of such decisions, they must be made by persons whom the people have elected and whom they can remove.[2]

The importation of this British case into Canadian jurisprudence effectively allowed the Court to circumvent the Charter. Although the United Kingdom has recently adopted the European Convention on Human Rights for domestic purposes, it does not have its own entrenched guarantee of rights and freedoms. The Court's use of this precedent reveals that our judges, gripped by the shock and grief aroused by September 11, were willing to dilute rights and freedoms in the name of national security.

The Court did not completely abdicate its second-order duties in *Suresh*. It emphasized the continuing importance of Charter values in the face of the terrorist threat: "In the end, it would be a Pyrrhic victory if terrorism were defeated at the cost of sacrificing our commitment to those values."[3] Nonetheless, the tenor of the judgment suggests that legislated violations of legal rights and fundamental freedoms will be upheld if they can be shown to be "rationally connected" to the "war on terror."[4] The terrorist threat confronting Western states, including Canada, will not disappear in the foreseeable future. As long as national security remains a central preoccupation of our policy-makers, including judges, Charter protection for unpopular minorities (e.g., Muslims) may be attenuated.

The first ruling on the constitutionality of the act itself, while narrow in scope, suggests that judicial willingness to defer to the executive branch in the context of national security was not a temporary reaction to the horror of 9/11. In June 2004, the Supreme Court upheld the "investigative hearing" provisions in

The 2001 Anti-Terrorism Act and the 2004 RCMP raid on the home of a journalist raised public fears about the security of Charter rights and freedoms.

Michael De Addar/artizans.com

s. 83.28 of the Anti-Terrorism Act.[5] Under those provisions, a police officer investigating a terrorism offence (past or potential) may ask a judge to issue "an order for the gathering of information." The person or persons named in the order must appear before the judge to answer questions about the terrorism offence under investigation. They may be ordered to produce "any thing in their possession or control" at the hearing. A "named person" is entitled to bring a lawyer to the hearing, but may not refuse to answer any question on the ground of self-incrimination. However, any incriminating information obtained at the hearing may not be introduced into evidence against that person at a subsequent criminal trial.

Section 83.28 represents a significant departure from Canada's common-law tradition. It takes away the freedom to decide whether or not to cooperate with a police investigation. It forces judges to collaborate with the executive branch, specifically police and prosecutors, in the investigation of alleged criminal offences. On these counts, it appears to infringe ss. 7 and 11(d) of the Charter.[6] The availability of counsel and the limited protection against self-incrimination have been described as "the bells and whistles of Charter-proofing"—intended to shield the law from nullification on Charter grounds, not to safeguard the due-process rights of the "named person."[7] If that was indeed the intention of the Department of Justice, it worked: the Court found no infringement of s. 7, although it had to "read in" procedural safeguards in order to uphold the law. The most important is the stipulation that any information obtained from a "named person" must not be used against him or her in a future deportation or extradition hearing.[8] The majority also ordered that lawyers for "named persons" be allowed to participate as fully in an investigative hearing as they would in a criminal trial, in order to protect their clients. Finally, the Court made it clear that judges must conduct "investigative hearings" in a way that conforms to Charter values.

The only major disagreement concerned the impact of s. 83.28 on judicial independence. Seven Justices argued that it did not turn judges into agents of the executive branch or the police: "The function of the judge in a judicial investigative hearing is not to act as 'an agent of the state', but rather, to protect the integrity of the investigation and, in particular, the

interests of the named person *vis-à-vis* the state."[9] The two dissenting Justices argued that the impugned provisions fused the judicial and executive branches, thus compromising the independence of the presiding judge and depriving him or her of "the means to effectively protect the rights and freedoms of the person being examined."[10]

The real significance of this ruling may lie in the interpretive approach adopted by the majority. Former Justices Arbour and Iacobucci based their ruling on the presumption of constitutionality, an important canon of judicial construction. They strove to find an interpretation of the impugned law that would allow them to uphold it. This has not always been the case in Charter challenges, where the protection of entrenched rights and freedoms has often taken priority over the presumption of constitutionality. One might conclude that the majority was determined to defer to Parliament if at all possible.

THE THREE BRANCHES OF GOVERNMENT IN THE CHARTER ERA

A second ongoing trend is the adaptation of governing institutions to their Charter duties, both independently and in relation to each other. The courts have forced the legislative and executive branches to overcome their initial resistance to entrenched limits on government action. Law-enforcement officers and prosecutors, often resentful of court rulings that tie their hands, have successfully lobbied Parliament to impose a different balance between due-process rights and public safety. Wrongful convictions and abuse of police powers have persisted in the Charter era, but it is almost certainly true that suspects are treated more fairly now than they would have been had Trudeau's entrenchment project failed.

In the future, it is to be hoped that Charter values will be balanced against competing policy considerations at all stages of the policy-making process, from the first proposal from the sponsoring government, through parliamentary scrutiny, to judicial review by the courts. The Supreme Court in particular has become more mindful of its deficiencies as a policy-making institution. After two decades of intragovernmental struggle, a consensus about the appropriate Charter duties of the various branches appears to be emerging, and with it a more consistent balance between protected rights and competing social values.

THE CHARTER GOES TO MARKET

In the 1980s, the majority of Justices refused to apply the Charter to economic issues—even though, in practice, they were willing to strike down laws that interfered with corporate profits. They refused to grant constitutional protection to collective bargaining. They insisted that the purpose of the Charter was to restrain government power, not to impose positive duties on the state to ensure the material security of the citizens. That approach is now under attack. The narrow meaning of associative freedom in s. 2(d) was abandoned in 2001, and labour-management relations were subjected to Charter review.[11] A year later, Justices L'Heureux-Dubé and Arbour argued (in dissent) that the phrase "security of the person" in s. 7 required governments to provide a minimum standard of living for the less fortunate.[12]

Despite the subsequent departure of both Justices, the Court might embrace positive rights in a future case. In June 2004, the Supreme Court heard two Charter challenges to the health-care system. One was brought by a doctor and his patient, who argued the Quebec law prohibiting the private delivery of medical services violated s. 7. The violation arose from the long waiting lists for treatment, which—the appellants argued—would be eliminated if private delivery were allowed in the province.[13] The other case concerned the refusal of the British Columbia government to cover the costs of a particular type of therapy for autism, which—the appellants argued—infringed the guarantee of security of the person and discriminated on the ground of mental disability (s. 15(1)).[14] Should either challenge succeed, it would constitute a serious judicial intrusion on the budgetary powers of Parliament. The generally cautious and deferential approach of the current Court makes it unlikely that the Justices would use the Charter to impose costly

new responsibilities on the legislative and executive branches.[15] However, further movement in the direction of positive rights cannot be ruled out.

These speculations may prove to be as inaccurate as the predictions occasioned by the creation of the Charter in the early 1980s. The only certainty is that judges will make unpredictable decisions, to which all of us—implementers, consumers, and the interested public—will have to respond. The next two decades of the Charter era will be fully as interesting, historic, and controversial as the events related in these pages.

DISCUSSION AND REVIEW QUESTIONS

1. In your opinion, should the courts be less vigilant in the protection of entrenched rights and freedoms in the interests of national security? Why or why not?

2. Do you believe that budgetary decisions that affect rights and freedoms should be left entirely to Parliament? Why or why not?

SUGGESTED READINGS

Daniels, Ronald J., Patrick Macklem, and Kent Roach, eds. *The Security of Freedom: Essays on Canada's Anti-Terrorism Bill.* Toronto: University of Toronto Press, 2002.

Roach, Kent. *September 11: Consequences for Canada.* Montreal and Kingston: McGill-Queen's University Press, 2003.

ENDNOTES

1. *Suresh v. Canada (Minister of Citizenship and Immigration)*, [2002] 1 S.C.R. 3, paragraph 107, *per curiam.*

2. *Secretary of State for the Home Department v. Rehman*, [2001] 3 W.L.R. 877, paragraph 62, *per* Lord Hoffmann, quoted in *Suresh*, paragraph 33 (emphasis added by the Supreme Court).

3. *Suresh*, paragraph 4.

4. Space does not permit a detailed analysis of the provisions in the Anti-Terrorism Act that infringe the Charter. The act contains clear violations of expressive and associative freedom (s. 83.18(4)), the principles of fundamental justice (e.g., s. 83–21(2)), and the due-process rights in ss. 8–12 (ss. 83.26 and 83.28). For more information, see Ronald J. Daniels, Patrick Macklem, and Kent Roach, eds., *The Security of Freedom: Essays on Canada's Anti-Terrorism Bill* (Toronto: University of Toronto Press, 2001), and Kent Roach, *September 11: Consequences for Canada* (Montreal and Kingston: McGill-Queen's University Press, 2003).

5. *Application under s. 83.28 of the Criminal Code (Re)*, 2004 SCC 42; *Vancouver Sun (Re)*, 2004 SCC 43. The latter case dealt with a specific judicial order issued under the provisions of the act; it will not be discussed here.

6. Roach, *September 11*, p. 50 and pp. 111–12; Kent Roach, "The Dangers of a Charter-Proof and Crime-Based Response to Terrorism," in Daniels, Macklem, and Roach, *The Security of Freedom*, pp. 135–36.

7. Roach, "The Dangers," p. 136.

8. *Application under s. 83.28, paragraphs 73–79, per* Iacobucci and Arbour JJ.

9. Ibid., *per* Iacobucci and Arbour JJ.

10. Ibid., paragraph 183, *per* Fish J.

11. *Dunmore v. Ontario*, [2001] 3 S.C.R. 1016 (see discussion in Dossier 8.12, pages 276–77).

12. *Gosselin v. Quebec (Attorney General)*, [2002] 4 S.C.R. 429.

13. *Jacques Chaoulli and Georges Zeliotis v. The Attorney General of Quebec and the Attorney General of Canada*, appeal to the Supreme Court of Canada, file number 29272, appeal heard June 8, 2004 (decision reserved).

14. *Attorney General of British Columbia, et al. v. Connor Auton, et al.*, appeal to the Supreme Court of Canada, file number 29508, appeal heard June 9, 2004 (decision reserved).

15. In October 2004, the Court unanimously upheld a 1991 Newfoundland law that suspended the government's pay-equity program for female hospital workers. Although the Court found that the law had violated s. 15(1), it held that the violation was justified under s. 1. The severity of the fiscal crisis, which had prompted the government of Newfoundland and Labrador to renege on its promises, was sufficient to outweigh the Charter claims of the affected workers. See *Newfoundland (Treasury Board) v. N.A.P.E.*, 2004 SCC 66.

List of Cases

Adler v. Ontario, [1996] 3 S.C.R. 609

R. v. Advance Cutting & Coring Ltd., [2001] 3 S.C.R. 209

A.G. (Canada) and Dupond v. Montreal, [1978] 2 S.C.R. 770

Ahani v. Canada (M.C.I.), [2002] 1 S.C.R. 72

R. v. Amway Corp., [1989] 1 S.C.R. 21

Andrews v. Law Society of British Columbia, [1989] 1 S.C.R. 143

Application under s. 83.28 of the Criminal Code (Re), 2004 SCC 42

Arsenault-Cameron v. Prince Edward Island, [2000] 1 S.C.R. 3

R. v. Askov, [1990] 2 S.C.R. 1199

Attorney General of Canada v. Lavell and Bedard, [1974] S.C.R. 1349

Attorney General of Quebec v. Quebec Association of Protestant School Boards, [1984] 2 S.C.R. 66

Authorson v. Canada (Attorney General), [2003] 2 S.C.R. 40

B. (R.) v. Children's Aid Society of Metropolitan Toronto, [1995] 1 S.C.R. 315

Barbeau v. British Columbia, 2003 BCCA 406

R. v. Bartle, [1994] 3 S.C.R. 173

BCGEU v. British Columbia (Attorney General), [1988] 2 S.C.R. 214

Benner v. Canada (Secretary of State), [1997] 1 S.C.R. 358

R. v. Bernard, [1988] 2 S.C.R. 833

Bhinder v. CN, [1985] 2 S.C.R. 561

R. v. Big M Drug Mart Ltd., [1985] 1 S.C.R. 295

Black v. Law Society of Alberta, [1989] 1 S.C.R. 591

Bliss v. Attorney General of Canada, [1979] 1 S.C.R. 183

Brown v. Board of Education of Topeka, 347 U.S. 483

Brownridge v. the Queen, [1972] S.C.R. 926

R. v. Broyles, [1991] 3 S.C.R. 595

R. v. Brydges, [1990] 1 S.C.R. 190

R. v. Buhay, [2003] 1 S.C.R. 631

R. v. Burlingham, [1995] 2 S.C.R. 206

R. v. Butler, [1992] 1 S.C.R. 452

Canada (Minister of Employment and Immigration) v. Chiarelli, [1992] 1 S.C.R. 711

Canadian Broadcasting Corp. v. Lessard, [1991] 3 S.C.R. 421

Canadian Council of Churches v. Canada (Minister of Employment and Immigration), [1992] 1 S.C.R. 236

Canadian Egg Marketing Agency v. Richardson, [1998] 3 S.C.R. 157

Canadian Foundation for Children, Youth and the Law v. Canada (Attorney General), 2004 SCC 4

Canadian Newspaper Co. v. Canada (A. G.), [1988] 2 S.C.R. 122

R. v. Carosella, [1997] 1 S.C.R. 80

R. v. Caslake, [1998] 1 S.C.R. 51

R. v. Chaulk, [1990] 3 S.C.R. 1303

Chromiak v. The Queen, [1980] 1 S.C.R. 471

Clarkson v. The Queen, [1986] 1 S.C.R. 383

R. v. Clay, [2003] 3 S.C.R. 735

R. v. Colarusso, [1994] 1 S.C.R. 20

R. v. Collins, [1987] 1 S.C.R. 265

Committee for the Commonwealth of Canada v. Canada, [1991] 1 S.C.R. 139

Conway v. Canada (Attorney General), [1993] 2 S.C.R. 872

Corbiere v. Canada (Minister of Indian and Northern Affairs), [1999] 2 S.C.R. 203

R. v. Creighton, [1993] 3 S.C.R. 3

Cuddy Chicks Ltd. v. Ontario (Labour Relations Board), [1991] 2 S.C.R. 5

Cunningham and Attorney General for British Columbia v. Tomey Homma, JCPC 1903

Dagenais v. Canadian Broadcasting Corp., [1994] 3 S.C.R. 835

R. v. Daviault, [1994] 3 S.C.R. 63

R. v. Demers, 2004 SCC 46

R. v. Dixon, [1998] 1 S.C.R. 244

Doucet-Boudreau v. Nova Scotia (Minister of Education), [2003] 3 S.C.R. 3

R. v. Downey, [1992] 2 S.C.R. 10

R. v. Drybones, [1970] S.C.R. 282

Dubois v. The Queen, [1985] 2 S.C.R. 350

R. v. Duguay, [1989] 1 S.C.R. 93

Dunmore v. Ontario, [2001] 3 S.C.R. 1016

Eaton v. Brant County Board of Education, [1997] 1 S.C.R. 241

Edmonton Journal v. Alberta (Attorney General), [1989] 2 S.C.R. 1326

R. v. Edwards, [1996] 1 S.C.R. 128

R. v. Edwards Books and Art Ltd., [1986] 2 S.C.R. 713

Egan v. Canada, [1995] 2 S.C.R. 513

Eldridge v. British Columbia (Attorney General), [1997] 3 S.C.R. 624

Error Muller v. Oregon, 208 U.S. 412

Escobedo v. Illinois, 378 U.S. 478 (1964)

R. v. Evans, [1991] 1 S.C.R. 869

R. v. Evans, [1996] 1 S.C.R. 8

R. v. Feeney, [1997] 2 S.C.R. 13

Figueroa v. Canada (Attorney General), [2003] 1 S.C.R. 912

Finlay v. Canada (Minister of Finance), [1986] 2 S.C.R. 607

R. v. Fitt (1995), 96 C.C.C. (3d) 341 (N.S.C.A.)

Ford v. Quebec (A. G.), [1988] 2 S.C.R. 712

R. v. Généreux, [1992] 1 S.C.R. 259

R. v. Goltz, [1991] 3 S.C.R. 485

R. v. Gonzales (1962), 32 D.L.R. (2d) 290

Gosselin v. Quebec (Attorney General), [2002] 4 S.C.R. 429

Granovsky v. Canada (Minister of Employment and Immigration), [2000] 1 S.C.R. 703

R. v. Grant, [1993] 3 S.C.R. 223

Haig v. Canada; Haig v. Canada (Chief Electoral Officer), [1993] 2 S.C.R. 995

Halpern v. Canada (Attorney General), ([2003]-06-10) ONCA

Harper v. Canada (Attorney General), 2004 SCC 33

Harrison v. Carswell, [1976] 2 S.C.R. 200

Harvey v. New Brunswick (Attorney General), [1996] 2 S.C.R. 876

R. v. Hebert, [1990] 2 S.C.R. 151

Hendricks v. Québec (Attorney General), [2002] J.Q. No. 3816

Henrietta Muir Edwards v. Attorney-General for Canada, JCPC, 1929 [the "Persons Case"]

R. v. Hess; R. v. Nguyen, [1990] 2 S.C.R. 906

R. v. Heywood, [1994] 3 S.C.R. 761

Hill v. Church of Scientology of Toronto, [1995] 2 S.C.R. 1130

Hogan v. the Queen, [1975] 2 S.C.R. 574

R. v. Holmes, [1988] 1 S.C.R. 914

Housen v. Nikolaisen, [2002], 2 S.C.R. 235

R. v. Hufsky, [1988] 1 S.C.R. 621

Hunter v. Southam Inc., [1984] 2 S.C.R. 145

Hyde v. Hyde and Woodmansee (1866), L.R. 1 P. & D. 130

Irwin Toy Ltd. v. Quebec (Attorney General), [1989] 1 S.C.R. 927

The Queen v. Jones, [1986] 2 S.C.R. 284

R. v. Keegstra, [1990] 3 S.C.R. 697

Kindler v. Canada (Minister of Justice), [1991] 2 S.C.R. 779

R. v. Kokesch, [1990] 3 S.C.R. 3

R. v. Kuldip, [1990] 3 S.C.R. 618

R. v. Latimer, [1997] 1 S.C.R. 217

R. v. Latimer, [2001] 1 S.C.R. 3

Lavigne v. Ontario Public Service Employees Union, [1991] 2 S.C.R. 211

Lavoie v. Canada, [2002] 1 S.C.R. 769

Law v. Canada (Minister of Employment and Immigration), [1999] 1 S.C.R. 497

Law Society of Upper Canada v. Skapinker, [1984] 1 S.C.R. 357

Libman v. Quebec (Attorney General), [1997] 3 S.C.R. 569

Little Sisters Book and Art Emporium v. Canada (Minister of Justice), [2000] 2 S.C.R. 1120

Lovelace v. Ontario, [2000] 1 S.C.R. 950

R. v. Luxton, [1990] 2 S.C.R. 711

R. v. Lyons, [1987] 2 S.C.R. 309

MacDonald v. City of Montreal, [1986] 1 S.C.R. 460

R. v. MacDougall, [1998] 3 S.C.R. 45

MacKay v. Manitoba, [1989] 2 S.C.R. 357

R. v. Malmo-Levine; R. v. Caine, [2003] 3 S.C.R. 571

R. v. Manninen, [1987] 1 S.C.R. 1233

R. v. Mannion, [1986] 2 S.C.R. 272

Mapp v. Ohio, 367 U.S. 643 (1961)

Marbury v. Madison, 5 U.S. 137 (1803)
McCulloch v. Maryland, 17 U.S. 316 (1819)
McKinney v. University of Guelph, [1990] 3 S.C.R. 229
R. v. Mellenthin, [1992] 3 S.C.R. 615
Mills v. The Queen, [1986] 1 S.C.R. 863
R. v. Mills, [1999] 3 S.C.R. 668
Miranda v. Arizona, 384 U.S. 436 (1966)
Miron v. Trudel, [1995] 2 S.C.R. 418
R. v. Morales, [1992] 3 S.C.R. 71
Morgentaler v. the Queen, [1976] 1 S.C.R. 616
R. v. Morgentaler, [1988] 1 S.C.R. 30
R. v. Morgentaler, [1993] 3 S.C.R. 463
R. v. Morin, [1992] 1 S.C.R. 771

New Brunswick Broadcasting Co. v. Nova Scotia (Speaker of the House of Assembly), [1993] 1 S.C.R. 319
New Brunswick (Minister of Health and Community Services) v. G. (J.), [1999] 3 S.C.R. 46
R. v. Noble, [1997] 1 S.C.R. 874
R. v. Noël, [2002] 3 S.C.R. 433
Nova Scotia (A.G.) v. Walsh, [2002] 4 S.C.R. 325
R. v. Nova Scotia Pharmaceutical Society, [1992] 2 S.C.R. 606

R. v. Oakes, [1986] 1 S.C.R. 103
R. v. O'Connor, [1995] 4 S.C.R. 411
Ontario (Attorney General) v. OPSEU, [1987] 2 S.C.R. 2
Operation Dismantle v. The Queen, [1985] 1 S.C.R. 441

R. v. P. (M.B.), [1994] 1 S.C.R. 555
R. v. Pearson, [1992] 3 S.C.R. 665
R. v. Plant, [1993] 3 S.C.R. 281
R. v. Potvin, [1993] 2 S.C.R. 880
R. v. Prosper, [1994] 3 S.C.R. 236

R. v. Quin, [1988] 2 S.C.R. 825

R. v. Rahey, [1987] 1 S.C.R. 588
Reference re Alberta Statutes, [1938] S.C.R. 100
Re: Anti-Inflation Act, [1976] 2 S.C.R. 373
Re B.C. Motor Vehicle Act, [1985] 2 S.C.R. 486
Reference re Bill 30, An Act to Amend the Education Act (Ont.), [1987] 1 S.C.R. 1148

Reference re Education Act (Que.), [1993] 2 S.C.R. 511
Reference re Legislative Authority of Parliament to Alter or Replace the Senate, [1980] 1 S.C.R. 54
Re Manitoba Language Rights, [1985] 1 S.C.R. 721
Reference re Prov. Electoral Boundaries (Sask.), [1991] 2 S.C.R. 158
Reference re Public Schools Act (Man.), s. 79(3), (4) and (7), [1993] 1 S.C.R. 839
Reference Re Public Service Employee Relations Act (Alta.), [1987] 1 S.C.R. 313 [the "Alberta Labour Reference"]
Reference re Remuneration of Judges of the Provincial Court (P.E.I.), [1997] 3 S.C.R. 3
Reference re Secession of Quebec, [1998] 2 S.C.R. 217
Reference re ss. 193 and 195.1(1)(c) of the Criminal Code (Man.), [1990] 1 S.C.R. 1123 [the "Prostitution Reference"]
Reference re Upper Churchill Water Rights Reversion Act, [1984] 1 S.C.R. 297
Reference re Workers' Compensation Act, 1983 (Nfld.) (Application to intervene), [1989] 2 S.C.R. 335
RJR-MacDonald Inc. v. Canada (Attorney General), [1995] 3 S.C.R. 199
Robertson and Rosetanni v. the Queen, [1963] S.C.R. 651
R. v. Robinson, [1996] 1 S.C.R. 683
Rocket v. Royal College of Dental Surgeons of Ontario, [1990] 2 S.C.R. 232
Rodriguez v. British Columbia (Attorney General), [1993] 3 S.C.R. 519
RWDSU v. Dolphin Delivery Ltd., [1986] 2 S.C.R. 573
RWDSU, Local 558 v. Pepsi-Cola Canada Beverages (West) Ltd., [2002] 1 S.C.R. 156

R. v. S.A.B., [2003] 2 S.C.R. 678
R. v. S. (R.J.), [1995] 1 S.C.R. 451
R. v. S. (S.), [1990] 2 S.C.R. 254
Saumur v. City of Quebec, [1953] 2 S.C.R. 299
Sauvé v. Canada (Attorney General), [1993] 2 S.C.R. 438
Sauvé v. Canada (Chief Electoral Officer), [2002] S.C.R. 519
Schachter v. Canada, [1992] 2 S.C.R. 679
R. v. Schwartz, [1988] 2 S.C.R. 443
R. v. Seaboyer; R. v. Gayme, [1991] 2 S.C.R. 577
R. v. Sellars, [1980] 1 S.C.R. 527

R. v. Sharpe, [2001] 1 S.C.R. 45

R. v. Simmons, [1988] 2 S.C.R. 495

Singh v. Minister of Employment and Immigration, [1985] 1 S.C.R. 177

R. v. Smith, [1987] 1 S.C.R. 1045

R. v. Smith, [1989] 2 S.C.R. 1120

R. v. Smith, [1991] 1 S.C.R. 714

R. v. Smith (Joey Leonard), [1989] 2 S.C.R. 368

Société des Acadiens v. Association of Parents, [1986] 1 S.C.R. 549

R. v. Stillman, [1997] 1 S.C.R. 607

R. v. Stinchcombe, [1991] 3 S.C.R. 326

Stoffman v. Vancouver General Hospital, [1990] 3 S.C.R. 483

R. v. Storrey, [1990] 1 S.C.R. 241

R. v. Strachan, [1988] 2 S.C.R. 980

Suresh v. Canada (Minister of Citizenship and Immigration), [2002] 1 S.C.R. 3

R. v. Swain, [1991] 1 S.C.R. 933

Switzman v. Elbling, [1957] S.C.R. 285

Symes v. Canada, [1993] 4 S.C.R. 695

R. v. Taillefer; R. v. Duguay, [2003] 3 S.C.R. 307

Tétreault-Gadoury v. Canada (Canada Employment and Immigration Commission), [1991] 2 S.C.R. 22

R. v. Therens, [1985] 1 S.C.R. 613

Thibaudeau v. Canada, [1995] 2 S.C.R. 627

Thomson Newspapers Co. v. Canada (Attorney General), [1998] 1 S.C.R. 877

R. v. Tran, [1994] 2 S.C.R. 951

R. v. Tremblay, [1987] 2 S.C.R. 435

Tremblay v. Daigle, [1989] 2 S.C.R. 530

Trociuk v. B.C. (A.G.), [2003] 1 S.C.R. 835

R. v. Turpin, [1989] 1 S.C.R. 1296

U.F.C.W., Local 1518 v. Kmart Canada, [1999] 2 S.C.R. 1083

United States v. Burns, [2001] 1 S.C.R. 283

R. v. Vaillancourt, [1987] 2 S.C.R. 636

Vancouver Sun (Re), 2004 SCC 43

Vriend v. Alberta, [1998] 1 S.C.R. 493

Waldman v. British Columbia (Medical Services Commission), 1999 BCCA 508

Weeks v. U.S., 232 U.S. 383 (1914)

R. v. Whittle, [1994] 2 S.C.R. 914

R. v. Whyte, [1988] 2 S.C.R. 3

Wigglesworth v. R., [1987] 2 S.C.R. 541

Winnipeg Child and Family Services (Northwest Area) v. G. (D.F.), [1997] 3 S.C.R. 925

R. v. Wise, [1992] 1 S.C.R. 527

R. v. Wray, [1971] S.C.R. 272

R. v. Zundel, [1992] 2 S.C.R. 731

Index